Arthur Carr

The Gospel According to St. Matthew

with maps, notes and introduction

Arthur Carr

The Gospel According to St. Matthew
with maps, notes and introduction

ISBN/EAN: 9783337285777

Printed in Europe, USA, Canada, Australia, Japan

Cover: Foto ©Lupo / pixelio.de

More available books at **www.hansebooks.com**

Cambridge Greek Testament for Schools and Colleges.

THE GOSPEL

ACCORDING TO

ST MATTHEW.

London: C. J. CLAY AND SONS,
CAMBRIDGE UNIVERSITY PRESS WAREHOUSE,
AVE MARIA LANE.
Glasgow: 263, ARGYLE STREET.

Leipzig: F. A. BROCKHAUS.
New York: THE MACMILLAN CO.
Bombay: GEORGE BELL AND SONS.

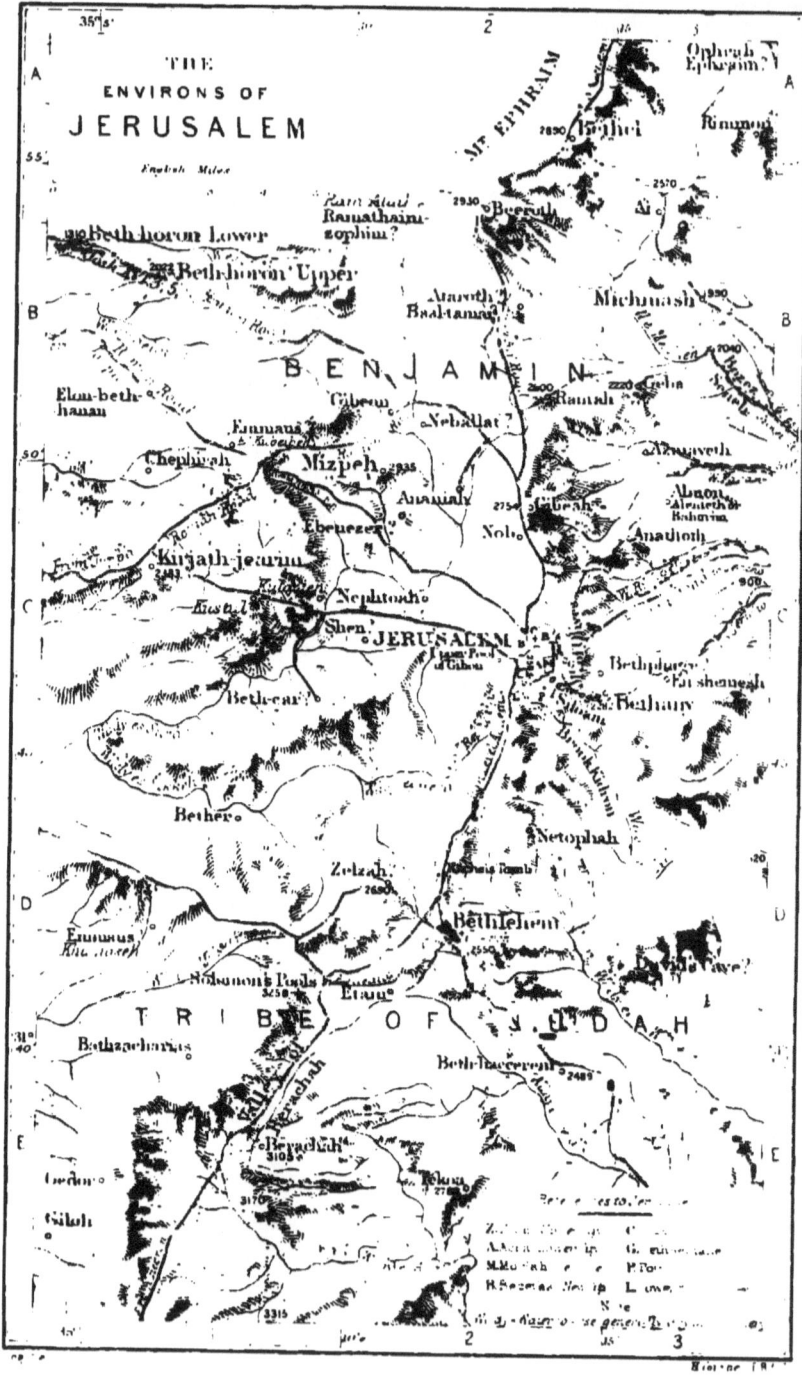

Cambridge Greek Testament for Schools and Colleges.

GENERAL EDITOR:—J. J. S. PEROWNE, D.D.,
BISHOP OF WORCESTER.

THE GOSPEL ACCORDING TO

ST MATTHEW,

WITH MAPS NOTES AND INTRODUCTION

BY

THE REV. A. CARR, M.A.

FORMERLY FELLOW OF ORIEL COLLEGE, OXFORD,
LATE ASSISTANT MASTER AT WELLINGTON COLLEGE.

STEREOTYPED EDITION

Cambridge:
AT THE UNIVERSITY PRESS
1896

[All Rights reserved.]

First Edition 1881.
Reprinted 1885, 1886, 1887, 1889 *(twice)*, 1892, 1894, 1896

PREFACE
BY THE GENERAL EDITOR.

THE General Editor of *The Cambridge Bible for Schools* thinks it right to say that he does not hold himself responsible either for the interpretation of particular passages which the Editors of the several Books have adopted, or for any opinion on points of doctrine that they may have expressed. In the New Testament more especially questions arise of the deepest theological import, on which the ablest and most conscientious interpreters have differed and always will differ. His aim has been in all such cases to leave each Contributor to the unfettered exercise of his own judgment, only taking care that mere controversy should as far as possible be avoided. He has contented himself chiefly with a careful revision of the notes, with pointing out omissions, with suggesting occasionally a reconsideration of some question, or a fuller treatment of difficult passages, and the like.

Beyond this he has not attempted to interfere, feeling it better that each Commentary should have its own individual character, and being convinced that freshness and variety of treatment are more than a compensation for any lack of uniformity in the Series.

EDITOR'S PREFACE.

THE general design of the Commentary, to which this is the first contribution, has been elsewhere stated. But it may be permitted me for the sake of clearness to name some of the points kept in view in the preparation of these notes.

One of the objects aimed at has been to connect more closely the study of the Classics with the reading of the New Testament. To recognise this connection and to draw it closer is the first task of the Christian scholar. The best thoughts as well as the words of Hellenic culture have a place, not of sufferance, but of right in the Christian system. This consideration will equally deepen the interest in the Greek and Latin Classics, and in the study of the New Testament. But the Greek Testament may become the centre towards which all lines of learning and research converge. Art, or the expressed thought of great painters, often the highest intellects of their day, once the great popular interpreters of Scripture, has bequeathed lessons which ought not to be neglected. Every advance in science, in philology, in grammar, in historical research, and every new phase of thought, throws its own light on the words of Christ. In this way, each successive age has a fresh contribution to bring to the interpretation of Scripture.

Another endeavour has been to bring in the aid of Modern Greek (which is in reality often very ancient Greek), in illustration of New Testament words and idioms. In this subject many suggestions have come from Geldart's *Modern Greek Language;* and among other works consulted have been: Clyde's *Romaic and Modern Greek*, Vincent and Bourne's *Modern Greek*, the Modern Greek grammars of J. Donaldson and Corfe and the Γραμματικὴ τῆς Ἀγγλικῆς γλώσσης ὑπὸ Γεωργίου Λαμπισῆ.

I have wished also to call attention to the form in which St Matthew has preserved our Lord's discourses. And here Bishop Jebb's *Sacred Literature* has been invaluable. His conclusions may not in every instance be accepted, but the line of investigation which he followed is very fruitful in interesting and profitable results. Of this more is said *infra*, Introd. ch. v. 2.

The works principally consulted have been: Bruder's *Concordance of the N. T.* and Trommius' of the LXX; Schleusner's *Lexicon*, Grimm's edition of Wilkii *Clavis*, the indices of Wyttenbach to Plutarch and of Schweighäuser to Polybius, E. A. Sophocles' *Greek Lexicon* (Roman and Byzantine period); Scrivener's *Introduction to the Criticism of the N. T.* (the references are to the second edition); Hammond's *Textual Criticism applied to the N. T.*; Dr Moulton's edition of Winer's *Grammar* (1870); Clyde's *Greek Syntax*, Goodwin's *Greek Moods and Tenses*; Westcott's *Introduction to the Study of the Gospels*; Bp Lightfoot, *On a Fresh Revision of the N. T.*; Lightfoot's *Horæ Hebraicæ*; Schöttgen's *Horæ Hebraicæ et Talmudicæ*, and various modern books of travel, to which references are given in the notes.

I have to thank very sincerely several friends who have helped me with suggestions, and have looked over the sheets as they passed through the press. In the preparation of the text and in the revision of the notes I owe a great deal to the kind assistance and accurate scholarship of Dr W. F. Moulton.

A. C.

WELLINGTON COLLEGE,
December 21, 1880.

ON THE GREEK TEXT.

IN undertaking an edition of the Greek text of the New Testament with English notes for the use of Schools, the Syndics of the Cambridge University Press have not thought it desirable to reprint the text in common use*. To have done this would have been to set aside all the materials that have since been accumulated towards the formation of a correct text, and to disregard the results of textual criticism in its application to MSS., Versions and Fathers. It was felt that a text more in accordance with the present state of our knowledge was desirable. On the other hand the Syndics were unable to adopt one of the more recent critical texts, and they were not disposed to make themselves responsible for the preparation of an

---

* The form of this text most used in England, and adopted in Dr Scrivener's edition, is that of the third edition of Robert Stephens (1550). The name "Received Text" is popularly given to the Elzevir edition of 1633, which is based on this edition of Stephens, and the name is borrowed from a phrase in the Preface, "Textum ergo habes nunc ab omnibus receptum."

entirely new and independent text: at the same time it would have been obviously impossible to leave it to the judgement of each individual contributor to frame his own text, as this would have been fatal to anything like uniformity or consistency. They believed however that a good text might be constructed by simply taking the consent of the two most recent critical editions, those of Tischendorf and Tregelles, as a basis. The same principle of consent could be applied to places where the two critical editions were at variance, by allowing a determining voice to the text of Stephens where it agreed with either of their readings, and to a third critical text, that of Lachmann, where the text of Stephens differed from both. In this manner readings peculiar to one or other of the two editions would be passed over as not being supported by sufficient critical consent; while readings having the double authority would be treated as possessing an adequate title to confidence.

A few words will suffice to explain the manner in which this design has been carried out.

In the *Acts*, the *Epistles*, and the *Revelation*, wherever the texts of Tischendorf and Tregelles agree, their joint readings are followed without any deviation. Where they differ from each other, but neither of them agrees with the text of Stephens as printed in Dr Scrivener's edition, the consensus of Lachmann with either is taken in preference to the text of Stephens. In all other cases the text of Stephens as represented in Dr Scrivener's edition has been followed.

In the *Gospels*, a single modification of this plan has been rendered necessary by the importance of the Sinai MS. (ℵ), which was discovered too late to be used by Tregelles except in the last chapter of St John's Gospel and in the following books. Accordingly, if a reading which Tregelles has put in his margin agrees with ℵ, it is considered as of the same authority as a reading which he has adopted in his text; and if any words which Tregelles has bracketed are omitted by ℵ, these words are here dealt with as if rejected from his text.

In order to secure uniformity, the spelling and the accentuation of Tischendorf have been adopted where he differs from other Editors. His practice has likewise been followed as regards the insertion or omission of Iota subscript in infinitives (as ζῆν, ἐπιτιμᾶν), and adverbs (as κρυφῇ, λάθρα), and the mode of printing such composite forms as διαπαντός, διατί, τουτέστι, and the like.

The punctuation of Tischendorf in his eighth edition has usually been adopted: where it is departed from, the deviation, together with the reasons that have led to it, will be found mentioned in the Notes. Quotations are indicated by a capital letter at the beginning of the sentence. Where a whole verse is omitted, its omission is noted in the margin (*e.g.* Matt. xvii. 21; xxiii. 12).

The text is printed in paragraphs corresponding to those of the English Edition.

Although it was necessary that the text of all the portions of the New Testament should be uniformly constructed in accordance with these general rules, each editor has been left at perfect liberty to express his preference for other readings in the Notes.

It is hoped that a text formed on these principles will fairly represent the results of modern criticism, and will at least be accepted as preferable to "the Received Text" for use in Schools.

J. J. STEWART PEROWNE.

CONTENTS.

I. INTRODUCTION.   PAGES
    Chapter I. Life of St Matthew .... xiii—xvii
    Chapter II. Authorship, Origin, and Characteristics of the Gospel.................... xvii—xxiv
    Chapter III. Analysis of the Gospel.............. xxiv—xxix
    Chapter IV. External History during the Life and Ministry of Jesus Christ .... xxix—xxxiv
    Chapter V. The Literary Form and Language of the Gospel .... xxxv—xlvii

II. TEXT.. 1—77

III. NOTES .... 79—320

IV. INDEX .... 321—330

MAPS—THE ENVIRONS OF JERUSALEM... *to face Title.*
    THE HOLY LAND
    THE CITY OF JERUSALEM } *to follow Introduction.*
    THE SEA OF GALILEE

INTRODUCTION.

CHAPTER I.

LIFE OF ST MATTHEW.

LEVI the son of Alphæus[1] was a tax-gatherer at Capernaum. His special duty would be to collect tolls from the fisheries on the Lake, and perhaps from the merchants travelling southward from Damascus. One day Jesus coming up from the Lake side passed near the custom-house where Levi was seated in Oriental fashion, and He saith unto him, Follow me, and he arose and followed Him (ch. ix. 9). That Jesus ever addressed Levi before, we are not told; but it is reasonable to suppose that he was expecting the summons, that he was already a disciple of Jesus, and prepared as soon as Christ gave the word to leave all for His sake. At any rate, Levi must have heard of the Great Rabbi and of His preaching, and have already resolved to adopt the view of the kingdom of God which Jesus taught.

When Levi became a follower of Jesus he changed his name from Levi to Matthew[2], which means "the Gift of God," and is the same as the Greek name Theodore. This practice was not unusual, and may be illustrated by the instances of Saul and of Simon, who also adopted new names in the new life.

The same day Matthew made a feast—perhaps a farewell feast to his old associates—to which he invited Jesus and His

---

[1] Alphæus being also the name of the father of James the Apostle it has been conjectured that James and Matthew were brethren. This is of course possible, but can hardly be called probable.

[2] This is indeed an inference, but one which is accepted by the best commentators to harmonize the "Levi" of the second and third Gospels with the "Matthew" of the first Gospel.

disciples. We may conceive what a joyous banquet that was for Matthew, when for the first time as an eye-witness he marked the words and acts of Jesus, and stored within his memory the scene and the conversation which he was inspired to write according to his clerkly ability for the instruction of the Church in all after ages.

After this Matthew is not once named in the Gospel history, except in the list of the Twelve; in the other Gospels he appears seventh on the list, in his own Gospel eighth—the last in the second division. In his own Gospel again—a further mark of humility—he designates himself as "Matthew the publican." His nearest companion seems to have been Thomas (whose surname Didymus has led to the belief that he was Matthew's twin-brother), and in the same group or division were Philip and Bartholomew. Such are the scanty details which the Gospels record of St Matthew. These few notices however suggest some inferences as to the religious position, character and teaching of the Evangelist.

Since Capernaum was in the tetrarchy of Herod Antipas, it may be inferred that Levi was an officer in the service of that prince, and not in the service of the Roman government, as is sometimes tacitly assumed. This is not unimportant in estimating the call and conversion of St Matthew.

A Hebrew who entirely acquiesced in the Roman supremacy could hardly have done so at this period without abandoning the national hopes. Jesus alone knew the secret of reconciling the highest aspirations of the Jewish race with submission to Cæsar. But to acknowledge the Herodian dynasty was a different thing from bowing to Rome. Herod was at least not a foreigner and a Gentile in the same sense as the Roman. Idumea had coalesced with Israel. It is therefore conceivable that a Jew who was waiting for the Messiah's reign may in very despair have learned to look for the fulfilment of his hopes in the Herodian family. If it was impossible to connect Messianic thoughts with an Antipas, or even with the more reputable Philip, still might not a prince hereafter spring from that house to restore the kingdom to Israel? Might not God in His providence fuse by some means the house and lineage of Herod with the house and lineage of David? It was not impossible, and probably the tyrannical Antipas owed the stability of his throne in some measure to a party among the Jews who cherished these ideas.

No one can read St Matthew's Gospel without perceiving that he was no Hellenist, but a Hebrew of the Hebrews, deeply learned in the history and prophecies of his race, and eagerly looking forward to their realization; but he had been content to find, or at least to expect, that realization in the family of Herod. These views were suited to his nature in two ways. For we may infer first, that he was influenced by what is almost an inherent passion in his race—the love of gain (had it not been so he would never have chosen a career which at its best was despised and odious); secondly, that he loved a life of contemplation and quiet, and was well pleased to separate himself from the fiery enthusiasm and headstrong schemes of the Galileans who surrounded him. Such may have been the hopes to which Levi clung. But when the plan and teaching of Jesus were unfolded to his mind stored with national memories, he instantly recognized the truth and beauty and completeness of that ideal, and gave himself up heart and soul to the cause of the Son of David. For that cause and for the kingdom of God he resigned all his hopes of advancement in Herod's kingdom, his lucrative calling, and the friends he had made.

It may be that Matthew's wealth was not in an absolute sense great, but it was great for the little Galilean town. It was great to him. And if like St Paul he had left a record of his personal religious feelings, he might have related how he counted up all the several items of gain, and found the sum total loss compared with the excellency of the knowledge of Christ Jesus[1].

If we may judge from the silence of the Gospels, the position which Matthew held among his fellow-disciples was a humble one. He was not among the chosen three. No incident connects itself with his name, as with the names of Andrew and Simon, of Philip, of Thomas, or of Bartholomew, of Judas [the brother] of James, of the sons of Zebedee. No one word of his

[1] Phil. iii. 7, 8.

to Christ is recorded. Even when he was called he rose and followed in silence.

We may picture Matthew to ourselves as a silent, unobtrusive, contemplative man, "swift to hear and slow to speak," unobservant of the minutiæ of outward action but with a mind teeming with the associations of his nation and deeply conscious of the momentous drama which was being enacted before him, of which he felt himself called upon to be the chronicler and interpreter to his own people.

No special mention is made of St Matthew in the Acts of the Apostles, or in the Epistles, but some light is thrown upon his after life by fragmentary notices of early Christian writers.

We gather that he remained in Palestine longer than the rest of the Apostles, and that he made his fellow-countrymen familiar with the words and works of Jesus. More will be said below as to the nature and special scope of his teaching; but an interesting point of Christian history, and one that bears upon St Matthew's character, recorded by Eusebius, may be mentioned here. St Matthew, says the historian, being about to depart for distant lands to preach to others also, left as a memorial to his Palestinian converts the story of the New Covenant committed to writing in their own tongue, the Aramaic or Hebrew dialect which they used. This parting gift of the Evangelist was the origin of the written Gospels.

Later authorities have named Æthiopia, Parthia, Egypt and Macedonia, as fields of his missionary work. Clement of Alexandria states that Matthew devoted himself to a strictly ascetic life, abstaining from the use of animal food.

By the most ancient testimony the death of this apostle is attributed to natural causes. The traditions of the Greek Church and the pictures of the Greek artists represent him dying peacefully. But the Western Church has placed Matthew on the list of martyrs, and in the works of Italian painters he is portrayed perishing by the executioner's sword. It is characteristic of this silent, unmarked life, in which the personality of the Evangelist is lost in the voice of the message which he was inspired to utter, that Matthew's name has been less prominent in the Churches and nations of Christendom than others of his co-apostles, or even than many saints, whose services to the Church of Christ have been infinitely less. None of the great Churches of Christendom have been called by his name, no guild or fraternity, no college in our great Universities, no state or nation, has chosen him for a patron. Scarcely one famous picture has taught the lesson of his call. The personal memory, like the personal life of St Matthew, withdraws itself from the observation of men.

CHAPTER II.

AUTHORSHIP, ORIGIN AND CHARACTERISTICS OF THE GOSPEL.

1. The authorship of the first Gospel has been ascribed by an unbroken tradition to the Apostle Matthew.

2. The date is uncertain. Irenæus however states that St Matthew wrote his Gospel when SS. Peter and Paul were founding the Church in Rome: and the fact that it was published first of the written Gospels rests upon early and uncontradicted testimony. The date of publication then should probably be fixed not many years after the Ascension.

3. St Matthew's Gospel was primarily intended for the use of the Jewish converts in Palestine. It is this fact that gives its special character to this Gospel. No other of the evangelists has so completely developed the idea that in Christ the nation lived again, that towards Christ all prophecy moved, that in Him all national aspirations were centred and satisfied. No other inspired writer has pictured so vividly the critical interest of the Messianic days as the meeting-point of the world's past and future.

According to St Matthew Jesus is from first to last Christ the King, the King of whom all the prophets spake in the past, but He is also the one figure round whom the historical interest of the future was destined to gather. Hence the twofold aspect of this Gospel; on the one hand it is the most national and the most retrospective of the Gospels; on the other it is the most universal and the most prophetic; in one sense St Matthew is more gentile than St Luke, in another he is truly a Hebrew of the Hebrews.

The very depth of St Matthew's patriotism impels him to glory in the universality of the Messianic reign. The Kingdom of God *must* over-pass the limits of the Chosen race. Hence it is no matter of surprise that the Hebrew historian should alone commemorate the coming of the Magi and the refuge in Egypt, and that he and not St Luke should tell the story of the Canaanitish woman.

The following points confirm the received account of the origin of this Gospel and indicate its special reference to the Jews.

(1) The numerous quotations from prophecy.

(2) The appeals to history as fulfilled in Christ.

(3) The rare explanation of Jewish words and customs.

(4) The strong and special denunciation of the Jews and of their rulers.

(5) The special reference to the Law in the Sermon on the Mount.

(6) The Genealogy traced from Abraham and David.

(7) The Mission of the Seventy omitted.

(8) The absence of Latin words, with very few exceptions.

(9) The prominence given to the Jewish thought of a Kingdom of Heaven: (*a*) in the general scope of the Gospel; (*b*) in the parables; (*c*) in the account of the Passion.

4. The style of St Matthew's Gospel is sufficiently distinctive in the use of special words and idioms, in constructions and transitional particles[1], to mark it as an original work, though in part derived from sources common to the other Synoptic Gospels. St Matthew has preserved faithfully and sympathetically the poetical beauty of the discourses of Christ; but in the descriptive passages his manner is less vivid and picturesque than St Mark's, more even and unvaried than St Luke's, whose diction is greatly influenced by the various sources whence he derived the details

---

[1] A list of such peculiarities is collected in Smith's *Bib. Dict.*, Vol. II. p. 277.

which he incorporates in his Gospel. Consequently although no passages in St Matthew's Gospel recall the classical ring like the introduction to St Luke's Gospel; on the other hand the Hebrew idiom never so manifestly shews itself in the first Gospel as in the opening chapters of the third.

St Matthew was an eyewitness of the events which he chronicles, yet it is often remarked that his descriptions are less graphic and full of detail than those of St Mark, who wrote what he had heard from the lips of others. This need not be a matter of surprise. It is indeed a phenomenon that meets us every day. It is not the contemporary and the eyewitness, but the historian of a succeeding age who takes the keenest interest in minute detail and records with faithful accuracy the less prominent circumstances of a great event. It is the Herodotus or the Macaulay—the historian, the 'questioner'—who gathers from every source materials for a minute and brilliant picture, rather than the actual spectator who is often too deeply absorbed by the one point of supreme interest in a scene to notice the looks and acts of other bystanders, or so impressed by the speaker's glowing thoughts as to deem them alone worthy of record.

But though St Mark enables us to realize more exactly the external accessories of the various incidents. St Matthew has treasured up for the Church more fully than the other synoptists the words and discourses of Jesus; such especially as present Him in the character of the Great Prophet, who, like the prophets of old time, denounces national sins and predicts the future of the nation and the Church. Instances of this characteristic are the full report of the Sermon on the Mount (ch. v. vi. vii.), the charge to the Apostles ch. x.; the great series of prophetic parables in ch. xiii. peculiar to this Gospel; the denunciation of the Scribes and Pharisees in ch. xxiii., the parables of the Passion ch. xxv., the predictions of the fall of Jerusalem, and of the second Advent, chs. xxiv. and xxv.

5. The ablest critics are agreed that St Matthew does not observe the chronological order of events. By the arrangement followed by this Evangelist, as may be seen by the accompanying analysis of the Gospel, special incidents and sayings are so

grouped together as to illustrate the different aspects of our Lord's life and teaching.

6. The most interesting literary question in connection with this Gospel concerns the language in which it was written. Is the Hellenistic Greek version which we possess, (1) the original Gospel, or (2) a translation from a Hebrew or Aramaic original; further, if a translation by whom was the translation made, by (*a*) St Matthew himself, or (*b*) by some other?

Apart from the antecedent probability of a Hebrew Gospel—a version of the New Covenant to correspond with the Hebrew of the Old Covenant, and to meet the requirements of those Jews who gloried in their knowledge of the Hebrew tongue, and their adhesion to Hebrew customs, who would listen more gladly to the Gospel if it were preached to them in the language of their fathers—direct testimony to the existence of an Aramaic original of St Matthew's Gospel is borne by a succession of the earliest Christian writers.

(1) Papias in the beginning of the second century writes:— '$Ματθαῖος\ μὲν\ οὖν\ \text{Ἑβραΐδι}\ διαλέκτῳ\ τὰ\ λόγια\ συνετάξατο·\ ἡρμήνευσε\ δ'\ αὐτὰ\ ὡς\ ἐδύνατο\ ἕκαστος.$' The best scholars are agreed that by τὰ λόγια the Gospel of St Matthew is meant.

(2) Irenæus says: '$ὁ\ μὲν\ Ματθαῖος\ ἐν\ τοῖς\ \text{Ἑβραίοις}\ τῇ\ ἰδίᾳ\ διαλέκτῳ\ αὐτῶν\ καὶ\ γραφὴν\ ἐξήνεγκεν\ εὐαγγελίου\ τοῦ\ Πέτρου\ καὶ\ τοῦ\ Παύλου\ ἐν\ \text{Ῥώμῃ}\ εὐαγγελιζομένων\ καὶ\ θεμελιούντων\ τὴν\ ἐκκλησίαν.$'

(3) Pantænus, according to Eusebius (*H. E.* v. 10), is said to have gone to preach to the Indians and to have found among them a copy of the Hebrew Gospel according to St Matthew which had been left by the Apostle Bartholomew.

(4) In later times evidence for the belief in a Hebrew original is drawn from the writings of Origen, Eusebius, Jerome, and many others.

Against this testimony in favour of a Hebrew original, arguments tending to an opposite conclusion are grounded on (1) the disappearance of the Hebrew Gospel: (2) the authority which the existing Version has always had in the Church: (3) the similarity of expression to certain portions of the other Gospels: (4) the apparent originality of style.

(1) That no copy of the Hebrew Gospel is extant need not excite surprise. With the destruction of Jerusalem the Hebrew-speaking Christians would be for the most part scattered far and wide over the limits of the Roman Empire. Necessity would impel them to become familiar with the Greek tongue. Their Jewish compatriots in foreign countries would be acquainted with no other. Everywhere the credit of the Greek version of St Matthew's Gospel would be fully established; to that version the original Hebrew edition would soon give place. It seems probable too that copies of this Gospel were purposely altered and mutilated to serve the ends of heretical sects, and thus the genuine Hebrew text would become more and more difficult to obtain, and finally would be discredited and lost to the Church. The preface of St Luke's Gospel suggests the thought that many more or less complete 'Gospels' once extant have disappeared. Moreover, most critics are agreed that the existing Epistles of St Paul do not comprise the whole number which he wrote to the Churches.

The points raised in the second (2) and third (3) arguments are considered below.

(4) The question of originality cannot be decisively settled by an appeal to the Greek style. There are, however, some characteristics that seem to indicate a translation, or rather, perhaps, a Greek edition of the Gospel by St Matthew himself or some other author of Apostolic authority. Such an inference would fall in with the tradition of the 'Hebrew Gospel,' and of St Matthew's preaching in other countries beyond the limits of Palestine. The style is uniform, and almost monotonous. Hebraisms are regularly and evenly distributed, not as in St Luke, prominent in some parts and altogether absent in others; and the number of actual Hebrew words is inconsiderable.

In citations from the Old Testament a distinction can be observed. When the narrative is closely parallel with the other Synoptic Gospels, the quotations are also parallel following generally the text of the LXX., but presenting the same variations from that text which appear in the other Synoptic Gospels. But in those portions of this Gospel which are independent of the others, the quotations approach more nearly to the Hebrew text.

Taking these features of the Gospel into account, we remark: 1. While they are not consistent with a literal translation of an Aramaic original, such as would have been produced by a scribe who wished to give an exact transcript of the idioms and even the words of his author: 2. They are consistent with a free rendering by the Evangelist versed in both tongues. 3. If the Gospel had been presented in a Greek form to the Hebrews of Palestine we should have expected citations from the Hebrew Bible throughout, and freer use of Aramaic diction. 4. On the other hand, Hebrew thought combined with freedom from literal Aramaic form is precisely what we should expect to find in a Hellenistic edition of an Aramaic original.

The following theory is advanced as a natural way of satisfying the traditional statements and the notes of style. St Matthew, in accordance with the patristic citations (p. **xx.**), composed in the first instance an Aramaic Gospel for the use of the Hebrew Christians in Palestine, to whom such a Gospel, and perhaps such only, would be fully acceptable. But on the disruption of the Jewish polity Aramaic would cease to be intelligible to many, and the demand would come for a Greek version of the Gospel according to St Matthew. How would this demand be met? Either St Matthew himself, or else some faithful scribe, would use the Hebrew Gospel as the basis of a Greek version. Many of the familiar parables and sayings of Jesus, which were orally afloat in all the Churches, he would (for the sake of old association) incorporate with little alteration, but he would preserve throughout the plan of the original, and, in passages where the special teaching of this Gospel came in, the version would be a close rendering of the Aramaic. This theory explains the verbal coincidence of some parts of St Matthew's Gospel with the parallel Synoptic passages, and accounts for the facts in regard to the quotations stated above.

Such a version, especially if made by St Matthew himself, would indeed be rather an original work than a translation, and would speedily in either case acquire the authority of the original Aramaic. Accordingly we find that even those writers who speak of the Hebrew Gospel themselves quote from the Greek version as authoritative[1].

Note I.

(A) *Miracles*, (B) *Parables*, (C) *Discourses*, (D) *Incidents peculiar to this Gospel.*

(A) *Miracles.*
  (1) Cure of two blind men......................ix. 27—31.
  (2) The stater in the fish's mouth ....xvii. 24—27.

(B) *Parables.*
  (1) The tares ....xiii. 24—30.
  (2) The hid treasure ....xiii. 44.
  (3) The pearl of great price ....xiii. 45, 46.
  (4) The draw-net....................................xiii. 47—50.
  (5) The unmerciful servant ....xviii. 23—35.
  (6) The labourers in the vineyard ....xx. 1—16.
  (7) The two sons....................................xxi. 28—32.
  (8) Marriage of the king's son ....xxii. 1—14.
  (9) The ten virgins.................................xxv. 1—13.
  (10) The talents ....xxv. 14—30.

(C) *Discourses.*
  (1) A large part of the sermon on the Mount.
  (2) Invitation to the heavy laden...............xi. 28—30.
  (3) Idle words......................................xii. 36, 37.
  (4) The blessing pronounced on Peter ......xvi. 17—19.
  (5) The greater part of ch. xviii. on humility and forgiveness.
  (6) The rejection of the Jews ....xxi. 43.
  (7) The denunciation of the Scribes and Pharisees as a connected discourse ...xxiii.
  (8) The description of the judgment ....xxv. 31—46.
  (9) The last commission and promise.........xxviii. 18—20.

---

[1] The further question as to the identity of the Aramaic Gospel of St Matthew and the 'Gospel according to the Hebrews' mentioned by several of the Fathers need not be argued here. It is really a distinct question. It may be well, however, to state that the fragments of the 'Gospel according to the Hebrews' which have been preserved, give ample evidence against identifying the 'Gospel according to the Hebrews' with the existing Gospel of St Matthew, and therefore with the Aramaic original of that Gospel, if such existed.

(D) *Incidents*.
- (1) The whole of ch. ii.
  - (α) The coming of the Magi, guided by the star in the east.
  - (β) The massacre of the innocents.
  - (γ) The flight into Egypt.
  - (δ) The return to Nazareth.
- (2) The coming of the Pharisees and Sadducees to John's baptism......iii. 7.
- (3) Peter's attempt to walk upon the water..xiv. 28—31.
- (4) Payment of the Temple Tax......xvii. 24—27.
- (5) In connection with the Passion:
  - (α) The covenant of Judas for thirty pieces of silver; his repentance, and his end ......xxvi. 14—16; xxvii. 3—10.
  - (β) The dream of Pilate's wife......xxvii. 19.
  - (γ) The appearance of Saints in Jerusalem......xxvii. 52.
- (6) In connection with the Resurrection:
  - (α) The watch placed at the sepulchre ..xxvii. 62—66.
  - (β) The soldiers bribed to spread a false report ......xxviii. 11—15.
  - (γ) The earthquake......xxviii. 2.

CHAPTER III.

ANALYSIS OF THE GOSPEL.

PART I.

The Birth and Childhood of the King :—i.—ii. 23.

- (1) The lineage of Jesus Christ ......i. 1—17.
- (2) His birth ......i. 18—25.
- (3) The visit of the Magi ......ii. 1—12.
- (4) The flight into Egypt and the return.....ii. 13—23.

According to St Matthew's plan Jesus Christ is represented as (α) the King; (β) descended from David; (γ) who fulfils the words of prophecy; (δ) whose Kingdom is recognized by the Gentiles; (ε) who is the representative of His nation, and fulfils their history.

PART II.

The beginning of the Kingdom :—iii.—iv. 11.

(1) The forerunner of the Kingdom .... iii. 1—12.
(2) The baptism of Jesus .... iii. 13—17.
(3) The Temptation .... iv. 1—11.

This part corresponds to the opening verses of St Mark's Gospel; it contains the announcement and victory of the King, and His entrance upon His reign; the true kingdom of God is opposed to the false conception of the Kingdom.

PART III.

The Works and Signs of the Kingdom of God :—iv. 12—xvi. 12.

Section (i). At Capernaum .... iv.—viii. 17.
(α) Preaching of repentance (*Metanoia*)....... iv. 17.
(β) Call of four disciples .... iv. 18—22.
(γ) Various diseases are cured................. iv. 23—25.
(δ) The sermon on the mount .... v., vi., vii.
(ε) Cleansing of a leper....................... viii. 1—4.
(ζ) Cure of the centurion's servant .... viii. 5—13.
(η) Cure of Peter's wife's mother............. viii. 14—17.

The preparation for the Kingdom is amendment of life, a changed heart. It is a kingdom of love shewn by deeds of mercy. The Law of the Kingdom is the highest fulfilment of the old Law.

Section (ii). Jesus crosses the Lake............... viii. 18—34.
(α) Fitness for discipleship .... viii. 18—22.
(β) The winds and the sea obey Him......... viii. 23—27.
(γ) The Gergesene demoniacs .... viii. 28—34.

Jesus shews that self-denial is essential to His subjects; He exhibits His power over nature, and over the spiritual world.

Section (iii). Return to Capernaum.............. ix.—xiii. 52.
(α) Cure of a paralytic .... ix. 1—8.
(β) Call of Levi .... ix. 9.
(γ) Feast in Levi's house. Jesus the friend
    of sinners .... ix. 10—13.
(δ) Fasting .... ix. 14—17.
(ε) The daughter of Jairus.—The woman
    with an issue................................ ix. 18—26.
(ζ) Two blind men cured .... ix. 27—31.
(η) The dumb demoniac .... ix. 32—34.

(θ)	The good works of Christ	ix. 35.
(ι)	The labourers are few	ix. 36—38.
(κ)	The choice and mission of the Twelve	x.
(λ)	John the Baptist—his message to Jesus —his position as a prophet	xi. 1—19.
(μ)	The unrepentant cities—The yoke of Christ	xi. 20—30.
(ν)	The observance of the Sabbath	xii. 1—13.
(ξ)	Plot of the Pharisees—Retirement of Jesus	xii. 14—21.
(ο)	Cure of the blind and dumb man— Blasphemy of the Pharisees	xii. 22—37.
(π)	Rebuke to those who ask for a sign	xii. 38—45.
(ρ)	The kinsfolk of Jesus	xii. 46—50.
(σ)	Teaching by parables	xiii. 1—52.

In these Chapters the teaching of the Kingdom is further developed in its relation (1) to John, as the greatest of the Prophets before the Kingdom; (2) to the religious system of the Pharisees. The Church of Christ is founded by the call of His disciples. Its future is foreshewn in the charge to the Twelve, and in the Parables of ch. xiii.

Section (iv). At Nazareth.
  His own receive Him not .... xiii. 53—58.
Section (v). In different parts of Galilee .... xiv.—xvi. 12.

(α)	Herod, who has slain John, asks concerning Christ	xiv. 1—12.
(β)	Jesus retires	xiv. 13, 14.
(γ)	The feeding of Five Thousand	xiv. 15—21.
(δ)	The passage to Gennesaret—Jesus walks on the sea	xiv. 22—36.
(ε)	The tradition of the elders—Hypocrisy	xv. 1—20.
(ζ)	The Canaanite woman	xv. 21—28.
(η)	Cure of many sick	xv. 29—31.
(θ)	The feeding of Four Thousand	xv. 32—38.
(ι)	A sign refused	xvi. 4.
(κ)	The leaven of the Pharisees	xvi. 5—12.

Here the Kingdom of God is brought into contrast with (1) the kingdom of Herod—a point of special interest to Matthew; and (2) with legal righteousness. Jesus indicates the extension of His Church to the Gentiles. He manifests His creative power.

INTRODUCTION.

PART IV.

The Predictions of the Passion :—xvi. 13—xx. 34.

Section (i). Near Cæsarea Philippi ....xvi. 13—28.
  (a) Peter's acknowledgment of the Son of
     God—The first prediction ....xvi. 13—20.
  (β) Peter rebuked—The true subjects of the
     King ....xvi. 21—28.

The Confession of St Peter is the central point of interest in the education of the disciples. The importance of the crisis is shewn by the expression *'from that time'* (xvi. 21). Possessing this truth the disciples may learn the other truth—the sufferings of the Son of Man. Each prediction presents the same contrast—a lesson of glory, and a lesson of humiliation.

Section (ii). The second prediction of the
    Passion ....xvii. 1—xviii. 35.
  (a) The Transfiguration ....xvii. 1—13.
  (β) Cure of the lunatic boy ....xvii. 14—21.
  (γ) The prediction ....xvii. 22, 23.
  (δ) The Temple Tax ....xvii. 24—27.
  (ε) Contention for greatness..............xviii. 1—6.
  (ς) Offences and forgiveness..............xviii. 7—35.

A glimpse of the glorified Kingdom of God contrasted with the misery of earth. All that follows the prediction shews the inability of the disciples to understand as yet the truth about the Kingdom.

Section (iii). The third prediction of the Passion...xix—xx. 34.
  (a) Journey through Peræa ....xix. 1, 2.
  (β) Question of divorce ....xix. 3—12.
  (γ) Children brought to Christ ....xix. 13—15.
  (δ) The rich young ruler ....xix. 16—22.
  (ε) Riches—Rewards of Christ's followers...xix. 23—30.
  (ς) Parable of the labourers in the vineyard...xx. 1—16.
  (η) The prediction ....xx. 17—19.
  (θ) The petition of Salome for her sons......xx. 20—28.
  (ι) Two blind men are cured..............xx. 29—34.

Compare the exactness of detail in this third Prediction with the less definite first and second Predictions.

The social life of the subjects of the King—marriage and the use of riches—must be moulded to the laws of the Kingdom. There are great rewards in store for Christ's faithful followers.

Part V.

The Triumph of the King:—xxi.—xxv.

Sunday and Monday, Nisan 9 and 10.

(α) The King enters the Holy City in triumph .... xxi. 1—11.
(β) The cleansing of the Temple .... xxi. 12—14.
(γ) The children's praise .... xxi. 15, 16.
(δ) Bethany—The cursing of the fig-tree..... xxi. 17—22.
(ε) The victories of the King .... xxi. 23—xxiii.
   (1) Over the Sanhedrin—The parables of the Two Sons, the Vineyard, and the Marriage Feast............ xxi. 23—xxii. 14.
   (2) Over the Pharisees—The tribute money .... xxii. 15—22.
   (3) Over the Sadducees—The Resurrection.. xxii. 23—33.
   (4) Over a certain lawyer—the greatest commandment .... xxii. 34—40.
   (5) By a counter-question — David's Son... xxii. 41—46.
   (6) Rebuke of the Pharisees .... xxiii.
(ζ) Discourse concerning the fall of Jerusalem and the end of the world—Type and antitype .... xxiv.

Here Jesus is set forth (1) as the King who triumphs; (2) as victorious over all adversaries; (3) as the Prophet who must perish in Jerusalem.

Part VI.

The Passion:—xxvi. xxvii.

Wednesday, Nisan 12—Friday, Nisan 14.

(α) A fourth prediction of the Passion ...... xxvi. 1, 2.
(β) A meeting of the Sanhedrin .... xxvi. 3—5.
(γ) The feast in Simon's house—Judas agrees to betray Jesus .... xxvi. 6—16.
(δ) The Last Supper .... xxvi. 17—30.
(ε) All shall be offended....................... xxvi. 31—35.
(ζ) The agony in the garden of Gethsemane.. xxvi. 36—46.
(η) The arrest of Jesus .... xxvi. 47—56.
(θ) The trial before Caiaphas .... xxvi. 57—68.
(ι) The denial of Peter .... xxvi. 69—72.
(κ) The formal trial before the Sanhedrin... xxvii. 1.

(λ) The remorse of Judas — The Roman trial...xxvii. 2—26.
(μ) The mockery by Roman soldiers ....xxvii. 27—30.
(ν) The crucifixion and death of Jesus .....xxvii. 31—56.
(ξ) The entombment..............................xxvii. 57—66.

The Triumph of the King is followed by the Humiliation, true to the Predictions of Jesus. "He humbled Himself even unto the death upon the Cross."

PART VII.

The Resurrection :— xxviii.

(α) The empty sepulchre ....xxviii. 1—8.
(β) The appearance of the Lord to the women..xxviii. 9, 10.
(γ) The soldiers bribed to silence..............xxviii. 11—15.
(δ) Jesus in Galilee................................xxviii. 16, 17.
(ε) The last commission ....xxviii. 18—20.

The Gospel of the Kingdom ends fittingly with the victory over death; with the declaration by the Lord Jesus of His universal power, and His commission to the disciples to teach all nations.

CHAPTER IV.

EXTERNAL HISTORY DURING THE LIFE AND MINISTRY OF JESUS CHRIST.

1. *Summary.*

B.C. 3. (see note ch. ii. 1) Octavianus Augustus had been sole ruler of the Roman Empire from B.C. 30.
Twice during that period the temple of Janus had been closed in sign of peace.

B.C. 1. Death of Herod. Rising of the Jews against the Procurator Sabinus. Repression of the revolt by Varus: 2000 Jews crucified.

A.D. 6. Resistance to the Census of Quirinus by Judas the Gaulonite and his Galilæan followers.

A.D.	7.	Banishment of Archelaus.
	1—12.	Campaigns against the Germans, Pannonians, and Dalmatians, conducted by Tiberius and Germanicus. The disastrous defeat of Varus in Germany. Final success and triumph of the Roman Generals.
	14.	Death of Augustus and succession of Tiberius.
	15—17.	Germanicus continues the war against the Germans, and triumphs.
	18.	Death of Ovid and of Livy.
	19.	Death of Germanicus. Jews banished from Italy.
	20—31.	Hateful tyranny of Tiberius. Ascendancy of Sejanus. Fall of Sejanus A.D. 30.
	26.	Pontius Pilate appointed as the sixth Procurator of Judæa.

2. *The Imperial Rule.*

It will be seen from this summary, that while Jesus was passing a quiet childhood in the Galilæan valley, few startling events disturbed the peace of the world. But it was an epoch of the greatest historical interest. It was a crisis in the kingdoms of the world as well as in the Kingdom of God. Rome had completed her conquests—no formidable rival was left to threaten her power in any direction. But the moment when the Roman people secured the empire of the world, they resigned their own liberties into the hands of a single master.

Cæsar Octavianus, afterwards named Augustus, the successor of the great Julius Cæsar, was the first to consolidate this enormous individual power; it was he who bequeathed to the world the proudest titles of despotic rule—Emperor—Kaiser—Czar. With him the true nature of the monarchy was veiled over by the retention of Republican forms, and by a nominal re-election at intervals. The justice and clemency of his rule kept out of sight the worst abuses of unlimited power. And partly owing to the fact that the most brilliant age of Roman literature coincided with the reign of Augustus, his name is associated rather with literary culture and refinement, than with despotic sway.

When Jesus grew up to manhood, the grace and culture and

the semblance of liberty which had gilded the despotism of Augustus vanished under the dark influence of the morose and cruel Tiberius. If ever men suffered from hopeless tyranny and wrong, it was in this reign. It is a miserable history of lives surrounded by suspicion and fear, and of the best and purest citizens yielding to despair or removed by secret assassination.

It can perhaps be scarcely a matter of surprise, that a Jewish patriot, alive to the horrors of this despotism and recalling the prophetic images of a triumphant Messiah, should sometimes have dreamed that the Kingdom of God would be manifested by the overthrow of this monstrous evil, and in turn establish itself as an external power stronger and more resistless than Rome. It is this thought that gives point to the third temptation presented to our Lord. (ch. iv. 8, 9.)

3. *The Provincial System.*

A glance at the Provincial system of Rome with especial reference to Palestine will shew how truly, in an external sense, Christ came in the fulness of time.

Under the Empire the condition of the provinces was happier than formerly. The rapacity of individual governors was checked by the imperial supervision. Moreover, great consideration was in many cases shewn to a conquered people. National customs were allowed to continue; even native princes were in several instances confirmed in their rule on condition of becoming tributary to Rome.

In accordance with this principle, the Herodian dynasty was tolerated in Palestine. Observe how the changes in that dynasty affected the life of Christ. When Jesus was born, Herod was reigning in Jerusalem; hence the events that led to the flight into Egypt. On the return of Jesus with Mary and Joseph, the kingdom was divided; hence the possibility of taking refuge from the cruelty of an Archelaus under the more tolerant Antipas in the home at Nazareth. The banishment of Archelaus a few years afterwards brought about the establishment in Judæa of the Roman government, which with its accustomed liberality left the national system represented by the Sanhedrin, not wholly unimpaired, indeed, but still influential.

Important consequences followed this precise political position. The Jewish nation was still responsible. It was Israel and not Rome that rejected the Messiah—Israel that condemned to death the Lord of Life. But it was Rome that executed the will of the Jewish people. Jesus suffered, by the law of Rome, death on the Roman cross, with all its significance, its agreement with prophecy, and its divine fitness. The point to be observed is that under no other political conditions could this event have taken place in that precise manner, which was wholly in accordance with the Scriptures that foretell the Messiah.

4. *A time of Peace.*

The lull of peace that pervaded the Roman world, was another element in the external preparation for the advent of Christ. In the generation which preceded and in that which followed the life of Christ on earth, Palestine, and indeed the whole empire, was disquieted by the greatest political confusion. In the generation before the Christian Era, Antony and Augustus were contending for the mastery of the world, and a disputed succession disturbed the peace of Palestine. The succeeding generation was filled with the horrors of the Jewish war, of which Galilee was the focus, and which culminated in the fall of Jerusalem. It is clear that the conditions of Christ's ministry could not have been fulfilled in either of these conjunctures.

5. *The various nationalities in Palestine.*

A further point of interest at the particular period when Jesus lived on earth, is the variety of nationalities which the special circumstances of the time brought together in Palestine.

A political epoch that found a Roman governor in the south (where the native ecclesiastical rule still prevailed), Idumean kings in the north and east, wild mountain and desert tribes pressing on the frontiers in one direction, peaceful Phœnicians in another, involved a mixture and gathering of populations which made Palestine an epitome of the whole world. The variety of life and thought, which must have resulted from these different social elements, is one of those external circumstances which have rendered the Gospel so fit to instruct every age and every condition of men.

6. *The religious condition of the Empire.*

The wider and more interesting question of the religious state of the world at this epoch, cannot be fully discussed here. In Greece and in Rome, the most civilized portions of the earth, Religion allowed, or at least was ineffectual to prevent, a state of morality which St Paul describes with terrible plainness in the first chapter of his Epistle to the Romans. Gross immorality entered even into the ritual of worship; Religion raised no voice against the butchery of gladiatorial shows, or against infanticide, or slavery, or suicide, or even against the horrors of human sacrifice.

Little real belief in the gods and goddesses remained; and though ancient superstitions still lingered among the vulgar, and interested motives on the part of priests and communities kept alive the cult of special deities, and supported shrines and temples in various parts of the world, and though, credulity gaining ground as true religious feeling passed away, the mysterious rites of Egypt and the East, the worship of Isis and of Mithras, flourished at Rome in spite of repressive edicts—all this was external and unreal, a thin cover for deep-seated and widespread scepticism.

Philosophy did but little to fill the void. Stoicism, the favourite creed with the practical Roman, though apparently nearest to Christianity in some respects, was deeply opposed to the Christian spirit by its pride, its self-sufficiency, its exclusiveness, its exaltation of human nature, its lack of love, its approval of suicide. Epicurism had degenerated from a high ideal to a mere pursuit of sensual pleasure.

It was in the midst of a world thus corrupt to the core, that the beautiful and novel conception rose of a religion which, recognizing no limits of race or language, should without distinction draw all men to itself by its appeal to the sin-stricken conscience, and by the satisfaction it brought to the deepest needs of humanity.

xxxiv *INTRODUCTION.*

Note II.

A GENEALOGICAL TABLE OF THE HERODIAN FAMILY, INCLUDING THOSE MEMBERS OF IT WHO ARE MENTIONED IN THE GOSPEL ACCORDING TO ST MATTHEW.

Herod the king (ch. ii. 1, 16, 19) married ten wives, among whom were:

1. Mariamne, grand-daughter of Hyrcanus and so connected with the Maccabees.

2. Mariamne, d. of Simon a high-priest.

3. Malthakè, a Samaritan.

4. Cleopatra of Jerusalem.

Aristobulus.
Herodias.
ch. xiv. 3—11.

Herod *Philip* I. = *Herodias.*
ch. xiv. 3 | ch. xiv. 3—11.
Salome.
ch. xiv. 6—11.

Archelaus.
ch. ii. 22.

Antipas = 1. d. of Aretas.
       = 2. *Herodias.*
            ch. xiv. 3.

Herod *Philip* II. = *Salome.*
the Tetrarch. ch. xiv. 6—11.
ch. xvi. 13.
Luke iii. 1.

CHAPTER V.

THE LITERARY FORM AND LANGUAGE OF THE GOSPEL.

1. Hellenistic Greek.

The Alexandrian Greek dialect or Hellenistic Greek in which the N.T. is written was a result of the Macedonian conquests which swept away the ancient barriers of many forms of Greek speech. The mingled fragments of diverse elements gradually took shape in the κοινὴ διάλεκτος or the New Macedonian dialect as distinguished from the old Doric Macedonian. This in turn gathered to itself fresh forms and peculiarities in the various communities which adopted it, and thus separated off into distinct dialects.

One of these offshoots growing up in the newly founded city of Alexandria with characteristics of its own in tense-forms in vocabulary and in construction became the language of those Jews who gathered in Alexandria in large numbers, partly attracted by the privileges granted them by its founder, partly driven to take refuge there from the cruelties of the Seleucidæ. It is probable that with these settlers Hebrew soon ceased to be the language of daily life. Constant intercourse with the Greek-speaking population that surrounded them would necessitate the use of a common language. To this fact the LXX. itself bears witness. That version was made at various periods not, as is sometimes said, to satisfy the curiosity of a Ptolemy, but to meet the religious necessities of the Jew. Thus from the first the Alexandrian dialect became strongly tinged by an infusion of Hebrew words and phraseology. The LXX. version stereotyped those new elements, and gave to the Greek of Alexandria a deep impress of Oriental idiom. This dialect thus dignified and consolidated by a great literary work was carried to all parts of the world by the Hellenist or Greek-speaking Jew.

At this stage Hellenistic Greek, as contrasted with Attic Greek, was distinguished by a simplicity of idioms and of syntax, by a restriction in the use of connecting particles, by less discrimination in the force of prepositions, by a growing disuse of the middle voice, and of the optative mood, by a preference for formulæ which, though rare in Greek, are common to that language and the Hebrew, by certain peculiar tense-forms, and by an increased employment of analytic tenses. The vocabulary was enriched by words unknown to the fastidious Attic of the literary style. 1. Vernacular words, which though long on the people's lips, now, for the first time, appear in literature; just as the vernacular Latin of Gaul rose to be the most polished European speech. 2. Words of ancient literature, Epic or Lyric, which had not held their own in Attic prose writers, emerging once more into the light of culture. 3. Words with a strong or a coarse meaning in classical days now weakened into the expression of gentler or more refined thoughts. 4. Outlandish words which could not have been in use when Marathon was fought—Macedonian—Persian—Egyptian—Hebrew, and later still, Latin.

When Hellenistic Greek became the language of the N.T. its vocabulary was further modified, partly by the rejection of words too deeply steeped in heathen vice or in false religious thought, partly by the addition of higher and holier ideas to the words which Christianity selected. In three ways at least such a tongue was admirably suited to the work of evangelizing the world. 1. It was universally recognized and understood. 2. It was the language of the common people, not of a refined and exclusive caste. 3. The very loss of the old subtlety has been a gain to it as the channel of religious ideas.

Thus, though the language has lost some of its charms for the scholar, and though it has ceased to give, as once it did, the most perfect expression to human conceptions, yet it has been the chosen instrument through which the thoughts have been conveyed, which, far beyond any other thoughts, have moved and influenced the world.

And it has a wonderful interest of its own. For the scholar

it is the stepping-stone between Classical and Modern Greek. To the theologian it is the starting-point of sacred terminology. Each is concerned to detect the exact force of a word, the drift and associations of every phrase. The variety in the word-history of the New Testament, the diverse fortunes and lives, so to speak, of Hellenistic terms make the search interesting and the solution difficult. Some words are purely Hellenistic, they begin and die with that stage of the language; others lived on to the present day and are still in the mouths of the Athenian citizens and Bœotian peasants, expressing daily wants and simple thoughts. Some existing obscurely for long, disclaimed by Attic culture, are now lifted to a diviner height than if Plato had employed them. Others, though known to the purest classical diction, out of an ancient variety and wide range of thought, survive in a single meaning. Some seem to have been kept especially sacred and intact from heathen association as by a particular providence to enshrine the pure conceptions of Christianity. Others, teeming with Pagan thought, have come to Christ to be purified, or to lay at His feet the riches of the Gentiles—the high and inspiring ideas which had been given to men who 'felt after' God in the dark heathen days.

2. The Poetical Element in this Gospel.

There are many *a priori* reasons which make it improbable that the poetry of the Bible would close with the canon of the O.T. It was not to be expected that the epoch which fulfilled the hopes expressed and vivified in successive ages by inspired odes of surpassing beauty should present the realization of them in a form less excellently perfect. Nor indeed was it to be expected that the greatest of Hebrew prophets should alone refrain from clothing His divine message in the glowing phrases, or in the exact and beautiful forms of Hebrew poetry. We should expect that in Him, who spake as never man spake, consummate excellence of thought and speech should be cast in the most perfect mould of human art.

Investigation shews that it is so. Poetry as real, as exquisite in art and feeling, as inventive and varied in device, as full of fancy and of pathos and delicate turns of expression, is to be found in the New as in the Old Testament. Indeed it is an interesting question how much of the literary charm of many parts of the N.T. is due to the latent influence of poetical form.

It is of course possible that much has been lost through translation from the Aramaic into Greek. If our knowledge of Hebrew poetry had come through the LXX. alone many a delicate turn and point of the poetical original would have been lost to view. But as St Matthew has rendered the passages cited from the Hebrew Scriptures more faithfully than the LXX., and with a truer sense of poetic beauty, it may be inferred that our Saviour's Aramaic speech has lost little by its transference to another language.

Here a question of great interest may present itself. How far, it may be asked, is this form due to the Evangelist? How far is it an exact transcript of the Saviour's words? The point might be argued at length, but the decision could scarcely fail to be that in the poetical discourses and sayings recorded by St Matthew we have not only the subject-matter of Christ's teaching, but the very manner in which the sacred truths were delivered.

At the same time it is manifest that St Matthew is the most appreciative among the Evangelists of the form of the Saviour's teaching. He is the Hebrew prophet of the N.T. His writings are λόγια—the prophetic oracles of God. If to any the gift of poetical expression were granted in those days surely it was granted to him, if to any the kindred soul to catch and retain the accents of poetry falling from the Master's lips surely to him.

One argument for the existence of the poetical element in the Gospel might be found in the *a priori* probability that Christ would deliver His laws in a form which would lend itself easily to the memory of His disciples; and in the observed fact that wherever the discourse rises to matters of the highest consideration—wherever maxims are delivered essential to the Christian life, in one or other of its many forms the element of poetry is discernible. Instances of this are:—the rule of devotion and of childlike humility (x. 37—42)—the new social laws in the Christian Commonwealth (xx. 25—28)—the sentence on the Last Day (xxv. 35—46).

If this decision be established its bearing on another subject of deep and mysterious import will at once suggest itself—the education of Jesus. We find Him, who is the end of all prophecy, not only trained or training Himself in the thoughts and aspirations of Hebrew prophecy, but growing familiar with the form in which it was couched—and here it may be noted that next to the words of Christ the most poetical expression in the N.T. is to be found in the epistle of James, the Lord's brother. The divine breath of Hebrew poetry lingered as an inheritance in the home of the Son of David.

Such are some of the inferences and underlying questions that indicate the interest of the subject.

Some remarks may now be made, (1) on the principles and mode of Hebrew poetry, (2) on its special laws.

(1) Hebrew poetry is not like classical poetry, Greek or Latin, or like modern European poetry, in having a fixed metre or measurement of words and a rhythm subject to strict laws, though it does possess a rhythmic structure. The chief characteristic of Hebrew poetry is parallelism—the correspondence of one clause to another, sometimes by way of antithesis, sometimes by way of gradation and climax. The response is sometimes effected in a very complicated and artistic way, sometimes in the simplest possible manner.

This system has the charm of greater variety than English rhyming poetry, more freedom and less danger of straining the sense to suit the rhyme. The ear is caught with the first line and eagerly listens for the response—one of sense and not of sound—perhaps the second, third and even fourth line keep up the suspense and tension, and the answering refrain falls line after line in perfect correspondence, often with a delicate difference of word or structure to give a fresh delight, or to draw attention to a special point. The restraining element in Hebrew poetry then does not consist in the exigency of rhyme or metre but the need of an antithetical expression—possibly one cause of ἅπαξ λεγόμενα and of new words.

(2) The special laws of Hebrew poetry. (The following remarks are founded to a great extent on the works of Bishop Lowth, who was the first English theologian to explain and apply the principles of Hebrew poetry in the interpretation of the O. T., and of Bishop Jebb, who extended the application of them to the N. T.)

Parallelisms are of three kinds. (a) *Synonymous*, or better *cognate*, where the second line or couplet or stanza answers to the first in expression or in structure, or in both, but enhances the effect of it by adding a further and deeper meaning. (β) *Antithetic*, where two propositions are contrasted with greater or less exactness. Sometimes they answer to one another, word for word, construction for construction; sometimes the opposition is only in general sense. (γ) *Constructive*, when the likeness or opposition does not turn upon the sense or meaning of the propositions, but consists in a balance and likeness of structure, word answering to word in the several lines.

Each of these classes of parallelisms admits of many variations. Sometimes the lines answer to each other alternately; sometimes there is a double parallelism; lines 1 and 3 and 2 and 4 answering to each other, as well as 1 and 2 and 3 and 4. Sometimes again a quatrain is so constructed that, besides the obvious way of reading the stanza lines 1 and 3 and 2 and 4, or 1 and 4 and 2 and 3, can be read continuously. A simple instance of this is ch. vii. 6, where the connection might be shewn by placing the fourth line second and reading thus:

> Give not that which is holy unto the dogs,
> Lest they turn again and rend you:
> Neither cast ye your pearls before swine,
> Lest they trample them under their feet.

This artifice is sometimes extended to stanzas of 8 lines.

Apart from this careful regard to form in Hebrew poetry great use is made of the climax. Of this many examples occur in this Gospel. It is at this point that it becomes difficult to draw the line with precision between rhetorical prose and poetry. There are passages of Cicero, for instance, where the balance of contrasted periods and the structure of the climax are so perfect and symmetrical that it would scarcely be possible to form a definition of Hebrew poetry which would exclude such passages as these. The distinction however between rhetoric and poetry is often one of feeling rather than of definition. Many of the ornaments of style and diction are common to both, and the difference consists not in the exclusive possession of these but in the use made of them.

Imagery and figurative language are characteristic of all poetry, but of Hebrew poetry they are eminently characteristic. Nature and all the objects of nature, the skies and the luminaries of heaven—man, his works and aims and several employments—his schemes and ambitions—the different social conditions—the various forms of government all enrich and exemplify the thoughts of Hebrew Christian poetry. This richness of imagery has even been a source of danger. It has given brightness and life to the expression of ideas, but it has led into error through tropes and figures familiar to an Oriental mind finding too literal an interpretation in the West.

The value of parallelism in exegesis.

It is clear that when a close relation of parallelism is established between two clauses they mutually elucidate one another. The effect of a seemingly slight change is deepened by the involuntary comparison. The absence or the presence of a corresponding word, which would otherwise pass unnoticed, throws into prominence the thought suppressed or added. A clause obscure from its position is made clear by referring it to the words with which the system of parallelism shews it to be really connected.

Contrasted ideas briefly expressed at the beginning or the end of a discourse will often prove the key to the right understanding of the whole. Again, this system has the power of throwing special words into prominence by placing corresponding emphatic terms first and last in their respective clauses, the less important expressions between. The meaning of such relative positions cannot be ignored by the interpreter of Scripture.

Comp. in illustration of these remarks, notes on ii. 18, v. 17—20, vii. 6, 7, 8, x. 34—39, 40—42, xii. 31, xix. 12, xx. 25, xxi. 5, xxv. 31—46.

3. The Literary Interpretation of the Gospels.

Two great questions must present themselves to every reader of the Gospels. (1) What did the words mean to those who first heard them? (2) What do they mean to us?

In one sense we dare not persuade ourselves that we know, or ever shall know, the exact import of all the expressions in the N.T. The gesture or the look that accompanied the speech, the tone in which it was said, the memories it stirred, its associations, depend on such very slight and delicate threads that we may not hope to have preserved intact and complete the whole thought that flashed on the souls of the men to whom Jesus spoke. To realize this it is only necessary to remember how a line half quoted, even a single passing phrase, recalls a whole poem, a chain of reasoning, a school of politics or theology, and the more familiar the conception the shorter the quotation needed to awaken it.

Some light of meaning must have vanished in this way, more still perhaps in the loss of the original words of Jesus. Few remember that, except here and there a word, the thoughts of Jesus have not reached us in the language in which (according to the most reasonable view) He first expressed them.

In part the New Testament is a translation of Aramaic speech, in part it is a transcript of Aramaic thought. Every word must be weighed with those considerations in view. The scholar must not be tempted to press the classical force too much in exegesis. So far as the moment of utterance is concerned only so much of the Greek thought should be taken into account as is covered by the meaning of the Hebrew or Aramaic word which it represents. Certainly other meanings soon flowed in upon the words of the Gospel, but such meanings would not be present to the minds of those who first listened to the preaching of Christ.

But this is only the first step. The word uttered by Christ meant more than the first group of listeners could fathom. The thought of the Cross—the sayings of the Last Supper—the Sacrifice of Christ—the baptism of fire—the gift of the Paraclete—the growth of the Kingdom,—all these conceptions and many more have received the interpretation of time, and we believe of the Holy Spirit moving through history. It is thus a part of the interpreter's task reverently in this light to search for the meaning of Christ and of His evangelists.

Here the work of interpretation might seem to have found a limit. But there are further steps. The interpreter of a classical work is concerned to discover the precise meaning of the text as it conveyed itself to the contemporaries of his author. The commentator on the N.T. must look on to mark the effect of the sacred words in successive epochs and in differing civilisations. The same discharge from the sky is snow when it touches the mountain-tops and rain when it reaches the warmer lowland, and there too it is coloured by the ground on which it falls. In like manner Scripture changes form and colour in different ages and in different hearts. Such changes must be noted in order that the abiding essence may remain. The stains of controversy, of passion and of ignorance must be removed and the native brightness of the gem restored to its original setting.

Again, because false interpretation has had enormous influence on history and religion, the commentator must take note even of false interpretation. In this point too Biblical criticism differs from the work of a classical annotator.

A further point must be noted. A Greek word, whatever its Hebrew or Aramaic equivalent may have been, must have carried much of the old Greek thought with it as it came in contact with Greek-speaking men. It is an interesting question how far this was *meant*, how far the thoughts thus infused into Christianity are true and wholesome thoughts, how far through that channel any harmful elements may have flowed in upon the original purity of truth.

This subject might be pursued, but enough has been said to shew the endless interest and usefulness of such researches, and the almost infinite directions in which they may be extended. In the limits of the brief notes which follow little more can be done than to indicate such lines of thought, and here and there to point to results.

NOTE III.

THE TEXT OF THE NEW TESTAMENT.

The evidence for the text of the N. T. is derived from three sources.

1. MSS. of the whole or portions of the N. T. Such portions are sometimes contained in lectionaries. 2. Patristic quotations. 3. Versions.

1. No classical work has so many valuable ancient MSS. on which to establish its text as the New Testament. The earliest of these MSS. are beautifully written on fine *vellum* (prepared skin of calves or kids) in *uncial* or large capital letters. The later MSS. are called *cursive*, from being written in a *cursive* (curro) or running hand.

The subjoined brief account of the more important uncial and cursive MSS. will explain the references in the Critical notes.

א. *Codex Sinaiticus.* This is probably the oldest MS. of the N. T. now extant, and is assigned to the *fourth* century. It was discovered by Tischendorf in the Convent of St Catharine on Mount Sinai, in 1859. "It contains both Old and New Testaments—the latter perfect without the loss of a single leaf. In addition it contains the entire Epistle of Barnabas and a portion of the 'Shepherd' of Hermas" (Tischendorf). This Codex is now at St Petersburg.

A. *Codex Alexandrinus.* This MS. belongs to the *fifth* century. It contains, with very few exceptions, the whole of the LXX. Version of the O. T.; in the N. T. the missing portions are Matt. i. 1—xxv. 6, John vi. 50—viii. 52, 2 Cor. iv. 13—xii. 6. It is now in the British Museum, having been presented to Charles I. by Cyrillus Lucaris, Patriarch of Constantinople, who had previously brought it from Alexandria in Egypt.

B. *Codex Vaticanus* also contains the LXX. Version of the O. T. with the exception of a large portion of Genesis and Psalms cv.—cxxxvii.; in the N. T. the latter part of the Epistle to the Hebrews is lacking (from ch. ix. 14—end), also the Pastoral Epistles and the Apocalypse. It is probably either contemporary with ℵ, or a little later. This MS. is now, as the name implies, in the Vatican Library.

C. *Codex Ephraemi rescriptus:* a *palimpsest;* i. e. on the vellum which contained the worn-out ancient letters (the value of the MS. not being recognised) were written the works of the Syrian Saint Ephraem. In the seventeenth century the older writing was observed beneath the more modern words, and a great portion of this valuable fifth-century Codex has been recovered and published. It contains portions of the LXX. Version of the O. T., and fragments of every book of the N. T. with the exception of 2 John and 2 Thessalonians, which are entirely lost. This Codex is in the National Library of Paris.

D. *Codex Bezæ:* a MS. of the sixth or seventh century, with a Latin Version as well as the Greek text, contains the Gospels and Acts, between which the Catholic Epistles once stood. Of these, 3 John, *vv.* 11—15, is the only extant portion. The interpolations and various readings of this MS. are of a remarkable character. There are several lacunæ. It is now in the Cambridge University Library, to which it was presented by Beza in 1581.

L. *Codex Regius,* written about the eighth century, though later than the foregoing should be named as of great critical value. It bears a strong resemblance to B and to the citations of Origen. It contains the four Gospels except Matt. iv. 22—v. 14, xxviii. 17—20; Mark x. 16—30, and v. 2—20; John xxi. 15—28.

The cursive MSS. date from the tenth century onward, of these the two numbered 1 and 33 respectively have the highest authority.

1. *Codex Basiliensis,* of tenth century according to Scrivener, who says of this MS.: 'In the Gospels the text is very remarkable, adhering pretty closely to the uncials BL and others of that class.'

33. Assigned to eleventh century. 'In text it resembles BDL more than any other cursive MS., and whatever may be thought of the character of its readings, they deserve the utmost attention.'—Scrivener.

209 may also be named as valuable in the Gospels. Its text resembles B. It belongs to the eleventh or twelfth century.

2. Quotations from the Fathers.

The full value of this source of evidence will not be reached until the early patristic writings shall have been critically edited. This has been only partially done. (See Dr Sanday's paper, *Expositor*, Vol. XI. 171 foll.) Patristic citations are valuable as affording testimony to the existence of a reading at a date fixed within certain limits. In some cases this evidence reaches an antiquity far beyond that of any existing MSS.; it is of special weight when an appeal is made in the patristic work from one MS. to another of greater authority, or where a reading is cited and defended in support of an argument, as in ch. i. 18 of this Gospel. But it often fails to render aid in the more delicate points of textual criticism.

3. Versions or translations from the original Greek into other languages.

The evidence of Versions is chiefly useful in determining questions of omission of words or passages. The literal character of some Versions indicates the order of the original language. But in many important questions as to connecting particles, tenses and construction, a translation brings precarious aid. In many cases the text of the Version is itself far from being critically settled, the language of others lies beyond the reach of most scholars. The following are among the more important Versions:

(1) Latin—(a) *Vetus Latina*. Made in Africa in the second century.

> The three principal codices are Cod. *Vercellensis* (fourth century), Cod. *Veronensis* (fourth or fifth century), Cod. *Colbertinus* (eleventh century).

(β) The Vulgate. The revision by St Jerome of the *Vetus Latina*. The best codices are Cod. *Amiaticus* and Cod. *Fuldensis*, both of the sixth century. The present authorised Vulgate is the result of a further revision at the end of the 16th century.

(2) Syriac or Aramaic Versions.
- (α) The Peshito (meaning 'simple,' perhaps = 'faithful'). This very ancient Version omits 2 Peter, 2 and 3 John, Jude, and the Apocalypse.
- (β) The Curetonian Syriac probably represents an older text than the Peshito. This MS. was discovered by Dr Cureton and published in 1858.
- (γ) The Philoxenian or Harclean Syriac. A literal rendering from the Greek made under Philoxenus, bishop of Hierapolis in Syria, A.D. 508, and revised by Thomas of Harkel A.D. 616. This is probably 'the most servile version of Scripture ever made.' The various readings in the margin are a valuable feature in this version.
- (δ) The Jerusalem Syriac (fifth or sixth century), also made from the Greek, and independent of the Peshito. It is written in a peculiar dialect, resembling the Chaldee rather than the Syriac.
- (ε) The Karkaphensian Syriac (so called probably from Carcuf, a city of Mesopotamia), discovered by Cardinal Wiseman in the Vatican, contains the same books as the Peshito, and bears a general resemblance to that Version.

Other Versions of critical value are—(3) The Coptic or Ægyptian, in which are included the Memphitic and the Thebaic Versions. For an account of these see a paper by Bp Lightfoot, printed in Scrivener's Introduction, &c., p. 319 foll. (4) The Gothic Version made by Ulfilas, bishop of the Goths, A.D. 348—388. The most valuable codex of this version is the Codex Argenteus (fifth or sixth century) preserved at Upsala. (5) The Æthiopic Version (date unknown). (6) The Armenian Version (fifth century).

Among easily accessible authorities on this subject are: Scrivener's *Introduction to the Criticism of the New Testament*; Prof. Westcott's articles in Smith's *Dictionary of the Bible* on the New Testament, and on the Vulgate; the Prolegomena to Alford's edition of the New Testament; Hammond's *Outlines of Textual Criticism applied to the N. T.*

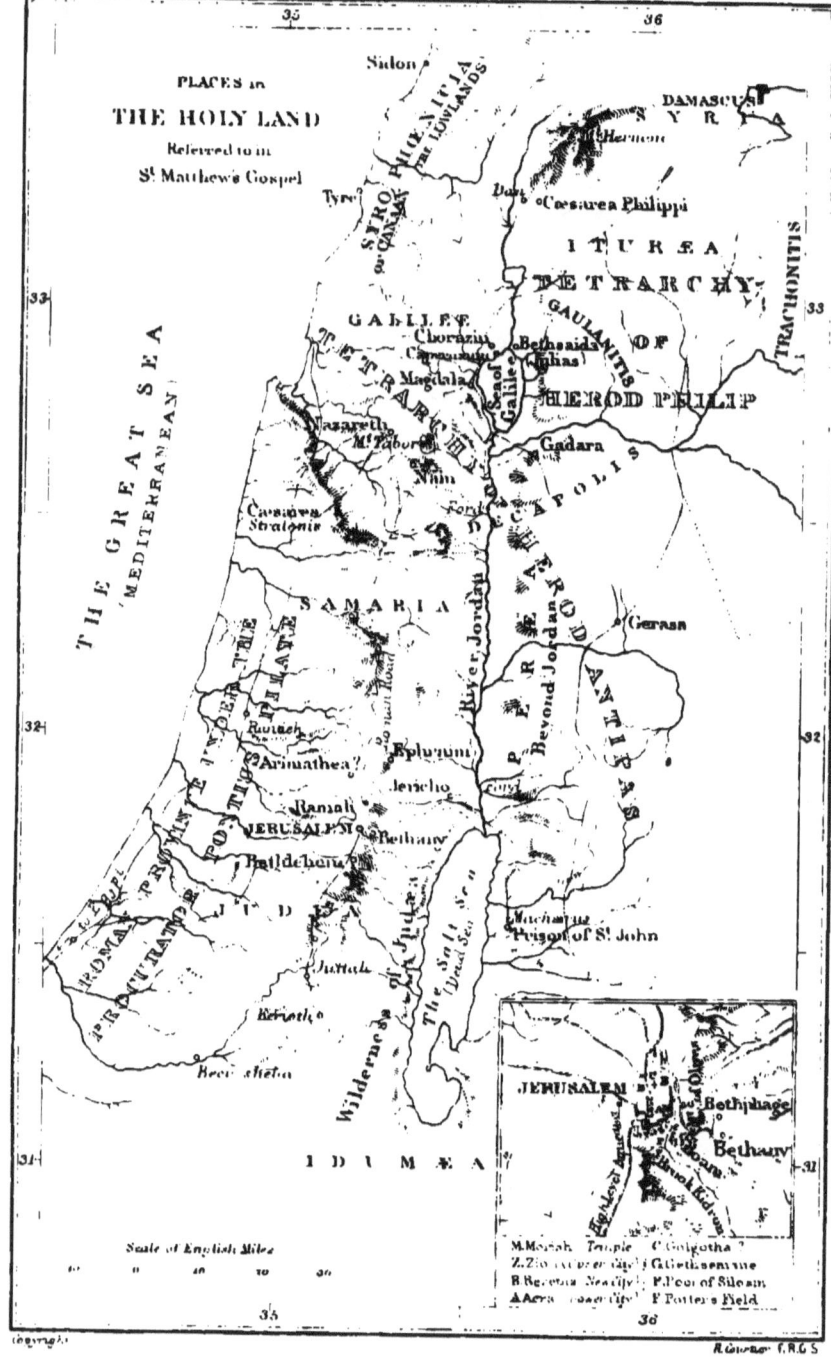

THE HOLY LAND.

Palestine (Philistia) or the Holy Land was about 140 miles in length. The distance from Dan to Beersheba was less than that between London and Manchester; the distance from Capernaum to Jerusalem was nearly the same as that from Rugby to London. The average breadth was 40 miles.

The political divisions are indicated as they existed during our Lord's ministry. At the date of His birth all the districts included in this map were comprised in the Kingdom of Herod the Great. After Herod's death, Archelaus ruled over Samaria and Judæa. When Archelaus was banished these divisions were placed under the rule of a Roman Procurator.

Mount Hermon, called also Sirion (the Glitterer), and Shenir (Deut. iii. 9), and Sion (Deut. iv. 48), ch. xvii. 1.

Cæsarea Philippi, ch. xvi. 13.

Syro-Phœnicia or *Canaan,* ch. xv. 22 and Mark vii. 26.

Nazareth, ch. ii. 23.

Mount Tabor, the traditional scene of the Transfiguration; at this time its summit was probably occupied by a fortress. Ch. xvii. 1.

Gerasa, not mentioned in this Gospel; see ch. viii. 28, and cp. Mark v. 1, where one reading is Gerasenes, inhabitants of a *different* Gerasa or Gergesa.

Ephraim, the supposed site of the Ephraim mentioned John xi. 54, to which Jesus retired shortly before His last Passover.

Ramah, ch. ii. 18.

Arimathæa, ch. xxvii. 57.

Jericho, ch. xx. 29.

Bethphage, ch. xxi. 1.

Bethany, ch. xxi. 17, xxvi. 6.

Bethlehem, ch. ii. 1.

Machærus, the scene of John Baptist's imprisonment and death, ch. iv. 12 and xiv. 10.

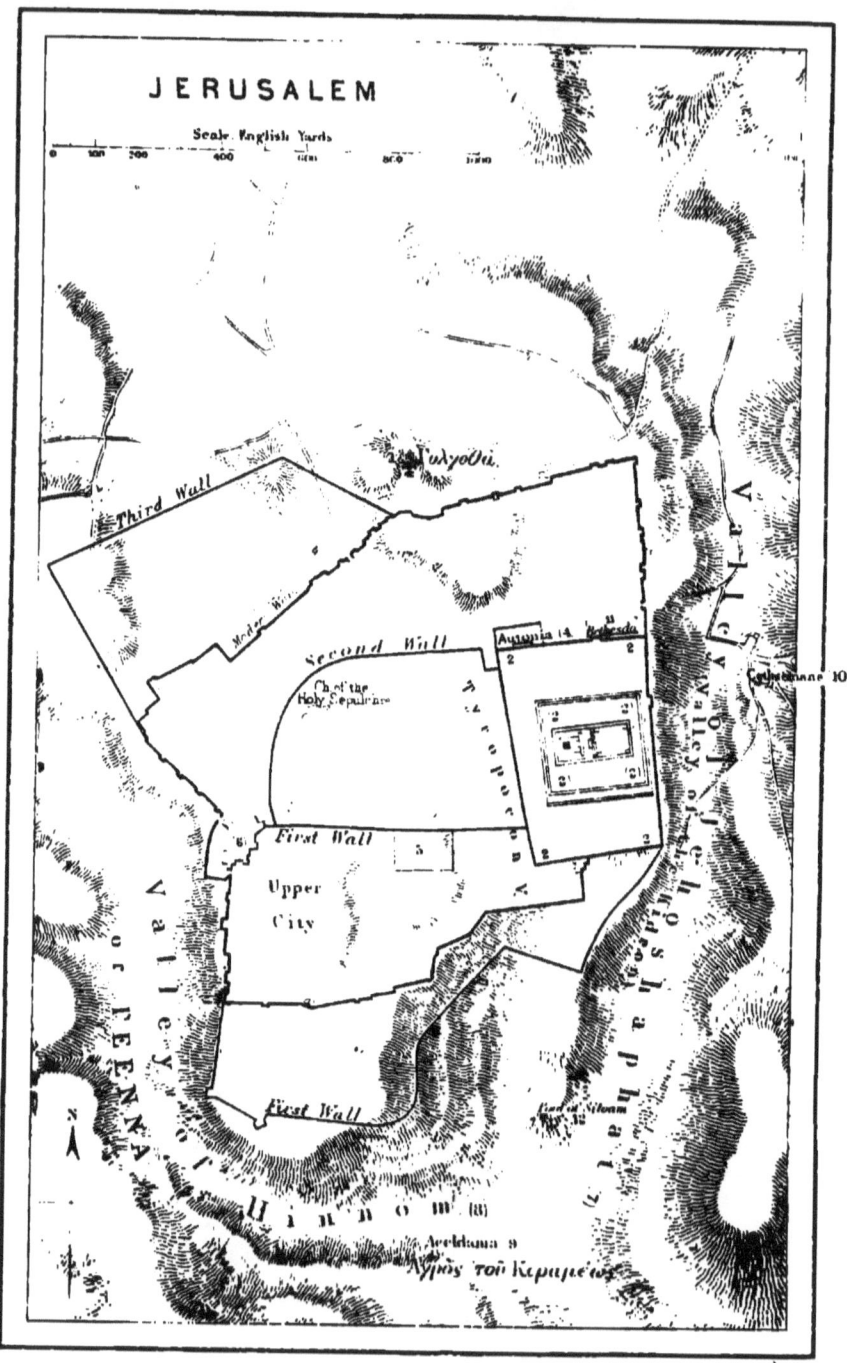

JERUSALEM.

1. Calvary and the Holy Sepulchre. Several explorers have pointed out the probability of the site indicated on the plan. It is outside the city gates. It is near one of the main roads, that leading to Shechem, and by the side of the road rises a rounded knoll (see note, ch. xxvii. 33) now called El Heidhemīyeh. Jewish and Christian tradition alike point to this as the ancient place of execution. It is named by the Jews Beth has Sekilah (the place of stoning). Near to this 'barren hillock' on either side of the road was the ancient Jewish burying-place (now a Mahometan cemetery), within which it is reasonable to place the site of the 'new tomb in the garden' (see Bædeker's *Palestine and Syria*, p. 189, and Conder, *Tent Work in Palestine*, ch. xii.). The Church of the Holy Sepulchre marks the traditional site, now abandoned.

2, 2, 2, 2. The *Haram* or Temple platform covered (a) wholly, or (β) in part by the Temple (τὸ ἱερόν), with its various courts. The first theory (a) is now held by few. But Col. Warren and others consider that the Temple occupied the whole of the Southern part (i.e. about ⅔) of the present enclosure. The mean measurement of the *Haram* is 982 feet by 1565 feet. (2), (2), (2), (2) represents the ἱερόν according to other authorities. Both the Talmud and Josephus describe the Temple area as square, but their measurements do not agree. The Temple was surrounded by porticos or arched colonnades. The substructures of massive stones surmounted by 'Solomon's Porch' on the eastern side were the οἰκοδομαί of ch. xxiv. 1 (see note). Here possibly was the πτερύγιον of ch. iv. 5.

In the north-west corner of the Temple area stood the Tower Antonia (4). It was built on a rock fifty cubits high (Joseph. *B. J.* v. 5. 8), and thus commanded the Temple. Here the Roman garrison was stationed. See ch. xxvii. 27.

3. ὁ ναός (indicated by the spot of darker colour), the Sanctuary or Holy House, to be carefully distinguished from the ἱερόν. See chs. xxiii. 16, 35, xxvi. 61, xxvii. 51. It was situated on the highest point of the Temple Hill, 2440 feet above the Mediterranean, now occupied by the Dome of the Rock. In front of the ναός, to the east of it, was the θυσιαστήριον, ch. xxiii. 35.

5. The Asmonean Palace, probably the residence of Herod Antipas while in Jerusalem. Joseph. *Ant.* xx. 8. 11.

6. The palace of Herod (Herodis Prætorium), in the Upper City, the residence of the Roman Procurator (Philo *de leg. ad Caium*, p. 1033 E; cp. p. 1034 E; Joseph. *B. .'.* ii. 14. 8, v. 4. 4). Between these two palaces Christ was led when Pilate 'remitted' Him to Herod. (For a description of this palace see Joseph. *B. J.* v. 4. 4, and Farrar's *Life of Christ*, ii. 364.)

7. Valley of the Kedron, or of Jehoshaphat. See note ch. xxvi. 31.
8. Valley of Hinnom or Gehenna [Γέεννα]. See note, ch. v. 22.
9. Aceldama (τὸν ἀγρὸν τοῦ κεραμέως, ch. xxvii. 7).
10. Gethsemane. Ch. xxvi. 36.
11. Bethesda, and 12, Pool of Siloam, not named in this Gospel.

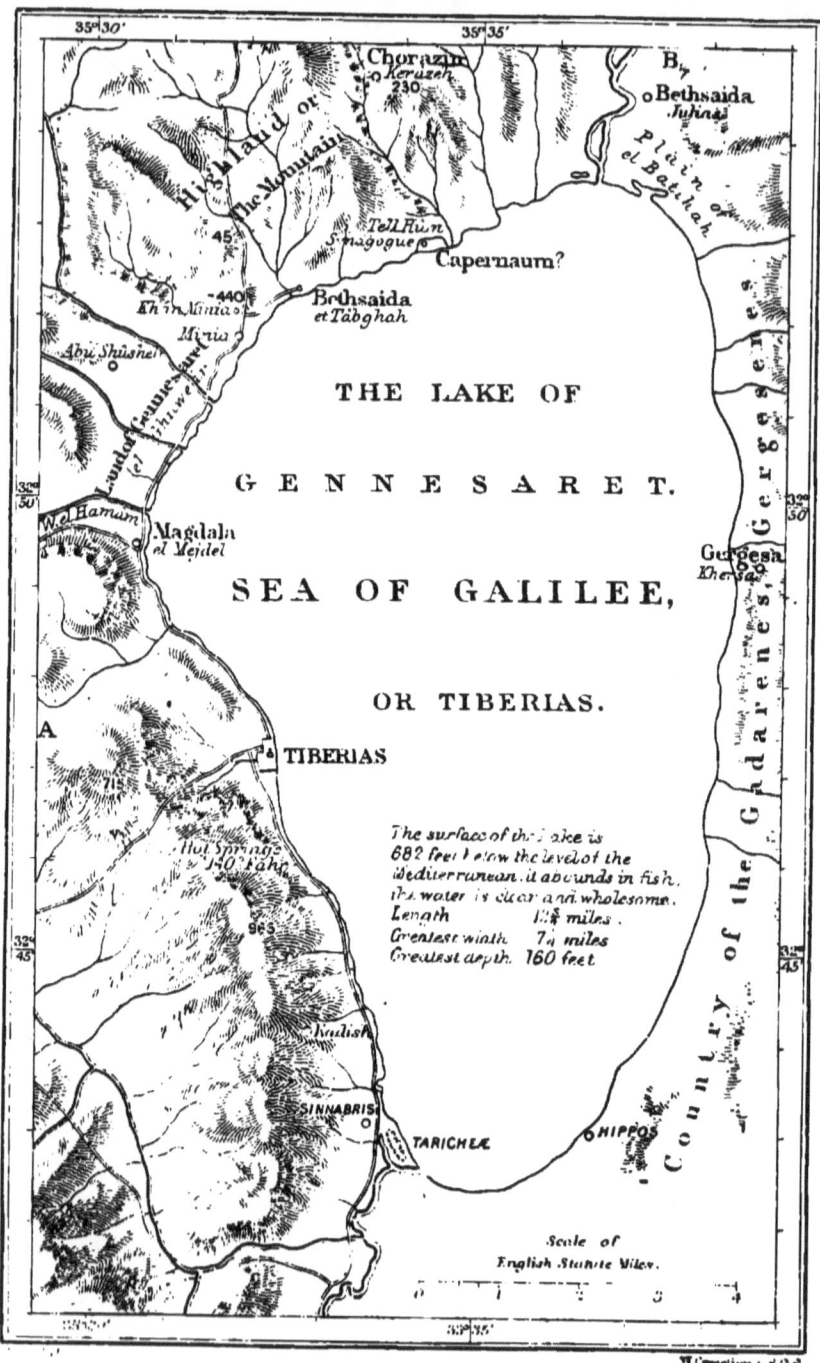

THE SEA OF GALILEE,

called the Lake of Gennesareth (Luke v. 1), the Sea of Tiberias (John vi. 1 and xxi. 1).

Bethsaida Julias, rebuilt by Herod Philip, the tetrarch, and called Julias after Julia, daughter of Augustus. See note, ch. xiv. 19.

Kerazeh, identified by Capt. Wilson with *Chorazin*. Ch. xi. 21.

Highland or *The Mountain*, the probable scene of the Sermon on the Mount and of the appearance of Jesus Christ, ch. xxviii. 16.

Tell Hûm, the site of *Capernaum*, according to Thomson (*Land and Book*), Capt. Wilson, Dean Stanley *latterly*, and others.

Et Tabigah, by some thought to be the *Bethsaida* ("House of Fish"), mentioned as being the home of Peter, Andrew and Philip (John i. 44); see chs. viii. 14 and xi. 21. Near Et Tabigah is a large fountain, probably "the fountain of Capharnaum" mentioned by Josephus, *B. J.* III. 10. 8, from which water was conveyed by an aqueduct to the plain of Gennesareth. Traces of this aqueduct and of an octagonal reservoir are distinctly visible. See *Recovery of Jerusalem*, p. 349.

Khan Minyeh, the site of Capernaum, according to Dean Stanley in *S. and P.* (in Preface to *Rec. of Jerusalem* the Dean inclines to the Tell Hûm site), Dr Robinson, Mr Macgregor (Rob Roy), and others.

El Ghuweir or *The Land of Gennesareth*, a fertile plain $2\frac{1}{2}$ miles in length, about 1 mile in breadth; ch. xiv. 34.

Mejdel, the Magdala of ch. xv. 39.

Tiberias. Not mentioned in this Gospel. But possibly Herod Antipas was holding his court here when John Baptist was put to death at Machærus; ch. xiv. 6 foll. It was built by Herod Antipas and named Tiberias in honour of the Emperor. See note, ch. xiv. 13—21, and cp. John vi. 1, 23.

K'hersa, identified with *Gergesa*. *Gerasa* (not the well-known Gerasa N. of the Jabbok; see Smith, *Bib. Dic.* sub voc.) is probably another form of the same name. See ch. viii. 23.

Gadara, the capital of "the country of the Gadarenes," to which district Gergesa belonged.

A and *B*, disputed sites for the miracle of feeding 5000; ch. xiv. 13—21.

ΕΥΑΓΓΕΛΙΟΝ ΚΑΤΑ ΜΑΘΘΑΙΟΝ

1 ¹ Βίβλος γενέσεως Ἰησοῦ Χριστοῦ υἱοῦ Δαυεὶδ υἱοῦ Ἀβραάμ. ² Ἀβραὰμ ἐγέννησεν τὸν Ἰσαάκ, Ἰσαὰκ δὲ ἐγέννησεν τὸν Ἰακώβ, Ἰακὼβ δὲ ἐγέννησεν τὸν Ἰούδαν καὶ τοὺς ἀδελφοὺς αὐτοῦ, ³ Ἰούδας δὲ ἐγέννησεν τὸν Φαρὲς καὶ τὸν Ζαρὰ ἐκ τῆς Θάμαρ, Φαρὲς δὲ ἐγέννησεν τὸν Ἐσρώμ, Ἐσρὼμ δὲ ἐγέννησεν τὸν Ἀράμ, ⁴ Ἀρὰμ δὲ ἐγέννησεν τὸν Ἀμιναδάβ, Ἀμιναδὰβ δὲ ἐγέννησεν τὸν Ναασσών, Ναασσὼν δὲ ἐγέννησεν τὸν Σαλμών, ⁵ Σαλμὼν δὲ ἐγέννησεν τὸν Βοὸς ἐκ τῆς Ῥαχάβ, Βοὸς δὲ ἐγέννησεν τὸν Ἰωβὴδ ἐκ τῆς Ῥούθ, Ἰωβὴδ δὲ ἐγέννησεν τὸν Ἰεσσαί, ⁶ Ἰεσσαὶ δὲ ἐγέννησεν τὸν Δαυεὶδ τὸν βασιλέα. Δαυεὶδ δὲ ἐγέννησεν τὸν Σολομῶνα ἐκ τῆς τοῦ Οὐρίου, ⁷ Σολομὼν δὲ ἐγέννησεν τὸν Ῥοβοάμ, Ῥοβοὰμ δὲ ἐγέννησεν τὸν Ἀβιά, Ἀβιὰ δὲ ἐγέννησεν τὸν Ἀσάφ, ⁸ Ἀσὰφ δὲ ἐγέννησεν τὸν Ἰωσαφάτ, Ἰωσαφὰτ δὲ ἐγέννησεν τὸν Ἰωράμ, Ἰωρὰμ δὲ ἐγέννησεν τὸν Ὀζείαν, ⁹ Ὀζείας δὲ ἐγέννησεν τὸν Ἰωάθαμ, Ἰωάθαμ δὲ ἐγέννησεν τὸν Ἄχαζ, Ἄχαζ δὲ ἐγέννησεν τὸν Ἐζεκίαν, ¹⁰ Ἐζεκίας δὲ ἐγέννησεν τὸν Μανασσῆ, Μανασσῆς δὲ ἐγέννησεν τὸν Ἀμώς, Ἀμὼς δὲ ἐγέννησεν τὸν Ἰωσείαν, ¹¹ Ἰωσείας δὲ ἐγέννησεν τὸν Ἰεχονίαν καὶ τοὺς ἀδελφοὺς αὐτοῦ ἐπὶ τῆς μετοικεσίας Βαβυλῶνος.

¹² Μετὰ δὲ τὴν μετοικεσίαν Βαβυλῶνος Ἰεχονίας ἐγέννησεν τὸν Σαλαθιήλ, Σαλαθιὴλ δὲ ἐγέννησεν τὸν Ζοροβάβελ, ¹³ Ζοροβάβελ δὲ ἐγέννησεν τὸν Ἀβιούδ, Ἀβιοὺδ δὲ ἐγέννησεν τὸν Ἐλιακείμ, Ἐλιακεὶμ δὲ ἐγέννησεν τὸν Ἀζώρ, ¹⁴ Ἀζὼρ δὲ ἐγέννησεν τὸν Σαδώκ, Σαδὼκ δὲ ἐγέννησεν τὸν Ἀχείμ, Ἀχεὶμ δὲ ἐγέννησεν τὸν Ἐλιούδ, ¹⁵ Ἐλιοὺδ δὲ ἐγέννησεν τὸν Ἐλεάζαρ, Ἐλεάζαρ δὲ ἐγέννησεν τὸν Ματθάν, Ματθὰν δὲ ἐγέννησεν τὸν Ἰακώβ, ¹⁶ Ἰακὼβ δὲ ἐγέννησεν τὸν Ἰωσὴφ τὸν ἄνδρα Μαρίας, ἐξ ἧς ἐγεννήθη Ἰησοῦς ὁ λεγόμενος Χριστός. ¹⁷ Πᾶσαι οὖν αἱ γενεαὶ ἀπὸ Ἀβραὰμ ἕως Δαυεὶδ γενεαὶ δεκατέσσαρες, καὶ ἀπὸ Δαυεὶδ ἕως τῆς μετοικεσίας Βαβυλῶνος γενεαὶ δεκατέσσαρες, καὶ ἀπὸ τῆς μετοικεσίας Βαβυλῶνος ἕως τοῦ Χριστοῦ γενεαὶ δεκατέσσαρες.

¹⁸ Τοῦ δὲ Ἰησοῦ Χριστοῦ ἡ γένεσις οὕτως ἦν. μνηστευθείσης τῆς μητρὸς αὐτοῦ Μαρίας τῷ Ἰωσήφ, πρὶν ἢ συνελθεῖν αὐτοὺς εὑρέθη ἐν γαστρὶ ἔχουσα ἐκ πνεύματος ἁγίου. ¹⁹ Ἰωσὴφ δὲ ὁ ἀνὴρ αὐτῆς, δίκαιος ὢν καὶ μὴ θέλων αὐτὴν δειγματίσαι, ἐβουλήθη λάθρα ἀπολῦσαι αὐτήν. ²⁰ ταῦτα δὲ αὐτοῦ ἐνθυμηθέντος, ἰδοὺ ἄγγελος κυρίου κατ' ὄναρ ἐφάνη αὐτῷ λέγων, Ἰωσὴφ υἱὸς Δαυείδ, μὴ φοβηθῇς παραλαβεῖν Μαριὰμ τὴν γυναῖκά σου· τὸ γὰρ ἐν αὐτῇ γεννηθὲν ἐκ πνεύματός ἐστιν ἁγίου. ²¹ τέξεται δὲ υἱόν, καὶ καλέσεις τὸ ὄνομα αὐτοῦ Ἰησοῦν· αὐτὸς γὰρ σώσει τὸν λαὸν αὐτοῦ ἀπὸ τῶν ἁμαρτιῶν αὐτῶν. ²² Τοῦτο δὲ ὅλον γέγονεν ἵνα πληρωθῇ τὸ ῥηθὲν ὑπὸ κυρίου διὰ τοῦ προφήτου λέγοντος, ²³ Ἰδοὺ ἡ παρθένος ἐν γαστρὶ ἕξει καὶ τέξεται υἱόν, καὶ καλέσουσιν τὸ ὄνομα αὐτοῦ Ἐμμανουήλ, ὅ ἐστιν μεθερμηνευόμενον μεθ' ἡμῶν ὁ θεός. ²⁴ ἐγερθεὶς

δὲ ὁ Ἰωσὴφ ἀπὸ τοῦ ὕπνου ἐποίησεν ὡς προσέταξεν αὐτῷ ὁ ἄγγελος κυρίου, καὶ παρέλαβεν τὴν γυναῖκα αὐτοῦ· ²⁵ καὶ οὐκ ἐγίνωσκεν αὐτὴν ἕως οὗ ἔτεκεν υἱόν, καὶ ἐκάλεσεν τὸ ὄνομα αὐτοῦ Ἰησοῦν.

2 ¹ Τοῦ δὲ Ἰησοῦ γεννηθέντος ἐν Βηθλεὲμ τῆς Ἰουδαίας ἐν ἡμέραις Ἡρώδου τοῦ βασιλέως, ἰδοὺ μάγοι ἀπὸ ἀνατολῶν παρεγένοντο εἰς Ἱεροσόλυμα ² λέγοντες, Ποῦ ἐστὶν ὁ τεχθεὶς βασιλεὺς τῶν Ἰουδαίων; εἴδομεν γὰρ αὐτοῦ τὸν ἀστέρα ἐν τῇ ἀνατολῇ, καὶ ἤλθομεν προσκυνῆσαι αὐτῷ. ³ ἀκούσας δὲ ὁ βασιλεὺς Ἡρώδης ἐταράχθη, καὶ πᾶσα Ἱεροσόλυμα μετ' αὐτοῦ, ⁴ καὶ συναγαγὼν πάντας τοὺς ἀρχιερεῖς καὶ γραμματεῖς τοῦ λαοῦ ἐπυνθάνετο παρ' αὐτῶν ποῦ ὁ Χριστὸς γεννᾶται. ⁵ οἱ δὲ εἶπον αὐτῷ, Ἐν Βηθλεὲμ τῆς Ἰουδαίας· οὕτως γὰρ γέγραπται διὰ τοῦ προφήτου, ⁶ Καὶ σὺ Βηθλεέμ, γῆ Ἰούδα, οὐδαμῶς ἐλαχίστη εἶ ἐν τοῖς ἡγεμόσιν Ἰούδα· ἐκ σοῦ γὰρ ἐξελεύσεται ἡγούμενος, ὅστις ποιμανεῖ τὸν λαόν μου τὸν Ἰσραήλ. ⁷ τότε Ἡρώδης λάθρα καλέσας τοὺς μάγους ἠκρίβωσεν παρ' αὐτῶν τὸν χρόνον τοῦ φαινομένου ἀστέρος, ⁸ καὶ πέμψας αὐτοὺς εἰς Βηθλεὲμ εἶπεν, Πορευθέντες ἐξετάσατε ἀκριβῶς περὶ τοῦ παιδίου· ἐπὰν δὲ εὕρητε, ἀπαγγείλατέ μοι, ὅπως κἀγὼ ἐλθὼν προσκυνήσω αὐτῷ. ⁹ οἱ δὲ ἀκούσαντες τοῦ βασιλέως ἐπορεύθησαν· καὶ ἰδοὺ ὁ ἀστήρ, ὃν εἶδον ἐν τῇ ἀνατολῇ, προῆγεν αὐτοὺς ἕως ἐλθὼν ἐστάθη ἐπάνω οὗ ἦν τὸ παιδίον. ¹⁰ ἰδόντες δὲ τὸν ἀστέρα ἐχάρησαν χαρὰν μεγάλην σφόδρα. ¹¹ καὶ ἐλθόντες εἰς τὴν οἰκίαν εἶδον τὸ παιδίον μετὰ Μαρίας τῆς μητρὸς αὐτοῦ, καὶ πεσόντες προσεκύνησαν αὐτῷ, καὶ ἀνοίξαντες τοὺς θησαυροὺς αὐτῶν προσήνεγκαν αὐτῷ δῶρα, χρυσὸν καὶ λίβανον καὶ σμύρναν. ¹² καὶ χρηματισθέντες κατ' ὄναρ μὴ ἀνακάμψαι πρὸς Ἡρώδην, δι' ἄλλης ὁδοῦ ἀνεχώρησαν εἰς τὴν χώραν αὐτῶν.

¹³ Ἀναχωρησάντων δὲ αὐτῶν, ἰδοὺ ἄγγελος κυρίου φαίνεται κατ' ὄναρ τῷ Ἰωσὴφ λέγων, Ἐγερθεὶς παράλαβε τὸ παιδίον καὶ τὴν μητέρα αὐτοῦ, καὶ φεῦγε εἰς Αἴγυπτον, καὶ ἴσθι ἐκεῖ ἕως ἂν εἴπω σοι· μέλλει γὰρ Ἡρώδης ζητεῖν τὸ παιδίον τοῦ ἀπολέσαι αὐτό. ¹⁴ ὁ δὲ ἐγερθεὶς παρέλαβεν τὸ παιδίον καὶ τὴν μητέρα αὐτοῦ νυκτός, καὶ ἀνεχώρησεν εἰς Αἴγυπτον, ¹⁵ καὶ ἦν ἐκεῖ ἕως τῆς τελευτῆς Ἡρώδου· ἵνα πληρωθῇ τὸ ῥηθὲν ὑπὸ κυρίου διὰ τοῦ προφήτου λέγοντος, Ἐξ Αἰγύπτου ἐκάλεσα τὸν υἱόν μου.

¹⁶ Τότε Ἡρώδης ἰδὼν ὅτι ἐνεπαίχθη ὑπὸ τῶν μάγων, ἐθυμώθη λίαν, καὶ ἀποστείλας ἀνεῖλεν πάντας τοὺς παῖδας τοὺς ἐν Βηθλεὲμ καὶ ἐν πᾶσι τοῖς ὁρίοις αὐτῆς ἀπὸ διετοῦς καὶ κατωτέρω, κατὰ τὸν χρόνον ὃν ἠκρίβωσεν παρὰ τῶν μάγων. ¹⁷ τότε ἐπληρώθη τὸ ῥηθὲν διὰ Ἱερεμίου τοῦ προφήτου λέγοντος, ¹⁸ Φωνὴ ἐν Ῥαμὰ ἠκούσθη, κλαυθμὸς καὶ ὀδυρμὸς πολύς, Ῥαχὴλ κλαίουσα τὰ τέκνα αὐτῆς, καὶ οὐκ ἤθελεν παρακληθῆναι, ὅτι οὐκ εἰσίν.

¹⁹ Τελευτήσαντος δὲ τοῦ Ἡρώδου, ἰδοὺ ἄγγελος κυρίου φαίνεται κατ' ὄναρ τῷ Ἰωσὴφ ἐν Αἰγύπτῳ ²⁰ λέγων, Ἐγερθεὶς παράλαβε τὸ παιδίον καὶ τὴν μητέρα αὐτοῦ, καὶ πορεύου εἰς γῆν Ἰσραήλ· τεθνήκασιν γὰρ οἱ ζητοῦντες τὴν ψυχὴν τοῦ παιδίου. ²¹ ὁ δὲ ἐγερθεὶς παρέλαβεν τὸ παιδίον καὶ τὴν μητέρα αὐτοῦ, καὶ εἰσῆλθεν εἰς γῆν Ἰσραήλ.

²² Ἀκούσας δὲ ὅτι Ἀρχέλαος βασιλεύει τῆς Ἰουδαίας ἀντὶ τοῦ πατρὸς αὐτοῦ Ἡρώδου, ἐφοβήθη ἐκεῖ

ἀπελθεῖν· χρηματισθεὶς δὲ κατ' ὄναρ ἀνεχώρησεν εἰς τὰ μέρη τῆς Γαλιλαίας. ²³ καὶ ἐλθὼν κατῴκησεν εἰς πόλιν λεγομένην Ναζαρέθ· ὅπως πληρωθῇ τὸ ῥηθὲν διὰ τῶν προφητῶν ὅτι Ναζωραῖος κληθήσεται.

3 ¹Ἐν δὲ ταῖς ἡμέραις ἐκείναις παραγίνεται Ἰωάννης ὁ βαπτιστὴς κηρύσσων ἐν τῇ ἐρήμῳ τῆς Ἰουδαίας, ²λέγων, Μετανοεῖτε· ἤγγικεν γὰρ ἡ βασιλεία τῶν οὐρανῶν. ³ οὗτος γάρ ἐστιν ὁ ῥηθεὶς διὰ Ἡσαΐου τοῦ προφήτου λέγοντος, Φωνὴ βοῶντος ἐν τῇ ἐρήμῳ, Ἑτοιμάσατε τὴν ὁδὸν κυρίου, εὐθείας ποιεῖτε τὰς τρίβους αὐτοῦ. ⁴ αὐτὸς δὲ ὁ Ἰωάννης εἶχεν τὸ ἔνδυμα αὐτοῦ ἀπὸ τριχῶν καμήλου καὶ ζώνην δερματίνην περὶ τὴν ὀσφὺν αὐτοῦ· ἡ δὲ τροφὴ ἦν αὐτοῦ ἀκρίδες καὶ μέλι ἄγριον. ⁵ Τότε ἐξεπορεύετο πρὸς αὐτὸν Ἱεροσόλυμα καὶ πᾶσα ἡ Ἰουδαία καὶ πᾶσα ἡ περίχωρος τοῦ Ἰορδάνου, ⁶ καὶ ἐβαπτίζοντο ἐν τῷ Ἰορδάνῃ ποταμῷ ὑπ' αὐτοῦ ἐξομολογούμενοι τὰς ἁμαρτίας αὐτῶν. ⁷ ἰδὼν δὲ πολλοὺς τῶν Φαρισαίων καὶ Σαδδουκαίων ἐρχομένους ἐπὶ τὸ βάπτισμα εἶπεν αὐτοῖς, Γεννήματα ἐχιδνῶν, τίς ὑπέδειξεν ὑμῖν φυγεῖν ἀπὸ τῆς μελλούσης ὀργῆς; ⁸ ποιήσατε οὖν καρπὸν ἄξιον τῆς μετανοίας, ⁹ καὶ μὴ δόξητε λέγειν ἐν ἑαυτοῖς, Πατέρα ἔχομεν τὸν Ἀβραάμ· λέγω γὰρ ὑμῖν ὅτι δύναται ὁ θεὸς ἐκ τῶν λίθων τούτων ἐγεῖραι τέκνα τῷ Ἀβραάμ. ¹⁰ ἤδη δὲ ἡ ἀξίνη πρὸς τὴν ῥίζαν τῶν δένδρων κεῖται· πᾶν οὖν δένδρον μὴ ποιοῦν καρπὸν καλὸν ἐκκόπτεται καὶ εἰς πῦρ βάλλεται. ¹¹ ἐγὼ μὲν ὑμᾶς βαπτίζω ἐν ὕδατι εἰς μετάνοιαν· ὁ δὲ ὀπίσω μου ἐρχόμενος ἰσχυρότερός μου ἐστίν, οὗ οὐκ εἰμὶ ἱκανὸς τὰ ὑποδήματα βαστάσαι· αὐτὸς ὑμᾶς βαπτίσει ἐν πνεύματι ἁγίῳ καὶ πυρί. ¹² οὗ τὸ πτύον ἐν τῇ χειρὶ αὐτοῦ, καὶ διακαθαριεῖ τὴν ἅλωνα αὐτοῦ, καὶ συνάξει τὸν σῖτον αὐτοῦ εἰς τὴν ἀποθήκην, τὸ δὲ ἄχυρον κατακαύσει πυρὶ ἀσβέστῳ.

¹³Τότε παραγίνεται ὁ Ἰησοῦς ἀπὸ τῆς Γαλιλαίας ἐπὶ τὸν Ἰορδάνην πρὸς τὸν Ἰωάννην τοῦ βαπτισθῆναι ὑπ᾽ αὐτοῦ. ¹⁴ὁ δὲ διεκώλυεν αὐτὸν λέγων, Ἐγὼ χρείαν ἔχω ὑπὸ σοῦ βαπτισθῆναι, καὶ σὺ ἔρχῃ πρός με; ¹⁵ἀποκριθεὶς δὲ ὁ Ἰησοῦς εἶπεν πρὸς αὐτόν, Ἄφες ἄρτι· οὕτως γὰρ πρέπον ἐστὶν ἡμῖν πληρῶσαι πᾶσαν δικαιοσύνην. τότε ἀφίησιν αὐτόν. ¹⁶βαπτισθεὶς δὲ ὁ Ἰησοῦς εὐθὺς ἀνέβη ἀπὸ τοῦ ὕδατος· καὶ ἰδοὺ ἀνεῴχθησαν αὐτῷ οἱ οὐρανοί, καὶ εἶδεν τὸ πνεῦμα τοῦ θεοῦ καταβαῖνον ὡσεὶ περιστεράν, ἐρχόμενον ἐπ᾽ αὐτόν. ¹⁷καὶ ἰδοὺ φωνὴ ἐκ τῶν οὐρανῶν λέγουσα, Οὗτός ἐστιν ὁ υἱός μου ὁ ἀγαπητός, ἐν ᾧ εὐδόκησα.

4 ¹Τότε ὁ Ἰησοῦς ἀνήχθη εἰς τὴν ἔρημον ὑπὸ τοῦ πνεύματος, πειρασθῆναι ὑπὸ τοῦ διαβόλου. ²καὶ νηστεύσας ἡμέρας τεσσεράκοντα καὶ νύκτας τεσσεράκοντα, ὕστερον ἐπείνασεν. ³καὶ προσελθὼν ὁ πειράζων εἶπεν αὐτῷ, Εἰ υἱὸς εἶ τοῦ θεοῦ, εἰπὲ ἵνα οἱ λίθοι οὗτοι ἄρτοι γένωνται. ⁴ὁ δὲ ἀποκριθεὶς εἶπεν, Γέγραπται, Οὐκ ἐπ᾽ ἄρτῳ μόνῳ ζήσεται ὁ ἄνθρωπος, ἀλλ᾽ ἐπὶ παντὶ ῥήματι ἐκπορευομένῳ διὰ στόματος θεοῦ. ⁵τότε παραλαμβάνει αὐτὸν ὁ διάβολος εἰς τὴν ἁγίαν πόλιν, καὶ ἔστησεν αὐτὸν ἐπὶ τὸ πτερύγιον τοῦ ἱεροῦ, ⁶καὶ λέγει αὐτῷ, Εἰ υἱὸς εἶ τοῦ θεοῦ, βάλε σεαυτὸν κάτω· γέγραπται γὰρ ὅτι Τοῖς ἀγγέλοις αὐτοῦ ἐντελεῖται περὶ σοῦ καὶ ἐπὶ χειρῶν ἀροῦσίν σε, μήποτε προσκόψῃς πρὸς λίθον τὸν πόδα σου. ⁷ἔφη αὐτῷ ὁ Ἰησοῦς, Πάλιν γέγραπται, Οὐκ ἐκπειράσεις κύριον τὸν θεόν σου. ⁸πάλιν παραλαμβάνει αὐτὸν ὁ διάβολος εἰς ὄρος ὑψηλὸν λίαν καὶ δείκνυσιν αὐτῷ πάσας τὰς βασιλείας τοῦ κόσμου καὶ τὴν δόξαν αὐτῶν, ⁰ καὶ εἶπεν αὐτῷ, Ταῦτά σοι πάντα δώσω, ἐὰν πεσὼν προσκυνήσῃς μοι. ¹⁰ τότε λέγει αὐτῷ ὁ Ἰησοῦς, Ὕπαγε σατανᾶ· γέγραπται γάρ, Κύριον τὸν θεόν σου προσκυνήσεις καὶ αὐτῷ μόνῳ λατρεύσεις. ¹¹ τότε ἀφίησιν αὐτὸν ὁ διάβολος, καὶ ἰδοὺ ἄγγελοι προσῆλθον καὶ διηκόνουν αὐτῷ.

¹² Ἀκούσας δὲ ὅτι Ἰωάννης παρεδόθη, ἀνεχώρησεν εἰς τὴν Γαλιλαίαν. ¹³ καὶ καταλιπὼν τὴν Ναζαρὰ ἐλθὼν κατῴκησεν εἰς Καφαρναοὺμ τὴν παραθαλασσίαν ἐν ὁρίοις Ζαβουλὼν καὶ Νεφθαλείμ, ¹⁴ ἵνα πληρωθῇ τὸ ῥηθὲν διὰ Ἡσαΐου τοῦ προφήτου λέγοντος, ¹⁵ Γῆ Ζαβουλὼν καὶ γῆ Νεφθαλείμ, ὁδὸν θαλάσσης, πέραν τοῦ Ἰορδάνου, Γαλιλαία τῶν ἐθνῶν, ¹⁶ ὁ λαὸς ὁ καθήμενος ἐν σκότει φῶς εἶδεν μέγα, καὶ τοῖς καθημένοις ἐν χώρᾳ καὶ σκιᾷ θανάτου φῶς ἀνέτειλεν αὐτοῖς.

¹⁷ Ἀπὸ τότε ἤρξατο ὁ Ἰησοῦς κηρύσσειν καὶ λέγειν, Μετανοεῖτε· ἤγγικεν γὰρ ἡ βασιλεία τῶν οὐρανῶν. ¹⁸ Περιπατῶν δὲ παρὰ τὴν θάλασσαν τῆς Γαλιλαίας εἶδεν δύο ἀδελφούς, Σίμωνα τὸν λεγόμενον Πέτρον καὶ Ἀνδρέαν τὸν ἀδελφὸν αὐτοῦ, βάλλοντας ἀμφίβληστρον εἰς τὴν θάλασσαν· ἦσαν γὰρ ἁλιεῖς. ¹⁹ καὶ λέγει αὐτοῖς, Δεῦτε ὀπίσω μου, καὶ ποιήσω ὑμᾶς ἁλιεῖς ἀνθρώπων. ²⁰ οἱ δὲ εὐθέως ἀφέντες τὰ δίκτυα ἠκολούθησαν αὐτῷ. ²¹ Καὶ προβὰς ἐκεῖθεν εἶδεν ἄλλους δύο ἀδελφούς, Ἰάκωβον τὸν τοῦ Ζεβεδαίου καὶ Ἰωάννην τὸν ἀδελφὸν αὐτοῦ, ἐν τῷ πλοίῳ μετὰ Ζεβεδαίου τοῦ πατρὸς αὐτῶν καταρτίζοντας τὰ δίκτυα αὐτῶν· καὶ ἐκάλεσεν αὐτούς. ²² οἱ δὲ εὐθέως ἀφέντες τὸ πλοῖον καὶ τὸν πατέρα αὐτῶν ἠκολούθησαν αὐτῷ.

²³ Καὶ περιῆγεν ὁ Ἰησοῦς ἐν ὅλῃ τῇ Γαλιλαίᾳ, διδά-

σκων ἐν ταῖς συναγωγαῖς αὐτῶν καὶ κηρύσσων τὸ εὐαγγέλιον τῆς βασιλείας καὶ θεραπεύων πᾶσαν νόσον καὶ πᾶσαν μαλακίαν ἐν τῷ λαῷ. ²⁴ καὶ ἀπῆλθεν ἡ ἀκοὴ αὐτοῦ εἰς ὅλην τὴν Συρίαν· καὶ προσήνεγκαν αὐτῷ πάντας τοὺς κακῶς ἔχοντας ποικίλαις νόσοις καὶ βασάνοις συνεχομένους καὶ δαιμονιζομένους καὶ σεληνιαζομένους καὶ παραλυτικούς, καὶ ἐθεράπευσεν αὐτούς. ²⁵ καὶ ἠκολούθησαν αὐτῷ ὄχλοι πολλοὶ ἀπὸ τῆς Γαλιλαίας καὶ Δεκαπόλεως καὶ Ἱεροσολύμων καὶ Ἰουδαίας καὶ πέραν τοῦ Ἰορδάνου.

5 ¹Ἰδὼν δὲ τοὺς ὄχλους ἀνέβη εἰς τὸ ὄρος· καὶ καθίσαντος αὐτοῦ προσῆλθαν αὐτῷ οἱ μαθηταὶ αὐτοῦ. ² καὶ ἀνοίξας τὸ στόμα αὐτοῦ ἐδίδασκεν αὐτοὺς λέγων,

³ Μακάριοι οἱ πτωχοὶ τῷ πνεύματι, ὅτι αὐτῶν ἐστὶν ἡ βασιλεία τῶν οὐρανῶν.

⁴ Μακάριοι οἱ πραεῖς, ὅτι αὐτοὶ κληρονομήσουσιν τὴν γῆν.

⁵ Μακάριοι οἱ πενθοῦντες, ὅτι αὐτοὶ παρακληθήσονται.

⁶ Μακάριοι οἱ πεινῶντες καὶ διψῶντες τὴν δικαιοσύνην, ὅτι αὐτοὶ χορτασθήσονται.

⁷ Μακάριοι οἱ ἐλεήμονες, ὅτι αὐτοὶ ἐλεηθήσονται.

⁸ Μακάριοι οἱ καθαροὶ τῇ καρδίᾳ, ὅτι αὐτοὶ τὸν θεὸν ὄψονται.

⁹ Μακάριοι οἱ εἰρηνοποιοί, ὅτι υἱοὶ θεοῦ κληθήσονται.

¹⁰ Μακάριοι οἱ δεδιωγμένοι ἕνεκεν δικαιοσύνης, ὅτι αὐτῶν ἐστὶν ἡ βασιλεία τῶν οὐρανῶν.

¹¹ Μακάριοί ἐστε ὅταν ὀνειδίσωσιν ὑμᾶς καὶ διώξωσιν καὶ εἴπωσιν πᾶν πονηρὸν καθ' ὑμῶν ψευδόμενοι ἕνεκεν ἐμοῦ.

¹² Χαίρετε καὶ ἀγαλλιᾶσθε, ὅτι ὁ μισθὸς ὑμῶν πολὺς ἐν τοῖς οὐρανοῖς· οὕτως γὰρ ἐδίωξαν τοὺς προφήτας τοὺς πρὸ ὑμῶν.

¹³ Ὑμεῖς ἐστὲ τὸ ἅλας τῆς γῆς· ἐὰν δὲ τὸ ἅλας μωρανθῇ, ἐν τίνι ἁλισθήσεται; εἰς οὐδὲν ἰσχύει ἔτι εἰ μὴ βληθὲν ἔξω καταπατεῖσθαι ὑπὸ τῶν ἀνθρώπων. ¹⁴ Ὑμεῖς ἐστὲ τὸ φῶς τοῦ κόσμου. οὐ δύναται πόλις κρυβῆναι ἐπάνω ὄρους κειμένη· ¹⁵ οὐδὲ καίουσιν λύχνον καὶ τιθέασιν αὐτὸν ὑπὸ τὸν μόδιον, ἀλλ' ἐπὶ τὴν λυχνίαν, καὶ λάμπει πᾶσιν τοῖς ἐν τῇ οἰκίᾳ. ¹⁶ οὕτως λαμψάτω τὸ φῶς ὑμῶν ἔμπροσθεν τῶν ἀνθρώπων, ὅπως ἴδωσιν ὑμῶν τὰ καλὰ ἔργα καὶ δοξάσωσιν τὸν πατέρα ὑμῶν τὸν ἐν τοῖς οὐρανοῖς.

¹⁷ Μὴ νομίσητε ὅτι ἦλθον καταλῦσαι τὸν νόμον ἢ τοὺς προφήτας· οὐκ ἦλθον καταλῦσαι ἀλλὰ πληρῶσαι. ¹⁸ ἀμὴν γὰρ λέγω ὑμῖν, ἕως ἂν παρέλθῃ ὁ οὐρανὸς καὶ ἡ γῆ, ἰῶτα ἓν ἢ μία κεραία οὐ μὴ παρέλθῃ ἀπὸ τοῦ νόμου, ἕως ἂν πάντα γένηται. ¹⁹ ὃς ἐὰν οὖν λύσῃ μίαν τῶν ἐντολῶν τούτων τῶν ἐλαχίστων καὶ διδάξῃ οὕτως τοὺς ἀνθρώπους, ἐλάχιστος κληθήσεται ἐν τῇ βασιλείᾳ τῶν οὐρανῶν. ὃς δ' ἂν ποιήσῃ καὶ διδάξῃ, οὗτος μέγας κληθήσεται ἐν τῇ βασιλείᾳ τῶν οὐρανῶν. ²⁰ λέγω γὰρ ὑμῖν ὅτι ἐὰν μὴ περισσεύσῃ ἡ δικαιοσύνη ὑμῶν πλεῖον τῶν γραμματέων καὶ Φαρισαίων, οὐ μὴ εἰσέλθητε εἰς τὴν βασιλείαν τῶν οὐρανῶν.

²¹ Ἠκούσατε ὅτι ἐρρέθη τοῖς ἀρχαίοις, Οὐ φονεύσεις· ὃς δ' ἂν φονεύσῃ, ἔνοχος ἔσται τῇ κρίσει. ²² ἐγὼ δὲ λέγω ὑμῖν ὅτι πᾶς ὁ ὀργιζόμενος τῷ ἀδελφῷ αὐτοῦ ἔνοχος ἔσται τῇ κρίσει· ὃς δ' ἂν εἴπῃ τῷ ἀδελφῷ αὐτοῦ, Ῥακά, ἔνοχος ἔσται τῷ συνεδρίῳ· ὃς δ' ἂν εἴπῃ, Μωρέ, ἔνοχος ἔσται εἰς τὴν γέενναν τοῦ πυρός.

²³ ἐὰν οὖν προσφέρῃς τὸ δῶρόν σου ἐπὶ τὸ θυσιαστήριον κἀκεῖ μνησθῇς ὅτι ὁ ἀδελφός σου ἔχει τι κατὰ σοῦ, ²⁴ ἄφες ἐκεῖ τὸ δῶρόν σου ἔμπροσθεν τοῦ θυσιαστηρίου καὶ ὕπαγε πρῶτον διαλλάγηθι τῷ ἀδελφῷ σου, καὶ τότε ἐλθὼν πρόσφερε τὸ δῶρόν σου. ²⁵ ἴσθι εὐνοῶν τῷ ἀντιδίκῳ σου ταχὺ ἕως ὅτου εἶ μετ' αὐτοῦ ἐν τῇ ὁδῷ· μήποτέ σε παραδῷ ὁ ἀντίδικος τῷ κριτῇ καὶ ὁ κριτὴς τῷ ὑπηρέτῃ, καὶ εἰς φυλακὴν βληθήσῃ. ²⁶ ἀμὴν λέγω σοι, οὐ μὴ ἐξέλθῃς ἐκεῖθεν ἕως ἂν ἀποδῷς τὸν ἔσχατον κοδράντην. ²⁷ Ἠκούσατε ὅτι ἐρρέθη, Οὐ μοιχεύσεις. ²⁸ ἐγὼ δὲ λέγω ὑμῖν ὅτι πᾶς ὁ βλέπων γυναῖκα πρὸς τὸ ἐπιθυμῆσαι αὐτὴν ἤδη ἐμοίχευσεν αὐτὴν ἐν τῇ καρδίᾳ αὐτοῦ. ²⁹ εἰ δὲ ὁ ὀφθαλμός σου ὁ δεξιὸς σκανδαλίζει σε, ἔξελε αὐτὸν καὶ βάλε ἀπὸ σοῦ· συμφέρει γάρ σοι ἵνα ἀπόληται ἓν τῶν μελῶν σου καὶ μὴ ὅλον τὸ σῶμά σου βληθῇ εἰς γέενναν. ³⁰ καὶ εἰ ἡ δεξιά σου χεὶρ σκανδαλίζει σε, ἔκκοψον αὐτὴν καὶ βάλε ἀπὸ σοῦ· συμφέρει γάρ σοι ἵνα ἀπόληται ἓν τῶν μελῶν σου καὶ μὴ ὅλον τὸ σῶμά σου εἰς γέενναν ἀπέλθῃ. ³¹ Ἐρρέθη δέ, Ὃς ἂν ἀπολύσῃ τὴν γυναῖκα αὐτοῦ, δότω αὐτῇ ἀποστάσιον. ³² ἐγὼ δὲ λέγω ὑμῖν ὅτι πᾶς ὁ ἀπολύων τὴν γυναῖκα αὐτοῦ παρεκτὸς λόγου πορνείας ποιεῖ αὐτὴν μοιχευθῆναι, καὶ ὃς ἐὰν ἀπολελυμένην γαμήσῃ, μοιχᾶται.

³³ Πάλιν ἠκούσατε ὅτι ἐρρέθη τοῖς ἀρχαίοις, Οὐκ ἐπιορκήσεις, ἀποδώσεις δὲ τῷ κυρίῳ τοὺς ὅρκους σου. ³⁴ ἐγὼ δὲ λέγω ὑμῖν μὴ ὀμόσαι ὅλως· μήτε ἐν τῷ οὐρανῷ, ὅτι θρόνος ἐστὶν τοῦ θεοῦ· ³⁵ μήτε ἐν τῇ γῇ, ὅτι ὑποπόδιόν ἐστιν τῶν ποδῶν αὐτοῦ· μήτε εἰς Ἱεροσόλυμα, ὅτι πόλις ἐστὶν τοῦ μεγάλου βασιλέως· ³⁶ μήτε ἐν τῇ κεφαλῇ σου ὀμόσῃς, ὅτι οὐ δύνασαι μίαν

τρίχα λευκὴν ποιῆσαι ἢ μέλαιναν. ³⁷ ἔστω δὲ ὁ λόγος ὑμῶν ναὶ ναί, οὒ οὔ· τὸ δὲ περισσὸν τούτων ἐκ τοῦ πονηροῦ ἐστίν.

³⁸ Ἠκούσατε ὅτι ἐρρέθη, Ὀφθαλμὸν ἀντὶ ὀφθαλμοῦ καὶ ὀδόντα ἀντὶ ὀδόντος. ³⁹ ἐγὼ δὲ λέγω ὑμῖν μὴ ἀντιστῆναι τῷ πονηρῷ· ἀλλ' ὅστις σε ῥαπίζει εἰς τὴν δεξιὰν σιαγόνα σου, στρέψον αὐτῷ καὶ τὴν ἄλλην· ⁴⁰ καὶ τῷ θέλοντί σοι κριθῆναι καὶ τὸν χιτῶνά σου λαβεῖν, ἄφες αὐτῷ καὶ τὸ ἱμάτιον· ⁴¹ καὶ ὅστις σε ἀγγαρεύσει μίλιον ἕν, ὕπαγε μετ' αὐτοῦ δύο. ⁴² τῷ αἰτοῦντί σε δός, καὶ τὸν θέλοντα ἀπὸ σοῦ δανείσασθαι μὴ ἀποστραφῇς.

⁴³ Ἠκούσατε ὅτι ἐρρέθη, Ἀγαπήσεις τὸν πλησίον σου καὶ μισήσεις τὸν ἐχθρόν σου. ⁴⁴ ἐγὼ δὲ λέγω ὑμῖν, ἀγαπᾶτε τοὺς ἐχθροὺς ὑμῶν καὶ προσεύχεσθε ὑπὲρ τῶν διωκόντων ὑμᾶς· ⁴⁵ ὅπως γένησθε υἱοὶ τοῦ πατρὸς ὑμῶν τοῦ ἐν οὐρανοῖς, ὅτι τὸν ἥλιον αὐτοῦ ἀνατέλλει ἐπὶ πονηροὺς καὶ ἀγαθοὺς καὶ βρέχει ἐπὶ δικαίους καὶ ἀδίκους. ⁴⁶ ἐὰν γὰρ ἀγαπήσητε τοὺς ἀγαπῶντας ὑμᾶς, τίνα μισθὸν ἔχετε; οὐχὶ καὶ οἱ τελῶναι τὸ αὐτὸ ποιοῦσιν; ⁴⁷ καὶ ἐὰν ἀσπάσησθε τοὺς ἀδελφοὺς ὑμῶν μόνον, τί περισσὸν ποιεῖτε; οὐχὶ καὶ οἱ ἐθνικοὶ τὸ αὐτὸ ποιοῦσιν; ⁴⁸ ἔσεσθε οὖν ὑμεῖς τέλειοι ὡς ὁ πατὴρ ὑμῶν ὁ οὐράνιος τέλειός ἐστιν.

6 ¹ Προσέχετε δὲ τὴν δικαιοσύνην ὑμῶν μὴ ποιεῖν ἔμπροσθεν τῶν ἀνθρώπων πρὸς τὸ θεαθῆναι αὐτοῖς· εἰ δὲ μήγε, μισθὸν οὐκ ἔχετε παρὰ τῷ πατρὶ ὑμῶν τῷ ἐν τοῖς οὐρανοῖς. ² ὅταν οὖν ποιῇς ἐλεημοσύνην, μὴ σαλπίσῃς ἔμπροσθέν σου, ὥσπερ οἱ ὑποκριταὶ ποιοῦσιν ἐν ταῖς συναγωγαῖς καὶ ἐν ταῖς ῥύμαις, ὅπως δοξασθῶσιν ὑπὸ τῶν ἀνθρώπων· ἀμὴν λέγω ὑμῖν, ἀπέχουσιν τὸν μισθὸν αὐτῶν. ³ σοῦ δὲ ποιοῦντος ἐλεημοσύνην μὴ γνώτω ἡ ἀριστερά σου τί ποιεῖ ἡ δεξιά σου, ⁴ ὅπως ᾖ σου ἡ ἐλεημοσύνη ἐν τῷ κρυπτῷ, καὶ ὁ πατήρ σου ὁ βλέπων ἐν τῷ κρυπτῷ ἀποδώσει σοι.

⁵ Καὶ ὅταν προσεύχησθε, οὐκ ἔσεσθε ὡς οἱ ὑποκριταί· ὅτι φιλοῦσιν ἐν ταῖς συναγωγαῖς καὶ ἐν ταῖς γωνίαις τῶν πλατειῶν ἑστῶτες προσεύχεσθαι, ὅπως φανῶσιν τοῖς ἀνθρώποις. ἀμὴν λέγω ὑμῖν, ἀπέχουσιν τὸν μισθὸν αὐτῶν. ⁶ σὺ δὲ ὅταν προσεύχῃ, εἴσελθε εἰς τὸ ταμιεῖόν σου καὶ κλείσας τὴν θύραν σου πρόσευξαι τῷ πατρί σου τῷ ἐν τῷ κρυπτῷ, καὶ ὁ πατήρ σου ὁ βλέπων ἐν τῷ κρυπτῷ ἀποδώσει σοι. ⁷ Προσευχόμενοι δὲ μὴ βαττολογήσητε ὥσπερ οἱ ἐθνικοί· δοκοῦσιν γὰρ ὅτι ἐν τῇ πολυλογίᾳ αὐτῶν εἰσακουσθήσονται. ⁸ μὴ οὖν ὁμοιωθῆτε αὐτοῖς· οἶδεν γὰρ ὁ πατὴρ ὑμῶν ὧν χρείαν ἔχετε πρὸ τοῦ ὑμᾶς αἰτῆσαι αὐτόν.

⁹ Οὕτως οὖν προσεύχεσθε ὑμεῖς· Πάτερ ἡμῶν ὁ ἐν τοῖς οὐρανοῖς, ἁγιασθήτω τὸ ὄνομά σου· ¹⁰ ἐλθάτω ἡ βασιλεία σου· γενηθήτω τὸ θέλημά σου ὡς ἐν οὐρανῷ καὶ ἐπὶ γῆς· ¹¹ τὸν ἄρτον ἡμῶν τὸν ἐπιούσιον δὸς ἡμῖν σήμερον· ¹² καὶ ἄφες ἡμῖν τὰ ὀφειλήματα ἡμῶν, ὡς καὶ ἡμεῖς ἀφήκαμεν τοῖς ὀφειλέταις ἡμῶν· ¹³ καὶ μὴ εἰσενέγκῃς ἡμᾶς εἰς πειρασμόν, ἀλλὰ ῥῦσαι ἡμᾶς ἀπὸ τοῦ πονηροῦ.

¹⁴ Ἐὰν γὰρ ἀφῆτε τοῖς ἀνθρώποις τὰ παραπτώματα αὐτῶν, ἀφήσει καὶ ὑμῖν ὁ πατὴρ ὑμῶν ὁ οὐράνιος· ¹⁵ ἐὰν δὲ μὴ ἀφῆτε τοῖς ἀνθρώποις τὰ παραπτώματα αὐτῶν, οὐδὲ ὁ πατὴρ ὑμῶν ἀφήσει τὰ παραπτώματα ὑμῶν.

¹⁶ Ὅταν δὲ νηστεύητε, μὴ γίνεσθε ὡς οἱ ὑποκριταὶ

σκυθρωποί· ἀφανίζουσιν γὰρ τὰ πρόσωπα αὐτῶν ὅπως φανῶσιν τοῖς ἀνθρώποις νηστεύοντες. ἀμὴν λέγω ὑμῖν, ἀπέχουσιν τὸν μισθὸν αὐτῶν. ¹⁷ σὺ δὲ νηστεύων ἄλειψαί σου τὴν κεφαλὴν καὶ τὸ πρόσωπόν σου νίψαι, ¹⁸ ὅπως μὴ φανῇς τοῖς ἀνθρώποις νηστεύων ἀλλὰ τῷ πατρί σου τῷ ἐν τῷ κρυφαίῳ, καὶ ὁ πατήρ σου ὁ βλέπων ἐν τῷ κρυφαίῳ ἀποδώσει σοι.

¹⁹ Μὴ θησαυρίζετε ὑμῖν θησαυροὺς ἐπὶ τῆς γῆς, ὅπου σὴς καὶ βρῶσις ἀφανίζει, καὶ ὅπου κλέπται διορύσσουσιν καὶ κλέπτουσιν· ²⁰ θησαυρίζετε δὲ ὑμῖν θησαυροὺς ἐν οὐρανῷ, ὅπου οὔτε σὴς οὔτε βρῶσις ἀφανίζει, καὶ ὅπου κλέπται οὐ διορύσσουσιν οὐδὲ κλέπτουσιν. ²¹ ὅπου γάρ ἐστιν ὁ θησαυρός σου, ἐκεῖ ἔσται καὶ ἡ καρδία σου. ²² Ὁ λύχνος τοῦ σώματός ἐστιν ὁ ὀφθαλμός. ἐὰν οὖν ὁ ὀφθαλμός σου ἁπλοῦς ᾖ, ὅλον τὸ σῶμά σου φωτεινὸν ἔσται· ²³ ἐὰν δὲ ὁ ὀφθαλμός σου πονηρὸς ᾖ, ὅλον τὸ σῶμά σου σκοτεινὸν ἔσται. εἰ οὖν τὸ φῶς τὸ ἐν σοὶ σκότος ἐστίν, τὸ σκότος πόσον; ²⁴ Οὐδεὶς δύναται δυσὶ κυρίοις δουλεύειν· ἢ γὰρ τὸν ἕνα μισήσει καὶ τὸν ἕτερον ἀγαπήσει, ἢ ἑνὸς ἀνθέξεται καὶ τοῦ ἑτέρου καταφρονήσει. οὐ δύνασθε θεῷ δουλεύειν καὶ μαμωνᾷ. ²⁵ Διὰ τοῦτο λέγω ὑμῖν, μὴ μεριμνᾶτε τῇ ψυχῇ ὑμῶν τί φάγητε ἢ τί πίητε· μηδὲ τῷ σώματι ὑμῶν τί ἐνδύσησθε. οὐχὶ ἡ ψυχὴ πλεῖόν ἐστιν τῆς τροφῆς καὶ τὸ σῶμα τοῦ ἐνδύματος; ²⁶ ἐμβλέψατε εἰς τὰ πετεινὰ τοῦ οὐρανοῦ, ὅτι οὐ σπείρουσιν οὐδὲ θερίζουσιν οὐδὲ συνάγουσιν εἰς ἀποθήκας, καὶ ὁ πατὴρ ὑμῶν ὁ οὐράνιος τρέφει αὐτά· οὐχ ὑμεῖς μᾶλλον διαφέρετε αὐτῶν; ²⁷ τίς δὲ ἐξ ὑμῶν μεριμνῶν δύναται προσθεῖναι ἐπὶ τὴν ἡλικίαν αὐτοῦ πῆχυν ἕνα; ²⁸ καὶ περὶ ἐνδύματος τί μεριμνᾶτε; καταμάθετε τὰ κρίνα τοῦ ἀγροῦ

πῶς αὐξάνουσιν· οὐ κοπιῶσιν οὐδὲ νήθουσιν. ²⁹λέγω δὲ ὑμῖν ὅτι οὐδὲ Σολομὼν ἐν πάσῃ τῇ δόξῃ αὐτοῦ περιεβάλετο ὡς ἓν τούτων. ³⁰εἰ δὲ τὸν χόρτον τοῦ ἀγροῦ σήμερον ὄντα καὶ αὔριον εἰς κλίβανον βαλλόμενον ὁ θεὸς οὕτως ἀμφιέννυσιν, οὐ πολλῷ μᾶλλον ὑμᾶς, ὀλιγόπιστοι; ³¹μὴ οὖν μεριμνήσητε λέγοντες, Τί φάγωμεν ἢ τί πίωμεν ἢ τί περιβαλώμεθα; ³²πάντα γὰρ ταῦτα τὰ ἔθνη ἐπιζητοῦσιν· οἶδεν γὰρ ὁ πατὴρ ὑμῶν ὁ οὐράνιος ὅτι χρῄζετε τούτων ἁπάντων. ³³ζητεῖτε δὲ πρῶτον τὴν βασιλείαν τοῦ θεοῦ καὶ τὴν δικαιοσύνην αὐτοῦ, καὶ ταῦτα πάντα προστεθήσεται ὑμῖν. ³⁴μὴ οὖν μεριμνήσητε εἰς τὴν αὔριον· ἡ γὰρ αὔριον μεριμνήσει ἑαυτῆς. ἀρκετὸν τῇ ἡμέρᾳ ἡ κακία αὐτῆς.

7 ¹Μὴ κρίνετε, ἵνα μὴ κριθῆτε· ²ἐν ᾧ γὰρ κρίματι κρίνετε κριθήσεσθε, καὶ ἐν ᾧ μέτρῳ μετρεῖτε μετρηθήσεται ὑμῖν. ³τί δὲ βλέπεις τὸ κάρφος τὸ ἐν τῷ ὀφθαλμῷ τοῦ ἀδελφοῦ σου, τὴν δὲ ἐν τῷ σῷ ὀφθαλμῷ δοκὸν οὐ κατανοεῖς; ⁴ἢ πῶς ἐρεῖς τῷ ἀδελφῷ σου, Ἄφες ἐκβάλω τὸ κάρφος ἐκ τοῦ ὀφθαλμοῦ σου, καὶ ἰδοὺ ἡ δοκὸς ἐν τῷ ὀφθαλμῷ σοῦ. ⁵ὑποκριτά, ἔκβαλε πρῶτον ἐκ τοῦ ὀφθαλμοῦ σοῦ τὴν δοκόν, καὶ τότε διαβλέψεις ἐκβαλεῖν τὸ κάρφος ἐκ τοῦ ὀφθαλμοῦ τοῦ ἀδελφοῦ σου.

⁶Μὴ δῶτε τὸ ἅγιον τοῖς κυσίν, μηδὲ βάλητε τοὺς μαργαρίτας ὑμῶν ἔμπροσθεν τῶν χοίρων, μήποτε καταπατήσουσιν αὐτοὺς ἐν τοῖς ποσὶν αὐτῶν καὶ στραφέντες ῥήξωσιν ὑμᾶς.

⁷Αἰτεῖτε, καὶ δοθήσεται ὑμῖν· ζητεῖτε, καὶ εὑρήσετε· κρούετε, καὶ ἀνοιγήσεται ὑμῖν. ⁸πᾶς γὰρ ὁ αἰτῶν λαμβάνει, καὶ ὁ ζητῶν εὑρίσκει, καὶ τῷ κρούοντι ἀνοιγήσεται. ⁹ἢ τίς ἐστιν ἐξ ὑμῶν ἄνθρωπος, ὃν αἰτήσει ὁ

υἱὸς αὐτοῦ ἄρτον, μὴ λίθον ἐπιδώσει αὐτῷ; ¹⁰ ἢ καὶ ἰχθὺν αἰτήσει, μὴ ὄφιν ἐπιδώσει αὐτῷ; ¹¹ εἰ οὖν ὑμεῖς πονηροὶ ὄντες οἴδατε δόματα ἀγαθὰ διδόναι τοῖς τέκνοις ὑμῶν, πόσῳ μᾶλλον ὁ πατὴρ ὑμῶν ὁ ἐν τοῖς οὐρανοῖς δώσει ἀγαθὰ τοῖς αἰτοῦσιν αὐτόν. ¹² πάντα οὖν ὅσα ἂν θέλητε ἵνα ποιῶσιν ὑμῖν οἱ ἄνθρωποι, οὕτως καὶ ὑμεῖς ποιεῖτε αὐτοῖς· οὗτος γάρ ἐστιν ὁ νόμος καὶ οἱ προφῆται.

¹³ Εἰσέλθατε διὰ τῆς στενῆς πύλης· ὅτι πλατεῖα ἡ πύλη καὶ εὐρύχωρος ἡ ὁδὸς ἡ ἀπάγουσα εἰς τὴν ἀπώλειαν, καὶ πολλοί εἰσιν οἱ εἰσερχόμενοι δι' αὐτῆς· ¹⁴ ὅτι στενὴ ἡ πύλη καὶ τεθλιμμένη ἡ ὁδὸς ἡ ἀπάγουσα εἰς τὴν ζωήν, καὶ ὀλίγοι εἰσὶν οἱ εὑρίσκοντες αὐτήν.

¹⁵ Προσέχετε ἀπὸ τῶν ψευδοπροφητῶν, οἵτινες ἔρχονται πρὸς ὑμᾶς ἐν ἐνδύμασιν προβάτων, ἔσωθεν δέ εἰσιν λύκοι ἅρπαγες. ¹⁶ ἀπὸ τῶν καρπῶν αὐτῶν ἐπιγνώσεσθε αὐτούς. μήτι συλλέγουσιν ἀπὸ ἀκανθῶν σταφυλὰς ἢ ἀπὸ τριβόλων σῦκα; ¹⁷ οὕτως πᾶν δένδρον ἀγαθὸν καρποὺς καλοὺς ποιεῖ, τὸ δὲ σαπρὸν δένδρον καρποὺς πονηροὺς ποιεῖ. ¹⁸ οὐ δύναται δένδρον ἀγαθὸν καρποὺς πονηροὺς ποιεῖν, οὐδὲ δένδρον σαπρὸν καρποὺς καλοὺς ποιεῖν. ¹⁹ πᾶν δένδρον μὴ ποιοῦν καρπὸν καλὸν ἐκκόπτεται καὶ εἰς πῦρ βάλλεται. ²⁰ ἄραγε ἀπὸ τῶν καρπῶν αὐτῶν ἐπιγνώσεσθε αὐτούς.

²¹ Οὐ πᾶς ὁ λέγων μοι, Κύριε, κύριε, εἰσελεύσεται εἰς τὴν βασιλείαν τῶν οὐρανῶν, ἀλλ' ὁ ποιῶν τὸ θέλημα τοῦ πατρός μου τοῦ ἐν τοῖς οὐρανοῖς. ²² πολλοὶ ἐροῦσίν μοι ἐν ἐκείνῃ τῇ ἡμέρᾳ, Κύριε, κύριε, οὐ τῷ σῷ ὀνόματι ἐπροφητεύσαμεν, καὶ τῷ σῷ ὀνόματι δαιμόνια ἐξεβάλομεν, καὶ τῷ σῷ ὀνόματι δυνάμεις πολλὰς ἐποιήσαμεν; ²³ καὶ τότε ὁμολογήσω αὐτοῖς ὅτι Οὐδέποτε

ἔγνων ὑμᾶς, ἀποχωρεῖτε ἀπ' ἐμοῦ οἱ ἐργαζόμενοι τὴν ἀνομίαν.

²⁴ Πᾶς οὖν ὅστις ἀκούει μου τοὺς λόγους τούτους καὶ ποιεῖ αὐτοὺς ὁμοιωθήσεται ἀνδρὶ φρονίμῳ, ὅστις ᾠκοδόμησεν αὐτοῦ τὴν οἰκίαν ἐπὶ τὴν πέτραν. ²⁵ καὶ κατέβη ἡ βροχὴ καὶ ἦλθον οἱ ποταμοὶ καὶ ἔπνευσαν οἱ ἄνεμοι καὶ προσέπεσαν τῇ οἰκίᾳ ἐκείνῃ, καὶ οὐκ ἔπεσεν· τεθεμελίωτο γὰρ ἐπὶ τὴν πέτραν. ²⁶ καὶ πᾶς ὁ ἀκούων μου τοὺς λόγους τούτους καὶ μὴ ποιῶν αὐτοὺς ὁμοιωθήσεται ἀνδρὶ μωρῷ, ὅστις ᾠκοδόμησεν αὐτοῦ τὴν οἰκίαν ἐπὶ τὴν ἄμμον. ²⁷ καὶ κατέβη ἡ βροχὴ καὶ ἦλθον οἱ ποταμοὶ καὶ ἔπνευσαν οἱ ἄνεμοι καὶ προσέκοψαν τῇ οἰκίᾳ ἐκείνῃ, καὶ ἔπεσεν, καὶ ἦν ἡ πτῶσις αὐτῆς μεγάλη. ²⁸ Καὶ ἐγένετο ὅτε ἐτέλεσεν ὁ Ἰησοῦς τοὺς λόγους τούτους, ἐξεπλήσσοντο οἱ ὄχλοι ἐπὶ τῇ διδαχῇ αὐτοῦ· ²⁹ ἦν γὰρ διδάσκων αὐτοὺς ὡς ἐξουσίαν ἔχων, καὶ οὐχ ὡς οἱ γραμματεῖς αὐτῶν.

8 ¹ Καταβάντι δὲ αὐτῷ ἀπὸ τοῦ ὄρους, ἠκολούθησαν αὐτῷ ὄχλοι πολλοί. ² καὶ ἰδοὺ λεπρὸς προσελθὼν προσεκύνει αὐτῷ λέγων, Κύριε, ἐὰν θέλῃς, δύνασαί με καθαρίσαι. ³ καὶ ἐκτείνας τὴν χεῖρα ἥψατο αὐτοῦ λέγων, Θέλω, καθαρίσθητι. καὶ εὐθέως ἐκαθαρίσθη αὐτοῦ ἡ λέπρα. ⁴ καὶ λέγει αὐτῷ ὁ Ἰησοῦς, Ὅρα μηδενὶ εἴπῃς, ἀλλὰ ὕπαγε σεαυτὸν δεῖξον τῷ ἱερεῖ καὶ προσένεγκον τὸ δῶρον ὃ προσέταξεν Μωϋσῆς, εἰς μαρτύριον αὐτοῖς.

⁵ Εἰσελθόντος δὲ αὐτοῦ εἰς Καφαρναούμ, προσῆλθεν αὐτῷ ἑκατόνταρχος παρακαλῶν αὐτὸν ⁶ καὶ λέγων, Κύριε, ὁ παῖς μου βέβληται ἐν τῇ οἰκίᾳ παραλυτικός, δεινῶς βασανιζόμενος. ⁷ λέγει αὐτῷ, Ἐγὼ ἐλθὼν θεραπεύσω αὐτόν. ⁸ ἀποκριθεὶς δὲ ὁ ἑκατόνταρχος

ἔφη, Κύριε, οὐκ εἰμὶ ἱκανὸς ἵνα μου ὑπὸ τὴν στέγην εἰσέλθῃς· ἀλλὰ μόνον εἰπὲ λόγῳ, καὶ ἰαθήσεται ὁ παῖς μου. ⁹καὶ γὰρ ἐγὼ ἄνθρωπός εἰμι ὑπὸ ἐξουσίαν, ἔχων ὑπ' ἐμαυτὸν στρατιώτας, καὶ λέγω τούτῳ, Πορεύθητι, καὶ πορεύεται, καὶ ἄλλῳ, Ἔρχου, καὶ ἔρχεται, καὶ τῷ δούλῳ μου, Ποίησον τοῦτο, καὶ ποιεῖ. ¹⁰ἀκούσας δὲ ὁ Ἰησοῦς ἐθαύμασεν καὶ εἶπεν τοῖς ἀκολουθοῦσιν, Ἀμὴν λέγω ὑμῖν, οὐδὲ ἐν τῷ Ἰσραὴλ τοσαύτην πίστιν εὗρον. ¹¹λέγω δὲ ὑμῖν ὅτι πολλοὶ ἀπὸ ἀνατολῶν καὶ δυσμῶν ἥξουσιν καὶ ἀνακλιθήσονται μετὰ Ἀβραὰμ καὶ Ἰσαὰκ καὶ Ἰακὼβ ἐν τῇ βασιλείᾳ τῶν οὐρανῶν· ¹²οἱ δὲ υἱοὶ τῆς βασιλείας ἐκβληθήσονται εἰς τὸ σκότος τὸ ἐξώτερον· ἐκεῖ ἔσται ὁ κλαυθμὸς καὶ ὁ βρυγμὸς τῶν ὀδόντων. ¹³καὶ εἶπεν ὁ Ἰησοῦς τῷ ἑκατοντάρχῃ, Ὕπαγε, ὡς ἐπίστευσας γενηθήτω σοι. καὶ ἰάθη ὁ παῖς ἐν τῇ ὥρᾳ ἐκείνῃ.

¹⁴Καὶ ἐλθὼν ὁ Ἰησοῦς εἰς τὴν οἰκίαν Πέτρου εἶδεν τὴν πενθερὰν αὐτοῦ βεβλημένην καὶ πυρέσσουσαν. ¹⁵καὶ ἥψατο τῆς χειρὸς αὐτῆς, καὶ ἀφῆκεν αὐτὴν ὁ πυρετός· καὶ ἠγέρθη, καὶ διηκόνει αὐτῷ. ¹⁶ὀψίας δὲ γενομένης προσήνεγκαν αὐτῷ δαιμονιζομένους πολλούς· καὶ ἐξέβαλεν τὰ πνεύματα λόγῳ, καὶ πάντας τοὺς κακῶς ἔχοντας ἐθεράπευσεν, ¹⁷ὅπως πληρωθῇ τὸ ῥηθὲν διὰ Ἡσαΐου τοῦ προφήτου λέγοντος, Αὐτὸς τὰς ἀσθενείας ἡμῶν ἔλαβεν καὶ τὰς νόσους ἐβάστασεν.

¹⁸Ἰδὼν δὲ ὁ Ἰησοῦς πολλοὺς ὄχλους περὶ αὐτὸν ἐκέλευσεν ἀπελθεῖν εἰς τὸ πέραν. ¹⁹καὶ προσελθὼν εἷς γραμματεὺς εἶπεν αὐτῷ, Διδάσκαλε, ἀκολουθήσω σοι ὅπου ἐὰν ἀπέρχῃ. ²⁰καὶ λέγει αὐτῷ ὁ Ἰησοῦς, Αἱ ἀλώπεκες φωλεοὺς ἔχουσιν καὶ τὰ πετεινὰ τοῦ οὐρανοῦ κατασκηνώσεις, ὁ δὲ υἱὸς τοῦ ἀνθρώπου οὐκ

ἔχει ποῦ τὴν κεφαλὴν κλίνῃ. ²¹ ἕτερος δὲ τῶν μαθητῶν εἶπεν αὐτῷ, Κύριε, ἐπίτρεψόν μοι πρῶτον ἀπελθεῖν καὶ θάψαι τὸν πατέρα μου. ²² ὁ δὲ Ἰησοῦς λέγει αὐτῷ, Ἀκολούθει μοι, καὶ ἄφες τοὺς νεκροὺς θάψαι τοὺς ἑαυτῶν νεκρούς.

²³ Καὶ ἐμβάντι αὐτῷ εἰς τὸ πλοῖον, ἠκολούθησαν αὐτῷ οἱ μαθηταὶ αὐτοῦ. ²⁴ καὶ ἰδοὺ σεισμὸς μέγας ἐγένετο ἐν τῇ θαλάσσῃ, ὥστε τὸ πλοῖον καλύπτεσθαι ὑπὸ τῶν κυμάτων· αὐτὸς δὲ ἐκάθευδεν. ²⁵ καὶ προσελθόντες ἤγειραν αὐτὸν λέγοντες, Κύριε σῶσον, ἀπολλύμεθα. ²⁶ καὶ λέγει αὐτοῖς, Τί δειλοί ἐστε, ὀλιγόπιστοι; τότε ἐγερθεὶς ἐπετίμησεν τοῖς ἀνέμοις καὶ τῇ θαλάσσῃ, καὶ ἐγένετο γαλήνη μεγάλη. ²⁷ οἱ δὲ ἄνθρωποι ἐθαύμασαν λέγοντες, Ποταπός ἐστιν οὗτος, ὅτι καὶ οἱ ἄνεμοι καὶ ἡ θάλασσα αὐτῷ ὑπακούουσιν;

²⁸ Καὶ ἐλθόντος αὐτοῦ εἰς τὸ πέραν εἰς τὴν χώραν τῶν Γαδαρηνῶν, ὑπήντησαν αὐτῷ δύο δαιμονιζόμενοι ἐκ τῶν μνημείων ἐξερχόμενοι, χαλεποὶ λίαν, ὥστε μὴ ἰσχύειν τινὰ παρελθεῖν διὰ τῆς ὁδοῦ ἐκείνης. ²⁹ καὶ ἰδοὺ ἔκραξαν λέγοντες, Τί ἡμῖν καὶ σοί, υἱὲ τοῦ θεοῦ; ἦλθες ὧδε πρὸ καιροῦ βασανίσαι ἡμᾶς; ³⁰ ἦν δὲ μακρὰν ἀπ' αὐτῶν ἀγέλη χοίρων πολλῶν βοσκομένη. ³¹ οἱ δὲ δαίμονες παρεκάλουν αὐτὸν λέγοντες, Εἰ ἐκβάλλεις ἡμᾶς, ἀπόστειλον ἡμᾶς εἰς τὴν ἀγέλην τῶν χοίρων. ³² καὶ εἶπεν αὐτοῖς, Ὑπάγετε. οἱ δὲ ἐξελθόντες ἀπῆλθον εἰς τοὺς χοίρους· καὶ ἰδοὺ ὥρμησεν πᾶσα ἡ ἀγέλη κατὰ τοῦ κρημνοῦ εἰς τὴν θάλασσαν, καὶ ἀπέθανον ἐν τοῖς ὕδασιν. ³³ οἱ δὲ βόσκοντες ἔφυγον, καὶ ἀπελθόντες εἰς τὴν πόλιν ἀπήγγειλαν πάντα καὶ τὰ τῶν δαιμονιζομένων. ³⁴ καὶ ἰδοὺ πᾶσα ἡ πόλις ἐξῆλθεν εἰς ὑπάντησιν τῷ Ἰησοῦ, καὶ ἰδόντες

αὐτὸν παρεκάλεσαν ὅπως μεταβῇ ἀπὸ τῶν ὁρίων αὐτῶν.

9 ¹Καὶ ἐμβὰς εἰς πλοῖον διεπέρασεν, καὶ ἦλθεν εἰς τὴν ἰδίαν πόλιν. ²καὶ ἰδοὺ προσέφερον αὐτῷ παραλυτικὸν ἐπὶ κλίνης βεβλημένον. καὶ ἰδὼν ὁ Ἰησοῦς τὴν πίστιν αὐτῶν εἶπεν τῷ παραλυτικῷ, Θάρσει τέκνον, ἀφίενταί σου αἱ ἁμαρτίαι. ³καὶ ἰδού τινες τῶν γραμματέων εἶπον ἐν ἑαυτοῖς, Οὗτος βλασφημεῖ. ⁴καὶ ἰδὼν ὁ Ἰησοῦς τὰς ἐνθυμήσεις αὐτῶν εἶπεν, Ἱνατί ἐνθυμεῖσθε πονηρὰ ἐν ταῖς καρδίαις ὑμῶν; ⁵τί γάρ ἐστιν εὐκοπώτερον εἰπεῖν, Ἀφίενταί σου αἱ ἁμαρτίαι, ἢ εἰπεῖν, Ἔγειρε καὶ περιπάτει; ⁶ἵνα δὲ εἰδῆτε ὅτι ἐξουσίαν ἔχει ὁ υἱὸς τοῦ ἀνθρώπου ἐπὶ τῆς γῆς ἀφιέναι ἁμαρτίας, τότε λέγει τῷ παραλυτικῷ, Ἐγερθεὶς ἆρόν σου τὴν κλίνην καὶ ὕπαγε εἰς τὸν οἶκόν σου. ⁷καὶ ἐγερθεὶς ἀπῆλθεν εἰς τὸν οἶκον αὐτοῦ. ⁸ἰδόντες δὲ οἱ ὄχλοι ἐφοβήθησαν καὶ ἐδόξασαν τὸν θεὸν τὸν δόντα ἐξουσίαν τοιαύτην τοῖς ἀνθρώποις.

⁹Καὶ παράγων ὁ Ἰησοῦς ἐκεῖθεν εἶδεν ἄνθρωπον καθήμενον ἐπὶ τὸ τελώνιον, Μαθθαῖον λεγόμενον, καὶ λέγει αὐτῷ, Ἀκολούθει μοι. καὶ ἀναστὰς ἠκολούθησεν αὐτῷ.

¹⁰Καὶ ἐγένετο αὐτοῦ ἀνακειμένου ἐν τῇ οἰκίᾳ, καὶ ἰδοὺ πολλοὶ τελῶναι καὶ ἁμαρτωλοὶ ἐλθόντες συνανέκειντο τῷ Ἰησοῦ καὶ τοῖς μαθηταῖς αὐτοῦ. ¹¹καὶ ἰδόντες οἱ Φαρισαῖοι ἔλεγον τοῖς μαθηταῖς αὐτοῦ, Διατί μετὰ τῶν τελωνῶν καὶ ἁμαρτωλῶν ἐσθίει ὁ διδάσκαλος ὑμῶν; ¹²ὁ δὲ ἀκούσας εἶπεν, Οὐ χρείαν ἔχουσιν οἱ ἰσχύοντες ἰατροῦ ἀλλ' οἱ κακῶς ἔχοντες. ¹³πορευθέντες δὲ μάθετε τί ἐστιν, Ἔλεος θέλω καὶ οὐ θυσίαν. οὐ γὰρ ἦλθον καλέσαι δικαίους ἀλλὰ ἁμαρτωλούς.

¹⁴ Τότε προσέρχονται αὐτῷ οἱ μαθηταὶ Ἰωάννου λέγοντες, Διατί ἡμεῖς καὶ οἱ Φαρισαῖοι νηστεύομεν πολλά, οἱ δὲ μαθηταί σου οὐ νηστεύουσιν; ¹⁵ καὶ εἶπεν αὐτοῖς ὁ Ἰησοῦς, Μὴ δύνανται οἱ υἱοὶ τοῦ νυμφῶνος πενθεῖν ἐφ' ὅσον μετ' αὐτῶν ἐστιν ὁ νυμφίος; ἐλεύσονται δὲ ἡμέραι ὅταν ἀπαρθῇ ἀπ' αὐτῶν ὁ νυμφίος, καὶ τότε νηστεύσουσιν. ¹⁶ οὐδεὶς δὲ ἐπιβάλλει ἐπίβλημα ῥάκους ἀγνάφου ἐπὶ ἱματίῳ παλαιῷ· αἴρει γὰρ τὸ πλήρωμα αὐτοῦ ἀπὸ τοῦ ἱματίου, καὶ χεῖρον σχίσμα γίνεται. ¹⁷ οὐδὲ βάλλουσιν οἶνον νέον εἰς ἀσκοὺς παλαιούς· εἰ δὲ μήγε, ῥήγνυνται οἱ ἀσκοί, καὶ ὁ οἶνος ἐκχεῖται καὶ οἱ ἀσκοὶ ἀπόλλυνται· ἀλλὰ βάλλουσιν οἶνον νέον εἰς ἀσκοὺς καινούς, καὶ ἀμφότεροι συντηροῦνται.

¹⁸ Ταῦτα αὐτοῦ λαλοῦντος αὐτοῖς, ἰδοὺ ἄρχων ἐλθὼν προσεκύνει αὐτῷ, λέγων ὅτι Ἡ θυγάτηρ μου ἄρτι ἐτελεύτησεν, ἀλλὰ ἐλθὼν ἐπίθες τὴν χεῖρά σου ἐπ' αὐτήν, καὶ ζήσεται. ¹⁹ καὶ ἐγερθεὶς ὁ Ἰησοῦς ἠκολούθει αὐτῷ καὶ οἱ μαθηταὶ αὐτοῦ. ²⁰ καὶ ἰδοὺ γυνὴ αἱμορροοῦσα δώδεκα ἔτη προσελθοῦσα ὄπισθεν ἥψατο τοῦ κρασπέδου τοῦ ἱματίου αὐτοῦ· ²¹ ἔλεγεν γὰρ ἐν ἑαυτῇ, Ἐὰν μόνον ἅψωμαι τοῦ ἱματίου αὐτοῦ, σωθήσομαι. ²² ὁ δὲ Ἰησοῦς στραφεὶς καὶ ἰδὼν αὐτὴν εἶπεν, Θάρσει θύγατερ, ἡ πίστις σου σέσωκέν σε. καὶ ἐσώθη ἡ γυνὴ ἀπὸ τῆς ὥρας ἐκείνης. ²³ καὶ ἐλθὼν ὁ Ἰησοῦς εἰς τὴν οἰκίαν τοῦ ἄρχοντος καὶ ἰδὼν τοὺς αὐλητὰς καὶ τὸν ὄχλον θορυβούμενον ²⁴ ἔλεγεν, Ἀναχωρεῖτε· οὐ γὰρ ἀπέθανεν τὸ κοράσιον ἀλλὰ καθεύδει. καὶ κατεγέλων αὐτοῦ. ²⁵ ὅτε δὲ ἐξεβλήθη ὁ ὄχλος, εἰσελθὼν ἐκράτησεν τῆς χειρὸς αὐτῆς, καὶ ἠγέρθη τὸ κοράσιον. ²⁶ καὶ ἐξῆλθεν ἡ φήμη αὕτη εἰς ὅλην τὴν γῆν ἐκείνην.

[²⁷ Καὶ παράγοντι ἐκεῖθεν τῷ Ἰησοῦ, ἠκολούθησαν

αὐτῷ δύο τυφλοὶ κράζοντες καὶ λέγοντες, Ἐλέησον ἡμᾶς, υἱὸς Δαυείδ. ²⁸ἐλθόντι δὲ εἰς τὴν οἰκίαν προσῆλθον αὐτῷ οἱ τυφλοί, καὶ λέγει αὐτοῖς ὁ Ἰησοῦς, Πιστεύετε ὅτι δύναμαι τοῦτο ποιῆσαι; λέγουσιν αὐτῷ, Ναί, κύριε. ²⁹τότε ἥψατο τῶν ὀφθαλμῶν αὐτῶν λέγων, Κατὰ τὴν πίστιν ὑμῶν γενηθήτω ὑμῖν. ³⁰καὶ ἀνεῴχθησαν αὐτῶν οἱ ὀφθαλμοί. καὶ ἐνεβριμήθη αὐτοῖς ὁ Ἰησοῦς λέγων, Ὁρᾶτε μηδεὶς γινωσκέτω. ³¹οἱ δὲ ἐξελθόντες διεφήμισαν αὐτὸν ἐν ὅλῃ τῇ γῇ ἐκείνῃ.] Rec

³²Αὐτῶν δὲ ἐξερχομένων, ἰδοὺ προσήνεγκαν αὐτῷ ἄνθρωπον κωφὸν δαιμονιζόμενον. ³³καὶ ἐκβληθέντος τοῦ δαιμονίου ἐλάλησεν ὁ κωφός. καὶ ἐθαύμασαν οἱ ὄχλοι λέγοντες, Οὐδέποτε ἐφάνη οὕτως ἐν τῷ Ἰσραήλ· ³⁴οἱ δὲ Φαρισαῖοι ἔλεγον, Ἐν τῷ ἄρχοντι τῶν δαιμονίων ἐκβάλλει τὰ δαιμόνια.

³⁵Καὶ περιῆγεν ὁ Ἰησοῦς τὰς πόλεις πάσας καὶ τὰς κώμας, διδάσκων ἐν ταῖς συναγωγαῖς αὐτῶν καὶ κηρύσσων τὸ εὐαγγέλιον τῆς βασιλείας καὶ θεραπεύων πᾶσαν νόσον καὶ πᾶσαν μαλακίαν. ³⁶ἰδὼν δὲ τοὺς ὄχλους ἐσπλαγχνίσθη περὶ αὐτῶν, ὅτι ἦσαν ἐσκυλμένοι καὶ ἐριμμένοι ὡσεὶ πρόβατα μὴ ἔχοντα ποιμένα. ³⁷τότε λέγει τοῖς μαθηταῖς αὐτοῦ, Ὁ μὲν θερισμὸς πολύς, οἱ δὲ ἐργάται ὀλίγοι· ³⁸δεήθητε οὖν τοῦ κυρίου τοῦ θερισμοῦ ὅπως ἐκβάλῃ ἐργάτας εἰς τὸν θερισμὸν αὐτοῦ.

10 ¹Καὶ προσκαλεσάμενος τοὺς δώδεκα μαθητὰς αὐτοῦ ἔδωκεν αὐτοῖς ἐξουσίαν πνευμάτων ἀκαθάρτων, ὥστε ἐκβάλλειν αὐτά, καὶ θεραπεύειν πᾶσαν νόσον καὶ πᾶσαν μαλακίαν. ²Τῶν δὲ δώδεκα ἀποστόλων τὰ ὀνόματά ἐστιν ταῦτα· πρῶτος Σίμων ὁ λεγόμενος Πέτρος καὶ Ἀνδρέας ὁ ἀδελφὸς αὐτοῦ, Ἰάκωβος ὁ τοῦ

Ζεβεδαίου καὶ Ἰωάννης ὁ ἀδελφὸς αὐτοῦ, ³ Φίλιππος καὶ Βαρθολομαῖος, Θωμᾶς καὶ Μαθθαῖος ὁ τελώνης, Ἰάκωβος ὁ τοῦ Ἀλφαίου καὶ Θαδδαῖος, ⁴ Σίμων ὁ Καναναῖος καὶ Ἰούδας Ἰσκαριώτης ὁ καὶ παραδοὺς αὐτόν.

⁵Τούτους τοὺς δώδεκα ἀπέστειλεν ὁ Ἰησοῦς παραγγείλας αὐτοῖς λέγων, Εἰς ὁδὸν ἐθνῶν μὴ ἀπέλθητε, καὶ εἰς πόλιν Σαμαρειτῶν μὴ εἰσέλθητε· ⁶ πορεύεσθε δὲ μᾶλλον πρὸς τὰ πρόβατα τὰ ἀπολωλότα οἴκου Ἰσραήλ. ⁷ πορευόμενοι δὲ κηρύσσετε λέγοντες ὅτι ἤγγικεν ἡ βασιλεία τῶν οὐρανῶν. ⁸ ἀσθενοῦντας θεραπεύετε, νεκροὺς ἐγείρετε, λεπροὺς καθαρίζετε, δαιμόνια ἐκβάλλετε· δωρεὰν ἐλάβετε, δωρεὰν δότε. ⁹ μὴ κτήσησθε χρυσὸν μηδὲ ἄργυρον μηδὲ χαλκὸν εἰς τὰς ζώνας ὑμῶν, ¹⁰ μὴ πήραν εἰς ὁδὸν μηδὲ δύο χιτῶνας μηδὲ ὑποδήματα μηδὲ ῥάβδον· ἄξιος γὰρ ὁ ἐργάτης τῆς τροφῆς αὐτοῦ. ¹¹ εἰς ἣν δ' ἂν πόλιν ἢ κώμην εἰσέλθητε, ἐξετάσατε τίς ἐν αὐτῇ ἄξιός ἐστιν· κἀκεῖ μείνατε ἕως ἂν ἐξέλθητε. ¹² εἰσερχόμενοι δὲ εἰς τὴν οἰκίαν ἀσπάσασθε αὐτήν. ¹³ καὶ ἐὰν μὲν ᾖ ἡ οἰκία ἀξία, ἐλθάτω ἡ εἰρήνη ὑμῶν ἐπ' αὐτήν· ἐὰν δὲ μὴ ᾖ ἀξία, ἡ εἰρήνη ὑμῶν πρὸς ὑμᾶς ἐπιστραφήτω. ¹⁴ καὶ ὃς ἂν μὴ δέξηται ὑμᾶς μηδὲ ἀκούσῃ τοὺς λόγους ὑμῶν, ἐξερχόμενοι ἔξω τῆς οἰκίας ἢ τῆς πόλεως ἐκείνης ἐκτινάξατε τὸν κονιορτὸν τῶν ποδῶν ὑμῶν. ¹⁵ ἀμὴν λέγω ὑμῖν, ἀνεκτότερον ἔσται γῇ Σοδόμων καὶ Γομόρρων ἐν ἡμέρᾳ κρίσεως ἢ τῇ πόλει ἐκείνῃ.

¹⁶ Ἰδοὺ ἐγὼ ἀποστέλλω ὑμᾶς ὡς πρόβατα ἐν μέσῳ λύκων· γίνεσθε οὖν φρόνιμοι ὡς οἱ ὄφεις καὶ ἀκέραιοι ὡς αἱ περιστεραί. ¹⁷ προσέχετε δὲ ἀπὸ τῶν ἀνθρώπων· παραδώσουσιν γὰρ ὑμᾶς εἰς συνέδρια, καὶ ἐν ταῖς συναγωγαῖς αὐτῶν μαστιγώσουσιν ὑμᾶς· ¹⁸ καὶ ἐπὶ ἡγεμόνας

δὲ καὶ βασιλεῖς ἀχθήσεσθε ἕνεκεν ἐμοῦ, εἰς μαρτύριον αὐτοῖς καὶ τοῖς ἔθνεσιν. ¹⁹ ὅταν δὲ παραδῶσιν ὑμᾶς, μὴ μεριμνήσητε πῶς ἢ τί λαλήσητε· δοθήσεται γὰρ ὑμῖν ἐν ἐκείνῃ τῇ ὥρᾳ τί λαλήσητε· ²⁰ οὐ γὰρ ὑμεῖς ἐστὲ οἱ λαλοῦντες, ἀλλὰ τὸ πνεῦμα τοῦ πατρὸς ὑμῶν τὸ λαλοῦν ἐν ὑμῖν. ²¹ παραδώσει δὲ ἀδελφὸς ἀδελφὸν εἰς θάνατον καὶ πατὴρ τέκνον, καὶ ἐπαναστήσονται τέκνα ἐπὶ γονεῖς καὶ θανατώσουσιν αὐτούς. ²² καὶ ἔσεσθε μισούμενοι ὑπὸ πάντων διὰ τὸ ὄνομά μου· ὁ δὲ ὑπομείνας εἰς τέλος, οὗτος σωθήσεται. ²³ ὅταν δὲ διώκωσιν ὑμᾶς ἐν τῇ πόλει ταύτῃ, φεύγετε εἰς τὴν ἑτέραν· ἀμὴν γὰρ λέγω ὑμῖν, οὐ μὴ τελέσητε τὰς πόλεις τοῦ Ἰσραὴλ ἕως ἂν ἔλθῃ ὁ υἱὸς τοῦ ἀνθρώπου. ²⁴ Οὐκ ἔστιν μαθητὴς ὑπὲρ τὸν διδάσκαλον, οὐδὲ δοῦλος ὑπὲρ τὸν κύριον αὐτοῦ. ²⁵ ἀρκετὸν τῷ μαθητῇ ἵνα γένηται ὡς ὁ διδάσκαλος αὐτοῦ, καὶ ὁ δοῦλος ὡς ὁ κύριος αὐτοῦ. εἰ τὸν οἰκοδεσπότην Βεελζεβοὺλ ἐπεκάλεσαν, πόσῳ μᾶλλον τοὺς οἰκιακοὺς αὐτοῦ. ²⁶ μὴ οὖν φοβηθῆτε αὐτούς· οὐδὲν γάρ ἐστιν κεκαλυμμένον ὃ οὐκ ἀποκαλυφθήσεται, καὶ κρυπτὸν ὃ οὐ γνωσθήσεται. ²⁷ ὃ λέγω ὑμῖν ἐν τῇ σκοτίᾳ, εἴπατε ἐν τῷ φωτί· καὶ ὃ εἰς τὸ οὖς ἀκούετε, κηρύξατε ἐπὶ τῶν δωμάτων. ²⁸ καὶ μὴ φοβεῖσθε ἀπὸ τῶν ἀποκτεννόντων τὸ σῶμα, τὴν δὲ ψυχὴν μὴ δυναμένων ἀποκτεῖναι· φοβήθητε δὲ μᾶλλον τὸν δυνάμενον καὶ ψυχὴν καὶ σῶμα ἀπολέσαι ἐν γεέννῃ. ²⁹ οὐχὶ δύο στρουθία ἀσσαρίου πωλεῖται; καὶ ἓν ἐξ αὐτῶν οὐ πεσεῖται ἐπὶ τὴν γῆν ἄνευ τοῦ πατρὸς ὑμῶν. ³⁰ ὑμῶν δὲ καὶ αἱ τρίχες τῆς κεφαλῆς πᾶσαι ἠριθμημέναι εἰσίν. ³¹ μὴ οὖν φοβεῖσθε· πολλῶν στρουθίων διαφέρετε ὑμεῖς. ³² Πᾶς οὖν ὅστις ὁμολογήσει ἐν ἐμοὶ ἔμπροσθεν τῶν ἀνθρώπων, ὁμολογήσω κἀγὼ ἐν αὐτῷ ἔμπροσθεν τοῦ πατρός μου τοῦ ἐν οὐρανοῖς· ³³ ὅστις δ' ἂν ἀρνήσηταί με ἔμπροσθεν τῶν ἀνθρώπων, ἀρνήσομαι κἀγὼ αὐτὸν ἔμπροσθεν τοῦ πατρός μου τοῦ ἐν οὐρανοῖς.

³⁴ Μὴ νομίσητε ὅτι ἦλθον βαλεῖν εἰρήνην ἐπὶ τὴν γῆν· οὐκ ἦλθον βαλεῖν εἰρήνην ἀλλὰ μάχαιραν. ³⁵ ἦλθον γὰρ διχάσαι ἄνθρωπον κατὰ τοῦ πατρὸς αὐτοῦ καὶ θυγατέρα κατὰ τῆς μητρὸς αὐτῆς καὶ νύμφην κατὰ τῆς πενθερᾶς αὐτῆς, ³⁶ καὶ ἐχθροὶ τοῦ ἀνθρώπου οἱ οἰκιακοὶ αὐτοῦ. ³⁷ Ὁ φιλῶν πατέρα ἢ μητέρα ὑπὲρ ἐμὲ οὐκ ἔστιν μου ἄξιος, καὶ ὁ φιλῶν υἱὸν ἢ θυγατέρα ὑπὲρ ἐμὲ οὐκ ἔστιν μου ἄξιος, ³⁸ καὶ ὃς οὐ λαμβάνει τὸν σταυρὸν αὐτοῦ καὶ ἀκολουθεῖ ὀπίσω μου, οὐκ ἔστιν μου ἄξιος. ³⁹ ὁ εὑρὼν τὴν ψυχὴν αὐτοῦ ἀπολέσει αὐτήν, καὶ ὁ ἀπολέσας τὴν ψυχὴν αὐτοῦ ἕνεκεν ἐμοῦ εὑρήσει αὐτήν.

⁴⁰ Ὁ δεχόμενος ὑμᾶς ἐμὲ δέχεται, καὶ ὁ ἐμὲ δεχόμενος δέχεται τὸν ἀποστείλαντά με. ⁴¹ ὁ δεχόμενος προφήτην εἰς ὄνομα προφήτου μισθὸν προφήτου λήμψεται, καὶ ὁ δεχόμενος δίκαιον εἰς ὄνομα δικαίου μισθὸν δικαίου λήμψεται. ⁴² καὶ ὃς ἐὰν ποτίσῃ ἕνα τῶν μικρῶν τούτων ποτήριον ψυχροῦ μόνον εἰς ὄνομα μαθητοῦ, ἀμὴν λέγω ὑμῖν, οὐ μὴ ἀπολέσῃ τὸν μισθὸν αὐτοῦ.

11 ¹ Καὶ ἐγένετο ὅτε ἐτέλεσεν ὁ Ἰησοῦς διατάσσων τοῖς δώδεκα μαθηταῖς αὐτοῦ, μετέβη ἐκεῖθεν τοῦ διδάσκειν καὶ κηρύσσειν ἐν ταῖς πόλεσιν αὐτῶν.

² Ὁ δὲ Ἰωάννης ἀκούσας ἐν τῷ δεσμωτηρίῳ τὰ ἔργα τοῦ Χριστοῦ, πέμψας διὰ τῶν μαθητῶν αὐτοῦ ³ εἶπεν αὐτῷ, Σὺ εἶ ὁ ἐρχόμενος, ἢ ἕτερον προσδοκῶμεν; ⁴ καὶ ἀποκριθεὶς ὁ Ἰησοῦς εἶπεν αὐτοῖς, Πορευθέντες ἀπαγγείλατε Ἰωάννῃ ἃ ἀκούετε καὶ βλέπετε· ⁵ τυφλοὶ ἀναβλέπουσιν καὶ χωλοὶ περιπατοῦσιν, λεπροὶ καθαρίζονται καὶ κωφοὶ ἀκούουσιν, καὶ νεκροὶ ἐγείρον-

ται καὶ πτωχοὶ εὐαγγελίζονται· ⁶ καὶ μακάριός ἐστιν ὃς ἐὰν μὴ σκανδαλισθῇ ἐν ἐμοί.

⁷ Τούτων δὲ πορευομένων ἤρξατο ὁ Ἰησοῦς λέγειν τοῖς ὄχλοις περὶ Ἰωάννου, Τί ἐξήλθατε εἰς τὴν ἔρημον θεάσασθαι; κάλαμον ὑπὸ ἀνέμου σαλευόμενον; ⁸ ἀλλὰ τί ἐξήλθατε ἰδεῖν; ἄνθρωπον ἐν μαλακοῖς ἠμφιεσμένον; ἰδοὺ οἱ τὰ μαλακὰ φοροῦντες ἐν τοῖς οἴκοις τῶν βασιλέων εἰσίν· ⁹ ἀλλὰ τί ἐξήλθατε; προφήτην ἰδεῖν; ναὶ λέγω ὑμῖν, καὶ περισσότερον προφήτου. ¹⁰ οὗτός ἐστιν περὶ οὗ γέγραπται, Ἰδοὺ ἐγὼ ἀποστέλλω τὸν ἄγγελόν μου πρὸ προσώπου σου, ὃς κατασκευάσει τὴν ὁδόν σου ἔμπροσθέν σου. ¹¹ ἀμὴν λέγω ὑμῖν, οὐκ ἐγήγερται ἐν γεννητοῖς γυναικῶν μείζων Ἰωάννου τοῦ βαπτιστοῦ· ὁ δὲ μικρότερος ἐν τῇ βασιλείᾳ τῶν οὐρανῶν μείζων αὐτοῦ ἐστίν. ¹² ἀπὸ δὲ τῶν ἡμερῶν Ἰωάννου τοῦ βαπτιστοῦ ἕως ἄρτι ἡ βασιλεία τῶν οὐρανῶν βιάζεται, καὶ βιασταὶ ἁρπάζουσιν αὐτήν. ¹³ πάντες γὰρ οἱ προφῆται καὶ ὁ νόμος ἕως Ἰωάννου ἐπροφήτευσαν, ¹⁴ καὶ εἰ θέλετε δέξασθαι, αὐτός ἐστιν Ἡλίας ὁ μέλλων ἔρχεσθαι. ¹⁵ ὁ ἔχων ὦτα ἀκούειν ἀκουέτω.

¹⁶ Τίνι δὲ ὁμοιώσω τὴν γενεὰν ταύτην; ὁμοία ἐστὶν παιδίοις καθημένοις ἐν ταῖς ἀγοραῖς, ἃ προσφωνοῦντα τοῖς ἑτέροις ¹⁷ λέγουσιν, Ηὐλήσαμεν ὑμῖν, καὶ οὐκ ὠρχήσασθε· ἐθρηνήσαμεν, καὶ οὐκ ἐκόψασθε. ¹⁸ ἦλθεν γὰρ Ἰωάννης μήτε ἐσθίων μήτε πίνων, καὶ λέγουσιν, Δαιμόνιον ἔχει. ¹⁹ ἦλθεν ὁ υἱὸς τοῦ ἀνθρώπου ἐσθίων καὶ πίνων, καὶ λέγουσιν, Ἰδοὺ ἄνθρωπος φάγος καὶ οἰνοπότης, τελωνῶν φίλος καὶ ἁμαρτωλῶν. καὶ ἐδικαιώθη ἡ σοφία ἀπὸ τῶν ἔργων αὐτῆς.

²⁰ Τότε ἤρξατο ὀνειδίζειν τὰς πόλεις ἐν αἷς ἐγένοντο αἱ πλεῖσται δυνάμεις αὐτοῦ, ὅτι οὐ μετενόησαν. ²¹ Οὐαί

σοι Χοραζείν, οὐαί σοι Βηθσαϊδάν, ὅτι εἰ ἐν Τύρῳ καὶ Σιδῶνι ἐγένοντο αἱ δυνάμεις αἱ γενόμεναι ἐν ὑμῖν, πάλαι ἂν ἐν σάκκῳ καὶ σποδῷ μετενόησαν. ²²πλὴν λέγω ὑμῖν, Τύρῳ καὶ Σιδῶνι ἀνεκτότερον ἔσται ἐν ἡμέρᾳ κρίσεως ἢ ὑμῖν. ²³καὶ σὺ Καφαρναούμ, μὴ ἕως οὐρανοῦ ὑψωθήσῃ; ἕως ᾅδου καταβιβασθήσῃ, ὅτι εἰ ἐν Σοδόμοις ἐγενήθησαν αἱ δυνάμεις αἱ γενόμεναι ἐν σοί, ἔμεινεν ἂν μέχρι τῆς σήμερον. ²⁴πλὴν λέγω ὑμῖν ὅτι γῇ Σοδόμων ἀνεκτότερον ἔσται ἐν ἡμέρᾳ κρίσεως ἢ σοί.

²⁵Ἐν ἐκείνῳ τῷ καιρῷ ἀποκριθεὶς ὁ Ἰησοῦς εἶπεν, Ἐξομολογοῦμαί σοι πάτερ, κύριε τοῦ οὐρανοῦ καὶ τῆς γῆς, ὅτι ἔκρυψας ταῦτα ἀπὸ σοφῶν καὶ συνετῶν, καὶ ἀπεκάλυψας αὐτὰ νηπίοις· ²⁶ναὶ ὁ πατήρ, ὅτι οὕτως ἐγένετο εὐδοκία ἔμπροσθέν σου. ²⁷Πάντα μοι παρεδόθη ὑπὸ τοῦ πατρός μου, καὶ οὐδεὶς ἐπιγινώσκει τὸν υἱὸν εἰ μὴ ὁ πατήρ, οὐδὲ τὸν πατέρα τις ἐπιγινώσκει εἰ μὴ ὁ υἱὸς καὶ ᾧ ἐὰν βούληται ὁ υἱὸς ἀποκαλύψαι.

²⁸Δεῦτε πρός με πάντες οἱ κοπιῶντες καὶ πεφορτισμένοι, κἀγὼ ἀναπαύσω ὑμᾶς. ²⁹ἄρατε τὸν ζυγόν μου ἐφ' ὑμᾶς καὶ μάθετε ἀπ' ἐμοῦ, ὅτι πραΰς εἰμι καὶ ταπεινὸς τῇ καρδίᾳ, καὶ εὑρήσετε ἀνάπαυσιν ταῖς ψυχαῖς ὑμῶν. ³⁰ὁ γὰρ ζυγός μου χρηστὸς καὶ τὸ φορτίον μου ἐλαφρόν ἐστιν.

12 ¹Ἐν ἐκείνῳ τῷ καιρῷ ἐπορεύθη ὁ Ἰησοῦς τοῖς σάββασιν διὰ τῶν σπορίμων· οἱ δὲ μαθηταὶ αὐτοῦ ἐπείνασαν, καὶ ἤρξαντο τίλλειν στάχυας καὶ ἐσθίειν. ²οἱ δὲ Φαρισαῖοι ἰδόντες εἶπαν αὐτῷ, Ἰδοὺ οἱ μαθηταί σου ποιοῦσιν ὃ οὐκ ἔξεστιν ποιεῖν ἐν σαββάτῳ. ³ὁ δὲ εἶπεν αὐτοῖς, Οὐκ ἀνέγνωτε τί ἐποίησεν Δαυείδ, ὅτε ἐπείνασεν καὶ οἱ μετ' αὐτοῦ; ⁴πῶς εἰσῆλθεν εἰς τὸν οἶκον τοῦ θεοῦ καὶ τοὺς ἄρτους τῆς προθέσεως ἔφαγεν, ὃ οὐκ ἐξὸν ἦν αὐτῷ φαγεῖν οὐδὲ τοῖς μετ' αὐτοῦ, εἰ μὴ τοῖς ἱερεῦσιν μόνοις; ⁵ἢ οὐκ ἀνέγνωτε ἐν τῷ νόμῳ ὅτι τοῖς σάββασιν οἱ ἱερεῖς ἐν τῷ ἱερῷ τὸ σάββατον βεβηλοῦσιν καὶ ἀναίτιοί εἰσιν; ⁶λέγω δὲ ὑμῖν ὅτι τοῦ ἱεροῦ μεῖζόν ἐστιν ὧδε. ⁷εἰ δὲ ἐγνώκειτε τί ἐστιν, Ἔλεος θέλω καὶ οὐ θυσίαν, οὐκ ἂν κατεδικάσατε τοὺς ἀναιτίους. ⁸κύριος γάρ ἐστιν τοῦ σαββάτου ὁ υἱὸς τοῦ ἀνθρώπου.

⁹Καὶ μεταβὰς ἐκεῖθεν ἦλθεν εἰς τὴν συναγωγὴν αὐτῶν. ¹⁰καὶ ἰδοὺ ἄνθρωπος χεῖρα ἔχων ξηράν· καὶ ἐπηρώτησαν αὐτὸν λέγοντες, Εἰ ἔξεστιν τοῖς σάββασιν θεραπεύειν; ἵνα κατηγορήσωσιν αὐτοῦ. ¹¹ὁ δὲ εἶπεν αὐτοῖς, Τίς ἔσται ἐξ ὑμῶν ἄνθρωπος ὃς ἕξει πρόβατον ἕν, καὶ ἐὰν ἐμπέσῃ τοῦτο τοῖς σάββασιν εἰς βόθυνον, οὐχὶ κρατήσει αὐτὸ καὶ ἐγερεῖ; ¹²πόσῳ οὖν διαφέρει ἄνθρωπος προβάτου· ὥστε ἔξεστιν τοῖς σάββασιν καλῶς ποιεῖν. ¹³τότε λέγει τῷ ἀνθρώπῳ, Ἔκτεινόν σου τὴν χεῖρα. καὶ ἐξέτεινεν, καὶ ἀπεκατεστάθη ὑγιὴς ὡς ἡ ἄλλη.

¹⁴Ἐξελθόντες δὲ οἱ Φαρισαῖοι συμβούλιον ἔλαβον κατ' αὐτοῦ, ὅπως αὐτὸν ἀπολέσωσιν. ¹⁵ὁ δὲ Ἰησοῦς γνοὺς ἀνεχώρησεν ἐκεῖθεν. καὶ ἠκολούθησαν αὐτῷ πολλοί, καὶ ἐθεράπευσεν αὐτοὺς πάντας, ¹⁶καὶ ἐπετίμησεν αὐτοῖς ἵνα μὴ φανερὸν αὐτὸν ποιήσωσιν· ¹⁷ἵνα πληρωθῇ τὸ ῥηθὲν διὰ Ἡσαΐου τοῦ προφήτου λέγοντος, ¹⁸Ἰδοὺ ὁ παῖς μου ὃν ᾑρέτισα, ὁ ἀγαπητός μου εἰς ὃν ηὐδόκησεν ἡ ψυχή μου· θήσω τὸ πνεῦμά μου ἐπ' αὐτόν, καὶ κρίσιν τοῖς ἔθνεσιν ἀπαγγελεῖ. ¹⁹οὐκ ἐρίσει οὐδὲ κραυγάσει, οὐδὲ ἀκούσει τις ἐν ταῖς πλατείαις τὴν φωνὴν αὐτοῦ. ²⁰κάλαμον συντετριμμένον οὐ κατεάξει καὶ λίνον τυφόμενον οὐ σβέσει, ἕως ἂν

ἐκβάλῃ εἰς νῖκος τὴν κρίσιν. ²¹ καὶ τῷ ὀνόματι αὐτοῦ ἔθνη ἐλπιοῦσιν.

²² Τότε προσηνέχθη αὐτῷ δαιμονιζόμενος τυφλὸς καὶ κωφός· καὶ ἐθεράπευσεν αὐτόν, ὥστε τὸν κωφὸν λαλεῖν καὶ βλέπειν. ²³ καὶ ἐξίσταντο πάντες οἱ ὄχλοι καὶ ἔλεγον, Μήτι οὗτός ἐστιν ὁ υἱὸς Δαυείδ; ²⁴ οἱ δὲ Φαρισαῖοι ἀκούσαντες εἶπον, Οὗτος οὐκ ἐκβάλλει τὰ δαιμόνια εἰ μὴ ἐν τῷ Βεελζεβοὺλ ἄρχοντι τῶν δαιμονίων. ²⁵ εἰδὼς δὲ τὰς ἐνθυμήσεις αὐτῶν εἶπεν αὐτοῖς, Πᾶσα βασιλεία μερισθεῖσα καθ' ἑαυτῆς ἐρημοῦται, καὶ πᾶσα πόλις ἢ οἰκία μερισθεῖσα καθ' ἑαυτῆς οὐ σταθήσεται. ²⁶ καὶ εἰ ὁ σατανᾶς τὸν σατανᾶν ἐκβάλλει, ἐφ' ἑαυτὸν ἐμερίσθη· πῶς οὖν σταθήσεται ἡ βασιλεία αὐτοῦ; ²⁷ καὶ εἰ ἐγὼ ἐν Βεελζεβοὺλ ἐκβάλλω τὰ δαιμόνια, οἱ υἱοὶ ὑμῶν ἐν τίνι ἐκβάλλουσιν; διὰ τοῦτο αὐτοὶ κριταὶ ἔσονται ὑμῶν. ²⁸ εἰ δὲ ἐν πνεύματι θεοῦ ἐγὼ ἐκβάλλω τὰ δαιμόνια, ἄρα ἔφθασεν ἐφ' ὑμᾶς ἡ βασιλεία τοῦ θεοῦ. ²⁹ ἢ πῶς δύναταί τις εἰσελθεῖν εἰς τὴν οἰκίαν τοῦ ἰσχυροῦ καὶ τὰ σκεύη αὐτοῦ ἁρπάσαι, ἐὰν μὴ πρῶτον δήσῃ τὸν ἰσχυρόν; καὶ τότε τὴν οἰκίαν αὐτοῦ διαρπάσει. ³⁰ ὁ μὴ ὢν μετ' ἐμοῦ κατ' ἐμοῦ ἐστίν, καὶ ὁ μὴ συνάγων μετ' ἐμοῦ σκορπίζει.

³¹ Διὰ τοῦτο λέγω ὑμῖν, πᾶσα ἁμαρτία καὶ βλασφημία ἀφεθήσεται τοῖς ἀνθρώποις, ἡ δὲ τοῦ πνεύματος βλασφημία οὐκ ἀφεθήσεται. ³² καὶ ὃς ἐὰν εἴπῃ λόγον κατὰ τοῦ υἱοῦ τοῦ ἀνθρώπου, ἀφεθήσεται αὐτῷ· ὃς δ' ἂν εἴπῃ κατὰ τοῦ πνεύματος τοῦ ἁγίου, οὐκ ἀφεθήσεται αὐτῷ οὔτε ἐν τούτῳ τῷ αἰῶνι οὔτε ἐν τῷ μέλλοντι. ³³ Ἢ ποιήσατε τὸ δένδρον καλὸν καὶ τὸν καρπὸν αὐτοῦ καλόν, ἢ ποιήσατε τὸ δένδρον σαπρὸν καὶ τὸν καρπὸν αὐτοῦ σαπρόν· ἐκ γὰρ τοῦ καρποῦ τὸ δένδρον γινώσκεται.

³⁴ γεννήματα ἐχιδνῶν, πῶς δύνασθε ἀγαθὰ λαλεῖν πονηροὶ ὄντες; ἐκ γὰρ τοῦ περισσεύματος τῆς καρδίας τὸ στόμα λαλεῖ. ³⁵ ὁ ἀγαθὸς ἄνθρωπος ἐκ τοῦ ἀγαθοῦ θησαυροῦ ἐκβάλλει τὰ ἀγαθά, καὶ ὁ πονηρὸς ἄνθρωπος ἐκ τοῦ πονηροῦ θησαυροῦ ἐκβάλλει πονηρά. ³⁶ λέγω δὲ ὑμῖν ὅτι πᾶν ῥῆμα ἀργὸν ὃ λαλήσουσιν οἱ ἄνθρωποι, ἀποδώσουσιν περὶ αὐτοῦ λόγον ἐν ἡμέρᾳ κρίσεως. ³⁷ ἐκ γὰρ τῶν λόγων σου δικαιωθήσῃ, καὶ ἐκ τῶν λόγων σου καταδικασθήσῃ.

³⁸ Τότε ἀπεκρίθησαν αὐτῷ τινὲς τῶν γραμματέων καὶ Φαρισαίων λέγοντες, Διδάσκαλε, θέλομεν ἀπὸ σοῦ σημεῖον ἰδεῖν. ³⁹ ὁ δὲ ἀποκριθεὶς εἶπεν αὐτοῖς, Γενεὰ πονηρὰ καὶ μοιχαλὶς σημεῖον ἐπιζητεῖ, καὶ σημεῖον οὐ δοθήσεται αὐτῇ εἰ μὴ τὸ σημεῖον Ἰωνᾶ τοῦ προφήτου. ⁴⁰ ὥσπερ γὰρ ἦν Ἰωνᾶς ἐν τῇ κοιλίᾳ τοῦ κήτους τρεῖς ἡμέρας καὶ τρεῖς νύκτας, οὕτως ἔσται ὁ υἱὸς τοῦ ἀνθρώπου ἐν τῇ καρδίᾳ τῆς γῆς τρεῖς ἡμέρας καὶ τρεῖς νύκτας. ⁴¹ ἄνδρες Νινευεῖται ἀναστήσονται ἐν τῇ κρίσει μετὰ τῆς γενεᾶς ταύτης καὶ κατακρινοῦσιν αὐτήν, ὅτι μετενόησαν εἰς τὸ κήρυγμα Ἰωνᾶ, καὶ ἰδοὺ πλεῖον Ἰωνᾶ ὧδε. ⁴² βασίλισσα νότου ἐγερθήσεται ἐν τῇ κρίσει μετὰ τῆς γενεᾶς ταύτης καὶ κατακρινεῖ αὐτήν, ὅτι ἦλθεν ἐκ τῶν περάτων τῆς γῆς ἀκοῦσαι τὴν σοφίαν Σολομῶνος, καὶ ἰδοὺ πλεῖον Σολομῶνος ὧδε.

⁴³ Ὅταν δὲ τὸ ἀκάθαρτον πνεῦμα ἐξέλθῃ ἀπὸ τοῦ ἀνθρώπου, διέρχεται δι' ἀνύδρων τόπων ζητοῦν ἀνάπαυσιν, καὶ οὐχ εὑρίσκει. ⁴⁴ τότε λέγει, Εἰς τὸν οἶκόν μου ἐπιστρέψω ὅθεν ἐξῆλθον. καὶ ἐλθὸν εὑρίσκει σχολάζοντα σεσαρωμένον καὶ κεκοσμημένον. ⁴⁵ τότε πορεύεται καὶ παραλαμβάνει μεθ' ἑαυτοῦ ἑπτὰ ἕτερα πνεύματα πονηρότερα ἑαυτοῦ, καὶ εἰσελθόντα κατοικεῖ ἐκεῖ,

καὶ γίνεται τὰ ἔσχατα τοῦ ἀνθρώπου ἐκείνου χείρονα τῶν πρώτων. οὕτως ἔσται καὶ τῇ γενεᾷ ταύτῃ τῇ πονηρᾷ.

⁴⁶ Ἔτι αὐτοῦ λαλοῦντος τοῖς ὄχλοις, ἰδοὺ ἡ μήτηρ καὶ οἱ ἀδελφοὶ αὐτοῦ εἱστήκεισαν ἔξω ζητοῦντες αὐτῷ λαλῆσαι. ⁴⁷ εἶπεν δέ τις αὐτῷ, Ἰδοὺ ἡ μήτηρ σου καὶ οἱ ἀδελφοί σου ἔξω ἑστήκασιν ζητοῦντές σοι λαλῆσαι. ⁴⁸ ὁ δὲ ἀποκριθεὶς εἶπεν τῷ λέγοντι αὐτῷ, Τίς ἐστιν ἡ μήτηρ μου, καὶ τίνες εἰσὶν οἱ ἀδελφοί μου; ⁴⁹ καὶ ἐκτείνας τὴν χεῖρα αὐτοῦ ἐπὶ τοὺς μαθητὰς αὐτοῦ εἶπεν, Ἰδοὺ ἡ μήτηρ μου καὶ οἱ ἀδελφοί μου· ⁵⁰ ὅστις γὰρ ἂν ποιήσῃ τὸ θέλημα τοῦ πατρός μου τοῦ ἐν οὐρανοῖς, αὐτός μου ἀδελφὸς καὶ ἀδελφὴ καὶ μήτηρ ἐστίν.

13 ¹ Ἐν τῇ ἡμέρᾳ ἐκείνῃ ἐξελθὼν ὁ Ἰησοῦς ἐκ τῆς οἰκίας ἐκάθητο παρὰ τὴν θάλασσαν. ² καὶ συνήχθησαν πρὸς αὐτὸν ὄχλοι πολλοί, ὥστε αὐτὸν εἰς πλοῖον ἐμβάντα καθῆσθαι, καὶ πᾶς ὁ ὄχλος ἐπὶ τὸν αἰγιαλὸν εἱστήκει. ³ καὶ ἐλάλησεν αὐτοῖς πολλὰ ἐν παραβολαῖς, λέγων, Ἰδοὺ ἐξῆλθεν ὁ σπείρων τοῦ σπείρειν. ⁴ καὶ ἐν τῷ σπείρειν αὐτὸν ἃ μὲν ἔπεσεν παρὰ τὴν ὁδόν, καὶ ἦλθεν τὰ πετεινὰ καὶ κατέφαγεν αὐτά. ⁵ ἄλλα δὲ ἔπεσεν ἐπὶ τὰ πετρώδη ὅπου οὐκ εἶχεν γῆν πολλήν, καὶ εὐθέως ἐξανέτειλεν διὰ τὸ μὴ ἔχειν βάθος γῆς· ⁶ ἡλίου δὲ ἀνατείλαντος ἐκαυματίσθη, καὶ διὰ τὸ μὴ ἔχειν ῥίζαν ἐξηράνθη. ⁷ ἄλλα δὲ ἔπεσεν ἐπὶ τὰς ἀκάνθας, καὶ ἀνέβησαν αἱ ἄκανθαι καὶ ἀπέπνιξαν αὐτά. ⁸ ἄλλα δὲ ἔπεσεν ἐπὶ τὴν γῆν τὴν καλὴν καὶ ἐδίδου καρπόν, ὃ μὲν ἑκατόν, ὃ δὲ ἑξήκοντα, ὃ δὲ τριάκοντα. ⁹ ὁ ἔχων ὦτα ἀκουέτω.

¹⁰ Καὶ προσελθόντες οἱ μαθηταὶ εἶπαν αὐτῷ, Διατί ἐν παραβολαῖς λαλεῖς αὐτοῖς; ¹¹ ὁ δὲ ἀποκριθεὶς εἶπεν

αὐτοῖς ὅτι Ὑμῖν δέδοται γνῶναι τὰ μυστήρια τῆς βασιλείας τῶν οὐρανῶν, ἐκείνοις δὲ οὐ δέδοται. ¹² ὅστις γὰρ ἔχει, δοθήσεται αὐτῷ καὶ περισσευθήσεται· ὅστις δὲ οὐκ ἔχει, καὶ ὃ ἔχει ἀρθήσεται ἀπ' αὐτοῦ. ¹³ διὰ τοῦτο ἐν παραβολαῖς αὐτοῖς λαλῶ, ὅτι βλέποντες οὐ βλέπουσιν καὶ ἀκούοντες οὐκ ἀκούουσιν οὐδὲ συνιοῦσιν. ¹⁴ καὶ ἀναπληροῦται αὐτοῖς ἡ προφητεία Ἡσαΐου ἡ λέγουσα, Ἀκοῇ ἀκούσετε καὶ οὐ μὴ συνῆτε, καὶ βλέποντες βλέψετε καὶ οὐ μὴ ἴδητε. ¹⁵ ἐπαχύνθη γὰρ ἡ καρδία τοῦ λαοῦ τούτου, καὶ τοῖς ὠσὶν βαρέως ἤκουσαν, καὶ τοὺς ὀφθαλμοὺς αὐτῶν ἐκάμμυσαν, μήποτε ἴδωσιν τοῖς ὀφθαλμοῖς καὶ τοῖς ὠσὶν ἀκούσωσιν καὶ τῇ καρδίᾳ συνῶσιν καὶ ἐπιστρέψωσιν, καὶ ἰάσομαι αὐτούς. ¹⁶ ὑμῶν δὲ μακάριοι οἱ ὀφθαλμοὶ ὅτι βλέπουσιν, καὶ τὰ ὦτα ὑμῶν ὅτι ἀκούουσιν. ¹⁷ ἀμὴν γὰρ λέγω ὑμῖν ὅτι πολλοὶ προφῆται καὶ δίκαιοι ἐπεθύμησαν ἰδεῖν ἃ βλέπετε, καὶ οὐκ εἶδαν, καὶ ἀκοῦσαι ἃ ἀκούετε, καὶ οὐκ ἤκουσαν.

¹⁸ Ὑμεῖς οὖν ἀκούσατε τὴν παραβολὴν τοῦ σπείραντος. ¹⁹ παντὸς ἀκούοντος τὸν λόγον τῆς βασιλείας καὶ μὴ συνιέντος, ἔρχεται ὁ πονηρὸς καὶ ἁρπάζει τὸ ἐσπαρμένον ἐν τῇ καρδίᾳ αὐτοῦ· οὗτός ἐστιν ὁ παρὰ τὴν ὁδὸν σπαρείς. ²⁰ ὁ δὲ ἐπὶ τὰ πετρώδη σπαρείς, οὗτός ἐστιν ὁ τὸν λόγον ἀκούων καὶ εὐθὺς μετὰ χαρᾶς λαμβάνων αὐτόν· ²¹ οὐκ ἔχει δὲ ῥίζαν ἐν ἑαυτῷ ἀλλὰ πρόσκαιρός ἐστιν, γενομένης δὲ θλίψεως ἢ διωγμοῦ διὰ τὸν λόγον εὐθὺς σκανδαλίζεται. ²² ὁ δὲ εἰς τὰς ἀκάνθας σπαρείς, οὗτός ἐστιν ὁ τὸν λόγον ἀκούων, καὶ ἡ μέριμνα τοῦ αἰῶνος καὶ ἡ ἀπάτη τοῦ πλούτου συμπνίγει τὸν λόγον, καὶ ἄκαρπος γίνεται. ²³ ὁ δὲ ἐπὶ τὴν καλὴν γῆν σπαρείς, οὗτός ἐστιν ὁ τὸν λόγον ἀκούων καὶ συνιείς,

ὃς δὴ καρποφορεῖ καὶ ποιεῖ ὁ μὲν ἑκατόν, ὁ δὲ ἑξήκοντα, ὁ δὲ τριάκοντα.

²⁴ Ἄλλην παραβολὴν παρέθηκεν αὐτοῖς λέγων, Ὡμοιώθη ἡ βασιλεία τῶν οὐρανῶν ἀνθρώπῳ σπείραντι καλὸν σπέρμα ἐν τῷ ἀγρῷ αὐτοῦ. ²⁵ ἐν δὲ τῷ καθεύδειν τοὺς ἀνθρώπους ἦλθεν αὐτοῦ ὁ ἐχθρὸς καὶ ἐπέσπειρεν ζιζάνια ἀνὰ μέσον τοῦ σίτου καὶ ἀπῆλθεν. ²⁶ ὅτε δὲ ἐβλάστησεν ὁ χόρτος καὶ καρπὸν ἐποίησεν, τότε ἐφάνη καὶ τὰ ζιζάνια. ²⁷ προσελθόντες δὲ οἱ δοῦλοι τοῦ οἰκοδεσπότου εἶπον αὐτῷ, Κύριε, οὐχὶ καλὸν σπέρμα ἔσπειρας ἐν τῷ σῷ ἀγρῷ; πόθεν οὖν ἔχει ζιζάνια; ²⁸ ὁ δὲ ἔφη αὐτοῖς, Ἐχθρὸς ἄνθρωπος τοῦτο ἐποίησεν. οἱ δὲ δοῦλοι αὐτῷ λέγουσιν, Θέλεις οὖν ἀπελθόντες συλλέξωμεν αὐτά; ²⁹ ὁ δὲ φησίν, Οὔ, μήποτε συλλέγοντες τὰ ζιζάνια ἐκριζώσητε ἅμα αὐτοῖς τὸν σῖτον. ³⁰ ἄφετε συναυξάνεσθαι ἀμφότερα μέχρι τοῦ θερισμοῦ, καὶ ἐν καιρῷ τοῦ θερισμοῦ ἐρῶ τοῖς θερισταῖς, Συλλέξατε πρῶτον τὰ ζιζάνια καὶ δήσατε αὐτὰ εἰς δεσμὰς πρὸς τὸ κατακαῦσαι αὐτά, τὸν δὲ σῖτον συναγάγετε εἰς τὴν ἀποθήκην μου.

³¹ Ἄλλην παραβολὴν παρέθηκεν αὐτοῖς λέγων, Ὁμοία ἐστὶν ἡ βασιλεία τῶν οὐρανῶν κόκκῳ σινάπεως, ὃν λαβὼν ἄνθρωπος ἔσπειρεν ἐν τῷ ἀγρῷ αὐτοῦ· ³² ὃ μικρότερον μέν ἐστιν πάντων τῶν σπερμάτων, ὅταν δὲ αὐξηθῇ, μεῖζον τῶν λαχάνων ἐστὶν καὶ γίνεται δένδρον, ὥστε ἐλθεῖν τὰ πετεινὰ τοῦ οὐρανοῦ καὶ κατασκηνοῦν ἐν τοῖς κλάδοις αὐτοῦ.

³³ Ἄλλην παραβολὴν ἐλάλησεν αὐτοῖς, Ὁμοία ἐστὶν ἡ βασιλεία τῶν οὐρανῶν ζύμῃ, ἣν λαβοῦσα γυνὴ ἐνέκρυψεν εἰς ἀλεύρου σάτα τρία, ἕως οὗ ἐζυμώθη ὅλον. ³⁴ Ταῦτα πάντα ἐλάλησεν ὁ Ἰησοῦς ἐν παρα-

βολαῖς τοῖς ὄχλοις, καὶ χωρὶς παραβολῆς οὐδὲν ἐλάλει αὐτοῖς, ³⁵ ὅπως πληρωθῇ τὸ ῥηθὲν διὰ τοῦ προφήτου λέγοντος, Ἀνοίξω ἐν παραβολαῖς τὸ στόμα μου, ἐρεύξομαι κεκρυμμένα ἀπὸ καταβολῆς.

³⁶ Τότε ἀφεὶς τοὺς ὄχλους ἦλθεν εἰς τὴν οἰκίαν. καὶ προσῆλθον αὐτῷ οἱ μαθηταὶ αὐτοῦ λέγοντες, Φράσον ἡμῖν τὴν παραβολὴν τῶν ζιζανίων τοῦ ἀγροῦ. ³⁷ ὁ δὲ ἀποκριθεὶς εἶπεν, Ὁ σπείρων τὸ καλὸν σπέρμα ἐστὶν ὁ υἱὸς τοῦ ἀνθρώπου, ὁ δὲ ἀγρός ἐστιν ὁ κόσμος· ³⁸ τὸ δὲ καλὸν σπέρμα, οὗτοί εἰσιν οἱ υἱοὶ τῆς βασιλείας· τὰ δὲ ζιζάνιά εἰσιν οἱ υἱοὶ τοῦ πονηροῦ, ³⁹ ὁ δὲ ἐχθρὸς ὁ σπείρας αὐτά ἐστιν ὁ διάβολος· ὁ δὲ θερισμὸς συντέλεια αἰῶνός ἐστιν, οἱ δὲ θερισταὶ ἄγγελοί εἰσιν. ⁴⁰ ὥσπερ οὖν συλλέγεται τὰ ζιζάνια καὶ πυρὶ κατακαίεται, οὕτως ἔσται ἐν τῇ συντελείᾳ τοῦ αἰῶνος. ⁴¹ ἀποστελεῖ ὁ υἱὸς τοῦ ἀνθρώπου τοὺς ἀγγέλους αὐτοῦ, καὶ συλλέξουσιν ἐκ τῆς βασιλείας αὐτοῦ πάντα τὰ σκάνδαλα καὶ τοὺς ποιοῦντας τὴν ἀνομίαν, ⁴² καὶ βαλοῦσιν αὐτοὺς εἰς τὴν κάμινον τοῦ πυρός· ἐκεῖ ἔσται ὁ κλαυθμὸς καὶ ὁ βρυγμὸς τῶν ὀδόντων. ⁴³ τότε οἱ δίκαιοι ἐκλάμψουσιν ὡς ὁ ἥλιος ἐν τῇ βασιλείᾳ τοῦ πατρὸς αὐτῶν. ὁ ἔχων ὦτα ἀκουέτω.

⁴⁴ Ὁμοία ἐστὶν ἡ βασιλεία τῶν οὐρανῶν θησαυρῷ κεκρυμμένῳ ἐν τῷ ἀγρῷ, ὃν εὑρὼν ἄνθρωπος ἔκρυψεν, καὶ ἀπὸ τῆς χαρᾶς αὐτοῦ ὑπάγει καὶ πωλεῖ πάντα ὅσα ἔχει καὶ ἀγοράζει τὸν ἀγρὸν ἐκεῖνον.

⁴⁵ Πάλιν ὁμοία ἐστὶν ἡ βασιλεία τῶν οὐρανῶν ἀνθρώπῳ ἐμπόρῳ ζητοῦντι καλοὺς μαργαρίτας· ⁴⁶ εὑρὼν δὲ ἕνα πολύτιμον μαργαρίτην ἀπελθὼν πέπρακεν πάντα ὅσα εἶχεν καὶ ἠγόρασεν αὐτόν.

⁴⁷ Πάλιν ὁμοία ἐστὶν ἡ βασιλεία τῶν οὐρανῶν

σαγήνη βληθείση εἰς τὴν θάλασσαν καὶ ἐκ παντὸς γένους συναγαγούση· ⁴⁸ ἣν ὅτε ἐπληρώθη ἀναβιβάσαντες ἐπὶ τὸν αἰγιαλὸν καὶ καθίσαντες συνέλεξαν τὰ καλὰ εἰς ἄγγη, τὰ δὲ σαπρὰ ἔξω ἔβαλον. ⁴⁹ οὕτως ἔσται ἐν τῇ συντελείᾳ τοῦ αἰῶνος· ἐξελεύσονται οἱ ἄγγελοι καὶ ἀφοριοῦσιν τοὺς πονηροὺς ἐκ μέσου τῶν δικαίων, ⁵⁰ καὶ βαλοῦσιν αὐτοὺς εἰς τὴν κάμινον τοῦ πυρός· ἐκεῖ ἔσται ὁ κλαυθμὸς καὶ ὁ βρυγμὸς τῶν ὀδόντων.

⁵¹ Συνήκατε ταῦτα πάντα; λέγουσιν αὐτῷ, Ναί. ⁵² ὁ δὲ εἶπεν αὐτοῖς, Διὰ τοῦτο πᾶς γραμματεὺς μαθητευθεὶς τῇ βασιλείᾳ τῶν οὐρανῶν ὅμοιός ἐστιν ἀνθρώπῳ οἰκοδεσπότῃ, ὅστις ἐκβάλλει ἐκ τοῦ θησαυροῦ αὐτοῦ καινὰ καὶ παλαιά.

⁵³ Καὶ ἐγένετο ὅτε ἐτέλεσεν ὁ Ἰησοῦς τὰς παραβολὰς ταύτας, μετῆρεν ἐκεῖθεν. ⁵⁴ καὶ ἐλθὼν εἰς τὴν πατρίδα αὐτοῦ ἐδίδασκεν αὐτοὺς ἐν τῇ συναγωγῇ αὐτῶν, ὥστε ἐκπλήσσεσθαι αὐτοὺς καὶ λέγειν, Πόθεν τούτῳ ἡ σοφία αὕτη καὶ αἱ δυνάμεις; ⁵⁵ οὐχ οὗτός ἐστιν ὁ τοῦ τέκτονος υἱός; οὐχ ἡ μήτηρ αὐτοῦ λέγεται Μαριὰμ καὶ οἱ ἀδελφοὶ αὐτοῦ Ἰάκωβος καὶ Ἰωσὴφ καὶ Σίμων καὶ Ἰούδας; ⁵⁶ καὶ αἱ ἀδελφαὶ αὐτοῦ οὐχὶ πᾶσαι πρὸς ἡμᾶς εἰσίν; πόθεν οὖν τούτῳ ταῦτα πάντα; ⁵⁷ καὶ ἐσκανδαλίζοντο ἐν αὐτῷ. ὁ δὲ Ἰησοῦς εἶπεν αὐτοῖς, Οὐκ ἔστιν προφήτης ἄτιμος εἰ μὴ ἐν τῇ πατρίδι καὶ ἐν τῇ οἰκίᾳ αὐτοῦ. ⁵⁸ καὶ οὐκ ἐποίησεν ἐκεῖ δυνάμεις πολλὰς διὰ τὴν ἀπιστίαν αὐτῶν.

14 ¹ Ἐν ἐκείνῳ τῷ καιρῷ ἤκουσεν Ἡρώδης ὁ τετράρχης τὴν ἀκοὴν Ἰησοῦ, ² καὶ εἶπεν τοῖς παισὶν αὐτοῦ, Οὗτός ἐστιν Ἰωάννης ὁ βαπτιστής· αὐτὸς ἠγέρθη ἀπὸ τῶν νεκρῶν, καὶ διὰ τοῦτο αἱ δυνάμεις ἐνεργοῦσιν ἐν αὐτῷ. ³ ὁ γὰρ Ἡρώδης κρατήσας τὸν Ἰωάννην ἔδησεν αὐτὸν καὶ ἐν τῇ φυλακῇ ἀπέθετο διὰ Ἡρωδιάδα τὴν γυναῖκα Φιλίππου τοῦ ἀδελφοῦ αὐτοῦ. ⁴ ἔλεγεν γὰρ αὐτῷ ὁ Ἰωάννης, Οὐκ ἔξεστίν σοι ἔχειν αὐτήν. ⁵ καὶ θέλων αὐτὸν ἀποκτεῖναι ἐφοβήθη τὸν ὄχλον, ὅτι ὡς προφήτην αὐτὸν εἶχον. ⁶ γενεσίοις δὲ γενομένοις τοῦ Ἡρώδου ὠρχήσατο ἡ θυγάτηρ τῆς Ἡρωδιάδος ἐν τῷ μέσῳ καὶ ἤρεσεν τῷ Ἡρώδῃ, ⁷ ὅθεν μεθ' ὅρκου ὡμολόγησεν αὐτῇ δοῦναι ὃ ἐὰν αἰτήσηται. ⁸ ἡ δὲ προβιβασθεῖσα ὑπὸ τῆς μητρὸς αὐτῆς, Δός μοι, φησίν, ὧδε ἐπὶ πίνακι τὴν κεφαλὴν Ἰωάννου τοῦ βαπτιστοῦ. ⁹ καὶ λυπηθεὶς ὁ βασιλεὺς διὰ τοὺς ὅρκους καὶ τοὺς συνανακειμένους ἐκέλευσεν δοθῆναι, ¹⁰ καὶ πέμψας ἀπεκεφάλισεν Ἰωάννην ἐν τῇ φυλακῇ. ¹¹ καὶ ἠνέχθη ἡ κεφαλὴ αὐτοῦ ἐπὶ πίνακι καὶ ἐδόθη τῷ κορασίῳ, καὶ ἤνεγκεν τῇ μητρὶ αὐτῆς. ¹² καὶ προσελθόντες οἱ μαθηταὶ αὐτοῦ ἦραν τὸ πτῶμα καὶ ἔθαψαν αὐτόν, καὶ ἐλθόντες ἀπήγγειλαν τῷ Ἰησοῦ. ¹³ ἀκούσας δὲ ὁ Ἰησοῦς ἀνεχώρησεν ἐκεῖθεν ἐν πλοίῳ εἰς ἔρημον τόπον κατ' ἰδίαν· καὶ ἀκούσαντες οἱ ὄχλοι ἠκολούθησαν αὐτῷ πεζῇ ἀπὸ τῶν πόλεων.

¹⁴ Καὶ ἐξελθὼν εἶδεν πολὺν ὄχλον, καὶ ἐσπλαγχνίσθη ἐπ' αὐτοῖς καὶ ἐθεράπευσεν τοὺς ἀρρώστους αὐτῶν. ¹⁵ ὀψίας δὲ γενομένης προσῆλθον αὐτῷ οἱ μαθηταὶ λέγοντες, Ἔρημός ἐστιν ὁ τόπος καὶ ἡ ὥρα ἤδη παρῆλθεν· ἀπόλυσον τοὺς ὄχλους, ἵνα ἀπελθόντες εἰς τὰς κώμας ἀγοράσωσιν ἑαυτοῖς βρώματα. ¹⁶ ὁ δὲ Ἰησοῦς εἶπεν αὐτοῖς, Οὐ χρείαν ἔχουσιν ἀπελθεῖν· δότε αὐτοῖς ὑμεῖς φαγεῖν. ¹⁷ οἱ δὲ λέγουσιν αὐτῷ, Οὐκ ἔχομεν ὧδε εἰ μὴ πέντε ἄρτους καὶ δύο ἰχθύας. ¹⁸ ὁ δὲ εἶπεν, Φέρετέ μοι ὧδε αὐτούς. ¹⁹ καὶ κελεύσας τοὺς ὄχλους

ἀνακλιθῆναι ἐπὶ τοῦ χόρτου, λαβὼν τοὺς πέντε ἄρτους καὶ τοὺς δύο ἰχθύας ἀναβλέψας εἰς τὸν οὐρανὸν εὐλόγησεν, καὶ κλάσας ἔδωκεν τοῖς μαθηταῖς τοὺς ἄρτους, οἱ δὲ μαθηταὶ τοῖς ὄχλοις. ²⁰ καὶ ἔφαγον πάντες καὶ ἐχορτάσθησαν, καὶ ἦραν τὸ περισσεῦον τῶν κλασμάτων δώδεκα κοφίνους πλήρεις. ²¹ οἱ δὲ ἐσθίοντες ἦσαν ἄνδρες ὡσεὶ πεντακισχίλιοι χωρὶς γυναικῶν καὶ παιδίων.

²² Καὶ εὐθέως ἠνάγκασεν τοὺς μαθητὰς ἐμβῆναι εἰς τὸ πλοῖον καὶ προάγειν αὐτὸν εἰς τὸ πέραν, ἕως οὗ ἀπολύσῃ τοὺς ὄχλους. ²³ καὶ ἀπολύσας τοὺς ὄχλους ἀνέβη εἰς τὸ ὄρος κατ' ἰδίαν προσεύξασθαι. ὀψίας δὲ γενομένης μόνος ἦν ἐκεῖ. ²⁴ τὸ δὲ πλοῖον ἤδη μέσον τῆς θαλάσσης ἦν βασανιζόμενον ὑπὸ τῶν κυμάτων· ἦν γὰρ ἐναντίος ὁ ἄνεμος. ²⁵ τετάρτῃ δὲ φυλακῇ τῆς νυκτὸς ἦλθεν πρὸς αὐτοὺς περιπατῶν ἐπὶ τὴν θάλασσαν. ²⁶ καὶ ἰδόντες αὐτὸν οἱ μαθηταὶ ἐπὶ τῆς θαλάσσης περιπατοῦντα ἐταράχθησαν λέγοντες ὅτι Φάντασμά ἐστιν, καὶ ἀπὸ τοῦ φόβου ἔκραξαν. ²⁷ εὐθὺς δὲ ἐλάλησεν αὐτοῖς λέγων, Θαρσεῖτε, ἐγώ εἰμι· μὴ φοβεῖσθε. ²⁸ ἀποκριθεὶς δὲ αὐτῷ ὁ Πέτρος εἶπεν, Κύριε, εἰ σὺ εἶ, κέλευσόν με ἐλθεῖν πρός σε ἐπὶ τὰ ὕδατα. ²⁹ ὁ δὲ εἶπεν, Ἐλθέ. καὶ καταβὰς ἀπὸ τοῦ πλοίου Πέτρος περιεπάτησεν ἐπὶ τὰ ὕδατα ἐλθεῖν πρὸς τὸν Ἰησοῦν. ³⁰ βλέπων δὲ τὸν ἄνεμον ἰσχυρὸν ἐφοβήθη, καὶ ἀρξάμενος καταποντίζεσθαι ἔκραξεν λέγων, Κύριε, σῶσόν με. ³¹ εὐθέως δὲ ὁ Ἰησοῦς ἐκτείνας τὴν χεῖρα ἐπελάβετο αὐτοῦ καὶ λέγει αὐτῷ, Ὀλιγόπιστε, εἰς τί ἐδίστασας; ³² καὶ ἀναβάντων αὐτῶν εἰς τὸ πλοῖον ἐκόπασεν ὁ ἄνεμος. ³³ οἱ δὲ ἐν τῷ πλοίῳ προσεκύνησαν αὐτῷ λέγοντες, Ἀληθῶς θεοῦ υἱὸς εἶ.

³⁴ Καὶ διαπεράσαντες ἦλθον ἐπὶ τὴν γῆν εἰς Γεννησαρέτ. ³⁵ καὶ ἐπιγνόντες αὐτὸν οἱ ἄνδρες τοῦ τόπου ἐκείνου ἀπέστειλαν εἰς ὅλην τὴν περίχωρον ἐκείνην, καὶ προσήνεγκαν αὐτῷ πάντας τοὺς κακῶς ἔχοντας, ³⁶ καὶ παρεκάλουν αὐτὸν ἵνα μόνον ἅψωνται τοῦ κρασπέδου τοῦ ἱματίου αὐτοῦ· καὶ ὅσοι ἥψαντο διεσώθησαν.

15 ¹ Τότε προσέρχονται τῷ Ἰησοῦ ἀπὸ Ἱεροσολύμων Φαρισαῖοι καὶ γραμματεῖς λέγοντες, ² Διατί οἱ μαθηταί σου παραβαίνουσιν τὴν παράδοσιν τῶν πρεσβυτέρων; οὐ γὰρ νίπτονται τὰς χεῖρας ὅταν ἄρτον ἐσθίωσιν. ³ ὁ δὲ ἀποκριθεὶς εἶπεν αὐτοῖς, Διατί καὶ ὑμεῖς παραβαίνετε τὴν ἐντολὴν τοῦ θεοῦ διὰ τὴν παράδοσιν ὑμῶν; ⁴ ὁ γὰρ θεὸς ἐνετείλατο λέγων, Τίμα τὸν πατέρα καὶ τὴν μητέρα, καί, Ὁ κακολογῶν πατέρα ἢ μητέρα θανάτῳ τελευτάτω· ⁵ ὑμεῖς δὲ λέγετε, Ὃς ἂν εἴπῃ τῷ πατρὶ ἢ τῇ μητρί, Δῶρον ὃ ἐὰν ἐξ ἐμοῦ ὠφεληθῇς, οὐ μὴ τιμήσει τὸν πατέρα αὐτοῦ ἢ τὴν μητέρα αὐτοῦ. ⁶ καὶ ἠκυρώσατε τὸν λόγον τοῦ θεοῦ διὰ τὴν παράδοσιν ὑμῶν. ⁷ ὑποκριταί, καλῶς ἐπροφήτευσεν περὶ ὑμῶν Ἡσαΐας λέγων, ⁸ Ὁ λαὸς οὗτος τοῖς χείλεσίν με τιμᾷ, ἡ δὲ καρδία αὐτῶν πόρρω ἀπέχει ἀπ' ἐμοῦ· ⁹ μάτην δὲ σέβονταί με διδάσκοντες διδασκαλίας ἐντάλματα ἀνθρώπων.

¹⁰ Καὶ προσκαλεσάμενος τὸν ὄχλον εἶπεν αὐτοῖς, Ἀκούετε καὶ συνίετε· ¹¹ οὐ τὸ εἰσερχόμενον εἰς τὸ στόμα κοινοῖ τὸν ἄνθρωπον, ἀλλὰ τὸ ἐκπορευόμενον ἐκ τοῦ στόματος, τοῦτο κοινοῖ τὸν ἄνθρωπον. ¹² τότε προσελθόντες οἱ μαθηταὶ λέγουσιν αὐτῷ, Οἶδας ὅτι οἱ Φαρισαῖοι ἀκούσαντες τὸν λόγον ἐσκανδαλίσθησαν; ¹³ ὁ δὲ ἀποκριθεὶς εἶπεν, Πᾶσα φυτεία ἣν οὐκ ἐφύ-

τευσεν ὁ πατήρ μου ὁ οὐράνιος ἐκριζωθήσεται. ¹⁴ ἄφετε αὐτούς· ὁδηγοί εἰσιν τυφλοὶ τυφλῶν· τυφλὸς δὲ τυφλὸν ἐὰν ὁδηγῇ, ἀμφότεροι εἰς βόθυνον πεσοῦνται. ¹⁵ ἀποκριθεὶς δὲ ὁ Πέτρος εἶπεν αὐτῷ, Φράσον ἡμῖν τὴν παραβολήν. ¹⁶ ὁ δὲ εἶπεν, Ἀκμὴν καὶ ὑμεῖς ἀσύνετοί ἐστε; ¹⁷ οὐ νοεῖτε ὅτι πᾶν τὸ εἰσπορευόμενον εἰς τὸ στόμα εἰς τὴν κοιλίαν χωρεῖ καὶ εἰς ἀφεδρῶνα ἐκβάλλεται; ¹⁸ τὰ δὲ ἐκπορευόμενα ἐκ τοῦ στόματος ἐκ τῆς καρδίας ἐξέρχεται, κἀκεῖνα κοινοῖ τὸν ἄνθρωπον. ¹⁹ ἐκ γὰρ τῆς καρδίας ἐξέρχονται διαλογισμοὶ πονηροί, φόνοι, μοιχεῖαι, πορνεῖαι, κλοπαί, ψευδομαρτυρίαι, βλασφημίαι. ²⁰ ταῦτά ἐστιν τὰ κοινοῦντα τὸν ἄνθρωπον· τὸ δὲ ἀνίπτοις χερσὶν φαγεῖν οὐ κοινοῖ τὸν ἄνθρωπον.

²¹ Καὶ ἐξελθὼν ἐκεῖθεν ὁ Ἰησοῦς ἀνεχώρησεν εἰς τὰ μέρη Τύρου καὶ Σιδῶνος. ²² καὶ ἰδοὺ γυνὴ Χαναναία ἀπὸ τῶν ὁρίων ἐκείνων ἐξελθοῦσα ἔκραζεν λέγουσα, Ἐλέησόν με, κύριε υἱὸς Δαυείδ· ἡ θυγάτηρ μου κακῶς δαιμονίζεται. ²³ ὁ δὲ οὐκ ἀπεκρίθη αὐτῇ λόγον. καὶ προσελθόντες οἱ μαθηταὶ αὐτοῦ ἠρώτουν αὐτὸν λέγοντες, Ἀπόλυσον αὐτήν, ὅτι κράζει ὄπισθεν ἡμῶν. ²⁴ ὁ δὲ ἀποκριθεὶς εἶπεν, Οὐκ ἀπεστάλην εἰ μὴ εἰς τὰ πρόβατα τὰ ἀπολωλότα οἴκου Ἰσραήλ. ²⁵ ἡ δὲ ἐλθοῦσα προσεκύνει αὐτῷ λέγουσα, Κύριε, βοήθει μοι. ²⁶ ὁ δὲ ἀποκριθεὶς εἶπεν, Οὐκ ἔστιν καλὸν λαβεῖν τὸν ἄρτον τῶν τέκνων καὶ βαλεῖν τοῖς κυναρίοις. ²⁷ ἡ δὲ εἶπεν, Ναί, κύριε· καὶ γὰρ τὰ κυνάρια ἐσθίει ἀπὸ τῶν ψιχίων τῶν πιπτόντων ἀπὸ τῆς τραπέζης τῶν κυρίων αὐτῶν. ²⁸ τότε ἀποκριθεὶς ὁ Ἰησοῦς εἶπεν αὐτῇ, Ὦ γύναι, μεγάλη σου ἡ πίστις· γενηθήτω σοι ὡς θέλεις. καὶ ἰάθη ἡ θυγάτηρ αὐτῆς ἀπὸ τῆς ὥρας ἐκείνης.

²⁹ Καὶ μεταβὰς ἐκεῖθεν ὁ Ἰησοῦς ἦλθεν παρὰ τὴν θάλασσαν τῆς Γαλιλαίας, καὶ ἀναβὰς εἰς τὸ ὄρος ἐκάθητο ἐκεῖ. ³⁰ καὶ προσῆλθον αὐτῷ ὄχλοι πολλοὶ ἔχοντες μεθ' ἑαυτῶν χωλούς, τυφλούς, κωφούς, κυλλοὺς καὶ ἑτέρους πολλούς, καὶ ἔρριψαν αὐτοὺς παρὰ τοὺς πόδας αὐτοῦ· καὶ ἐθεράπευσεν αὐτούς, ³¹ ὥστε τοὺς ὄχλους θαυμάσαι βλέποντας κωφοὺς λαλοῦντας, κυλλοὺς ὑγιεῖς καὶ χωλοὺς περιπατοῦντας καὶ τυφλοὺς βλέποντας· καὶ ἐδόξασαν τὸν θεὸν Ἰσραήλ.

³² Ὁ δὲ Ἰησοῦς προσκαλεσάμενος τοὺς μαθητὰς αὐτοῦ εἶπεν, Σπλαγχνίζομαι ἐπὶ τὸν ὄχλον, ὅτι ἤδη ἡμέραι τρεῖς προσμένουσίν μοι καὶ οὐκ ἔχουσιν τί φάγωσιν· καὶ ἀπολῦσαι αὐτοὺς νήστεις οὐ θέλω, μήποτε ἐκλυθῶσιν ἐν τῇ ὁδῷ. ³³ καὶ λέγουσιν αὐτῷ οἱ μαθηταί, Πόθεν ἡμῖν ἐν ἐρημίᾳ ἄρτοι τοσοῦτοι ὥστε χορτάσαι ὄχλον τοσοῦτον; ³⁴ καὶ λέγει αὐτοῖς ὁ Ἰησοῦς, Πόσους ἄρτους ἔχετε; οἱ δὲ εἶπον, Ἑπτά, καὶ ὀλίγα ἰχθύδια. ³⁵ καὶ παραγγείλας τῷ ὄχλῳ ἀναπεσεῖν ἐπὶ τὴν γῆν, ³⁶ ἔλαβεν τοὺς ἑπτὰ ἄρτους καὶ τοὺς ἰχθύας, εὐχαριστήσας ἔκλασεν καὶ ἐδίδου τοῖς μαθηταῖς, οἱ δὲ μαθηταὶ τοῖς ὄχλοις. ³⁷ καὶ ἔφαγον πάντες καὶ ἐχορτάσθησαν, καὶ τὸ περισσεῦον τῶν κλασμάτων ἦραν ἑπτὰ σπυρίδας πλήρεις. ³⁸ οἱ δὲ ἐσθίοντες ἦσαν τετρακισχίλιοι ἄνδρες χωρὶς γυναικῶν καὶ παιδίων.

³⁹ Καὶ ἀπολύσας τοὺς ὄχλους ἐνέβη εἰς τὸ πλοῖον, καὶ ἦλθεν εἰς τὰ ὅρια Μαγαδάν. **16** ¹ Καὶ προσελθόντες οἱ Φαρισαῖοι καὶ Σαδδουκαῖοι πειράζοντες ἐπηρώτησαν αὐτὸν σημεῖον ἐκ τοῦ οὐρανοῦ ἐπιδεῖξαι αὐτοῖς. ² ὁ δὲ ἀποκριθεὶς εἶπεν αὐτοῖς, Ὀψίας γενομένης λέγετε, Εὐδία, πυρράζει γὰρ ὁ οὐρανός· ³ καὶ πρωΐ,

Σήμερον χειμών, πυρράζει γὰρ στυγνάζων ὁ οὐρανός. τὸ μὲν πρόσωπον τοῦ οὐρανοῦ γινώσκετε διακρίνειν, τὰ δὲ σημεῖα τῶν καιρῶν οὐ δύνασθε; ⁴ γενεὰ πονηρὰ καὶ μοιχαλὶς σημεῖον ἐπιζητεῖ, καὶ σημεῖον οὐ δοθήσεται αὐτῇ εἰ μὴ τὸ σημεῖον Ἰωνᾶ. καὶ καταλιπὼν αὐτοὺς ἀπῆλθεν.

⁵ Καὶ ἐλθόντες οἱ μαθηταὶ εἰς τὸ πέραν ἐπελάθοντο ἄρτους λαβεῖν. ⁶ ὁ δὲ Ἰησοῦς εἶπεν αὐτοῖς, Ὁρᾶτε καὶ προσέχετε ἀπὸ τῆς ζύμης τῶν Φαρισαίων καὶ Σαδδουκαίων. ⁷ οἱ δὲ διελογίζοντο ἐν ἑαυτοῖς λέγοντες ὅτι Ἄρτους οὐκ ἐλάβομεν. ⁸ γνοὺς δὲ ὁ Ἰησοῦς εἶπεν, Τί διαλογίζεσθε ἐν ἑαυτοῖς, ὀλιγόπιστοι, ὅτι ἄρτους οὐκ ἐλάβετε; ⁹ οὔπω νοεῖτε, οὐδὲ μνημονεύετε τοὺς πέντε ἄρτους τῶν πεντακισχιλίων καὶ πόσους κοφίνους ἐλάβετε; ¹⁰ οὐδὲ τοὺς ἑπτὰ ἄρτους τῶν τετρακισχιλίων καὶ πόσας σπυρίδας ἐλάβετε; ¹¹ πῶς οὐ νοεῖτε ὅτι οὐ περὶ ἄρτων εἶπον ὑμῖν; προσέχετε δὲ ἀπὸ τῆς ζύμης τῶν Φαρισαίων καὶ Σαδδουκαίων. ¹² τότε συνῆκαν ὅτι οὐκ εἶπεν προσέχειν ἀπὸ τῆς ζύμης τῶν ἄρτων, ἀλλὰ ἀπὸ τῆς διδαχῆς τῶν Φαρισαίων καὶ Σαδδουκαίων.

¹³ Ἐλθὼν δὲ ὁ Ἰησοῦς εἰς τὰ μέρη Καισαρείας τῆς Φιλίππου ἠρώτα τοὺς μαθητὰς αὐτοῦ λέγων, Τίνα λέγουσιν οἱ ἄνθρωποι εἶναι τὸν υἱὸν τοῦ ἀνθρώπου; ¹⁴ οἱ δὲ εἶπαν, Οἱ μὲν Ἰωάννην τὸν βαπτιστήν, ἄλλοι δὲ Ἡλίαν, ἕτεροι δὲ Ἰερεμίαν ἢ ἕνα τῶν προφητῶν. ¹⁵ λέγει αὐτοῖς, Ὑμεῖς δὲ τίνα με λέγετε εἶναι; ¹⁶ ἀποκριθεὶς δὲ Σίμων Πέτρος εἶπεν, Σὺ εἶ ὁ Χριστὸς ὁ υἱὸς τοῦ θεοῦ τοῦ ζῶντος. ¹⁷ ἀποκριθεὶς δὲ ὁ Ἰησοῦς εἶπεν αὐτῷ, Μακάριος εἶ, Σίμων Βὰρ Ἰωνᾶ, ὅτι σὰρξ καὶ αἷμα οὐκ ἀπεκάλυψέν σοι ἀλλ' ὁ πατήρ μου ὁ ἐν τοῖς οὐρανοῖς. ¹⁸ κἀγὼ δέ σοι λέγω ὅτι σὺ εἶ Πέτρος,

καὶ ἐπὶ ταύτῃ τῇ πέτρᾳ οἰκοδομήσω μου τὴν ἐκκλησίαν, καὶ πύλαι ᾅδου οὐ κατισχύσουσιν αὐτῆς. ¹⁹ καὶ δώσω σοὶ τὰς κλεῖδας τῆς βασιλείας τῶν οὐρανῶν, καὶ ὃ ἐὰν δήσῃς ἐπὶ τῆς γῆς ἔσται δεδεμένον ἐν τοῖς οὐρανοῖς, καὶ ὃ ἐὰν λύσῃς ἐπὶ τῆς γῆς ἔσται λελυμένον ἐν τοῖς οὐρανοῖς. ²⁰ τότε διεστείλατο τοῖς μαθηταῖς ἵνα μηδενὶ εἴπωσιν ὅτι αὐτός ἐστιν ὁ Χριστός.

²¹ Ἀπὸ τότε ἤρξατο ὁ Ἰησοῦς δεικνύειν τοῖς μαθηταῖς αὐτοῦ ὅτι δεῖ αὐτὸν εἰς Ἱεροσόλυμα ἀπελθεῖν καὶ πολλὰ παθεῖν ἀπὸ τῶν πρεσβυτέρων καὶ ἀρχιερέων καὶ γραμματέων καὶ ἀποκτανθῆναι καὶ τῇ τρίτῃ ἡμέρᾳ ἐγερθῆναι. ²² καὶ προσλαβόμενος αὐτὸν ὁ Πέτρος ἤρξατο ἐπιτιμᾶν αὐτῷ λέγων, Ἵλεώς σοι, κύριε· οὐ μὴ ἔσται σοι τοῦτο. ²³ ὁ δὲ στραφεὶς εἶπεν τῷ Πέτρῳ, Ὕπαγε ὀπίσω μου, σατανᾶ· σκάνδαλον εἶ ἐμοῦ, ὅτι οὐ φρονεῖς τὰ τοῦ θεοῦ ἀλλὰ τὰ τῶν ἀνθρώπων.

²⁴ Τότε ὁ Ἰησοῦς εἶπεν τοῖς μαθηταῖς αὐτοῦ, Εἴ τις θέλει ὀπίσω μου ἐλθεῖν, ἀπαρνησάσθω ἑαυτὸν καὶ ἀράτω τὸν σταυρὸν αὐτοῦ, καὶ ἀκολουθείτω μοι. ²⁵ ὃς γὰρ ἐὰν θέλῃ τὴν ψυχὴν αὐτοῦ σῶσαι, ἀπολέσει αὐτήν· ὃς δ' ἂν ἀπολέσῃ τὴν ψυχὴν αὐτοῦ ἕνεκεν ἐμοῦ, εὑρήσει αὐτήν. ²⁶ τί γὰρ ὠφεληθήσεται ἄνθρωπος, ἐὰν τὸν κόσμον ὅλον κερδήσῃ, τὴν δὲ ψυχὴν αὐτοῦ ζημιωθῇ; ἢ τί δώσει ἄνθρωπος ἀντάλλαγμα τῆς ψυχῆς αὐτοῦ; ²⁷ μέλλει γὰρ ὁ υἱὸς τοῦ ἀνθρώπου ἔρχεσθαι ἐν τῇ δόξῃ τοῦ πατρὸς αὐτοῦ μετὰ τῶν ἀγγέλων αὐτοῦ, καὶ τότε ἀποδώσει ἑκάστῳ κατὰ τὴν πρᾶξιν αὐτοῦ. ²⁸ ἀμὴν λέγω ὑμῖν, εἰσίν τινες τῶν ὧδε ἑστώτων οἵτινες οὐ μὴ γεύσωνται θανάτου ἕως ἂν ἴδωσιν τὸν υἱὸν τοῦ ἀνθρώπου ἐρχόμενον ἐν τῇ βασιλείᾳ αὐτοῦ.

17 ¹Καὶ μεθ' ἡμέρας ἓξ παραλαμβάνει ὁ Ἰησοῦς τὸν Πέτρον καὶ Ἰάκωβον καὶ Ἰωάννην τὸν ἀδελφὸν αὐτοῦ, καὶ ἀναφέρει αὐτοὺς εἰς ὄρος ὑψηλὸν κατ' ἰδίαν. ²καὶ μετεμορφώθη ἔμπροσθεν αὐτῶν, καὶ ἔλαμψεν τὸ πρόσωπον αὐτοῦ ὡς ὁ ἥλιος, τὰ δὲ ἱμάτια αὐτοῦ ἐγένετο λευκὰ ὡς τὸ φῶς. ³καὶ ἰδοὺ ὤφθη αὐτοῖς Μωϋσῆς καὶ Ἠλίας συνλαλοῦντες μετ' αὐτοῦ. ⁴ἀποκριθεὶς δὲ ὁ Πέτρος εἶπεν τῷ Ἰησοῦ, Κύριε, καλόν ἐστιν ἡμᾶς ὧδε εἶναι· εἰ θέλεις, ποιήσω ὧδε τρεῖς σκηνάς, σοὶ μίαν καὶ Μωϋσεῖ μίαν καὶ Ἠλίᾳ μίαν. ⁵ἔτι αὐτοῦ λαλοῦντος, ἰδοὺ νεφέλη φωτεινὴ ἐπεσκίασεν αὐτούς, καὶ ἰδοὺ φωνὴ ἐκ τῆς νεφέλης λέγουσα, Οὗτός ἐστιν ὁ υἱός μου ὁ ἀγαπητός, ἐν ᾧ εὐδόκησα· ἀκούετε αὐτοῦ. ⁶καὶ ἀκούσαντες οἱ μαθηταὶ ἔπεσαν ἐπὶ πρόσωπον αὐτῶν καὶ ἐφοβήθησαν σφόδρα. ⁷καὶ προσῆλθεν ὁ Ἰησοῦς καὶ ἁψάμενος αὐτῶν εἶπεν, Ἐγέρθητε καὶ μὴ φοβεῖσθε. ⁸ἐπάραντες δὲ τοὺς ὀφθαλμοὺς αὐτῶν οὐδένα εἶδον εἰ μὴ τὸν Ἰησοῦν μόνον.

⁹Καὶ καταβαινόντων αὐτῶν ἐκ τοῦ ὄρους ἐνετείλατο αὐτοῖς ὁ Ἰησοῦς λέγων, Μηδενὶ εἴπητε τὸ ὅραμα ἕως οὗ ὁ υἱὸς τοῦ ἀνθρώπου ἐκ νεκρῶν ἐγερθῇ. ¹⁰Καὶ ἐπηρώτησαν αὐτὸν οἱ μαθηταὶ λέγοντες, Τί οὖν οἱ γραμματεῖς λέγουσιν ὅτι Ἠλίαν δεῖ ἐλθεῖν πρῶτον; ¹¹ὁ δὲ ἀποκριθεὶς εἶπεν, Ἠλίας μὲν ἔρχεται καὶ ἀποκαταστήσει πάντα. ¹²λέγω δὲ ὑμῖν ὅτι Ἠλίας ἤδη ἦλθεν, καὶ οὐκ ἐπέγνωσαν αὐτόν, ἀλλ' ἐποίησαν ἐν αὐτῷ ὅσα ἠθέλησαν. οὕτως καὶ ὁ υἱὸς τοῦ ἀνθρώπου μέλλει πάσχειν ὑπ' αὐτῶν. ¹³τότε συνῆκαν οἱ μαθηταὶ ὅτι περὶ Ἰωάννου τοῦ βαπτιστοῦ εἶπεν αὐτοῖς.

¹⁴Καὶ ἐλθόντων πρὸς τὸν ὄχλον, προσῆλθεν αὐτῷ ἄνθρωπος γονυπετῶν αὐτὸν ¹⁵καὶ λέγων, Κύριε,

ἐλέησόν μου τὸν υἱόν, ὅτι σεληνιάζεται καὶ κακῶς πάσχει· πολλάκις γὰρ πίπτει εἰς τὸ πῦρ καὶ πολλάκις εἰς τὸ ὕδωρ. ¹⁶ καὶ προσήνεγκα αὐτὸν τοῖς μαθηταῖς σου, καὶ οὐκ ἠδυνήθησαν αὐτὸν θεραπεῦσαι. ¹⁷ ἀποκριθεὶς δὲ ὁ Ἰησοῦς εἶπεν, Ὦ γενεὰ ἄπιστος καὶ διεστραμμένη, ἕως πότε μεθ' ὑμῶν ἔσομαι; ἕως πότε ἀνέξομαι ὑμῶν; φέρετέ μοι αὐτὸν ὧδε. ¹⁸ καὶ ἐπετίμησεν αὐτῷ ὁ Ἰησοῦς, καὶ ἐξῆλθεν ἀπ' αὐτοῦ τὸ δαιμόνιον, καὶ ἐθεραπεύθη ὁ παῖς ἀπὸ τῆς ὥρας ἐκείνης. ¹⁹ Τότε προσελθόντες οἱ μαθηταὶ τῷ Ἰησοῦ κατ' ἰδίαν εἶπον, Διὰ τί ἡμεῖς οὐκ ἠδυνήθημεν ἐκβαλεῖν αὐτό; ²⁰ ὁ δὲ λέγει αὐτοῖς, Διὰ τὴν ὀλιγοπιστίαν ὑμῶν· ἀμὴν γὰρ λέγω ὑμῖν, ἐὰν ἔχητε πίστιν ὡς κόκκον σινάπεως, ἐρεῖτε τῷ ὄρει τούτῳ, Μετάβα ἔνθεν ἐκεῖ, καὶ μεταβήσεται, καὶ οὐδὲν ἀδυνατήσει ὑμῖν.*

²² Συστρεφομένων δὲ αὐτῶν ἐν τῇ Γαλιλαίᾳ εἶπεν αὐτοῖς ὁ Ἰησοῦς, Μέλλει ὁ υἱὸς τοῦ ἀνθρώπου παραδίδοσθαι εἰς χεῖρας ἀνθρώπων, ²³ καὶ ἀποκτενοῦσιν αὐτόν, καὶ τῇ τρίτῃ ἡμέρᾳ ἐγερθήσεται. καὶ ἐλυπήθησαν σφόδρα.

²⁴ Ἐλθόντων δὲ αὐτῶν εἰς Καφαρναοὺμ προσῆλθον οἱ τὰ δίδραχμα λαμβάνοντες τῷ Πέτρῳ καὶ εἶπαν, Ὁ διδάσκαλος ὑμῶν οὐ τελεῖ τὰ δίδραχμα; ²⁵ λέγει, Ναί. καὶ εἰσελθόντα εἰς τὴν οἰκίαν προέφθασεν αὐτὸν ὁ Ἰησοῦς λέγων, Τί σοι δοκεῖ, Σίμων; οἱ βασιλεῖς τῆς γῆς ἀπὸ τίνων λαμβάνουσιν τέλη ἢ κῆνσον; ἀπὸ τῶν υἱῶν αὐτῶν ἢ ἀπὸ τῶν ἀλλοτρίων; ²⁶ εἰπόντος δέ, Ἀπὸ τῶν ἀλλοτρίων, ἔφη αὐτῷ ὁ Ἰησοῦς, Ἄραγε ἐλεύθεροί εἰσιν οἱ υἱοί. ²⁷ ἵνα δὲ μὴ σκανδαλίσωμεν αὐτούς, πορευθεὶς εἰς θάλασσαν βάλε ἄγκι-

* Verse 21 omitted on the best MS. authority.

στρον καὶ τὸν ἀναβάντα πρῶτον ἰχθὺν ἆρον, καὶ ἀνοίξας τὸ στόμα αὐτοῦ εὑρήσεις στατῆρα· ἐκεῖνον λαβὼν δὸς αὐτοῖς ἀντὶ ἐμοῦ καὶ σοῦ.

18 ¹ Ἐν ἐκείνῃ τῇ ὥρᾳ προσῆλθον οἱ μαθηταὶ τῷ Ἰησοῦ λέγοντες, Τίς ἄρα μείζων ἐστὶν ἐν τῇ βασιλείᾳ τῶν οὐρανῶν; ² καὶ προσκαλεσάμενος παιδίον ἔστησεν αὐτὸ ἐν μέσῳ αὐτῶν ³ καὶ εἶπεν, Ἀμὴν λέγω ὑμῖν, ἐὰν μὴ στραφῆτε καὶ γένησθε ὡς τὰ παιδία, οὐ μὴ εἰσέλθητε εἰς τὴν βασιλείαν τῶν οὐρανῶν. ⁴ ὅστις οὖν ταπεινώσει ἑαυτὸν ὡς τὸ παιδίον τοῦτο, οὗτός ἐστιν ὁ μείζων ἐν τῇ βασιλείᾳ τῶν οὐρανῶν.

⁵ Καὶ ὃς ἐὰν δέξηται ἓν παιδίον τοιοῦτον ἐπὶ τῷ ὀνόματί μου, ἐμὲ δέχεται. ⁶ ὃς δ' ἂν σκανδαλίσῃ ἕνα τῶν μικρῶν τούτων τῶν πιστευόντων εἰς ἐμέ, συμφέρει αὐτῷ ἵνα κρεμασθῇ μύλος ὀνικὸς περὶ τὸν τράχηλον αὐτοῦ καὶ καταποντισθῇ ἐν τῷ πελάγει τῆς θαλάσσης.

⁷ Οὐαὶ τῷ κόσμῳ ἀπὸ τῶν σκανδάλων· ἀνάγκη γάρ ἐστιν ἐλθεῖν τὰ σκάνδαλα, πλὴν οὐαὶ τῷ ἀνθρώπῳ δι' οὗ τὸ σκάνδαλον ἔρχεται. ⁸ εἰ δὲ ἡ χείρ σου ἢ ὁ πούς σου σκανδαλίζει σε, ἔκκοψον αὐτὸν καὶ βάλε ἀπὸ σοῦ· καλόν σοί ἐστιν εἰσελθεῖν εἰς τὴν ζωὴν χωλὸν ἢ κυλλόν, ἢ δύο χεῖρας ἢ δύο πόδας ἔχοντα βληθῆναι εἰς τὸ πῦρ τὸ αἰώνιον. ⁹ καὶ εἰ ὁ ὀφθαλμός σου σκανδαλίζει σε, ἔξελε αὐτὸν καὶ βάλε ἀπὸ σοῦ· καλόν σοί ἐστιν μονόφθαλμον εἰς τὴν ζωὴν εἰσελθεῖν, ἢ δύο ὀφθαλμοὺς ἔχοντα βληθῆναι εἰς τὴν γέενναν τοῦ πυρός.

¹⁰ Ὁρᾶτε μὴ καταφρονήσητε ἑνὸς τῶν μικρῶν τούτων· λέγω γὰρ ὑμῖν ὅτι οἱ ἄγγελοι αὐτῶν ἐν οὐρανοῖς διὰ παντὸς βλέπουσιν τὸ πρόσωπον τοῦ πατρός μου τοῦ ἐν οὐρανοῖς. * ¹² Τί ὑμῖν δοκεῖ; ἐὰν γένηταί τινι

---

* Verse 11 omitted on the best MS. authority.

ἀνθρώπῳ ἑκατὸν πρόβατα καὶ πλανηθῇ ἓν ἐξ αὐτῶν, οὐχὶ ἀφεὶς τὰ ἐνενήκοντα ἐννέα ἐπὶ τὰ ὄρη πορευθεὶς ζητεῖ τὸ πλανώμενον; ¹³ καὶ ἐὰν γένηται εὑρεῖν αὐτό, ἀμὴν λέγω ὑμῖν ὅτι χαίρει ἐπ' αὐτῷ μᾶλλον ἢ ἐπὶ τοῖς ἐνενήκοντα ἐννέα τοῖς μὴ πεπλανημένοις. ¹⁴ οὕτως οὐκ ἔστιν θέλημα ἔμπροσθεν τοῦ πατρὸς ὑμῶν τοῦ ἐν οὐρανοῖς ἵνα ἀπόληται ἓν τῶν μικρῶν τούτων.

¹⁵ Ἐὰν δὲ ἁμαρτήσῃ ὁ ἀδελφός σου, ὕπαγε ἔλεγξον αὐτὸν μεταξὺ σοῦ καὶ αὐτοῦ μόνου· ἐάν σου ἀκούσῃ, ἐκέρδησας τὸν ἀδελφόν σου. ¹⁶ ἐὰν δὲ μὴ ἀκούσῃ, παράλαβε μετὰ σοῦ ἔτι ἕνα ἢ δύο, ἵνα ἐπὶ στόματος δύο μαρτύρων ἢ τριῶν σταθῇ πᾶν ῥῆμα. ¹⁷ ἐὰν δὲ παρακούσῃ αὐτῶν, εἰπὲ τῇ ἐκκλησίᾳ· ἐὰν δὲ καὶ τῆς ἐκκλησίας παρακούσῃ, ἔστω σοι ὥσπερ ὁ ἐθνικὸς καὶ ὁ τελώνης. ¹⁸ Ἀμὴν λέγω ὑμῖν, ὅσα ἐὰν δήσητε ἐπὶ τῆς γῆς ἔσται δεδεμένα ἐν τῷ οὐρανῷ, καὶ ὅσα ἐὰν λύσητε ἐπὶ τῆς γῆς ἔσται λελυμένα ἐν οὐρανῷ. ¹⁹ Πάλιν λέγω ὑμῖν ὅτι ἐὰν δύο συμφωνήσουσιν ἐξ ὑμῶν ἐπὶ τῆς γῆς περὶ παντὸς πράγματος οὗ ἐὰν αἰτήσωνται, γενήσεται αὐτοῖς παρὰ τοῦ πατρός μου τοῦ ἐν οὐρανοῖς. ²⁰ οὗ γάρ εἰσιν δύο ἢ τρεῖς συνηγμένοι εἰς τὸ ἐμὸν ὄνομα, ἐκεῖ εἰμὶ ἐν μέσῳ αὐτῶν.

²¹ Τότε προσελθὼν ὁ Πέτρος εἶπεν αὐτῷ, Κύριε, ποσάκις ἁμαρτήσει εἰς ἐμὲ ὁ ἀδελφός μου καὶ ἀφήσω αὐτῷ; ἕως ἑπτάκις; ²² λέγει αὐτῷ ὁ Ἰησοῦς, Οὐ λέγω σοι ἕως ἑπτάκις, ἀλλ' ἕως ἑβδομηκοντάκις ἑπτά. ²³ διὰ τοῦτο ὡμοιώθη ἡ βασιλεία τῶν οὐρανῶν ἀνθρώπῳ βασιλεῖ, ὃς ἠθέλησεν συνᾶραι λόγον μετὰ τῶν δούλων αὐτοῦ. ²⁴ ἀρξαμένου δὲ αὐτοῦ συναίρειν, προσηνέχθη αὐτῷ εἷς ὀφειλέτης μυρίων ταλάντων. ²⁵ μὴ ἔχοντος δὲ αὐτοῦ ἀποδοῦναι, ἐκέλευσεν αὐτὸν ὁ κύριος πραθῆναι

καὶ τὴν γυναῖκα αὐτοῦ καὶ τὰ τέκνα καὶ πάντα ὅσα εἶχεν καὶ ἀποδοθῆναι. ²⁶ πεσὼν οὖν ὁ δοῦλος προσεκύνει αὐτῷ λέγων, Μακροθύμησον ἐπ' ἐμοί, καὶ πάντα ἀποδώσω σοι. ²⁷ σπλαγχνισθεὶς δὲ ὁ κύριος τοῦ δούλου ἐκείνου ἀπέλυσεν αὐτόν, καὶ τὸ δάνειον ἀφῆκεν αὐτῷ. ²⁸ ἐξελθὼν δὲ ὁ δοῦλος ἐκεῖνος εὗρεν ἕνα τῶν συνδούλων αὐτοῦ ὃς ὤφειλεν αὐτῷ ἑκατὸν δηνάρια, καὶ κρατήσας αὐτὸν ἔπνιγεν λέγων, Ἀπόδος εἴ τι ὀφείλεις. ²⁹ πεσὼν οὖν ὁ σύνδουλος αὐτοῦ παρεκάλει αὐτὸν λέγων, Μακροθύμησον ἐπ' ἐμοί, καὶ ἀποδώσω σοι. ³⁰ ὁ δὲ οὐκ ἤθελεν, ἀλλὰ ἀπελθὼν ἔβαλεν αὐτὸν εἰς φυλακὴν ἕως ἀποδῷ τὸ ὀφειλόμενον. ³¹ ἰδόντες οὖν οἱ σύνδουλοι αὐτοῦ τὰ γενόμενα ἐλυπήθησαν σφόδρα, καὶ ἐλθόντες διεσάφησαν τῷ κυρίῳ ἑαυτῶν πάντα τὰ γενόμενα. ³² τότε προσκαλεσάμενος αὐτὸν ὁ κύριος αὐτοῦ λέγει αὐτῷ, Δοῦλε πονηρέ, πᾶσαν τὴν ὀφειλὴν ἐκείνην ἀφῆκά σοι, ἐπεὶ παρεκάλεσάς με· ³³ οὐκ ἔδει καὶ σὲ ἐλεῆσαι τὸν σύνδουλόν σου, ὡς κἀγὼ σὲ ἠλέησα; ³⁴ καὶ ὀργισθεὶς ὁ κύριος αὐτοῦ παρέδωκεν αὐτὸν τοῖς βασανισταῖς ἕως οὗ ἀποδῷ πᾶν τὸ ὀφειλόμενον αὐτῷ. ³⁵ οὕτως καὶ ὁ πατήρ μου ὁ οὐράνιος ποιήσει ὑμῖν, ἐὰν μὴ ἀφῆτε ἕκαστος τῷ ἀδελφῷ αὐτοῦ ἀπὸ τῶν καρδιῶν ὑμῶν.

19 ¹ Καὶ ἐγένετο ὅτε ἐτέλεσεν ὁ Ἰησοῦς τοὺς λόγους τούτους, μετῆρεν ἀπὸ τῆς Γαλιλαίας καὶ ἦλθεν εἰς τὰ ὅρια τῆς Ἰουδαίας πέραν τοῦ Ἰορδάνου. ² καὶ ἠκολούθησαν αὐτῷ ὄχλοι πολλοί, καὶ ἐθεράπευσεν αὐτοὺς ἐκεῖ.

³ Καὶ προσῆλθον αὐτῷ οἱ Φαρισαῖοι πειράζοντες αὐτὸν καὶ λέγοντες, Εἰ ἔξεστιν ἀνθρώπῳ ἀπολῦσαι τὴν γυναῖκα αὐτοῦ κατὰ πᾶσαν αἰτίαν; ⁴ ὁ δὲ ἀποκριθεὶς εἶπεν, Οὐκ ἀνέγνωτε ὅτι ὁ ποιήσας ἀπ'

ἀρχῆς ἄρσεν καὶ θῆλυ ἐποίησεν αὐτούς; ⁵ καὶ εἶπεν, Ἕνεκα τούτου καταλείψει ἄνθρωπος τὸν πατέρα καὶ τὴν μητέρα καὶ κολληθήσεται τῇ γυναικὶ αὐτοῦ, καὶ ἔσονται οἱ δύο εἰς σάρκα μίαν. ⁶ ὥστε οὐκέτι εἰσὶν δύο ἀλλὰ σὰρξ μία. ὃ οὖν ὁ θεὸς συνέζευξεν, ἄνθρωπος μὴ χωριζέτω. ⁷ λέγουσιν αὐτῷ, Τί οὖν Μωϋσῆς ἐνετείλατο δοῦναι βιβλίον ἀποστασίου καὶ ἀπολῦσαι; ⁸ λέγει αὐτοῖς ὅτι Μωϋσῆς πρὸς τὴν σκληροκαρδίαν ὑμῶν ἐπέτρεψεν ὑμῖν ἀπολῦσαι τὰς γυναῖκας ὑμῶν· ἀπ' ἀρχῆς δὲ οὐ γέγονεν οὕτως. ⁹ λέγω δὲ ὑμῖν ὅτι ὃς ἂν ἀπολύσῃ τὴν γυναῖκα αὐτοῦ μὴ ἐπὶ πορνείᾳ καὶ γαμήσῃ ἄλλην, μοιχᾶται. ¹⁰ λέγουσιν αὐτῷ οἱ μαθηταὶ αὐτοῦ, Εἰ οὕτως ἐστὶν ἡ αἰτία τοῦ ἀνθρώπου μετὰ τῆς γυναικός, οὐ συμφέρει γαμῆσαι. ¹¹ ὁ δὲ εἶπεν αὐτοῖς, Οὐ πάντες χωροῦσιν τὸν λόγον τοῦτον, ἀλλ' οἷς δέδοται. ¹² εἰσὶν γὰρ εὐνοῦχοι οἵτινες ἐκ κοιλίας μητρὸς ἐγεννήθησαν οὕτως, καὶ εἰσὶν εὐνοῦχοι οἵτινες εὐνουχίσθησαν ὑπὸ τῶν ἀνθρώπων, καὶ εἰσὶν εὐνοῦχοι οἵτινες εὐνούχισαν ἑαυτοὺς διὰ τὴν βασιλείαν τῶν οὐρανῶν. ὁ δυνάμενος χωρεῖν χωρείτω.

¹³ Τότε προσηνέχθησαν αὐτῷ παιδία, ἵνα τὰς χεῖρας ἐπιθῇ αὐτοῖς καὶ προσεύξηται· οἱ δὲ μαθηταὶ ἐπετίμησαν αὐτοῖς. ¹⁴ ὁ δὲ Ἰησοῦς εἶπεν, Ἄφετε τὰ παιδία καὶ μὴ κωλύετε αὐτὰ ἐλθεῖν πρός με· τῶν γὰρ τοιούτων ἐστὶν ἡ βασιλεία τῶν οὐρανῶν. ¹⁵ καὶ ἐπιθεὶς τὰς χεῖρας αὐτοῖς ἐπορεύθη ἐκεῖθεν.

¹⁶ Καὶ ἰδοὺ εἷς προσελθὼν αὐτῷ εἶπεν, Διδάσκαλε, τί ἀγαθὸν ποιήσω ἵνα σχῶ ζωὴν αἰώνιον; ¹⁷ ὁ δὲ εἶπεν αὐτῷ, Τί με ἐρωτᾷς περὶ τοῦ ἀγαθοῦ; εἷς ἐστιν ὁ ἀγαθός. εἰ δὲ θέλεις εἰς τὴν ζωὴν εἰσελθεῖν, τήρησον τὰς ἐντολάς. ¹⁸ λέγει αὐτῷ, Ποίας; ὁ δὲ Ἰησοῦς

εἶπεν, Τὸ οὐ φονεύσεις, οὐ μοιχεύσεις, οὐ κλέψεις, οὐ ψευδομαρτυρήσεις, ¹⁹ τίμα τὸν πατέρα καὶ τὴν μητέρα, καὶ ἀγαπήσεις τὸν πλησίον σου ὡς σεαυτόν. ²⁰ λέγει αὐτῷ ὁ νεανίσκος, Πάντα ταῦτα ἐφύλαξα· τί ἔτι ὑστερῶ; ²¹ ἔφη αὐτῷ ὁ Ἰησοῦς, Εἰ θέλεις τέλειος εἶναι, ὕπαγε πώλησόν σου τὰ ὑπάρχοντα καὶ δὸς πτωχοῖς, καὶ ἕξεις θησαυρὸν ἐν οὐρανῷ, καὶ δεῦρο ἀκολούθει μοι. ²² ἀκούσας δὲ ὁ νεανίσκος τὸν λόγον ἀπῆλθεν λυπούμενος· ἦν γὰρ ἔχων κτήματα πολλά.

²³ Ὁ δὲ Ἰησοῦς εἶπεν τοῖς μαθηταῖς αὐτοῦ, Ἀμὴν λέγω ὑμῖν ὅτι πλούσιος δυσκόλως εἰσελεύσεται εἰς τὴν βασιλείαν τῶν οὐρανῶν. ²⁴ πάλιν δὲ λέγω ὑμῖν εὐκοπώτερόν ἐστιν κάμηλον διὰ τρυπήματος ῥαφίδος εἰσελθεῖν ἢ πλούσιον εἰς τὴν βασιλείαν τῶν οὐρανῶν. ²⁵ ἀκούσαντες δὲ οἱ μαθηταὶ ἐξεπλήσσοντο σφόδρα λέγοντες, Τίς ἄρα δύναται σωθῆναι; ²⁶ ἐμβλέψας δὲ ὁ Ἰησοῦς εἶπεν αὐτοῖς, Παρὰ ἀνθρώποις τοῦτο ἀδύνατόν ἐστιν, παρὰ δὲ θεῷ πάντα δυνατά.

²⁷ Τότε ἀποκριθεὶς ὁ Πέτρος εἶπεν αὐτῷ, Ἰδοὺ ἡμεῖς ἀφήκαμεν πάντα καὶ ἠκολουθήσαμέν σοι· τί ἄρα ἔσται ἡμῖν; ²⁸ ὁ δὲ Ἰησοῦς εἶπεν αὐτοῖς, Ἀμὴν λέγω ὑμῖν ὅτι ὑμεῖς οἱ ἀκολουθήσαντές μοι, ἐν τῇ παλινγενεσίᾳ, ὅταν καθίσῃ ὁ υἱὸς τοῦ ἀνθρώπου ἐπὶ θρόνου δόξης αὐτοῦ, καθίσεσθε καὶ αὐτοὶ ἐπὶ δώδεκα θρόνους κρίνοντες τὰς δώδεκα φυλὰς τοῦ Ἰσραήλ. ²⁹ καὶ πᾶς ὅστις ἀφῆκεν ἀδελφοὺς ἢ ἀδελφὰς ἢ πατέρα ἢ μητέρα ἢ τέκνα ἢ ἀγροὺς ἢ οἰκίας ἕνεκεν τοῦ ὀνόματός μου, πολλαπλασίονα λήμψεται καὶ ζωὴν αἰώνιον κληρονομήσει. ³⁰ πολλοὶ δὲ ἔσονται πρῶτοι ἔσχατοι καὶ ἔσχατοι πρῶτοι.

20 ¹Ὁμοία γάρ ἐστιν ἡ βασιλεία τῶν οὐρανῶν ἀνθρώπῳ οἰκοδεσπότῃ, ὅστις ἐξῆλθεν ἅμα πρωῒ μισθώσασθαι ἐργάτας εἰς τὸν ἀμπελῶνα αὐτοῦ. ²συμφωνήσας δὲ μετὰ τῶν ἐργατῶν ἐκ δηναρίου τὴν ἡμέραν ἀπέστειλεν αὐτοὺς εἰς τὸν ἀμπελῶνα αὐτοῦ. ³καὶ ἐξελθὼν περὶ τρίτην ὥραν εἶδεν ἄλλους ἑστῶτας ἐν τῇ ἀγορᾷ ἀργούς, ⁴κἀκείνοις εἶπεν, Ὑπάγετε καὶ ὑμεῖς εἰς τὸν ἀμπελῶνα, καὶ ὃ ἐὰν ᾖ δίκαιον δώσω ὑμῖν. ⁵οἱ δὲ ἀπῆλθον. πάλιν δὲ ἐξελθὼν περὶ ἕκτην καὶ ἐνάτην ὥραν ἐποίησεν ὡσαύτως. ⁶περὶ δὲ τὴν ἑνδεκάτην ἐξελθὼν εὗρεν ἄλλους ἑστῶτας, καὶ λέγει αὐτοῖς, Τί ὧδε ἑστήκατε ὅλην τὴν ἡμέραν ἀργοί; ⁷λέγουσιν αὐτῷ ὅτι Οὐδεὶς ἡμᾶς ἐμισθώσατο. λέγει αὐτοῖς, Ὑπάγετε καὶ ὑμεῖς εἰς τὸν ἀμπελῶνα. ⁸ὀψίας δὲ γενομένης λέγει ὁ κύριος τοῦ ἀμπελῶνος τῷ ἐπιτρόπῳ αὐτοῦ, Κάλεσον τοὺς ἐργάτας καὶ ἀπόδος τὸν μισθόν, ἀρξάμενος ἀπὸ τῶν ἐσχάτων ἕως τῶν πρώτων. ⁹καὶ ἐλθόντες οἱ περὶ τὴν ἑνδεκάτην ὥραν ἔλαβον ἀνὰ δηνάριον. ¹⁰ἐλθόντες δὲ οἱ πρῶτοι ἐνόμισαν ὅτι πλεῖον λήμψονται· καὶ ἔλαβον τὸ ἀνὰ δηνάριον καὶ αὐτοί. ¹¹λαβόντες δὲ ἐγόγγυζον κατὰ τοῦ οἰκοδεσπότου ¹²λέγοντες, Οὗτοι οἱ ἔσχατοι μίαν ὥραν ἐποίησαν, καὶ ἴσους αὐτοὺς ἡμῖν ἐποίησας τοῖς βαστάσασι τὸ βάρος τῆς ἡμέρας καὶ τὸν καύσωνα. ¹³ὁ δὲ ἀποκριθεὶς εἶπεν ἑνὶ αὐτῶν, Ἑταῖρε, οὐκ ἀδικῶ σε· οὐχὶ δηναρίου συνεφώνησάς μοι; ¹⁴ἆρον τὸ σὸν καὶ ὕπαγε. θέλω δὲ τούτῳ τῷ ἐσχάτῳ δοῦναι ὡς καὶ σοί· ¹⁵ἢ οὐκ ἔξεστίν μοι ὃ θέλω ποιῆσαι ἐν τοῖς ἐμοῖς; ἢ ὁ ὀφθαλμός σου πονηρός ἐστιν ὅτι ἐγὼ ἀγαθός εἰμι; ¹⁶οὕτως ἔσονται οἱ ἔσχατοι πρῶτοι καὶ οἱ πρῶτοι ἔσχατοι.

¹⁷ Καὶ ἀναβαίνων ὁ Ἰησοῦς εἰς Ἱεροσόλυμα παρέλαβεν τοὺς δώδεκα κατ' ἰδίαν, καὶ ἐν τῇ ὁδῷ εἶπεν αὐτοῖς, ¹⁸ Ἰδοὺ ἀναβαίνομεν εἰς Ἱεροσόλυμα, καὶ ὁ υἱὸς τοῦ ἀνθρώπου παραδοθήσεται τοῖς ἀρχιερεῦσιν καὶ γραμματεῦσιν, καὶ κατακρινοῦσιν αὐτὸν θανάτῳ. ¹⁹ καὶ παραδώσουσιν αὐτὸν τοῖς ἔθνεσιν εἰς τὸ ἐμπαῖξαι καὶ μαστιγῶσαι καὶ σταυρῶσαι, καὶ τῇ τρίτῃ ἡμέρᾳ ἐγερθήσεται.

²⁰ Τότε προσῆλθεν αὐτῷ ἡ μήτηρ τῶν υἱῶν Ζεβεδαίου μετὰ τῶν υἱῶν αὐτῆς, προσκυνοῦσα καὶ αἰτοῦσά τι παρ' αὐτοῦ. ²¹ ὁ δὲ εἶπεν αὐτῇ, Τί θέλεις; λέγει αὐτῷ, Εἰπὲ ἵνα καθίσωσιν οὗτοι οἱ δύο υἱοί μου εἷς ἐκ δεξιῶν σου καὶ εἷς ἐξ εὐωνύμων σου ἐν τῇ βασιλείᾳ σου. ²² ἀποκριθεὶς δὲ ὁ Ἰησοῦς εἶπεν, Οὐκ οἴδατε τί αἰτεῖσθε. δύνασθε πιεῖν τὸ ποτήριον ὃ ἐγὼ μέλλω πίνειν; λέγουσιν αὐτῷ, Δυνάμεθα. ²³ λέγει αὐτοῖς, Τὸ μὲν ποτήριόν μου πίεσθε, τὸ δὲ καθίσαι ἐκ δεξιῶν μου καὶ ἐξ εὐωνύμων, οὐκ ἔστιν ἐμὸν δοῦναι, ἀλλ' οἷς ἡτοίμασται ὑπὸ τοῦ πατρός μου. ²⁴ καὶ ἀκούσαντες οἱ δέκα ἠγανάκτησαν περὶ τῶν δύο ἀδελφῶν. ²⁵ ὁ δὲ Ἰησοῦς προσκαλεσάμενος αὐτοὺς εἶπεν, Οἴδατε ὅτι οἱ ἄρχοντες τῶν ἐθνῶν κατακυριεύουσιν αὐτῶν καὶ οἱ μεγάλοι κατεξουσιάζουσιν αὐτῶν. ²⁶ οὐχ οὕτως ἔσται ἐν ὑμῖν· ἀλλ' ὃς ἐὰν θέλῃ ἐν ὑμῖν μέγας γενέσθαι, ἔσται ὑμῶν διάκονος, ²⁷ καὶ ὃς ἂν θέλῃ ἐν ὑμῖν εἶναι πρῶτος, ἔσται ὑμῶν δοῦλος· ²⁸ ὥσπερ ὁ υἱὸς τοῦ ἀνθρώπου οὐκ ἦλθεν διακονηθῆναι, ἀλλὰ διακονῆσαι καὶ δοῦναι τὴν ψυχὴν αὐτοῦ λύτρον ἀντὶ πολλῶν.

²⁹ Καὶ ἐκπορευομένων αὐτῶν ἀπὸ Ἰεριχὼ ἠκολούθησεν αὐτῷ ὄχλος πολύς. ³⁰ καὶ ἰδοὺ δύο τυφλοὶ καθήμενοι παρὰ τὴν ὁδόν, ἀκούσαντες ὅτι Ἰησοῦς παράγει, ἔκραξαν λέγοντες, Κύριε, ἐλέησον ἡμᾶς, υἱὲ Δαυείδ. ³¹ ὁ

δὲ ὄχλος ἐπετίμησεν αὐτοῖς ἵνα σιωπήσωσιν· οἱ δὲ μεῖζον ἔκραξαν λέγοντες, Κύριε, ἐλέησον ἡμᾶς, υἱὲ Δαυείδ. ³²καὶ στὰς ὁ Ἰησοῦς ἐφώνησεν αὐτοὺς καὶ εἶπεν, Τί θέλετε ποιήσω ὑμῖν; ³³λέγουσιν αὐτῷ, Κύριε, ἵνα ἀνοιγῶσιν οἱ ὀφθαλμοὶ ἡμῶν. ³⁴σπλαγχνισθεὶς δὲ ὁ Ἰησοῦς ἥψατο τῶν ὀμμάτων αὐτῶν, καὶ εὐθέως ἀνέβλεψαν, καὶ ἠκολούθησαν αὐτῷ.

21 ¹Καὶ ὅτε ἤγγισαν εἰς Ἱεροσόλυμα καὶ ἦλθον εἰς Βηθφαγὴ εἰς τὸ ὄρος τῶν ἐλαιῶν, τότε ὁ Ἰησοῦς ἀπέστειλεν δύο μαθητὰς ²λέγων αὐτοῖς, Πορεύεσθε εἰς τὴν κώμην τὴν κατέναντι ὑμῶν, καὶ εὐθέως εὑρήσετε ὄνον δεδεμένην καὶ πῶλον μετ' αὐτῆς· λύσαντες ἀγάγετέ μοι. ³καὶ ἐάν τις ὑμῖν εἴπῃ τι, ἐρεῖτε ὅτι Ὁ κύριος αὐτῶν χρείαν ἔχει· εὐθὺς δὲ ἀποστελεῖ αὐτούς. ⁴τοῦτο δὲ γέγονεν ἵνα πληρωθῇ τὸ ῥηθὲν διὰ τοῦ προφήτου λέγοντος, ⁵Εἴπατε τῇ θυγατρὶ Σιών, Ἰδοὺ ὁ βασιλεύς σου ἔρχεταί σοι πραῢς καὶ ἐπιβεβηκὼς ἐπὶ ὄνον καὶ ἐπὶ πῶλον υἱὸν ὑποζυγίου. ⁶πορευθέντες δὲ οἱ μαθηταὶ καὶ ποιήσαντες καθὼς προσέταξεν αὐτοῖς ὁ Ἰησοῦς, ⁷ἤγαγον τὴν ὄνον καὶ τὸν πῶλον, καὶ ἐπέθηκαν ἐπ' αὐτῶν τὰ ἱμάτια, καὶ ἐπεκάθισεν ἐπάνω αὐτῶν. ⁸ὁ δὲ πλεῖστος ὄχλος ἔστρωσαν ἑαυτῶν τὰ ἱμάτια ἐν τῇ ὁδῷ, ἄλλοι δὲ ἔκοπτον κλάδους ἀπὸ τῶν δένδρων καὶ ἐστρώννυον ἐν τῇ ὁδῷ. ⁹οἱ δὲ ὄχλοι οἱ προάγοντες αὐτὸν καὶ οἱ ἀκολουθοῦντες ἔκραζον λέγοντες, Ὡσαννὰ τῷ υἱῷ Δαυείδ, εὐλογημένος ὁ ἐρχόμενος ἐν ὀνόματι κυρίου, ὡσαννὰ ἐν τοῖς ὑψίστοις.

¹⁰Καὶ εἰσελθόντος αὐτοῦ εἰς Ἱεροσόλυμα ἐσείσθη πᾶσα ἡ πόλις λέγουσα, Τίς ἐστιν οὗτος; ¹¹οἱ δὲ ὄχλοι ἔλεγον, Οὗτός ἐστιν ὁ προφήτης Ἰησοῦς ὁ ἀπὸ Ναζαρὲθ τῆς Γαλιλαίας.

¹² Καὶ εἰσῆλθεν Ἰησοῦς εἰς τὸ ἱερὸν τοῦ θεοῦ, καὶ ἐξέβαλεν πάντας τοὺς πωλοῦντας καὶ ἀγοράζοντας ἐν τῷ ἱερῷ, καὶ τὰς τραπέζας τῶν κολλυβιστῶν κατέστρεψεν καὶ τὰς καθέδρας τῶν πωλούντων τὰς περιστεράς, ¹³ καὶ λέγει αὐτοῖς, Γέγραπται, Ὁ οἶκός μου οἶκος προσευχῆς κληθήσεται, ὑμεῖς δὲ αὐτὸν ποιεῖτε σπήλαιον λῃστῶν. ¹⁴ Καὶ προσῆλθον αὐτῷ τυφλοὶ καὶ χωλοὶ ἐν τῷ ἱερῷ, καὶ ἐθεράπευσεν αὐτούς.

¹⁵ Ἰδόντες δὲ οἱ ἀρχιερεῖς καὶ οἱ γραμματεῖς τὰ θαυμάσια ἃ ἐποίησεν καὶ τοὺς παῖδας τοὺς κράζοντας ἐν τῷ ἱερῷ καὶ λέγοντας, Ὡσαννὰ τῷ υἱῷ Δαυείδ, ἠγανάκτησαν, ¹⁶ καὶ εἶπαν αὐτῷ, Ἀκούεις τί οὗτοι λέγουσιν; ὁ δὲ Ἰησοῦς λέγει αὐτοῖς, Ναί· οὐδέποτε ἀνέγνωτε ὅτι Ἐκ στόματος νηπίων καὶ θηλαζόντων κατηρτίσω αἶνον; ¹⁷ καὶ καταλιπὼν αὐτοὺς ἐξῆλθεν ἔξω τῆς πόλεως εἰς Βηθανίαν, καὶ ηὐλίσθη ἐκεῖ.

¹⁸ Πρωῒ δὲ ἐπαναγαγὼν εἰς τὴν πόλιν ἐπείνασεν. ¹⁹ καὶ ἰδὼν συκῆν μίαν ἐπὶ τῆς ὁδοῦ ἦλθεν ἐπ' αὐτήν, καὶ οὐδὲν εὗρεν ἐν αὐτῇ εἰ μὴ φύλλα μόνον, καὶ λέγει αὐτῇ, Μηκέτι ἐκ σοῦ καρπὸς γένηται εἰς τὸν αἰῶνα. καὶ ἐξηράνθη παραχρῆμα ἡ συκῆ. ²⁰ καὶ ἰδόντες οἱ μαθηταὶ ἐθαύμασαν λέγοντες, Πῶς παραχρῆμα ἐξηράνθη ἡ συκῆ; ²¹ ἀποκριθεὶς δὲ ὁ Ἰησοῦς εἶπεν αὐτοῖς, Ἀμὴν λέγω ὑμῖν, ἐὰν ἔχητε πίστιν καὶ μὴ διακριθῆτε, οὐ μόνον τὸ τῆς συκῆς ποιήσετε, ἀλλὰ κἂν τῷ ὄρει τούτῳ εἴπητε, Ἄρθητι καὶ βλήθητι εἰς τὴν θάλασσαν, γενήσεται· ²² καὶ πάντα ὅσα ἂν αἰτήσητε ἐν τῇ προσευχῇ πιστεύοντες λήμψεσθε.

²³ Καὶ ἐλθόντος αὐτοῦ εἰς τὸ ἱερόν, προσῆλθον αὐτῷ διδάσκοντι οἱ ἀρχιερεῖς καὶ οἱ πρεσβύτεροι τοῦ λαοῦ λέγοντες, Ἐν ποίᾳ ἐξουσίᾳ ταῦτα ποιεῖς; καὶ τίς

σοι ἔδωκεν τὴν ἐξουσίαν ταύτην; ²⁴ ἀποκριθεὶς δὲ ὁ Ἰησοῦς εἶπεν αὐτοῖς, Ἐρωτήσω ὑμᾶς κἀγὼ λόγον ἕνα, ὃν ἐὰν εἴπητέ μοι, κἀγὼ ὑμῖν ἐρῶ ἐν ποίᾳ ἐξουσίᾳ ταῦτα ποιῶ· ²⁵ τὸ βάπτισμα τὸ Ἰωάννου πόθεν ἦν; ἐξ οὐρανοῦ ἢ ἐξ ἀνθρώπων; οἱ δὲ διελογίζοντο παρ' ἑαυτοῖς λέγοντες, ²⁶ Ἐὰν εἴπωμεν, Ἐξ οὐρανοῦ, ἐρεῖ ἡμῖν, Διὰ τί οὖν οὐκ ἐπιστεύσατε αὐτῷ; ἐὰν δὲ εἴπωμεν, Ἐξ ἀνθρώπων, φοβούμεθα τὸν ὄχλον· πάντες γὰρ ὡς προφήτην ἔχουσιν τὸν Ἰωάννην. ²⁷ καὶ ἀποκριθέντες τῷ Ἰησοῦ εἶπον, Οὐκ οἴδαμεν. ἔφη αὐτοῖς καὶ αὐτός, Οὐδὲ ἐγὼ λέγω ὑμῖν ἐν ποίᾳ ἐξουσίᾳ ταῦτα ποιῶ.

²⁸ Τί δὲ ὑμῖν δοκεῖ; ἄνθρωπος εἶχεν τέκνα δύο· καὶ προσελθὼν τῷ πρώτῳ εἶπεν, Τέκνον, ὕπαγε σήμερον ἐργάζου ἐν τῷ ἀμπελῶνι. ²⁹ ὁ δὲ ἀποκριθεὶς εἶπεν, Οὐ θέλω, ὕστερον δὲ μεταμεληθεὶς ἀπῆλθεν. ³⁰ προσελθὼν δὲ τῷ δευτέρῳ εἶπεν ὡσαύτως. ὁ δὲ ἀποκριθεὶς εἶπεν, Ἐγὼ κύριε, καὶ οὐκ ἀπῆλθεν. ³¹ τίς ἐκ τῶν δύο ἐποίησεν τὸ θέλημα τοῦ πατρός; λέγουσιν, Ὁ πρῶτος. λέγει αὐτοῖς ὁ Ἰησοῦς, Ἀμὴν λέγω ὑμῖν ὅτι οἱ τελῶναι καὶ αἱ πόρναι προάγουσιν ὑμᾶς εἰς τὴν βασιλείαν τοῦ θεοῦ. ³² ἦλθεν γὰρ Ἰωάννης πρὸς ὑμᾶς ἐν ὁδῷ δικαιοσύνης, καὶ οὐκ ἐπιστεύσατε αὐτῷ· οἱ δὲ τελῶναι καὶ αἱ πόρναι ἐπίστευσαν αὐτῷ· ὑμεῖς δὲ ἰδόντες οὐ μετεμελήθητε ὕστερον τοῦ πιστεῦσαι αὐτῷ.

³³ Ἄλλην παραβολὴν ἀκούσατε. ἄνθρωπος ἦν οἰκοδεσπότης, ὅστις ἐφύτευσεν ἀμπελῶνα, καὶ φραγμὸν αὐτῷ περιέθηκεν καὶ ὤρυξεν ἐν αὐτῷ ληνὸν καὶ ᾠκοδόμησεν πύργον, καὶ ἐξέδοτο αὐτὸν γεωργοῖς, καὶ ἀπεδήμησεν. ³⁴ ὅτε δὲ ἤγγισεν ὁ καιρὸς τῶν καρπῶν, ἀπέστειλεν τοὺς δούλους αὐτοῦ πρὸς τοὺς γεωργοὺς λαβεῖν τοὺς καρποὺς αὐτοῦ. ³⁵ καὶ λαβόντες οἱ γεωργοὶ τοὺς δούλους

αὐτοῦ ὃν μὲν ἔδειραν, ὃν δὲ ἀπέκτειναν, ὃν δὲ ἐλιθοβόλησαν. ³⁶ πάλιν ἀπέστειλεν ἄλλους δούλους πλείονας τῶν πρώτων, καὶ ἐποίησαν αὐτοῖς ὡσαύτως. ³⁷ ὕστερον δὲ ἀπέστειλεν πρὸς αὐτοὺς τὸν υἱὸν αὐτοῦ, λέγων, Ἐντραπήσονται τὸν υἱόν μου. ³⁸ οἱ δὲ γεωργοὶ ἰδόντες τὸν υἱὸν εἶπον ἐν ἑαυτοῖς, Οὗτός ἐστιν ὁ κληρονόμος· δεῦτε ἀποκτείνωμεν αὐτὸν καὶ σχῶμεν τὴν κληρονομίαν αὐτοῦ. ³⁹ καὶ λαβόντες αὐτὸν ἐξέβαλον ἔξω τοῦ ἀμπελῶνος καὶ ἀπέκτειναν. ⁴⁰ ὅταν οὖν ἔλθῃ ὁ κύριος τοῦ ἀμπελῶνος, τί ποιήσει τοῖς γεωργοῖς ἐκείνοις ; ⁴¹ λέγουσιν αὐτῷ, Κακοὺς κακῶς ἀπολέσει αὐτούς, καὶ τὸν ἀμπελῶνα ἐκδώσεται ἄλλοις γεωργοῖς, οἵτινες ἀποδώσουσιν αὐτῷ τοὺς καρποὺς ἐν τοῖς καιροῖς αὐτῶν. ⁴² λέγει αὐτοῖς ὁ Ἰησοῦς, Οὐδέποτε ἀνέγνωτε ἐν ταῖς γραφαῖς, Λίθον ὃν ἀπεδοκίμασαν οἱ οἰκοδομοῦντες, οὗτος ἐγενήθη εἰς κεφαλὴν γωνίας· παρὰ κυρίου ἐγένετο αὕτη, καὶ ἔστιν θαυμαστὴ ἐν ὀφθαλμοῖς ἡμῶν; ⁴³ διὰ τοῦτο λέγω ὑμῖν ὅτι ἀρθήσεται ἀφ' ὑμῶν ἡ βασιλεία τοῦ θεοῦ καὶ δοθήσεται ἔθνει ποιοῦντι τοὺς καρποὺς αὐτῆς. ⁴⁴ καὶ ὁ πεσὼν ἐπὶ τὸν λίθον τοῦτον συνθλασθήσεται· ἐφ' ὃν δ' ἂν πέσῃ, λικμήσει αὐτόν. ⁴⁵ ἀκούσαντες δὲ οἱ ἀρχιερεῖς καὶ οἱ Φαρισαῖοι τὰς παραβολὰς αὐτοῦ ἔγνωσαν ὅτι περὶ αὐτῶν λέγει· ⁴⁶ καὶ ζητοῦντες αὐτὸν κρατῆσαι ἐφοβήθησαν τοὺς ὄχλους, ἐπεὶ εἰς προφήτην αὐτὸν εἶχον.

22 ¹ Καὶ ἀποκριθεὶς ὁ Ἰησοῦς πάλιν εἶπεν ἐν παραβολαῖς αὐτοῖς, λέγων, ² Ὡμοιώθη ἡ βασιλεία τῶν οὐρανῶν ἀνθρώπῳ βασιλεῖ, ὅστις ἐποίησεν γάμους τῷ υἱῷ αὐτοῦ. ³ καὶ ἀπέστειλεν τοὺς δούλους αὐτοῦ καλέσαι τοὺς κεκλημένους εἰς τοὺς γάμους, καὶ οὐκ ἤθελον ἐλθεῖν. ⁴ πάλιν ἀπέστειλεν ἄλλους δούλους λέγων, Εἴπατε τοῖς κεκλημένοις, Ἰδοὺ τὸ ἄριστόν μου ἡτοίμακα, οἱ ταῦροί μου καὶ τὰ σιτιστὰ τεθυμένα, καὶ πάντα ἕτοιμα· δεῦτε εἰς τοὺς γάμους. ⁵ οἱ δὲ ἀμελήσαντες ἀπῆλθον, ὃς μὲν εἰς τὸν ἴδιον ἀγρόν, ὃς δὲ ἐπὶ τὴν ἐμπορίαν αὐτοῦ· ⁶ οἱ δὲ λοιποὶ κρατήσαντες τοὺς δούλους αὐτοῦ ὕβρισαν καὶ ἀπέκτειναν. ⁷ ὁ δὲ βασιλεὺς ὠργίσθη, καὶ πέμψας τὰ στρατεύματα αὐτοῦ ἀπώλεσεν τοὺς φονεῖς ἐκείνους καὶ τὴν πόλιν αὐτῶν ἐνέπρησεν. ⁸ τότε λέγει τοῖς δούλοις αὐτοῦ, Ὁ μὲν γάμος ἕτοιμός ἐστιν, οἱ δὲ κεκλημένοι οὐκ ἦσαν ἄξιοι. ⁹ πορεύεσθε οὖν ἐπὶ τὰς διεξόδους τῶν ὁδῶν, καὶ ὅσους ἐὰν εὕρητε καλέσατε εἰς τοὺς γάμους. ¹⁰ καὶ ἐξελθόντες οἱ δοῦλοι ἐκεῖνοι εἰς τὰς ὁδοὺς συνήγαγον πάντας ὅσους εὗρον, πονηρούς τε καὶ ἀγαθούς, καὶ ἐπλήσθη ὁ νυμφὼν ἀνακειμένων. ¹¹ εἰσελθὼν δὲ ὁ βασιλεὺς θεάσασθαι τοὺς ἀνακειμένους εἶδεν ἐκεῖ ἄνθρωπον οὐκ ἐνδεδυμένον ἔνδυμα γάμου. ¹² καὶ λέγει αὐτῷ, Ἑταῖρε, πῶς εἰσῆλθες ὧδε μὴ ἔχων ἔνδυμα γάμου; ὁ δὲ ἐφιμώθη. ¹³ τότε ὁ βασιλεὺς εἶπεν τοῖς διακόνοις, Δήσαντες αὐτοῦ πόδας καὶ χεῖρας ἐκβάλετε αὐτὸν εἰς τὸ σκότος τὸ ἐξώτερον· ἐκεῖ ἔσται ὁ κλαυθμὸς καὶ ὁ βρυγμὸς τῶν ὀδόντων. ¹⁴ πολλοὶ γάρ εἰσιν κλητοί, ὀλίγοι δὲ ἐκλεκτοί.

¹⁵ Τότε πορευθέντες οἱ Φαρισαῖοι συμβούλιον ἔλαβον ὅπως αὐτὸν παγιδεύσωσιν ἐν λόγῳ. ¹⁶ καὶ ἀποστέλλουσιν αὐτῷ τοὺς μαθητὰς αὐτῶν μετὰ τῶν Ἡρωδιανῶν λέγοντας, Διδάσκαλε, οἴδαμεν ὅτι ἀληθὴς εἶ καὶ τὴν ὁδὸν τοῦ θεοῦ ἐν ἀληθείᾳ διδάσκεις, καὶ οὐ μέλει σοι περὶ οὐδενός, οὐ γὰρ βλέπεις εἰς πρόσωπον ἀνθρώπων· ¹⁷ εἰπὲ οὖν ἡμῖν, τί σοι δοκεῖ; ἔξεστιν δοῦναι κῆνσον Καίσαρι ἢ οὔ; ¹⁸ γνοὺς δὲ ὁ Ἰησοῦς τὴν πονηρίαν αὐτῶν εἶπεν, Τί με πειράζετε, ὑποκριταί; ¹⁹ ἐπι-

δείξατέ μοι τὸ νόμισμα τοῦ κήνσου. οἱ δὲ προσήνεγκαν αὐτῷ δηνάριον. ²⁰ καὶ λέγει αὐτοῖς, Τίνος ἡ εἰκὼν αὕτη καὶ ἡ ἐπιγραφή; ²¹ λέγουσιν αὐτῷ, Καίσαρος. τότε λέγει αὐτοῖς, Ἀπόδοτε οὖν τὰ Καίσαρος Καίσαρι καὶ τὰ τοῦ θεοῦ τῷ θεῷ. ²² καὶ ἀκούσαντες ἐθαύμασαν, καὶ ἀφέντες αὐτὸν ἀπῆλθαν.

²³ Ἐν ἐκείνῃ τῇ ἡμέρᾳ προσῆλθον αὐτῷ Σαδδουκαῖοι λέγοντες μὴ εἶναι ἀνάστασιν, καὶ ἐπηρώτησαν αὐτὸν ²⁴ λέγοντες, Διδάσκαλε, Μωϋσῆς εἶπεν, Ἐάν τις ἀποθάνῃ μὴ ἔχων τέκνα, ἐπιγαμβρεύσει ὁ ἀδελφὸς αὐτοῦ τὴν γυναῖκα αὐτοῦ καὶ ἀναστήσει σπέρμα τῷ ἀδελφῷ αὐτοῦ. ²⁵ ἦσαν δὲ παρ' ἡμῖν ἑπτὰ ἀδελφοί, καὶ ὁ πρῶτος γήμας ἐτελεύτησεν, καὶ μὴ ἔχων σπέρμα ἀφῆκεν τὴν γυναῖκα αὐτοῦ τῷ ἀδελφῷ αὐτοῦ. ²⁶ ὁμοίως καὶ ὁ δεύτερος καὶ ὁ τρίτος, ἕως τῶν ἑπτά. ²⁷ ὕστερον δὲ πάντων ἀπέθανεν ἡ γυνή. ²⁸ ἐν τῇ ἀναστάσει οὖν τίνος τῶν ἑπτὰ ἔσται γυνή; πάντες γὰρ ἔσχον αὐτήν. ²⁹ ἀποκριθεὶς δὲ ὁ Ἰησοῦς εἶπεν αὐτοῖς, Πλανᾶσθε, μὴ εἰδότες τὰς γραφὰς μηδὲ τὴν δύναμιν τοῦ θεοῦ. ³⁰ ἐν γὰρ τῇ ἀναστάσει οὔτε γαμοῦσιν οὔτε γαμίζονται, ἀλλ' ὡς ἄγγελοι θεοῦ ἐν τῷ οὐρανῷ εἰσίν. ³¹ περὶ δὲ τῆς ἀναστάσεως τῶν νεκρῶν οὐκ ἀνέγνωτε τὸ ῥηθὲν ὑμῖν ὑπὸ τοῦ θεοῦ λέγοντος, ³² Ἐγώ εἰμι ὁ θεὸς Ἀβραὰμ καὶ ὁ θεὸς Ἰσαὰκ καὶ ὁ θεὸς Ἰακώβ; οὐκ ἔστιν ὁ θεὸς νεκρῶν ἀλλὰ ζώντων. ³³ καὶ ἀκούσαντες οἱ ὄχλοι ἐξεπλήσσοντο ἐπὶ τῇ διδαχῇ αὐτοῦ.

³⁴ Οἱ δὲ Φαρισαῖοι ἀκούσαντες ὅτι ἐφίμωσεν τοὺς Σαδδουκαίους συνήχθησαν ἐπὶ τὸ αὐτό, ³⁵ καὶ ἐπηρώτησεν εἷς ἐξ αὐτῶν νομικὸς πειράζων αὐτόν, ³⁶ Διδάσκαλε, ποία ἐντολὴ μεγάλη ἐν τῷ νόμῳ; ³⁷ ὁ δὲ ἔφη αὐτῷ, Ἀγαπήσεις κύριον τὸν θεόν σου ἐν ὅλῃ τῇ

καρδία σου καὶ ἐν ὅλῃ τῇ ψυχῇ σου καὶ ἐν ὅλῃ τῇ διανοίᾳ σου. ³⁸ αὕτη ἐστὶν ἡ μεγάλη καὶ πρώτη ἐντολή. ³⁹ δευτέρα δὲ ὁμοία αὐτῇ, Ἀγαπήσεις τὸν πλησίον σου ὡς σεαυτόν. ⁴⁰ ἐν ταύταις ταῖς δυσὶν ἐντολαῖς ὅλος ὁ νόμος κρέμαται καὶ οἱ προφῆται.

⁴¹ Συνηγμένων δὲ τῶν Φαρισαίων ἐπηρώτησεν αὐτοὺς ὁ Ἰησοῦς ⁴² λέγων, Τί ὑμῖν δοκεῖ περὶ τοῦ Χριστοῦ; τίνος υἱός ἐστιν; λέγουσιν αὐτῷ, Τοῦ Δαυείδ. ⁴³ λέγει αὐτοῖς, Πῶς οὖν Δαυεὶδ ἐν πνεύματι καλεῖ αὐτὸν κύριον, λέγων, ⁴⁴ Εἶπεν κύριος τῷ κυρίῳ μου, Κάθου ἐκ δεξιῶν μου ἕως ἂν θῶ τοὺς ἐχθρούς σου ὑποκάτω τῶν ποδῶν σου. ⁴⁵ εἰ οὖν Δαυεὶδ καλεῖ αὐτὸν κύριον, πῶς υἱὸς αὐτοῦ ἐστίν; ⁴⁶ καὶ οὐδεὶς ἐδύνατο ἀποκριθῆναι αὐτῷ λόγον, οὐδὲ ἐτόλμησέν τις ἀπ' ἐκείνης τῆς ἡμέρας ἐπερωτῆσαι αὐτὸν οὐκέτι.

23 ¹ Τότε ὁ Ἰησοῦς ἐλάλησεν τοῖς ὄχλοις καὶ τοῖς μαθηταῖς αὐτοῦ ² λέγων, Ἐπὶ τῆς Μωϋσέως καθέδρας ἐκάθισαν οἱ γραμματεῖς καὶ οἱ Φαρισαῖοι. ³ πάντα οὖν ὅσα ἂν εἴπωσιν ὑμῖν ποιήσατε καὶ τηρεῖτε, κατὰ δὲ τὰ ἔργα αὐτῶν μὴ ποιεῖτε· λέγουσιν γὰρ καὶ οὐ ποιοῦσιν. ⁴ δεσμεύουσιν δὲ φορτία βαρέα καὶ ἐπιτιθέασιν ἐπὶ τοὺς ὤμους τῶν ἀνθρώπων, αὐτοὶ δὲ τῷ δακτύλῳ αὐτῶν οὐ θέλουσιν κινῆσαι αὐτά. ⁵ πάντα δὲ τὰ ἔργα αὐτῶν ποιοῦσιν πρὸς τὸ θεαθῆναι τοῖς ἀνθρώποις· πλατύνουσιν γὰρ τὰ φυλακτήρια αὐτῶν καὶ μεγαλύνουσιν τὰ κράσπεδα, ⁶ φιλοῦσιν δὲ τὴν πρωτοκλισίαν ἐν τοῖς δείπνοις καὶ τὰς πρωτοκαθεδρίας ἐν ταῖς συναγωγαῖς ⁷ καὶ τοὺς ἀσπασμοὺς ἐν ταῖς ἀγοραῖς καὶ καλεῖσθαι ὑπὸ τῶν ἀνθρώπων ῥαββί. ⁸ ὑμεῖς δὲ μὴ κληθῆτε ῥαββί· εἷς γάρ ἐστιν ὑμῶν ὁ διδάσκαλος, πάντες δὲ ὑμεῖς ἀδελφοί ἐστε. ⁹καὶ πατέρα μὴ καλέσητε ὑμῶν ἐπὶ τῆς γῆς· εἷς γάρ ἐστιν ὑμῶν ὁ πατὴρ ὁ οὐράνιος. ¹⁰μηδὲ κληθῆτε καθηγηταί, ὅτι καθηγητὴς ὑμῶν ἐστὶν εἷς ὁ Χριστός. ¹¹ὁ δὲ μείζων ὑμῶν ἔσται ὑμῶν διάκονος. ¹²ὅστις δὲ ὑψώσει ἑαυτὸν ταπεινωθήσεται, καὶ ὅστις ταπεινώσει ἑαυτὸν ὑψωθήσεται.*

¹⁴Οὐαὶ δὲ ὑμῖν, γραμματεῖς καὶ Φαρισαῖοι ὑποκριταί, ὅτι κλείετε τὴν βασιλείαν τῶν οὐρανῶν ἔμπροσθεν τῶν ἀνθρώπων· ὑμεῖς γὰρ οὐκ εἰσέρχεσθε, οὐδὲ τοὺς εἰσερχομένους ἀφίετε εἰσελθεῖν.

¹⁵Οὐαὶ ὑμῖν, γραμματεῖς καὶ Φαρισαῖοι ὑποκριταί, ὅτι περιάγετε τὴν θάλασσαν καὶ τὴν ξηρὰν ποιῆσαι ἕνα προσήλυτον, καὶ ὅταν γένηται, ποιεῖτε αὐτὸν υἱὸν γεέννης διπλότερον ὑμῶν.

¹⁶Οὐαὶ ὑμῖν, ὁδηγοὶ τυφλοὶ οἱ λέγοντες, Ὃς ἂν ὀμόσῃ ἐν τῷ ναῷ, οὐδέν ἐστιν· ὃς δ᾽ ἂν ὀμόσῃ ἐν τῷ χρυσῷ τοῦ ναοῦ, ὀφείλει. ¹⁷μωροὶ καὶ τυφλοί, τίς γὰρ μείζων ἐστίν, ὁ χρυσὸς ἢ ὁ ναὸς ὁ ἁγιάσας τὸν χρυσόν; ¹⁸καί, Ὃς ἂν ὀμόσῃ ἐν τῷ θυσιαστηρίῳ, οὐδέν ἐστιν· ὃς δ᾽ ἂν ὀμόσῃ ἐν τῷ δώρῳ τῷ ἐπάνω αὐτοῦ, ὀφείλει. ¹⁹τυφλοί, τί γὰρ μεῖζον, τὸ δῶρον ἢ τὸ θυσιαστήριον τὸ ἁγιάζον τὸ δῶρον; ²⁰ὁ οὖν ὀμόσας ἐν τῷ θυσιαστηρίῳ ὀμνύει ἐν αὐτῷ καὶ ἐν πᾶσιν τοῖς ἐπάνω αὐτοῦ· ²¹καὶ ὁ ὀμόσας ἐν τῷ ναῷ ὀμνύει ἐν αὐτῷ καὶ ἐν τῷ κατοικοῦντι αὐτόν· ²²καὶ ὁ ὀμόσας ἐν τῷ οὐρανῷ ὀμνύει ἐν τῷ θρόνῳ τοῦ θεοῦ καὶ ἐν τῷ καθημένῳ ἐπάνω αὐτοῦ.

²³Οὐαὶ ὑμῖν, γραμματεῖς καὶ Φαρισαῖοι ὑποκριταί, ὅτι ἀποδεκατοῦτε τὸ ἡδύοσμον καὶ τὸ ἄνηθον καὶ τὸ κύμινον, καὶ ἀφήκατε τὰ βαρύτερα τοῦ νόμου, τὴν

* Verse 13 omitted on the best MS. authority.

κρίσιν καὶ τὸ ἔλεος καὶ τὴν πίστιν· ταῦτα ἔδει ποιῆσαι κἀκεῖνα μὴ ἀφεῖναι. ²⁴ ὁδηγοὶ τυφλοί, οἱ διϋλίζοντες τὸν κώνωπα, τὴν δὲ κάμηλον καταπίνοντες.

²⁵ Οὐαὶ ὑμῖν, γραμματεῖς καὶ Φαρισαῖοι ὑποκριταί, ὅτι καθαρίζετε τὸ ἔξωθεν τοῦ ποτηρίου καὶ τῆς παροψίδος, ἔσωθεν δὲ γέμουσιν ἐξ ἁρπαγῆς καὶ ἀκρασίας. ²⁶ Φαρισαῖε τυφλέ, καθάρισον πρῶτον τὸ ἐντὸς τοῦ ποτηρίου καὶ τῆς παροψίδος, ἵνα γένηται καὶ τὸ ἐκτὸς αὐτοῦ καθαρόν.

²⁷ Οὐαὶ ὑμῖν, γραμματεῖς καὶ Φαρισαῖοι ὑποκριταί, ὅτι παρομοιάζετε τάφοις κεκονιαμένοις, οἵτινες ἔξωθεν μὲν φαίνονται ὡραῖοι, ἔσωθεν δὲ γέμουσιν ὀστέων νεκρῶν καὶ πάσης ἀκαθαρσίας. ²⁸ οὕτως καὶ ὑμεῖς ἔξωθεν μὲν φαίνεσθε τοῖς ἀνθρώποις δίκαιοι, ἔσωθεν δέ ἐστε μεστοὶ ὑποκρίσεως καὶ ἀνομίας.

²⁹ Οὐαὶ ὑμῖν, γραμματεῖς καὶ Φαρισαῖοι ὑποκριταί, ὅτι οἰκοδομεῖτε τοὺς τάφους τῶν προφητῶν καὶ κοσμεῖτε τὰ μνημεῖα τῶν δικαίων, ³⁰ καὶ λέγετε, Εἰ ἤμεθα ἐν ταῖς ἡμέραις τῶν πατέρων ἡμῶν, οὐκ ἂν ἤμεθα κοινωνοὶ αὐτῶν ἐν τῷ αἵματι τῶν προφητῶν. ³¹ ὥστε μαρτυρεῖτε ἑαυτοῖς ὅτι υἱοί ἐστε τῶν φονευσάντων τοὺς προφήτας. ³² καὶ ὑμεῖς πληρώσατε τὸ μέτρον τῶν πατέρων ὑμῶν. ³³ ὄφεις, γεννήματα ἐχιδνῶν, πῶς φύγητε ἀπὸ τῆς κρίσεως τῆς γεέννης;

³⁴ Διὰ τοῦτο ἰδοὺ ἐγὼ ἀποστέλλω πρὸς ὑμᾶς προφήτας καὶ σοφοὺς καὶ γραμματεῖς· ἐξ αὐτῶν ἀποκτενεῖτε καὶ σταυρώσετε, καὶ ἐξ αὐτῶν μαστιγώσετε ἐν ταῖς συναγωγαῖς ὑμῶν καὶ διώξετε ἀπὸ πόλεως εἰς πόλιν· ³⁵ ὅπως ἔλθῃ ἐφ᾽ ὑμᾶς πᾶν αἷμα δίκαιον ἐκχυννόμενον ἐπὶ τῆς γῆς ἀπὸ τοῦ αἵματος Ἅβελ τοῦ δικαίου ἕως τοῦ αἵματος Ζαχαρίου υἱοῦ Βαραχίου, ὃν ἐφονεύσατε

μεταξὺ τοῦ ναοῦ καὶ τοῦ θυσιαστηρίου. ³⁶ ἀμὴν λέγω ὑμῖν, ἥξει ταῦτα πάντα ἐπὶ τὴν γενεὰν ταύτην.

³⁷ Ἱερουσαλὴμ Ἱερουσαλήμ, ἡ ἀποκτείνουσα τοὺς προφήτας καὶ λιθοβολοῦσα τοὺς ἀπεσταλμένους πρὸς αὐτήν, ποσάκις ἠθέλησα ἐπισυναγαγεῖν τὰ τέκνα σου, ὃν τρόπον ὄρνις ἐπισυνάγει τὰ νοσσία αὐτῆς ὑπὸ τὰς πτέρυγας, καὶ οὐκ ἠθελήσατε. ³⁸ ἰδοὺ ἀφίεται ὑμῖν ὁ οἶκος ὑμῶν ἔρημος. ³⁹ λέγω γὰρ ὑμῖν, οὐ μή με ἴδητε ἀπ' ἄρτι ἕως ἂν εἴπητε, Εὐλογημένος ὁ ἐρχόμενος ἐν ὀνόματι κυρίου.

24 ¹ Καὶ ἐξελθὼν ὁ Ἰησοῦς ἀπὸ τοῦ ἱεροῦ ἐπορεύετο, καὶ προσῆλθον οἱ μαθηταὶ αὐτοῦ ἐπιδεῖξαι αὐτῷ τὰς οἰκοδομὰς τοῦ ἱεροῦ. ² ὁ δὲ ἀποκριθεὶς εἶπεν αὐτοῖς, Οὐ βλέπετε ταῦτα πάντα; ἀμὴν λέγω ὑμῖν, οὐ μὴ ἀφεθῇ ὧδε λίθος ἐπὶ λίθον, ὃς οὐ καταλυθήσεται. ³ καθημένου δὲ αὐτοῦ ἐπὶ τοῦ ὄρους τῶν ἐλαιῶν προσῆλθον αὐτῷ οἱ μαθηταὶ κατ' ἰδίαν λέγοντες, Εἰπὲ ἡμῖν, πότε ταῦτα ἔσται, καὶ τί τὸ σημεῖον τῆς σῆς παρουσίας καὶ συντελείας τοῦ αἰῶνος; ⁴ καὶ ἀποκριθεὶς ὁ Ἰησοῦς εἶπεν αὐτοῖς, Βλέπετε μή τις ὑμᾶς πλανήσῃ. ⁵ πολλοὶ γὰρ ἐλεύσονται ἐπὶ τῷ ὀνόματί μου λέγοντες, Ἐγώ εἰμι ὁ Χριστός, καὶ πολλοὺς πλανήσουσιν. ⁶ μελλήσετε δὲ ἀκούειν πολέμους καὶ ἀκοὰς πολέμων· ὁρᾶτε μὴ θροεῖσθε· δεῖ γὰρ γενέσθαι, ἀλλ' οὔπω ἐστὶν τὸ τέλος. ⁷ ἐγερθήσεται γὰρ ἔθνος ἐπὶ ἔθνος καὶ βασιλεία ἐπὶ βασιλείαν, καὶ ἔσονται λιμοὶ καὶ σεισμοὶ κατὰ τόπους. ⁸ πάντα δὲ ταῦτα ἀρχὴ ὠδίνων.

⁹ Τότε παραδώσουσιν ὑμᾶς εἰς θλῖψιν καὶ ἀποκτενοῦσιν ὑμᾶς, καὶ ἔσεσθε μισούμενοι ὑπὸ πάντων τῶν ἐθνῶν διὰ τὸ ὄνομά μου. ¹⁰ καὶ τότε σκανδαλισθήσονται

πολλοὶ καὶ ἀλλήλους παραδώσουσιν καὶ μισήσουσιν ἀλλήλους. ¹¹ καὶ πολλοὶ ψευδοπροφῆται ἐγερθήσονται καὶ πλανήσουσιν πολλούς. ¹² καὶ διὰ τὸ πληθυνθῆναι τὴν ἀνομίαν ψυγήσεται ἡ ἀγάπη τῶν πολλῶν. ¹³ ὁ δὲ ὑπομείνας εἰς τέλος, οὗτος σωθήσεται. ¹⁴ καὶ κηρυχθήσεται τοῦτο τὸ εὐαγγέλιον τῆς βασιλείας ἐν ὅλῃ τῇ οἰκουμένῃ εἰς μαρτύριον πᾶσιν τοῖς ἔθνεσιν, καὶ τότε ἥξει τὸ τέλος.

¹⁵ Ὅταν οὖν ἴδητε τὸ βδέλυγμα τῆς ἐρημώσεως τὸ ῥηθὲν διὰ Δανιὴλ τοῦ προφήτου ἑστὸς ἐν τόπῳ ἁγίῳ, ὁ ἀναγινώσκων νοείτω, ¹⁶ τότε οἱ ἐν τῇ Ἰουδαίᾳ φευγέτωσαν ἐπὶ τὰ ὄρη, ¹⁷ ὁ ἐπὶ τοῦ δώματος μὴ καταβάτω ἆραι τὰ ἐκ τῆς οἰκίας αὐτοῦ, ¹⁸ καὶ ὁ ἐν τῷ ἀγρῷ μὴ ἐπιστρεψάτω ὀπίσω ἆραι τὸ ἱμάτιον αὐτοῦ. ¹⁹ οὐαὶ δὲ ταῖς ἐν γαστρὶ ἐχούσαις καὶ ταῖς θηλαζούσαις ἐν ἐκείναις ταῖς ἡμέραις. ²⁰ προσεύχεσθε δὲ ἵνα μὴ γένηται ἡ φυγὴ ὑμῶν χειμῶνος μηδὲ σαββάτῳ. ²¹ ἔσται γὰρ τότε θλῖψις μεγάλη, οἵα οὐ γέγονεν ἀπ' ἀρχῆς κόσμου ἕως τοῦ νῦν οὐδ' οὐ μὴ γένηται. ²² καὶ εἰ μὴ ἐκολοβώθησαν αἱ ἡμέραι ἐκεῖναι, οὐκ ἂν ἐσώθη πᾶσα σάρξ· διὰ δὲ τοὺς ἐκλεκτοὺς κολοβωθήσονται αἱ ἡμέραι ἐκεῖναι.

²³ Τότε ἐάν τις ὑμῖν εἴπῃ, Ἰδοὺ ὧδε ὁ Χριστός, ἤ Ὧδε, μὴ πιστεύσητε. ²⁴ ἐγερθήσονται γὰρ ψευδόχριστοι καὶ ψευδοπροφῆται, καὶ δώσουσιν σημεῖα μεγάλα καὶ τέρατα, ὥστε πλανῆσαι, εἰ δυνατόν, καὶ τοὺς ἐκλεκτούς. ²⁵ ἰδοὺ προείρηκα ὑμῖν. ²⁶ ἐὰν οὖν εἴπωσιν ὑμῖν, Ἰδοὺ ἐν τῇ ἐρήμῳ ἐστίν, μὴ ἐξέλθητε· Ἰδοὺ ἐν τοῖς ταμείοις, μὴ πιστεύσητε. ²⁷ ὥσπερ γὰρ ἡ ἀστραπὴ ἐξέρχεται ἀπὸ ἀνατολῶν καὶ φαίνεται ἕως δυσμῶν, οὕτως ἔσται ἡ παρουσία τοῦ υἱοῦ τοῦ ἀνθρώπου. ²⁸ ὅπου ἐὰν ᾖ τὸ πτῶμα, ἐκεῖ συναχθήσονται οἱ ἀετοί.

²⁹ Εὐθέως δὲ μετὰ τὴν θλίψιν τῶν ἡμερῶν ἐκείνων ὁ ἥλιος σκοτισθήσεται καὶ ἡ σελήνη οὐ δώσει τὸ φέγγος αὐτῆς, καὶ οἱ ἀστέρες πεσοῦνται ἀπὸ τοῦ οὐρανοῦ, καὶ αἱ δυνάμεις τῶν οὐρανῶν σαλευθήσονται. ³⁰ καὶ τότε φανήσεται τὸ σημεῖον τοῦ υἱοῦ τοῦ ἀνθρώπου ἐν οὐρανῷ, καὶ τότε κόψονται πᾶσαι αἱ φυλαὶ τῆς γῆς καὶ ὄψονται τὸν υἱὸν τοῦ ἀνθρώπου ἐρχόμενον ἐπὶ τῶν νεφελῶν τοῦ οὐρανοῦ μετὰ δυνάμεως καὶ δόξης πολλῆς. ³¹ καὶ ἀποστελεῖ τοὺς ἀγγέλους αὐτοῦ μετὰ σάλπιγγος φωνῆς μεγάλης, καὶ ἐπισυνάξουσιν τοὺς ἐκλεκτοὺς αὐτοῦ ἐκ τῶν τεσσάρων ἀνέμων ἀπ᾽ ἄκρων οὐρανῶν ἕως ἄκρων αὐτῶν.

³² Ἀπὸ δὲ τῆς συκῆς μάθετε τὴν παραβολήν. ὅταν ἤδη ὁ κλάδος αὐτῆς γένηται ἁπαλὸς καὶ τὰ φύλλα ἐκφύῃ, γινώσκετε ὅτι ἐγγὺς τὸ θέρος· ³³ οὕτως καὶ ὑμεῖς ὅταν ἴδητε ταῦτα πάντα, γινώσκετε ὅτι ἐγγύς ἐστιν ἐπὶ θύραις. ³⁴ ἀμὴν λέγω ὑμῖν, οὐ μὴ παρέλθῃ ἡ γενεὰ αὕτη ἕως ἂν πάντα ταῦτα γένηται. ³⁵ ὁ οὐρανὸς καὶ ἡ γῆ παρελεύσεται, οἱ δὲ λόγοι μου οὐ μὴ παρέλθωσιν.

³⁶ Περὶ δὲ τῆς ἡμέρας ἐκείνης καὶ ὥρας οὐδεὶς οἶδεν, οὐδὲ οἱ ἄγγελοι τῶν οὐρανῶν, εἰ μὴ ὁ πατὴρ μόνος. ³⁷ ὥσπερ δὲ αἱ ἡμέραι τοῦ Νῶε, οὕτως ἔσται ἡ παρουσία τοῦ υἱοῦ τοῦ ἀνθρώπου. ³⁸ ὡς γὰρ ἦσαν ἐν ταῖς ἡμέραις ταῖς πρὸ τοῦ κατακλυσμοῦ τρώγοντες καὶ πίνοντες, γαμοῦντες καὶ γαμίζοντες, ἄχρι ἧς ἡμέρας εἰσῆλθεν Νῶε εἰς τὴν κιβωτόν, ³⁹ καὶ οὐκ ἔγνωσαν ἕως ἦλθεν ὁ κατακλυσμὸς καὶ ἦρεν ἅπαντας, οὕτως ἔσται καὶ ἡ παρουσία τοῦ υἱοῦ τοῦ ἀνθρώπου.

⁴⁰ Τότε δύο ἔσονται ἐν τῷ ἀγρῷ, εἷς παραλαμβάνεται καὶ εἷς ἀφίεται· ⁴¹ δύο ἀλήθουσαι ἐν τῷ μύλῳ, μία παραλαμβάνεται καὶ μία ἀφίεται. ⁴² γρηγορεῖτε οὖν, ὅτι οὐκ οἴδατε ποίᾳ ἡμέρᾳ ὁ κύριος ὑμῶν ἔρχεται.

⁴³ Ἐκεῖνο δὲ γινώσκετε, ὅτι εἰ ᾔδει ὁ οἰκοδεσπότης ποίᾳ φυλακῇ ὁ κλέπτης ἔρχεται, ἐγρηγόρησεν ἂν καὶ οὐκ ἂν εἴασεν διορυχθῆναι τὴν οἰκίαν αὐτοῦ. ⁴⁴ διὰ τοῦτο καὶ ὑμεῖς γίνεσθε ἕτοιμοι, ὅτι ᾗ οὐ δοκεῖτε ὥρᾳ ὁ υἱὸς τοῦ ἀνθρώπου ἔρχεται.

⁴⁵ Τίς ἄρα ἐστὶν ὁ πιστὸς δοῦλος καὶ φρόνιμος, ὃν κατέστησεν ὁ κύριος ἐπὶ τῆς οἰκετείας αὐτοῦ τοῦ δοῦναι αὐτοῖς τὴν τροφὴν ἐν καιρῷ; ⁴⁶ μακάριος ὁ δοῦλος ἐκεῖνος ὃν ἐλθὼν ὁ κύριος αὐτοῦ εὑρήσει οὕτως ποιοῦντα. ⁴⁷ ἀμὴν λέγω ὑμῖν ὅτι ἐπὶ πᾶσιν τοῖς ὑπάρχουσιν αὐτοῦ καταστήσει αὐτόν. ⁴⁸ ἐὰν δὲ εἴπῃ ὁ κακὸς δοῦλος ἐκεῖνος ἐν τῇ καρδίᾳ αὐτοῦ, Χρονίζει μου ὁ κύριος, ⁴⁹ καὶ ἄρξηται τύπτειν τοὺς συνδούλους αὐτοῦ, ἐσθίῃ δὲ καὶ πίνῃ μετὰ τῶν μεθυόντων· ⁵⁰ ἥξει ὁ κύριος τοῦ δούλου ἐκείνου ἐν ἡμέρᾳ ᾗ οὐ προσδοκᾷ καὶ ἐν ὥρᾳ ᾗ οὐ γινώσκει, ⁵¹ καὶ διχοτομήσει αὐτόν, καὶ τὸ μέρος αὐτοῦ μετὰ τῶν ὑποκριτῶν θήσει· ἐκεῖ ἔσται ὁ κλαυθμὸς καὶ ὁ βρυγμὸς τῶν ὀδόντων.

25 ¹ Τότε ὁμοιωθήσεται ἡ βασιλεία τῶν οὐρανῶν δέκα παρθένοις, αἵτινες λαβοῦσαι τὰς λαμπάδας αὐτῶν ἐξῆλθον εἰς ὑπάντησιν τοῦ νυμφίου. ² πέντε δὲ ἐξ αὐτῶν ἦσαν μωραὶ καὶ πέντε φρόνιμοι. ³ αἱ γὰρ μωραὶ λαβοῦσαι τὰς λαμπάδας αὐτῶν οὐκ ἔλαβον μεθ' ἑαυτῶν ἔλαιον· ⁴ αἱ δὲ φρόνιμοι ἔλαβον ἔλαιον ἐν τοῖς ἀγγείοις μετὰ τῶν λαμπάδων αὐτῶν. ⁵ χρονίζοντος δὲ τοῦ νυμφίου ἐνύσταξαν πᾶσαι καὶ ἐκάθευδον. ⁶ μέσης δὲ νυκτὸς κραυγὴ γέγονεν, Ἰδοὺ ὁ νυμφίος, ἐξέρχεσθε εἰς ἀπάντησιν αὐτοῦ. ⁷ τότε ἠγέρθησαν πᾶσαι αἱ παρθένοι ἐκεῖναι καὶ ἐκόσμησαν τὰς λαμπάδας ἑαυτῶν. ⁸ αἱ δὲ μωραὶ ταῖς φρονίμοις εἶπαν, Δότε ἡμῖν ἐκ τοῦ ἐλαίου ὑμῶν, ὅτι αἱ λαμπάδες ἡμῶν σβέννυνται. ⁹ ἀπεκρίθησαν δὲ αἱ φρόνιμοι λέγουσαι, Μήποτε οὐκ ἀρκέσῃ ἡμῖν καὶ ὑμῖν· πορεύεσθε μᾶλλον πρὸς τοὺς πωλοῦντας καὶ ἀγοράσατε ἑαυταῖς. [10] ἀπερχομένων δὲ αὐτῶν ἀγοράσαι ἦλθεν ὁ νυμφίος, καὶ αἱ ἕτοιμοι εἰσῆλθον μετ' αὐτοῦ εἰς τοὺς γάμους, καὶ ἐκλείσθη ἡ θύρα. [11] ὕστερον δὲ ἔρχονται καὶ αἱ λοιπαὶ παρθένοι λέγουσαι, Κύριε κύριε, ἄνοιξον ἡμῖν. [12] ὁ δὲ ἀποκριθεὶς εἶπεν, Ἀμὴν λέγω ὑμῖν, οὐκ οἶδα ὑμᾶς. [13] γρηγορεῖτε οὖν, ὅτι οὐκ οἴδατε τὴν ἡμέραν οὐδὲ τὴν ὥραν.

[14] Ὥσπερ γὰρ ἄνθρωπος ἀποδημῶν ἐκάλεσεν τοὺς ἰδίους δούλους καὶ παρέδωκεν αὐτοῖς τὰ ὑπάρχοντα αὐτοῦ, [15] καὶ ᾧ μὲν ἔδωκεν πέντε τάλαντα, ᾧ δὲ δύο, ᾧ δὲ ἕν, ἑκάστῳ κατὰ τὴν ἰδίαν δύναμιν, καὶ ἀπεδήμησεν. [16] εὐθέως πορευθεὶς ὁ τὰ πέντε τάλαντα λαβὼν εἰργάσατο ἐν αὐτοῖς καὶ ἐποίησεν ἄλλα πέντε τάλαντα. [17] ὡσαύτως ὁ τὰ δύο ἐκέρδησεν ἄλλα δύο. [18] ὁ δὲ τὸ ἓν λαβὼν ἀπελθὼν ὤρυξεν γῆν καὶ ἔκρυψεν τὸ ἀργύριον τοῦ κυρίου αὐτοῦ. [19] μετὰ δὲ πολὺν χρόνον ἔρχεται ὁ κύριος τῶν δούλων ἐκείνων καὶ συναίρει λόγον μετ' αὐτῶν. [20] καὶ προσελθὼν ὁ τὰ πέντε τάλαντα λαβὼν προσήνεγκεν ἄλλα πέντε τάλαντα λέγων, Κύριε, πέντε τάλαντά μοι παρέδωκας, ἴδε ἄλλα πέντε τάλαντα ἐκέρδησα. [21] ἔφη αὐτῷ ὁ κύριος αὐτοῦ, Εὖ, δοῦλε ἀγαθὲ καὶ πιστέ, ἐπὶ ὀλίγα ἦς πιστός, ἐπὶ πολλῶν σε καταστήσω· εἴσελθε εἰς τὴν χαρὰν τοῦ κυρίου σου. [22] προσελθὼν δὲ καὶ ὁ τὰ δύο τάλαντα εἶπεν, Κύριε, δύο τάλαντά μοι παρέδωκας, ἴδε ἄλλα δύο τάλαντα ἐκέρδησα. [23] ἔφη αὐτῷ ὁ κύριος αὐτοῦ, Εὖ, δοῦλε ἀγαθὲ καὶ πιστέ, ἐπὶ ὀλίγα ἦς πιστός, ἐπὶ πολλῶν σε καταστήσω· εἴσελθε εἰς τὴν χαρὰν τοῦ κυρίου σου. [24] προσελθὼν δὲ καὶ ὁ τὸ ἓν τάλαντον εἰληφὼς εἶπεν, Κύριε,

ἔγνων σε ὅτι σκληρὸς εἶ ἄνθρωπος, θερίζων ὅπου οὐκ ἔσπειρας, καὶ συνάγων ὅθεν οὐ διεσκόρπισας· ²⁵ καὶ φοβηθεὶς ἀπελθὼν ἔκρυψα τὸ τάλαντόν σου ἐν τῇ γῇ· ἴδε ἔχεις τὸ σόν. ²⁶ ἀποκριθεὶς δὲ ὁ κύριος αὐτοῦ εἶπεν αὐτῷ, Πονηρὲ δοῦλε καὶ ὀκνηρέ, ᾔδεις ὅτι θερίζω ὅπου οὐκ ἔσπειρα, καὶ συνάγω ὅθεν οὐ διεσκόρπισα; ²⁷ ἔδει σε οὖν βαλεῖν τὸ ἀργύριόν μου τοῖς τραπεζίταις, καὶ ἐλθὼν ἐγὼ ἐκομισάμην ἂν τὸ ἐμὸν σὺν τόκῳ. ²⁸ ἄρατε οὖν ἀπ' αὐτοῦ τὸ τάλαντον καὶ δότε τῷ ἔχοντι τὰ δέκα τάλαντα. ²⁹ τῷ γὰρ ἔχοντι παντὶ δοθήσεται καὶ περισσευθήσεται· τοῦ δὲ μὴ ἔχοντος, καὶ ὃ ἔχει ἀρθήσεται ἀπ' αὐτοῦ. ³⁰ καὶ τὸν ἀχρεῖον δοῦλον ἐκβάλετε εἰς τὸ σκότος τὸ ἐξώτερον· ἐκεῖ ἔσται ὁ κλαυθμὸς καὶ ὁ βρυγμὸς τῶν ὀδόντων.

³¹ Ὅταν δὲ ἔλθῃ ὁ υἱὸς τοῦ ἀνθρώπου ἐν τῇ δόξῃ αὐτοῦ καὶ πάντες οἱ ἄγγελοι μετ' αὐτοῦ, τότε καθίσει ἐπὶ θρόνου δόξης αὐτοῦ· ³² καὶ συναχθήσονται ἔμπροσθεν αὐτοῦ πάντα τὰ ἔθνη, καὶ ἀφοριεῖ αὐτοὺς ἀπ' ἀλλήλων, ὥσπερ ὁ ποιμὴν ἀφορίζει τὰ πρόβατα ἀπὸ τῶν ἐρίφων, ³³ καὶ στήσει τὰ μὲν πρόβατα ἐκ δεξιῶν αὐτοῦ, τὰ δὲ ἐρίφια ἐξ εὐωνύμων.

³⁴ Τότε ἐρεῖ ὁ βασιλεὺς τοῖς ἐκ δεξιῶν αὐτοῦ, Δεῦτε οἱ εὐλογημένοι τοῦ πατρός μου, κληρονομήσατε τὴν ἡτοιμασμένην ὑμῖν βασιλείαν ἀπὸ καταβολῆς κόσμου. ³⁵ ἐπείνασα γὰρ καὶ ἐδώκατέ μοι φαγεῖν, ἐδίψησα καὶ ἐποτίσατέ με, ξένος ἤμην καὶ συνηγάγετέ με, ³⁶ γυμνὸς καὶ περιεβάλετέ με, ἠσθένησα καὶ ἐπεσκέψασθέ με, ἐν φυλακῇ ἤμην καὶ ἤλθατε πρός με. ³⁷ τότε ἀποκριθήσονται αὐτῷ οἱ δίκαιοι λέγοντες, Κύριε, πότε σε εἴδομεν πεινῶντα καὶ ἐθρέψαμεν; ἢ διψῶντα καὶ ἐποτίσαμεν; ³⁸ πότε δέ σε εἴδομεν ξένον καὶ συνηγάγομεν; ἢ γυμνὸν

καὶ περιεβάλομεν; ³⁹ πότε δέ σε εἴδομεν ἀσθενοῦντα ἢ ἐν φυλακῇ καὶ ἤλθομεν πρός σε; ⁴⁰ καὶ ἀποκριθεὶς ὁ βασιλεὺς ἐρεῖ αὐτοῖς, Ἀμὴν λέγω ὑμῖν, ἐφ' ὅσον ἐποιήσατε ἑνὶ τούτων τῶν ἀδελφῶν μου τῶν ἐλαχίστων, ἐμοὶ ἐποιήσατε.

⁴¹ Τότε ἐρεῖ καὶ τοῖς ἐξ εὐωνύμων, Πορεύεσθε ἀπ' ἐμοῦ κατηραμένοι εἰς τὸ πῦρ τὸ αἰώνιον τὸ ἡτοιμασμένον τῷ διαβόλῳ καὶ τοῖς ἀγγέλοις αὐτοῦ. ⁴² ἐπείνασα γὰρ καὶ οὐκ ἐδώκατέ μοι φαγεῖν, ἐδίψησα καὶ οὐκ ἐποτίσατέ με, ⁴³ ξένος ἤμην καὶ οὐ συνηγάγετέ με, γυμνὸς καὶ οὐ περιεβάλετέ με, ἀσθενὴς καὶ ἐν φυλακῇ καὶ οὐκ ἐπεσκέψασθέ με. ⁴⁴ τότε ἀποκριθήσονται καὶ αὐτοὶ λέγοντες, Κύριε, πότε σε εἴδομεν πεινῶντα ἢ διψῶντα ἢ ξένον ἢ γυμνὸν ἢ ἀσθενῆ ἢ ἐν φυλακῇ, καὶ οὐ διηκονήσαμέν σοι; ⁴⁵ τότε ἀποκριθήσεται αὐτοῖς λέγων, Ἀμὴν λέγω ὑμῖν, ἐφ' ὅσον οὐκ ἐποιήσατε ἑνὶ τούτων τῶν ἐλαχίστων, οὐδὲ ἐμοὶ ἐποιήσατε. ⁴⁶ καὶ ἀπελεύσονται οὗτοι εἰς κόλασιν αἰώνιον, οἱ δὲ δίκαιοι εἰς ζωὴν αἰώνιον.

26 ¹ Καὶ ἐγένετο ὅτε ἐτέλεσεν ὁ Ἰησοῦς πάντας τοὺς λόγους τούτους, εἶπεν τοῖς μαθηταῖς αὐτοῦ, ² Οἴδατε ὅτι μετὰ δύο ἡμέρας τὸ πάσχα γίνεται, καὶ ὁ υἱὸς τοῦ ἀνθρώπου παραδίδοται εἰς τὸ σταυρωθῆναι. ³ Τότε συνήχθησαν οἱ ἀρχιερεῖς καὶ οἱ πρεσβύτεροι τοῦ λαοῦ εἰς τὴν αὐλὴν τοῦ ἀρχιερέως τοῦ λεγομένου Καϊάφα, ⁴ καὶ συνεβουλεύσαντο ἵνα τὸν Ἰησοῦν δόλῳ κρατήσωσιν καὶ ἀποκτείνωσιν. ⁵ ἔλεγον δέ, Μὴ ἐν τῇ ἑορτῇ, ἵνα μὴ θόρυβος γένηται ἐν τῷ λαῷ.

⁶ Τοῦ δὲ Ἰησοῦ γενομένου ἐν Βηθανίᾳ ἐν οἰκίᾳ Σίμωνος τοῦ λεπροῦ, ⁷ προσῆλθεν αὐτῷ γυνὴ ἔχουσα ἀλάβαστρον μύρου πολυτίμου καὶ κατέχεεν ἐπὶ τῆς

κεφαλῆς αὐτοῦ ἀνακειμένου. ⁸ ἰδόντες δὲ οἱ μαθηταὶ ἠγανάκτησαν λέγοντες, Εἰς τί ἡ ἀπώλεια αὕτη; ⁹ ἠδύνατο γὰρ τοῦτο πραθῆναι πολλοῦ καὶ δοθῆναι πτωχοῖς. ¹⁰ γνοὺς δὲ ὁ Ἰησοῦς εἶπεν αὐτοῖς, Τί κόπους παρέχετε τῇ γυναικί; ἔργον γὰρ καλὸν εἰργάσατο εἰς ἐμέ. ¹¹ πάντοτε γὰρ τοὺς πτωχοὺς ἔχετε μεθ᾽ ἑαυτῶν, ἐμὲ δὲ οὐ πάντοτε ἔχετε. ¹² βαλοῦσα γὰρ αὕτη τὸ μύρον τοῦτο ἐπὶ τοῦ σώματός μου πρὸς τὸ ἐνταφιάσαι με ἐποίησεν. ¹³ ἀμὴν λέγω ὑμῖν, ὅπου ἐὰν κηρυχθῇ τὸ εὐαγγέλιον τοῦτο ἐν ὅλῳ τῷ κόσμῳ, λαληθήσεται καὶ ὃ ἐποίησεν αὕτη εἰς μνημόσυνον αὐτῆς.

¹⁴ Τότε πορευθεὶς εἷς τῶν δώδεκα, ὁ λεγόμενος Ἰούδας Ἰσκαριώτης, πρὸς τοὺς ἀρχιερεῖς ¹⁵ εἶπεν, Τί θέλετέ μοι δοῦναι, κἀγὼ ὑμῖν παραδώσω αὐτόν; οἱ δὲ ἔστησαν αὐτῷ τριάκοντα ἀργύρια. ¹⁶ καὶ ἀπὸ τότε ἐζήτει εὐκαιρίαν ἵνα αὐτὸν παραδῷ.

¹⁷ Τῇ δὲ πρώτῃ τῶν ἀζύμων προσῆλθον οἱ μαθηταὶ τῷ Ἰησοῦ λέγοντες, Ποῦ θέλεις ἑτοιμάσωμέν σοι φαγεῖν τὸ πάσχα; ¹⁸ ὁ δὲ εἶπεν, Ὑπάγετε εἰς τὴν πόλιν πρὸς τὸν δεῖνα καὶ εἴπατε αὐτῷ, Ὁ διδάσκαλος λέγει, Ὁ καιρός μου ἐγγύς ἐστιν, πρὸς σὲ ποιῶ τὸ πάσχα μετὰ τῶν μαθητῶν μου. ¹⁹ καὶ ἐποίησαν οἱ μαθηταὶ ὡς συνέταξεν αὐτοῖς ὁ Ἰησοῦς, καὶ ἡτοίμασαν τὸ πάσχα.

²⁰ Ὀψίας δὲ γενομένης ἀνέκειτο μετὰ τῶν δώδεκα. ²¹ καὶ ἐσθιόντων αὐτῶν εἶπεν, Ἀμὴν λέγω ὑμῖν ὅτι εἷς ἐξ ὑμῶν παραδώσει με. ²² καὶ λυπούμενοι σφόδρα ἤρξαντο λέγειν αὐτῷ εἷς ἕκαστος, Μήτι ἐγώ εἰμι, κύριε; ²³ ὁ δὲ ἀποκριθεὶς εἶπεν, Ὁ ἐμβάψας μετ᾽ ἐμοῦ τὴν χεῖρα ἐν τῷ τρυβλίῳ, οὗτός με παραδώσει. ²⁴ ὁ μὲν υἱὸς τοῦ ἀνθρώπου ὑπάγει καθὼς γέγραπται περὶ αὐτοῦ. οὐαὶ δὲ τῷ ἀνθρώπῳ ἐκείνῳ δι᾽ οὗ ὁ υἱὸς τοῦ

ἀνθρώπου παραδίδοται· καλὸν ἦν αὐτῷ εἰ οὐκ ἐγεννήθη ὁ ἄνθρωπος ἐκεῖνος. ²⁵ ἀποκριθεὶς δὲ Ἰούδας ὁ παραδιδοὺς αὐτὸν εἶπεν, Μήτι ἐγώ εἰμι, ῥαββί; λέγει αὐτῷ, Σὺ εἶπας.

²⁶ Ἐσθιόντων δὲ αὐτῶν λαβὼν ὁ Ἰησοῦς ἄρτον καὶ εὐλογήσας ἔκλασεν καὶ δοὺς τοῖς μαθηταῖς εἶπεν, Λάβετε φάγετε· τοῦτό ἐστιν τὸ σῶμά μου. ²⁷ καὶ λαβὼν ποτήριον καὶ εὐχαριστήσας ἔδωκεν αὐτοῖς λέγων, Πίετε ἐξ αὐτοῦ πάντες· ²⁸ τοῦτο γάρ ἐστιν τὸ αἷμά μου τῆς καινῆς διαθήκης τὸ περὶ πολλῶν ἐκχυννόμενον εἰς ἄφεσιν ἁμαρτιῶν. ²⁹ λέγω δὲ ὑμῖν, οὐ μὴ πίω ἀπ' ἄρτι ἐκ τούτου τοῦ γενήματος τῆς ἀμπέλου ἕως τῆς ἡμέρας ἐκείνης ὅταν αὐτὸ πίνω μεθ' ὑμῶν καινὸν ἐν τῇ βασιλείᾳ τοῦ πατρός μου. ³⁰ Καὶ ὑμνήσαντες ἐξῆλθον εἰς τὸ ὄρος τῶν ἐλαιῶν.

³¹ Τότε λέγει αὐτοῖς ὁ Ἰησοῦς, Πάντες ὑμεῖς σκανδαλισθήσεσθε ἐν ἐμοὶ ἐν τῇ νυκτὶ ταύτῃ. γέγραπται γάρ, Πατάξω τὸν ποιμένα, καὶ διασκορπισθήσονται τὰ πρόβατα τῆς ποίμνης. ³² μετὰ δὲ τὸ ἐγερθῆναί με προάξω ὑμᾶς εἰς τὴν Γαλιλαίαν. ³³ ἀποκριθεὶς δὲ ὁ Πέτρος εἶπεν αὐτῷ, Εἰ πάντες σκανδαλισθήσονται ἐν σοί, ἐγὼ οὐδέποτε σκανδαλισθήσομαι. ³⁴ ἔφη αὐτῷ ὁ Ἰησοῦς, Ἀμὴν λέγω σοι ὅτι ἐν ταύτῃ τῇ νυκτὶ πρὶν ἀλέκτορα φωνῆσαι τρὶς ἀπαρνήσῃ με. ³⁵ λέγει αὐτῷ ὁ Πέτρος, Κἂν δέῃ με σὺν σοὶ ἀποθανεῖν, οὐ μή σε ἀπαρνήσομαι. ὁμοίως καὶ πάντες οἱ μαθηταὶ εἶπον.

³⁶ Τότε ἔρχεται μετ' αὐτῶν ὁ Ἰησοῦς εἰς χωρίον λεγόμενον Γεθσημανεί, καὶ λέγει τοῖς μαθηταῖς, Καθίσατε αὐτοῦ ἕως οὗ ἀπελθὼν ἐκεῖ προσεύξωμαι. ³⁷ καὶ παραλαβὼν τὸν Πέτρον καὶ τοὺς δύο υἱοὺς Ζεβεδαίου ἤρξατο λυπεῖσθαι καὶ ἀδημονεῖν. ³⁸ τότε λέγει αὐτοῖς,

Περίλυπός ἐστιν ἡ ψυχή μου ἕως θανάτου· μείνατε ὧδε καὶ γρηγορεῖτε μετ' ἐμοῦ. ³⁹ καὶ προσελθὼν μικρὸν ἔπεσεν ἐπὶ πρόσωπον αὐτοῦ προσευχόμενος καὶ λέγων, Πάτερ μου, εἰ δυνατόν ἐστιν, παρελθάτω ἀπ' ἐμοῦ τὸ ποτήριον τοῦτο· πλὴν οὐχ ὡς ἐγὼ θέλω ἀλλ' ὡς σύ. ⁴⁰ καὶ ἔρχεται πρὸς τοὺς μαθητὰς καὶ εὑρίσκει αὐτοὺς καθεύδοντας, καὶ λέγει τῷ Πέτρῳ, Οὕτως οὐκ ἰσχύσατε μίαν ὥραν γρηγορῆσαι μετ' ἐμοῦ; ⁴¹ γρηγορεῖτε καὶ προσεύχεσθε ἵνα μὴ εἰσέλθητε εἰς πειρασμόν. τὸ μὲν πνεῦμα πρόθυμον, ἡ δὲ σὰρξ ἀσθενής. ⁴² πάλιν ἐκ δευτέρου ἀπελθὼν προσηύξατο λέγων, Πάτερ μου, εἰ οὐ δύναται τοῦτο παρελθεῖν ἐὰν μὴ αὐτὸ πίω, γενηθήτω τὸ θέλημά σου. ⁴³ καὶ ἐλθὼν πάλιν εὗρεν αὐτοὺς καθεύδοντας· ἦσαν γὰρ αὐτῶν οἱ ὀφθαλμοὶ βεβαρημένοι. ⁴⁴ καὶ ἀφεὶς αὐτοὺς πάλιν ἀπελθὼν προσηύξατο ἐκ τρίτου, τὸν αὐτὸν λόγον εἰπών. ⁴⁵ τότε ἔρχεται πρὸς τοὺς μαθητὰς καὶ λέγει αὐτοῖς, Καθεύδετε τὸ λοιπὸν καὶ ἀναπαύεσθε. ἰδοὺ ἤγγικεν ἡ ὥρα καὶ ὁ υἱὸς τοῦ ἀνθρώπου παραδίδοται εἰς χεῖρας ἁμαρτωλῶν. ⁴⁶ ἐγείρεσθε, ἄγωμεν· ἰδοὺ ἤγγικεν ὁ παραδιδούς με.

⁴⁷ Καὶ ἔτι αὐτοῦ λαλοῦντος, ἰδοὺ Ἰούδας εἷς τῶν δώδεκα ἦλθεν, καὶ μετ' αὐτοῦ ὄχλος πολὺς μετὰ μαχαιρῶν καὶ ξύλων ἀπὸ τῶν ἀρχιερέων καὶ πρεσβυτέρων τοῦ λαοῦ. ⁴⁸ ὁ δὲ παραδιδοὺς αὐτὸν ἔδωκεν αὐτοῖς σημεῖον λέγων, Ὃν ἂν φιλήσω, αὐτός ἐστιν· κρατήσατε αὐτόν. ⁴⁹ καὶ εὐθέως προσελθὼν τῷ Ἰησοῦ εἶπεν, Χαῖρε ῥαββί, καὶ κατεφίλησεν αὐτόν. ⁵⁰ ὁ δὲ Ἰησοῦς εἶπεν αὐτῷ, Ἑταῖρε, ἐφ' ὃ πάρει; τότε προσελθόντες ἐπέβαλον τὰς χεῖρας ἐπὶ τὸν Ἰησοῦν καὶ ἐκράτησαν αὐτόν. ⁵¹ καὶ ἰδοὺ εἷς τῶν μετὰ Ἰησοῦ ἐκτείνας τὴν χεῖρα ἀπέσπασεν τὴν μάχαιραν αὐτοῦ, καὶ πατάξας τὸν

δοῦλον τοῦ ἀρχιερέως ἀφεῖλεν αὐτοῦ τὸ ὠτίον. ⁵² τότε λέγει αὐτῷ ὁ Ἰησοῦς, Ἀπόστρεψόν τὴν μάχαιράν σου εἰς τὸν τόπον αὐτῆς· πάντες γὰρ οἱ λαβόντες μάχαιραν ἐν μαχαίρῃ ἀπολοῦνται. ⁵³ ἢ δοκεῖς ὅτι οὐ δύναμαι παρακαλέσαι τὸν πατέρα μου, καὶ παραστήσει μοι ἄρτι πλείω δώδεκα λεγεῶνας ἀγγέλων; ⁵⁴ πῶς οὖν πληρωθῶσιν αἱ γραφαί, ὅτι οὕτως δεῖ γενέσθαι; ⁵⁵ ἐν ἐκείνῃ τῇ ὥρᾳ εἶπεν ὁ Ἰησοῦς τοῖς ὄχλοις, Ὡς ἐπὶ λῃστὴν ἐξήλθατε μετὰ μαχαιρῶν καὶ ξύλων συλλαβεῖν με· καθ' ἡμέραν ἐν τῷ ἱερῷ ἐκαθεζόμην διδάσκων, καὶ οὐκ ἐκρατήσατέ με. ⁵⁶ τοῦτο δὲ ὅλον γέγονεν ἵνα πληρωθῶσιν αἱ γραφαὶ τῶν προφητῶν. τότε οἱ μαθηταὶ πάντες ἀφέντες αὐτὸν ἔφυγον.

⁵⁷ Οἱ δὲ κρατήσαντες τὸν Ἰησοῦν ἀπήγαγον πρὸς Καϊάφαν τὸν ἀρχιερέα, ὅπου οἱ γραμματεῖς καὶ οἱ πρεσβύτεροι συνήχθησαν. ⁵⁸ ὁ δὲ Πέτρος ἠκολούθει αὐτῷ ἀπὸ μακρόθεν ἕως τῆς αὐλῆς τοῦ ἀρχιερέως, καὶ εἰσελθὼν ἔσω ἐκάθητο μετὰ τῶν ὑπηρετῶν ἰδεῖν τὸ τέλος. ⁵⁹ Οἱ δὲ ἀρχιερεῖς καὶ τὸ συνέδριον ὅλον ἐζήτουν ψευδομαρτυρίαν κατὰ τοῦ Ἰησοῦ, ὅπως αὐτὸν θανατώσουσιν, ⁶⁰ καὶ οὐχ εὗρον πολλῶν προσελθόντων ψευδομαρτύρων. ὕστερον δὲ προσελθόντες δύο ⁶¹ εἶπον, Οὗτος ἔφη, Δύναμαι καταλῦσαι τὸν ναὸν τοῦ θεοῦ καὶ διὰ τριῶν ἡμερῶν αὐτὸν οἰκοδομῆσαι. ⁶² καὶ ἀναστὰς ὁ ἀρχιερεὺς εἶπεν αὐτῷ, Οὐδὲν ἀποκρίνῃ; τί οὗτοί σου καταμαρτυροῦσιν; ⁶³ Ὁ δὲ Ἰησοῦς ἐσιώπα. καὶ ἀποκριθεὶς ὁ ἀρχιερεὺς εἶπεν αὐτῷ, Ἐξορκίζω σε κατὰ τοῦ θεοῦ τοῦ ζῶντος, ἵνα ἡμῖν εἴπῃς εἰ σὺ εἶ ὁ Χριστὸς ὁ υἱὸς τοῦ θεοῦ. ⁶⁴ λέγει αὐτῷ ὁ Ἰησοῦς, Σὺ εἶπας· πλὴν λέγω ὑμῖν, ἀπ' ἄρτι ὄψεσθε τὸν υἱὸν τοῦ ἀνθρώπου καθήμενον ἐκ δεξιῶν τῆς δυνάμεως καὶ ἐρχόμενον

ἐπὶ τῶν νεφελῶν τοῦ οὐρανοῦ. ⁶⁵ τότε ὁ ἀρχιερεὺς διέρρηξεν τὰ ἱμάτια αὐτοῦ λέγων, Ἐβλασφήμησεν· τί ἔτι χρείαν ἔχομεν μαρτύρων; ἴδε νῦν ἠκούσατε τὴν βλασφημίαν. ⁶⁶ τί ὑμῖν δοκεῖ; οἱ δὲ ἀποκριθέντες εἶπον, Ἔνοχος θανάτου ἐστίν. ⁶⁷ Τότε ἐνέπτυσαν εἰς τὸ πρόσωπον αὐτοῦ καὶ ἐκολάφισαν αὐτόν, οἱ δὲ ἐράπισαν ⁶⁸ λέγοντες, Προφήτευσον ἡμῖν, Χριστέ, τίς ἐστιν ὁ παίσας σε;

⁶⁹ Ὁ δὲ Πέτρος ἐκάθητο ἔξω ἐν τῇ αὐλῇ· καὶ προσῆλθεν αὐτῷ μία παιδίσκη λέγουσα, Καὶ σὺ ἦσθα μετὰ Ἰησοῦ τοῦ Γαλιλαίου. ⁷⁰ ὁ δὲ ἠρνήσατο ἔμπροσθεν πάντων λέγων, Οὐκ οἶδα τί λέγεις. ⁷¹ ἐξελθόντα δὲ αὐτὸν εἰς τὸν πυλῶνα, εἶδεν αὐτὸν ἄλλη καὶ λέγει τοῖς ἐκεῖ, Οὗτος ἦν μετὰ Ἰησοῦ τοῦ Ναζωραίου. ⁷² καὶ πάλιν ἠρνήσατο μετὰ ὅρκου ὅτι Οὐκ οἶδα τὸν ἄνθρωπον. ⁷³ μετὰ μικρὸν δὲ προσελθόντες οἱ ἑστῶτες εἶπον τῷ Πέτρῳ, Ἀληθῶς καὶ σὺ ἐξ αὐτῶν εἶ· καὶ γὰρ ἡ λαλιά σου δῆλόν σε ποιεῖ. ⁷⁴ τότε ἤρξατο καταθεματίζειν καὶ ὀμνύειν ὅτι Οὐκ οἶδα τὸν ἄνθρωπον· καὶ εὐθέως ἀλέκτωρ ἐφώνησεν. ⁷⁵ καὶ ἐμνήσθη ὁ Πέτρος τοῦ ῥήματος Ἰησοῦ εἰρηκότος ὅτι Πρὶν ἀλέκτορα φωνῆσαι τρὶς ἀπαρνήσῃ με· καὶ ἐξελθὼν ἔξω ἔκλαυσεν πικρῶς.

27 ¹ Πρωΐας δὲ γενομένης συμβούλιον ἔλαβον πάντες οἱ ἀρχιερεῖς καὶ οἱ πρεσβύτεροι τοῦ λαοῦ κατὰ τοῦ Ἰησοῦ, ὥστε θανατῶσαι αὐτόν. ² καὶ δήσαντες αὐτὸν ἀπήγαγον καὶ παρέδωκαν Πιλάτῳ τῷ ἡγεμόνι.

³ Τότε ἰδὼν Ἰούδας ὁ παραδιδοὺς αὐτὸν ὅτι κατεκρίθη, μεταμεληθεὶς ἔστρεψεν τὰ τριάκοντα ἀργύρια τοῖς ἀρχιερεῦσιν καὶ πρεσβυτέροις ⁴ λέγων, Ἥμαρτον παραδοὺς αἷμα ἀθῷον. οἱ δὲ εἶπον, Τί πρὸς ἡμᾶς;

σὺ ὄψῃ. ⁵ καὶ ῥίψας τὰ ἀργύρια εἰς τὸν ναὸν ἀνεχώρησεν, καὶ ἀπελθὼν ἀπήγξατο. ⁶ οἱ δὲ ἀρχιερεῖς λαβόντες τὰ ἀργύρια εἶπαν, Οὐκ ἔξεστιν βαλεῖν αὐτὰ εἰς τὸν κορβανᾶν, ἐπεὶ τιμὴ αἵματός ἐστιν. ⁷ συμβούλιον δὲ λαβόντες ἠγόρασαν ἐξ αὐτῶν τὸν ἀγρὸν τοῦ κεραμέως εἰς ταφὴν τοῖς ξένοις. ⁸ διὸ ἐκλήθη ὁ ἀγρὸς ἐκεῖνος ἀγρὸς αἵματος ἕως τῆς σήμερον. ⁹ τότε ἐπληρώθη τὸ ῥηθὲν διὰ Ἰερεμίου τοῦ προφήτου λέγοντος, Καὶ ἔλαβον τὰ τριάκοντα ἀργύρια, τὴν τιμὴν τοῦ τετιμημένου ὃν ἐτιμήσαντο ἀπὸ υἱῶν Ἰσραήλ, ¹⁰ καὶ ἔδωκαν αὐτὰ εἰς τὸν ἀγρὸν τοῦ κεραμέως, καθὰ συνέταξέν μοι κύριος.

¹¹ Ὁ δὲ Ἰησοῦς ἐστάθη ἔμπροσθεν τοῦ ἡγεμόνος· καὶ ἐπηρώτησεν αὐτὸν ὁ ἡγεμὼν λέγων, Σὺ εἶ ὁ βασιλεὺς τῶν Ἰουδαίων; ὁ δὲ Ἰησοῦς ἔφη αὐτῷ, Σὺ λέγεις. ¹² καὶ ἐν τῷ κατηγορεῖσθαι αὐτὸν ὑπὸ τῶν ἀρχιερέων καὶ τῶν πρεσβυτέρων οὐδὲν ἀπεκρίνατο. ¹³ τότε λέγει αὐτῷ ὁ Πιλᾶτος, Οὐκ ἀκούεις πόσα σου καταμαρτυροῦσιν; ¹⁴ καὶ οὐκ ἀπεκρίθη αὐτῷ πρὸς οὐδὲ ἓν ῥῆμα, ὥστε θαυμάζειν τὸν ἡγεμόνα λίαν.

¹⁵ Κατὰ δὲ ἑορτὴν εἰώθει ὁ ἡγεμὼν ἀπολύειν ἕνα τῷ ὄχλῳ δέσμιον ὃν ἤθελον. ¹⁶ εἶχον δὲ τότε δέσμιον ἐπίσημον, λεγόμενον Βαραββᾶν. ¹⁷ συνηγμένων οὖν αὐτῶν εἶπεν αὐτοῖς ὁ Πιλᾶτος, Τίνα θέλετε ἀπολύσω ὑμῖν, Βαραββᾶν ἢ Ἰησοῦν τὸν λεγόμενον Χριστόν; ¹⁸ ᾔδει γὰρ ὅτι διὰ φθόνον παρέδωκαν αὐτόν. ¹⁹ καθημένου δὲ αὐτοῦ ἐπὶ τοῦ βήματος ἀπέστειλεν πρὸς αὐτὸν ἡ γυνὴ αὐτοῦ λέγουσα, Μηδὲν σοὶ καὶ τῷ δικαίῳ ἐκείνῳ· πολλὰ γὰρ ἔπαθον σήμερον κατ' ὄναρ δι' αὐτόν. ²⁰ οἱ δὲ ἀρχιερεῖς καὶ οἱ πρεσβύτεροι ἔπεισαν τοὺς ὄχλους ἵνα αἰτήσωνται τὸν Βαραββᾶν, τὸν δὲ Ἰησοῦν ἀπολέσωσιν. ²¹ ἀποκριθεὶς δὲ ὁ ἡγεμὼν εἶπεν αὐτοῖς, Τίνα

θέλετε ἀπὸ τῶν δύο ἀπολύσω ὑμῖν; οἱ δὲ εἶπαν, Τὸν Βαραββᾶν. ²² λέγει αὐτοῖς ὁ Πιλᾶτος, Τί οὖν ποιήσω Ἰησοῦν τὸν λεγόμενον Χριστόν; λέγουσιν πάντες, Σταυρωθήτω. ²³ ὁ δὲ ἔφη, Τί γὰρ κακὸν ἐποίησεν; οἱ δὲ περισσῶς ἔκραζον λέγοντες, Σταυρωθήτω. ²⁴ ἰδὼν δὲ ὁ Πιλᾶτος ὅτι οὐδὲν ὠφελεῖ ἀλλὰ μᾶλλον θόρυβος γίνεται, λαβὼν ὕδωρ ἀπενίψατο τὰς χεῖρας ἀπέναντι τοῦ ὄχλου λέγων, Ἀθῷός εἰμι ἀπὸ τοῦ αἵματος τοῦ δικαίου τούτου· ὑμεῖς ὄψεσθε. ²⁵ καὶ ἀποκριθεὶς πᾶς ὁ λαὸς εἶπεν, Τὸ αἷμα αὐτοῦ ἐφ' ἡμᾶς καὶ ἐπὶ τὰ τέκνα ἡμῶν. ²⁶ τότε ἀπέλυσεν αὐτοῖς τὸν Βαραββᾶν, τὸν δὲ Ἰησοῦν φραγελλώσας παρέδωκεν ἵνα σταυρωθῇ.

²⁷ Τότε οἱ στρατιῶται τοῦ ἡγεμόνος παραλαβόντες τὸν Ἰησοῦν εἰς τὸ πραιτώριον συνήγαγον ἐπ' αὐτὸν ὅλην τὴν σπεῖραν. ²⁸ καὶ ἐκδύσαντες αὐτὸν χλαμύδα κοκκίνην περιέθηκαν αὐτῷ, ²⁹ καὶ πλέξαντες στέφανον ἐξ ἀκανθῶν ἐπέθηκαν ἐπὶ τῆς κεφαλῆς αὐτοῦ καὶ κάλαμον ἐν τῇ δεξιᾷ αὐτοῦ, καὶ γονυπετήσαντες ἔμπροσθεν αὐτοῦ ἐνέπαιξαν αὐτῷ λέγοντες, Χαῖρε ὁ βασιλεὺς τῶν Ἰουδαίων, ³⁰ καὶ ἐμπτύσαντες εἰς αὐτὸν ἔλαβον τὸν κάλαμον καὶ ἔτυπτον εἰς τὴν κεφαλὴν αὐτοῦ.

³¹ Καὶ ὅτε ἐνέπαιξαν αὐτῷ, ἐξέδυσαν αὐτὸν τὴν χλαμύδα καὶ ἐνέδυσαν αὐτὸν τὰ ἱμάτια αὐτοῦ, καὶ ἀπήγαγον αὐτὸν εἰς τὸ σταυρῶσαι. ³² Ἐξερχόμενοι δὲ εὗρον ἄνθρωπον Κυρηναῖον, ὀνόματι Σίμωνα· τοῦτον ἠγγάρευσαν ἵνα ἄρῃ τὸν σταυρὸν αὐτοῦ.

³³ Καὶ ἐλθόντες εἰς τόπον λεγόμενον Γολγοθᾶ, ὅ ἐστιν κρανίου τόπος λεγόμενος, ³⁴ ἔδωκαν αὐτῷ πιεῖν οἶνον μετὰ χολῆς μεμιγμένον· καὶ γευσάμενος οὐκ ἠθέλησεν πιεῖν. ³⁵ σταυρώσαντες δὲ αὐτὸν διεμερίσαντο τὰ ἱμάτια

αὐτοῦ βαλόντες κλῆρον, ³⁶ καὶ καθήμενοι ἐτήρουν αὐτὸν ἐκεῖ. ³⁷ καὶ ἐπέθηκαν ἐπάνω τῆς κεφαλῆς αὐτοῦ τὴν αἰτίαν αὐτοῦ γεγραμμένην, Οὗτός ἐστιν Ἰησοῦς ὁ βασιλεὺς τῶν Ἰουδαίων. ³⁸ Τότε σταυροῦνται σὺν αὐτῷ δύο λῃσταί, εἷς ἐκ δεξιῶν καὶ εἷς ἐξ εὐωνύμων.

³⁹ Οἱ δὲ παραπορευόμενοι ἐβλασφήμουν αὐτόν, κινοῦντες τὰς κεφαλὰς αὐτῶν ⁴⁰ καὶ λέγοντες, Ὁ καταλύων τὸν ναὸν καὶ ἐν τρισὶν ἡμέραις οἰκοδομῶν, σῶσον σεαυτόν, εἰ υἱὸς εἶ τοῦ θεοῦ, κατάβηθι ἀπὸ τοῦ σταυροῦ. ⁴¹ ὁμοίως καὶ οἱ ἀρχιερεῖς ἐμπαίζοντες μετὰ τῶν γραμματέων καὶ πρεσβυτέρων ἔλεγον, ⁴² Ἄλλους ἔσωσεν, ἑαυτὸν οὐ δύναται σῶσαι· βασιλεὺς Ἰσραήλ ἐστιν, καταβάτω νῦν ἀπὸ τοῦ σταυροῦ καὶ πιστεύσομεν ἐπ᾽ αὐτόν· ⁴³ πέποιθεν ἐπὶ τὸν θεόν, ῥυσάσθω νῦν εἰ θέλει αὐτόν· εἶπεν γὰρ ὅτι θεοῦ εἰμὶ υἱός. ⁴⁴ τὸ δ᾽ αὐτὸ καὶ οἱ λῃσταὶ οἱ συνσταυρωθέντες σὺν αὐτῷ ὠνείδιζον αὐτόν.

⁴⁵ Ἀπὸ δὲ ἕκτης ὥρας σκότος ἐγένετο ἐπὶ πᾶσαν τὴν γῆν ἕως ὥρας ἐνάτης. ⁴⁶ περὶ δὲ τὴν ἐνάτην ὥραν ἀνεβόησεν ὁ Ἰησοῦς φωνῇ μεγάλῃ λέγων, Ἠλὶ ἠλὶ λεμὰ σαβαχθανεί; τοῦτ᾽ ἔστιν· θεέ μου θεέ μου, ἱνατί με ἐγκατέλιπες; ⁴⁷ τινὲς δὲ τῶν ἐκεῖ ἑστηκότων ἀκούσαντες ἔλεγον ὅτι Ἠλίαν φωνεῖ οὗτος. ⁴⁸ καὶ εὐθέως δραμὼν εἷς ἐξ αὐτῶν καὶ λαβὼν σπόγγον πλήσας τε ὄξους καὶ περιθεὶς καλάμῳ ἐπότιζεν αὐτόν. ⁴⁹ οἱ δὲ λοιποὶ ἔλεγον, Ἄφες ἴδωμεν εἰ ἔρχεται Ἡλίας σώσων αὐτόν.

⁵⁰ Ὁ δὲ Ἰησοῦς πάλιν κράξας φωνῇ μεγάλῃ ἀφῆκεν τὸ πνεῦμα.

⁵¹ Καὶ ἰδοὺ τὸ καταπέτασμα τοῦ ναοῦ ἐσχίσθη ἀπὸ ἄνωθεν ἕως κάτω εἰς δύο, καὶ ἡ γῆ ἐσείσθη, καὶ αἱ πέτραι ἐσχίσθησαν, ⁵² καὶ τὰ μνημεῖα ἀνεῴχθησαν καὶ

πολλὰ σώματα τῶν κεκοιμημένων ἁγίων ἠγέρθησαν· ⁵³ καὶ ἐξελθόντες ἐκ τῶν μνημείων μετὰ τὴν ἔγερσιν αὐτοῦ εἰσῆλθον εἰς τὴν ἁγίαν πόλιν καὶ ἐνεφανίσθησαν πολλοῖς. ⁵⁴ ὁ δὲ ἑκατόνταρχος καὶ οἱ μετ' αὐτοῦ τηροῦντες τὸν Ἰησοῦν ἰδόντες τὸν σεισμὸν καὶ τὰ γινόμενα ἐφοβήθησαν σφόδρα, λέγοντες, Ἀληθῶς θεοῦ υἱὸς ἦν οὗτος. ⁵⁵ Ἦσαν δὲ ἐκεῖ γυναῖκες πολλαὶ ἀπὸ μακρόθεν θεωροῦσαι, αἵτινες ἠκολούθησαν τῷ Ἰησοῦ ἀπὸ τῆς Γαλιλαίας διακονοῦσαι αὐτῷ· ⁵⁶ ἐν αἷς ἦν Μαρία ἡ Μαγδαληνή, καὶ Μαρία ἡ τοῦ Ἰακώβου καὶ Ἰωσὴφ μήτηρ, καὶ ἡ μήτηρ τῶν υἱῶν Ζεβεδαίου.

⁵⁷ Ὀψίας δὲ γενομένης ἦλθεν ἄνθρωπος πλούσιος ἀπὸ Ἀριμαθαίας, τοὔνομα Ἰωσήφ, ὃς καὶ αὐτὸς ἐμαθητεύθη τῷ Ἰησοῦ· ⁵⁸ οὗτος προσελθὼν τῷ Πιλάτῳ ᾐτήσατο τὸ σῶμα τοῦ Ἰησοῦ. τότε ὁ Πιλᾶτος ἐκέλευσεν ἀποδοθῆναι. ⁵⁹ καὶ λαβὼν τὸ σῶμα ὁ Ἰωσὴφ ἐνετύλιξεν αὐτὸ σινδόνι καθαρᾷ, ⁶⁰ καὶ ἔθηκεν αὐτὸ ἐν τῷ καινῷ αὐτοῦ μνημείῳ ὃ ἐλατόμησεν ἐν τῇ πέτρᾳ, καὶ προσκυλίσας λίθον μέγαν τῇ θύρᾳ τοῦ μνημείου ἀπῆλθεν. ⁶¹ ἦν δὲ ἐκεῖ Μαρία ἡ Μαγδαληνὴ καὶ ἡ ἄλλη Μαρία, καθήμεναι ἀπέναντι τοῦ τάφου.

⁶² Τῇ δὲ ἐπαύριον, ἥτις ἐστὶν μετὰ τὴν παρασκευήν, συνήχθησαν οἱ ἀρχιερεῖς καὶ οἱ Φαρισαῖοι πρὸς Πιλᾶτον ⁶³ λέγοντες, Κύριε, ἐμνήσθημεν ὅτι ἐκεῖνος ὁ πλάνος εἶπεν ἔτι ζῶν, Μετὰ τρεῖς ἡμέρας ἐγείρομαι. ⁶⁴ κέλευσον οὖν ἀσφαλισθῆναι τὸν τάφον ἕως τῆς τρίτης ἡμέρας, μήποτε ἐλθόντες οἱ μαθηταὶ αὐτοῦ κλέψωσιν αὐτὸν καὶ εἴπωσιν τῷ λαῷ, Ἠγέρθη ἀπὸ τῶν νεκρῶν, καὶ ἔσται ἡ ἐσχάτη πλάνη χείρων τῆς πρώτης. ⁶⁵ ἔφη αὐτοῖς ὁ Πιλᾶτος, Ἔχετε κουστωδίαν· ὑπάγετε ἀσφαλίσασθε ὡς οἴδατε. ⁶⁶ οἱ δὲ πορευθέντες ἠσφαλίσαντο

τὸν τάφον, σφραγίσαντες τὸν λίθον μετὰ τῆς κουστωδίας.

28 ¹ Ὀψὲ δὲ σαββάτων, τῇ ἐπιφωσκούσῃ εἰς μίαν σαββάτων, ἦλθεν Μαρία ἡ Μαγδαληνὴ καὶ ἡ ἄλλη Μαρία θεωρῆσαι τὸν τάφον. ² καὶ ἰδοὺ σεισμὸς ἐγένετο μέγας· ἄγγελος γὰρ κυρίου καταβὰς ἐξ οὐρανοῦ καὶ προσελθὼν ἀπεκύλισεν τὸν λίθον καὶ ἐκάθητο ἐπάνω αὐτοῦ. ³ ἦν δὲ ἡ εἰδέα αὐτοῦ ὡς ἀστραπή, καὶ τὸ ἔνδυμα αὐτοῦ λευκὸν ὡς χιών. ⁴ ἀπὸ δὲ τοῦ φόβου αὐτοῦ ἐσείσθησαν οἱ τηροῦντες καὶ ἐγενήθησαν ὡς νεκροί. ⁵ ἀποκριθεὶς δὲ ὁ ἄγγελος εἶπεν ταῖς γυναιξίν, Μὴ φοβεῖσθε ὑμεῖς· οἶδα γὰρ ὅτι Ἰησοῦν τὸν ἐσταυρωμένον ζητεῖτε. ⁶ οὐκ ἔστιν ὧδε· ἠγέρθη γάρ, καθὼς εἶπεν· δεῦτε ἴδετε τὸν τόπον ὅπου ἔκειτο. ⁷ καὶ ταχὺ πορευθεῖσαι εἴπατε τοῖς μαθηταῖς αὐτοῦ ὅτι ἠγέρθη ἀπὸ τῶν νεκρῶν, καὶ ἰδοὺ προάγει ὑμᾶς εἰς τὴν Γαλιλαίαν, ἐκεῖ αὐτὸν ὄψεσθε. ἰδοὺ εἶπον ὑμῖν. ⁸ καὶ ἀπελθοῦσαι ταχὺ ἀπὸ τοῦ μνημείου μετὰ φόβου καὶ χαρᾶς μεγάλης ἔδραμον ἀπαγγεῖλαι τοῖς μαθηταῖς αὐτοῦ.

⁹ Καὶ ἰδοὺ ὁ Ἰησοῦς ὑπήντησεν αὐταῖς λέγων, Χαίρετε. αἱ δὲ προσελθοῦσαι ἐκράτησαν αὐτοῦ τοὺς πόδας καὶ προσεκύνησαν αὐτῷ. ¹⁰ τότε λέγει αὐταῖς ὁ Ἰησοῦς, Μὴ φοβεῖσθε· ὑπάγετε ἀπαγγείλατε τοῖς ἀδελφοῖς μου ἵνα ἀπέλθωσιν εἰς τὴν Γαλιλαίαν, κἀκεῖ με ὄψονται.

¹¹ Πορευομένων δὲ αὐτῶν, ἰδοὺ τινὲς τῆς κουστωδίας ἐλθόντες εἰς τὴν πόλιν ἀπήγγειλαν τοῖς ἀρχιερεῦσιν ἅπαντα τὰ γενόμενα. ¹² καὶ συναχθέντες μετὰ τῶν πρεσβυτέρων συμβούλιόν τε λαβόντες ἀργύρια ἱκανὰ ἔδωκαν τοῖς στρατιώταις, ¹³ λέγοντες, Εἴπατε ὅτι Οἱ μαθηταὶ αὐτοῦ νυκτὸς ἐλθόντες ἔκλεψαν αὐτὸν ἡμῶν κοιμωμένων. ¹⁴ καὶ ἐὰν ἀκουσθῇ τοῦτο ἐπὶ τοῦ

ἡγεμόνος, ἡμεῖς πείσομεν καὶ ὑμᾶς ἀμερίμνους ποιήσομεν. ¹⁵ οἱ δὲ λαβόντες τὰ ἀργύρια ἐποίησαν ὡς ἐδιδάχθησαν· καὶ διεφημίσθη ὁ λόγος οὗτος παρὰ Ἰουδαίοις μέχρι τῆς σήμερον.

¹⁶ Οἱ δὲ ἕνδεκα μαθηταὶ ἐπορεύθησαν εἰς τὴν Γαλιλαίαν, εἰς τὸ ὄρος οὗ ἐτάξατο αὐτοῖς ὁ Ἰησοῦς, ¹⁷ καὶ ἰδόντες αὐτὸν προσεκύνησαν, οἱ δὲ ἐδίστασαν.

¹⁸ Καὶ προσελθὼν ὁ Ἰησοῦς ἐλάλησεν αὐτοῖς λέγων, Ἐδόθη μοι πᾶσα ἐξουσία ἐν οὐρανῷ καὶ ἐπὶ γῆς. ¹⁹ πορευθέντες μαθητεύσατε πάντα τὰ ἔθνη, βαπτίζοντες αὐτοὺς εἰς τὸ ὄνομα τοῦ πατρὸς καὶ τοῦ υἱοῦ καὶ τοῦ ἁγίου πνεύματος, ²⁰ διδάσκοντες αὐτοὺς τηρεῖν πάντα ὅσα ἐνετειλάμην ὑμῖν. καὶ ἰδοὺ ἐγὼ μεθ᾽ ὑμῶν εἰμὶ πάσας τὰς ἡμέρας ἕως τῆς συντελείας τοῦ αἰῶνος.

NOTES.

CHAPTER I.

In the remarks on the results of textual revision prefixed to the Notes on each Chapter, it is not intended to enter minutely into each critical point, but to indicate generally the drift and import of the corrections, and occasionally to state the grounds on which a reading is preferred.

κατὰ Ματθαῖον is adopted in preference to κατὰ Ματθαῖον by the best recent editors on the authority of ℵBD. The evidence, however, is not conclusive, for in the text even these MSS. admit the other forms in some instances. See Scrivener's *Introd.* p. 488.

2. ἐγέννησεν. In accordance with all the uncial MSS. the final ν (called ἐφελκυστικόν or 'attached') is added in the best critical editions before vowels and consonants alike. To this rule Tischendorf admits a few exceptions, as δυσί (ch. vi. 24), βαστάσασι (ch. xx. 12). It is probable that 'ν' ἐφελκυστικόν appeared invariably in the written prose language even in Attic Greek. See Winer, 43, 44, note 2, and Scrivener's *Introd.* p. 486, 487.

18. (a) Ἰησοῦ, now read by Tisch. (ed. 8), though absent from editions 5 and 7, is supported by all the *Greek* codices, but rejected by some critics, chiefly on the evidence of Irenaeus, who (as appears from the Latin version of his works) read τοῦ Χριστοῦ and sustained it on special grounds; but also because the collocation ὁ Ἰησοῦς Χριστός is hardly defensible from the position of the adjective χριστός, and is not found elsewhere in the genuine text of the N.T. See Hammond (*Text. Crit.* p. 66 foll.), who discusses this reading at length: and Scrivener's *Introd.* p. 493.

The reading τοῦ δὲ Χριστοῦ ἡ γένεσις, 'the birth of the Messiah,' is theologically valuable as denoting that the Messiah was born, against the false teaching that Jesus became the Messiah, or the Messiah entered into Him at baptism. Hence the interest of the discussion.

(β) After μνηστευθείσης the received text has γάρ—the usual particle for beginning a narrative in explanation of a statement: cp.

τοιοῦτον ἦν τὸ πρᾶγμ', ὅπως γὰρ ἤλθομεν κ.τ.λ.

Soph. *Ant.* 407.

Nam is similarly used in Latin. The insertion of γάρ in the text was probably the unconscious error of a copyist familiar with classical usage.

22. κυρίου not τοῦ κυρίου. Κύριος, in the sense of Jehovah—the triune God—is almost invariably without the article.

25. υἱόν (א B) for τὸν υἱὸν αὐτῆς τὸν πρωτότοκον. The reading of the *textus receptus* is probably due to Luke ii. 7, where πρωτότοκον is unchallenged. The insertion may have been made for controversial reasons, as slightly favouring the view that 'the brethren of the Lord' were his full brethren. But this is unlikely.

Εὐαγγέλιον, like χριστός (see ch. i. 18), is rare in the classics. The history of it is that of many Hellenistic words—first Homeric, then vernacular, then again found in literature. It occurs twice in Homer, in the sense of 'reward for good news,' *Od.* xiv. 152 εὐαγγέλιον δέ μοι ἔστω | αὐτίκ' ἐπεί κεν κεῖνος ἰὼν τὰ ἃ δώμαθ' ἵκηται: and again in the same passage l. 166. In Aristoph. *Eq.* 656 εὐαγγέλια θύειν is 'to sacrifice for good news,' *Eq.* 647 εὐαγγέλια στεφανοῦν, 'to crown for good news.' In later Greek εὐαγγέλιον acquires the more familiar sense of 'good news,' as distinct from 'reward for good news.' The LXX. has the word in both senses. It was a familiar term to educated Romans: cp. 'Primum ut opinor εὐαγγέλια. Valerius absolutus est,' Cic. *ad Att.* ii. 3. In its N.T. use εὐαγγέλιον is closely allied to the thought of the Kingdom of God, it is distinctively the announcement of the Messianic hopes fulfilled. The word is not used by St John except in one passage of the Apocalypse, ch. xiv. 6, or by St James, and once only by St Peter, it does not occur in St Luke's Gospel. With St Paul, however, εὐαγγέλιον is very frequent, and to him is due its leading place in the Christian vocabulary. For the verb see ch. xi. 5. The English equivalent 'gospel' (A.-Saxon Godspell) is a felicitous rendering, though it fails to convey all that belongs to εὐαγγέλιον. The Continental languages have naturalised the Greek word: *évangile* (French), *evangelium* (German), *evangelio* (Italian).

κατά, 'according to.' The gospel is presented according to the plan and aims of the different writers inspired to meet the requirements of particular readers and to satisfy special needs.

1. Βίβλος γενέσεως, 'Book of generation,' i.e. the pedigree extracted from the public archives which were carefully preserved and placed under the special care of the Sanhedrin. The expression recalls, perhaps designedly, Gen. v. 1 αὕτη ἡ βίβλος γενέσεως ἀνθρώπων.

(1) The genealogy is an answer to the question which would be asked by every Jew of any one who claimed to be the Messiah, 'Is he of the house of David?' for by no name was the Messiah more frequently spoken of by Jews and by foreigners (see ch. xv. 22), and designated in the Talmud, than by that of the Son of David.

(2) Both this genealogy and that in St Luke's Gospel trace Joseph's descent. But see below, *v.* 16.

(3) St Matthew traces the pedigree from Abraham, the Father of the Chosen Race, through David, from whose house the Messiah was expected; St Luke, true to the scope of his Gospel, traces it from the common Father of Jew and Gentile.

(4) St Matthew gives the *royal succession*, St Luke, the *family lineage*. This accounts for many variations in names.

(5) This genealogy *descends* from father to son, and is therefore probably the more exact transcript of the original document. St Luke's *ascends* from son to father.

2. τὸν Ἰσαάκ. The article is generally used with indeclinable proper names for the sake of perspicuity. See Winer, p. 141.

3. Θάμαρ. St Matthew also differs from St Luke in naming women in the genealogy. Of the four mentioned two—Rahab and Ruth—are foreigners, and three—Thamar, Rahab and Bathsheba—were stained with sin. The purpose of the Evangelist in recording their names may be to show that He who came to save 'that which was lost,' the Friend of sinners, does not scorn such descent.

5. Σαλμών...Ἰεσσαί. According to the received chronology the space of time between Salmon and Jesse was not less than 400 years. In that space there are only four generations recorded in the text. Either then the received chronology is wrong or the genealogy not complete. In all probability the former is at fault, and the shortening of the period named would bring 'Jewish history into harmony with Egyptian and with the internal evidence of the Israelitish history itself.' See Art. 'Genealogy' in *Bib. Dict.* for this and other points.

6. Δαυεὶδ τὸν βασιλέα. A special hint of Christ the king, of whom David was the type.

ἐκ τῆς τοῦ Οὐρίου. For the omission of γυναικὸς cp. 'Hectoris Andromache,' *Æn.* III. 319: such ellipse is natural where there would be no difficulty in supplying the missing word.

It is at this point that St Luke's genealogy branches off. According to *natural* descent Joseph was a descendant of *Nathan*, not of *Solomon*. The genealogies meet again in the names of Zorobabel and Salathiel. See below, *v.* 12.

8. Ἰωράμ δὲ ἐγέννησεν τὸν Ὀζείαν (Uzziah). The names of Ahaziah, Joash and Amaziah are here omitted; see note, *v.* 17.

11. Ἰωσείας δὲ ἐγέννησεν τὸν Ἰεχονίαν (Jehoiakim); but in the next *v.* Jechonias = Jehoiachin. A step is thus wanting in the genealogy, which is supplied by a very early though probably not genuine reading: Ἰωσείας δὲ ἐγέννησεν τὸν Ἰωακείμ· Ἰωακείμ δὲ ἐγέννησεν τὸν Ἰεχονίαν (Jehoiachin). The insertion would make fifteen steps in this portion of the genealogy and would not remove the difficulty unless τοὺς ἀδελφοὺς were placed after Ἰωακείμ.

Ἰεχονίαν καὶ τοὺς ἀδελφοὺς αὐτοῦ. No brethren of Jehoiachin are mentioned, but Jehoiakim had three (1 Chr. iii. 15): a further indication that Ἰεχονίας in this verse = Jehoiakim.

ἐπὶ τῆς μετοικεσίας Βαβυλῶνος. 'At the time of the migration or transportation to Babylon' (606 B.C.). For ἐπὶ in this sense cp. ἐπὶ Κλαυδίου, Acts xi. 28; ἐπὶ ἀρχιερέως Ἄννα, Luke iii. 2. This use of the preposition comes from the conception that one event rests on, but not wholly on, a person or other events. μετοικεσία, the LXX. word for the Babylonish exile, for which the classical μετοικία is also used. For the genitive Βαβυλῶνος see Winer, p. 234. Cp. French 'chemin de Paris,' road to Paris.

12. Ἰεχονίας ἐγέννησεν τὸν Σαλαθιήλ. Jehoiachin had no children of his own, 'write ye this man childless' (Jer. xxii. 30). Salathiel was the son of Neri (Luke), but heir to Jehoiachin.

13. Ζοροβάβελ δὲ ἐγέννησεν τὸν Ἀβιούδ. Here a step is omitted, Abiud—the Hodaiah of 1 Chron. iii. 24—being the grandson of Zerubbabel. Rhesa, who is named as Zerubbabel's son (Luke iii. 27), is conjectured to be a title (Rhesa or Rosh = a Prince): in that case the text in Luke should run, 'which was the son of Rhesa Zorobabel.' The Juda of Luke is the same as Abiud.

16. Ἰακὼβ δὲ ἐγέννησεν τὸν Ἰωσήφ. 'Joseph which was the son of Heli' (Luke), see last note; probably Joseph was the son of Heli and the heir to Jacob. It is conjectured with much probability that Jacob was Mary's father. In that case, although both genealogies show Joseph's descent, they are in fact equally genealogies of Mary's family.

```
                        Matthan or Matthat
                      ┌─────────────────────┐
(According to Matthew) Jacob              Heli (according to Luke)
                       │                    │
                    Mary (?)            Joseph
```

17. This division into three sets, each containing fourteen steps of descent, is an instance of a practice familiar to readers of Jewish antiquities. Lightfoot says, 'They do so very much delight in such kind of concents, that they oftentimes screw up the strings beyond the due measure and stretch them till they crack.' Such a system necessitates the omission of steps in the descent: see notes vv. 8 and 13.

18—25. THE BIRTH OF JESUS CHRIST. Luke i. 26—56 and ii. 4—7.

St Mark and St John give no account of the birth of Jesus, St Luke narrates several particulars not recorded by St Matthew, (1) the annunciation, (2) Mary's salutation of Elizabeth in a city of Juda (or Juttah), and (3) the journey from Galilee to Bethlehem.

18. Ἰησοῦ Χριστοῦ. See v. 21.

Χριστοῦ. As a classical word χριστός is very rare (Æsch. *Prom. Vinct.* 480 and Eur. *Hipp.* 516 are among the few instances where it occurs) and thus belongs to a class of words that have passed into Christian use without any debasing pagan associations. In the LXX. it is frequent as a translation of the Hebrew *Mashiach* (anointed). To the Jew it would suggest the thought of (1) Prophet, μὴ ἅψησθε τῶν χριστῶν μου καὶ ἐν τοῖς προφήταις μου μὴ πονηρεύεσθε, Ps. civ. 15; (2) Priest, καὶ εἰσοίσει ὁ ἱερεὺς ὁ χριστὸς ἀπὸ τοῦ αἵματος, Levit. iv. 16; (3) King, ποιῶν ἔλεος τῷ χριστῷ αὐτοῦ τῷ Δαβίδ, Ps. xvii. 54. As a proper name it was the Messiah, the Χριστὸς ἡγούμενος of Dan. ix. 25— the only passage where the term *Mashiach* is applied directly to the coming Deliverer. In the N. T. the Hebrew form is used twice (John i. 41 and iv. 25), where it is explained: εὑρήκαμεν τὸν Μεσσίαν ὅ ἐστιν μεθερμηνευόμενον χριστός (ch. i. 42) and οἶδα ὅτι Μεσσίας ἔρχεται ὁ λεγόμενος χριστός. Note that one title—Messiah or Christ—has been adopted almost to the exclusion of others quite as common in the O. T., 'The Branch,' 'He that cometh' (ὁ ἐρχόμενος, Hebr. *Habba*), 'The Prophet.' This is partly due to the great influence of Daniel's prophecy, partly to the appropriateness of the title to the Son of David.

μνηστευθείσης, 'betrothed.' Among the Jews the betrothal took place a year before marriage, and during the interval the betrothed maiden remained with her own family. But from the day of betrothal the pair were regarded as man and wife. For the genitive absolute μνηστ....Μαρίας instead of the nominative as subject to εὑρέθη see Winer, p. 260.

Μαρίας. The Hebrew form is Miriam.

19. δίκαιος ὤν, 'since he was a just man,' i.e. one who observed the law, and, therefore, feeling bound to divorce Mary. But two courses were open to him. He could either summon her before the law-courts to be judicially condemned and punished, or he could put her away by a bill of divorcement before witnesses, but without assigning cause. This is meant by λάθρα ἀπολῦσαι αὐτήν, the more merciful course which Joseph resolved to adopt. The tradition of mediæval art that Joseph was an old man at this time rests on no scriptural evidence, but the fact that he disappears from the Gospel history after Luke ii. 51, and the inference that he died before our Lord's ministry began are adduced in support of that view.

καὶ μὴ θέλων. καί appears to have a restrictive force and to be equivalent to καίτοι. See Jelf, 759. 3, and Campbell's Soph. *Introd.* § 25. 2. 6. Cp. ὦ στέφανε χαίρων ἄπιθι καὶ σ' ἄκων ἐγὼ | λείπω, Aristoph. *Eq.* 1250, and καὶ θεὸς ἐμμὶ καὶ οὐ δύναμαί σε διώκειν, Bion, *Id.* I. 53. In all these passages, however, it is better to see the restrictive or adversative force not in the connecting particle but in the contrasted clauses and to regard καί as simply conjunctive. See Winer, 545.

μὴ θέλων, 'since he was unwilling,' *quum nollet*. In modern Greek μή is always the negative used with participles. Perhaps the origin of the usage may be traced to the fact that the participle generally explains the motive or condition of an action and so would require μή rather than οὐ. Then from the tendency to grammatical uniformity the usage became universal. In the N. T. there is a close approach in this respect to the rule of modern Greek.

δειγματίσαι, 'to display,' 'exhibit,' here 'to expose in open court,' as opposed to λάθρα ἀπολῦσαι. παραδειγματίσαι—the reading of the received text—is used by Polybius of punishing the guilty for an example to others, II. 60. 7, xv. 32. 5, et alibi, see Schweighäuser sub voc. The simple verb which does not appear to be classical is found in the sense of 'displaying' as in a triumph in Col. ii. 15, τὰς ἐξουσίας

F 2

ἐδειγμάτισεν ἐν παρρησίᾳ, see Bp Lightfoot on the passage. The modern Greek version νὰ θεατρίσῃ conveys the idea of exposure simply.

20. ἰδού. Used like the Hebr. *hinneh* as a particle of transition. See note ch. ii. 7.

κατ' ὄναρ for classical ὄναρ.

παραλαβεῖν, the technical word for receiving a bride from her parents: καὶ τί ἄν, ἔφη ὁ Σωκράτης, ἐπισταμένην αὐτὴν παρέλαβες (Xen. Œcon.).

21. καλέσεις τὸ ὄνομα αὐτοῦ Ἰησοῦν. *Jesus* represents the Greek form, while *Joshua* represents the Hebrew form of the same name. The same Hebrew root occurs in the salutation *Hosanna*: see note, ch. xxi. 9. Joshua who led the Israelites into the Promised Land, and Joshua or Jeshua, who was high priest at the time of the return from the Babylonish Captivity, are types of Jesus Christ in respect both of work and name.

αὐτός, with some emphasis, he will not only preach σωτηρία, but will himself confer it.

σώσει τὸν λαὸν αὐτοῦ ἀπὸ τῶν ἁμαρτιῶν αὐτῶν. An announcement of a spiritual Kingdom. Contrary to the thought of many Jews the salvation which Jesus brought was not to be a saving from the Roman or Herodian rule, but a life protected from sin.

22. ὅλον. For the Hellenistic use of ὅλος in preference to πᾶς cp. French '*tout*' from *totus*, adopted rather than any word derived from *omnis*. Possibly the similarity to Hebr. *col* (all) may have influenced the Hellenistic writers in their choice.

γέγονεν, 'has come to pass.' The Evangelist speaks as a contemporary. The tense is a note of the early date of this gospel.

ἵνα πληρωθῇ. By this formula the Evangelist recognises in the event described a fulfilment of a type or prophecy. It matters little whether we regard ἵνα as (1) *final*, 'in order that,' or (2) by a late use *consecutive*, 'so that,' in other words (1) as marking the conscious intention of the prophet or of God speaking through the prophet, or (2) a reflection of the Evangelist viewing the historical fact in connection with the prophecy—and finding in the prophecy an analogy, if not a definite prediction. For in regard to divine action the intention and result are identical, that is, we cannot conceive of any result being unintentional with God. It has been disputed whether ἵνα is ever used in a consecutive sense. Meyer and Alford deny this use (see his note 1 Thess. v. 4), and Winer with perhaps one exception, Rev. xiii. 13. On the other side see Bp Ellicott on Eph. i. 17 and Bp Lightfoot on Gal. v. 17, and comp. 1 Thess. v. 4. In these and other passages ἵνα undoubtedly marks the result as distinct from conscious purpose. In confirmation of this view take into account (1) The Jewish mode of thought, according to which all results are regarded as purposed by God. The absence of τύχη from the N. T. vocabulary is striking evidence of this. (2) The influence of Latin, in which the same particle *ut* is used to express aim and result. (3)

The analogy of the genitive of the infinitive (e.g. τοῦ πιστεύειν) insensibly passing from an idea of aim to that of result. (4) The usage of modern Greek, towards which Hellenistic Greek is a step, which finds νά (ἵνα) too weak to express the idea of purpose and strengthens that particle by the addition of διά, so that διὰ νά = 'in order that.' (5) The general tendency of language in a later stage, especially on its popular side, to make special words serve a manifold use.

The use of ἵνα is further extended in Hellenistic Greek

(1) to oblique petition after words of entreaty, command, &c. instead of ὅπως or infinitive. Cp. εἰπὲ ἵνα γένηται, Luke iv. 3.

(2) to substantival clauses, where ὅτι or ὡς with the indicative would be the regular classical construction; cp. John xvii. 3, αὕτη δέ ἐστιν ἡ αἰώνιος ζωή, ἵνα γινώσκωσίν σε κ.τ.λ., and Epict. II. 1. 1, εἰ ἀληθές ἐστι τόδε ἵνα ᾖ ἅμα μὲν...πάντα ποιεῖν, si verum hoc est fieri posse &c. (Schweighäuser).

Comp. the indices of Schweighäuser to Epictetus and of Wyttenbach to Plutarch, where examples are given of ἵνα consecutive.

ὑπὸ...διά. See note ch. ii. 5.

23. ἡ παρθένος ἐν γαστρὶ ἕξει. Not *a* Virgin as A.V. but *the* Virgin: so also the Hebrew, which differs from this quotation only in having the singular 'she shall call.' The citation agrees with the LXX. where however the reading varies between ἕξει and λήψεται and between καλέσεις and καλέσουσιν. See Is. vii. 14.

The historical crisis was this, Ahaz is alarmed by the threatened invasion of Pekah and Rezin—the confederate kings of Samaria and Damascus. Isaiah reassures Ahaz, who hypocritically refuses to ask for a sign. Yet a sign is given. She, who is now unmarried, shall bear a son, probably a scion of the royal house of David; he shall be called Emmanuel, and before he arrives at years of discretion the deliverance shall come, though a heavier distress is at hand.

The prophecy is distinctly Messianic, but the sign in Isaiah is not concerned with the *manner* of the child's birth, but with the name, and the deliverance which should happen in his infancy. Therefore, the weight of the reference is to the name 'Emmanuel' and to the true Son of David, whose birth was the sign of His people's deliverance.

μεθερμηνευόμενον, a late word (Polyb. and Diod. Sic.). Cp. τοὺς καλουμένους ἐξτραορδιναρίους ὃ μεθερμηνευόμενον ἐπιλέκτους δηλοῖ. Polyb. VI. 26. 6. The explanation would not of course appear in the original Aramaic gospel.

25. οὐκ ἐγίνωσκεν κ.τ.λ. This expression cannot be considered as in any way decisive of the question, whether the Virgin Mary had or had not children besides our blessed Lord.

CHAPTER II.

9. ἐστάθη for ἔστη (אBCD). The passive implies agency, here divine agency: see ch. xxvii. 11.

11. εἶδον for εὗρον, with all the leading MSS. and versions. εὗρον influenced by v. 8.

15. κυρίου for τοῦ κυρίου. See ch. i. 22.

17. διά for ὑπό, the reading of all the more ancient authorities. The prophet is regarded as the instrument, not the agent.

18. θρῆνος καὶ omitted before κλαυθμός with אB against many later authorities. The omission brings the quotation into closer verbal agreement with the Hebrew; but the words are found in the LXX., and were probably meant to express the Hebrew intensive word by an addition.

23. Ναζαρέθ. The MSS. vary wherever this name occurs between Ναζαρέθ, Ναζαρέτ, Ναζαράθ and Ναζαρά, so that the orthography cannot be determined.

1—12. THE VISIT OF THE MAGI. Recorded by St Matthew only.

1. τοῦ δὲ Ἰησοῦ γεννηθέντος. The year 3 before the Christian era has been fixed almost beyond a doubt as the date of the Nativity. The present year—1881—is therefore correctly A.D. 1884. The data on which the computation is founded are: (1) The first rule of Quirinus (Luke ii. 2), which should probably be placed between the years B.C. 4 and A.D. 1 of the common era. Josephus mentions Quirinus as Governor in A.D. 6—nine or ten years after the true date of the nativity. The conjecture of a previous *first* governorship of Quirinus was made and ably supported by A. W. Zumpt. His conclusions are generally accepted. (2) The accession of Tiberius A.D. 14; thus the fifteenth year of Tiberius, in which Jesus was baptized (Luke iii. 1, 2) ended Aug. 19, A.D. 29. (3) The Paschal full moon; which fell on a Friday, 15th Nisan in A.D. 30 and also in A.D. 33. On one of these two dates the Crucifixion must have taken place. If the second be adopted as agreeing best with the other chronological notes in the gospels, Jesus was crucified on April 3 [O.S.], A.D. 33, when he may have been between 34 and 35 years of age. (4) The reign of Herod; which began in B.C. 36 and ended in B.C. 1. The last-named date has been accurately determined in a paper read before the Society of Biblical Archæology (June, 1871) by Mr J. W. Bosanquet,—which see for a learned discussion of the whole question.

ἐν Βηθλεέμ. St Matthew omits the circumstances which brought Mary to Bethlehem.

Βηθλεέμ ('The House of Bread,' cp. John vi. 51), the city of David, situate on a limestone ridge a few miles S. of Jerusalem. The old name of Bethlehem was Ephrath or Ephratah; it is now called Beit-lahm. It is worthy of remark that no visit of Jesus or of his disciples to Bethlehem, his birthplace and the cradle of his race, is recorded.

Ἡρώδου τοῦ βασιλέως. Called afterwards, but not in his lifetime, Herod the Great; he was an Idumæan (Edomite) who, chiefly through the friendship of M. Antony, became king of Judæa. For date of reign see above. The title of βασιλεύς distinguishes him from the other Herods named in the gospels. Antipas, who tried in vain to obtain the title, is called King by courtesy, Mark vi. 14.

Herod was not an absolute monarch, but subject to the Roman empire, much in the same way as some of the Indian princes are subject to the British government, or as Servia was till recently subject to the Porte.

ἰδού. See note ch. i. 20.

μάγοι, originally the name of a Median tribe, who, according to Herodotus, possessed the power of interpreting dreams. Their religion consisted in the worship of the heavenly bodies and of the elements. At this date the name implied a religious caste—the followers of Zoroaster, who were the astrologers of the East. Their tenets had spread widely; and as the East is a vague term, it is difficult to determine from what country these Magi came. A theory, stated below, connects them with Egypt, or at least with an Egyptian system of chronology. The common belief that the Magi were three in number is a mere tradition, which has been perpetuated by great painters. It was probably an inference from *v.* 11. Every reader of the Classics knows how common a failing it is with ancient annotators to state deductions from the text as proved facts. An equally groundless tradition has designated the Magi as kings, and has assigned names to them. The first part of this tradition is probably due to the words of Ps. lxviii. 29, lxxii. 11; Is. xlix. 23 and other passages. The special names Caspar, Balthasar, and Melchior are supposed to indicate the three countries of Babylon, Assyria, and Egypt.

ἀπὸ ἀνατολῶν, plural, as always in later Greek (Polyb. and Plut.) in the sense of 'the East,' i.e. the quarter in which the sun rises, cp. αἱ δυσμαί, αἱ ἄρκτοι (Schweighäuser). Here for 'the Eastern lands,' cp. Anglo-French 'the levant.' This use is later, the classical meaning is 'the rising,' of the sun, moon, or stars, see note on next verse. By another later use ἀνατολή = 'a branch' or 'shoot,' hence 'The Branch' as a Messianic title.

2. τεχθείς. This form is rarely if ever found in classical Attic; see Veitch sub voc. τίκτω and cp. Luke ii. 11—the only other passage where this tense-form occurs in N. T.

ὁ τεχθεὶς βασιλεύς. One who was *born* king—whose title was hereditary—would bring special fear to Herod.

βασιλεὺς τῶν Ἰουδαίων. A title unknown to the earlier history of Israel and applied to no one except the Messiah. It reappears in the inscription over the Cross (ch. xxvii. 37).

In estimating the Jewish conception of the 'kingdom of heaven' and of the Messiah who is the central figure of that thought, account should be taken of the awe with which the Oriental regarded the person of a king, who was far more highly exalted above his subjects than Western ideas admit (cp. Rawlinson's Herod. vii. 13). The βασιλεύς in this sense is to be distinguished from the petty prince or *regulus* who, like Herod, assumed the imperial title of βασιλεύς.

εἴδομεν...ἤλθομεν, keep the strict aoristic force 'we saw'...'we came.'

αὐτοῦ τὸν ἀστέρα. The simplest explanation of this is that a star or meteor appeared in the sky to guide the Magi on their way first to Jerusalem, then to Bethlehem. It is, however, quite possible that the Magi were divinely led to connect some calculated phenomenon with the birth of the 'King of the Jews.' Among many conjectures may be mentioned one recently propounded by Prof. Lauth of Munich. It appears to be proved that the dog-star Sirius rose heliacally, i.e. appeared at sunrise, on the first of the Egyptian month Mesori, for four years in succession, viz. 5, 4, 3, 2 before our era. The rising of this star of special brilliance on the first of this special month (Mesori=birth of the prince) would have a marked significance. By the Magi it might well be connected with the prophecy of 'the star of Jacob' (Numb. xxiv. 17), and become the cause of their journey to Jerusalem. This theory explains Herod's edict, *v.* 16, for the destruction of all male children 'from two years old and under,' for, as according to the date assigned to the Nativity of Christ, the arrival of the Magi at Jerusalem would coincide with the year 3 before the Christian era, the star had appeared for two years.

The theory, supported by Alford, which identifies this 'star' with a conjunction of Jupiter and Saturn, forces the meaning of the word 'star,' is inconsistent with the latest chronological results, and is shown to be scientifically impossible by Prof. Pritchard in *Dict. of the Bible*, *sub voc.* 'Star of the Magi.'

The connection of the birth of the Messiah with the appearance of a star is illustrated by the name Barcochab ('Son of a Star'), assumed by a false Messiah who appeared in the year 120 A.D. It has also been noticed that in the *Cartouche* or Egyptian royal symbol of Vespasian (see note ch. ii. 6 *ad fin.*), the word 'God' is for the first time expressed by a star. (Dr Lauth, *Trans. Bib. Arch. Soc.* IV. 2.)

ἐν τῇ ἀνατολῇ. Probably 'at its rising.' If the ordinary interpretation 'in the East' be adopted, it would be an unusual, perhaps an unexampled, instance of the singular in this sense. The suggested rendering suits the technical language of the astrologers.

προσκυνῆσαι. A favourite word with St Matthew as with St John. Its occurrence thus early in the Gospel strikes the note of the Gospel of the Great King. προσκυνεῖν is used of the servile prostration before an Oriental monarch. Cp. Herod. VII. 13, where a striking instance of this subservience is recorded: οἱ Πέρσαι μὲν ὡς ἤκουσαν ταῦτα (views entirely opposed to their own) κεχαρηκότες προσεκύνεον. This connection gives point to the word as used ch. xx. 20, where see note.

3. ἐταράχθη. Herod, with the instincts of a tyrant, would be alarmed for his throne. His subjects (πᾶσα Ἱεροσόλυμα) had learnt

to dread his outbreaks of passion. μετ' αὐτοῦ not σὺν αὐτῷ, they did not sympathise in *his* alarm.

πᾶσα Ἱεροσόλυμα. The feminine form which occurs here and possibly ch. iii. 5, is remarkable. Elsewhere Ἱεροσόλυμα is a neuter plural. St Matthew uses this form in preference to Ἱερουσαλήμ, except in one passage, ch. xxiii. 37, where see note. St Luke, both in his Gospel and in the Acts and St Paul, each with few exceptions, adopt the Hebraic form in -ήμ. St John has the Greek termination only in his Gospel, the Hebrew only in the Apocalypse.

For a similar variety of gender in the name of a town, cp. Verg. *Æn.* VII. 682 altum Præneste, with *Æn.* VIII. 511 Præneste sub alta, and Thuc. II. 99 τόν τε Ἀνθεμοῦντα, with Dem. *Phil.* II. 20 Ἀνθεμοῦντα ἧς ἀντεποιοῦντο.

4. πάντας τοὺς ἀρχιερεῖς καὶ γραμματεῖς τοῦ λαοῦ, i. e. summoned a meeting of the Sanhedrin. But from the omission of τοὺς πρεσβυτέρους, who are generally included in the designation of the Sanhedrin it is contended by some that this was an irregular meeting of the chief priests and learned men. With this view it is difficult to explain πάντας.

For an account of the Sanhedrin see note ch. xxvi. 3, for γραμματεῖς see notes on ch. vii. 29, and for ἀρχιερεῖς, note ch. xxi. 15.

ποῦ ὁ Χριστὸς γεννᾶται. Lit. 'where the Christ or Messiah is born.' Where do your sacred writings represent him to be born? For this use of the pres. indic. cp. ἐκ τῆς Γαλ. προφ. οὐκ ἐγείρεται, John vii. 52.

5. Βηθλεέμ τῆς Ἰουδαίας. To distinguish this Bethlehem from the Bethlehem in the tribe of Zebulun (Josh. xix. 15).

γέγραπται, well expressed by Luther's translation, *stehet geschrieben*. The tense marks the continued validity of a law or a prophecy; so also in the classics, ἐν τοῖς φονικοῖς γέγραπται νόμοις...καὶ ἄτιμος τεθνάτω. Dem. *Phil.* 3. 44.

διὰ τοῦ προφήτου, 'by means of,' 'through'—the prophet is regarded as the instrument. In v. 17 and iii. 3, some MSS. have the preposition signifying personal agency (ὑπό), instead of the instrumental preposition (διά); but the usual formula is as in v. 15, ὑπὸ Κυρίου διὰ τοῦ προφήτου.

6. καὶ σὺ Βηθλεέμ κ.τ.λ. Micah v. 2. The quotation (as usually in passages cited by St Matthew alone) nearly corresponds with the Hebrew text, the literal translation of which is: 'But thou Bethlehem Ephratah, though thou be little to be among the thousands of Judah, yet out of thee shall come forth unto me he that is to be ruler in Israel.'

A note of interrogation in the Hebrew would entirely reconcile the quotation with the original passage. Others have conjectured the loss of a negative in the Hebrew text, which seems to have been cited by some of the fathers with the negative. See Bp Jebb, *Sacr. Lit.* p. 99.

The LXX. differs widely both in words and construction—an indication of a Hebrew original of this gospel; for the Greek translation of the prophecy is evidently independent of the LXX. It stands thus in A. καὶ σὺ Βηθλεέμ, οἶκος τοῦ Ἐφραθά, ὀλιγοστὸς εἶ τοῦ εἶναι ἐν χιλιάσιν Ἰούδα· ἐκ σοῦ μοι ἐξελεύσεται ἡγούμενος, τοῦ εἶναι εἰς ἄρχοντα ἐν τῷ Ἰσραήλ. Note here the greater excellence of the Gospel version and the poetical touch in ποιμανεῖ (cp. the Homeric ποιμένα λαῶν) not found in the Hebrew original or in the LXX. ὀλιγοστὸς appears to be used in the LXX. as superlative of ὀλίγος for ὀλίγιστος· the classical meaning 'one of few,' i.e. 'among the mightiest,' 'considerable' (see Campbell's note on Soph. *Ant.* 625 and cp. πολλοστός) would bring the LXX. more nearly in accord with St Matthew's citation. The substitution of ἡγεμόσιν for the technical word χιλιάσιν may mark the form in which the message was actually conveyed to Herod, or it may be an adaptation for the sake of clearness. ἡγούμενος, modern Greek, in this sense, see Geldart, *Mod. Greek*, p. 103.

A reflection of this prophecy became prevalent in the East. Accordingly the Roman historians designate the Emperor Vespasian as the Eastern Prince who was destined to rule the world: 'Percrebuerat Oriente toto vetus et constans opinio esse in fatis ut eo tempore Judæa profecti rerum potirentur. Id de Imperatore Romano quantum postea eventu paruit prædictum Judæi ad se trahentes rebellarunt.' Suet. *Vesp.* IV. Similarly Tac. *Hist.* v. 13. Comp. Joseph. *B. J.* VI. 5. 4. See above, *v.* 2.

7. τότε, a favourite word of transition with St Matthew. It occurs more frequently in this gospel alone than in all the rest of the N.T. The modes of transition in the several Evangelists are interesting as notes of style. Thus τότε is characteristic of St Matthew, εὐθύς (εὐθέως) of St Mark, καὶ ἐγένετο of St Luke, καὶ ἰδού is about equally common in Luke and Matthew.

ἠκρίβωσεν, 'accurately ascertained,' used of scientific exactness, σοφοὶ μὲν οὖν εἶσ' οἱ τάδ' ἠκριβωκότες, Eur. *Hec.* 1192. The reason of Herod's enquiry appears in *v.* 16.

τὸν χρόνον τοῦ φαιν. ἀστ. Literally, 'the time of the star which was appearing,' i.e. when it first appeared and how long it would continue. The χρόνος was astrologically important.

8. πέμψας αὐτοὺς εἰς Βηθλεέμ. Up to this time the Magi are not said to have been guided by the star; they go to Bethlehem in accordance with Herod's directions, which were based on the report of the Sanhedrin; as they went the star again appeared in the East.

ἐξετάζειν, 'to enquire into the reality or essence of a thing' (ἐτεός, ἐτός, εἰμί.) Used by Plato of the Socratic Elenchus: φιλοσοφοῦντά με ζῆν καὶ ἐξετάζοντα ἐμαυτὸν καὶ τοὺς ἄλλους. (*Apol. Socr.*)

10. ἐχάρησαν χαρὰν κ.τ.λ. The cognate noun becomes far more frequent in Hellenistic Greek under the influence of Hebrew expression. Observe the intensity of the joy expressed by the combination of cognate noun, adjective and adverb. To them it was a triumph at once of science and religion.

11. εἰς τὴν οἰκίαν. St Matthew gives no hint that 'the house' was an inn, or that the babe was lying in a manger. Perhaps here as in other places we are misled by the ideas suggested by great pictures; and in truth the visit of the Magi should be placed at least some days after the events recorded in Luke ii. 1—38.

τοὺς θησαυρούς. 'Caskets' or 'chests' in which treasures were placed. Such offerings to kings were quite in accordance with Eastern usage: Reges Parthos non potest quisquam salutare sine munere. Sen. *Ep.* XVII. Cp. Ps. lxviii. 29, lxxii. 10.

λίβανον καὶ σμύρναν. Frankincense and myrrh were products of Arabia, and, according to Herodotus, of that country only. They were both used for medicinal purposes and for embalming; cp. John xix. 39.

12. χρηματισθέντες κατ' ὄναρ, 'divinely warned by a dream.' χρηματίζειν. (1) 'To transact business,' 'to deal or act or confer' with any one. (2) Of divine dealings with men, 'to answer,' 'warn' or 'command,'—a late use frequent in Diod. Sic., Plutarch and Polyb., e.g. θεοὺς αὐτοῖς ταῦτα κεχρηματικέναι. Diod. Sic. I. 177. Hence ὁ χρηματισμός (Rom. xi. 4), 'the divine word,' 'the oracle.' With Diod. Sic. who retains the classical use of χρησμός, χρηματισμός = 'a judicial decree.' (3) From the notion of transacting business under a particular name χρηματίζειν has the meaning of 'to assume a title,' 'to be named,' τὸ λοιπὸν ἐχρημάτισε βασιλεύς. Diod. Sic. XX. 789. βασιλεὺς ἐτόλμιζε χρηματίζειν. Polyb. V. 57. 5. χρηματίσαι τε πρώτως ἐν Ἀντιοχείᾳ τοὺς μαθητὰς Χριστιανούς. Acts xi. 26. Hence still later χρηματισμός means 'a name.' (4) In modern Greek χρηματίζειν is used for the substantive verb 'to be.'

κατ' ὄναρ. See ch. i. 20.

13—15. The Flight into Egypt.

13. τὸ παιδίον. Named first as the most precious charge and the most exposed to danger.

εἰς Αἴγυπτον. Egypt was at all times the readiest place of refuge for the Israelites, whether from famine or from political oppression. It had sheltered many thousands of Jews from the tyranny of the Syrian kings. Consequently large settlements of Jews were to be found in various cities of Egypt and Africa. In Alexandria the Jews numbered a fifth of the population. Wherever therefore the infant Saviour's home was in Egypt, it would be in the midst of his brethren according to the flesh.

At this time Egypt was a Roman province. This incident of Christ's stay in Egypt would be regarded as a precious memory by the African Church—the church of Cyprian, Origen and Augustine.

τοῦ ἀπολέσαι, 'in order to slay it.' A classical idiom which became frequent in the N.T. especially with St Paul and St Luke; it is still more frequent in the LXX.

(1) Denoting *purpose*, as here. Cp. εἰσῆλθεν τοῦ μεῖναι σὺν αὐτοῖς, Luke xxiv. 29. τοῦ μηκέτι δουλεύειν τῇ ἁμαρτίᾳ, Rom. vi. 6. These instances are best referred to the use of the partitive genitive with verbs signifying aim or striving for, or to the genitive of cause denoting that from which the action springs. Comp. the final use of the genitive of the gerund and gerundive in Latin.

(2) *Result*—a usage closely connected with the last, as the ideas of purpose and result are nearly related, particularly according to the Hebraic modes of thought. (See note ch. i. 22 on ἵνα.) Cp. ἐλευθέρα ἐστὶν ἀπὸ τοῦ νόμου τοῦ μὴ εἶναι αὐτὴν μοιχαλίδα, Rom. vii. 2. Possibly ἐκρίθη τοῦ ἀποπλεῖν ἡμᾶς (Acts xxvii. 1) belongs to this head, —the decision resulted in sailing—cp. πέρας...τοῦ ἀπαλλάσσεσθαι, 'an end that consisted or resulted in escape.' See also Gossrau's note on *aram sepulchri*, Verg. Æn. vi. 177.

(3) In many cases τοῦ with the infinitive is regularly used after words requiring a genitive, as ἐὰν ᾖ ἄξιον τοῦ κἀμὲ πορεύεσθαι, 1 Cor. xvi. 4.

(4) In some passages it appears (α) as the object of verbs where the accusative would be required in Classical Greek, as οὐ γὰρ ἔκρινα τοῦ εἰδέναι τι ἐν ὑμῖν, 1 Cor. ii. 2. Or (β) as the subject of the verb: ὡς δὲ ἐγένετο τοῦ εἰσελθεῖν τὸν Πέτρον, Acts x. 25. These and similar expressions may indeed be explained as extensions of recognised genitival uses, but it is better to regard them as illustrating the gradual forgetfulness in language of the origin of idioms. In illustration of this, comp. the use in French of the infinitive with *de* either as subject or as object; e.g. il est triste de vous voir,—on craint d'y aller; the adoption of the (Latin) accusative in the same language as the sole representative of the Latin cases; and the extension of ἵνα (νά) with the subjunctive in modern Greek to the various uses of the infinitive.

Hebrew scholars also note the widely-extended use of ל as influencing this formula. See Winer 407—412. Jelf 492. 678. 3 *b*. Arnold's Thuc. viii. 14.

14. ἀναχωρεῖν (1) 'to retire' from danger as here, and chs. iv. 12, xii. 16, and elsewhere; (2) in the later Classics 'to retire from business or public life;' (3) in Ecclesiastical writers 'to retire from the world,' 'become a hermit, or anchoret' (ἀναχωρητής).

This word, which occurs much more frequently in this Gospel than elsewhere in N.T. seems to connect itself with two points in the traditional life of St Matthew. 1. His stay in Egypt—the cradle of the anchoret life. 2. His asceticism, to which the notion of 'retirement' is closely related.

15. ἕως τῆς τελευτῆς Ἡρώδου. According to the chronology adopted above this would be for a space of less than two years.

ἵνα πληρωθῇ. See note on ch. i. 22.

ἐξ Αἰγύπτου ἐκάλεσα τὸν υἱόν μου. The history of Israel is regarded as typical of the Messiah's life. He alone gives significance to that history. He is the true seed of Abraham. In him the blessing promised to Abraham finds its highest fulfilment. (See Lightfoot on

Gal. iii. 16.) Even particular incidents in the Gospel narrative have their counterpart in the O.T. history. Accordingly St Matthew, who naturally reverts to this thought more constantly than the other Evangelists, from the very nature of his gospel, recognises in this incident an analogy to the call of Israel from Egypt.

The quotation is again from the original Hebrew of Hosea xi. 2, and again the LXX. differs considerably. It runs ἐξ Αἰγύπτου μετεκάλεσα τὰ τέκνα αὐτοῦ. Cp. Exod. iv. 22, 23 υἱὸς πρωτότοκός μου Ἰσραήλ· εἶπα δέ σοι ἐξαπόστειλον τὸν λαόν μου ἵνα μοι λατρεύσῃ, where τὸν υἱόν μου would be a closer rendering of the Hebrew than τὸν λαόν μου.

16. ἀνεῖλεν, 'slew.' The verb occurs here only in Matthew. It is frequent in the Acts, occurring rarely elsewhere. Out of a great variety of classical meanings the Hellenistic usage nearly confines the word to its force here. The two instances of a different meaning in N.T. are Acts vii. 21 and Hebr. x. 9.

πάντας τοὺς παῖδας, 'all the male children.'

ἀπὸ διετοῦς. Either (1) there is an ellipse of παιδός, or (2) more probably διετοῦς is neuter. If we adopt the hypothesis regarding the star mentioned above, a satisfactory explanation is given for Herod's directions, which otherwise it is difficult to explain. Even if the above theory is not the true one, the two years mentioned in the text are clearly connected with the astronomical appearances described by the Magi, in answer to Herod's 'diligent enquiries.'

Profane history passes over this atrocity in silence. But Josephus may well have found his pages unequal to contain a complete record of all the cruel deeds of a tyrant like Herod. Macaulay relates that the massacre of Glencoe is not even alluded to in the pages of Evelyn, a most diligent recorder of passing political events. Besides, the crime was executed with secrecy, the number of children slain was probably very inconsiderable, for Bethlehem was but a small town; and though it was possibly crowded at the time (Luke ii. 7), the number of very young children would not have been considerably augmented by those strangers.

The whole scene must have been very different from that which is presented to us on the canvas of the great mediæval artists.

17. τότε ἐπληρώθη. This turn of expression may be regarded as identical with the more usual 'that it might be fulfilled.'

18. Jer. xxxi. 15, in LXX. xxxviii. 15. In a singularly touching passage, Rachel, the mother of the tribe of Benjamin (whose tomb was close to Bethlehem; Gen. xxxv. 19), is conceived of as weeping for her captive sons at Ramah—some of whom were possibly doomed to die; cp. Jer. xl. 1.

The Evangelist pictures Rachel's grief re-awakened by the slaughter of the infants at Bethlehem.

The Ramah alluded to by Jeremiah, generally identified with the modern Er-Rama, was about five miles N. of Jerusalem, and in the tribe of Benjamin. There is no proof of another Ramah near Bethlehem. The analogy therefore must not be pressed.

As the text now stands emended St Matthew's citation agrees with the Hebrew (the repetition of 'for her children' in the last line in the Hebrew text is doubtful), and preserves the beauty of the parallelism. In the quatrain each couplet is in cognate parallelism [see Introduction, p. xxxviii.]; the second line advancing on the first, and further there is a parallel relation between lines 1 and 3 and 2 and 4. In the LXX. this beauty is lost; the reading of the Vatican codex is: φωνὴ ἐν Ῥαμὰ ἠκούσθη | θρήνου καὶ κλαυθμοῦ καὶ ὀδυρμοῦ | Ῥαχὴλ ἀποκλαιομένη [codex A. -ης ἐπὶ τῶν υἱῶν αὐτῆς] | οὐκ ἤθελε παύσασθαι ἐπὶ τοῖς υἱοῖς αὐτῆς [codex A. παρακληθῆναι and om. ἐπὶ τ. υἱ. αὐ.] ὅτι οὐκ εἰσίν | .

Observe here the loss of the parallelism by the genitive cases, line 2. It is an interesting example of St Matthew's sense of poetical form, and of the greater excellence and beauty of his version as compared with the LXX.

19—21. THE RETURN FROM EGYPT.

20. οἱ ζητοῦντες. Plural used sometimes where there is no need or no wish to individualise. Others however joined Herod in his design to slay the young child; but with the death of Herod the whole plot would fall to the ground.

22. Ἀρχέλαος. A son of Herod the Great. His mother was Malthaké, a Samaritan. After a cruel and disturbed reign (under the title of Ethnarch) of about eight years he was banished to Vienna in Gaul—the modern Vienne. His dominions, including Samaria, Judæa, and Idumæa, then passed into the direct government of Rome. See note, ch. xiv. 1, and Introduction, p. xxix.

ἐκεῖ for ἐκεῖσε, as in English there for thither: cp. Soph *O. C.* 1019, ὁδοῦ κατάρχειν τῆς ἐκεῖ. Hdt. VII. 147, καὶ ἡμεῖς ἐκεῖ πλέομεν.

τὰ μέρη τῆς Γαλιλαίας. Now under the government of Herod Antipas, full brother of Archelaus. For the extent of his dominions see *Map*.

23. εἰς πόλιν λεγομένην Ναζαρέθ. St Matthew gives no intimation of any previous residence of Mary and Joseph at Nazareth.

If the Son of David, full of wisdom and of grace, had continued to live on at Bethlehem, the home of his ancestors, hopes and schemes, and therefore dangers, might have gathered round him, rendering impossible such quiet life as he led at Nazareth.

Ναζαρέθ. Said to signify 'the Protectress' (Hebr. *natsar*), a small town of central Galilee, on the edge of the plain of Esdraelon, beautifully situated on the side of a steep hill within a sheltered valley.

Ναζωραῖος κληθήσεται. The meaning of this passage was probably as clear to the contemporaries of St Matthew, as the other references to prophecy *vv.* 15, 17; for us it is involved in doubt. First, it may be said Nazarene cannot=Nazarite: the word differs in form, and in no sense could Christ be called a Nazarite. Secondly, the quotation is probably not from a lost prophecy. One meaning of the word

Nazoræus is an inhabitant of Nazareth, but the word either (1) recalls the Hebrew word *netser* a Branch, a title by which the Messiah is designated Isai. xi. 1, or (2) connects itself in thought with the Hebr. *natsar*, to save or protect (see above), and so has reference to the name and work of Jesus, or (3) is a synonym for 'contemptible' or 'lowly,' from the despised position of Nazareth. Of these (3) is perhaps the least probable explanation. The play upon words which (1) and (2) involve is quite characteristic of Hebrew phraseology. The sound of the original would be either (1) He whom the prophet called the 'Netser' dwells at 'Netser'—(for this form of Nazareth see Smith's *Bib. Dict.*), or (2) He who is called 'Notsri' (my protector) dwells at 'Natsaret' (the protectress).

In any case the passage gains fresh interest from the fact that the early Christians were called Nazarenes in scorn. Cp. Acts xxiv. 5. For them it would be a point of triumph that their enemies thus unconsciously connected them with a prophetic title of their Master.

CHAPTER III.

3. διά for ὑπό, see ch. ii. 17.

1—12. JOHN BAPTIST PREACHES IN THE WILDERNESS OF JUDÆA. Mark i. 2—8; Luke iii. 1—18; John i. 15—34.

St Matthew alone names the coming of the Pharisees and Sadducees. St Mark's brief account contains no additional particulars. St Luke adds the special directions to the various classes—people—publicans and soldiers. The fourth gospel reports more fully the Baptist's disclaimer of Messiahship—he recognises the Messiah by the descent of the Holy Spirit—he points him out as the Lamb of God. Again (ch. iii. 25—36) John shows his own disciples the true relation between Christ and himself—Christ is the Bridegroom, John is the friend of the Bridegroom.

1. ἐν ταῖς ἡμέραις ἐκείναις. See Luke iii. 1, where the time is defined.

Ἰωάννης ὁ βαπτιστής. So named by the other Synoptists and by Josephus: in the fourth gospel he is called simply John, a note of the authenticity of St John's gospel. Josephus mentions the great influence of John and speaks of the crowds that flocked to hear him preach and to be baptized of him. He says John taught men ἀρετὴν ἐπασκοῦντας καὶ τῇ πρὸς ἀλλήλους δικαιοσύνῃ καὶ πρὸς τὸν θεὸν εὐσεβείᾳ χρωμένους βαπτισμῷ συνιέναι· οὕτω γὰρ καὶ τὴν βάπτισιν ἀποδεκτὴν αὐτῷ φανεῖσθαι, μὴ ἐπί τινων ἁμαρτάδων παραιτήσει χρωμένων ἀλλ' ἐφ' ἁγνείᾳ τοῦ σώματος ἅτε δὴ καὶ τῆς ψυχῆς δικαιοσύνῃ προεκκεκαθαρμένης. *Ant.* XVIII. v. 2. Compare this view of John's baptism by the Pharisee Josephus with John's own statement of the end of baptism—εἰς μετάνοιαν (v. 11).

κηρύσσων. Heralding, a word appropriate to the thought of the proclamation of a King.

ἐν τῇ ἐρήμῳ τῆς Ἰουδαίας, i.e. the uncultivated Eastern frontier of Judah. The term also includes the cliffs and Western shore of the Dead Sea. In this wild and nearly treeless district there were formerly a few cities, and there are still some luxuriant spots. See Tristram's *Topog. of H. L.* Ch. IV.

The wilderness has a threefold significance (α) as the desolate scene of John's ascetic life, (β) as the battle-field of the Temptation (see notes ch. iv.), (γ) as the pathway of the Royal Advent. In this last aspect John fitly appears in the wilderness as the herald of a promised deliverance foreshadowed by two great prophetic types—the deliverance from Egypt (Numb. xxiii. 21, 22; Ps. lxviii. 4—7), and the deliverance from Babylon, each associated with a march through the desert. Isaiah speaks of both (ch. xliii. 18, 19), 'Remember not the former things, and the things of ancient times regard not' (the return from Egypt). 'Behold I make a new thing...yea, I will make in the wilderness a way' (the return from Babylon). See Bp Lowth on Is. xl.

2. μετανοεῖτε. More than 'feel sorrow or regret for sin,' it is rather 'change the life, the heart, the *motive* for action.' It was a call to self-examination and reality of life.

ἡ βασιλεία τῶν οὐρανῶν. St Matthew alone uses this expression, but he also employs the equivalent phrase, ἡ βασιλεία τοῦ θεοῦ, in common with the other N.T. writers. In itself the expression was not new. It connected itself in Jewish thought with the theocracy—the direct rule of God—of which the earthly Kingdom was a shadow. It implied the reign of the Messiah (cp. Dan. vii. 14). It became the watchword of the zealots 'no king but God.' Jesus took up the word and gave it a new deep and varied spiritual significance, which is rather illustrated than defined.

The principal meanings of the Kingdom of Heaven in N.T. are (1) The presence of Christ on earth. (2) His Second Advent. (3) His influence in the heart. (4) Christianity, (a) as a Church, (b) as a faith. (5) The life eternal.

3. διά. See note on ch. ii. 5.

διὰ Ἡσαΐου τοῦ προφήτου. The reference in Is. xl. 3 is to the promised return from Babylon. A herald shall proclaim the joyous news on mountains and in the desert through which the return should be. This incident in the national history is transferred to the more glorious deliverance from bondage and to the coming of the true King.

With the exception of αὐτοῦ for τοῦ θεοῦ ἡμῶν the quotation follows the LXX., as, with few exceptions, in passages cited by all the Synoptists. Bp Lowth's version of the Hebrew is: 'A voice crieth in the wilderness, Prepare ye the way of Jehovah, make straight in the desert a high way for our God,' where the parallelism is more perfect than in the Greek versions.

φωνή. The message is more than the messenger, the prophet's personality is lost in the prophetic voice.

εὐθείας ποιεῖτε τὰς τρίβους. The image would be familiar to Eastern thought, a Semiramis or a Xerxes orders the mountains to be levelled or cut through, and causeways to be raised in the valleys. Cp. Diod. Sic. II. 101, διόπερ τούς τε κρημνοὺς κατακόψασα (Semiramis) καὶ τοὺς κοίλους τόπους χώσασα σύντομον καὶ πολυτελῆ κατεσκεύασεν ὁδόν.

4. τὸ ἔνδυμα αὐτοῦ κ.τ.λ. A kind of tunic or shirt coarsely woven of camel's hair, 'one of the most admirable materials for clothing, it keeps out the heat, cold and rain.' *Recovery of Jerusalem*, p. 445.

ἀκρίδες καὶ μέλι ἄγριον. Thomson, *Land and Book*, pp. 419, 420, states that though tolerated, as an article of food, only by the very poorest people, locusts are still eaten by the Bedawin. Burckhardt mentions having seen locust shops at Medina and Tayf. After being dried in the sun the locusts are eaten with butter and honey. Sometimes they are sprinkled with salt and either boiled or roasted. Thomson adds that wild honey is still gathered from trees in the wilderness and from rocks in the Wadies.

Diod. Sic., speaking of the Nabatæans, an Arabian tribe living near this very region, says part of their fare was μέλι πολὺ τὸ καλούμενον ἄγριον ᾧ χρῶνται ποτῷ μεθ' ὕδατος. The clothing and dress of John were in fact those of the poorest of his fellow countrymen. The description would recall—is probably intended to recall—that of Elijah, 2 Kings i. 8.

6. ἐβαπτίζοντο were 'immersed;' (the tense marks the successive instances). βαπτίζω, a strengthened form of βάπτω, like some other leading Christian words (e. g. Χριστός, ἀγάπη, μετάνοια), is rare in the Classics; it is used in different figurative senses by Plato, e. g. of a boy 'drowned with questions,' *Euthyd.* 277 D; in Polyb. literally of ships sinking, in Diod. Sic. both literally and metaphorically: ὁ ποταμὸς πολλοὺς ἐβάπτιζε, II. 143; and οὐ βαπτίζουσι ταῖς εἰσφοραῖς τοὺς ἰδιώτας, I. 85. Note the revival of the literal meaning in the later stage of the language.

In baptizing John introduced no new custom, for ceremonial ablution or baptism was practised in all ancient religions. Cp. Soph. *Aj.* 654—656, ἀλλ' εἶμι πρός τε λουτρὰ καὶ παρακτίους | λειμῶνας, ὡς ἂν λύμαθ' ἁγνίσας ἐμὰ | μῆνιν βαρεῖαν ἐξαλύξωμαι θεᾶς, where see Prof. Jebb's note. Among the Jews proselytes were baptized on admission to the Mosaic covenant. John's baptism was the outward sign of the purification and 'life-giving change,' and contained the promise of forgiveness of sins. Christ too adopted the ancient custom and enriched it with a new significance, and a still mightier efficacy. From the history of the word it is clear that the primitive idea of baptism was immersion. This was for long the only recognised usage in the Christian Church, and much of the figurative force was lost when sprinkling was substituted for immersion. The convert who entered the clear rushing stream, soiled, weary, and scorched by the hot Eastern sun, and then after being hidden from the sight for a few moments 'buried in baptism' reappeared, fresh, vigorous, and cleansed, having put off 'the filth of the flesh,' seemed indeed to have risen to a new and purified life in Christ. ἐν τῷ Ἰορδάνῃ ποταμῷ. Two points on the Jordan are named in John. See note on *v.* 13.

ἐξομολογεῖσθαι. 'To acknowledge or declare fully,' used either (1) of confession as here, and Mark i. 5; Acts xix. 18; or (2) of thanks and praise as in ch. xi. 25; Luke x. 21; Rom. xv. 9.

7. Φαρισαίων. The name signifies 'Separatists;' the party dates from the revival of the National life, and observances of the Mosaic Law under the Maccabees. Their ruling principle was a literal obedience to the written law and to an unwritten tradition. Originally they were leaders of a genuine reform. But in the hands of less spiritual successors their system had become little else than a formal observance of carefully prescribed rules. 'The real virtues of one age become the spurious ones of the next.' Prof. Mozley, *Sermon on Pharisees*. The 'hypocrisy' of the Pharisees, which stifled conscience and made them '*incapable of repentance*,' is the special sin of the day rebuked more than any other by the Saviour.

Politically they were the popular party, supporters of an isolating policy, who would make no terms with Rome or any other foreign power. The *Zealots* may be regarded as the extreme section of the Pharisees.

The *Sadducees* were the aristocratic and priestly party, they acquiesced in foreign rule, and foreign civilisation. They refused to give the same weight as the Pharisees to unwritten tradition, but adhered strictly to the written law of Moses. Their religious creed excluded belief in a future life, or in angels and spirits (Acts xxiii. 8). The name is probably derived from Zadok the priest in David's time. Others with less probability connect it with Zadok, a disciple of Antigonus of Socho, who lived in the second century B.C. The derivation from *tsaddik* (righteous) is untenable.

γεννήματα, 'offspring,' 'brood,' of vipers.

ἐχιδνῶν. ἔχιδνα not the 'seeing creature,' ὄφις (see note ch. x. 16), but lit. the pernicious and dangerous beast that 'strangles;' from the same root as *anguis*, 'ango' (Curtius, *Etym.*). The word suggests the harmful teaching of the Pharisees that 'strangled' truth.

φυγεῖν ἀπό. Cp. ἀπὸ Σκύλλης φεύγειν. Xen. *Mem.* II. p. 31.

τῆς μελλούσης ὀργῆς. Cp. τῆς ὀργῆς τῆς ἐρχομένης. 1 Thess. i. 10. ὀργή, or 'wrath,' is the human conception by which the divine attitude towards sin is 'expressed;' hence, the divine judgment upon sin. Cp. Rom. ii. 5, θησαυρίζεις σεαυτῷ ὀργὴν ἐν ἡμέρᾳ ὀργῆς καὶ δικαιοκρισίας τοῦ θεοῦ; Rev. xi. 18, ἦλθεν ἡ ὀργή σου; and Luke xxi. 23, ὀργὴ τῷ λαῷ τούτῳ, of the divine judgment in relation to the fall of Jerusalem. ὀργή belongs rather to the O. T. than to the New. It does not occur again in this gospel, and is very rare in the others. But St Paul frequently introduces the conception of ὀργή in illustration of δικαιοσύνη, cp. Rom. i. 17, 18, δικαιοσύνη γὰρ θεοῦ ἀποκαλύπτεται...ἀποκαλύπτεται γὰρ ὀργὴ θεοῦ κ.τ.λ.

For this judicial sense of ὀργή in Classical Greek cp. τὸ τρίτον ὕδωρ ἐγχεῖται τῇ τιμήσει καὶ τῷ μεγέθει τῆς ὀργῆς τῆς ὑμετέρας, Plato *Lys.* XXIII. 4. 8; and Strabo c. 67, 4, ἐλεγχόμενος δ' ὑπὸ τῶν κατηγόρων ἐπὶ τοῦ Ἀντωνίου παρῃτεῖτο τὴν ὀργήν. 'Fleeing from the wrath to come' implies agreeing with God's view of sin and therefore 'repentance' or change of heart.

8. ποιήσατε. Aorist imperative, denoting complete and immediate action. See Donaldson *Gk. Gram.* 427 (a).

μετάνοια. Rare in classical writers, joined by Thuc. with ἀναλογισμός (III. 36). Cp. also μετάνοια δεινὴ τοὺς Ἀθηναίους καὶ πόθος ἔσχε τοῦ Κίμωνος, and Plut. p. 452, ἡ νουθεσία καὶ ὁ ψόγος ἐμποιεῖ μετάνοιαν καὶ αἰσχύνην. The meaning deepens with Christianity. It is not adequately translated by 'repentance.' The marginal reading of A.V. 'amendment of life' is better. It implies that revolution in the religious life which Christianity effected and still effects. It is the starting point in the faith—a rudimentary doctrine: μὴ πάλιν θεμέλιον καταβαλλόμενοι μετανοίας ἀπὸ νεκρῶν ἔργων. Heb. vi. 1. The Vulgate translates μετάνοια 'poenitentia,' Beza's rendering, resipiscentia, raised a stormy controversy. Neither word entirely covers μετάνοια, which implies both sorrow for the past and change of heart.

9. μὴ δόξητε λέγειν, 'do not presume to say.' For this use of δοκεῖν cp. Phil. iii. 4, εἴ τις δοκεῖ ἄλλος πεποιθέναι ἐν σαρκί, ἐγὼ μᾶλλον.

πατέρα ἔχομεν τὸν Ἀβραάμ. The Jewish doctors taught that no one who was circumcised should enter Gehenna.

ἐκ τῶν λίθων. Stones are regarded as the most insensate, the furthest removed from life of created things. May there not be a play on the words *banim* (children) *abanim* (stones)?

10. μὴ ποιοῦν, 'if it bring not forth.'

ἐκκόπτεται, 'is being cut down,' the work has already begun. ἐκκόπτειν, used specially of cutting down trees. Cp. ἔκκοψον αὐτήν, Luke xiii. 7, and πίτυς μούνη πάντων δενδρέων ἐκκοπεῖσα βλαστὸν οὐδένα μετίει, Hdt. VI. 37. ἐκ denotes completion of act.

καρπὸν καλόν. The Oriental values trees only as productive of fruit, all others are cut down as cumberers of the ground. He lays his axe literally at the root. *Land and Book*, p. 341.

11. ἐν ὕδατι. Either (1) 'in water,' the surrounding element is water; or better (2) 'with water,' ἐν being used of the instrument as frequently in Hellenistic Greek. Cp. ἐν μαχαίρᾳ ἀπολοῦνται, ch. xxvi. 52. ἐν τίνι αὐτὸ ἀρτύσετε; Mark ix. 50. And occasionally in the classical period, as ἐν τόμᾳ σιδάρου, Soph. *Tr.* 887, 'by cutting with steel,' and ἐν κερτομίοις γλώσσαις, *Ant.* 961, 'with reviling tongue.' See Campbell's Soph. on the last passage. The best supported reading ὕδατι in the parallel passage, Mark i. 8, is in favour of the instrumental sense here, but the other would not be excluded from the mind of a Greek reader.

εἰς, 'with a view to.' εἰς with a noun = a final sentence. In order that we may live the changed life.

τὰ ὑποδήματα βαστάσαι. The work of the meanest slaves (a pedibus pueri). John, great prophet as he was, with influence sufficient to make even Herod tremble for his throne, is unworthy to be the meanest slave of the Stronger One—the Son of God.

This figure gives to αὐτός its proper force, the 'Master,' in contrast with the slave.

ἐν πνεύματι ἁγίῳ. It must be remembered that the matured Christian conception of the Holy Ghost would not be present to the mind of John. Some of his disciples at Ephesus said to St Paul, 'We have not so much as heard whether there be any Holy Ghost,' Acts xix. 2.

πνεῦμα is the Greek representative of Hebr. *ruach* which meant 'breath' or 'wind.' This then was the earthly likeness or parable by which the thought of the Holy Spirit was brought home to men. In the O.T. πνεῦμα signifies, (1) Breath (2) Wind (3) Spirit or soul —the invisible and immortal part of a man conceived as breathed into him by God, called πνοὴν ζωῆς, Gen. iv. 7. (4) The faculty of thought and volition; this is either (α) evil or (β) good, cp. καὶ πνεῦμα Κυρίου ἀπέστη ἀπὸ Σαούλ, καὶ ἔπνιγεν αὐτὸν πνεῦμα πονηρὸν παρὰ Κυρίου. (5) The highest spiritual intelligence; the faculty of insight. (6) The divine Personal Spirit. Of these meanings classical Greek hardly includes more than (1) and (2), but cp. Soph. *Œd. Col.* 612, where πνεῦμα = 'feeling,' and the beautiful cognate expression ἠνεμόεν φρόνημα, 'wind-swift thought,' *Ant.* 354. In the N.T. the sense of 'wind' has nearly passed away, except in immediate connection with the figurative application, as John iii. 8, τὸ πνεῦμα ὅπου θέλει πνεῖ, κ.τ.λ., but the thought of the wind is never quite lost sight of in the derived meaning, and the verbs used in connection with the various senses of πνεῦμα often recall the original sense of the word; nor could any natural phenomenon more strikingly illustrate the manifestations of the Holy Spirit than the viewless, searching, all-penetrating force of wind, or than the breath of man, which is the essence of life and of speech. In a sense the Holy Spirit not only gives but is the highest life of the soul, and the divine prophetic breath. (Acts iv. 25.)

It may be further noted that as *ruach*, the Hebr. equivalent for πνεῦμα, was the only generic term for 'wind,' the figurative or parabolic sense would be more vividly present to the Jew than to the Greek, whose language possesses other words for 'wind,' e.g. ἄνεμος is often used in the LXX. to translate *ruach* in this sense.

In the Latin '*spiritus*' the thought of 'breathing' would be retained throughout the derived senses, but not that of 'wind.' In English the thought of the Spirit of God and the thought of the movement of air or of breath are kept separate as far as language goes. It is therefore needful to recall the original image. For the literal meaning of a word is often a parable through which the knowledge of the unseen is approached.

πυρί. This metaphor implies: (1) Purification, (2) Fiery zeal or enthusiasm, (3) Enlightenment; all which are gifts of the Holy

Spirit. In the ancient hymn by Robert II. of France the third point is brought out:

> "Et emitte cælitus
> Lucis tuæ radium
> * * * *
> Veni lumen cordium."

12. πτύον, also called λικμός or λίκνον, Lat. *vannus*, was the instrument by which the corn after being threshed was thrown up against the wind to clear it of chaff. Cp. *Il.* XIII. 588—90.

> ὡς δ' ὅτ' ἀπὸ πλατέος πτυόφιν μεγάλην κατ' ἀλωὴν
> θρώσκωσιν κύαμοι μελανόχροες ἢ ἐρέβινθοι
> πνοιῇ ὑπὸ λιγυρῇ καὶ λικμητῆρος ἐρωῇ.

αὐτοῦ...αὐτοῦ...αὐτοῦ. The thrice repeated αὐτοῦ marks forcibly what are Christ's—the hand, the floor, and the corn are His, but the chaff is not His. Cp. a similar prominence given to the sense of possession, Luke xii. 18, 19.

ἅλωνα. (From a root signifying 'whirl,' &c.) 'A threshing-floor,' a broad flat place, usually on a rocky hill-top exposed to the breeze, or in a wind-swept valley. ἅλωνα is here put for the contents of the threshing-floor, the mingled grain and chaff. Observe how the thought of the πνεῦμα ἅγιον and the πῦρ rises again in this verse, a different use being made of the metaphor. It is the divine wind—the Spirit of God that clears the grain ('Thou shalt fan them and the wind shall carry them away.' Isai. xli. 16); and the divine fire that burns the chaff.

The separation by Christ's winnowing fan is sometimes a separation between individuals, sometimes a separation between the good and evil in the heart of a man or in a society or nation.

ἄχυρον. Cp. Aristoph. *Ach.* 471, 472.

> ἀλλ' ἐσμὲν αὐτοὶ νῦν γε περιεπτισμένοι
> τοὺς γὰρ μετοίκους ἄχυρα τῶν ἀστῶν λέγω.

The 'metics' are the worthless 'residuum' of the citizens.

St Matthew represents the picturesque side of John's preaching. These verses are full of imagery, the vipers, the stones, the trees, the slave, the threshing-floor, are all used to illustrate his discourse. St Luke throws into prominence the great teacher's keen discrimination of character. St John has recorded a fragment of the Baptist's deeper teaching as to the nature and mission of the Son of God.

13—17. JESUS COMES TO BE BAPTIZED OF JOHN. Mark i. 9—11; Luke iii. 21, 22; John i. 32—34.

St Luke adds two particulars: that the Holy Spirit descended on Jesus (1) "in a bodily shape," and (2) "while He was praying."

In the fourth Gospel, where John Baptist's own words are quoted, the act of baptism is not named; a touch of the Baptist's characteristic humility.

13. ἐπὶ τὸν Ἰορδάνην. Probably at "Ænon near to Salim" (John

iii. 23), a day's journey from Nazareth, 'close to the passage of the Jordan near Succoth and far away from that near Jericho.' *Sinai and Palestine*, p. 311. Cp. also John i. 28, where the correct reading is: ταῦτα ἐν Βηθανίᾳ ἐγένετο πέραν τοῦ Ἰορδάνου, ὅπου ἦν ὁ Ἰωάννης βαπτίζων. Lt. Conder (*Tent Work in Palestine*, II. 67) states that 'Bathania was the well-known form used in the time of Christ of the old name Bashan.' He adds that the name Abârah is given by the natives to one of the main fords 'where the Jalûd river, flowing down the Valley of Jezreel, and by Beisân (Bethshean) debouches into the Jordan.' This accounts for the reading 'Bethabara,' and probably fixes the site.

τοῦ βαπτισθῆναι. For construction see note, ch. ii. 13. Jesus who is the pattern of the New life submits to the baptism which is a symbol of the New life (μετάνοια). He who has power to forgive sins seems to seek through baptism forgiveness of sins. But in truth by submitting to baptism Jesus shows the true efficacy of the rite. He who is most truly man declares what man may become through baptism—clothed and endued with the Holy Spirit, and touched by the fire of zeal and purity.

There is no hint in the Gospel narrative of that beautiful companionship and intercourse in childhood between Jesus and the Baptist with which Art has familiarised us. See John i. 31, a passage which tends to an opposite conclusion.

14. διεκώλυεν, 'was preventing,' or, 'endeavoured to prevent.'

15. ἀποκριθείς. ἀποκρίνομαι is the Attic word in this sense. (ὑποκρίνοιντο, Thuc. VII. 4, is a possible exception.) ὑποκρίνομαι Homeric and Ionic. Alexandrine Greek here, contrary to the general rule, follows the Attic rather than the Homeric use. ὑποκρίνομαι occurs once only in the N.T. (Luke xx. 20), and there in the sense of 'feigning.' The aor. 1. passive (ἀποκριθείς) in middle sense is late. It occurs in Plato *Alc.* II. 149 B, but the genuineness of that dialogue is doubtful; see Lid. and Scott. The aor. 1. mid. is rare in the N.T. See ch. xxvii. 12.

ἄφες. Sc. ἐμὲ βαπτισθῆναι.

ἡμῖν, *us*. It was the privilege of John to share the work of the Messiah.

δικαιοσύνην. Here = 'the requirements of the law.'

16. οἱ οὐρανοί. A literal translation of the Hebrew word, which is a plural form.

καὶ εἶδεν. We should infer from the text that the vision was to Jesus alone, but the Baptist also was a witness as we learn from John i. 32, "And John bare record, I saw the Spirit descending from heaven like a dove, and it abode upon him." This was to John the sign by which the Messiah should be recognised.

17. φωνὴ ἐκ τῶν οὐρανῶν. Thrice during our Lord's ministry it is recorded that a voice from heaven came to Him. The two other occasions were at the Transfiguration and in the week of the Passion (John xii. 28).

ἀγαπητός, in the Gospels always in reference to Christ the beloved Son of God, (Mark xii. 6 and Luke xx. 13 cannot be regarded as exceptions). In this connection it is closely related to μονογενής, cp. John i. 14—18, iii. 16—18. (ἀγαπητὸς does not occur in the fourth Gospel.) Gen. xxii. 2, λάβε τὸν υἱόν σου τὸν ἀγαπητόν. The Scholiast on *Il.* vi. 401, Ἑκτορίδην ἀγαπητόν, notes the same connection. See Bp Lightfoot on Col. i. 13.

In the Epistles the word is applied to the Christian brotherhood united by the common bond of ἀγάπη.

εὐδοκεῖν. A late word (see Sturz. *de dial. Mac.* 168) not found in the Attic writers, constructed (1) with the infinitive in the sense of 'to be pleased,' i.e. 'to resolve,' εὐδοκοῦμεν μᾶλλον ἐκδημῆσαι, 2 Cor. v. 8; (2) with accusative (see ch. xii. 18), 'to be pleased with,' 'take delight in:' ὁλοκαυτώματα οὐκ εὐδόκησας, Hebr. x. 8; εὐδόκησας, κύριε, τὴν γῆν σου, Ps. lxxxiv. 1; (3) with εἰς and ἐν with the same meaning as (2) or 'to be pleased in,' i.e. to place one's purpose, decision, or resolution in a thing or person. Here the sense is: My Son, the Beloved in whom my pleasure rests, in whom my plan for the salvation of mankind is centred. Cp. Eph. i. 9, γνωρίσας ἡμῖν τὸ μυστήριον τοῦ θελήματος αὐτοῦ κατὰ τὴν εὐδοκίαν αὐτοῦ ἣν προέθετο ἐν αὐτῷ. εὐδοκεῖν answers to εὐδοκίαν προθέσθαι.

CHAPTER IV.

5. ἔστησεν for ἵστησιν with the four oldest uncials and the cursives 1, 33, 209. The reading of the *textus receptus* may be due to the present, παραλαμβάνει.

9. εἶπεν for λέγει with the same weight of authority.

12 and 23. ὁ Ἰησοῦς omitted in v. 12 after ἀκούσας δέ, and by Tischendorf also in v. 23. The instances of this insertion in the text of the N.T. from the margin or from lectionaries are very numerous.

13. Καφαρναούμ. This form is found in ℵBD and versions, on the other side are CEL and the majority of MSS.

16. σκότει, the reading of *textus receptus* retained in preference to σκοτίᾳ. The question of reading is interesting, the great MSS. being divided. ℵ*CEL and the majority of uncials are in favour of σκότει. ℵᵇBD read σκοτίᾳ. Of the leading editors Lachmann and Tregelles (neither of whom had seen ℵ) read σκοτίᾳ, Tischendorf reads σκότει.

1—11. THE TEMPTATION OF JESUS. Mark i. 12, 13; Luke iv. 1—13.

St Mark's account is short; the various temptations are not specified; he adds the striking expression ἦν μετὰ τῶν θηρίων. St Luke places the temptation of the Kingdoms of the World before that of the Pinnacle of the Temple.

Generally it may be remarked that the account can have come from no other than Jesus Himself. The words of the Evangelist describe an actual scene—not a dream. The devil *really* came to Jesus, but in what manner he came is not stated. These were not isolated temptations in the life of Jesus. Cp. Luke xxii. 28, 'Ye are they which have continued with me in my *temptations*.' But they are typical temptations, representative of the various forms of temptation by which human nature can be assailed. For, as it has often been said, the three temptations cover the same ground as 'the lust of the flesh, the lust of the eyes, and the pride of life' (1 John ii. 16) in which St John sums up the evil of the world.

Viewing the temptation in a personal reference to Jesus Christ we discern Him tempted (1) As the Son of man—the representative of humanity—in whom human nature in its perfection triumphs over sin. An important element in the Atonement. (2) As the second Adam regaining for man what the first Adam lost for man. (3) As the Son of Abraham following the fortunes of his race, tempted in the wilderness as the Hebrews were tempted: a thought present implicitly in our Lord's answers. (4) As the true Messiah or Christos rejecting the unreal greatness which was the aim of false Messiahs. He would not win popular enthusiasm by becoming a wonder-working γόης or μάγος greater than Theudas or than Simon Magus, or a prince more powerful than the Maccabees or than Cæsar.

Hence a warning for the Church as a *Missionary* Church. She is tempted to win her conquests by forbidden ways, by lying signs and wonders, by grasping at the dominion of this world, by alliance with the powers of the world, by craft and policy, not by submission and suffering.

The lesson of each and all of the temptations is trust in God and submission to God's will—the result in us of μετάνοια.

1. **τότε**. The εὐθὺς of St Mark i. 12 points still more clearly to the significant nearness of the Temptation to the Baptism.

ἀνήχθη...ὑπὸ τοῦ πνεύματος. The agency of the Spirit of God is named in each of the Synoptists. St Mark uses the strong expression 'the Spirit driveth him forth.' St Luke uses the preposition ἐν (in) denoting the influence in which Jesus passed into the wilderness.

εἰς τὴν ἔρημον. See note on ch. iii. 1, but the locality of the temptation is not known.

The desert as the scene of the temptation has a peculiar significance. It was the waste and waterless tract (ἄνυδροι τόποι, ch. xii. 43) which unpeopled by men was thought to be the abode of demons. So Jesus meets the evil spirit in his own domains, the Stronger One coming upon the strong man who keepeth his palace (Luke xi. 21, 22). The retirement preparatory to the great work may be compared with that of Elijah and of Paul. It is perhaps an invariable experience in deeply religious lives to be taken into the desert of their own hearts and there to meet and resist the temptations that assailed Christ.

πειρασθῆναι. The final infinitive is very usual with St Matthew. In the other Synoptic Gospels the purpose is not expressly noted.

τοῦ διαβόλου. The Hebrew word 'Satan' of which διάβολος is a rendering means 'one who meets or opposes,' 'an adversary.' διάβολος had originally the same meaning. Thus διαβάλλειν in the LXX. = 'to meet,' cp. Numbers xxii. 22 and 32, ἀνέστη ὁ ἄγγελος τοῦ θεοῦ διαβαλεῖν αὐτόν, and ἰδοὺ ἐγὼ ἐξῆλθον εἰς διαβολήν σου.

To this original meaning of διάβολος the classical force of διαβάλλειν and its derivatives added the ideas of (1) deceiving, (2) calumniating, (3) accusing. In Rev. xx. 2, we find both the Greek and Hebrew forms—ὅς ἐστιν διάβολος καὶ Σατανᾶς—a proof that the meanings of the two words, synonymous at first, had already been severed, and one among many instances of the influence of translation on religious ideas.

2. **ὕστερον ἐπείνασεν.** The words imply that the particular temptations named were offered at the end of the forty days during which he had fasted. But the parallel accounts represent the temptation as enduring throughout the whole period: ἦν ἐν τῇ ἐρήμῳ...πειραζόμενος (Mark); ἤγετο ἐν τῇ ἐρήμῳ πειραζόμενος (Luke).

So far as fasting rests on the facts of human nature it may be regarded as (1) a result of sorrow, (a) either the natural sorrow for the loss of those we love, or (β) sorrow for sin—contrition. (2) The effect of deep absorption. (3) A means to secure self-mastery and a test of it. Such signs and natural uses of it are deepened and sanctified by the example of Christ.

3. **ἵνα οἱ λίθοι οὗτοι ἄρτοι γένωνται.** The temptation is addressed to the appetite, Use thy divine power to satisfy the desire of the flesh. The very discipline by which He fortified his human soul against temptation is sought to be made an inlet to temptation—a frequent incident in religious experience.

4. **γέγραπται.** See note ch. ii. 5. Jesus answers by a quotation from Deut. viii. 3. The chapter sets forth the teaching of the wilderness. The forty years were to the Jews what the forty days are to Jesus. The Lord God proved Israel 'to know what was in thine heart, whether thou wouldest keep his commandments or no. And he humbled thee and suffered thee to hunger, and fed thee with manna...that he might make thee know that man doth not live by bread only, but by every [word, omitted in Hebr.] that proceedeth out of the mouth of the Lord doth man live.'

Christ's test of sonship is obedience and entire trust in God who alone is the giver of every good gift. The devil's test of sonship is supply of bodily wants, external prosperity, &c.

5. **ἁγίαν πόλιν.** This designation used of the actual Jerusalem by St Matthew alone is transferred to the heavenly Jerusalem, Rev. xi. 2, xxi. 2, xxii. 19.

τὸ πτερύγιον. Not as in A.V. 'a pinnacle,' but either (1) 'the pinnacle,' or winglike projection (πτερύγιον = 'a little wing'), i.e. some well-known pinnacle of the Temple, probably on one of the lofty porticoes overlooking the deep Valley of Kidron or Hinnom; or (2) 'the roof' of the Temple or one of the porticoes—a sense which πτερὸν bears in the classics; cp. Scholiast on Aristoph. *Aves* 1110. διὰ τὰ ἐν τοῖς ναοῖς ἀετώματα—τὰς γὰρ τῶν ἱερῶν στέγας πτερὰ καὶ ἀετοὺς καλοῦσιν. πτερύγιον itself does not appear to be classical in this sense. Eus. *H. E.* II. 23 names in the same definite way τὸ πτερ. τοῦ ἱεροῦ.

6. βάλε σεαυτὸν κάτω. The depth was immense: Josephus speaking of the 'Royal Porch' (στοὰ βασιλική) says 'if anyone looked down from the top of the battlements he would be giddy, while his sight could not reach to such an immense depth.' *Antiq.* xv. 11. 5.

γέγραπται. Ps. xci. [xc. LXX.] 11, 12. The quotation follows the LXX. version, but the words τοῦ διαφυλάξαι σε ἐν πάσαις ταῖς ὁδοῖς σου are omitted in the text. The omission distorts the meaning of the original, which is that God will keep the righteous on their journeys. No inducement is offered by them to tempt God by rash venture or needless risk. The Psalmist himself probably quotes Prov. iii. 23. 'Thus [i.e. by obedience: see preceding verses] shalt thou walk in thy way safely, and thy foot shall not stumble.'

7. οὐκ ἐκπειράσεις κύριον τὸν θεόν σου. Deut. vi. 16. The verse ends 'as ye tempted him in Massah.' The reference to Massah (Numb. xx. 7—12) shows the true meaning of the Saviour's answer. Moses and Aaron displayed distrust in God when they tried to draw to themselves the glory of the miracle instead of 'sanctifying the Lord.' Jesus will not glorify Himself in the eyes of the Jews by a conspicuous miracle. His work as the Son of Man is to glorify the Father's name through obedience. Cp. John xii. 28.

8. εἰς ὄρος ὑψηλὸν λίαν. It is idle to ask what this mountain was, or in what sense Jesus saw the kingdoms of the world. It is enough that the thought and the temptation of earthly despotism and glory were present to the mind of Jesus. The Galilæans put the same temptation to Jesus when they wished to make Him a king (John vi. 15), and even the disciples shared the hope of an earthly Messianic kingdom. The picture of the expected Deliverer was drawn by the popular imagination from the memory of the Maccabees or from the actual power of Cæsar, and this was the thought which the tempter presented to Christ.

9. ταῦτά σοι πάντα δώσω. Satan, the 'prince of this world' (John xii. 31), claims the disposal of earthly thrones. This is more clearly brought out by St Luke (ch. iv. 6), 'All this power will I give thee and the glory of them, for that is delivered unto me, and to whomsoever I will I give it.' The arrogance, selfishness and cruelty of contemporary rulers would give force to such an assumption. A Tiberius or a Herod Antipas might indeed be thought to have worshipped Satan.

ἐὰν πεσὼν προσκυνήσῃς μοι, i.e. acknowledge as sovereign, as the lesser kings acknowledged Cæsar: jus imperiumque Phraates | Cæsaris accepit *genibus minor*. Hor. *Ep.* I. 12. 27.

10. ὕπαγε σατανᾶ. It is instructive to find these words addressed to Peter (ch. xvi. 23) when he put himself as it were in the place of the tempter. See note *ad loc.*

In Homer ὑπάγειν is used of bringing cattle under the yoke, ὕπαγε ζύγον ὤκεας ἵππους, a force which some have given to the word in this passage 'bow thyself to the yoke of God;' against this is the early gloss ὀπίσω μου found in some MSS., and the entirely prevalent use of the verb in other passages.

καὶ αὐτῷ μόνῳ λατρεύσεις. Deut. vi. 10—13. Idolatry, multiplicity of aims, and forgetfulness of God are the dangers of prosperity and ambition. See context of passage in Deut.

11. διηκόνουν, from διακονέω. The Attic form of the imperfect is ἐδιακόνουν; but διηκόνουν is possibly a right reading, Eur. *Cycl.* 406. διακονεῖν is strictly to 'serve at table,' 'minister food,' hence the appropriateness of the word in its use, Acts vi. 2.

12—16. JESUS RETURNS INTO GALILEE.

Mark i. 14; Luke iv. 14, who assigns no reason; John iv. 1—3. St John gives a further reason 'when the Lord knew how the Pharisees had heard that Jesus made and baptized more disciples than John, he left Judæa,' &c.

12. ἀκούσας δέ, 'having heard,' not only *when* but also *because* He heard. It was a needful precaution against the cruel treachery of Herod Antipas. At Capernaum He would be close to the dominions of Herod Philip.

παρεδόθη. παραδιδόναι is used of 'delivering' to death (Acts iii. 13), to a judge (ch. v. 25), or of casting into prison (Luke xii. 58 τῷ πράκτορι; Acts viii. 3 and here); but it is possible that the idea of treachery and betrayal may also be present as in ch. x. 4, xxvii. 3, 4; 1 Cor. xi. 23.

The place of imprisonment was Machærus. The cause of John's imprisonment is stated at length ch. xiv. 3, 4 (where see note) and Luke iii. 19, 20.

On hearing of the *death* of John the Baptist Jesus retired into the wilderness. See ch. xiv. 13.

ἀνεχώρησεν εἰς τὴν Γαλιλαίαν. By the shortest route through Samaria. John iv. 4. During this journey must be placed the conversation with the woman of Samaria. This was after a ministry in Judæa, which had lasted eight months (Ellicott, *Lectures on the life of our Lord*, p. 130), some incidents of which are related by St John, ii. and iii.

Γαλιλαία = a circle or circuit, originally confined to a 'circle' of 20 cities given by Solomon to Hiram, 1 Kings ix. 11. Cp. Josh. xx. 7 and Josh. viii. 2 (where the Vulgate reads Galilæa Philistim 'the circle' or 'district' of the Philistines). From this small beginning the name spread to a larger district, just as the name of Asia spread from a district near the Mæander, first to the Roman Province, then to a quarter of the Globe. The Jews were in a minority in those parts. The population mainly consisted of Phœnicians, Arabs, and Greeks.

13. καταλιπὼν τὴν Ναζαρά. Partly because of the unbelief of the Nazarenes, partly (we may infer) in order to be in a frontier town from which He might easily pass from the jurisdiction of Antipas.

Καφαρναούμ, a town on the N.W. shore of the Sea of Galilee. It was the scene of a considerable traffic, and had a large Gentile element in its population. The exact site is keenly disputed. It was, perhaps, at Khan Minyeh (see map), not quite on the sea, but on the plain of Gennesaret, at a short distance from the sea.

Others, with greater probability, identify Capernaum with the modern Tell Hûm, at the N. end of the Lake in the plain of the Jordan. The name Tell Hûm nearly corresponds with Kefr na Hum, thought by some to have been the ancient form of Capernaum. The most interesting point in the identification is that among the ruins at Tell Hûm are remains of a synagogue, in which some of the Saviour's 'mighty works' may have been wrought. See map.

Whatever the truth may be in this question it is certain that in passing from Nazareth to Capernaum Jesus left a retired mountain home for a busy and populous neighbourhood, 'the manufacturing district of Palestine.'

14. διὰ Ἡσαΐου. Read the whole of the prophecy (Is. viii. 11—ix. 6) which is unfortunately broken in the E.V. by the division into chapters, and is more mistranslated than any other passage of like importance.

15. Γαλιλαία τῶν ἐθνῶν. See above, v. 12.

ὁδὸν θαλάσσης. The accusative may be explained either by the regimen of the omitted Hebrew words or by taking ὁδὸν as an adverbial accusative influenced by a similar use of the Hebrew *derech*.

The immediate historical reference of the prophecy was to the invasion of Tiglathpileser, whom Ahaz called in to assist him against Rezin and Pekah. It fell with great severity on the northern tribes (2 Kings xv. 29). Yet even they are promised a great deliverance ['As in the former time, he brought into contempt the land of Zebulun and the land of Naphtali, so in the latter time he hath made it glorious,' Is. ix. 1], in the first instance, by the destruction of Sennacherib, from temporal distress (cp. Is. chs. x. and xi. with ch. ix. 1—6); secondly, by the advent of the Messiah, from spiritual darkness.

16. ὁ λαὸς ὁ καθήμενος, κ.τ.λ. The quotation nearly follows the Hebrew of Isaiah ix. 1, 2 (two lines of the original being omitted). The LXX. presents a wide difference in form.

The repeated καθήμενος...καθημένοις of the text represents two distinct Hebrew words, the first signifying literally 'walking.' The parallelism suffers by the Greek translation, 'to sit' being an advance on 'to walk,' as implying a more settled condition. Cp. Ps. i. 1, 'walked...stood...sat.' In like manner σκιὰ θανάτου is an advance on σκότος, and φῶς ἀνέτειλεν αὐτοῖς implies a great deal more than φῶς εἶδεν μέγα.

17—22. THE CALL OF PETER AND ANDREW AND OF THE SONS OF ZEBEDEE. See Mark i. 16—20.

In Luke, Simon is mentioned without any introduction, ch. iv. 38. The narrative of Luke v. 3—11 must be referred to a different occasion, though v. 11 corresponds with v. 22 of this chapter. St Luke adds that the sons of Zebedee were partners with Simon. John i. 35—42 refers to a previous summons. We learn there that Andrew was a disciple of John the Baptist, and that Bethsaida was the city of Andrew and Peter.

17. ἀπὸ τότε, for classical ἐξ ἐκείνου [χρόνου].

For μετάνοια and βασιλεία, which are the key-notes of our Saviour's preaching, see note, ch. iii. 2.

18. ἀμφίβληστρον, 'a casting-net,' here only in N.T. (in Mark i. 16 the true reading is ἀμφιβάλλοντας ἐν τῇ θαλάσσῃ). The word occurs Herod. I. 141. Cp. Soph. *Antig.* 343, κουφονόων τε φῦλον ὀρνίθων ἀμφιβαλὼν ἄγει...πόντου τ' εἰναλίαν φύσιν. Virgil alludes to the same kind of net, *Georg.* I. 141. Alius latum *funda* jam verberat amnem.

ἦσαν γὰρ ἁλιεῖς. The fisheries on the Sea of Galilee, once so productive, are now deserted. It seems that the Bedawin have an invincible dislike and dread of the sea. Consequently there is scarcely a boat to be seen, and the Lake yields no harvest. See *Land and Book*, 401.

ἁλιεῖς, lit. 'sea-folk' (ἅλς), Homeric but not in Attic writers, one of the many words that disappear from literature in the long interval between Homer and the Alexandrine epoch.

ἁλιέων βίος is quoted as a proverbial expression for a life of extreme poverty. (See Wetstein.) Such it undoubtedly was in general, but see below, v. 22. No fitter training than that of the fisherman could be imagined for the perils and privations of the apostle's life.

19. δεῦτε. Frequent in Homer and in lyric poets. It was used as an 'animating interjection' (Buttmann), without any necessary connection with movement, as ἔρως με δεῦτε Κύπριδος ἔκατι | γλυκὺς κατείβων καρδίαν ἰαίνει. Alcman. (Buttmann, *Lex.* 316—319.) This word is an instance of epic influence on Alexandrine Greek as it is not Attic: in N.T. it is rare except in this Gospel.

ἁλιεῖς ἀνθρώπων. A condensed parable explicitly drawn out, ch. xiii. 47—50. Cp. Jer. xvi. 16, ἰδοὺ ἐγὼ ἀποστέλλω τοὺς ἁλιεῖς τοὺς πολλούς, λέγει κύριος, καὶ ἁλιεύσουσιν αὐτούς.

22. καὶ τὸν πατέρα. St Mark (i. 20) adds 'with the hired servants.' We may infer that Zebedee and his sons and their partners were raised above the lowest social rank.

Two modernisms may be noticed in this verse, ἀφέντες preferred in Hellenistic Greek to λείπω and compounds of λείπω: and ἀκολουθεῖν used in the N.T. to the exclusion of ἕπεσθαι which does not occur (the compound συνέπεσθαι is found in one passage, Acts xx. 4).

23—25. JESUS PREACHES THE GOSPEL AND CURES DISEASES IN GALILEE.

Special instances of cure are recorded in Mark i. 13 and foll.; Luke v. 31 and foll.

23. ἐν ταῖς συναγωγαῖς. The synagogue, built on a hill or on the highest place in the city, distinguished sometimes by a tall pole corresponding to a modern steeple, was as familiar and conspicuous in a Jewish town as the Church is in an English village. Sometimes, however, the synagogue was placed on the bank of a river. Sometimes it was constructed without a roof and open to the sky.

1. Divine service was held in the synagogue on the Sabbath and also on the second and fifth day of each week.

2. The service consisted in reading the Law and the Prophets by those who were called upon by the 'Angel of the Church,' and in prayers offered up by the minister for the people; the people responding 'Amen' as with us.

3. But the synagogues were not churches alone. Like Turkish mosques they were also Courts of Law in which the sentence was not only pronounced but executed, 'they shall scourge you in their synagogues.' Further, the synagogues were Public Schools, 'the boys that were scholars were wont to be instructed before their masters in the synagogue' (Talmud). Lastly, the synagogues were the Divinity Schools or Theological Colleges among the Jews.

4. The affairs of the synagogue were administered by ten men, of whom three, called 'Rulers of the Synagogue,' acted as judges, admitted proselytes and performed other important functions. A fourth was termed the 'Angel of the Church' or bishop of the congregation; three others were deacons or almoners. An eighth acted as 'interpreter,' rendering the Hebrew into the vernacular; the ninth was the master of the Divinity School, the tenth his interpreter; see ch. x. 27.

It is interesting to trace in the arrangements of the synagogue the germs of the organization of the Christian Church. This note is chiefly due to Lightfoot *Hor. Hebr.* ad loc.

αὐτῶν. Often used of the Jews without any definite antecedent, cp. οἱ γραμματεῖς αὐτῶν. Luke v. 30.

νόσον...μαλακίαν. Probably to be distinguished as 'acute' and 'chronic' diseases, μαλακίαν implying general prostration of the bodily powers. It is not classical in this sense. The word is confined to St Matthew in N.T.

ἐν τῷ λαῷ, i.e. among the Jews.

24. εἰς ὅλην τὴν Συρίαν. The fame passes to the north and east, rather than to the south. Galilee is connected by trade and affinity with Damascus rather than with Jerusalem.

βασάνοις...συνεχομένους. βάσανος is (1) a 'touch-stone,' the lapis Lydius by which the quality of gold and other metals was tested,

The process is alluded to Herod. VII. 10. Cp. also Theognis 417, ἐς βάσανον δ' ἐλθὼν παρατρίβομαι ὥστε μολίβδῳ | χρυσός. (2) Then 'torture' the touch-stone of justice, because no testimony was believed unless elicited by this means, comp. the same sequence of thought in the expression 'to put to the question.' (3) Hence a disease that racks and agonizes the limbs like the torture which many a poor Galilæan had experienced in the courts of law.

For the question of 'demoniacal possession' see ch. vii. 22.

συνέχειν is used specially of the pressure and constraint of disease and pain; cp. Luke iv. 38, συνεχομένη πυρετῷ μεγάλῳ.

σεληνιαζομένους, 'affected by the moon;' the changes of the moon being thought to influence mad persons. The passage is important as distinguishing demoniacal possession from lunacy.

The only special instance of curing a lunatic is recorded in ch. xvii. 14—21 and in the parallel passages, where the symptoms described are those of epilepsy. The origin of mental disease may often be traced to licentious living. Observe the frequent instances of unclean spirits met with in these districts.

The Christian Church has followed her divine Founder's example in this tendance of bodily ailment. The founding of hospitals and the care of the sick are distinguishing features of Christianity and among the most blessed fruits of it. A deeper respect for life and a deeper sense of purity have followed as necessary consequences.

It is contended by some that the 'several house' of 2 Chron. xxvi. 21 was a hospital. Possibly this was so, but the spirit of Judaism in this respect was not the spirit of Christianity. It may readily be acknowledged, however, that the Jews of the present day are the foremost in works of charity and tender regard for the sick.

25. Δεκάπολις, a group of ten cities. The cities included in this group are variously named by different authors, they lay to the E. and S. of the Sea of Galilee; by some Damascus is mentioned as belonging to the group. See map.

For the form of the word cp. Herod. I. 144, καθάπερ οἱ ἐκ τῆς Πενταπόλιος νῦν χώρης Δωριέες, πρότερον δὲ Ἑξαπόλιος τῆς αὐτῆς ταύτης καλεομένης.

CHAPTER V.

In this and the two following chapters the textual criticism rises to higher importance; the precise words spoken by our Lord being in question.

4, 5. These verses are transposed by the leading critics following Origen, Eusebius and other fathers, but not on the very highest MS. authority, viz. D. 33 and some versions. On the effect of this change see notes.

22. The insertion of εἰκῇ after αὐτοῦ dates from very ancient MSS., but ℵ and B omit, also Vulgate and Æth. Verss. and Origen twice. The feeling which prompted its insertion as a marginal note would tend to retain it in the text.

27. The reading of τοῖς ἀρχαίοις after ἐρρέθη is due to the tendency to introduce uniformity of structure; other instances of the same kind in this chapter are ὃς ἂν ἀπολύσῃ for πᾶς ὁ ἀπολύων v. 32, βληθῇ εἰς γέενναν for ἀπέλθῃ εἰς γέενναν v. 31, to agree with previous verse.

28. In αὐτῆς read for αὐτὴν we trace the probably unconscious emendation of a scholar.

32. μοιχευθῆναι for μοιχᾶσθαι. The change to the passive is supported by ℵ B D and approves itself as the truer to fact, but perhaps for that very reason is open to some suspicion.

44. Here we miss the beautiful words undoubtedly spoken by Christ but omitted in this passage by ℵ B and many of the fathers and versions, εὐλογεῖτε τοὺς καταρωμένους ὑμᾶς καλῶς ποιεῖτε τοὺς μισοῦντας ὑμᾶς. After προσεύχεσθε ὑπὲρ τῶν the *textus receptus* has ἐπηρεαζόντων ὑμᾶς καί, the evidence is especially weighty against the three last words. The passage is probably an insertion borrowed from Luke vi. 27, 28.

47. ἐθνικοὶ for τελῶναι of the *textus receptus*, on the highest authority.

Chs. V.—VII. Sermon on the Mount.

It is instructive to find the Sermon on the Mount following close upon the works of mercy which would open men's hearts to receive the Saviour's words. It is a discourse about the changed life or μετάνοια, showing its conditions; and about the Kingdom or βασιλεία showing its nature, legislation, and privileges.

The description of the Kingdom here given may be compared with the thoughts suggested by Satan in the Temptation. Jesus makes no promise to conquer the world, or to dazzle men by a display of power, or to satisfy bodily wants, making poverty cease.

In regard to *heathenism* the sermon is a contrast, in regard to the *Jewish Law* it is a sublime fulfilment. Again, instead of curses there are blessings, instead of penalties, reward.

Two questions are raised in regard to the Sermon on the Mount. (1) Is it a connected discourse, and not merely a collection of our Lord's sayings? (2) Is it to be identified with the Sermon on the Plain, Luke vi. 17—49?

The first of these questions may without doubt be answered in the affirmative, the second with less certainty. 1. (*a*) This is the most natural inference from the Evangelist's words and from the manner in which the discourse is introduced. (*b*) An analysis points to a close connection of thought and to a systematic arrangement of the different sections of the Sermon. It is true that some of the sayings are found in a different connection in St Luke's Gospel, but it is more than probable that our Lord repeated portions of His teaching on various occasions. 2. In favour of the identity of the two discourses it may be noted that: (*a*) The beginning and end are identical as well as much of the intervening matter. (*b*) The portions omitted—a comparison between the old and the new legislation—are such as would be less adapted for St Luke's readers than for St Matthew's. On the other hand it is urged that (a) St Matthew describes the sermon as being delivered on the mountain (ἀνέβη εἰς τὸ ὄρος) while St Luke's words are ἔστη ἐπὶ τόπου πεδινοῦ. But the 'mount' and the 'plain' are not necessarily distinct localities. The τόπος πεδινὸς was probably a platform on the high land. Summoque in vertice montis | planities ignota jacet tutique receptus. Verg. Æn. XI. 526. (β) The place in the order of events differs in St Luke. But it is probable that here as well as elsewhere St Matthew does not observe the order of time.

Here the question of time is important as bearing on a further question, whether Matthew was himself among the audience. Was the Sermon delivered after the call of the twelve (Luke) or before (Matthew)?

The following analysis may be of use in shewing the connection.

A. The Subjects of the Kingdom, v. 3—16.
    (1) Their character and privileges, v. 3—12.
    (2) Their responsibility, v. 13—16.

B. The Kingdom of Heaven in relation (1) to the Law, v. 17—48; and (2) to Pharisaic rules, vi. 1—34.

(1) It is the highest fulfilment of the law in regard to (a) The Decalogue, v. 21—37. (b) The law of Retaliation, 38—42. (c) Love or Charity, 43—48.

(2) It exceeds the righteousness of the Pharisees in regard to (a) Almsgiving, vi. 1—4; (b) Prayer, vi. 5—15; (c) Fasting, vi. 16—18; (d) Earthly possessions and daily cares, vi. 19—34.

C. Characteristics of the Kingdom, vii. 1—27. (a) Judgment on others, vii. 1—6. (b) The Father's love for the Children of the Kingdom, 7—12. (c) The narrow entrance therein, 13, 14. (d) The danger of false guides to the narrow entrance, and the test of the true, 15—23. (e) A description of the true subjects of the Kingdom, as distinguished from the false, 24—27.

ὄχλους. The plural indicates either (1) the separate groups of listeners; or (2) the people the several units of which the whole was composed. This use of the plural to signify the parts which together form the whole may be illustrated by εὔνοιαι 'marks of favour,' μανίαι 'fits of madness,' (Clyde, *Gk. Synt.* § 10); and by *ars* 'art,' *artes* 'works of art,' *regnum* 'kingdom,' *regna* 'royal prerogatives.'

τὸ ὄρος, 'the mountain', the high land bordering on the Lake, behind Tell Hûm or Ain et Tâbigah, which the inhabitants of those places would naturally call 'the mountain' (see map). It was the Sinai of the New Law. Cp. Ps. lxxii. 3.

καθίσαντος αὐτοῦ. The usual position of a Jewish teacher. In the Talmud 'to sit' is nearly synonymous with 'to teach.'

Christ is not preaching a sermon or heralding the Gospel as in ch. iv. 23. 'The Sermon on the Mount' is more properly the 'New

Law.' Therefore he does not stand like a modern or mediæval preacher as often represented, but sits like an Oriental monarch or teacher. The difference seems slight, but in the Ceremonial East it would mean a great deal.

In Mediæval art the Sermon on the Mount is an illustration of 'Practical Theology.' (See Ruskin, *Mornings in Florence*, v. 145.)

προσῆλθαν. This aoristic form, of which ἔλαβα, ἔφαγα, ἔπεσα are examples, is rightly restored on the highest MS. authority in many passages. Sturz (*Dial. Mac. et Alex.* § 9) regards it as a Cilician form—a point of some interest in relation to St Paul's Greek.

The *anacoluthon* καθίσαντος αὐτοῦ......προσῆλθαν αὐτῷ is frequent in the N.T. and not very uncommon in the Classics, cp. εἰκὸς γὰρ ὀργὰς θῆλυ ποιεῖσθαι γένος, | γάμους παρεμπολῶντος ἀλλοίους πόσει. Eur. *Med.* 909. ὕπεστί μοι θράσος, | ἀδυπνόων κλύουσαν | ἀρτίως ὀνειράτων. Soph. *El.* 479. See also Æsch. *Suppl.* 437.

A. The Subjects of the Kingdom, v. 3—16.

(1) Their character and privileges, v. 3—12.

3—9. The transposition of verses 4 and 5 to their order in the text is on the authority of the leading textual critics without however conclusive MS. support. The logical gradation of thought is in favour of the change. Of the 'Beatitudes'—so called from the opening word 'beati' in the Vulgate—the first seven may be regarded as groups of characters, or as a scheme of Christian ethics on an ascending scale, tracing the Christian growth step by step; the two last have special reference to the disciples—they supply the tests and the hopes of discipleship.

The subjoined scheme is suggested in explanation of the order.

The quest for Righteousness	{ πτωχοὶ τῷ πνεύματι πραεῖς }	Passive qualities or conditions of the Soul.
	{ πενθοῦντες πεινῶντες καὶ διψῶντες τ.δ. }	Movement of the Soul from Sin to Righteousness.
The Attainment	ἐλεήμονες	Practical action.
The Christian Life	καθαροὶ τῇ καρδίᾳ	The inner principle.
	εἰρηνοποιοί	Spiritual energy.

First, two passive qualities 'lowliness and meekness,' which mark the character receptive of Christianity, then two activities or movements of the soul; 'mourning,' which alienates it from earth, tending 'to loose the chain | that binds us to a world of pain.' Then divine 'hungering and thirsting' which draw it to heaven. This fourth Beatitude is the central point: δικαιοσύνη is the coping-stone of the soul seeking God, the foundation of the soul which has found Him. Three graces of the Christian life follow, 'mercy,' the first-fruits of righteousness, (see the close connection between the two ch. vi. 1 and comp. the fruits of righteousness in the judgment-scene ch. xxv.,) 'purity of heart,' the soul cleansed from all defilement sees God, and 'peace-making', wherein the soul that has seen God imitates the work of God—reconciliation.

πτωχοὶ τῷ πνεύματι. St Luke omits τῷ πνεύματι, showing that the literal poor are primarily meant, St Matthew shows that they are not exclusively meant. The πτωχοί (nearly i.q. ταπεινοί) are opposed to the spiritually proud and the self-sufficient; they have need of the riches of Christ and feel their need. To reckon ταπεινότης or ταπεινοφροσύνη as a virtue is a Christian thought and opposed to heathen ethics, τίς θέλει ζῆν ταπεινός; Epict. Dissert. IV. 1. 2.

αὐτῶν ἐστὶν ἡ βασιλεία. By a kind of divine irony the unsought reward is the most diverse from the character that wins it: the least ambitious shall have the prize of the most ambitious.

4. πραότης, as an ethical term, is concerned with anger, it means absence from resentment, meekness in suffering; it is mentioned with very faint praise by Aristotle who says, ἐπὶ τὸν μέσον τὴν πραότητα φέρομεν πρὸς τὴν ἔλλειψιν ἀποκλίνουσαν, and again, εἴπερ δὴ ἡ πραότης ἐπαινεῖται, Eth. Nic. IV. 5. 1—3. In the Christian scheme πραότης is the root of ἀγάπη, absence of resentment grows into perfect love through ἐπιείκεια. Jesus who was πραΰς loved (ἠγάπησεν) his enemies.

κληρονομήσουσιν τὴν γῆν. Ps. xxxvii. 11. In a literal sense the meek have inherited the earth. History has no example of higher exaltation than that of the Apostles, and the code which they promulgated rules the world. To this thought may possibly be referred, 1 Cor. vi. 2, οὐκ οἴδατε ὅτι οἱ ἅγιοι τὸν κόσμον κρινοῦσιν;

5. οἱ πενθοῦντες. Those who mourn for sin are primarily intended, but the secondary meaning of 'all who are sorrowful' is not excluded. Sorrow is in itself neutral, cp. 2 Cor. vii. 9, νῦν χαίρω οὐχ ὅτι ἐλυπήθητε ἀλλ' ὅτι ἐλυπήθητε εἰς μετάνοιαν.

παρακληθήσονται. The supreme παράκλησις is Christ.

6. αὐτοί, they in their turn.

χορτασθήσονται. χορτάζειν is one of those words strong and even coarse in their origin which came to be used by the Jews at Alexandria with a softened and more refined meaning. It is properly used of cattle 'to feed,' βοσκημάτων δίκην...βόσκονται χορταζόμενοι, Plato, Rep. 586, then in mid. voice in comedy of men 'to eat'; cp. German *fressen* and see Thuc. VII. 48 and Arnold's note there on βόσκονται. In late Greek as here χορτάζειν = 'to satisfy' for the classical κορεννύναι. It is curious to note how completely the distinction between χορτάζεσθαι and ἐσθίειν has vanished. In Mark vii. 27, 28 both verbs are used, but their proper application is reversed, ἐσθίειν being used of the κυνάρια, and χορτάζεσθαι of the τέκνα.

7. ἐλεήμονες. With the Stoics ἔλεος was reckoned among the defects or vices, it was a disturbing element that broke in upon the philosophic calm, cp. the following passage which gives the Stoic view of most of the moral ideas of the Beatitudes: ὁ ἀπειθῶν τῇ θείᾳ διοικήσει ἔστω ταπεινός, ἔστω δοῦλος, λυπείσθω, φθονείτω, ἐλεείτω· τὸ κεφάλαιον πάντων δυστυχείτω, θρηνείτω. Epict. Diss. III. 24. 43.

ἐλεηθήσονται. This principle in the divine government that men shall be dealt with as they deal with their fellow-men is taught in the parable of the Unmerciful Servant, ch. xviii., and underlies the fifth petition in the Lord's Prayer, ch. vi. 12.

8. καθαροὶ τῇ καρδίᾳ. Purity is a distinguishing virtue of Christianity. It finds no place even in the teaching of Socrates, or in the system of Aristotle. Pure *in heart* 'non sufficit puritas ceremonialis,' Bengel.

τὸν θεὸν ὄψονται. The Christian education is a gradual unveiling of God (ἀποκάλυψις), all have glimpses of Him, to the pure He appears quite plainly; cp. Heb. xii. 14, τὸν ἁγιασμὸν οὗ χωρὶς οὐδεὶς ὄψεται τὸν κύριον, and see 1 John iii. 2, 3. In a further sense the unveiled sight of God is reserved for the Eternal life.

9. εἰρηνοποιοί, this is the highest energy of the perfected soul that has seen God, has had the deepest insight into the divine nature and is thereby moved to do a divine work. εἰρήνη in its lower sense is the absence of dissension or difference between men, in a higher sense it is reconciliation of man with God—the peace made by Christ.

εἰρηνοποιὸς does not occur elsewhere in N.T., but εἰρηνοποιεῖν is used Col. i. 20 in the latter sense, cp. also Ephes. ii. 15, αὐτὸς γάρ ἐστιν ἡ εἰρήνη ἡμῶν ὁ ποιήσας τὰ ἀμφότερα ἐν...τὴν ἔχθραν...καταργήσας ἵνα τοὺς δύο κτίσῃ ἐν ἑαυτῷ εἰς ἕνα καινὸν ἄνθρωπον.

υἱοὶ θεοῦ. These are most akin to the divine nature, perfect as their Father which is in heaven is perfect, *v.* 48, cp. 1 John iii. 1, ἴδετε ποταπὴν ἀγάπην δέδωκεν ἡμῖν ὁ πατὴρ ἵνα τέκνα θεοῦ κληθῶμεν, καὶ ἐσμέν.

κληθήσονται. καλεῖσθαι is not merely equivalent to the substantive verb, but implies (1) prestige, as ὁ πᾶσι κλεινὸς Οἰδίπους καλούμενος, Soph. *Œd. R.* 8. (2) permanence in a class, τάδε γὰρ ἄλυτα κεκλήσεται, Soph. *El.* 230. See Jebb on the last passage and Ellendt's *Lex.* sub. voc. (3) recognition by others, cp. Luke i. 76. Rom. ix. 26. James ii. 23.

10. οἱ δεδιωγμένοι. 'Those who have been persecuted,' not as in A.V. 'they which are persecuted'. The tense brings the past action into close relation with the present, and implies either (1) generally Blessed are the prophets and other servants of God, who in all past time have been persecuted, i. e. the results of persecution are good, or persecution is a test of good: or (2) specially and with direct reference to the present hour, Blessed are my followers who have already suffered such persecution for my sake as is indicated in *v.* 11, see next note. According to the second view (2) Jesus after enumerating the excellencies of the kingdom of God turns to His own followers, comforting them with the thought that their very troubles have already given them a claim to the title of 'Blessed.'

The turn to the passive is very beautiful in this connection, the quality itself is veiled but the result is given; not blessed are the δίκαιοι, but blessed are those that have been persecuted ἕνεκεν δικαιοσύνης. Persecution is the seal of perfect δικαιοσύνη.

11. The nature of the persecution is indicated in this verse; not torture, imprisonment, and death, but reproach and calumny, precisely the form of persecution to which the disciples must have been now subjected.

12. ἀγαλλιᾶσθε, of excessive and demonstrative joy. Neither the verb nor its derivatives are classical. St Luke in his parallel passage (vi. 23), has χάρητε ἐν ἐκείνῃ τῇ ἡμέρᾳ καὶ σκιρτήσατε.

Such contrasts as this which the kingdom of heaven presents have their counterpart in the εἰρωνεία of Greek tragedy.

τοὺς προφήτας τοὺς πρὸ ὑμῶν. Implying that the disciples too were προφῆται.

(2) *Their responsibility*, v. 13—16

The disciples, though lowly and meek, are heirs of the world. They must claim their inheritance, and not shrink from a foremost position either from fear of persecution or from a false idea of Christian πτωχεία and ταπεινότης.

13. τὸ ἅλας τῆς γῆς. Salt (1) preserves from corruption; (2) gives taste to all that is insipid; (3) is essential to all organised life. So the Apostles alone can save the world from corruption; the gospel alone can give zest and meaning to society; it is essential to the life of the world.

ἅλας. Late as a literary word for ἅλς, but it occurs in the adage ἅλασιν ὕει. In Mark ix. 49 both forms are used according to the best reading, τὸ ἅλας and accus. ἅλα, dat. ἁλί from ἅλς. In Col. iv. 6, the dat. ἅλατι of the neuter form is used. Attic prose has the plural only.

ἐὰν μωρανθῇ. The causal force of μωραίνω is Hellenistic; in the classical period the meaning is 'to be foolish.' For the use of the word in a literal sense cp. Rom. i. 22, φάσκοντες εἶναι σοφοὶ ἐμωράνθησαν. And for the interchange of meaning between folly and insipidity cp. *sapere, sapientia, insipidus; sal, sales*, 'salt', then 'wit' (so in late Greek ἅλες); *insulsus*, 'unsalted,' then 'stupid'.

ἐν τίνι. ἐν is here clearly instrumental, see ch. iii. 11.

καταπατεῖσθαι ὑπὸ τῶν ἀνθρώπων. Thomson, *Land and Book*, 382, describes 'the sweeping out of the spoiled salt and casting it into the streets' as 'actions familiar to all men.'

14. τὸ φῶς τοῦ κόσμου. See John viii. 12, where Jesus says of Himself ἐγώ εἰμι τὸ φῶς τοῦ κόσμου. Cp. Phil. ii. 15, φαίνεσθε ὡς φωστῆρες ἐν κόσμῳ.

τοῦ κόσμου, i.e. of the whole world, not of Israel only; or of the dark and evil world. κόσμος has an interesting history: (1) 'order,' 'propriety' (Homer); (2) 'the divine order and arrangement of nature' (Heracleitus and Anaxagoras); (3) 'celestial order' (Plato); (4) 'order celestial and terrestrial'—the universe (Plato, see Bruder's

Concordance); (5) 'the habitable world,' ἡ πίστις ὑμῶν καταγγέλλεται ἐν ὅλῳ τῷ κόσμῳ, Rom. i. 8; (6) the world around us, society; (7) especially 'the evil world', so frequently in John as μισεῖ ὑμᾶς ὁ κόσμος, xv. 19; (8) in modern Greek a 'crowd,' 'rabble.' κόσμος ἄπειρος 'a countless multitude' would have seemed to Heracleitus a contradiction in terms (Geldart, *Mod. Greek*, 94). In LXX. κόσμος is not used in this later sense of 'the world,' it there means 'ornament' or 'order (host) of heaven': καὶ συνετελέσθησαν καὶ πᾶς ὁ κόσμος αὐτῶν, Gen. ii. 1.

πόλις ἐπάνω ὄρους κειμένη. Stanley remarks (*S. and P.* 337) that in Northern Palestine 'the plain and mountain-sides are dotted with villages...situated for the most part (not like those of Judæa, on hill-tops, or Samaria, in deep valleys, but) as in Philistia, on the slopes of the ranges which intersect or bound the plain.' The image in the text therefore recalls Judæa rather than Galilee, Bethlehem rather than Nazareth. Some however have conjectured that the lofty Safed was in sight, and was pointed to by our Lord. *Land and Book*, 273.

κρυβῆναι. This 2nd aor. form is late: in Soph. *Aj.* 1145, κρυφείς is now read for κρυβείς.

15. τὸν μόδιον. 'The bushel,' i.e. the common measure found in every Jewish house. The article generalises. Strictly speaking, the *modius* denoted a smaller measure equal to about two gallons.

λύχνος...λυχνία. 'Lamp,' 'lampstand.' The lamp in a Jewish house was not set on a table, but on a tall pedestal or stand, sometimes made with a sliding shaft.

πᾶσιν τοῖς ἐν τῇ οἰκίᾳ, i.e. the Jews. St Luke, true to the character of his gospel, says 'that they which enter in', i.e. the Gentiles, 'may see the light'.

B. (1) The Kingdom of Heaven is a fulfilment of the law, v. 17—48. Stated generally, v. 17—20.

17. οὐκ ἦλθον καταλῦσαι κ.τ.λ. 'I came not to destroy', a divine *captatio* which would instantly soothe the possible fear that Christ was a καταλυτὴς τοῦ νόμου. For the word cp. Polyb. III. 2, καταλύσαντα τοὺς νόμους εἰς μοναρχίαν περιστῆσαι τὸ πολίτευμα τῶν Καρχηδονίων.

17—20. The poetical form traceable throughout the Sermon on the Mount is especially observable here. οὐ καταλῦσαι and πληρῶσαι are the key-words. The γάρ in v. 18 (ἀμὴν γάρ) introduces an explanation of οὐ καταλῦσαι: the second γάρ in v. 20 (λέγω γάρ) carries out the thought of πληρῶσαι. Then note to what a height the contrasting climax rises. So far from being a κατάλυσις of the whole law, not a jot or tittle shall pass from it (v. 18). So far from Christ himself destroying (καταλῦσαι) the whole law, if his followers break even (λῦσαι, a weaker word) a single one of the least of the commandments he shall be least in the Kingdom. So also in v. 20, περισσεύῃ is an advance even on πληρῶσαι, which in itself is more than οὐ καταλῦσαι.

πληρῶσαι. To give the full and true meaning to the law: not to extend or develop it so much as to teach the deep underlying principles of it. Thus St Paul says, πλήρωμα οὖν νόμου ἡ ἀγάπη, Rom. xiii. 10.

18. ἀμήν. Strictly a verbal adjective, 'firm,' 'true,' from Hebr. *aman* to 'support,' 'confirm'; thus used, Rev. iii. 14, ὁ ἀμὴν ὁ μάρτυς ὁ πιστὸς καὶ ἀληθινός. (2) An adverb of affirmation preceding or concluding a statement or prayer. The familiar use of the word in the Christian liturgy is derived from the service of the synagogue.

ἰῶτα. '*yod*' (') the smallest of the Hebr. characters, generally a silent letter, rather the adjunct of a letter than an independent letter. Still a critical interpretation might turn on the presence or absence of *yod* in a word. The controversy as to the meaning of Shiloh, Gen. xlix. 10, is an instance of this. The letter *yod* makes the difference between Sarai and Sarah. It is the first letter in Jehovah and in the Hebrew form of Jesus or Joshua.

κεραία, lit. 'a horn.' Here the extremity of a letter, a little point or a turn, in which one letter differs from another, as e.g. כ [*caph* or c] differs from ב [*beth* or b], or as ד [*daleth* or d] differs from ר [*resch* or r]. The Rabbinical writers point out that a confusion between the first two would change the sense of 'none holy as the Lord' (1 Sam. ii. 2) to 'nought is holy in the Lord'; and a confusion between the second pair of letters would change 'one Lord' (Deut. vi. 4) to 'false Lord.' Schöttgen *ad loc*. The Greek grammarians used the word for 'a mark over a letter,' as ᾱ.

19. λύσῃ...διδάξῃ. Recall in this connection St Paul's attitude in relation to the law. διδάσκειν points to the Presbyter or Teacher, λύσῃ, a more general term, to the people.

ποιήσῃ καὶ διδάξῃ. Again addressed to the Apostles as teachers. The union of doing and teaching is essential. It was the grave sin of the Pharisees that they taught without doing. See ch. xxiii. 2, 3. This explains the *for* of next verse.

20. δικαιοσύνη, 'observance of the law.' Unless ye observe the law with greater exactness than the Pharisees, ye shall not enter the kingdom of heaven. The Pharisaic δικαιοσύνη consisted in extended and minute external observances, Christ's περίσσευμα in reaching the spiritual meaning of the law.

(*a*) Instances from the Decalogue, v. 21—37. (*a*) Murder, v. 21—26.

21. ἠκούσατε, 'ye heard,' a use of the Greek aorist to express frequentative action where in English it would be natural to use the present tense; 'ye hear' daily in the Synagogue the law as it was delivered to them of old time. See note ch. xi. 27.

τοῖς ἀρχαίοις, 'to them of old time.' This rendering is made almost certain by the dativial force of ὑμῖν in the antithetic clause, *v.* 22.

22. ἔνοχος, lit. 'held fast by,' (ἐνέχω) so 'liable to' with dative. It is frequently used in this technical judicial sense by Plato, the Attic Orators and the later historians, as Polybius and Diod. Siculus. When ἔνοχος is followed by a genitive some word like δίκη or γραφῇ should be supplied. See ch. xxvi. 66 and Mark iii. 26 (where ἁμαρτήματος not κρίσεως is the true reading). εἰς τὴν γέενναν is not a change for the dative, but denotes the extent to which the sentence might go 'subject to a penalty extending to the Gehenna of fire'—usque ad pœnam Gehennæ. The extremity of human punishment is meant with the underlying thought of the figurative sense of Gehenna. See *infra*.

τῇ κρίσει, to the judgment of the lower court, whose jurisdiction was limited.

ῥακά. A word of contempt, said to be from a root meaning to 'spit'. The distinction between *Raca* and *Thou fool* is lost, and naturally, for they belong to that class of words, the meaning of which depends entirely on the usage of the day. An expression innocent and unmeaning in one age becomes the watchword of a revolution in another. There is, however, clearly a climax. (1) Feeling of anger without words. (2) Anger venting itself in words. (3) Insulting anger. The gradation of punishment corresponds; liable (1) to the local court; (2) to the Sanhedrin; (3) to Gehenna.

συνεδρίῳ. See note ch. xxvi. 3.

γέενναν τοῦ πυρός. 'Gehenna of fire, i.e. burning Gehenna'. Gehenna is the Greek form of the Hebrew Ge-Hinnom or 'Valley of Hinnom,' sometimes called 'Valley of the sons of Hinnom', also 'Tophet' (Jer. vii. 31). It was a deep narrow glen S.W. of Jerusalem, once the scene of the cruel worship of Moloch; but Josiah, in the course of his reformation, 'defiled Tophet, that no man might make his son or his daughter to pass through the fire to Moloch' (2 Kings xxiii. 10). Cp. Milton, *Paradise Lost*, I.

> 'First Moloch, horrid king, besmeared with blood
> Of human sacrifice and parents' tears;
> Though, for the noise of drums and timbrels loud,
> Their children's cries unheard that passed through fire
> To his grim idol'.

After that time pollutions of every kind, among them the bodies of criminals who had been executed, were thrown into the valley. From this defilement and from its former desecration Gehenna was used to express the abode of the wicked after death. The words 'of fire' are added, either because of the ancient rites of Moloch, or, if a Rabbinical tradition is to be credited, because fires were always burning in the valley.

τοῦ πυρός. The adjectival genitive may be illustrated from classical Greek ἄστρων εὐφρόνη, 'the starry night,' Soph. *El.* 19. χιόνος πτέρυγι, 'a snowy wing,' *Antig.* 114. τραύματα αἵματος, 'bloody wounds,' Eur. *Phœn.* 1616. See Donaldson's *Greek Grammar*, § 454.

But in this and other instances in the N.T. this genitive may be referred to a Hebrew usage due partly to the comparative scarcity of adjectives in the Hebrew language, partly to the vividness and poetry of oriental speech.

23. οὖν. In consequence of this truth that anger makes you liable to the extremity of punishment.

προσφέρῃς τὸ δῶρον, 'make thy offering.' Cp. Levit. ii. 1, ἐὰν δὲ ψυχὴ προσφέρῃ δῶρον θυσίαν τῷ κυρίῳ, where the Hebrew words are *korban minchah*; for *korban* see note ch. xvii. 6. *Minchah* literally means 'a gift,' and technically denoted vegetable offerings as distinguished from the animal offerings. δῶρον is used to translate both *korban* and *minchah*. It is adopted in the Talmud as a Hebrew word. μνημόσυνον or 'memorial,' another translation for *minchah*, Levit. ii. 2, seems to form a link with the use of μνησθῇς in this connection. See *Speaker's Commentary*, ad loc. cit.

μνησθῇς. The word itself reminds us that true observance of the law lies in thought not in act.

ὅτι ὁ ἀδελφός σου ἔχει τι κατὰ σοῦ. That thy brother hath cause of complaint against thee, just or unjust.

24. ἔμπροσθεν τοῦ θυσιαστηρίου. Stay the sacrifice, though begun, for God will not accept it unless the heart be free from anger, and the conscience from offence. It is an application of the great principle summed up in 'I will have mercy and not sacrifice.' Cp. also Ps. xxvi. 6, 'I will wash my hands in innocency, O Lord, and so will I go to thine altar.'

25, 26. The illustration is drawn from a legal process. It would be wise for the debtor to arrange with the creditor while he is on the way to the Court; otherwise the judge's sentence and a hopeless imprisonment await him.

Sin is the debt (here especially anger the source of murder), the sense of sin or the conscience is the adversary. Let the sinner come to terms with his conscience by confession of sin and prayer for forgiveness while he has opportunity, lest he be brought unrepentant and unforgiven to the tribunal of the judge.

ἴσθι εὐνοῶν. The participle conveys the idea of continuance: be at peace with conscience all through life.

26. κοδράντην. Cp. Mark xii. 42, λεπτὰ δύο ὅ ἐστιν κοδράντης. κοδράντης = Lat. *quadrans*, the fourth part of an *as*, and the smallest Roman coin. τὸ λεπτὸν in the parallel passage in Luke is the *prutah* or smallest Jewish coin. For this view of sin as a debt cp. ὀφειλήματα in the Lord's Prayer, and the parable of the Unmerciful Servant, ch. xviii. 23 foll., and the Lord's question to Simon the Pharisee, Luke vii. 42.

See Luke xii. 57—59, where the same illustration is used in reference to the divine judgment which was swiftly overtaking the Jewish people.

(β) *Adultery*, 27—32.

28. πρὸς τὸ ἐπιθυμῆσαι, i.e. 'with a view to lust after her.'

ἐν τῇ καρδίᾳ. Contrast with the pure *in heart*, v. 8.

29. ὁ ὀφθαλμός σου, suggested by the preceding verse. The eye and the hand are not only in themselves good and serviceable, but *necessary*. Still they may become the occasion of sin to us. So pursuits and pleasures innocent in themselves may bring temptation, and involve us in sin. These must be resigned, however great the effort implied in 'cast it from thee.'

σκανδαλίζει σε, 'allure thee to destruction.' This verb which is confined to Hellenistic Greek is derived from σκάνδαλον also Hellenistic; the classical form σκανδάληθρον, itself very rare, is defined as, 'the crooked stick forming the part of a trap on which the bait is placed' (the root-meaning of the word is swift darting movement, as of falling or gliding away, Curtius, *Greek Etymology*, 166). Hence σκάνδαλον and its cognates have first the meaning of temptation, combined with those of entrapping and swift destruction. Cp. σκανδαληθρ᾽ ἱστὰς ἐπῶν, Arist. *Ach.* 647, 'setting word-traps.' κρεάδιον τῆς σκανδάλης ἀφάψας, Alciphr. III. 22, 'having attached a bait to the trap.' ἐσκανδαλίσθη εἰς ἐμέ. Joan. Mosch. 3049 c. (quoted E. A. Soph. *Greek Lex.* and there rendered 'tempted to fall in love with me'). This sense of the word conveying, by a vivid and apt imagery, the idea of temptation or allurement to ruin, is applicable to the use of σκάνδαλον in most passages of the N.T. See notes, chs. xiii. 41, xvi. 23, xviii. 7. It appears also to be the primary thought in σκανδαλίζειν. In other passages the notion of 'entrapping' is prominent. Hence to 'impede,' 'bring into difficulties'; so to 'irritate,' 'offend.' At this point begins the correspondence with the figurative sense of προσκόπτειν and πρόσκομμα, the Latin rendering of which supplies the English words to offend, offence, &c., by which σκανδαλίζειν and σκάνδαλον are translated in the A.V. And though differing in their origin and literal meaning σκάνδαλον appears in parallelism with πρόσκομμα in Rom. ix. 31 and 1 Pet. ii. 7, and σκανδαλίζεσθαι is nearly synonymous with the figurative sense of προσκόπτειν.

συμφέρει γάρ σοι κ.τ.λ. Cp. Cic. *Phil.* VIII. 15, In corpore si quid ejusmodi est quod reliquo corpori noceat, uri necarique patimur; ut membrorum aliquod potius quam totum corpus intereat.

31. ἀποστάσιον. See note on ch. i. 19. The greatest abuses had arisen in regard to divorce, which was permitted on very trivial grounds. One Rabbinical saying was 'If any man hate his wife, let him put her away.' Copies of these bills of divorce are still preserved. The formula may be seen in Lightfoot, *Hor. Hebr.* ad loc. The same facility of divorce prevails in Mohammedan countries.

32. παρεκτός. A rare word in N.T. and condemned by the Atticists. See Sturz, *Dial. Mac.* 210.

λόγου πορνείας. A Hebraism, 'the case of adultery.'

ἀπολελυμένην, 'when she hath been divorced.'

(γ) Oaths, 33—37.

33. οὐκ ἐπιορκήσεις. The special reference may be to the third commandment. Cp. also Levit. xix. 12, 'Ye shall not swear by my name falsely, neither shalt thou profane the name of thy God.' In the kingdom of God no external act or profession as distinct from the thought of the heart can find a place. But such words as those of the Apostle, 'The God and Father of our Lord Jesus Christ, which is blessed for evermore, knoweth that I lie not' (2 Cor. xi. 31), will prevent Christians observing the letter rather than the spirit of our Blessed Saviour's words.

34. μὴ ὀμόσαι ὅλως. The prohibition must be understood of rash and careless oaths in conversation, not of solemn asseveration in Courts of Justice.

ὅτι θρόνος ἐστὶν τοῦ θεοῦ. Such was the prevalent hypocrisy that the Jews of the day thought that they escaped the sin of perjury if in their oaths they avoided using the name of God. One of the Rabbinical sayings was 'As heaven and earth shall pass away, so passeth away the oath taken by them.' Our Lord shows that a false oath taken by heaven, by earth, or by Jerusalem is none the less a profanation of God's name.

Hypocrisy reproduces itself. Louis XI. 'admitted to one or two peculiar forms of oath the force of a binding obligation which he denied to all others, strictly preserving the secret, which mode of swearing he really accounted obligatory, as one of the most valuable of state mysteries.' Introd. to *Quentin Durward*.

35. εἰς. The change from ἐν τῇ γῇ to εἰς Ἱερ. is to be explained by the etymological identity of εἰς (ἐνς) and ἐν. εἰς is used in late Greek where there is no idea of motion, as ὁ ὢν εἰς τὸν κόλπον τοῦ πατρός, John i. 18...where ἐν would be required in Classical Greek; other instances are ἀποθανεῖν εἰς Ἱερουσαλήμ, Acts xviii. 21, τὰ παιδία μου μετ' ἐμοῦ εἰς τὴν κοίτην εἰσίν, Luke xi. 7. εἰς τὸ κήρυγμα, Luke xi. 32. εἰς διαταγὰς ἀγγέλων, Acts vii. 53. ἵν' αὐτὸ λούσῃ εἰς σκάφην, Epict. III. 22. 71. Conversely ἐν is found for εἰς, Epict. II. 20. 23, ἀπελθεῖν ἐν βαλανείῳ and Id. I. 11. 32, νῦν ἐν Ῥώμῃ ἀνέρχῃ. In the common spoken dialect of modern Greek εἰς is used to the exclusion of ἐν. Clyde, *Greek Gram.* § 83, Obs. 4. Vincent and Dickson, *Handbook to Modern Greek*, § 80.

The construction of ὄμνυμι in classical Greek is τι or κατά τινος. The first is found in James v. 12, a passage closely parallel to this, μὴ ὀμνύετε μήτε τὸν οὐρανὸν κ.τ.λ.; the second Heb. vi. 16, ἄνθρωποι γὰρ κατὰ τοῦ μείζονος ὀμνύουσιν. The construction with ἐν and εἰς is a rendering of the Hebrew idiom.

36. ἐν τῇ κεφαλῇ σου. A common form of oath in the ancient world: cp. 'Per caput hoc juro per quod pater ante solebat.' Verg. *Æn.* IX. 300.

37. ἐκ τοῦ πονηροῦ. (1) 'of evil', (2) or perhaps better 'from the evil one.'

(b) The law of retaliation, 38—42.

38. ὀφθαλμὸν ἀντὶ ὀφθαλμοῦ. See Exod. xxi. 24. The Scribes drew a false inference from the letter of the law. As a legal remedy the *lex talionis* was probably the best possible in a rude state of society. The principle was admitted in all ancient nations. But the retribution was exacted by a judicial sentence for the good of the community, not to gratify personal vengeance. The deduction that it was morally right for individuals to indulge revenge could not be justified.

Jewish history however records no instance of the law being literally carried out. A fine was substituted for the retributive penalty. But the principle of the *lex talionis* underlay the enactments of the law, and it is against the principle that Christ's words are directed.

39. μὴ ἀντιστῆναι τῷ πονηρῷ, i.e. do not seek to retaliate evil.

ῥαπίζει. See ch. xxvi. 67.

στρέψον αὐτῷ καὶ τὴν ἄλλην. To be understood with the limitation imposed on the words by our Lord's personal example, John xviii. 22, 23.

The gradation of the examples given is from the greater to the less provocation.

40. κριθῆναι. In Attic κρίνειν = 'to bring to trial.' For the construction of κρίνομαι with dat. cp. Eur. *Med.* 609, ὡς οὐ κρινοῦμαι τῶνδε σοί τὰ πλείονα.

χιτῶνα, 'tunic,' the under-garment. It had sleeves, and reached below the knees, somewhat like a modern shirt. ἱμάτιον, the upper garment. A large square woollen robe, resembling the modern Arab *abba* or *abayeh*. The poorest people wore a tunic only. Among the richer people many wore two tunics besides the upper garment. Wealth is often shown in the East not only by the quality but also by the amount of clothing worn. For the general sense cp. 1 Cor. vi. 7, 'There is utterly a fault...suffer yourselves to be defrauded.'

41. ἀγγαρεύειν, from a Persian word which is probably a corruption of *hakkáreh*, 'an express messenger' (see Rawlinson, Herod. VIII. 98, note 1), signifies 'to press into service as a courier' for the royal post, then, generally, 'to force to be a guide,' 'to requisition,' men or cattle. This was one of the exactions which the Jews suffered under the Romans. Alford quotes Joseph. *Ant.* XIII. 2, 3, where Demetrius promises not to press into the service the beasts of burden belonging to the Jews. For an instance of this forced service see ch. xxvii. 32.

For the Greek word cp. ἄγγαρον πῦρ, 'the courier fire,' Æsch. *Agam.* 282. The verb is not classical.

μίλιον. Here only in N.T. Used by Strabo = Lat. *miliare*.

42. τὸν θέλοντα ἀπὸ σοῦ δανείσασθαι. St Luke has, δανείζετε μηδὲν ἀπελπίζοντες (vi. 35). Forced loans have been a mode of oppression in every age, from which, perhaps, no people have suffered more than the Jews.

(c) Love or Charity, 43—48.

43. ἀγαπήσεις τὸν πλησίον σου. Levit. xix. 18, 'Thou shalt love thy neighbour as thyself.' The second clause does not occur in Levit., but was a Rabbinical inference. ἐχθρούς, all who are outside the chosen race, the etymological force of the word. Heathen writers bear testimony to this unsocial characteristic of the Jews. Juvenal says it was their rule—

'Non monstrare vias eadem nisi sacra colenti,
Quæsitum ad fontem solos deducere verpos.'—*Sat.* xiv. 104.

44. See critical notes *supra*.

45. ὅπως γένησθε κ.τ.λ. See note on *v.* 9. To act thus would be to act like God, who blesses those who curse Him and are his enemies, by the gifts of sun and rain. This is divine. Mere return of love for love is a human, even a heathen virtue.

Shakespeare beautifully and most appropriately reproduces this thought in the appeal to the Jew on the Christian principle of mercy, which 'droppeth like the gentle rain from heaven.' *Merchant of Venice*, Act. iv. sc. 1. Comp. also Seneca, *de Ben.* i. 1. 9, Quam multi indigni luce sunt et tamen dies oritur.

The illustration would be far more telling in a hot eastern climate than with us. In the Hindoo mythology two out of the three manifestations of deity are Sun and Rain. The thought of God as giver of rain and fruitful seasons is seized upon by St Paul as a conception common to Jew and Gentile on which to found his argument at Lystra. Acts xiv. 17.

βρέχει, used in this sense in the older Greek poets: βρέχε χρυσέαις νιφάδεσσιν (Pindar), afterwards it passed into the vernacular, but reappears in Polybius, it is frequent in the LXX., and in modern Greek the usual phrases are βρέχει, 'it is raining,' θὰ βρέξῃ, 'it is going to rain.'

46. οἱ τελῶναι, tax-gatherers; not collectors of a regular tax fixed by government, as with us, but men who farmed or contracted for the *publicum* (state revenue), hence called Publicani. At Rome the equestrian order enjoyed almost exclusively the lucrative privilege of farming the state revenues.

The publicans of the N.T. however are a lower class of tax-gatherers, (*exactores*), to whom the contractors sublet the collection of taxes. These men repaid themselves by cruel and oppressive exactions. Only the least patriotic and most degraded of the population undertook these functions which naturally rendered them odious to their fellow-citizens.

It is this system pursued in the Turkish Empire that produces much frightful misery and illegal oppression.

47. τοὺς ἀδελφοὺς ὑμῶν μόνον. See *v.* 43. The Hebrew salutation was *Shalom* (peace).

48. ἔσεσθε τέλειοι. Lit. 'ye shall be perfect.' Either (1) in reference to a future state, 'if ye have this true love or charity ye shall be perfect hereafter'; or (2) the future has an imperative force, and τέλειοι is limited by the preceding words = perfect in respect of love, i.e. 'love your enemies as well as your neighbours,' because your Father being perfect in respect of love does this. This use of the future is in accordance with the Hebrew idiom.

CHAPTER VI.

1. δικαιοσύνην (ℵ*BD, 1. 209) for ἐλεημοσύνην of the *textus receptus*. ἐλεημοσύνην was doubtless a marginal explanation.

4. αὐτός omitted before ἀποδώσει, (ℵBL and others) its presence emphasises the reward.

ἐν τῷ φανερῷ inserted in *textus receptus* after ἀποδώσει σοι, a rhetorical gloss arising from a search after antithesis. For the real antithesis see note.

5. προσεύχησθε οὐκ ἔσεσθε, instead of the singular προσεύχῃ οὐκ ἔσῃ, the singular introduced to harmonise with context ὅταν ποιῇς v. 2, ὅταν προσεύχῃ v. 6.

6. ταμεῖον has high authority (ℵBDE) for ταμιεῖον; cp. the late form ὑγεία for ὑγίεια.

12. ἀφήκαμεν for ἀφίεμεν or ἀφίομεν: this important change has the highest support (ℵBZ). See notes.

13. The doxology was an early insertion from the liturgy, it is absent from the oldest MSS. (ℵBD). The *textus receptus* reads ὅτι σοῦ ἐστιν ἡ βασιλεία καὶ ἡ δύναμις καὶ ἡ δόξα εἰς τοὺς αἰῶνας. ἀμήν.

18. κρυπτῷ is read for κρυφαίῳ from the occurrence of the word in verses 4 and 6.

21. σου is rightly restored for ὑμῶν. The sing. individualises the action.

28. In the *textus receptus* the verbs are in the sing. according to rule: this and τὰ ἑαυτῆς v. 34 are grammatical corrections.

---

(2) The Kingdom of Heaven exceeds the righteousness of the Pharisees in regard to

(a) ALMSGIVING, 1—4.

1. δικαιοσύνην for ἐλεημοσύνην. See crit. notes for the evidence for the reading. The two words were nearly synonymous with the Jews, partly because the poor had a right to share in the produce of the land; partly because almsgiving is the most natural and obvious external work of righteousness. In the same way ἀγάπη, the leading Christian virtue, has lost its original breadth of meaning and has sunk to the modern and restricted sense of 'charity.'

2. ἐλεημοσύνη, not classical: it occurs in a poem by Callimachus of Cyrene, librarian of the famous Alexandrian library, *circa* 260 B.C. Elsewhere it seems to be confined to LXX. and to two writers in the N.T., St Matthew and St Luke. With Christianity the word became frequent and is found in all western languages in different forms— aumône, almosen, alms.

μὴ σαλπίσῃς. The chests for alms in the Synagogue and also in the Temple treasury were called *shopharoth* (trumpets) from their shape. Possibly the words of the text contain a reference to these *shopharoth*. Those who dropped their coins into the 'trumpets' with a ringing sound might be said σαλπίζειν. Schöttgen *ad loc.* But perhaps the expression means simply 'avoid ostentation in almsgiving.'

οἱ ὑποκριταί. ὑποκριτής (1) lit. 'one who answers,' then from dialogues on the stage (2) 'an actor,' hence (3) in a sense confined to LXX. (Job xxxiv. 30, xxxvi. 13) and N.T. and there with one exception (Mark vii. 6) to Matthew and Luke, 'hypocrites,' those who play a part in life, whose actions are not the true reflection of their thoughts, whose religion is external and unreal. Such men begin by deceiving others, but end in self-deception. It is against these that our Lord's severest reproofs are delivered. ὑπόκρισις occurs in late authors (Polyb., Lucian) in the sense of 'dissimulation,' 'hypocrisy.'

ἐν ταῖς ῥύμαις. ῥύμη passed from its classical force of 'a rush,' 'impetus', through the softened meaning of 'going', to that of a narrow lane or street, like English 'alley' from French *aller*. Polybius uses the word for the streets in a camp. In Luke xiv. 21 the ῥύμαι are contrasted with the πλατεῖαι or broad open spaces in an Eastern city. Schöttgen suggests that the meaning here may be the narrow 'passages' in a synagogue.

ἀπέχουσιν, 'have in full.' Their reward is *now* and *on earth*, cp. Luke vi. 24, ἀπέχετε τὴν παράκλησιν. Phil. iv. 18, ἀπέχω πάντα, and for the thought, ἀπέλαβες τὰ ἀγαθά σου ἐν τῇ ζωῇ σου, Luke xvi. 25.

3. σοῦ δὲ ποιοῦντος. Observe the singular number here and *v.* 6; the duties of prayer and almsgiving are taught in their personal and individual aspect. The teaching of the Talmud commends secrésy in almsgiving in such sayings as 'he that doeth alms in secret is greater than Moses.' But the spirit of hypocrisy prevailed; the Pharisees taught and did not.

4. The restored reading in this verse (see above crit. notes) gives the real antithesis which lies in the contrast between reward by God and reward by man, not between secret act and open reward. The repeated ἐν τῷ κρυπτῷ links together the thoughts of the secret act and of the eye that sees things secret.

(b) PRAYER, 5—15.

5. προσεύχησθε. Plural, because here the reference is to public worship. It is a rule for the Church.

τῶν πλατειῶν. See note *v.* 2, ῥύμαις. πλατεῖαι not classical in this sense is a literal translation of a Hebrew word.

ἑστῶτες. There is no stress on this word, for the posture of standing was as closely connected with prayer as that of sitting was with teaching.

6. ταμιεῖον. A private oratory or place of prayer. These were usually in the upper part of the house; in classical Greek 'storehouse' or 'treasury', the meaning of the word Luke xii. 24. See Matt. xxiv. 26.

πρόσευξαι τῷ πατρί σου τῷ ἐν τῷ κρυπτῷ. Christ was the first to enjoin clearly secret and silent prayer. Certainly to pray aloud and in public appears to have been the Jewish practice (see however 1 Sam. i. 13); it is still the practice with the heathen and Mahommedans. The Roman looked with suspicion on private prayer: 'quod scire hominem nolunt deo narrant' (Seneca). Cp. Hor. *Ep.* I. 16. 59—62, where see Macleane's note. Cp. also Soph. *Electra* 638, where Clytemnestra apologises for offering up a secret prayer.

7. μὴ βαττολογήσητε. It is not the length of time spent in prayer or the fervent or reasonable repetition of forms of prayer that is forbidden, but the mechanical repetition of set words, and the belief that the efficacy of prayer consists in such repetition.

βαττολογεῖν, not classical, and ἅπαξ λεγ. in N.T. 'to stammer,' so 'to repeat words again and again.' The word is generally derived from Battus founder of Cyrene who stammered and had a lisp in his speech, ἰσχνόφωνος καὶ τραυλός, Herod. IV. 155, where the story is given. Possibly it was a Cyrenian term, in which case the meaning 'to stammer like your founder Battus' would popularise the word. According to Herod. *loc. cit.* Battus was Libyan for 'king.'

ὥσπερ οἱ ἐθνικοί. The Jews also had a saying 'every one that multiplies prayer is heard.'

8. οἶδεν γὰρ ὁ πατὴρ κ.τ.λ. Our Father knows our wants, still we are bound to express them. Why? because this is a proof of our faith and dependence upon God, which are the conditions of success in prayer.

9—13. THE LORD'S PRAYER.

St Luke xi. 2—4, where the prayer is found in a different connection, and is given by our Lord in answer to a request from the disciples to teach them to pray, 'even as John taught his disciples.' The text of St Luke as it stands in E.V. has probably been supplemented by additions from St Matthew.

πάτερ ἡμῶν. It is of the essence of Christian prayer that God should be addressed as a Father to whose love we appeal, not as a God whose anger we appease. The analogy removes nearly all the real difficulties on the subject of prayer. A wise earthly father does not grant *all* requests, but all which are for the good of his children and which are in his power to grant. Again, the child asks without fear, yet no refusal shakes his trust in his father's love or power.

ἁγιασθήτω, 'held sacred,' 'revered.' Each of these petitions implies an obligation to carry out on our own part what we pray God to accomplish.

10. ἐλθάτω ἡ βασιλεία σου. Note the loss in the A.V. of the emphasis given by the position of ἁγιασθήτω—ἐλθάτω—γενηθήτω. See note ch. iii. 2. Lightfoot (*Hor. Heb.*) quotes an axiom from the Jewish Schools, 'that prayer wherein there is not mention of the Kingdom of God is not prayer.'

11. ἄρτον, 'Bread,' primarily in a literal sense, subsistence as distinct from luxury; but the spiritual meaning cannot be excluded, Christ the Bread of Life is the Christian's daily food.

The address to God as Father influences each petition—to feed, to forgive and to protect his children, are special acts of a father's love.

ἐπιούσιον. This word is unknown to the Classics and in N.T. occurs in the Lord's Prayer only. For a full discussion of the meaning and history of this word see Bp Lightfoot, *On a Fresh Revision of the N.T.*, Appendix 195. His ultimate decision is, "that the familiar rendering 'daily'...is a fairly adequate representation of the original; nor indeed does the English language furnish any one word which would answer the purpose so well." Dr McClellan has also written an exhaustive treatise on ἐπιούσιος (*Notes on the Four Gospels*, p. [632]); he translates, 'give us to-day,' and 'give us day by day [Luke] our bread of life eternal.'

Two derivations have been given. A. ἐπί and οὐσία. B. The participle of ἐπιέναι, either *masc.* ἐπιών, or *fem.* ἡ ἐπιοῦσα (ἡμέρα).

A. The principal meanings which rely on this etymology are: (1) 'for subsistence,' so 'necessary,' 'needful,' or (2) 'supersubstantial,' i.e. above all essences, so 'excellent' or 'preeminent.' Both these renderings are open to exception; for οὐσία is very rare in the sense required by (1), and (2) belongs to a much later theological terminology, and is foreign to the simplicity of the Lord's Prayer. But the form of the compound ἐπιούσιος rather than ἐπούσιος affords the most conclusive argument against any interpretation founded on a derivation from οὐσία. περιούσιος, sometimes adduced in support of such a form, is not to the point (for the ι in περί regularly remains unelided), nor are ἐπιανδάνω, ἐπιεικής, ἐπίορκος, and the like (see Bp Lightfoot's *Dissertation*); for the words which here follow ἐπί originally began with a digamma.

B. (a) Derived immediately from the *masc.* participle ἐπιών, as ἐθελούσιος from ἐθέλων, ἑκούσιος from ἑκών, the adjective has received the meaning of 'coming,' 'succeeding' or 'future,' 'futurus,' 'veniens,' 'adveniens,' a meaning which by a very early interpretation of the word is extended to 'belonging to the future, eternal life,' so 'heavenly' or 'spiritual.'

Against this meaning of the noun and adjective it may be argued: (1) A word made for the occasion could not have received the succession of meanings implied by this sense; (2) There would be no need to coin a word to express a meaning already conveyed by ἐπουράνιος, αἰώνιος, &c.; (3) ἐπιών implies the nearer future as distinct from μέλλων which relates to a more distant future; (4) The one petition for the supply of simple temporal wants is essential to this, the model of all Christian prayer. Therefore, though the spiritual sense is not excluded, it is present as a secondary and not as a primary meaning.

(β) Another line of interpretation connects ἐπιούσιος with the quasi-substantive ἡ ἐπιοῦσα (ἡμέρα) and gives the following meanings: (1) '*for the morrow*,' 'crastinum'; (2) '*daily*,' 'quotidianum' of the Vetus Itala and of the Vulgate in Luke (not in Matthew where Jerome renders the word 'supersubstantialem'); (3) '*continual*,' 'assiduum,' perhaps from the notion of succeeding days.

Of these, (1) and (2) approach very nearly to the true meaning of the word, but against all these the same objection holds which was urged above, viz. that the ideas were expressed by existing adjectival forms. The necessity of a new word arises from the necessity of expressing a new idea, and the new idea expressed by ἐπιούσιος and by no other Greek adjective is that of the closely impending future, the moment, the hour, or the day that succeeds the present instant. Translate therefore 'bread for instant need.' For this precise thought no other adjective exists but ἐπιούσιος; but it is the thought that distinguishes ἡ ἐπιοῦσα from ἡ αὔριον. ἡ αὔριον implies the interval of a night, it implies delay, it excludes the present and is contrasted with it; ἡ ἐπιοῦσα (ἡμέρα, νύξ [Acts xxiii. 11] or ὥρα) implies absence of interval and immediate succession. See Bp Lightfoot's *Dissertation*, p. 203, where this distinction is clearly shown, and comp. the following instances: Hdt. III. 85, ὥρη μηχανᾶσθαι καὶ μὴ ἀναβάλλεσθαι ὡς τῆς ἐπιούσης ἡμέρης ὁ ἀγὼν ἡμῖν ἐστι; Polyb. III. 42. 9, παρασκευαζόμενοι πρὸς τὴν ἐπιοῦσαν χρείαν, 'ad instans negotium' (Schweighäuser). ἡ ἐπιοῦσα occurs once only in the LXX., Prov. xxvii. 1 and in N.T. in the Acts only, where in three instances out of five it is used of pursuing a voyage on the 'succeeding' day, in one, ch. xxiii. 11, of the Lord appearing to Paul τῇ ἐπιούσῃ νυκτί, i.e. without an interval.

Thus this interesting word ἐπιούσιος beautifully and alone expresses our dependence, each succeeding day and hour, on our Father for the supply of needs temporal, and in a secondary sense, of needs spiritual. It is the thought expressed by Dr Newman:

'Keep thou my feet; I do not ask to see
The distant scene, one step enough for me.'

12. **ἄφες ἡμῖν τὰ ὀφειλήματα ἡμῶν.** ἀφιέναι and ἄφεσις are the words used in the N.T. to express the act of forgiveness whether on the part of God or of man. It is important to fix as precisely as possible the meaning of terms intimately bound up with the thought of the Atonement. To the Jewish mind the figure would connect itself with the year of jubilee or release (ἔτος or ἐνιαυτὸς τῆς ἀφέσεως or simply ἄφεσις, Levit. xxv. 31, 40, xxvii. 24) in which all debts were remitted. See Trench, *N.T. Syn.* p. 131. To the Greek mind it would denote the thought of 'letting go' from a charge (ἐγκλήματα, φόνον, Demosth. passim), or from penalties (πληγάς, Aristoph. *Nubes*, 1426), but also the idea of forgiveness of debt and generally of condoning faults: ἀπῆκέ τ' ἂν αὐτῷ τὴν αἰτίην, Hdt. VI. 30.

ὀφειλήματα. Sin is a debt—a shortcoming in the service due to God or a harm to fellow-men that requires reparation. St Paul gives vivid expression to the thought Col. ii. 14, ἐξαλείψας τὸ καθ' ἡμῶν χειρόγραφον, 'the bond against us'—'the account standing against us.' It is contemplated as a thing left undone, rather than an act of transgression.

ἀφήκαμεν. The force of the aorist (see Crit. Notes) is that the act of forgiveness on man's part is past before he prays to receive forgiveness. Cp. ch. v. 23, 24, also the parable of the Unforgiving Servant, ch. xviii. 23 seqq.

13. μὴ εἰσενέγκῃς ἡμᾶς εἰς πειρασμόν. The statement of James, i. 2, πᾶσαν χαρὰν ἡγήσασθε ὅταν πειρασμοῖς περιπέσητε ποικίλοις, is not really contradictory. The Christian character is strengthened and purified by temptation, but no one can think of temptation without dread.

ῥῦσαι. Lit. 'draw to thyself,' 'rescue,' as from an enemy. Cp. 1 Thess. i. 10, Ἰησοῦν τὸν ῥυόμενον ἡμᾶς ἀπὸ τῆς ὀργῆς τῆς ἐρχομένης, where the act of rescuing is regarded as continuous, and Col. i. 13, ὃς ἐρύσατο ἡμᾶς ἐκ τῆς ἐξουσίας τοῦ σκότους, where the reference is to a single act of salvation. The aorist imperative (ῥῦσαι) indicates a prayer for instant and special deliverance, not continued preservation from danger, cp. δὸς and ἄφες above and σῶσον, ἀπολλύμεθα, ch. viii. 25.

ἀπὸ τοῦ πονηροῦ. (1) From the evil one, i.e. Satan, or (2) from evil. The Greek bears either rendering, but the neuter is preferable and gives a deeper sense. We pray to be delivered from all that is included under the name of evil, not only from external evil but from the principle of evil within us.

The Formal Structure of the Lord's Prayer.

The Lord's Prayer falls naturally into two divisions answering to one another. The thought of the first line—God addressed as Father—is felt in each petition. The next three lines correspond to one another precisely in structure and in rhythm. Note the sense of earnestness expressed by the aorist imperative with which each line begins, and the sense of devotion expressed by the thrice repeated σου.

These three petitions are in gradation, forming a climax. (1) The preparation for the Kingdom; (2) the coming of it; (3) the perfection of it. This answers to three historical stages: the acknowledgement of Jehovah in the O.T.; the advent of the Kingdom in the N.T.; the realised Kingdom in the Church of Christ.

The addition to the third petition ὡς ἐν οὐρ. καὶ ἐπὶ γῆς at once recalls the address in the first line ὁ ἐν οὐρ, and connects the second division of the prayer with the first by linking οὐρανὸς and γῆ.

In the three last petitions there is also a climax. (1) Prayer for the supply of present temporal need—the necessary condition of earthly life. (2) Prayer for forgiveness of past sin—the necessary condition of spiritual life. (3) Prayer for future exemption from evil, even from temptation to evil, i.e. σωτηρία or salvation. Cp. with the three points of time thus faintly indicated, Soph. *Ant.* 607, τό τ' ἔπειτα καὶ τὸ μέλλον | καὶ τὸ πρὶν ἐπαρκέσει, 'shall hold good for future near and far as through the past,' where τὸ ἔπειτα=ἐπιούσιον, see note *supra*.

Last, observe the correspondence of the several clauses in each division: (1) God's name hallowed, with the food and sustenance of the Christian life. (2) The Kingdom of God, with forgiveness of sins (cp. Matt. iii. 2 with Mark i. 4). (3) The will of God, with freedom from evil (1 Thess. iv. 3, Heb. x. 10). In accordance with this interpretation a spiritual sense is given to ἄρτον also, as Christ, the Bread of Life.

14. παραπτώματα. Another conception of sin, either (1) a false step, a blunder, or (2) a fall beside the way (cp. παραπεσόντες, Heb. vi. 6), so a transgression. In ὀφειλήματα sin is viewed in its aspect toward another, in παραπτώματα in its relation to the offender himself, παράπτωμα is later and rarer than παράπτωσις. Polybius uses the word with the same meaning as in the text; in Diod. Sic. it means 'a defeat.' For the force of παρά cp. παρακόπτειν and παράσημος of coins struck on the side instead of in the centre.

(c) Fasting, 16—18.

16. Fasting, in itself a natural result of grief, as any one who has witnessed deep sorrow knows, easily degenerates into a form without reality.

ἀφανίζουσιν. Either (1) make unseen, 'veil,' or (2) cause to disappear, so 'destroy', hence (3) 'mar,' by leaving the face unwashen, or by throwing ashes on the head. The first meaning (1) is well established, that of (2) 'destroying' is the prevailing one in LXX., the sense of (3) 'disfiguring,' or 'marring' has less support. Wetstein quotes *Etym. M.* ἀφανίσαι, οἱ πάλαι οὐχὶ τὸ μολῦναι ὡς νῦν ἀλλὰ τὸ τελέως ἀφανῆ ποιῆσαι, and Chrys. ἀφανίζουσιν, τοῦτό ἐστιν διαφθείρουσιν, scil. *cinere*.

The apparent play upon the Greek words ἀφανίζουσιν...φανῶσιν has been adduced in support of their view by those who consider Greek to have been the original language of the gospel; but it is more than doubtful that the antithesis is intended.

ὅπως φανῶσιν. Not as in A.V. 'that they may appear' but 'that they may be seen to be fasting.'

17. σὺ δὲ νηστεύων ἄλειψαι, as if feasting rather than fasting: cp. τῷ δὲ λοεσσαμένῳ καὶ ἀλειψαμένῳ λίπ' ἐλαίῳ | δείπνῳ ἐφιζανέτην, *Il.* x. 577.

(d) Earthly possessions and daily cares.

19. θησαυροὺς ἐπὶ τῆς γῆς. Cp. ἐκ γῆς γὰρ τάδε πάντα καὶ ἐς γῆν πάντα τελευτᾷ (Xenophanes). Love of amassing wealth has been characteristic of the Jews in all ages.

Oriental wealth consisted to a great extent in stores of linen, embroidered garments, &c., which were handed down and left as heirlooms.

σής. The English word 'moth'='the devourer'.

βρῶσις. Money was frequently buried in the ground in those unsettled times, and so would be more liable to rust. Banks in the modern sense were unknown. Cp. ὁ πλοῦτος ὑμῶν σέσηπεν καὶ τὰ ἱμάτια ὑμῶν σητόβρωτα γέγονεν, James v. 2, 3. One of the many references to the Sermon on the Mount in that epistle. Elsewhere in N.T. βρῶσις means 'eating,' as John iv. 32, ἐγὼ βρῶσιν ἔχω φαγεῖν ἣν ὑμεῖς οὐκ οἴδατε, and Rom. xiv. 17, οὐ γάρ ἐστιν ἡ βασιλεία τοῦ θεοῦ βρῶσις καὶ πόσις, with this cp. Hom. Od. x. 167 ὄφρ' ἐν νηὶ θοῇ βρῶσίς τε πόσις τε. This force remains in late Greek. Here either (1) of metals 'rust,' or (2) 'eating away' with special reference to σής, with which it would form a kind of hendiadys (cp. σητόβρωτα in the citation from St James above), or (3) decay in general. On the whole the second (2) is probably the kind of spoiling or decay chiefly thought of, but the other meanings need not be excluded. The word βρῶσις is doubtless influenced by the Hebr. *achal* as used Mal. iii. 11.

διορύσσουσιν. An expression applicable to the mud walls of Oriental huts. Cp. Job xxiv. 26, διώρυξεν ἐν σκότει οἰκίας, and Thuc. II. 3, διορύσσοντες τοὺς κοινοὺς τοίχους. τοιχώρυχος = 'a housebreaker.'

21. ὅπου...ὁ θησαυρός. The words gain point if we think of the hoards buried in the *earth*.

22. ὁ λύχνος. 'The lamp.' See ch. v. 15, where the A.V. gives to λύχνος the meaning of 'candle'; the translation here 'light' is still less correct. The eye is not itself the light, but contains the light; it is the 'lamp' of the body, the light-conveying principle. If the eye or lamp is single, it admits the influx of the pure light only; if an eye be evil, i.e. affected with disease, the body can receive no light at all. The whole passage is on the subject of the *singleness* of service to God. There can be but one treasure, one source of light, one master. The eye is the spiritual faculty, through which the light of God's truth is recognised and admitted into the soul.

In the current phraseology 'a good eye' meant a bountiful heart, 'an evil eye' a covetous heart (Lightfoot, *Hor. Hebr.* ad loc.). This gives to our Lord's words the thought, 'covetousness darkens the soul more than anything else, it is a medium through which the light cannot pass'; cp. 1 Tim. vi. 10, where the same truth is taught in a different figure, ῥίζα γὰρ πάντων τῶν κακῶν ἐστὶν ἡ φιλαργυρία.

The connection in which the words occur in Luke xi. 34 is instructive. The inference there is that the spiritual perception of the Pharisees is dimmed, so that they cannot recognise Christ.

23. τὸ φῶς, here correctly in A.V. 'the light.' If the light be darkened by the diseased and impervious medium which prevents it gaining an entrance all will be darkness within. Covetousness permits no ray of divine light to enter.

24. Another illustration of the singleness of the Christian character, 'the simplicity that is in Christ' (2 Cor. xi. 3), drawn from the relation of master and slave.

δυσὶ κυρίοις δουλεύειν. Strictly, be a slave to two masters. The absolute subjection of the slave must be considered. The interests of the 'two masters' are presupposed to be diverse.

δυσί, a form condemned by the Atticists (Lob. *Phryn.* p. 210). In Thuc. VIII. 101, δυσὶν ἡμέραις is read by some editors, see Arnold *ad loc.* He reads δυοῖν, observing that the words practically differ only in accent.

μαμωνᾷ. An Aramaic and a Punic word (see Wetstein) signifying 'wealth,' probably connected with Hebr. *Aman.* So that the literal meaning would be, 'that in which one trusts' (*Wilkii Clavis*). It is said, on hardly sufficient authority, to have been personified as a god. This would strengthen the antithesis. See Schleusner *sub voc.* It stands here for all that mostly estranges men from God: cp. τὴν πλεονεξίαν ἥτις ἐστὶν εἰδωλολατρεία, Col. iii. 5.

25—34. The parallel passage (Luke xii. 22—31) follows immediately the parable of the Rich Fool.

25. διὰ τοῦτο, i.e. because this double service is impossible there must be no distraction of thought.

μὴ μεριμνᾶτε. 'Do not be anxious,' which was the meaning of 'take no thought,' when the E. V. was made. The same word occurs Phil. iv. 6, μηδὲν μεριμνᾶτε, where, as here, the tense marks continuance, 'do not be ever anxious.' Cp. 1 Pet. v. 7, πᾶσαν τὴν μέριμναν ὑμῶν ἐπιρίψαντες ἐπ' αὐτόν. See Bp Lightfoot, *On a Fresh Revision of the New Testament*, &c., p. 171.

The argument in the verse is: such anxiety is unnecessary; God gave the life and the body; will He not give the smaller gifts of food and clothing?

Socrates describes this to be the object of his mission: 'to persuade young and old,' μήτε σωμάτων ἐπιμελεῖσθαι μήτε χρημάτων πρότερον μηδὲ οὕτω σφόδρα ὡς τῆς ψυχῆς ὅπως ὡς ἀρίστη ἔσται. See v. 34 for a continuation of this quotation.

26. ἐμβλέψατε. The aorist implies the instantaneous glance possibly at large flocks of birds whirling at that moment in the sky, just as Canon Tristram observed on that very spot 'myriads of rock pigeons. In absolute clouds they dashed to and fro in the ravine, whirling round with a rush and a whirr that could be felt like a rush of wind.' The cliffs too are full of caves, the secure resting-places of 'noble griffons, lammergeyers, lanner falcons, and several species of eagles' (*Land of Israel*, p. 446). From this description and from the emphatic ἓν στρουθίον, ch. x. 29, it seems that the multitude of the birds is a leading thought in this illustration just as the colour and brightness of the flowers is the most prominent point in the other.

οὐ σπείρουσιν κ.τ.λ. There is no argument here against forethought or labour. In one sense 'trusting to providence' is idleness and a sin. God has appointed labour as the means whereby man provides for his wants. Even birds shew forethought, and search for the food which God has provided for them.

διαφέρειν, to differ by way of excellence, i.e. 'to excel': μᾶλλον redundant strengthens the verb.

27. προσθεῖναι ἐπὶ τὴν ἡλικίαν αὐτοῦ πῆχυν ἕνα. ἡλικία, either 'stature' or 'duration of life,' so that the meaning may be 'add a cubit to his life.' Comp. Ps. xxxix. 5, 'Thou hast made my days as an handbreadth.' This rendering falls in better with the connection. With all his anxiety man cannot add to his length of days, or clothe himself like the flowers.

Some reasons however may be adduced in favour of the rendering of the A.V., which coincides with the Vulgate. (1) It is better to retain the literal meaning of πῆχυν. (2) The rapid growth of vegetation in the East would make the thought more natural than with us. Comp. the well-known story in Herod. VIII. 55, δευτέρῃ δὲ ἡμέρῃ ἀπὸ τῆς ἐμπρήσιος Ἀθηναίων οἱ θύειν ὑπὸ βασιλέος κελευόμενοι...ὥρων βλαστὸν ἐκ τοῦ στελέχεος ὅσον τε πηχυαῖον ἀναδεδραμηκότα. See Godet on Luke xii. 25, and Maldonatus *ad loc.*

28. ἐνδύματος. The birds are an example of God's care in providing food, the flowers of His care in providing apparel. The Creator promises that the care shown to the lowliest of his works shall be extended to the noblest.

τὰ κρίνα τοῦ ἀγροῦ, identified by Dr Thomson (*Land and Book*, p. 256) with a species of lily found in the neighbourhood of Hûlêh. He speaks of having met with 'this incomparable flower, in all its loveliness...around the northern base of Tabor, and on the hills of Nazareth, where our Lord spent His youth.' Canon Tristram (*Nat. Hist. of the Bible*) claims this honour for the beautiful and varied *anemone coronaria*. 'If in the wondrous richness of bloom which characterises the Land of Israel in spring any one plant can claim pre-eminence, it is the anemone, the most natural flower for our Lord to pluck and seize upon as an illustration, whether walking in the fields or sitting on the hill-side.'

αὐξάνουσιν...κοπιῶσιν...νήθουσιν. Two reasons are assigned for the use of the plural verb after a neuter plural signifying *material* objects: either (1) the various parts of the subject are thought of separately rather than collectively; or (2) the action predicated of the subject is conceived as being repeated at successive periods. It may perhaps be a refinement to appeal to these reasons in this particular case, though both apply: probably the preceding structure, *v.* 26, influences the syntax here. Other instances of this anomaly in the N. T. are 1 Tim. v. 25, τὰ ἄλλως ἔχοντα (ἔργα) κρυβῆναι οὐ δύνανται. Rev. i. 19, ἃ εἶδες καὶ ἃ εἰσίν.

29. περιεβάλετο, 'arrayed himself.' The middle voice has a special force. Though he arrayed himself, the lilies, who trusted to God for their array, are more beautiful than he.

30. χόρτος, lit. (1) 'an enclosed place,' especially for feeding cattle, hence (2) 'provender,' grass, hay, (3) then generally 'vegetation,' flowers and grass growing in the fields, which when dried are used for fuel in the East. For the first sense cp. Hom. *Il.* xi. 774, αὐλῆς ἐν χόρτῳ; for the second Eur. *Alc.* 495, θηρῶν ὀρείων χόρτον οὐχ ἵππων λέγεις. The third sense is not classical.

εἰς κλίβανον βαλλόμενον. The κλίβανος was a vessel of baked clay wider at the bottom than the top. The process of baking meal-cakes or *Chupatties* in India, as a friend describes it to me, illustrates this passage and also the meaning of ἄρτοι (ch. xiv. 17 and elsewhere) and the expression κλάσαι ἄρτον (ch. xv. 36, Acts xx. 7). "The 'oven' is a jar-shaped vessel formed of tempered clay sunk in the ground. The fuel (χόρτος of the text) is 'cast into the oven' and lighted. The meal is first made into cakes, which are then taken up and whirled round between the two hands edgeways, and patted until they are as thin and about the size of a pancake, when by a dexterous movement the hand is introduced into the oven and the *chupattie* thrown against the side. There it sticks of its own adhesion; as it bakes, the edges curl and peel off, when nearly done and in danger of falling, a stick with a curved spike holds it until the correct moment, and serves to withdraw it from the oven. The result is a crisp thin cake, not unlike our oat-cake."

The Attic form of the word is κρίβανος: in later Greek both forms are retained and used indiscriminately. For this interchange of λ and ρ cp. σιγηρὸς for σιγηλός, βουκόλος and αἰγικορεύς. Lob. *Phryn.* 652.

ἀμφιέννυσιν. This word is used appropriately of the delicate membrane that clothes and protects the flower. Accordingly the thought suggested is not only the brilliant colour of the flower, but also the protection of the surrounding cuticle or sheath, which thin and delicate as it is is yet 'little sensitive to external and even chemical agencies.' The *periblem* (cp. περιεβάλετο above) is a technical term with botanists for the cortical tissue or inner membrane underlying the *epidermis*. See Thomé's *Struct. and Phys. Botany* (translated), Ch. III.

ὀλιγόπιστοι. A translation of a common Rabbinical expression.

32. ἐπιζητοῦσιν. Either (1) 'seek with eagerness'; ἐπί having the force of 'on,' 'further,' so earnestly. See Vaughan on Rom. xi. 7. Or (2) 'make special objects of pursuit,' from the sense of direction or aim in ἐπί. Cp. ἐπικωμῳδεῖν, 'to select for caricature.' Riddell, Plato, *Apol. Socr.* 31 D. With the general thought of the passage cp. Rom. xiv. 17, οὐ γάρ ἐστιν ἡ βασιλεία τοῦ Θεοῦ βρῶσις καὶ πόσις ἀλλὰ δικαιοσύνη καὶ εἰρήνη καὶ χαρὰ ἐν πνεύματι ἁγίῳ.

33. τὴν δικ. αὐτοῦ, i.e. τὴν δικ. Θεοῦ (Rom. i. 17), the leading thought in that epistle. It is the aim (ζητεῖτε) of the Christian life. Note how Christians are taught at least to *aim* at (ζητεῖν) righteousness, when the heathen *earnestly* aim at (ἐπιζητεῖν) lower objects.

ταῦτα πάντα προστεθήσεται ὑμῖν. One of the traditional sayings of Christ is closely parallel to this: αἰτεῖτε τὰ μεγάλα καὶ τὰ μικρὰ ὑμῖν προστεθήσεται, καὶ αἰτεῖτε τὰ ἐπουράνια καὶ τὰ ἐπίγεια προστεθήσεται ὑμῖν. Orig. *de Orat.* 2.

For a corresponding sentiment in Greek philosophy cp. Plato, *Apol. Socr.* p. 30, ἐξ ἀρετῆς χρήματα καὶ τἆλλα ἀγαθὰ τοῖς ἀνθρώποις ἅπαντα καὶ ἰδίᾳ καὶ δημοσίᾳ. The whole passage is worth reading in this connection. Such passages bear witness that what the best heathen recognised as their best thoughts were in fact the nearest to Christianity. The same Spirit led Gentile as well as Jew.

34. μὴ οὖν μεριμνήσητε εἰς τὴν αὔριον. Lightfoot, *Hor. Hebr.*, quotes a Rabbinical saying in illustration: 'there is enough of trouble in the very moment.'

ἡ κακία. Here in the unclassical sense of 'trouble,' 'sorrow,' cp. Amos iii. 6, εἰ ἔσται κακία ἐν πόλει ἣν Κύριος οὐκ ἐποίησεν;

CHAPTER VII.

2. μετρηθήσεται for ἀντιμετρηθήσεται taken from parallel passage Luke vi. 38. In *v.* 28 again the simple verb is preferred on good authority to the compound συνετέλεσεν.

4. ἐκ τοῦ ὀφθαλμοῦ for ἀπὸ τ. ὀφθ. ἀπὸ denoting removal from the *surface*, perhaps introduced from a note to mark and heighten the contrast. But the evidence for ἐκ is not decisive.

6. καταπατήσουσιν for καταπατήσωσιν the subjunctive was a correction to a more regular construction.

9. ὃν ἐὰν αἰτήσῃ for ὃν αἰτήσει and ἐὰν αἰτήσῃ for ἢ καὶ αἰτήσει (*v.* 10) are also grammatical corrections tending to explain the structure.

13. εἰσέλθετε for εἰσέλθατε was a change to a more regular form.

14. ὅτι is rightly adopted, though τί has a great preponderance of external authority; of the uncials, ℵ* B* and X alone exhibit ὅτι. The variant probably illustrates an interesting cause of error, by which the initial letter was sometimes overlooked through being reserved for subsequent revision and more careful work. Scrivener's *Introd.*, p. 15.

24. ὁμοιώσω, the reading of *textus receptus* for ὁμοιωθήσεται, has considerable, but not the most ancient evidence to support it. The variation from the passive ὁμοιωθήσεται, *v.* 26, has some point. Christ Himself sanctions the first part of the comparison, but leaves the other as a generally accepted and obvious fact without any special sanction on his part. See Jebb, *Sacr. Lit.* p. 217.

C. CHARACTERISTICS OF THE KINGDOM, 1—27.

After contrasting the New Law with the Mosaic Law and with Pharisaic rules and conduct, Jesus proceeds to lay down rules for the guidance of His disciples in the Christian life.

(a) *Judgment on others*, 1—6.

The passage occurs in St Luke's report of the Sermon on the Mount (ch. vi. 37, 38), with a different context, and a further illustration of 'full measure.'

1. μὴ κρίνετε κ.τ.λ. This is the form which the '*lex talionis*,' or law of reciprocity, takes in the kingdom of heaven.

The censorious spirit is condemned, it is opposed to the ἐπιείκεια, 'forbearance,' 'fairness in judgment,' that allows for faults, a characteristic ascribed to Jesus Christ Himself, 2 Cor. x. 1; cp. also Rom. xiv. 3 foll.

ἵνα μὴ κριθῆτε. By Christ on the Last Day.

2. κρίμα, 'judgment' either (1) in the sense of a judicial sentence as Rom. ii. 2, τὸ κρίμα τοῦ θεοῦ ἐστὶν κατὰ ἀλήθειαν, or (2) a rule or principle of judging, apparently the meaning here. The notion of 'censure' or 'condemnation' passes into the word from the context as: οὗτοι λήμψονται περισσότερον κρίμα. Mark xii. 40. The word is somewhat rare in the classics. In Æsch. *Supp.* 397 it means 'the question in dispute,' οὐκ εὔκριτον τὸ κρῖμα. For the accent see Winer's *Grammar*, 57. 2 and note 2. Penultimates long in Attic were sometimes shortened in later Greek, as θλίψις, ch. xxiv. 9.

3. βλέπεις. Of seeing the external surface of a thing contrasted with κατανοεῖς, which implies thoughtful perception. It is the contrast between judging from the outside and examination of the heart.

κάρφος. A 'twig,' 'splinter,' dry particle of hay (κάρφη Xen. *Anab.* I. 5, 10), straw, &c. Cp. Aristoph. *Av.* 641, εἰσέλθετ' ἐς νεοττιάν τε τὴν ἐμὴν | καὶ τἀμὰ κάρφη καὶ τὰ παρόντα φρύγανα.

τὴν ἐν τῷ σῷ ὀφθαλμῷ δοκόν. Which (1) ought to prevent condemnation of another for a less grave offence; and which (2) would obscure the spiritual discernment, and so render thee an incapable judge. The Pharisaic sin of hypocrisy (see next verse) was deeper and more fatal to the spiritual life than the sins which the Pharisee condemned.

δοκόν. From δέχομαι, in the sense of receiving, = 'a beam *let in*'; cp. ἱστοδόκη, and Hom. *Il.* XVII. 744, ἢ δοκὸν ἠὲ δόρυ μέγα νήϊον. See also Aristoph. *Vesp.* 201. The word appears to be Homeric and vernacular, not used in literary language.

4. ἄφες ἐκβάλω. 'Let me cast out.' See Winer, p. 356 *b*, and note 3, where instances of this case of ἄφες with conjunctive are quoted from Epictetus, e.g. ἄφες ἴδω, ἄφες δείξωμεν. The expression belongs to the vernacular. In modern Greek ἆς, a corruption of ἄφες, is used with the subjunctive whenever *let* occurs in the English imperative. Clyde's *Modern Greek*, p. 17.

τὸ κάρφος ἐκ τοῦ ὀφθ. ἀπό for ἐκ, though probably not the true reading, has considerable MS. support (see Crit. Notes). The gloss if it be a gloss shows a sense of the contrast already indicated by βλέπειν and κατανοεῖν. ἀπό implies removal from the surface, ἐκ removal from deep within.

(b) *The Father's love for the children of the Kingdom shown by answering prayer,* 7—11.

6. The connection between this verse and the preceding section is not quite obvious. It seems to be this. Although evil and censorious judgment is to be avoided, discrimination is needful. The Christian must be judicious, not judicial.

τὸ ἅγιον, i.e. 'spiritual truths.' Some have seen in the expression a reference to the holy flesh of the offering (Hag. ii. 12). But this allusion is very doubtful; see Meyer on this passage.

κυσίν...χοίρων. Unclean animals; see the proverb quoted 2 Pet. ii. 22; cp. Phil. iii. 2, βλέπετε τοὺς κύνας, βλέπετε τοὺς κακοὺς ἐργάτας; also Hor. *Ep.* I. 2. 25, '*vel canis immundus vel amica luto sus.*' See note on ch. xv. 26.

μαργαρίτας. The only gems mentioned in the Gospels, twice named by Jesus: here, where they signify the deepest spiritual thoughts of God and heaven, and ch. xiii. 46, where 'the pearl of great price' is the kingdom of heaven itself. The general sense is 'use discrimination, discern between holy and unholy, between those who are receptive of these high truths and those who are not.' The profane will despise the gift and put the giver to shame. Want of common sense does great harm to religion.

μήποτε καταπατήσουσιν. The future indicative is sometimes used in final clauses in place of the subjunctive after ὅπως and ὄφρα, very rarely (in Classics) after μή. Goodwin, *Greek Moods and Tenses,* § 44, note 1.

ἐν τοῖς ποσίν. (1) 'with their feet,' or (2) 'at their feet.'
This verse is a good example of Hebrew poetical form; the fourth line, καὶ στραφέντες ῥήξωσιν ὑμᾶς, being in parallel relation to the first, μὴ δῶτε κ.τ.λ.; the third, μήποτε καταπατήσουσιν κ.τ.λ. in relation to the second. Thus the appropriate actions are ascribed to the κύνες and the χοῖροι.

7, 8. Here each verse contains a triplet with ascending climax, αἰτεῖτε—ζητεῖτε—κρούετε. Each line of the one answers to the corresponding line of the other, with which it might be read continuously. It is a simple instance of a special characteristic of Hebrew poetry, of which examples sometimes elaborated with the greatest skill may be seen in Jebb's *Sacred Lit.* sec. IV. Comp. with this triple climax of rising earnestness in prayer, the triple climax of things desired in the Lord's Prayer. A close relation between the two might be shewn.

αἰτεῖτε, καὶ δοθήσεται. The connection is again difficult. The verse may be the answer to the disciples' unspoken questions: (1) 'How shall *we* discriminate?' or (2) 'Who are fit to receive these divine truths?' The words of Christ teach, (1) that discernment will be given, among other 'good things,' in answer to prayer; (2) that prayer in itself implies fitness, because it implies desire for such truths.

αἰτεῖτε. αἰτεῖν used of the petition to a superior. ἐρωτᾶν, in its unclassical sense of 'requesting,' is used of equals, a distinction which is strictly observed in the N.T. Trench (*N.T. Syn.* p. 169) remarks, 'our Lord never uses αἰτεῖν or αἰτεῖσθαι of Himself in respect of that which He asks on behalf of His disciples from God.'

9. Translate: 'Or what man is there from among you of whom his son shall ask a loaf—he will not give him a stone, will he?' Here the regular interrogative form of the sentence is checked and gives place to a fresh form of interrogation which is more pointed as definitely involving the reply. μή asks affirmatively and expects a negative answer.

ἄρτον...λίθον...ἰχθύν...ὄφιν. The things contrasted have a certain superficial resemblance, but in each case one thing is good, the other unclean or even dangerous.

10. **ἢ καὶ ἰχθὺν αἰτήσει.** See Critical Notes. Regarding the construction as independent, translate (1) 'Or again (the son) will ask a fish—will (the father) give him a serpent?' or (2) understanding the relative ὅν from the previous clause, 'or will he of whom his son shall ask,' &c.

It may be noted that both ἄρτος and ἰχθύς became for different reasons symbols of Christ.

11. **πονηροί.** 'Evil' as compared with the perfect righteousness of God.

ἀγαθά. For this St Luke (xi. 13) has 'the Holy Spirit,' shewing that spiritual rather than temporal 'good things' are intended.

12. **οὖν.** The practical result of what has been said both in regard to judgment and to prayer is mutual charity. The thought of the divine judgment teaches forbearance; the thought of the divine goodness teaches kindness.

(c) *The narrow entrance to the Kingdom*, 13, 14.

These verses are linked to the preceding by the thought of prayer, for it is by prayer chiefly that the narrow entrance must be gained.

13. **εἰσέλθατε...πύλης.** Luke xiii. 24, 25. The illustration seems to be drawn from a mansion having a large portal at which many enter, and a narrow entrance known to few, with broad and narrow ways leading respectively to each. One is the gate and the way of destruction (ἀπώλεια), the other is the gate and the way of life (ζωή or σωτηρία). Cp. the contrast between οἱ ἀπολλύμενοι, 'those in the way of destruction,' and οἱ σωζόμενοι, 'those on the way of salvation or life,' 1 Cor. i. 18. The πύλαι are probably the palace or city gates, not, as some have inferred from the position of the words, the entrances to the two ways. πύλη is named before ὁδός according to a not uncommon Greek usage, as being first in thought though second in point of fact; cp. Plato, *Apol. Soc.* p. 18, where παῖδες is named before μειράκια, and p. 32, where ἠναντιώθην is named before ἐψηφισάμην.

To the use of ὁδός in this passage we may probably refer ἡ ὁδός and αὕτη ἡ ὁδός, meaning the Christian Church (Acts ix. 2, xix. 9). Such usage was however influenced by the philosophic meaning of ὁδός, and the common Hebraisms 'the way of the Lord,' 'the paths of righteousness,' &c.

14. ὅτι. This ὅτι equally with the first, v. 13, is in construction with εἰσέλθατε διὰ τῆς στενῆς πύλης.

For the reading τί στενή see Crit. Notes. The internal evidence against it is strong. (1) The meaning assigned to τί, '*how* narrow,' is unexampled in the N.T.; Luke xii. 49 is not an instance. (2) The reading is harsh and breaks the constructive rhythm of the passage.

τεθλιμμένη. (θλίβω), lit. 'pressed,' 'confined.' Cp. Theocr. xxi. 18, παρ' αὐτὰν | θλιβομέναν καλύβαν (*angustam casam*).

ὀλίγοι οἱ εὑρίσκοντες. An answer to one of the disputed questions of the day, εἰ ὀλίγοι οἱ σωζόμενοι, Luke xiii. 43, the parallel passage to this (St Luke has instead of εἰσέλθατε the stronger phrase ἀγωνίζεσθε εἰσελθεῖν). It was a question that had been canvassed most earnestly in the reflective period after the cessation of prophecy. An answer to it would be demanded of every great teacher. See Prof. Westcott's *Introduction to N. T.*, p. 105, especially the quotation from 2 Esdras vii. 1—13. 'The entrance to the fair city was made by one only path, even between fire and water, so small that there could but one man go there at once.' Before Adam's transgression it was wide and sure.

(d) *The false guides to the narrow entrance, and the test of the true*, 15—23.

15. προσέχετε ἀπό. The classical constructions of προσέχειν (νοῦν) are τινί, πρός τι, πρός τινι: from the idea of attention to a thing comes that of caution about a thing, and ἀπό denotes the source of expected danger, cp. φοβεῖσθαι ἀπό. St Luke has this unclassical usage xii. 1, προσέχετε ἑαυτοῖς ἀπὸ τῆς ζύμης, and xx. 46, ἀπὸ τῶν γραμματέων. The construction is not used in N.T. except by St Matthew and St Luke.

ψευδοπροφητῶν, who will not help you to find the narrow way.

ἐν ἐνδύμασιν προβάτων. Not in a literal sense, but figuratively, 'wearing the appearance of guilelessness and truth.'

λύκοι ἅρπαγες. Cp. Acts xx. 29, where St Paul, possibly with this passage in his thoughts, says to the presbyters of Ephesus, ἐγὼ οἶδα ὅτι ἐλεύσονται μετὰ τὴν ἄφιξίν μου λύκοι βαρεῖς εἰς ὑμᾶς μὴ φειδόμενοι τοῦ ποιμνίου. Cp. Ezek. xxii. 27, οἱ ἄρχοντες αὐτῆς ἐν μέσῳ αὐτῆς ὡς λύκοι ἁρπάζοντες ἁρπάγματα τοῦ ἐκχέαι αἷμα κ.τ.λ. Such images as this contain implicitly a whole range of thoughts which would be present to the instructed disciples of the Lord—the fold of Christ—the Good Shepherd—the thief 'whose own the sheep are not.'

Wolves are still common in Palestine. Canon Tristram observes that they are larger than any European wolf and of a lighter colour.

16. ἄκανθα. A thorn tree, a kind of acacia. Athenæus describes it as having a round fruit on small stalks. It would give additional point to the saying if there were a distant but deceptive likeness between grapes and the berries of the *ἄκανθα*.

τρίβολος. The caltrop, a prickly plant reckoned by Virgil among the farmer's plagues, *Lappæque tribulique interque nitentia culta | infelix lolium et steriles dominantur avenæ.* Georg. I. 153.

19. μὴ ποιοῦν. 'If it does not produce.' To this day in the East trees are valued only so far as they produce fruit.

20. ἀπὸ τῶν καρπῶν κ.τ.λ. Re-echoed by a beautiful poetical figure from v. 16. See Jebb's *Sacred Lit.* p. 195—197. The well-known lines of Dryden, ' What passion cannot music raise and quell'; and those of Southey in a passage beginning and ending ' How beautiful is night!' are quoted in illustration.

22. ἐν ἐκείνῃ τῇ ἡμέρᾳ. A well-known Hebraism for 'the last day.' This is a forecast far into the distant future, when it would be worth while to assume Christianity, when hypocrisy would take the form of pretending to be a follower of the now despised Jesus. (See Canon Mozley's sermon, *On the reversal of human judgment.*)

Κύριε, κύριε. The iteration implies affection and reverence; it was usual in an address to a Rabbi. Here it is the repetition of hypocrisy. The chain of meanings in *φάσκειν* shows that reiterated assertion brings no impression of truthfulness.

ἐπροφητεύσαμεν, i.e. preached. The greatest of preachers dreads such a sentence. 1 Cor. ix. 27, 'Lest that by any means, when I have preached to others, I myself should be a castaway.' There is a reference to these words in the so-called second epistle of Clement, § 4: μὴ μόνον οὖν αὐτὸν καλῶμεν Κύριον· οὐ γὰρ τοῦτο σώσει ὑμᾶς· λέγει γὰρ οὐ πᾶς ὁ λέγων μοι, Κύριε Κύριε, σωθήσεται ἀλλὰ ὁ ποιῶν τὴν δικαιοσύνην. See at v. 23.

For the position of the augment see Winer, p. 84, and note; Tisch. and Treg. place the augment before the preposition wherever the word occurs, Lach. excepts Jude 14, *προεφήτευσεν.* With later authors the position in the text is not unusual, and as there is no simple verb *φητεύω* it must be regarded as regular.

23. ὁμολογεῖν. Properly to 'agree,' 'admit': in late Greek to 'assert,' 'affirm.'

οὐδέποτε ἔγνων. 'Never recognised you as being my disciples, with my name on your lips your heart was far from me.' Each false claim is answered by the Judge. As prophets he does not recognise them. He bids the false casters-forth of demons begone as though they themselves were demons,—the workers of *δυνάμεις* were really workers of *ἀνομία.* Comp. Clem. *Ep.* II. *loc. cit.* above: εἶπεν ὁ Κύριος ἐὰν ἦτε μετ' ἐμοῦ συνηγμένοι ἐν τῷ κόλπῳ μου καὶ μὴ ποιῆτε τὰς ἐντολάς μου ἀποβαλῶ ὑμᾶς καὶ ἐρῶ ὑμῖν· ὑπάγετε ἀπ' ἐμοῦ, οὐκ οἶδα ὑμᾶς πόθεν ἐστέ, ἐργάται ἀνομίας.

24. πᾶς ὅστις ἀκούει. Cp. v. 26, every one that heareth. Both classes of men hear the word. So far they are alike. Moreover the two houses have externally the same appearance. The great day of trial shews the difference. The imagery is from a mountain-country where the torrent-beds, sometimes more than half a mile in width in the plain below the mountain, are dry in summer, and present a level waste of sand and stones. We may picture the foolish man building on this sandy bottom, while the wise or prudent man builds on a rock planted on the shore, or rising out of the river-bed, too high to be affected by the rush of waters. In the autumn the torrents stream down, filling the sandy channel and carrying all before them. For the spiritual sense of the parable see 1 Cor. iii. 10 foll.

The effect of the two pictures is heightened by the poetical form. Observe the three long slow lines that describe the building of the houses succeeded by the brief vivid sentences that recall the beating of a fierce tropical tempest, and then the lasting result when the tempest passes away described by another long line.

The points of similarity in the two descriptions give prominence to the points of difference. ἄμμον and πέτραν are contrasted in the third line of each stanza. But the fatal and infinite distinction is reserved for the close. Like line and like condition succeed each other in the parallel images, and all seems safe and well for each alike until the fatal last line falls on heart and ear with a crash.

27. κατέβη...ἦλθον...ἔπνευσαν. Both the tense and the emphatic position of the verbs give great vivacity to the description.

οἱ ποταμοί. 'Streams,' rather than 'floods,' A.V. ἦλθαν, 'came,' because before there had been only a dry channel.

28. ἐξεπλήσσοντο. The tense implies the continuance of the astonishment, or the passing of it from group to group.

The meaning of this astonishing discourse was not lost upon the audience. No word could express more clearly the wonder and sense of novelty excited by the language and (as we may believe) the looks and bearing of Jesus. It was the astonishment of men who find themselves listening to the proclamation of a revolution set forth with marvellous force and beauty of language, who quite unconsciously find themselves face to face with a national crisis, the greatness of which was recognised by the listeners with a swiftness of spiritual perception only paralleled by the intellectual quickness of an Athenian crowd.

οἱ ὄχλοι. The crowds, i.e. the various groups that composed the assemblage.

τῇ διδαχῇ αὐτοῦ. 'His teaching,' both the matter and the manner of it.

29. ἦν γὰρ διδάσκων. The analytic imperfect indicates vividly the continuance of the action, 'He was teaching,' not as A.V. 'taught.' The thought of the listeners was: 'While He was teaching we felt all along that He was a lawgiver, not merely an interpreter of the law.'

ὡς οἱ γραμματεῖς αὐτῶν. Whose highest boast it was that they never spoke save in the words of a Rabbi.

οἱ γραμματεῖς. *Sopherim* = either (1) 'those who count' (Heb. *saphar*); because the Scribes counted each word and letter of the Scriptures; or

(2) 'those occupied with books' (Heb. *sepher*). The Scribes, as an organised body, originated with Ezra, who was in a special sense the '*Sopher*' or Scribe. This order of *Sopherim*, strictly so called, terminated B.C. 300. Their successors in our Lord's time were usually termed *Tanaim*, 'those who repeat, i.e. teach the Law.' They are called 'lawyers' (ch. xxii. 35; Luke v. 17; Acts v. 34), also 'the wise,' 'Elders,' and 'Rabbis.'

A scribe's education began as early as in his fifth year. At thirteen he became a 'son of the law,' *Bar-mitsvah*. If deemed fit, he became a disciple. At thirty he was admitted as a teacher, having tablets and a key given him. See note, ch. xvi. 19. His functions were various; he transcribed the law (here the greatest accuracy was demanded); he expounded the law, always with reference to authority —he acted as judge in family litigation, and was employed in drawing up various legal documents, such as marriage-contracts, writings of divorce, &c. (See Kitto's *Cycl. Bib. Lit.* and Smith's *Bib. Dict.* Art. 'Scribes.')

The alliance between Scribes and Pharisees was very close, each taught that the law could be interpreted, 'fenced round' and aided by tradition, in opposition to the Sadducees, who adhered to the strict letter of the written law.

CHAPTER VIII.

2. προσελθών for ἐλθών. The termination of λεπρὸς caused the omission of πρὸς before ἐλθών.

3. The name Ἰησοῦς occurs in this chapter four times against MS. authority,—*vv.* 3, 5, 7, 29. Such insertions are principally due to the Church lectionaries, the proper name being introduced at the commencement of a passage selected for reading.

8. λόγῳ for λόγον. The accusative inserted as the more usual case after εἶπε.

28. Γαδαρηνῶν. (ℵ* B C &c.), Γεργεσηνῶν (E K L &c.), Γερασηνῶν stated by Origen to be the prevailing reading.

31. ἀπόστειλον ἡμᾶς for ἐπίτρεψον ἡμῖν ἀπελθεῖν, doubtless influenced by Luke viii. 32.

32. εἰς τοὺς χοίρους (ℵ B C*) for εἰς τὴν ἀγέλην τῶν χοίρων.

34. ὑπάντησιν for συνάντησιν. See notes *infra*.

1—4. A LEPER IS CLEANSED.

St Mark i. 40—44; where this incident is placed in the course of a Galilæan circuit, and before the return to Capernaum. St Luke v. 12, where the cure is placed ἐν μιᾷ τῶν πόλεων, and precedes the Sermon on the Mount. With these discrepancies which meet us at every turn in the Gospels, it appears to be a hopeless task to construct a chronological arrangement of our Lord's ministry. On the other hand such divergences of plan form the strongest evidence of the independence of the narratives.

2. λεπρός. St Luke has ἀνὴρ πλήρης λέπρας, a term implying the gravity of the disease. In Levit. xiii. 13, where a man appears to be pronounced clean if 'the leprosy have covered all his flesh,' there is probably, as it is pointed out in the Speaker's Commentary, a misconception which has caused much difficulty to commentators. The plague there described is not true leprosy or elephantiasis, but the common white leprosy. The priest shall consider and pronounce clean the plague, i.e. declare that it is not true leprosy. Leprosy is to be regarded as especially symbolic of sin: (1) the beginning of the disease is almost unnoticed, (2) it is contagious (this point is disputed, but see in *Speaker's Commentary* note preceding Levit. xiii. 13, and Belcher, *Our Lord's Miracles of Healing*, ch. IV., also Meyer *ad loc.* who takes the same view), (3) in its worst form it is incurable except by the touch of Christ; (4) it separated a man and classed him with the dead.

προσεκύνει. The imperfect marks that persistency in prayer, which Jesus had just promised should win acceptance; while the leper's words imply a faith which is another condition of acceptance.

For the word see note ch. ii. 2. Κύριε bears out the idea of Oriental sovereignty conveyed by the verb. In Mark the reading γονυπετῶν is doubtful, St Luke has πεσὼν ἐπὶ πρόσωπον.

3. ἥψατο. An act that would bring with it legal defilement. St Mark gives the motive of Jesus in the cure σπλαγχνισθείς, 'from compassion;' both he and St Luke express the healing somewhat more vividly: ἀπῆλθεν ἀπ' αὐτοῦ ἡ λέπρα.

4. λέγει αὐτῷ. St Mark has ἐμβριμησάμενος ἐξέβαλεν αὐτὸν καὶ εἶπεν.

ὅρα μηδενὶ εἴπῃς. Christ enjoins the cleansed leper to tell no one, thus instructing us that He would not have people converted by His miracles. Christ addresses Himself to men's hearts, not to their eyes or ears. He will not fling Himself from the height of the temple to persuade men. But the injunction was doubtless also for the sake of the cured leper. It was not for his soul's health to publish to others the work that Christ had done on him.

προσένεγκον 1 aor. προσένεγκε 2 aor. (Mark and Luke). For the classical use of these two aorists see Veitch *sub voc.* φέρω.

ὃ προσέταξεν Μωϋσῆς. 'Two birds alive and clean, and cedar wood, and scarlet and hyssop.' And on the eighth day 'two he lambs without blemish, and one ewe lamb of the first year without blemish, and three tenth deals of fine flour for a meat offering, mingled with oil, and one log of oil;' or if poor, 'he shall take one lamb for a trespass offering to be waved, and one tenth deal of flour mingled with oil for a meat offering, and a log of oil and two turtle doves or two young pigeons such as he is able to get.' Levit. xiv. 4, 10, 21, 22.

Dr Edersheim says of this twofold rite that the first was to restore the leper to fellowship with the congregation, the second to introduce him anew into communion with God.

αὐτοῖς. Either (1) to the priests, or (2) to the people who were following Jesus; in either case to shew that Jesus came to fulfil the law, and as an evidence that the cure was real and complete.

5—13. CURE OF A CENTURION'S SERVANT.

St Luke vii. 1—10, where the incident is placed immediately after the Sermon on the Mount. The centurion sends a deputation of Jewish elders to Jesus, who speak of the worthiness of the centurion and of his love to the nation, 'he built us a synagogue.' St Luke does not introduce our Lord's comparison between Jew and Gentile, and the promises to the latter. This last point is characteristic—the rejection of the Jews is not dwelt upon when the Gospel is preached to the Gentiles. This might be further illustrated from the Acts.

5. ἑκατόνταρχος, i.e. a captain or commander of a century—a company nominally composed of a hundred men, the sixtieth part of a legion in the Roman army. This centurion was probably an officer in the army of Herod Antipas, which would be modelled after the Roman fashion, and not, as is often understood, a Roman Centurion.

This form appears to be used indifferently with the form in -ης which the best criticism has restored in *v.* 13.

6. ὁ παῖς. 'Slave,' not 'son;' the meaning is determined by the parallel passages; in Luke vii. where though the centurion himself uses the more affectionate term παῖς (*v.* 7), the messenger (*v.* 3) and the Evangelist (*v.* 10) call the servant δοῦλος.

παραλυτικός. Stricken with palsy or paralysis, a disease often free from acute suffering, but when it is accompanied by contraction of the muscles, the pain, as in this case, is very grievous. St Luke does not name the nature of the disease.

δεινῶς βασανιζόμενος. 'Terribly tortured.' For βάσανος see ch. iv. 24. The invariable practice of extracting evidence from slaves by torture gives βασανίζεσθαι the secondary force 'to torture,' 'to put to the question.'

Possibly the actual experience of this poor slave suggested the word; by no other could he describe to his master the agony he was enduring; it was the agony of torture.

8. ἀποκριθεὶς δὲ ὁ ἑκατόνταρχος. The argument lies in a comparison between the centurion's command and the authority of Jesus. 'If I who am under authority command others, how much more hast thou power to command who art under no authority? If I can send my soldiers or my slave to execute my orders, how much more canst thou send thy ministering spirits to do thy bidding?' The centurion was doubtless acquainted with the Jewish belief on the subject of angels, their subordination and their office as ministers of God.

ἱκανὸς ἵνα. The construction belongs to the consecutive and later use of ἵνα. The classical idiom would require the infinitive.

9. καὶ γάρ, 'for indeed.' καί connects the reason why Christ should not enter more closely with the facts of the centurion's position.

ὑπὸ ἐξουσίαν, 'under authority,' e.g. that of the χιλίαρχος or *tribunus militum*: cp. Acts xxi. 32, ὃς (χιλίαρχος) παραλαβὼν στρατιώτας καὶ ἑκατοντάρχας.

τούτῳ [στρατιώτῃ]...τῷ δούλῳ μου. Observe a distinction in the centurion's orders, his *soldiers* come and go, i.e. march when he bids them. His *slave* he orders to do this, i.e. perform any servile work. In the household of the centurion Cornelius we find as here οἰκέται and στρατιῶται (Acts x. 7).

Mark this as the first contact of Jesus with slavery. With such relations between master and slave as these slavery would soon pass away.

It was no express enactment of Christ, but the Spirit of Christ, which this centurion had caught, that abolished slavery.

11. ἀνατολῶν. See note ch. ii. 1.

ἀνακλιθήσονται, i.e. recline at a feast. The image of a banquet is often used to represent the joy of the kingdom of heaven. Luke xiv. 15, xxii. 29, 30; Rev. xix. 9. Cp. Isaiah xxv. 6.

12. τὸ σκότος τὸ ἐξώτερον, i.e. the darkness outside the house in which the banquet is going on.

ὁ κλαυθμὸς καὶ ὁ βρυγμός. The article, ignored in A.V., means 'that wailing and gnashing of teeth which you speak of;' τὸ λεγόμενον, it was a common figure.

13. ὕπαγε, 'go,' the ordinary modern word in this sense, and so used colloquially before it was established in literary language. Cp. Aristoph. *Ranæ*, 174, ὑπάγεθ' ὑμεῖς τῆς ὁδοῦ. See note ch. iv. 10. ὑπάγειν is especially frequent in St John's gospel.

14—17. THE CURE OF PETER'S MOTHER-IN-LAW OF A FEVER, Mark i. 29—31; Luke iv. 38, 39.

St Luke's description bears special marks of scientific accuracy. Both St Mark and St Luke mention that the incident took place when 'he came out of the synagogue;' and St Mark adds that he went into the house of Simon and Andrew with James and John.

14. εἰς τὴν οἰκίαν Πέτρου. From John i. 44 we learn that Bethsaida was the city of Andrew and Simon Peter. Either then (1) they had changed their home to Capernaum, or (2) Bethsaida was close to Capernaum.

τὴν πενθεράν. St Peter alone of the Apostles is expressly named as being married. It is however a probable inference from 1 Cor. ix. 5, that all the Apostles were married: μὴ οὐκ ἔχομεν ἐξουσίαν ἀδελφὴν γυναῖκα περιάγειν ὡς καὶ οἱ λοιποὶ ἀπόστολοι καὶ οἱ ἀδελφοὶ τοῦ Κυρίου καὶ Κηφᾶς. It is worthy of note that no wives or children of Apostles are known to Church history.

βεβλημένην καὶ πυρέσσουσαν. St Luke has συνεχομένη πυρετῷ μεγάλῳ. συνεχ. is a technical word implying the 'constraint' of sickness; the symptoms of πυρετὸς μέγας as described by ancient physicians resemble those of typhus fever.

βεβλημένην denotes the great and sudden prostration characteristic of this kind of fever.

15. ἥψατο. The touch of Jesus is not mentioned in Luke.

ἀφῆκεν αὐτήν. The addition of εὐθέως in Mark is probably a gloss. St Luke however has παραχρῆμα ἀναστᾶσα. To the physician the completeness and suddenness of the cure proves the miraculous nature of it.

διηκόνει. In the proper sense of serving at table; see note ch. iv. 11.

16. λόγῳ. Not by a touch, as in the case of leprosy and fever. Christ never laid his hand on demoniacs.

17. Isaiah liii. 4.

18—22. FITNESS FOR DISCIPLESHIP. Luke ix. 57—62.

St Luke names three instances, and places the scene of the incident in Samaria.

The instances are typical of the way in which Jesus deals with different characters. To one attracted by the promises of the Gospel and full of eagerness, Jesus presents the darker side—the difficulties of the Christian life; the half-hearted discipleship of the other is confronted with the necessity of absolute self-renunciation.

19. εἷς. To be taken in connection with ἕτερος δέ, the first in the enumeration.

γραμματεύς. The accession of a Scribe to the cause of Christ must have appeared to the people as a great success. Language of the most extravagant adulation is used to express the dignity and influence of the Scribes. Yet Jesus discourages him. No secondary motives are named, but the Scribe may have expected a high position in the kingdom of a temporal Messiah. We are not told whether, thus brought face to face with privation and hardship, he was daunted like the young ruler (ch. xix. 16), or persevered like the sons of Zebedee (ch. xx. 22).

20. φωλεούς. A word used by Plutarch and other late authors. Theocritus has φωλάδες ἄρκτοι, I. 115, and κνώδαλα φωλεύοντα, xxiv. 83, a heteroclite plural φωλεά is found.

κατασκηνώσεις. Cp.

'In which all trees of honour stately stood,
And did all winter as in summer bud,
Spreading pavilions for the birds to bower.'

E. SPENSER.

ὁ υἱὸς τοῦ ἀνθρώπου. The origin of this expression as a Messianic title is found in Dan. vii. 13: 'I saw in the night visions, and, behold, one like the Son of man came with (in) the clouds of heaven, and came to the Ancient of days, and they brought him near before him.' Hence to the Jews it would be a familiar designation of the Messiah—the King whose 'everlasting dominion' is described in the next verse (Dan. vii. 14). (See Dr Pusey, *On Daniel*, Lecture II.)

The Hebraism may be considered in the light of similar expressions, 'sons of light,' 'son of perdition,' 'son of peace,' &c., in all of which the genitive denotes a quality inherent in the subject. Sons of light = the spiritually enlightened, sons of wisdom = the wise. By the Son of man then is meant He who is essentially man, who took man's nature upon Him, who is man's representative before God, shewing the possibilities of purified human nature, and so making atonement practicable.

The title 'Son of man,' so frequently used by our Lord of Himself, is not applied to Him except by Stephen (Acts vii. 56), 'I see the heavens opened, and the Son of man standing on the right hand of God.' In Rev. i. 13 and xiv. 14, where the expression occurs without the definite article the reference to the Messianic title is not certain.

οὐκ ἔχει ποῦ τὴν κεφαλὴν κλίνῃ. A saying attributed to Tib. Gracchus is sometimes quoted as parallel: τὰ μὲν θηρία τὰ τὴν Ἰταλίαν νεμόμενα καὶ φωλεὸν ἔχει καὶ κοιταῖόν ἐστὶν αὐτῶν ἑκάστῳ καὶ καταδύσεις· τοῖς δὲ ὑπὲρ τῆς Ἰταλίας μαχομένοις καὶ ἀποθνήσκουσιν ἀέρος καὶ φωτὸς ἄλλου δὲ οὐδένος μέτεστιν, Plut. p. 828, c.

22. θάψαι τοὺς ἑαυτῶν νεκρούς. The exact force of this is not quite clear. The word 'dead' is used first in a figurative, secondly, in a literal sense, as in John xi. 25, 26. In a figurative sense by the 'dead' are intended those who are outside the kingdom, who are dead to the true life. Perhaps a brother or brothers of the disciple had rejected Christ, 'let them bury their father.'

St Luke, after 'let the dead bury their dead,' adds, 'but go thou and preach the kingdom of God.'

Perhaps no incident marks more decisively the height of self-abandonment required by Jesus of His followers. In this instance the disciple is called upon to renounce for Christ's sake the last and most sacred of filial duties. The unswerving devotion to Christ is illustrated in the parallel passage (Luke ix. 62) by 'the man who puts his hand to the plough.'

23—27. THE STORM ON THE LAKE. Mark iv. 35—41; Luke viii. 22—25.

St Mark, as usual, adds some interesting details: 'it was evening—there were other boats with Him—a great storm (λαῖλαψ) of wind—the waves beat into the boat—He was asleep on the cushion (τὸ προσκεφάλαιον) in the hinder part of the boat.'

With all these points of difference in seven short verses, how can it be said that St Mark's Gospel is an abridgment of St Matthew's?

23. τὸ πλοῖον. The ship or fishing-boat, i.e. the boat which Jesus always used.

24. σεισμός, elsewhere of earthquakes, Luke and Mark have the more descriptive λαῖλαψ.

αὐτὸς ἐκάθευδεν. 'He—the Master—continued to sleep.' It is the only place where the sleep of Jesus is named.

The nominative of αὐτὸς is very rare in Matthew and Mark but very common in Luke. It has the proper classical force of contrast in this passage, but there is also some evidence that αὐτὸς was used of Christ in relation to his disciples as the Master in the sense of αὐτὸς ἔφα, cp. 2 Peter iii. 4; 1 John ii. 12; 2 John 6, where αὐτοῦ is used of Christ without any expressed antecedent.

25. σῶσον, ἀπολλύμεθα. The brevity of speech that wastes no words adds to the impression of danger. Cp. ch. xxvi. 45, 46. St Luke has ἐπιστάτα repeated. St Mark the pathetic διδάσκαλε οὐ μέλει σοι ὅτι ἀπολλύμεθα. Cp. with σῶσον,—the aorist of earnest and instant request—the aorists in the Lord's prayer.

26. δειλοί, 'cowardly:' ὁ δὲ τῷ φοβεῖσθαι ὑπερβάλλων δειλός, Arist. *Eth. Nic.* III. 7, 10. The sea was a recognised test of courage, οὐ μὴν ἀλλὰ καὶ ἐν θαλάττῃ...ἀδεὴς ὁ ἀνδρεῖος (Arist.). Neither ἀνδρεῖος nor θρασὺς occur in N. T. Cowardice and want of faith are classed together as grievous sins in Rev. xxi. 8, δειλοῖς καὶ ἀπίστοις.

ἐπετίμησεν τοῖς ἀνέμοις. Cp. ἐπετίμησεν τῷ πυρετῷ (Luke iv. 39). The vivacity of Eastern speech personifies the disease as well as winds and waves. ἐπιτιμᾶν, first of fixing a penalty (τιμή), then of judicial rebuke, then of rebuke generally.

27. οἱ ἄνθρωποι. The disciples, and other fishermen who were also on the Lake: see account in Mark.

28—34. THE GADARENE DEMONIACS. St Mark v. 1—20; St Luke viii. 26—39.

St Mark and St Luke make mention of one demoniac only. St Mark relates the incident at greater length and with more particularity. St Matthew omits the name 'legion,' the prayer not to be sent into the 'abyss' (Luke), the request of one of the demoniacs to be with Jesus, and the charge which Jesus gives him to tell his friends what great things the Lord had done for him.

28. Γαδαρηνῶν. The readings vary between Γερασηνῶν, Γαδαρηνῶν and Γεργεσηνῶν in the Synoptic accounts. Gerasa and Gergesa are forms of the same name. Gadara was some distance to the south of the Lake. It was, however, the capital of Peræa, and the more important place; possibly Gergesa was under its jurisdiction. Gergesa is identified with the modern Khersa; in the neighbourhood of which 'rocks with caves in them very suitable for tombs, a verdant sward with bulbous roots on which the swine might feed' (Macgregor, *Rob Roy*), and a steep descent to the verge of the Lake, exactly correspond with the circumstances of the miracle. (See Map.)

IX.] *NOTES.* 151

ὑπήντησαν. The force of ὑπό in this word may be illustrated by ὑποκρίνεσθαι, 'to answer back,' ὑπολογίζεσθαι, 'to reckon on the opposite side' (*per contra*), ὑποστρέφειν, 'to turn in an opposite direction;' here ὑπαντᾶν is to meet from an opposite direction. ὑπωμοσία and ὑποτιμᾶσθαι are similar instances of the use of ὑπό cited by Riddell, Plato, *Apol. Socr.*, Digest. 131.

μνημείων. Tombs hewn out of the mountain-sides formed convenient dwelling-places for the demoniacs.

29. ἰδοὺ ἔκραξαν. Cp. Verg. *Aen.* IV. 490, Mugire *videbis* | sub pedibus terram; but ἰδού in Hellenistic Greek is little more than a vivid transitional particle, drawing attention to what follows.

31. δαίμονες. The masculine form occurs nowhere else in N.T. In the parallel passages Mark v. 12 and Luke viii. 29, the best criticism rejects this form. It is an interesting instance of the tendency with copyists to assimilate parallel passages even in minor particulars.

32. τοῦ κρημνοῦ. Translate, *the* steep place. The slope of Gergesa, familiar to Matthew and to the readers of his Gospel.

33. οἱ δὲ βόσκοντες. It does not appear whether these were Jews or Gentiles, more probably the latter; if the former, they were transgressing the law.

(1) This narrative may be regarded as a signal instance of μετάνοια, or change from the old evil state to the new life. (2) It recalls the connection between sin and disease. The majority of cases of *mania* may be traced to sins of impurity; the impurity expelled, the man becomes sound in body as well as in mind. (3) The destruction of the swine should present no difficulty. The same God, who, for purposes often hidden, allows men to die by thousands in war or by pestilence, here, by the destruction of a herd of swine, enforces a moral lesson which the world has never forgotten.

34. ὅπως μεταβῇ. The motive for the request was fear lest a greater disaster should follow (Meyer).

CHAPTER IX.

2. ἀφίενται for ἀφέωνται. This important change (see notes *infra*) is supported by ℵ B and Origen, and is adopted by the leading editors. In Luke v. 23, ἀφέωνται is unquestioned.

5. ἔγειρε for ἔγειραι. An example of *itacism*, errors arising from similarity of sound. 'In all the passages in which ἔγειρε occurs, there is found, as a different reading, ἔγειραι.' (Meyer.)

8. ἐφοβήθησαν. ἐθαύμασαν of *textus receptus* is a gloss.

13. εἰς μετάνοιαν after καλέσαι. An insertion due to the parallel passage, Luke v. 32. The tendency to harmonise is a frequent source of error.

30. ἐνεβριμήθη, the true reading for ἐνεβριμήσατο, is an instance of the forms of the middle voice gradually giving place to passive forms. In modern Greek there is no middle voice.

35. The words ἐν τῷ λαῷ, limiting the action to Israel, are rightly elided after μαλακίαν.

36. ἐσκυλμένοι. A certain change for ἐκλελυμένοι.

ἐριμμένοι, for ἐρριμμένοι, in accordance with the more ancient MSS; but D* has ρεριμμένοι.

1—8. CURE OF A MAN AFFLICTED WITH PARALYSIS.
Mark ii. 1—12; Luke v. 18—26.

Both St Mark and St Luke notice the crowding of the people to hear Jesus, and narrate the means by which the sufferer was brought into His presence.

1. εἰς πλοῖον. In such adverbial expressions the article is often absent, as εἰς οἶκον. Cp. English 'to take ship,' 'to go home.'

τὴν ἰδίαν πόλιν. Capernaum, the city where He dwelt, thus designated here only: cp. ἕκαστος εἰς τὴν ἑαυτοῦ πόλιν (Luke ii. 3), his ancestral city.

2—6. When Jesus said 'Thy sins are forgiven thee' the young man did not immediately rise (see *v.* 7). Instantly the Scribes thought with a sneer 'this fellow blasphemes,' i.e. pretends to a divine power which he does not possess. They said in their hearts it is easy to say, 'Thy sins are forgiven,' let him say, 'Arise, and walk,' then we shall discover his blasphemy. Jesus answers their thoughts. His words are not '*whether*' as in A.V., but '*why* is it easier to say, Thy sins are forgiven thee, than to say, Arise, and walk?' In truth it was not easier to say, 'Thy sins are forgiven' as Jesus says those words, for to say them implied the cure of soul and of body too; but in order to convince the Scribes of His power He adds the words, 'Arise, and walk;' and implicitly bids them infer that the inner work of forgiveness had as surely followed the first words as the outward and visible result followed the command to rise and walk.

2. παραλυτικόν, not in this case δεινῶς βασανιζόμενος (see ch. viii. 6), therefore suffering from a less severe type of paralysis.

τὴν πίστιν αὐτῶν: the faith of those who brought him as well as his own. Cp. Mark ix. 23, 24.

ἀφίενται, 'are being forgiven,' for ἀφέωνται of received text (see Crit. Notes). Comp. with this passage John xx. 23, where ἀφέωνται is the true reading for ἀφίενται of the received text. The reversal of the readings in the two cases is important. With the divine Saviour the act of forgiveness is present and in progress, with the Apostles it is the spiritual gift to see, and authority to declare a sentence passed in heaven.

3. βλασφημεῖν. Construction τινά, εἰς τινα, τι or abs. (1) to speak evil of God or of sacred things βλ. εἰς τὸ πνεῦμα τὸ ἅγιον, Mark iii. 29

and Luke xii. 10; *ἠνάγκαζον βλασφημεῖν*, Acts xxvi. 11; *ἵνα μὴ ὁ λόγος τοῦ Θεοῦ βλασφημῆται*, Tit. ii. 5. (2) to disparage the divine nature, to usurp the honour due to God, as here and generally in the Gospels. (3) 'to calumniate men' *τί βλασφημοῦμαι ὑπὲρ οὗ ἐγὼ εὐχαριστῶ;* 1 Cor. x. 30. As a classical word *βλασφημεῖν* is opposed to *εὐφημεῖν*: so *βλασφημία*, Eur. *Ion.* 1189, *βλασφημίαν τις οἰκετῶν ἐφθέγξατο*, 'spake word of evil omen.' The derivation is uncertain, perhaps from the same root as *βλάξ, βλάζειν*, see Buttmann, *Lex*, *sub voc. βλίττειν*, § 6. Others connect the word with *βλάπτειν*, cp. 'all words that may do hurt.'

5. **εὐκοπώτερον.** A post-classical word, used only in the Synoptic Gospels, and always in the comparative degree.

6. **ἆρόν σου τὴν κλίνην.** The Oriental frequently spreads a mat upon the ground and sleeps in the open air, in the morning he rolls up his mat and carries it away.

9. THE CALL OF ST MATTHEW. Mark ii. 14; Luke v. 27, 28.

St Mark has 'Levi, the son of Alphæus,' St Luke 'a publican named Levi.' The identification of Matthew with Levi can scarcely be seriously disputed. The circumstances of the call are precisely similar as narrated by the Synoptists; and it was too usual for a Jew to have more than one name for this difference to be a difficulty. Probably the name Matthew, 'Gift of Jehovah,' was adopted by the Apostle when he became a follower of Jesus.

παράγων. 'As he passed by,' not passed *forth*, as A. V.

τὸ τελώνιον, the toll- or custom-house. For a longer notice of the call of St Matthew, see Introduction.

10—13. A MEAL IN THE EVANGELIST'S HOUSE. Mark ii. 15—17; Luke v. 29—32.

10. **καὶ ἐγένετο.** See note, ch. xi. 1.

ἀνακεῖσθαι, late in this sense for the classical *κατακεῖσθαι*, 'to recline at table.'

ἐν τῇ οἰκίᾳ. St Luke says 'and Levi made him a great feast,' which makes it clear that the meal was in Levi's house.

πολλοὶ τελῶναι. The fact that the tax-gatherers were numerous enough to form a large class of society points significantly to the oppression of the country. **ἁμαρτωλοί**, men of impure lives, or esteemed impure by the Pharisees.

11. **ἰδόντες οἱ Φαρισαῖοι.** The Pharisees were not guests, but came into the house,—a custom still prevalent in the East. A traveller writes from Damietta, 'In the room where we were received, besides the divan on which we sat, there were seats all round the walls. Many came in and took their place on those side-seats, uninvited and yet unchallenged. They spoke to those at table on business, or the news of the day, and our host spoke freely to them. We afterwards saw this custom at Jerusalem...first one and then another stranger opened the door and came in, taking seats by the wall. They leaned forward and spoke to those at table.' *Scripture Manners and Customs*, p. 185.

Διατί κ.τ.λ. St Mark represents the question to be asked by οἱ γραμματεῖς τῶν Φαρισαίων, St Luke by οἱ Φαρισαῖοι καὶ οἱ γραμματεῖς αὐτῶν.

12. οἱ ἰσχύοντες κ.τ.λ. There is a touch of irony in the words. They that are 'whole' are they who think themselves whole. So below, the 'righteous' are those who are righteous in their own eyes.

13. πορευθέντες μάθετε. A translation of a common Rabbinical formula.

Ἔλεος θέλω. 'I desire mercy.' I require mercy rather than sacrifice, Hosea vi. 6. It is a protest by the prophet against the unloving, insincere formalist of his day. It is closely parallel to our Lord's injunction, ch. v. 23, 24. Sacrifice without mercy is no acceptable sacrifice. To love sinners is a better fulfilling of the law than to stand aloof from them. See note ch. xii. 7, where our Lord again quotes these words.

The neuter form ἔλεος is late: cp. κατὰ τὸ πλοῦτος corrected from κατὰ τὸν πλοῦτον, Phil. iv. 19.

καλέσαι. The underlying thought is invitation to a banquet; the word has a special significance in the circumstances: cp. the important Christian derived terms κλῆσις, (1) 'the invitation,' 2 Pet. i. 10; (2) the body of the 'called,' 1 Cor. i. 26, and κλητὸς as Rom. i. 1, κλητὸς ἀπόστολος.

It was from scenes like this that Jesus was named φάγος καὶ οἰνοπότης τελωνῶν φίλος καὶ ἁμαρτωλῶν, ch. xi. 19.

14—17. A QUESTION ABOUT FASTING. Mark ii. 18—22; Luke v. 33—39.

It is not quite clear whether this further incident took place at Levi's feast. St Luke leads us to draw that inference.

15. οἱ υἱοὶ τοῦ νυμφῶνος. See note, v. 6. 'The children of the bridechamber' were the bridegroom's friends or groomsmen who went to conduct the bride from her father's house (see note, ch. xxv. 1). The procession passed through the streets, gay with festive dress, and enlivened with music and joyous shouts, and with the brilliant light of lamps and flambeaux. With the same pomp and gladness the bride was conducted to her future home, where the marriage-supper was prepared.

ὁ νυμφίος. The Jews symbolised the 'congregation' or 'church' by the image of a bride. Jesus sets himself forth as the Bridegroom of the Christian Church. See Herschell, *Sketch of the Jews*, pp. 92—97.

ὅταν ἀπαρθῇ. For the first time in this gospel Jesus alludes to his death.

νηστεύσουσιν. Herschell (quoted in *Scripture Manners and Customs*) observes that many Jews who keep voluntary fasts, if invited to a marriage are specially exempted from the observance of them. Jesus first gives a special answer to the question about fasting. There is a time of sorrow in store for my disciples when fasting will have a real meaning, *now* in my presence they can but rejoice. Note that fasting and mourning are regarded as quite synonymous. This they are to the perfectly sincere only. The words of Jesus are true also of Christian experience. There are joyous times when the presence of Christ is felt to be near. Then fasting would be out of harmony. But there are also seasons of despondency and depression, when Christ seems to be taken away, when fasting is natural and appropriate.

16. **οὐδεὶς δέ**, but no man. The particle δέ is omitted in A.V.; it marks a turn in the argument which is indicated still more clearly in Luke (v. 36), ἔλεγεν δὲ καὶ παραβολὴν πρὸς αὐτούς. The words of Jesus here take a wider range. He says in effect to John's disciples: 'Your question implies ignorance of my teaching. My doctrine is not merely a reformed Judaism like the teaching of John and Pharisaism, it is a new life to which such questions as these concerning ceremonial fasting are quite alien.'

ἀγνάφου, 'new;' literally, uncarded, from γνάπτω. The old garment is Judaism. Christianity is not to be pieced on to Judaism to fill up its deficiencies. This would make the rent—the divisions of Judaism—still more serious.

σχίσμα is used of the 'schisms' in the Corinthian Church, 1 Cor. i. 10, and has so passed into ecclesiastical language.

17. **οἶνον νέον εἰς ἀσκοὺς παλαιούς**. The Oriental bottles are skins of sheep or goats. Old bottles would crack and leak. This may be regarded as a further illustration of the doctrine taught in the preceding verse. But it is better to give it an individual application. The new wine is the new law, the freedom of Christianity. The new bottles are those fitted to live under that law. The old wine is Judaism, the old bottles those, who trained in Judaism, cannot receive the new law, who say 'the old is better' (or 'good'), Luke v. 39.

Our Lord's answer then is threefold, (1) specially as to fasting, (2) as to Christianity in regard to Judaism, (3) as to individuals trained in Judaism.

(1) This is a joyous time, not a season for fasting, which is a sign of sorrow.
(2) Christianity is not a sect of Judaism, or to be judged according to rules of Judaism.
(3) It is not every soul that is capable of receiving the new and spiritual law. The new wine of Christianity requires new vessels to contain it.

εἰ δὲ μήγε, 'otherwise.' Literally, 'unless he acts thus.' Cp. Epict. Diss. I. 15, οὐκ ἐπαγγέλλεται ἔφη φιλοσοφία τῶν ἐκτός τι περιποιήσειν τῷ ἀνθρώπῳ εἰ δὲ μὴ κ.τ.λ., where εἰ δὲ μή=*nisi ita esset ut ego dico*. (Schweighäuser).

οἶνον νέον. 'New wine,' i.e. wine of this vintage. ἀσκοὺς καινούς, 'new skins,' i.e. that have not been used before; cp. καινὸν μνημεῖον, a sepulchre that had never been used, not one that had been lately hewn out; νέα διαθήκη, a covenant that is quite recent; καινὴ διαθήκη, one that is distinct from the old covenant. See Trench, *Synonyms*, part 2, § 10.

18—26. The Daughter of Jairus, 18, 19 and 23—26; Mark v. 22—24 and 35—43. Luke viii. 41, 42 and 49—56.

The Woman cured of an Issue of Blood, 20—22. Mark v. 25—34; Luke viii. 43—48.

Related with more detail by St Mark and St Luke. She had spent all her living on physicians. Jesus perceives that virtue has gone out of him. The woman tells all the truth before the people.

18. ἄρχων. From Mark and Luke we learn that he was a chief ruler of the synagogue (ἀρχισυνάγωγος, Mark), Jairus by name. ἡ θυγάτηρ μου. τὸ θυγάτριόν μου (Mark). θυγάτηρ μονογενής (Luke). ἄρτι ἐτελεύτησεν. ἐσχάτως ἔχει (Mark). ἀπέθνησκεν (Luke).

20. τοῦ κρασπέδου. See ch. xiv. 36 and xxii. 5.

21. ἔλεγεν γὰρ ἐν ἑαυτῇ. The imperfect denotes intensity of feeling, 'she kept saying over and over to herself.'

22. Eusebius (*H. E.* vii. 18) states that in the city of Caesarea-Philippi stood a bronze statue of this woman kneeling before the Saviour, who was represented extending his hand to her.

23. St Mark and St Luke mention the message to Jairus on the way, that his daughter was already dead, and name the three disciples whom Jesus permits to enter the house with him.

τοὺς αὐλητάς. The minstrels are mentioned by St Matthew only. Lane (*Modern Egyptians*) says 'the women of the family raise the cries of lamentations called '*welweleh*' or '*wilwal;*' uttering the most piercing shrieks and calling upon the name of the deceased.' The employment of hired minstrels for funeral lamentations seems to have been universal in the ancient world. Cp. *Cantabat maestis tibia funeribus,* Ov. *Trist.* v. 1. 14; τί με ὁ κωκυτὸς ὑμῶν ὀνίνησι, Lucian, *de luctu*. 10. 'Even the poorest among the Israelites will afford her not less than two pipes and one woman to make lamentation.' (Talmud.)

τὸν ὄχλον θορυβούμενον. To join in lamentation for the dead and to assist in the preparation for the funeral rites were reckoned among the most meritorious works of charity.

24. τὸ κοράσιον. Diminutive of affection. This form is rejected by the Atticists in favour of κόριον, κορίδιον, κορίσκη, κορίσκιον. It is frequent in Epictetus, Lucian, and other late authors. See Lob. *Phryn.* 73, and Sturz, *De dial. Maced.* p. 42.

οὐ γὰρ ἀπέθανεν ἀλλὰ καθεύδει. These words are reported without variation by the three Synoptists; it is open to question whether they ought not to be taken literally. For although κοιμᾶσθαι is frequently used both by classical authors and in the N.T. of the sleep of death, it is doubtful whether this metaphorical sense is ever attached to καθεύδειν in the N.T. or elsewhere. Λάζαρος ὁ φίλος ἡμῶν κεκοίμηται (not καθεύδει) John xi. 11; καὶ τοῦτο εἰπὼν ἐκοιμήθη, Acts vii. 60.

The Jews also spoke of death as sleep, but it is clear that in this instance they understood Jesus to speak of natural sleep.

κατεγέλων. For the force of κατὰ cp. καταφιλεῖν, ch. xxvi. 49; Acts xx. 37, and Thuc. III. 83, καταγελασθὲν ἠφανίσθη.

25. ἐξεβλήθη ὁ ὄχλος. The crowd which paid no regard to the repeated bidding (ἔλεγεν, v. 24, imperf.) of Jesus was now thrust forth.

27—31. A Cure of two Blind Men.

Peculiar to St Matthew. Archbp. Trench alludes to the fact that cases of blindness are far more numerous in the East than in Western countries. 'The dust and flying sand enter the eyes, causing inflammations......the sleeping in the open air, and the consequent exposure of the eyes to the noxious nightly dews, is another source of this malady.'

27. υἱὸς Δαυείδ. See note ch. i. 1. The thought of the kingdom of heaven had been closely linked with the reign of a son of David, but doubtless with many Jews the glory of the Asmonean dynasty (the Maccabees) and the established power of the Herods had tended to obscure this expectation. To have clung to it was an act of faith.

28. For ναί see Bp. Ellicott on Phil. iv. 8. Here of assent to a question, as ch. xvii. 25, and as always in John. Sometimes of assent to a statement, as ch. xv. 27, or strongly asseverative as always in Luke and ch. xi. 9, 26.

30. ἐμβριμᾶσθαι. Lit. 'to roar,' *leonis voce uti* (Schleusner), then (1) 'to charge with vehement threats:' cp. εἰ σὺ βριμήσαιο, Aristoph. *Knights*, 851, where the Scholiast explains the word τὸ ὀργίζεσθαι καὶ ἀπειλεῖν, implying 'fretful impatience,' (Jebb on Soph. *Ajax*, 322); (2) 'to enjoin strictly' (here and Mark i. 43); (3) to be loudly indignant (Mark xiv. 5). In John xi. 33, ἐνεβριμήσατο τῷ πνεύματι probably means, 'felt indignation in his spirit,' possibly, expressed indignation, 'groaned in his spirit;' so also John xi. 38.

32—34. Cure of a Dumb Man possessed by an Evil Spirit.
St Luke xi. 14, 15.

33. ἐκβληθέντος τοῦ δαιμονίου. An expression like this raises the question of demoniacal possession. We ask whether the instances described by the Evangelists point to forms of disease recognised in modern medical practice or to a distinct class of phenomena.

Jewish belief indeed appears to have attributed diseases, cases of insanity and even bodily infirmities such as dumbness, to the agency of indwelling personal evil spirits or δαιμόνια. The distinguishing feature of such demoniacal possession may be described as the phenomenon of a double consciousness. The occult spiritual power became as it were a second self ruling and checking or injuring the better and healthier self.

But on the other hand the use by the evangelists of a word or expression with which a theory is bound up, or even vivid and picturesque description in accordance with it, does not necessarily imply their acquiescence in that theory much less the actual truth of it.

Accordingly the adoption of the word δαιμόνιον and its cognates cannot be considered as decisive on the point of the real existence of personal spiritual agents in disease. A hundred words and phrases implicitly containing false theories, are yet not rejected by correct thinkers. Christ left many truths to come to light in the course of ages, not needlessly breaking into the order by which physical facts are revealed.

At the same time not only is there nothing in the result of science (which does not deal with ultimate causes) inconsistent with *some* form of the belief in demoniacal possession, but certain phenomena of madness and infatuation are more naturally described by the words of the evangelists in their accounts of demoniacal possession than by any other; and our Lord's own words, 'This kind *goeth not out* but by prayer and fasting,' seem more than a mere concession to vulgar beliefs; for it is obvious a less definite expression might have been used if the belief itself was mistaken.

In the classical writers δαιμόνιος is used of acts, agencies, or powers that lie beyond human control or observation. Demosthenes e.g. in a striking passage speaks of the divine power or force which he sometimes fancied to be hurrying on the Hellenic race to destruction: ἐπελήλυθε καὶ τοῦτο φοβεῖσθαι, μή τι δαιμόνιον τὰ πράγματα ἐλαύνῃ, Phil. III. § 54. Of the return of Orestes, Electra says δαιμόνιον τίθημ' ἐγώ, Soph. *El.* 1270. The δαιμόνιον of Socrates was the divine warning voice which apart from his own reasoning faculties checked him from entering upon dangerous enterprizes. Again δαιμόνιον had the meaning of a divine being or agent, a divinity or demi-god. The enemies of Socrates in their indictment used the word in this secondary sense not intended by him. He was charged with introducing καινὰ δαιμόνια (cp. Acts xvii. 18). It is in this sense of demigods or intermediate divine agencies that δαιμόνια is used 1 Cor. x. 20, 21, where the argument is obscured by the rendering of the A.V. 'devils.' As a classical word δαιμόνιον never means '*evil* spirit.'

34. ἔλεγον. 'Used to say;' this was their habitual argument. The answer to it is given, ch. xii. 25—30.

35—38. The Preaching of Jesus. The Harvest of the World.

This passage forms the preface to the mission of the twelve. The connection points to a regular sequence of thought in St Matthew's plan. The work of Christ is described as the model for the work of the twelve; cp. *v.* 35 with ch. x. 7, 8. The pity of Jesus for the lost and shepherdless flock was the *motive* for the mission; cp. *v.* 36 with ch. x. 6. The thought of the harvest of God and the labourers, *vv.* 37 and 38, is raised again in the charge ch. x. 10. The A.V. unfortunately translates ἐργάτης by 'labourer' ix. 37, and 'workman' x. 10.

35. νόσον...μαλακίαν. See ch. iv. 23.

36. ἐσπλαγχνίσθη. σπλάγχνα = the nobler organs, heart, liver, lungs, then specially the heart as the seat of various emotions. In a literal sense Acts i. 18; in the sense of 'pity' frequent in St Paul's epistles. In the classics the meaning is extended to other feelings: μὴ πρὸς ὀργὴν σπλάγχνα θερμήνῃς, Aristoph. *Ranæ*, 844. ἀνδρὸς σπλάγχνον ἐκμαθεῖν, Eur. *Med.* 220. The verb, which is post-classical, is confined to the sense of 'feeling pity,' and occurs in the Synoptic Gospels only.

ἐσκυλμένοι. 'Worn out, harassed.' The literal meaning of σκύλλειν is 'to flay,' then to 'vex,' or 'harass,' τί ἔτι σκύλλεις τὸν διδάσκαλον, Mark v. 35. It is a striking instance of the softening and refining process in the meaning of words: cp. ἐρεύγομαι, χορτάζω.

ἐριμμένοι. Either (1) 'prostrate,' or (2) 'neglected,' set at naught by the national teachers.

μὴ ἔχοντα. 'When they have no shepherd,' the condition that excites pity is expressed by μή, οὐκ ἔχοντα would indicate the fact simply.

37. ὁ μὲν θερισμὸς πολύς. The same expression occurs Luke x. 2 on the occasion of sending forth the Seventy: cp. also John iv. 35, θεάσασθε τὰς χώρας, ὅτι λευκαί εἰσιν πρὸς θερισμὸν ἤδη.

38. ὅπως ἐκβάλῃ. The verb ἐκβάλλειν, to thrust forth, send out, denotes the enthusiastic impulse of mission work: cp. Mark i. 12, τὸ πνεῦμα ἐκβάλλει αὐτὸν εἰς τὴν ἔρημον—driveth him like a wind; and Matt. xiii. 52, of the enthusiastic teacher, ὅστις ἐκβάλλει ἐκ τοῦ θησαυροῦ αὐτοῦ καινὰ καὶ παλαιά.

CHAPTER X.

3. Θαδδαῖος (ℵ B and several versions). The other reading Λεββαῖος has however the authority of D, and it is difficult to account for the presence of the word (which occurs here only) unless it was the original reading.

8. νεκροὺς ἐγείρετε (ℵ B C D), omitted in most of the later uncials and by many cursives and versions. Tischendorf has replaced the words in his text, ed. 8.

25. ἐπεκάλεσαν, a certain correction for ἐκάλεσαν. For the difference of meaning see notes *infra*.

28. ἀποκτεννόντων. Reduplication of consonants was characteristic of the Alexandrine dialect; Sturz (*de dial. Al. et Mac.* p. 128), quotes as instances, ἁμαρτάννειν, φθάννειν, καταβέννειν, &c.

41. λήμψεται (ℵ B C D). The non-assimilation of consonants was also characteristic of the Alexandrine dialect, as ἐνγύς, σύνκεισθε, συνπάτει. On the other hand assimilation takes place in the Alexandrine dialect in the case of ν, contrary to the usage of other dialects, as ἐμμέσῳ, ἐμ Πάρῳ ἐγ Κυβέλοις, though, as might be expected, the MSS. differ considerably in these readings (Sturz, 130—134).

THE MISSION OF THE TWELVE 1—4, AND THE CHARGE TO THEM, 5—42. Mark iii. 14—19, and vi. 7—13. Luke vi. 12—16; ix. 1—6.

1. τοὺς δώδεκα μαθητάς. The first passages in St Mark and St Luke record the *choice* or *calling* of the Twelve, this chapter and Mark vi. and Luke ix. narrate *the* mission or *a* mission of the disciples. Possibly they were sent forth more than once. The number twelve was doubtless in reference to the twelve tribes of Israel, which, as the type of the Christian Church, survive unbroken and undispersed.

νόσον...μαλακίαν. See note ch. iv. 23, and ix. 35.

2. ἀποστόλων, the only passage in this Gospel where the word occurs. The literal meaning, 'sent forth,' or 'envoys,' though scarcely recognised by classical authors, was not new. It seems to have been a 'title borne by those who were despatched from the mother city by the rulers of the race on any foreign mission, especially such as were charged with collecting the tribute paid to the temple service' (Lightfoot, *Gal.* p. 90). The title of ἀπόστολοι was given in a special sense to the Twelve, but was not confined to them. Matthias was added to the number of the twelve, Paul was 'called to be an apostle,' James the Lord's brother, and Barnabas, are designated by the same title. It had even a wider signification: cp. among other passages Rom. xvi. 7. The name is applied to Jesus Christ, Heb. iii. 1, κατανοήσατε τὸν ἀπόστολον καὶ ἀρχιερέα τῆς ὁμολογίας ἡμῶν Χριστὸν Ἰησοῦν. He came to do the will of Him that sent Him.

There are four lists of the Apostles recorded, one by each of the Synoptic Evangelists, one in the Acts of the Apostles. No two of these lists perfectly coincide. This will be seen from the tabular view below.

Matt. x. 3.	*Mark* iii. 16.	*Luke* vi. 14.	*Acts* i. 13.
1. Simon Peter.	Simon Peter.	Simon Peter.	Peter.
2. Andrew.	James the son of Zebedee.	Andrew.	James.
3. James the son of Zebedee.	John the brother of James.	James.	John.
4. John his brother.	Andrew.	John.	Andrew.
5. Philip.	Philip.	Philip.	Philip.
6. Bartholomew.	Bartholomew.	Bartholomew.	Thomas.
7. Thomas.	Matthew.	Matthew.	Bartholomew.
8. Matthew the Publican.	Thomas.	Thomas.	Matthew.
9. James the son of Alphæus.	James son of Alphæus.	James the son of Alphæus.	James son of Alphæus.
10. Lebbæus surnamed Thaddæus.	Thaddæus.	Simon Zelotes.	Simon Zelotes.
11. Simon the Cananite.	Simon the Cananite.	Judas (son) of James.	Judas (son) of James.
12. Judas Iscariot.	Judas Iscariot.	Judas Iscariot.	

It will be observed from a comparison of these lists that the twelve names fall into three divisions, each containing four names which remain in their respective divisions in all the lists. Within these divisions however, the order varies. But Simon Peter is placed first, and Judas Iscariot last, in all. Again, Philip invariably heads the second, and James the son of Alphæus the third division. The classification of the apostolate is the germ of Christian Organisation. It implies diversity of work and dignity suited to differences of intelligence and character. The first group of four are twice named as being alone with Jesus, Mark i. 29, and xiii. 3; Peter and the sons of Zebedee on three occasions, see ch. xvii. 1.

Andrew, a Greek name; see John xii. 21, 22, where the Greeks in the temple address themselves to Philip, 'Philip cometh and telleth Andrew and Andrew and Philip tell Jesus.' An incident that seems to point to some Greek connection besides the mere name.

3. Philip, also a Greek name prevalent at the time, partly through the influence of the Macedonian monarchy, whose real founder was Philip, father of Alexander the Great; partly owing to its adoption by the Herodian family.

Lebbæus, Thaddæus, Jude the [son] of James, are all names of one and the same person. He was the son in all probability of a James or Jacob, not, as usually translated, brother of James. The name 'Lebbæus'='courageous' from a Hebrew word (*leb*) signifying 'heart.'

This Jude or Judas must not be confused with Jude or Judas the 'brother' of our Lord; nor must James the son of Alphæus be confused with James the brother of our Lord. The 'brethren of the Lord' believed not on Him, and could not have been among His apostles. James and Judas were both common names, and the variety of names seems to have been small at this epoch. According to this theory there are four persons named James—(1) the son of Zebedee, (2) the son of Alphæus, (3) the father of Jude, (4) 'The less' or rather 'the little' (ὁ μικρός), the brother of the Lord: and three named Judas—(1) the brother of the Lord, (2) the apostle, son of James, (3) Iscariot.

Matthew or Levi also was son of an Alphæus, but there is no evidence or hint that he was connected with James son of Alphæus.

Bartholomew=son of Tolmai, probably to be identified with Nathanael. (1) St John, who twice mentions the name of Nathanael, never mentions that of Bartholomew; (2) the three Synoptists mention Bartholomew but not Nathanael. (3) Philip is closely connected with Nathanael and also with Bartholomew. (4) Lastly, Nathanael is mentioned with six other disciples as if like them he belonged to the Twelve. (John xxi. 2.)

4. Simon ὁ Καναναῖος, (Aramaic *Kanani*, Hebr. *Kannah*, 'jealous,' Ex. xx. 5), or ζηλωτής, equivalent terms. The fierce party of the Zealots professed a rigid attachment to the Mosaic law; they acknowledged no king save God. Under Judas the Gaulonite they rose in rebellion at the time of the census.

We hear of a Theudas (which is another form of Thaddæus) who rose in rebellion (Acts v. 36). Is it not possible that this Lebbæus or Jude may owe his third name to this patriot, as a Galilæan might regard him? It may be observed that Simon (Joseph. *Ant.* xvii. 10, 5) and

Judas (*Ant.* XVIII. 1, 1) were also names of zealous patriots who rose against the Roman government.

Iscariot = Man of Kerioth, in the tribe of Judah; accordingly (if this be the case) the only non-Galilæan among the Apostles. For other accounts of the name see *Dict. of Bible*.

The choice of the disciples is an instance of the winnowing of Christ, the sifting of the wheat from the chaff. In these men the new life had manifested itself. Their faith, or at least their capacity for faith, was intense, and sufficient to bear them through the dangers that confronted them by their Master's side. [*Editor's notes on Greek text of St Luke's Gospel.*]

5—42. CHRIST'S CHARGE TO THE APOSTLES.

This discourse falls naturally into two divisions; of which the first (*vv.* 5—15) has reference to the immediate present, the second relates rather to the church of the future. The subdivisions of the first part are: (1) Their mission field, 5, 6. (2) Their words and works, 7, 8. (3) Their equipment, 9, 10. (4) Their approach to cities and houses, 11—15.

5. εἰς ὁδὸν ἐθνῶν μὴ ἀπέλθητε. For the expression 'way of the Gentiles,' cp. ch. iv. 15, 'the way of the sea.'

This prohibition is not laid on the Seventy (St Luke x. 1—16), they are expressly commissioned to carry tidings of the gospel to cities and places which our Lord Himself proposed to visit.

εἰς πόλιν Σαμαρειτῶν. The Samaritans were foreigners descended from the alien population introduced by the Assyrian king (probably Sargon), 2 Kings xvii. 24, to supply the place of the exiled Israelites. In Luke xvii. 18, our Lord calls a Samaritan 'this stranger,' i.e. this man of alien or foreign race. The bitterest hostility existed between Jew and Samaritan, which has not died out to this day. The origin of this international ill-feeling is related Ezra iv. 2, 3. Their religion was a corrupt form of Judaism. For being plagued with lions, the Samaritans summoned a priest to instruct them in the religion of the Jews. Soon, however, they lapsed from a pure worship, and in consequence of their hatred to the Jews, purposely introduced certain innovations. Their rival temple on Mount Gerizim was destroyed by John Hyrcanus about 129 B.C. See Nutt's *Sketch of the Samaritans*, p. 19.

About twenty years previous to our Lord's ministry the Samaritans had intensified the national antipathy by a gross act of profanation. During the celebration of the Passover they stole into the Temple Courts when the doors were opened after midnight and strewed the sacred enclosure with dead men's bones (Jos. *Ant.* XVIII. 2, 2). Even after the siege of Jerusalem, when the relations between Jews and Samaritans were a little less hostile, the latter were still designated by the Jews as the 'Proselytes of the lions,' from the circumstance mentioned above.

Samaria was the stepping stone to the Gentile world. After the Ascension the charge to the Apostles was to be witnesses, ἔν τε Ἱερουσαλὴμ καὶ πάσῃ Ἰουδαίᾳ καὶ Σαμαρείᾳ καὶ ἕως ἐσχάτου τῆς γῆς, Acts i. 8. The Acts of the Apostles contain the history of this successive widening of the gospel.

6. πρὸς τὰ πρόβατα τὰ ἀπολωλότα. See note ch. ix. 36.

8. λεπροὺς καθαρίζετε. Leprosy is not classed with the other diseases. As especially symbolical of a sin-stricken man, the leper requires cleansing or purification.

9. μὴ κτήσησθε. 'Do not get, acquire,' εἰς τὰς ζώνας ὑμῶν 'for your girdles.' The disciples must not furnish themselves with the ordinary equipment of an Eastern traveller.

χρυσὸν...ἄργυρον...χαλκόν. Of the three metals named the brass or copper represents the native currency. The coinage of Herod the Great was copper only. But Greek and Roman money was also current. The Roman *denarius*, a silver coin, is frequently mentioned (ch. xviii. 28, xx. 2). The farthing, v. 29, is the Roman *as*, the 16th part of a denarius; the Greek *drachma* of nearly the same value as a denarius, and the *stater* (ch. xvii. 27), were also in circulation.

ζώνας. Literally, girdles or money-belts, cp. 'Ibit eo quo vis qui zonam perdidit,' Hor. *Ep.* II. 2. 40. Sometimes a fold of the tunic held up by the girdle served for a purse, 'quando | major avaritiæ patuit sinus?' Juv. *Sat.* I. 88.

10. δύο χιτῶνας. See ch. v. 40. In like manner the philosopher Socrates wore one tunic only, went without sandals, and lived on the barest necessaries of life. See Xen. *Mem.* 1. 6. 2, where Antiphon, addressing Socrates, says: ζῇς γοῦν οὕτως, ὡς οὐδ' ἂν εἷς δοῦλος ὑπὸ δεσπότῃ διαιτώμενος μείνειε, σιτία τε σιτῇ καὶ ποτὰ πίνεις τὰ φαυλότατα καὶ ἱμάτιον ἠμφίεσαι οὐ μόνον φαῦλον ἀλλὰ τὸ αὐτὸ θέρους τε καὶ χειμῶνος, ἀνυπόδητός τε καὶ ἀχίτων διατελεῖς. καὶ μὴν χρήματά γε οὐ λαμβάνεις ἃ καὶ κτωμένους εὐφραίνει καὶ κεκτημένους ἐλευθεριώτερόν τε καὶ ἥδιον ποιεῖ ζῆν. Epiphanius relates that James the Lord's brother never wore two tunics but only a cloak of fine linen (σινδόνα).

ὑποδήματα, 'shoes.' From Mark vi. 9 it appears that the apostles were enjoined to wear sandals (σανδάλια). This distinction is dwelt upon in the Talmud. Shoes were of softer leather, and therefore a mark of more luxurious living. Sandals were often made with soles of wood, or rushes, or bark of palm-trees. Lightfoot, *Hor. Hebr.* ad loc.

ἐργάτης. See on ch. ix. 35—38.

These directions correspond to the Rabbinical rules for approach to the Temple: 'Let no man enter into the Mount of the Temple, neither with his staff in his hand, nor with his shoes upon his feet, nor with money bound up in his linen, nor with a purse hanging on his back' (Lightfoot, *Hor. Hebr. ad loc.*). In some sense this connection must have been meant by Christ, and present to the minds of the disciples. It would intensify the thought of the sacredness of their mission, and suggest the thought of a Spiritual Temple.

12. εἰσερχόμενοι εἰς τὴν οἰκίαν. 'When ye are entering into the house,' i.e. the house of him who is indicated as 'worthy.' The injunction to remain in the same house was, perhaps, partly to avoid feasting from house to house, partly for the sake of secrecy—a necessary precaution in after times. Such 'worthy' hosts of the Church afterwards were Lydia at Philippi ('If ye have judged me to be faithful to the Lord, come into my house and abide there,' Acts xvi. 15), Jason at Thessalonica, Gaius perhaps at Derbe, see Rom. xvi. 23. This kind of general hospitality is still recognised as a duty in the East, where indeed it may be regarded as a necessity.

ἀσπάσασθε. 'Salute it,' saying 'Peace (εἰρήνη) be unto you' (*Shalom l'cha*), the usual salutation at this day. This of course explains εἰρήνη in the next verse. The ordinary and conventional salutation acquires a sacred depth of meaning on the lips of Christ, Luke xxiv. 36 and John xiv. 27.

14. ἐκτινάξατε τὸν κονιορτόν, as St Paul did at Antioch in Pisidia, Acts xiii. 51. The cities of Israel that rejected the Gospel should be regarded as heathen. The very dust of them was a defilement as the dust of a heathen land. See Lightfoot, *ad loc.*

15. Comp. ch. xi. 24.

16—42. THE CHURCH OF THE FUTURE.

(1) The Apostolic character, 16. (2) Persecution, 17—25. (3) Consolation—the care of the Father, 26—31. (4) The reward, 32. (5) The Christian choice, 33—39. (6) The hosts of the Church, 40—42.

16. ὡς πρόβατα ἐν μέσῳ λύκων] Clemens Rom. (II. 5), who quotes these words, adds to them: ἀποκριθεὶς δὲ ὁ Πέτρος αὐτῷ λέγει, Ἐὰν οὖν διασπαράξωσιν οἱ λύκοι τὰ ἀρνία; Εἶπεν ὁ Ἰησοῦς τῷ Πέτρῳ, Μὴ φοβείσθωσαν τὰ ἀρνία τοὺς λύκους μετὰ τὸ ἀποθανεῖν αὐτά.

φρόνιμοι ..ἀκέραιοι. The qualities required for the safety of the unarmed traveller. Prudence and simplicity are the defence of the weak. φρόνιμοι = 'prudent,' full of precaution, possessing such 'practical wisdom' as Paul had when he claimed the rights of Roman citizenship at Philippi. But the wisdom of a serpent is often to escape notice. With this thought the etymology of ὄφις agrees, whether it is the 'seeing creature' (ὀπ- as in ὄπωπα) quick to discern danger, or 'the creature that hides' (ὀπή, a hole). Comp. the expression in Rom. xvi. 19, θέλω δὲ ὑμᾶς σοφοὺς εἶναι εἰς τὸ ἀγαθόν, ἀκεραίους δὲ εἰς τὸ κακόν, and note the change from φρόνιμοι of the text to σοφούς, denoting intellectual discernment of the good. The difference in the directions precisely meets the difference of the two occasions. ἀκέραιοι (κεράννυμι) means unmixed, so 'pure,' 'simple,' 'sincere,' not 'harmless,' as in A.V. The disciples who were 'simple' as doves might hope to share the immunity of doves. Tibullus says (I. 7. 17):

Quid referam ut volitet crebras intacta per urbes
 Alba Palestino sancta columba Syro.

The epithet *alba* helps to explain ἀκέραιοι.

17. προσέχετε ἀπὸ τῶν ἀνθρώπων. Perhaps with a reference to the serpents and the doves, which shun the approach of men; but comp. ch. xvii. 22, μέλλει ὁ υἱὸς τοῦ ἀνθρώπου παραδίδοσθαι εἰς χεῖρας ἀνθρώπων.

συνέδρια. i.e. provincial synagogue-tribunals. See note, ch. iv. 23.

18. ἡγεμόνας. Such as Felix and Festus at Cæsarea, the Praetors or Duumviri at Philippi (Acts xvi. 20), the Politarchs at Thessalonica (Acts xvii. 6).

βασιλεῖς. As Herod Agrippa or the Roman Emperor.

19. μὴ μεριμνήσητε πῶς ἢ τί λαλήσητε. Curiously enough this has been quoted as if it justified want of preparation for sermons or addresses to a Christian congregation. The direction points definitely to the Christian 'apologies,' of which specimens have come down to us in the Acts (iv. 8—12, v. 29—32, vii. 1—53, xxvi. 2—29) and in the records of the Early Church.

20. τὸ πνεῦμα τοῦ πατρὸς ὑμῶν. The Christian 'apologist' shall not stand alone. The same Spirit instructs him which inspires the universal Church. St Paul experienced such consolation: ἐν τῇ πρώτῃ μου ἀπολογίᾳ οὐδείς συμπαρεγένετο...ὁ δὲ Κύριός μοι παρέστη. 2 Tim. iv. 16, 17. It is to this work of the Holy Spirit that the word παράκλητος may be especially referred. He is the Advocate in court standing by the martyr's side. This is the classical force of παράκλητος.

21. ἀδελφὸς...ἀδελφόν...πατὴρ τέκνον. The history of persecutions for religion affords many instances of this. It is true even of civil disputes. Thucydides, describing the horrors of the Corcyrean sedition, says (III. 81, 82), καὶ γὰρ πατὴρ παῖδα ἀπέκτεινε...καὶ τὸ ξυγγενὲς τοῦ ἑταιρικοῦ ἀλλοτριώτερον ἐγένετο.

ἐπαναστήσονται. ἐπανάστασις is defined by the Scholiast on Thuc. III. 39 to be ὅταν τινες τιμώμενοι καὶ μὴ ἀδικούμενοι στασιάσωσι καὶ ἐχθρεύσωσι τοῖς μηδὲν ἀδικήσασι—inexcusable and heartless rebellion.

22. ὁ δὲ ὑπομείνας εἰς τέλος κ.τ.λ. The parallel expression Luke xxi. 19 is made clear by this verse, ἐν τῇ ὑπομονῇ ὑμῶν κτήσεσθε τὰς ψυχὰς ὑμῶν, 'by your patience ye shall win for yourselves your souls,' i.e. win your true life by enduring to the end. Comp. Rom. v. 3—5, καυχώμεθα ἐν ταῖς θλίψεσιν ·εἰδότες ὅτι ἡ θλῖψις ὑπομονὴν κατεργάζεται ἡ δὲ ὑπομονὴ δοκιμήν, ἡ δὲ δοκιμὴ ἐλπίδα ἡ δὲ ἐλπὶς οὐ καταισχύνει.

σωθήσεται. 'Shall be saved,' shall win σωτηρία. In classical Greek σωτηρία means, 'safety,' 'welfare,' i.e. life secure from evil, cp. Luke i. 71; in the Christian sense it is a life of secured happiness, hence 'salvation' is the highest sense. So σώζεσθαι = 'to live securely' with an additional notion of rescue from surrounding danger, οἱ σωζόμενοι means those who are enjoying this life of blessed security.

23. ὅταν δὲ διώκωσιν ὑμᾶς. Such words indicate that these ' instructions' have a far wider range than the immediate mission of the Apostles. They are prophetic, bringing both warning and consolation to all ages of the Church.

ἕως ἄν ἔλθῃ ὁ υἱὸς τοῦ ἀνθρώπου. The passage in Luke xxi., which is to a great extent parallel to this, treats of the destruction of Jerusalem; and no one who carefully weighs our Lord's words can fail to see that in a real sense He came in the destruction of Jerusalem. That event was in truth the judgment of Christ falling on the unrepentant nation. In this sense the Gospel had not been preached to all the cities of Israel before Christ came. But all these words point to a more distant future. The work of Christian missions is going on, and will still continue until Christ comes again to a final judgment.

24. οὐκ ἔστιν μαθητὴς ὑπὲρ τὸν διδάσκαλον. The disciples of Jesus can expect no other treatment than that which befell their Master Christ. The same proverb occurs in a different connection Luke vi. 40, where Christ is speaking of the responsibility of the Apostles as *teachers;* 'as they are, their disciples shall be.'

25. ἀρκετὸν ἵνα, comp. 'sufficit ut exorari te sinas.' Plin. Such use of *ut* in Latin will illustrate and indeed may have influenced the extended use of ἵνα in later Greek.

Βεελζεβούλ. Baal Zebub = 'Lord of flies,' i.e. 'averter of flies,' a serious plague in hot countries. By a slight change of letter the Jews threw contempt on their enemies' god, calling him Baal Zebel—'Lord of mire'—and lastly identified him with Satan. The changes from Bethel ('House of God') to Bethaven ('House of naught or evil'), (Hos. iv. 15), from Nahash ('serpent') to Nehushtan (2 Kings xviii. 4), and from the name Barcochab ('Son of a star'), assumed by a false Messiah, to Barcozab ('Son of a lie'), are instances of the same quaint humour.

Another derivation of Beelzebul makes it equivalent to 'Lord of the dwelling,' i.e. of the abode of evil spirits. This meaning would be very appropriate in relation to 'the master of the house;' and the form Baalzebul is a nearer approach to the Greek word than Baalzebel.

ἐπεκάλεσαν. 'Surnamed;' more than 'called' A.V.: cp. ὁ ἐπικληθεὶς Θαδδαῖος, v. 3; ὁ ἐπικληθεὶς Βαρνάβας, Acts iv. 36. Probably the enemies of Jesus had actually added the name in derision.

26. οὐδὲν γάρ ἐστιν κεκαλυμμένον κ.τ.λ. Two reasons against fear are implied: (1) If you fear, a day will come which will reveal your disloyalty; (2) Fear not, for one day the unreality of the things that terrify you will be made manifest.

27. ὁ εἰς τὸ οὖς ἀκούετε. Lightfoot (*Hor. Heb.*) refers this to a custom in the 'Divinity School' of the synagogue (see ch. iv. 23), where the master whispered into the ear of the interpreter, who repeated in a loud voice what he had heard.

ἐπὶ τῶν δωμάτων. Travellers relate that in the village districts of Syria proclamations are frequently made from the housetops at the present day. The announcement of the approaching Sabbath was made by the minister of the Synagogue from the roof of an exceeding high house (Lightfoot, *Hor. Heb.*) just as the Turkish 'Muezzin' proclaims the hour of prayer from the top of the mosque.

28. ἀποκτεννόντων. Among other instances of this Alexandrine form quoted by Sturz (*de dial. Mac. et Alex.*) are ἁμαρτάννειν (1 Kings ii. 25) and ἀναβέννειν (Deut. i. 41). See Crit. Notes, ch. x. 28.

τὸν δυνάμενον...ἀπολέσαι. Either (1) God, whose power extends beyond this life. Comp. Clem. Rom. *Ep.* II. 4, where there is a probable reference to this passage, οὐ δεῖ ἡμᾶς φοβεῖσθαι τοὺς ἀνθρώπους μᾶλλον ἀλλὰ τὸν θεόν. Or (2) Satan, into whose power the wicked surrender themselves.

ἐν γεέννῃ. See note, ch. v. 22.

29. στρουθία, translated 'sparrows' (A.V.) means any kind of small bird.

καὶ ἓν ἐξ αὐτῶν κ.τ.λ. Two deductions may be drawn—(1) That human life is more precious in God's sight than the life of the lower animals (*v.* 31); (2) That kindness to animals is part of God's law.

32. ὁμολογήσει ἐν ἐμοί. Confess *in* me: make me the central point and object of his confession.

34—39. These verses exhibit beautifully three characteristics of Hebrew poetry, antithesis, climax, refrain. The first four lines μὴ νομίσητε...οἱ οἰκιακοὶ αὐτοῦ, which reflect the words of Micah vii. 6, indicate the separating influence of Christianity. Note here, as in all great revolutions of thought, the change begins from the young. The separation is *against* father, mother, mother-in-law. The remaining lines indicate the *cause* of division. Absolute devotion to Christ implies (or may imply) severance from the nearest and dearest of earthly ties. This is set forth in a climax of three couplets each ending with the refrain οὐκ ἔστιν μου ἄξιος, followed by an antithetic quatrain.

ἦλθον βαλεῖν. The infinitive expressing a purpose is specially characteristic of this Gospel. The idea of aim is not prominent in the construction, as the infinitive might equally well express result.

35. διχάσαι. ἅπαξ λεγ. in N.T. carries on the idea of separation involved in μάχαιρα, for which Luke in parallel passage xii. 52 has διαμερισμόν.

37. The connection is this: there will be divisions in families; My disciples must not hesitate to side with *Me* rather than with father or mother, or son or daughter. The new life changes the old relationships: everything is viewed now in reference to Christ, to whom His followers are related as mother and sisters and brethren.

This absolute self-surrender and subordination of all meaner interests to the higher law and the one great Master find parallels in Greek conceptions. Hector prefers honour and duty to love of Andromache (*Il.* vi. 441 foll.). The interest of the *Antigone* turns on the conflict between obedience to the supreme law of conscience and the respect to human law and human relations:

> οὐδὲ σθένειν τοσοῦτον ᾠόμην τὰ σὰ
> κηρύγμαθ' ὥστ' ἄγραπτα κἀσφαλῆ θεῶν
> νόμιμα δύνασθαι θνητὸν ὄνθ' ὑπερδραμεῖν.
>
> *Ant.* 453.

Thus it is that Christ sets his seal on all that is noblest in the uninspired thought of the world.

38. ὃς οὐ λαμβάνει τὸν σταυρὸν αὐτοῦ. A further advance in the devotion and self-abandonment required in the disciples of Jesus. These are deeply interesting and solemn words. The cross is named for the first time by the Saviour. The expression recurs ch. xvi. 24, following upon the announcement of the Passion to the disciples. By the Roman custom criminals were compelled to bear the cross to the place of execution. The Galilæans would know too well what was meant by 'taking the cross.' Many hundreds had paid that forfeiture for rebellion that had not prospered under Judas the Gaulonite and others. (See Introduction, Chapter IV.)

39. ὁ εὑρὼν τὴν ψυχὴν κ.τ.λ. ψυχή embraces every form of life from mere vegetative existence to the highest spiritual life of the soul. Sometimes this variety of meaning is found within the limits of a single sentence—'He that findeth the life of external comfort and pleasure, shall lose the eternal life of spiritual joy; and conversely, he who loseth his earthly life for my sake shall find the truer and more blessed life in heaven.' Even in a lower sense this is true: ὁπόσοι μὲν μαστεύουσιν ζῆν ἐκ παντὸς τρόπου ἐν τοῖς πολεμικοῖς οὗτοι κακῶς τε καὶ αἰσχρῶς ὡς ἐπὶ τὸ πολὺ ἀποθνήσκουσιν. Xen. *Cyr. Exped.* III. i. 43.

40—42. THE RECEPTION OF THE APOSTLES AND MINISTERS OF JESUS CHRIST.

In respect of poetical form, note first the ascending climax ὑμᾶς.. ἐμέ...τὸν πέμψαντα ἐμέ. And then the descending climax, προφήτην... δίκαιον...ἕνα τῶν μικρῶν. The privilege rises to the highest point conceivable; the reward is not only for welcome to a prophet but for the slightest service to the lowliest child of God (see Bp. Jebb, *Sacr. Lit.*, on the whole passage). For a similar rise and fall in a poetical passage see ch. xx. 25—28.

40. ὁ δεχόμενος. In the sense of receiving as a teacher, and of welcoming as a guest, see v. 14. Whoever welcomes the Apostles and listens to them, listens to the voice of Jesus Christ and of God the Father Himself, and They 'will make their abode with him,' John xiv. 23.

41. εἰς ὄνομα προφήτου. A Hebraism: for the sake of, out of regard to the prophet's character. In translating the Hebr. *l'shem* the Hellenistic writers use indifferently εἰς [τὸ] ὄνομα, ἐν [τῷ] ὀνόματι, ἐπὶ [τῷ] ὀνόματι.

μισθὸν προφήτου. Such reward as a prophet or preacher of the gospel hath.

δίκαιον. The righteous are those who fulfil the requirements of the *Christian* law (comp. ch. i. 19), true members of the Christian Church—the saints.

42. ἕνα τῶν μικρῶν. The reference may be to the disciples. But there appears to be a gradation, in the lowest step of which are 'these little ones.' Possibly some children standing near were then addressed, or, perhaps, some converts less instructed than the Apostles had gathered round. 'The little ones' then would mean the young disciples, who are babes in Christ. The lowest in the scale—apostles—prophets—the saints—the young disciples. The simplest act of kindness done to one of Christ's little ones *as such* shall have its reward.

ψυχροῦ (ὕδατος). As *aqua* is understood in Latin 'Frigida non desit, non deerit calda petenti.' Mart. XIV. 103.

οὐ μὴ ἀπολέσῃ. οὐ μή expresses an emphatic denial. οὐ denies the fact, μή the very conception of it; οὐ denies a thing absolutely, μή as it presents itself to us. The explanation usually given of an ellipse of δέος ἐστιν fails to satisfy all instances. See Goodwin's *Greek Moods and Tenses*, § 89.

CHAPTER XI.

2. διά for δύο of *textus receptus* on the highest evidence.

16. The *textus receptus* here has καὶ προσφωνοῦσι τοῖς ἑταίροις αὐτῶν καὶ λέγουσιν. The authority for the correction is decisive.

19. The change from τέκνων to ἔργων is not certain, it is however supported by אB*, by Jerome's testimony, and by some Versions.

23. Here the correction is partly a question of punctuation. The received text has καὶ σύ, Καπερναούμ, ἡ ἕως τοῦ οὐρανοῦ ὑψωθεῖσα, ἕως ᾅδου καταβιβασθήσῃ. The best editors give the reading of this text: but there is some authority for ἢ ὑψώθης in place of μὴ ὑψωθήσῃ.

The earliest MSS. afford little guidance as to punctuation. 'The Greek interrogation now in use (;) first occurs about the ninth century, and (,) used as a stop a little later.' Scrivener's *Introduction*, p. 45.

---

1. JESUS PREACHES THE GOSPEL, PROBABLY UNACCOMPANIED BY THE TWELVE.

2—19. CONCERNING JOHN THE BAPTIST.

His message to Jesus 2—6. His position as a Prophet 7—14. His relation to Jesus and to his contemporaries 15—19.

St Luke vii. 18—35.

1. καὶ ἐγένετο. A translation of a Hebrew transitional formula; the verb which follows (1) is sometimes connected with καί, as ch. ix. 10, καὶ ἐγένετο αὐτοῦ ἀνακειμένου...καὶ ἰδού, (2) sometimes, as here, has

no connecting particle; (3) sometimes the infinitive is used, as καὶ ἐγένετο παραπορεύεσθαι αὐτόν, Mark ii. 23. This formula varied by ἐγένετο δὲ is especially frequent in St Luke, and does not occur in St John. The particular phrase καὶ ἐγένετο, ὅτε ἐτέλεσεν, is confined to St Matthew; see ch. vii. 28 (συνετ.), xiii. 53, xix. 1, xxvi. 1. (Winer, p. 406 c, and p. 760 e, and note 2.)

ἐκεῖθεν. The place where Jesus delivered the charge to the Apostles is not named.

2. ἐν τῷ δεσμωτηρίῳ. At Machærus. See note, ch. xiv. 3.

τὰ ἔργα, which were not the works which John might have expected from a Messiah, in whose hand was the separating fan, and at whose coming the axe was laid at the root of the trees.

διὰ τῶν μαθητῶν. See critical note *supra*, and cp. Luke vii. 19.

3. ὁ ἐρχόμενος. Hebr. *Habba*, one of the designations of the Messiah; in every age the prophet said 'He cometh.' See note ch. i. 18.

ἕτερον, another—a different Messiah, whose 'works' shall not be those of love and healing. προσδοκῶμεν, probably conjunctive, 'are we to expect.'

It is often disputed whether John sent this message (1) from a sense of hope deferred and despondency in his own soul; he would ask himself: (a) Is this the Christ whom I knew and whom I baptized? (b) Are these works of which I hear, the works of the promised Messiah? or (2) to confirm the faith of his disciples, or (3) to induce Jesus to make a public confession of His Messiahship. (1) The first motive is the most natural and the most instructive. In the weary constraint and misery of the prison the faith of the strongest fails for a moment. It is not doubt, but faith wavering: 'Lord, I believe; help Thou mine unbelief.' (2) The second has been suggested, and found support rather from the wish to uphold the consistency of the Baptist's character than because it is the clearest inference from the text; note especially the words ἀπαγγείλατε, Ἰωάννῃ. (3) The third motive would have been hardly less derogatory to John's faith than the first. And would not our Lord's rebuke, v. 6, have taken a different form, as when he said to Mary, 'Mine hour is not yet come?'

5. Comp. Isaiah xxxv. 5 and lxi. 1. The first passage describes the work of God, who '*will come and save you*.'

πτωχοὶ εὐαγγελίζονται. In earthly kingdoms envoys are sent to the rich and great. Compare the thought implied in the disciple's words, 'Who then can be saved?' If it is difficult for the rich to enter the kingdom, how much more for the poor?

For the construction see Winer 287. 5, and 326. 1, a. It falls under one or other of the following rules: (1) a verb governing dative of person and accusative of thing in active voice retains the accusative of the thing in the passive. Cp. πεπίστευμαι τὸ εὐαγγέλιον from πιστεύω τινί τι. (2) A verb governing a genitive or dative in the active has for subject in the passive the object of the active verb.

6. καὶ μακάριος, κ.τ.λ. Blessed are all who see that these works of mine are truly the works of the Messiah. Some had thought only of an avenging and triumphant Christ.

μακάριος. A term that denotes spiritual insight and advance in the true life.

σκανδαλισθῇ. See note, ch. v. 29. In this passage σκανδαλίζεσθαι has the force of being entrapped or deceived by false notions.

7—14. The position of John as a prophet. The message of the Baptist must have made a deep and a mournful impression on the bystanders. It may have caused some of them to lose their faith in Christ or in John, and to ask, like John, whether this was indeed the Christ. Jesus restores their belief in John by an appeal to their own thoughts concerning him. It was no fickle waverer or courtier that they went out to see.

7. Some editors place the interrogative after ἔρημον, but the correction seems harsh and unnecessary.

κάλαμον ὑπὸ ἀνέμου σαλ. If the first suggestion (v. 3) be adopted, the words have a corroborative force. It was no waverer that ye went out to see—his message was clear, his faith was strong *then*.

Others give the words a literal sense—the reeds on the banks of Jordan—and observe a climax, a reed—a man—a prophet—more than a prophet—the greatest of them.

8. ἐν μαλακοῖς ἠμφιεσμένον. Prof. Plumptre (Smith's *Bib. Dic.* I. 1166) suggests that there may be a historical allusion in these words. A certain Menahem, who had been a colleague of the great teacher Hillel, 'was tempted by the growing power of Herod, and with a large number of his followers entered the king's service...they appeared publicly in gorgeous apparel, glittering with gold.' (See Lightfoot, *Hor. Hebr.*, on Matt. xxii. 16.)

9. περισσότερον προφήτου. Other prophets foresaw the Messiah, the Baptist beheld Him, and ushered in His kingdom: he was the herald of the King. Further, John was himself the subject of prophecy.

περισσότερον, late for πλέον. As περισσὸς has in itself a comparative force, the form περισσότερον is due to the redundance of expression characteristic of the later stage of a language.

10. γέγραπται. See note ch. ii. 5.

ἰδοὺ ἐγὼ ἀποστέλλω κ.τ.λ. Mal. iii. 1. The quotation is nearly a literal translation of the Hebrew, except that for the second person, ἔμπροσθέν σου, the Hebrew has the first person, 'before me.' The same change is made in the parallel passage Luke vii. 27, and where the words are cited by St Mark i. 2. By such change the Lord quotes the prophecy as addressed to Himself. The σου of the N.T. represents the μου of the O.T. Possibly the reading is due to the Aramaic Version of the Scriptures familiar to the contemporaries of Christ. But in any case only the divine Son of God could apply to Himself what was spoken of Jehovah.

11. ὁ δὲ μικρότερος. He that is less, either (1) than John or (2) than others. Those who are in the kingdom, who are brought nearer to God and have clearer spiritual knowledge of God, have higher privileges than the greatest of those who lived before the time of Christ.

12. ἀπὸ δὲ τῶν ἡμερῶν κ.τ.λ. Another point shewing the greatness of John, and also the beginning of the Kingdom: it was from the time of John's preaching that men began to press into the kingdom, and the earnest won their way in. For the preaching of John was the epoch to which all prophecy tended.

βιάζεται. Is forced, broken into, as a ship enters a harbour by breaking the boom stretched across the harbour's mouth. Cp. *βιάσασθαι τὸν ἔκπλουν* (Thuc. VII. 72) of the Athenian fleet forcing its way out of the harbour at Syracuse. John's preaching was the signal for men to press into the kingdom—to adopt eagerly the new rule and life heralded by John and set forth by Christ.

καὶ βιασταὶ ἁρπάζουσιν. The invaders, those who force their way in—the eager and enthusiastic followers of Christ seize the kingdom—win it as a prize of war.

βιασταί. Here only in N.T. one other instance of its occurrence is quoted (Philo, *de Agricultura*, p. 314, A.D. 40). Cp. the Pindaric *βιατάς*.

13. γάρ gives the reason why the wonderful growth of the kingdom should be witnessed *now*.

14. εἰ θέλετε δέξασθαι. 'The present unhappy circumstances in which John was placed seemed inconsistent with such a view of his mission' (Meyer).

16. ὁμοία ἐστὶν παιδίοις κ.τ.λ. If the grammatical form of the comparison be closely pressed, the interpretation must be that the children who complain of the others are the Jews who are satisfied neither with Jesus nor with John. The men of the existing generation appealed in turn to John and to Christ, and found no response in either. They blamed John for too great austerity, Jesus for neglect of Pharisaic exclusiveness and of ceremonial fasting.

But if the comparison be taken as applicable generally to the two terms, it may be explained by John first making an appeal, then Christ, and neither finding a response in the nation. This is the ordinary interpretation, and certainly agrees better with the facts, inasmuch as Christ and John made the appeal to the nation, not the nation to them.

It has been remarked that the joyous strain of the children, and the more genial mood of Christ, begin and end the passage, pointing to joyousness as the appropriate note of the Christian life.

18. μήτε ἐσθίων μήτε πίνων. *μήτε* not *οὔτε*, because it is not only that a matter of fact is stated, but the view which was taken of John's conduct.

Demosthenes was reproached for being a water drinker, ὡς ἐγὼ μὲν ὕδωρ πίνων εἰκότως δύστροπος καὶ δύσκολός εἰμί τις ἄνθρωπος. *Phil.* II. 30.

19. For this adversative use of καί, see note ch. i. 19.

δικαιοῦν. Lit. 'to make right,' of a person to do him justice, give him what he deserves, either punishment (Thuc. III. 40. Herod. I. 100), or (later) acquittal: here, 'was acquitted of folly.' The aorist marks the result, or is the aorist of a customary act—a meaning expressed by the present tense in English.

ἡ σοφία is 'divine wisdom,' God regarded as the All-wise. The conception of a personified Wisdom is a growth of later Jewish thought, bringing with it many beautiful associations of Jewish literature, and hallowed by the use of the word in this sense by Christ.

ἀπὸ τῶν ἔργων. See critical notes, *supra*. ἀπό, which strictly marks result, is used of the instrument and of the agent in later Greek. Here the sense is: 'the results justify the plan or method of divine providence.'

If the reading of the *textus receptus* be taken, τέκνα τῆς σοφίας = 'the divinely wise.' The spiritual recognise the wisdom of God, both in the austerity of John and in the loving mercy of Jesus, who condescends to eat with publicans and sinners.

20—24. THE CITIES THAT REPENTED NOT.

St Luke x. 13—15, where the words form part of the charge to the seventy disciples. It is instructive to compare the connection suggested by the two evangelists. In St Matthew the link is the rejection of Christ by the Jews—then by these favoured cities; in St Luke, the rejection of the Apostles as suggestive of the rejection of Jesus.

21. Χοραζείν is identified with Kerazeh, two and a half miles N. of Tell Hum. The ruins here are extensive and interesting; among them a synagogue built of hard black basalt and houses with walls still six feet high. *Recovery of Jerusalem*, p. 347.

Βηθσαϊδάν (House of Fish), either on the Western shore of the Lake near Capernaum (see Map); or, in case there was only one place of that name (see note, chap. xiv. 13), it is Bethsaida Julias, so named by Herod Philip in honour of Julia, daughter of Augustus.

22. πλήν. Connected probably with πλέον, πλεῖν. So 'more than,' 'moreover,' 'further' (Curtius, *Grk. Etym.*; Ellicott, Phil. i. 18; Winer, p. 552); or with πέλας, 'besides,' 'apart from this,' 'only' (Hartung, Lightfoot, Phil. iii. 16). (1) The rendering 'moreover' would suit this passage. (2) In others πλήν almost = ἀλλά, 'notwithstanding' (the additional fact being often adversative); or (3) 'except,' constructed with genitive, or ὅτι, or with ἤ. The first and last of these constructions favour the derivation from πλέον.

23. Καφαρναούμ. See map. Although Capernaum was truly exalted unto heaven in being our Lord's 'own city,' the thought is rather of self-exaltation. The expressions recall Isaiah xiv. 13—15. Capernaum has exalted herself like Babylon—like Babylon she shall be brought low. The idea that Capernaum was literally on a height does not appear to be borne out by facts. Both the conjectural sites are marked low in the map published by the Palestine Exploration Fund.

25—27. THE REVELATION TO 'BABES.'

St Luke x. 21—22, where the words are spoken on the return of the Seventy.

The close connection between this section and that which follows has been pointed out by Dean Perowne (*Expositor*, Vol. VIII.). In this section two divine moral laws are set forth: (1) The revelation is made to humility. (2) The revelation is made through Christ alone. The invitation which follows (*vv.* 28—30) is given (1) not to the self-assertion of man, but to his need and the confession of that need, by One who is 'meek and lowly in heart;' (2) with a promise of rest to those, and those only, who take upon them Christ's yoke and learn of Him.

25. ἀποκριθείς. This use of ἀποκριθείς, 'answering,' where no question precedes, is a Hebraism.

ἐξομολογοῦμαι. Strictly, 'to speak forth,' 'confess,' τὰς ἁμαρτίας, ch. iii. 6; cp. Phil. ii. 11, then to 'utter aloud' praise or thanks, as here and Rom. xiv. 11 (quoted from Is. xiv. 23), ὅτι ἐμοὶ κάμψει πᾶν γόνυ καὶ πᾶσα γλῶσσα ἐξομολογήσεται τῷ θεῷ.

τοῦ οὐρανοῦ καὶ τῆς γῆς. The expression points to God as the author of law in nature and in religion.

ὅτι ἔκρυψας. 'That thou hidest,' not by an arbitrary and harsh will, but in accordance with a law of divine wisdom. Truth is not revealed to the philosophical theorist, but the humility that submits to observe and follow the method of nature and working of God's laws is rewarded by the discovery of truth. For this use of the aorist see note *v.* 27, last clause.

ἀπὸ σοφῶν καὶ συνετῶν, for the classical construction, κρύπτειν τί τινα, or τι πρός τινα. There is a sense of separation in 'concealment' denoted by ἀπό. The secrets of the kingdom are not revealed to those who are wise in their own conceit, but to those who have the meekness of infants and the child-like eagerness for knowledge. In a special Jewish sense 'the wise and prudent' are the Scribes and Pharisees. In a purely Greek sense, σοφοὶ καὶ συνετοί are they to whom especially the apprehension of the highest truths belonged. σοφία is wisdom in its highest philosophic sense; it is the most exact of sciences—ἀκριβεστάτη τῶν ἐπιστημῶν, and is said μὴ μόνον τὰ ἐκ τῶν ἀρχῶν εἰδέναι ἀλλὰ καὶ περὶ τὰς ἀρχὰς ἀληθεύειν (Arist. *Eth. Nic.* VI. 7). σύνεσις is 'critical intelligence.'

26. ναὶ ὁ πατήρ. 'Yea, Father (I thank thee), that,' &c. Not as in A. V., 'Even so, Father, for,' &c. For the nominative in place of vocative cp. Soph. *El.* 634,

ἔπαιρε δὴ σὺ θύμαθ' ἡ παροῦσά μοι.

εὐδοκία. 'Pleasure,' in the sense of resolve or determination (see note, ch. iii. 17). The divine plan of discovery and revelation is a subject of thankfulness.

27. παρεδόθη. Strictly, '*were* delivered.' The A. V. translates the aorist by a present in this passage, by a perfect definite the similar expression, ch. xxviii. 18, ἐδόθη μοι πᾶσα ἐξουσία ἐν οὐρανῷ καὶ ἐπὶ τῆς γῆς. It is not always easy to determine the force of the aorist in the N. T. (1) In classical Greek the aorist is occasionally used where the English idiom would require the perfect definite. But in such cases it is not correct to say that the English perfect and the Greek aorist denote precisely the same temporal idea, but rather that in some instances the Greeks marked an action only as past where our idiom connects the past action with the present by the use of the perfect definite. (2) Again, when the Greek aorist *seems* to be used for the present, the explanation is: (a) either that the action is past, but only just past—a point of time expressed by the English present, but more accurately indicated in Greek by the use of the aorist; e. g. the Greeks said accurately τί ἔλεξας; what didst thou say? when the words have scarcely passed the speaker's lips; in English it is natural to translate this by the less exact 'what sayest thou?' (β) Or the action is one of indefinite frequency. Here again the English present takes the place of the Greek aorist. But in this idiom also the aorist retains its proper force. The Greeks only cared to *express* a single occurrence of the act, but from that single occurrence *inferred* the repetition of it. It will be observed that these usages are due to the singular (a) exactness and (β) rapidity of Greek thought.

In later Greek some of this exactness was doubtless lost, the aorist coming more and more into use, being an 'aggressive tense,' as Buttmann calls it, till in modern Greek the synthetic perfect has disappeared.

It is, however, possible probably in every instance in the N. T. to refer the aorist to one or other of the above-named classical uses, even where (1) the perfect and aorist are used in the same clause. As in Acts xxii. 15, ἑώρακας = 'hast seen' (the image is still vividly present just now—past action connected with present time); καὶ ἤκουσας, 'and didst hear' (act regarded merely as past); so also in Jas. i. 24, κατενόησεν γὰρ ἑαυτὸν καὶ ἀπελήλυθεν, the aorist marks the momentary act, the perfect the continuing effect. Cp. *Medea*, 293, οὐ νῦν με πρῶτον ἀλλὰ πολλάκις, Κρέον, | ἔβλαψε δόξα μεγάλα τ' εἴργασται κακά, the effects of the evil remain *now*. Or (2) where the relation to the present is very close, as Luke xiv. 18, ἀγρὸν ἠγόρασα...γυναῖκα ἔγημα = 'I have bought...married;' see above (1). Or (3) where νῦν or νυνί is joined to the aorist. Here the temporal particle denotes the present order or state of things as contrasted with the past, *not* the present moment; as Col. i. 21, νυνὶ δὲ ἀποκατηλλάγητε [or ἀποκατήλλαξεν]. See Bp. Lightfoot, *ad loc.* Cp. 1 Peter ii. 25.

In this passage and ch. xxviii. 18, the act indicated by the aorist is placed in the eternal past, where the notion of time is lost, but as an eternal fact may be regarded as ever present, this aspect of the aorist is properly represented by the English present tense.

ἐπιγινώσκει, as distinguished from the simple verb, implies a further and therefore a more perfect and thorough knowledge. ἵνα ἐπιγνῷς, Luke i. 4, 'that thou mayest perfectly know.' ἐπίγνωσις is used especially of the knowledge of God and of Christ as being the perfection of knowledge. Bp. Lightfoot, Col. i. 9.

28—30. REST FOR THE HEAVY LADEN.

These words of Jesus are preserved by St Matthew only. The connecting thought is, those alone shall know who desire to learn, those alone shall have rest who feel their burden. The babes are those who feel ignorant, the laden those who feel oppressed.

28. Δεῦτε πρός με. Jesus does not give rest to all the heavy laden, but to those of them who shew their want of relief by coming to Him. For δεῦτε see note ch. iv. 19.

κοπιῶντες καὶ πεφορτισμένοι. Answering through parallelism to the last line of the stanza—ὁ γὰρ ζυγὸς κ.τ.λ. The figure is from beasts of burden which either plough or draw chariots, wagons, &c., for which κοπιῶντες and ζυγὸς are appropriate words; or else carry burdens (φορτία).

29. μάθετε ἀπ' ἐμοῦ. i.e. 'become my disciples;' an idea also conveyed by the word ζυγός, which was used commonly among the Jews for the yoke of instruction. Stier quotes from the Mishna, 'Take upon you the yoke of the holy kingdom.' Men of Belial = 'Men without the yoke,' 'the uninstructed.'

ὅτι πραΰς εἰμι καὶ ταπεινὸς τῇ καρδίᾳ. The character of Jesus described by Himself: cp. 2 Cor. x. 1, παρακαλῶ ὑμᾶς διὰ τῆς πραΰτητος καὶ ἐπιεικείας τοῦ Χριστοῦ. It is this character that brings rest to the soul, and therefore gives us a reason why men should become His disciples.

ἀνάπαυσιν ταῖς ψυχαῖς ὑμῶν. Cp. Jer. vi. 16, 'Thus saith the Lord, Stand ye in the ways, and see, and ask for the old paths, where is the good way, and walk therein, and ye shall find rest for your souls. But they said, We will not walk therein.'

ταῖς ψυχαῖς] Not relief from *external* bodily toil.

30. τὸ φορτίον μου ἐλαφρόν ἐστιν. Contrast with this the burden of the Pharisees, ch. xxiii. 4, φορτία βαρέα [καὶ δυσβάστακτα].

CHAPTER XII.

4. ὁ for οὕς. **6.** μεῖζον for μείζων. **7.** ἔλεος for ἔλεον; in these instances the *textus receptus* represents an unauthorised change to an easier construction or a more usual grammatical form.

31. The omission of τοῖς ἀνθρώποις after οὐκ ἀφεθήσεται is on the authority of the leading editors and has the sanction of the oldest MSS. and several versions. But, with the exception of ℵ B, all the important Uncials contain the words, and their retention gives weight and solemnity to the clause.

35. τῆς καρδίας after θησαυροῦ is rightly rejected as a gloss.

1—13. THE OBSERVANCE OF THE SABBATH.

1. The disciples pluck ears of corn on the Sabbath. 2. A man with a withered hand cured on the Sabbath.

St Mark ii. 23—28, iii. 1—5; St Luke vi. 1—11.

1. ἐπορεύθη. St Luke has the less classical ἐγένετο διαπορεύεσθαι.

τοῖς σάββασιν. For the form as if from a sing. σάββας -ατος see Winer 73. τὸ σάββατον and τὰ σάββατα, whether in singular or plural, mean (1) the sabbath, ἐν τῷ σαββάτῳ, Luke vi. 7. ὀψὲ δὲ σαββάτων, Matt. xxviii. 1. (2) The week, πρώτῃ σαββάτου, Mark xvi. 9. εἰς μίαν σαββάτων, Matt. xxviii. 1.

ἐπείνασαν. A late form for ἐπείνησαν. So πεινᾶν and πεινᾷ for Attic πεινῆν and πεινῇ.

ἤρξαντο τίλλειν στάχυας. The Pharisees, who seem to have been watching their opportunity, make the objection as soon as the disciples *began* what by Pharisaic rules was an unlawful act.

2. ὃ οὐκ ἔξεστιν ποιεῖν ἐν σαββάτῳ. This prohibition is a Pharisaic rule not found in the Mosaic Law. It was a principle with the Pharisees to extend the provisions of the Law and make minute regulations over and beyond what Moses commanded, in order to avoid the possibility of transgression. To pluck ears of corn was in a sense, the Pharisees said, to reap, and to reap on the Sabbath day was forbidden and punishable by death. These regulations did in fact make void the Law; e.g. the result of this particular prohibition was to contravene the intention or *motive* of the Sabbath. If sabbatical observances prevented men from satisfying hunger, the Sabbath was no longer a blessing but an injury to man.

3. Ahimelech, the priest at Nob, gave David and his companions five loaves of the shewbread (1 Sam. xxi. 1—7). 'It is no improbable conjecture that David came to Nob either on the Sabbath itself, or when the Sabbath was but newly gone.' Lightfoot, *Hor. Heb. ad loc.*

4. τοὺς ἄρτους τῆς προθέσεως. Literally, 'loaves of the setting forth,' i.e. the bread that was set forth in the sanctuary. It was also called 'continual bread' as being set forth perpetually before the Lord, hence the Hebrew name, 'bread of the presence.' Twelve loaves or cakes were placed in two 'piles' (rather than 'rows,' Lev. xxiv. 6) on the 'pure table' every Sabbath. On each pile was put a golden cup of frankincense. See Exod. xxv. 30; Lev. xxiv. 6—8; Josephus, *Ant.* III. 10. 7.

τῆς προθέσεως. This use of the attribute genitive is very frequent in the Hebrew language, which has few adjectives in proportion to the substantives. Adjectives of material are almost entirely wanting (Rödiger's *Gesenius Hebr. Gram.* p. 236). The construction however belongs also to Greek syntax, μέλαινα δ' ἄστρων...εὐφρόνη 'starry night.' Soph. *El.* 19. λευκῆς χιόνος πτέρυγι. *Ant.* 114. 'a snowy wing.' See Donaldson, *Grk. Gr.* 454.

ἐξὸν ἦν. A late analytic form for ἐξῆν.

5. ἀνέγνωτε. For the aor. see ch. v. 21 and xi. 27.

βεβηλοῦσιν. By labour in removing the shewbread, preparing fire for the sacrifice, and performing the whole temple service. 'Not merely does the sacred *history* relate exceptional instances of *necessity*, but the *Law* itself ordains labour on the Sabbath as a duty' (Stier).

βεβηλοῦσιν. The verb is late. βέβηλος (βάω, βαίνω, βηλός, 'a threshold') lit. = 'allowable for all to tread,' so common, profane.

6. μεῖζον. The neuter gives the sense of indefinite greatness; cp. Luke xi. 32, πλεῖον Σολομῶνος ὧδε, and Eur. *Ion*, 973, καὶ πῶς τὰ κρείσσω θνητὸς οὖσ' ὑπερδράμω, where τὰ κρείσσω is equivalent to τὸν θεόν.

7. εἰ δὲ ἐγνώκειτε. This form of the conditional sentence implies that the action of the protasis did not take place. The Pharisees did not recognise the true meaning of the prophet.

Ἔλεος θέλω καὶ οὐ θυσίαν. Quoted a second time, see ch. ix. 13. There is something more binding than the Law, and that is the principle which underlies the Law. The law rightly understood is the expression of God's love to man. That love allowed the act of David, and the labour of the priests; 'Shall it not permit my disciples to satisfy their hunger?'

The MSS. vary between ἔλεος and ἔλεον. In the classics ἔλεος is always masc., in Hellenistic Greek generally neuter, similar instances are πλοῦτος neut. 2 Cor. viii. 2; Phil. iv. 19 *alibi*, and ζῆλος neut. Phil. iii. 6 (Lachmann and Tischendorf).

10. χεῖρα ἔχων ξηράν, i.e. paralysed or affected by atrophy. St Luke has ἡ χεὶρ αὐτοῦ ἡ δεξιά.

εἰ does not introduce direct questions in Attic Greek. For this later use, compare Latin *an* and even *si*. The construction is probably due to an ellipse. Winer, 639.

11. In the other Synoptic Gospels the argument is different. 'Is it lawful to do good on the Sabbath days, or to do evil? to save life or to kill?' St Matthew states the argument that bears specially on the Jewish Law. St Luke, however, mentions the application of the same argument by our Lord on a different occasion, ch. xiv. 5. Our Lord's answer is thrown into the form of a syllogism, the minor premiss and conclusion of which are left to be inferred in St Luke *loc. cit.*

12. διαφέρει. Cp. ch. x. 31, πολλῶν στρουθίων διαφέρετε ὑμεῖς.

13. ἀπεκατεστάθη. For the double augment see Winer, P. ii., xii. 7.

14—21. THE PHARISEES PLOT AGAINST JESUS, WHO RETIRES.

Mark iii. 6—12; Luke vi. 11, 12.

14. συμβούλιον ἔλαβον κατ' αὐτοῦ. St Mark adds that the Herodians joined the Pharisees.

ὅπως αὐτὸν ἀπολέσωσιν. This sequence of the subjunctive on the historic tenses is the established usage in Hellenistic Greek. For instances in the Classics see note, ch. xiv. 36. The use of the subjunctive gradually displaced the optative mood, which does not exist in Modern Greek. In the N.T. it is somewhat rare. It occurs, (1) in conditional sentences; as, ἀλλ' εἰ καὶ πάσχοιτε διὰ δικαιοσύνην, μακάριοι, 1 Pet. iii. 14. (2) In the expression of a wish; as, μηδεὶς καρπὸν φάγοι, Mark xi. 14, and the formula, μὴ γένοιτο. (3) In indirect questions; as, ἤρξαντο συζητεῖν...τὸ τίς ἄρα εἴη ἐξ αὐτῶν, Luke xxii. 23. (4) In a temporal sentence; once only, in oratio obliqua, Acts xxv. 16. (5) With ἄν, 'when subjective possibility is connected with a condition' (Winer), as Acts xvii. 18. (6) In strictly final sentences it does not occur; on the apparent instances, (α) Mark ix. 30, and xiv. 10, where there are strong reasons for regarding γνοῖ and παραδοῖ as subjunctive forms; and (β) Eph. i. 17, where the sentence introduced by ἵνα expresses the object of the prayer or wish; see Winer. p. 360, note 2, and p. 363.

15. ἀνεχώρησεν ἐκεῖθεν. See ch. x. 23. Jesus follows the principle which He laid down for his disciples' guidance.

17. τὸ ῥηθὲν διὰ Ἡσαΐου. Is. xlii. 1—4. The quotation follows the Hebr. with slight variation. After ἕως ἂν ἐκβάλῃ...κρίσιν a clause follows, expanding the thought of those words: 'His force shall not be abated nor broken. Until he hath firmly seated judgment in the earth' (Lowth's trans.). In the LXX., Ἰακὼβ and Ἰσραὴλ are inserted as subjects in the first clauses, and there are many verbal discrepancies.

18. ὁ παῖς μου. 'My servant.' In Isaiah's prophecy, either (1) 'the chosen one,' whom Jehovah raised 'from the north' (Is. xli. 25) *to do his will*, and bring about His people's deliverance from the Babylonish Captivity, or (2) the nation of Israel the worker out of Jehovah's purposes, in either case in an ultimate sense the Messiah.

κρίσιν. The Hebrew word (*mishpat*) is used in a wider sense than κρίσις denoting 'rule,' 'plan,' 'ordinance,' &c. Adhering, however, to the strict force of the Greek, we may regard κρίσις as the 'divine sentence or decree,' so the 'purpose' of God in the Gospel.

τοῖς ἔθνεσιν. Possibly our Lord in His retirement addressed Himself more especially to the Gentiles—the Greeks, Phœnicians, and others, settled near the lake. 'They about Tyre and Sidon, a great multitude,...came unto Him,' Mark iii. 8.

19, 20. These verses describe the gentleness and forbearance of Christ. He makes no resistance or loud proclamation like an earthly prince. The bruised reed and the feebly-burning wick may be referred to the failing lives which Jesus restores and the sparks of faith which He revives.

19. ἐρίσει. Here, only in N.T., it may be noted that in this citation there are three ἅπαξ λεγόμενα in N.T. αἱρετίζειν—ἐρίζειν—τύφομαι, none of which occur in the LXX. version of the prophecy; the fut. κατεάξει is extremely rare, and the construction of ἐλπίζειν is found here only in N.T. The divergence from the LXX. points to an independent version, and the divergence from St Matthew's vocabulary points to some translator other than the Evangelist.

ἀκούσει. Late for middle form ἀκούσεται.

ἐν ταῖς πλατείαις. 'In the open spaces' of the city. Jesus had retired to the desert.

20. ἕως ἂν ἐκβάλῃ εἰς νῖκος τὴν κρίσιν, i.e. 'until he makes his judgment triumph—until he brings it to victory.' ἐκβάλλειν denotes the impulse of enthusiasm. See ch. ix. 38.

For εἰς νῖκος the lit. rendering of the Hebr. is 'to truth.' Maldonatus suggests as an explanation of the discrepancy, a corruption in the Chaldæan text. But, on the other hand, εἰς νῖκος expresses the general sense of the omitted words.

21. τῷ ὀνόματι αὐτοῦ. The LXX. reading, ἐπὶ τῷ ὀνόματι, nearly agrees with this. The Hebrew text has 'for his law.' It is hardly probable that the mistake should have arisen, as Maldonatus suggests, from the similarity of νόμῳ and ὀνόματι.

22, 23. CURE OF A MAN WHO WAS BLIND AND DUMB.
Luke xi. 14—16.

St Luke omits to mention that the man was blind as well as dumb.

23. μήτι οὗτός ἐστιν ὁ υἱὸς Δαυείδ; This form of interrogation implies a negative answer. Those who can scarcely hope for an affirmative reply, naturally give a negative cast to their question. 'Can this possibly (τι) be the son of David?' But the question itself implies a hope. See Winer, p. 641, note 3, and p. 642; Jelf, § 873. 4, and Goodwin, *Moods and Tenses*, p. 84.

24—30. THE CHARGE, 'HE CASTETH OUT DEVILS BY BEELZEBUB.'
THE ANSWER OF JESUS.
Mark iii. 22—27; Luke xi. 15.

24. Βεελζεβούλ. See ch. x. 25.

25. πᾶσα βασιλεία μερισθεῖσα κ.τ.λ. Not that civil disputes destroy a nation, but a nation disunited, rent by factions, in the presence of a common enemy must fall. Here Satan's kingdom is regarded as warring against the kingdom of God.

Observe the gradation of βασιλεία—πόλις—οἰκία—Σατανᾶς; it is a climax; the smaller the community the more fatal the division. Division in an individual is a contradiction in terms.

27. οἱ υἱοὶ ὑμῶν ἐν τίνι ἐκβάλλουσιν; The children are the disciples of the Pharisees, who either really possessed the power of casting out evil spirits, or pretended to have that power. In either case the argument of Jesus was unanswerable.

28. ἐν πνεύματι θεοῦ. ἐν δακτύλῳ θεοῦ (Luke).

ἔφθασεν ἐφ' ὑμᾶς. 'Came upon you,' surprised you; aorist of immediate past. φθάνειν, from its classical force of 'anticipating,' or 'coming before others,' passes to that of simply coming and arriving at a place. This was indeed probably the original meaning of the word (Geldart, *Mod. Greek*, p. 206). It is also the modern meaning; προφθάνειν being used in the sense of 'to anticipate.' But in such a phrase as ἔφθασα τὸ ἀτμόπλοιον, 'I caught the steamer,' a trace of the prevailing classical use is discerned. Both senses are found in N.T. For the first, 1 Thess. iv. 15, οὐ μὴ φθάσωμεν τοὺς κοιμηθέντας, for the second, Rom. ix. 31, Ἰσραὴλ δὲ διώκων νόμον δικαιοσύνης εἰς νόμον οὐκ ἔφθασεν. In 2 Cor. x. 14, φθάνειν is synonymous with ἐφικνεῖσθαι.

29. Not only is Satan not an ally, but he is an enemy and a vanquished enemy.

τὰ σκεύη. Including τὴν πανοπλίαν ἐφ' ᾗ ἐπεποίθει, as well as the τὰ ὑπάρχοντα of St Luke—his goods and furniture, his armour and equipment generally. Cp. Is. liii. 12, τῶν ἰσχυρῶν μεριεῖ σκῦλα (LXX).

30. **ὁ μὴ ὢν μετ' ἐμοῦ κατ' ἐμοῦ ἐστίν**] The thought of the contest between Christ and Satan is continued. Satan is not divided against himself, neither can Christ be. Neutrality is impossible in the Christian life. It must be for Christ or against Christ. The metaphor of gathering and scattering may be from collecting and scattering a flock of sheep, as καὶ ὁ λύκος ἁρπάζει αὐτὰ καὶ σκορπίζει τὰ πρόβατα (John x. 12), or from gathering and squandering wealth, money, &c., the resources given by God to his stewards to spend for him: cp. Luke xvi. 1, διεβλήθη αὐτῷ ὡς διασκορπίζων τὰ ὑπάρχοντα αὐτοῦ.

σκορπίζειν, an Ionic word for the Attic σκεδάννυμι. It is found in Lucian, Strabo and other late writers (Lob. *Phryn.* 218).

31—37. BLASPHEMING AGAINST THE HOLY GHOST.

31. **διὰ τοῦτο.** The conclusion of the whole is—you are on Satan's side, and *knowingly* on Satan's side, in this decisive struggle between the two kingdoms, and this is blasphemy against the Holy Ghost—an unpardonable sin.

This answer is thrown into a poetical form, often observable in the more solemn, or (in human language) the more studied utterances of Christ. Two couplets are followed by a fifth line (οὔτε ἐν τούτῳ .. μέλλοντι) which affects each one of the preceding lines.

This charge was not brought forward for the first time. For a while it may have been passed over in silence. When the season for utterance came the manner as well as the meaning of the words would fix themselves for ever in the memory of the listeners.

32. **ὃς δ' ἂν εἴπῃ κατὰ τοῦ πνεύματος τοῦ ἁγίου.** To speak against the Holy Ghost is to speak against the clear voice of conscience, to call good evil and light darkness, to pursue goodness as such with malignity and hatred. Such sin, or sinful state, cannot be forgiven since from its very nature it excludes the idea of repentance. Jesus, who saw the heart, knew that the Pharisees were insincere in the charge which they brought against Him. They were attributing to Satan what they knew to be the work of God. Their former

attacks against the Son of man had excuse; for instance, they might have differed conscientiously on the question of sabbath observance, now they have no excuse.

33. ἢ ποιήσατε τὸ δένδρον καλόν κ.τ.λ. The meaning and connection are; 'Be honest for once; represent the tree as good, and its fruit as good, or the tree as evil and its fruit as evil; either say that I am evil and that my works are evil, or, if you admit that my works are good, admit that I am good also and not in league with Beelzebub.'

34. γεννήματα ἐχιδνῶν. Cp. ch. iii. 7. Here the argument is turned round against the Pharisees: 'your words and works are evil, and spring from an evil source.'

The burst of indignation after an argument calmly stated resembles the turn in St Stephen's speech (Acts vii. 51) σκληροτράχηλοι, καὶ ἀπερίτμητοι κ.τ.λ.

πῶς δύνασθε ἀγαθὰ λαλεῖν κ.τ.λ. Closely connected with the preceding thought, but further illustrated by two figures—the overflow as of a cistern, and the abundance of a treasury.

περίσσευμα. Cp. περισσεύματα κλασμάτων. Mark viii. 8. Here words are regarded as the overflow of the heart.

35. ἐκβάλλει expresses vigorous and enthusiastic teaching and influence.

θησαυροῦ. Treasury or storehouse. Cp. ch. ii. 11.

36. ἀργόν, without result (a and ἔργον, cp. the frequent rhetorical contrast between λόγος and ἔργον, also between ῥῆμα and ἔργον, as Soph. *O. C.* 873; Thuc. v. 111), so 'useless,' 'ineffective,' and by *litotes* 'harmful,' 'pernicious.' Cp. τοῖς ἔργοις τοῖς ἀκάρποις τοῦ σκότους. Eph. v. 11. Words must be not only not evil, but they must be actively good. The same principle rules the decision at the final judgment (ch. xxv. 45).

ἀποδώσουσιν λόγον...ἐκ γὰρ τῶν λόγων σου...ἐκ τῶν λόγων σου. Note the repeated λόγον...λόγων...λόγων. The English Version by translating ῥῆμα, 'word,' and ἐκ τῶν λόγων σου, 'from thy words,' regards ῥῆμα as synonymous with λόγος, and translates as if ἐκ τῶν ῥημάτων were read. But a different explanation may suggest itself if the passage be read thus: 'every idle ῥῆμα that men shall speak, they shall render a λόγος thereof in the day of judgment; for from thy own λόγοι thou shalt be acquitted and by thy own λόγοι thou shalt be condemned.' The sound and rhythm of the sentence almost compel the reader to refer the same meaning to λόγον and λόγων and to distinguish between ῥῆμα and λόγων. λόγος is the 'reasoned word,' the defence put forth by the individual in the day of judgment for this special thing—'the idle expression;' the plural λόγοι denotes the various points in the defence. In this view γὰρ introduces the reason for ἀποδώσουσιν λόγον. Acquittal or condemnation shall be the result (ἐκ) of each man's defence, ἐκ τοῦ στόματός σου κρινῶ σε πονηρὲ δοῦλε, Luke xix. 22. Cp. too the description of the actual scene of judgment, Matt. xxv. 34—45. For the change from the generic ἄνθρωποι to the specializing 2nd person sing. in *v.* 37 see ch. vii. 7, 8.

The above interpretation harmonises better with facts, for ἔργα as well as ῥήματα will come into account on the last day.

38—42. THE PHARISEES ASK FOR A SIGN.

St Luke xi. 16, 29—32. St Luke omits, or at least does not state explicitly, the special application of the sign given in *v.* 40, to understand which required a knowledge of the Jewish prophets which would be lacking to St Luke's readers.

38. θέλομεν ἀπὸ σοῦ σημεῖον ἰδεῖν. This is the second expedient taken by the Pharisees after their resolution to destroy Jesus.

39. μοιχαλίς, estranged from God; a figure often used by the Prophets to express the defection of Israel from Jehovah. Cp. ch. xvi. 4 and Is. i. 21, πῶς ἐγένετο πόρνη πόλις πιστὴ Σιὼν πλήρης κρίσεως; and Is. lvii. 3.

40. Jonah is a sign (1) as affording a type of the Resurrection, (2) as a preacher of righteousness to a people who needed repentance as this generation needs it.

ἐν τῇ κοιλίᾳ τοῦ κήτους. The A.V. introduces a needless difficulty by translating κήτους, 'whale.' κῆτος (probably from a root meaning 'cleft,' so 'hollow,' &c., perhaps connected with *squatus*, 'a shark') means a 'sea monster:' δελφῖνάς τε κύνας τε καὶ εἴποτε μεῖζον ἔληται | κῆτος. *Od.* XII. 97.

The O.T. rendering is more accurate, 'the fish's belly' (Jonah ii. 1), 'a great fish,' (Jonah i. 17). It is scarcely needful to note that there are no whales in the Mediterranean.

41. ἀναστήσονται κ.τ.λ., 'Shall stand up in the judgment, (i.e. in the day of judgment) beside.' When on the day of judgment the Ninevites stand side by side with the men of that generation, they will by their penitence condemn the impenitent Jews.

εἰς τὸ κήρυγμα. Cp. εἰς διαταγὰς ἀγγέλων, Acts vii. 53. In both instances εἰς appears to be equivalent to ἐν. The two prepositions were originally identical in form and meaning -ενς. In proof of this cp. ἄμειψεν ἐν κοιλόπεδον νάπος θεοῦ. Pind. *Pyth.* v. 37. In later Greek the two forms are interchanged: ὁ ὢν εἰς τὸν κόλπον τοῦ πατρός, John i. 18. ἵν' αὐτὸ λούσῃ εἰς σκάφην, Epict. III. 22, 71. On the other hand, ἐν for εἰς, as ἐπιστρέψαι ἀπειθεῖς ἐν φρονήσει δικαίων, Luke i. 17. ἀπελθεῖν ἐν βαλανείῳ, Epict. I. 11, 32. See Donaldson's *Greek Grammar*, p. 510. Clyde's *Greek Syntax*, § 83, obs. 4.

42. βασίλισσα νότου. 'The Queen of the South.' So correctly and not *a* queen of the South as some translate. The absence of the definite article in the original is due to the influence of the Hebrew idiom. For an account of the queen of Sheba or Southern Arabia, see 1 Kings x. 1.

βασίλισσα. This form is found in all the late authors for the classical βασίλεια. See Lob. *Phryn.* 96.

43—45. A Figure to illustrate the surpassing Wickedness of the day.

Luke xi. 24—26, where the connection is different. St Luke, as usual, omits the direct application to Israel.

This short parable explains the supreme wickedness of the present generation. And herein lies the connection. The Jews of former times were like a man possessed by a single demon, the Jews of the day are like a man possessed by many demons. And this is in accordance with a moral law. If the expulsion of sin be not followed by real amendment of life, and perseverance in righteousness, a more awful condition of sinfulness will result. See note v. 45.

43. δέ, 'but,' introducing the explanation of the facts stated. The connection is obscured in A.V. by the omission of the particle.

ἀνύδρων τόπων. The waterless desert uninhabited by man was regarded by the Jews as the especial abode of evil spirits.

44. σχολάζοντα. Properly 'at leisure.' There must be no leisure in the Christian life; to have cast out a sin does not make a man safe from sin. Christians are οἱ σωζόμενοι not οἱ σεσωσμένοι.

45. οὕτως ἔσται καὶ τῇ γενεᾷ ταύτῃ. Israel had cast forth the demon of idolatry—the sin of its earlier history, but worse demons had entered in—the more insidious and dangerous sins of hypocrisy and hardness of heart.

46—50. Jesus is sought by His Mother and Brethren. The true Mother and Brethren of Jesus.

Mark iii. 31—35; Luke viii. 19—21.

The account is given with very slight variation by the three Synoptists. But see Mark iii. 21 and 30, 31, where a *motive* is suggested—'When his friends heard of it, they went out to lay hold on Him: for they said, He is beside Himself' (v. 21). It would seem that the Pharisees, on the pretext that Jesus had a demon, had persuaded His friends to secure Him. This was another device to destroy Jesus, see vv. 14 and 38.

47. οἱ ἀδελφοί σου. It is a point of controversy whether these were (1) the own brothers of Jesus, sons of Joseph and Mary, or (2) sons of Joseph by a former marriage, or (3) cousins, sons of a sister of Mary.

The names of the 'brethren' are given ch. xiii. 55, where see note.

It may be observed in regard to this question that the nearer the relationship of the ἀδελφοί to Jesus is held to be, the more gracious are the words of Christ, and the nearer the spiritual kinship which is compared to the human brotherhood.

49. ἰδοὺ ἡ μήτηρ μου καὶ οἱ ἀδελφοί μου. The new life subverts the old relationships. By the spiritual birth new ties of kindred are established.

50. ὅστις γὰρ ἂν ποιήσῃ κ.τ.λ. 'These which hear the word of God and do it' (Luke viii. 21).

τοῦ ἐν οὐρανοῖς. The addition is important. 'Not those who do the will of my earthly father, but those who do the will of my heavenly Father are brethren.' The essence of sonship is obedience, and obedience to God constitutes brotherhood to Jesus who came to do τὸ θέλημα τοῦ πέμψαντος. John vi. 38.

CHAPTER XIII.

2. πλοῖον, for τὸ πλοῖον. Here there is no mention of the particular boat used by Christ and his disciples.

15. ἰάσομαι, for ἰάσωμαι. The latter reading is due to the influence of grammatical uniformity, or an *itacism*, confusion of vowels that have a similar sound.

18. σπείραντος, for σπείροντος. **24.** σπείραντι for σπείροντι. The first change is less well supported than the second, but the tendency to assimilate in the first case to ὁ σπείρων (v. 3) would be greater.

25. ἐπέσπειρεν for ἔσπειρεν. The simple verb has large MS. support, but there would be great probability of losing the preposition in transcribing, and very little of its insertion if not in original text. For effect on sense see note *infra*.

35. The insertion of Ἡσαίου before τοῦ προφήτου, a mistaken gloss, has very slender authority, א being the only uncial that contains the reading.

40. There is strong support for καίεται instead of κατακαίεται which *may* have been influenced by v. 30.

48. ἄγγη for ἀγγεῖα, on good authority. ἀγγεῖα an explanation of the rarer form ἄγγη.

51. λέγει αὐτοῖς ὁ Ἰησοῦς. Omitted in the oldest uncials א B D, appears in C and with the later uncials. The harshness of the construction without these words goes to prove a later insertion.

52. τῇ βασιλείᾳ has the best authority and is the more difficult reading. εἰς τὴν βασιλείαν was probably a marginal note.

1—9. JESUS TEACHES IN PARABLES. THE PARABLE OF THE SOWER.

Mark iv. 1—9; Luke viii. 4—9.

1. ἐκάθητο. The usual position of a Jewish teacher.

παρὰ τὴν θάλασσαν. At the N. end of the Lake of Gennesaret there are small creeks or inlets 'where the ship could ride in safety only a few feet from the shore, and where the multitudes seated on both sides and before the boat could listen without distraction or fatigue. As if on purpose to furnish seats, the shore on both sides of these narrow inlets is piled up with smooth boulders of basalt.' Thomson, *Land and Book*, p. 356.

2. εἰς πλοῖον. See crit. notes, and compare such expressions as ἔρχονται εἰς οἶκον, Mark iii. 19.

3. ἐν παραβολαῖς. Up to this time Jesus had preached repentance, proclaiming the kingdom, and setting forth the laws of it in direct terms. He now indicates by parables the reception, growth, characteristics, and future of the kingdom. The reason for this manner of teaching is given below, *vv.* 10—15.

παραβολή, from παραβάλλειν, 'to put side by side,' 'compare' (Hebr. *mashal*)='a likeness' or 'comparison.' The meaning of the Hebrew word extends to proverbial sayings: 1 Sam. x. 12; Prov. i. 1, and to poetical narration, Ps. lxxviii. 2 (see Dean Perowne's note). Parables differ from fables in being pictures of possible occurrences—frequently of actual daily occurrences,—and in teaching *religious* truths rather than *moral* truths. See below *v.* 10 and *v.* 33.

4. ἃ μὲν...ἄλλα δέ. For this use of the relative as a demonstrative cp. ὃν μὲν ἔδειραν ὃν δὲ ἀπέκτειναν, ch. xxi. 35. οὓς μὲν ἐξέβαλον τῶν πολιτῶν οὓς δὲ ἀπέσφαξαν (Dem.); and for ἄλλα δέ, following ἃ μέν, cp. οἱ μέν...ἄλλοι δέ...ἕτεροι δέ, ch. xvi. 14; Winer, p. 130. ὅς ἥ ὅ like ὁ ἡ τό was originally demonstrative, but the relative and the article are traced to independent originals. Clyde's *Greek Syntax*, § 30. (Ed. 5.)

παρὰ τὴν ὁδόν, i.e. along the narrow footpath dividing one field from another.

5. τὰ πετρώδη. Places where the underlying rock was barely covered with earth. The hot sun striking on the thin soil and warming the rock beneath would cause the corn to spring up rapidly and then as swiftly to wither.

7. αἱ ἄκανθαι. Virgil mentions among the 'plagues' of the wheat,

'Ut mala culmos
Esset robigo segnisque horreret in arvis
Carduus.' *Georg.* i. 150—153.

8. ὃ μὲν ἑκατόν, κ.τ.λ. Thomson, *Land and Book*, p. 83, ascribes the different kinds of fertility to different kinds of grain; 'barley yields more than wheat, and white maize sown in the neighbourhood, often yields several hundred fold.' It is however better to refer the difference of yield to differences in particular parts of the good soil. The highest in the kingdom of God differ in receptivity and fruitfulness. As to the fact, cf. Strabo, xv. p. 1063 c.: πολύσιτος δ' ἄγαν ἐστι ὥστε ἑκατοντάχουν δι' ὁμαλοῦ καὶ κριθὴν καὶ πυρὸν ἐκτρέφειν ἐστι δ' ὅτε καὶ διακοσιοντάχουν.

10—17. THE REASON WHY JESUS TEACHES IN PARABLES.
Mark iv. 10—12; Luke viii. 10.

10. ἐν παραβολαῖς. The parable is suited (1) to the uninstructed, as being attractive in form and as revealing spiritual truth exactly in proportion to the capacity of the hearer; and (2) to the divinely wise as wrapping up a secret which he can penetrate by his spiritual insight. In this it resembles the Platonic myth; it was the form in which many philosophers clothed their deepest thoughts. (3) It fulfils the condition of all true knowledge. He alone who seeks finds. In relation to Nature, Art, God Himself, it may be said the dull 'seeing see not.' The commonest and most obvious things hide the greatest truths. (4) The divine Wisdom has been justified in respect to this mode of teaching. The parables have struck deep into the thought and language of men (not of Christians only), as no other teaching could have done; in proof of which it is sufficient to name such words and expressions as 'talents,' 'dispensation,' 'leaven,' 'prodigal son,' 'light under a bushel,' 'building on sand.'

11. τὰ μυστήρια τῆς βασιλείας τῶν οὐρανῶν. Secrets known only to the initiated—the inner teaching of the gospel. St Paul regards as 'mysteries,' the spread of the gospel to the Gentiles, Eph. iii. 3. 4, 9; the doctrine of the resurrection, 1 Cor. xv. 51, the conversion of the Jews, Rom. xi. 25; the relation of Christ to His Church; Eph. v. 32.

To the Greek, μυστήρια would recall the associations of Eleusis and Samothrace, and so necessarily bring a part of the mystic thought into Christianity; only, however, to contrast the true Christian mysticism, which is open to all (νῦν δὲ ἐφανερώθη τοῖς ἁγίοις αὐτοῦ, Col. i. 27), with the secresy and exclusiveness of the pagan mysteries. Bp. Lightfoot on Col. i. 21—28. The derivation is from μύειν, 'to close the lips.' The initiated are called μεμυημένοι or τέλειοι (fully instructed); the use of the latter word may be applied to the same conception in 1 Cor. ii. 6, σοφίαν λαλοῦμεν ἐν τοῖς τελείοις...θεοῦ σοφίαν ἐν μυστηρίῳ κεκρυμμένην. See also Phil. iii. 15; Hebr. v. 14.

12. Cp. ch. xxv. 29.

13. διὰ τοῦτο...ὅτι. Jesus teaches in parables, *because*, as it is, the people do not understand, &c., i.e. (1) either He teaches them in the simplest and most attractive form so as by degrees to lead them on to deeper knowledge, or (2) He teaches in parables because it is not fitting that divine truths should be at once patent to the unreflective and indifferent multitude.

In the parallel passages a final clause takes the place of the causal sentence: Mark iv. 11, ἐκείνοις δὲ τοῖς ἔξω ἐν παραβολαῖς τὰ πάντα γίνεται ἵνα βλέποντες βλέπωσιν κ.τ.λ. Luke viii. 10, τοῖς δὲ λοιποῖς ἐν παραβολαῖς ἵνα βλέποντες βλέπωσιν κ.τ.λ. The final particle ἵνα denotes intention or aim. But in regard to God's dealing, all results are *intended* results, and the usual distinction between consecutive and final clauses is lost. The result of teaching by parables was that the careless and indifferent did not understand, it was the intention of God; in other words it is a spiritual law that those only who have πίστις shall learn. The form and thought of the original Hebrew corresponds with this view.

14. Is. vi. 9, 10. The words form part of the mission of Isaiah.

15. ἐπαχύνθη ἡ καρδία. The heart, regarded by the ancients as the seat of intelligence, has become gross or fat, and so closed against the perception of spiritual truth.

μήποτε ἴδωσιν...ἰάσομαι. For the sequence of the subjunctive and future indicative co-ordinately after a final particle, cp. Rev. xxii. 14, μακάριοι οἱ πλύνοντες τὰς στολὰς αὐτῶν, ἵνα ἔσται ἡ ἐξουσία αὐτῶν...καὶ εἰσέλθωσιν. For the future, among other passages, cp. Gal. ii. 4, where the best editors read ἵνα ἡμᾶς καταδουλώσουσιν. See Winer, p. 361. In the classics the future indicative in pure final clauses is found after ὅπως and ὄφρα, never after ἵνα or ὡς, and very seldom after the simple μή. Goodwin's *Moods and Tenses*, p. 68. Elmsley, however (Eur. *Bacch.*, p. 164) does not admit the exception of ἵνα. See Winer, *loc. cit.* above. In the N.T. ὅπως occurs with the future, Matt. ch. xxvi. 59, and, on good MS. authority, Rom. iii. 4. As distinguished from the subjunctive in such instances the future indicative implies a more permanent condition.

16. ὑμῶν δὲ μακάριοι οἱ ὀφθαλμοί. The disciples have discernment to understand the explanation which would be thrown away on the unistructed multitude.

18—23. THE PARABLE OF THE SOWER IS EXPLAINED.
Mark iv. 14—20; Luke viii. 11—15.

19. On some the word of God makes no *impression*, as we say; some hearts are quite unsusceptible of good.

παντὸς ἀκούοντος. Si quis audit, quisquis est, for the classical ἐάν τις ἀκούσῃ. πᾶς here follows the usage of Hebr. *kol*, 'all,' or 'any.' See note ch. xxiv. 22.

20, 21. εὐθύς...εὐθύς. The unstable and volatile nature is as quick to be attracted by the gospel at first, as it is to abandon it afterwards when the trial comes.

ὁ δὲ σπαρείς. 'He that was sown.' The man is compared to the seed. Comp. the more definite expression in Luke viii. 14, τὸ δὲ εἰς τὰς ἀκάνθας πεσόν οὗτοί εἰσιν οἱ ἀκούσαντες. For a defence of the A.V. 'He that receiveth the seed' (σπαρείς being taken in the sense of τὴν σπειρομένην Αἴγυπτον), see McClellan, New Testament, &c., *ad loc.*

21. γενομένης δὲ θλίψεως ἢ διωγμοῦ. Jesus forecasts the persecution of Christians, and the time when 'the love of many shall wax cold,' ch. xxiv. 12.

σκανδαλίζεται. 'Falls,' is ensnared by attempting to avoid persecution. See note, ch. v. 29.

22. ἡ μέριμνα τοῦ αἰῶνος καὶ ἡ ἀπάτη τοῦ πλούτου. St Mark adds αἱ περὶ τὰ λοιπὰ ἐπιθυμίαι, St Luke ἡδονῶν τοῦ βίου. These things destroy the 'singleness' of the Christian life. Compare with this the threefold employment of the world as described by Christ, at the time of the Flood, at the destruction of Sodom and Gomorrah, and at the coming of the Son of man. (Luke xvii. 26—30.)

μέριμνα, 'absorbing care,' from a root that connects it with μερμηρίζω, μάρτυς, memoria, mora.

23. The word will be more fruitful in some hearts than in others. Even the Apostles exemplified this. The triple division in their number seems to point to differences of gifts and spiritual fruitfulness.

24—30. THE PARABLE OF THE TARES. Confined to St Matthew.

24. παρέθηκεν here and v. 31 only in this sense. Elsewhere of 'setting meat before a guest'—the usual Homeric use of the word—Mark vi. 41, viii. 6, 7; Luke xi. 6. Of committing a charge to a person, Luke xii. 48; 2 Tim. ii. 2. In mid. voice, of 'proving' by comparison, Acts xvii. 3. Here the word might be taken in a similar sense 'made a similitude,' παραβολήν regarded as cognate.

σπείραντι, not 'which sowed,' A.V. but when he sowed.

25. ἐν δὲ τῷ καθεύδειν τοὺς ἀνθρώπους, i.e. during the night. The expression is not introduced into the Lord's explanation of the parable.

ἐπέσπειρεν ζιζάνια. Travellers mention similar instances of spiteful conduct in the East, and elsewhere, in modern times. ἐπί gives the force of an *after* sowing or sowing *over* the good seed.

ζιζάνια. Probably the English 'darnel;' Latin, *lolium*; in the earlier stages of its growth this weed very closely resembles wheat, indeed can scarcely be distinguished from it. This resemblance gives an obvious point to the parable. The good and the evil are often indistinguishable in the visible church. The Day of Judgment will separate. Men have tried in every age to make the separation beforehand, but have failed. For proof of this read the history of the Essenes or the Donatists. The Lollards—as the followers of Wyckliffe were called—were sometimes by a play on the word *lolium* identified by their opponents with the tares of this parable. A friend suggests the reflection: 'How strange it was that the very men who applied the word "Lollard" from this parable, acted in direct opposition to the great lesson which it taught, by being persecutors.'

The parable of the Tares has a sequence in thought on the parable of the Sower. The latter shows that the kingdom of God will not be coextensive with the world; all men have not sufficient faith to receive the word. This indicates that the kingdom of God—the true Church—is not coextensive with the visible Church. Some who seem to be subjects of the Kingdom are not really subjects.

26. ἐφάνη, 'was manifest,' when the good corn made fruit: before that they were indistinguishable.

31—33. (1) The Parable of the Mustard Seed. (2) The Parable of the Leaven which leavened the Meal.
(1) Mark iv. 30—32. (1) and (2) Luke xiii. 18—21.

The 'mystery' or secret of the future contained in these two parables has reference to the growth of the Church; the first regards the growth in its external aspect, the second in its inner working.

The power that plants possess of absorbing within themselves, and assimilating the various elements of the soil in which they are planted, and the surrounding gases—not by one channel but by many—the conditions too under which this is done—the need of water, of the breath of heaven and of sunlight—find a close parallel in the history and influence of the Church of Christ. It is an instance where the thought of the illustration is deepened by fresh knowledge.

31. ὃν λαβὼν ἄνθρωπος ἔσπειρεν. ὅταν σπαρῇ, St Mark, who thus does not name an agent, the planter of the seed.

ἐν τῷ ἀγρῷ αὐτοῦ. εἰς κῆπον ἑαυτοῦ (Luke), 'his own garden,' with special reference to the land of Israel.

32. μικρότερον πάντων τῶν σπερμάτων. Not absolutely the least, but least in proportion to the plant that springs from the seed. Moreover the mustard seed was used proverbially of anything excessively minute.

κατασκηνοῖν ἐν τοῖς κλάδοις αὐτοῦ, i.e. settle for the purpose of rest or shelter or to eat the seeds, of which goldfinches and linnets are very fond. (Tristram, *Nat. Hist. of Bible*, p. 473.) κατασκηνοῖν. Literally, dwell in tents. If we think of the leafy huts constructed for the feast of tabernacles the propriety of the word will be seen. The mustard plant does not grow to a very great height, so that St Luke's expression ἐγένετο εἰς δένδρον [μέγα] must not be pressed. Dr Thomson (*Land and Book*) mentions as an exceptional instance that he found it on the plain of Akkar as tall as a horse and its rider.

κατασκηνοῖν. For the infinitive termination see Winer, p. 92. Cp. the contraction χρυσόει = χρυσοῖ, though in infin. generally χρυσόειν = χρυσοῦν, also the Pindaric forms ἔχοισιν for ἔχουσιν, &c. δίδοι for δίδου. (Donaldson's *Pindar, de Stilo Pindari*, p. liv) and the Thessalian genitive form is -οι for -ου (Papillon, *Compar. Phil.* 112 note).

33. ζύμη. Except in this one parable, leaven is used of the working of evil; cp. μικρὰ ζύμη ὅλον τὸ φύραμα ζυμοῖ, Gal. v. 9; 1 Cor. v. 6; and ἐκκαθάρατε οὖν τὴν παλαιὰν ζύμην, 1 Cor. v. 7. So, too, in the Rabbinical writings. This thought probably arose from the prohibition of leaven during the paschal season. But the secrecy and the all-pervading character of leaven aptly symbolize the growth of Christianity, (1) as a society penetrating everywhere by a subtle and mysterious operation until in this light—as a secret brotherhood—it appeared dangerous to the Roman empire; (2) as an influence unfelt at *first* growing up within the human soul.

Sir Bartle Frere on *Indian Missions*, p. 9; speaking of the gradual change wrought by Christianity in India, says, in regard to religious innovations in general: 'They are always subtle in operation, and generally little noticeable at the outset in comparison with the power of their ultimate operation.'

σάτα τρία, 'three seahs.' In Gen. xviii. 6, Abraham bids Sarah 'make ready three "seahs" of fine meal, knead it and make cakes upon the hearth.'

34. ἐν παραβολαῖς. In reference to the teaching by parables it may be remarked, (1) that the variety in the subject-matter not only gives great vivacity and fulness to the instruction, but the several illustrations would interest specially particular classes and persons—the fisherman on the lake, the farmer and the merchant would each in turn find his own pursuit furnishing a figure for divine things, even the poor woman standing on the outskirts of the crowd learns that her daily task is fruitful in spiritual lessons. (2) As descriptive of the kingdom of heaven they set it forth as incapable of definition, as presenting many aspects, as suggested by a variety of external things, though not itself external. (3) For the general effect on the imagination and for variety comp. the series of images by which Homer describes the march of the Achæan host. *Il.* II. 455—484.

35. ὅπως πληρωθῇ, For the meaning of this formula cp. note, ch. i. 22.

διὰ τοῦ προφήτου, Asaph, the author of Ps. lxxviii. from which this quotation is taken. He is called 'Asaph the seer,' 2 Chron. xxix. 30.

The quotation does not agree verbally with the LXX. where the last clause is φθέγξομαι προβλήματα ἀπ' ἀρχῆς. It is a direct translation of the Hebrew. The psalm which follows these words is a review of the history of Israel from the Exodus to the reign of David. This indicates the somewhat wide sense given to 'parables' and 'dark sayings.' Here the *mashal*, παραβολή, or 'comparison,' implies the teachings of history. Though possibly the term may apply only to the antithetical form of Hebrew poetry. See Dean Perowne *ad loc.*

ἐρεύγεσθαι. Ionic form for Attic ἐρυγγάνω, cp. τυγχάνω for τεύχω, λανθάνω for λήθω. Cp. ἐρεύγετο οἰνοβαρείων, *Od.* IX. 374. (κύματα) ἐρεύγεται ἠπειρόνδε, *Od.* v. 438. The word is similarly used in Pindar and Theocritus, and in the LXX. of lions roaring, Hos. xi. 11; Amos iii. 4, 8; of water bursting forth, Lev. xi. 10, and in Ps. xviii. 2 figuratively ἡμέρα τῇ ἡμέρᾳ ἐρεύγεται ῥῆμα. Here only in the softened sense of 'speaking;' such softening of coarse and strong meanings is characteristic of Alexandrine Greek, cp. σκύλλειν.

καταβολή, foundation, beginning. So used by Pindar and Polyb. ἐκ καταβολῆς κατηγορεῖν, Polyb. xxvi. 1, 9. καταβολὴν ἐποιεῖτο καὶ θεμέλιον ὑπεβάλλετο πολυχρονίου τυραννίδος, XIII. 6, 2. Cp. μὴ πάλιν θεμέλιον καταβαλλόμενοι μετανοίας ἀπὸ νεκρῶν ἔργων. Heb. vi. 1.

36—43. EXPLANATION OF THE PARABLE OF THE TARES, in St Matthew only.

39. συντέλεια. In classical Greek 'a joint subscription, or association for paying state dues,' &c. later the 'completion' of a scheme opposed to ἀρχή or ἐπιβολή, cp. συντέλειαν ἐπιθεῖναι τοῖς ἔργοις, Polyb. XI. 33, 7.

συντέλεια αἰῶνος. 'Completion of the Æon,' the expression is confined to this Gospel; see below, *vv.* 40 and 49 and ch. xxiv. 3, but compare Hebr. ix. 26, ἐπὶ συντελείᾳ τῶν αἰώνων, 'at the completion of the Æons,' and 1 Cor. x. 11, τὰ τέλη τῶν αἰώνων, the ends or the final result of the Æons. In the two last passages the '*Æons*' are the successive periods previous to the advent of Christ, the '*Æon*' of the text is the period introduced by Christ, which will not be completed till his second Advent.

41. πάντα τὰ σκάνδαλα. Everything that ensnares or tempts men to destruction; see ch. v. 29.

42. ὁ κλαυθμὸς καὶ ὁ βρυγμὸς τῶν ὀδόντων. For the force of the article see ch. viii. 12. 'The grinding of the teeth and the uttering of piercing shrieks give relief in an agony of pain.' Darwin, *Expression of the Emotions*, p. 177.

43. τότε οἱ δίκαιοι κ.τ.λ. Cp. Dan. xii. 3, 'Then they that be wise shall shine as the brightness of the firmament.'

44. THE PARABLE OF THE HID TREASURE, in this Gospel only.

In ancient times, and in an unsettled country like Palestine, where there were no banks, in the modern sense, it was a common practice to conceal treasures in the ground. Even at this day the Arabs are keenly alive to the chance of finding such buried stores. The dishonesty of the purchaser must be excluded from the thought of the parable. The *unexpected* discovery, the consequent excitement and joy, and the eagerness to buy at any sacrifice, are the points to be observed in the interpretation.

εὑρών. Here the kingdom of heaven presents itself unexpectedly, 'Christ is found of one who sought Him not.' The woman of Samaria, the jailer at Philippi, the centurion by the Cross are instances,

πωλεῖ πάντα ὅσα ἔχει. This is the renunciation which is always needed for the winning of the kingdom, cp. ch. x. 38. Thus Paul gave up position, Matthew wealth, Barnabas lands.

ἀγοράζει τὸν ἀγρὸν ἐκεῖνον. Puts himself in a position to attain the kingdom.

45, 46. THE PARABLE OF THE PEARL OF GREAT PRICE, in St Matthew only.

Here the story is of one who succeeds in getting what he strives to obtain. The Jewish or the Greek 'seekers after God,' possessing many pearls, but still dissatisfied, sought others yet more choice, and finding one, true to the simplicity in Christ, renounce all for that; the one his legalism, the other his philosophy. Nathaniel, Apollos, Timotheus, Justin Martyr are amongst those who thus sought and found.

46. πέπρακεν, 'sells at once.' The perfect marks the quickness of the transaction, cp. Dem. *Phil.* I. 19, δεδόχθαι, 'instantly determined upon.' Soph. *Aj.* 275, νῦν δ' ὡς ἔληξε κἀπέπνευσε τῆς νόσου, | κεῖνός τε λύπῃ πᾶς ἐλήλαται κακῇ, and 479, ἦ καλῶς τεθνηκέναι, ' or *at once* nobly die.' See Jebb on both passages. τὸ μὴ ἐμποδὼν ἀνανταγωνίστῳ εὐνοίᾳ τετίμηται, (Thuc. II. 45) '*is at once* held in honour.' Donaldson, *Greek Grammar*, p. 409, (cc.)

47—50. THE PARABLE OF THE NET, in St Matthew only.

7. σαγήνη. A drag-net or *seine* (the English word comes from the Greek through *sagena* of the Vulgate). One end of the *seine* is held on the shore, the other is hauled off by a boat and then returned to the land. In this way a large number of fishes of all kinds is enclosed. Seine-fishing is still practised on the coasts of Devonshire and Cornwall.

The teaching of this parable partly coincides with that of the parable of the Tares (*vv.* 24—30). In both are exhibited the mixture of good and evil in the visible Church, and the final separation of them. But here the thought is specially directed to the ingathering of the Church. The ministers of Christ will of necessity draw converts of diverse character, good and evil, and actuated by different motives. From the parable of the tares we learn not to reject any from within the Church, in the hope of expelling the element of evil. It is a parable of the settled Church. This is a missionary parable. It teaches that as a matter of history or of fact, no barrier or external test will serve to exclude the unworthy convert.

50. εἰς τὴν κάμινον τοῦ πυρός. The article has the same force as in ὁ κλαυθμός. The figure may be generally drawn from an oriental mode of punishment, or there may be special reference to Dan. iii. 6.

51, 52. THE SCRIBES OF THE KINGDOM OF HEAVEN.

51. συνήκατε. σύνεσις, 'intelligent apprehension,' is used specially of spiritual intelligence, Col. i. 9. Cp. ch. xvi. 12, xvii. 13.

52. μαθητευθεὶς τῇ βασιλείᾳ. The new law requires a new order of Scribes who shall be instructed in the kingdom of heaven—instructed in its mysteries, its laws, its future—as the Jewish Scribes are instructed in the observances of the Mosaic law.

καινὰ καὶ παλαιά. (1) Just as the householder brings from his stores or treasury precious things which have been heir-looms for generations, as well as newly acquired treasures; the disciples following their master's example will exhibit the true teaching of the old law, and add thereto the new lessons of Christianity. (2) Another interpretation finds a reference to Jewish sacrificial usage by which sometimes the newly-gathered fruit or corn, sometimes the produce of a former year furnished the offering. The wise householder was ready for all emergencies. So the Christian teacher will have an apt lesson on each occasion.

As applied to the teaching of Christ Himself καινὰ points to the fresh revelation, παλαιὰ to the Law and the Prophets on which the new truths rested and from which they were evolved. Instances are, the extended and deeper meaning given to the decalogue, and to the law of forgiveness, &c., the fresh light thrown on prophecy and on Rabbinical sayings, the confirmation of the ancient dealings of God combined with the revelation of entirely new truths, as that of the resurrection,—of the Christian Church,—of the Sacraments,—of the extension of the Gospel to the Gentiles.

53—58. The Prophet in his own Country
Mark vi. 1—6; Luke iv. 16—30.

In Mark the incident is placed between the cure of Jairus' daughter and the mission of the Twelve; in Luke our Lord's discourse in the synagogue is given at length. But many commentators hold with great probability that St Luke's narrative refers to a different and earlier visit to Nazareth.

53. μετῆρεν. Only here and ch. xix. 1 in N.T. The seemingly intransitive use of αἴρειν comes from the familiar phrase αἴρειν στόλον, 'to start an expedition,' then, the object being omitted, as in many English nautical phrases, 'to start.' This use of the compound μεταίρειν however does not appear to be classical.

54. τὴν πατρίδα αὐτοῦ. Nazareth and the neighbourhood.

55. οὐχ οὗτός ἐστιν ὁ τοῦ τέκτονος υἱός; In Mark vi. 3, ὁ υἱὸς Μαρίας καὶ ἀδελφὸς Ἰακώβου καὶ Ἰωσῆτος καὶ Ἰούδα καὶ Σίμωνος; No allusion being made to the father, as in the other synoptists, possibly Joseph was no longer living. For ὁ τέκτονος υἱὸς Mark has ὁ τέκτων. As every Jew was taught a trade there would be no improbability in the carpenter's son becoming a scribe. But it was known that Jesus had not had the ordinary education of a scribe.

οἱ ἀδελφοὶ αὐτοῦ. Probably the sons of Joseph and Mary. It is certain that no other view would ever have been propounded except for the assumption that the blessed Virgin remained ever-virgin.

Two theories have been mooted in support of this assumption. (1) The 'brethren of the Lord' were His cousins, being sons of Cleophas (or Alphæus), and Mary, a sister of the Virgin Mary. (2) They were sons of Joseph by a former marriage.

Neither of these theories derives any support from the direct words of Scripture, and some facts tend to disprove either. The second theory is the least open to objection on the ground of language, and of the facts of the gospel.

The brethren of the Lord were probably not in the number of the Twelve. This seems to be rendered nearly certain by St John's assertion (vii. 5) οὐδὲ γὰρ οἱ ἀδελφοὶ αὐτοῦ ἐπίστευον εἰς αὐτόν, and is strengthened by the way in which the brethren's names are introduced, as though they were more familiar than Jesus to the men of Nazareth; it seems to be implied that they were still living there.

James afterwards became president or bishop of the Church at Jerusalem: he presided at the first Council and pronounced the decision: διὸ ἐγὼ κρίνω κ.τ.λ. (Acts xv. 19). The authorship of the Epistle is generally ascribed to him. His manner of life and his death are described by Hegesippus (Eus. *H. E.* II. 23, p. 58, 59, Bright's ed.). Of Joses nothing further is known. Jude is most probably to be identified with the author of the Epistle bearing his name. Tradition has an interesting story concerning his two grandsons, who being arrested as descendants of the royal house and therefore possible leaders of sedition, and brought before the Emperor Domitian, described their poverty, and shewed him their hands, rough and horny from personal toil, and so dispelled the idea of danger and regained their freedom (Eus. *H. E.* III. 21). Of Simeon tradition has nothing certain or trustworthy to report.

For the many difficult and intricate questions involved in the controversy as to the 'brethren of the Lord,' see the various articles in *Dict. of the Bible*, and Bp. Lightfoot's dissertation in his edition of the *Epistle to the Galatians*.

CHAPTER XIV.

3. ἀπέθετο, probably right (א B), for ἔθετο.

6. γενεσίοις γενομένοις, for γενεσίων γενομένων. The dative has decisive authority. The gen. abs. a grammatical note, which has come into the text as the easier reading.

14, 22, 25. The subject Ἰησοῦς omitted, insertion due to lectionaries or marginal note.

19. τοῦ χόρτου. The plural τοὺς χόρτους ('grassy places') has the support of the late MSS.: the gen. sing. is the reading of אBC*.

25, 26. The true reading ἐπὶ τὴν θάλ....ἐπὶ τῆς θαλ. reverses the *textus receptus*. The change of case after ἐπί, and of the order of the participle, is suggestive: περιπ. ἐπὶ τὴν θάλ. 'walking over the sea,' ἐπὶ τῆς θαλ. περιπ. 'upon the sea,' (the wonder that first struck the disciples,) 'walking,' a secondary thought.

30. ἰσχυρόν, omitted by Tischendorf on the evidence of א B* 33. Lachmann and Tregelles, who retain it, did not know of א.

1—12. HEROD THE TETRARCH PUTS TO DEATH JOHN THE BAPTIST.

Mark vi. 14—29, where the further conjectures as to the personality of Jesus are given, 'Elias, a [or the] prophet, or as one of the prophets,' and the whole account is narrated in the vivid dramatic manner of St Mark. St Luke relates the cause of the imprisonment, iii. 19, 20; the conjectures as to Jesus, ix. 7—9.

1. ἐν ἐκείνῳ τῷ καιρῷ. During the missionary journey of the Twelve. See Mark *loc. cit.*

Ἡρώδης. Herod Antipas, tetrarch of Galilee and Peræa. He was a son of Herod the Great, and Malthakè, a Samaritan, who was also the mother of Archelaus and Olympias. He was thus of Gentile origin, and his early associations were Gentile, for he was brought up at Rome with his brother Archelaus. He married first a daughter of Aretas, king of Arabia, and afterwards, while his first wife was still living, he married Herodias, wife of his half-brother Philip,—who was living in a private station, and must not be confused with Philip the tetrarch of Ituræa. Cruel, scheming, irresolute, and wicked, he was a type of the worst of tyrants. He intrigued to have the title of tetrarch changed for the higher title of king; very much as Charles the Bold of Burgundy endeavoured to change his dukedom into a kingdom. In pursuance of this scheme Antipas went to Rome 'to receive for himself a kingdom and return' (Luke xix. 12). He was however foiled in this attempt by the arts of his nephew Agrippa, and was eventually banished to Lyons, being accused of confederacy with Sejanus, and of an intention to revolt. Herodias was his worst enemy: she advised the two most fatal errors of his reign: the execution of John Baptist, which brought him into enmity with the Jews, and the attempt to gain the royal title, the result of which was his fall and banishment. But there is a touch of nobility in the determination she took to share her husband's exile as she had shared his days of prosperity. For Herod's design against our Lord, see Luke xiii. 31; and for the part which he took in the Passion, see Luke xxiii. 6—12.

τετράρχης. Literally, the ruler of a fourth part or district into which a province was divided, ἕκαστα (ἔθνη) διελόντες εἰς τέσσαρας μερίδας τετραρχίαν ἑκάστην ἐκάλεσεν (Strabo XII. p. 850). Afterwards the name was extended to denote generally a petty king, '(tetrarchiæ regnorum instar,' Plin. *H. N.* v. 16) the ruler of a provincial district. Deiotarus, whose cause Cicero supported, was tetrarch of Galatia. He is called king by Appian, just as Herod Antipas is called king, *v.* 9, and Mark vi. 14.

The relation of these principalities to the Roman Empire resembled that of the feudal dependencies to the Suzerain in mediæval times, or that of the Indian native states to the British Crown—political independence and the liberty of raising troops, imposing taxes, maintaining courts of justice, only conditional on the payment of tribute into the imperial exchequer.

2. αὐτός. Emphatic, 'he himself,' 'in his own person.'

ἠγέρθη ἀπὸ τῶν νεκρῶν. A proof that Herod did not hold the Sadducaean doctrine, that there is no resurrection.

διὰ τοῦτο. In consequence of having risen from the dead he is thought to be possessed of larger powers. Alford remarks that this incidentally confirms St John's statement (ch. x. 41), that John wrought no miracle while living.

αἱ δυνάμεις. 'The works of power' of which Herod had heard. δυνάμεις, miracles regarded as marks of divine power; as proofs or signs of the divine presence they are σημεῖα, as exciting wonder they are τέρατα. The latter word is never used *alone* of miracles: this is not the side on which the Gospel dwells. Trench. *Syn. of N. T.* 177 foll.

ἐνεργοῦσιν. Not 'shew themselves forth,' A.V., but, 'are active in him.' The verb is frequent in Aristotle, the substantive ἐνέργεια is an important philosophical term in relation to δύναμις. The same contrast is suggested here. In Polybius ἐνεργεῖν is sometimes (1) transitive, as πάντα κατὰ δύναμιν ἐνεργεῖν, xviii. 14. 8. Sometimes (2) intransitive, as τῶν αἰτίων ἐνεργούντων κατὰ τὸ συνεχές, iv. 40. 4. Both these uses are found in N.T. (1) ὁ αὐτὸς θεὸς ὁ ἐνεργῶν τὰ πάντα ἐν πᾶσιν, 1 Cor. xii. 6. (2) τοῦ νῦν ἐνεργοῦντος ἐν τοῖς υἱοῖς τῆς ἀπειθείας. Eph. ii. 2.

3. **ἐν τῇ φυλακῇ.** At Machærus, in Peræa, on the eastern side of the Dead Sea, near the southern frontier of the tetrarchy. Here Antipas had a palace and a prison under one roof, as was common in the East. Cp. Nehemiah iii. 25, 'The tower which lieth out from the king's high house that was by the court of the prison.' It was the ordinary arrangement in feudal castles. At Machærus, now M'khaur, remains of buildings are still visible. These are probably the ruins of the Baptist's prison. Herod was living in this border fortress in order to prosecute the war with his offended father-in-law, Aretas. He was completely vanquished—a disaster popularly ascribed to his treatment of John the Baptist.

4. **ἔλεγεν.** Imperfect, 'told him repeatedly.'

ἔχειν, 'to marry' her. ἔχειν has this special force, 1 Cor. v. 1, τοιαύτη πορνεία...ὥστε γυναῖκά τινα τοῦ πατρὸς ἔχειν. ch. xxii. 28, πάντες γὰρ ἔσχον αὐτήν. Xen. *Cyrop.* I, Κυαξάρης ἔπεμψε πρὸς Καμβύσην τὸν τὴν ἀδελφὴν ἔχοντα.

οὐκ ἔξεστίν σοι ἔχειν αὐτήν. St Luke adds, iii. 19, that Herod was also reproved 'περὶ πάντων ὧν ἐποίησεν πονηρῶν.' 'Boldly to rebuke vice' is fixed upon as the leading characteristic of the Baptist in the collect for St John the Baptist's day.

5. **θέλων.** From St Mark we learn that Herodias was eager to kill John, while Herod, partly from fear of his prisoner, partly from interest in him, refused to take away his life. St Mark's narrative gives a picture of the inner court intrigues, and bears evidence of keen questioning of some eye-witness as to facts. Possibly some of Herod's own household were secret adherents of John.

ἐφοβήθη τὸν ὄχλον. The same motive that held the tyrant's hand, checked the arguments of the Pharisees, ch. xxi. 26.

6. **γενεσίοις γενομένοις.** Dative of time, 'marking *precisely* time when' (Clyde); cp. τοῖς σάββασιν, ch. xii. 2, Winer, p. 274. Plural,

as usual in names of festivals, ἐγκαίνια, ἄζυμα, Παναθήναια, *Saturnalia*. Here τὰ γενέσια retains what must have been its original sense, 'a birthday festival;' but in classical Greek it meant a memorial feast in honour of the dead, celebrated on the anniversary of birth, and so distinguished from τὰ νεκύσια, the feast observed on the anniversary of death. See Rawlinson's note on Herod. IV. 26. The classical word for a birthday feast was τὰ γενέθλια, this in turn came through the process of Christian thought to mean a festival commemorative of a martyr's death—his birth into the new life—ἐπιτελεῖν τὴν τοῦ μαρτυρίου αὐτοῦ ἡμέραν γενέθλιον, *Martyr. Polyc.* 18, p. 1044 A. See Sophocles' *Lexicon* on γενέθλιος and γενέσιος and Lob. *Phryn.* 104.

ὠρχήσατο. Some sort of pantomimic dance is meant. Horace notes as one of the signs of national decay that even highborn maidens learnt the voluptuous dances of the East, Hor. Od. III. 6. 21. Herod would recall similar scenes at Rome. See note v. 1.

ἡ θυγάτηρ τῆς Ἡρωδιάδος. Salome; she was afterwards married to her uncle Herod-Philip, the tetrarch, and on his death to Aristobulus, grandson of Herod the Great.

8. προβιβασθεῖσα. 'Impelled,' 'instigated;' cp. Xen. *Mem.* 1. 5. 1, ἐπισκεψώμεθα εἴ τι προυβίβαζε λέγων εἰς αὐτὴν τοιάδε.

πίναξ = 'a flat wooden trencher' on which meat was served, δαιτρὸς δὲ κρειῶν πίνακας παρέθηκεν ἀείρας, Hom. Od. I. 141. This appears to have been the meaning of the old English word 'charger' (A.V.), which is connected with *cargo* and with French *charger*, and signified originally that on which a load is placed, hence a dish.

9. λυπηθείς, 'though vexed;' he still feared the popular vengeance, and perhaps did not himself desire the death of John, see Mark vi. 20.

ὁ βασιλεύς. A title which Antipas had in vain tried to acquire: it was probably addressed to him by his courtiers.

διὰ τοὺς ὅρκους. 'Because of the *oaths;*' he had sworn repeatedly.

11. ἤνεγκεν τῇ μητρὶ αὐτῆς. The revenge of Herodias recalls the story of Fulvia, who treated with great indignity the head of her murdered enemy Cicero, piercing the tongue once so eloquent against her. Both are instances of 'furens quid femina possit.' The perpetration of the deed on the occasion of a birthday feast would heighten the atrocity of it in the eyes of the ancient world: it was an acknowledged rule, 'ne die qua ipsi lumen accepissent aliis demerent.'

The great Florentine and other mediæval painters have delighted to represent the contrasts suggested by this scene at Machærus. The palace and the prison—Greek refinement and the preacher's simplicity—Oriental luxury and Oriental despotism side by side—the cause of the world and the cause of Christ. In all this the 'irony' of the Greek dramatists is present. The real strength is on the side that seems weakest.

12. ἦραν τὸ πτῶμα καὶ ἔθαψαν αὐτόν. There is in this some proof of forbearance, if not of kindness, on Herod's part. He did not persecute John's disciples, or prevent them paying the last offices to their master.

πτῶμα. Lat. *cadaver*, in this sense πτῶμα is followed by νεκροῦ, or by genitive of person in classical period as, 'Ετεοκλέους δὲ πτῶμα Πολυνείκους τε τοῦ; Eur. *Phoen.* 1697.

13—21. JESUS RETIRES TO A DESERT PLACE, WHERE HE FEEDS FIVE THOUSAND.

Mark vi. 31—44; Luke ix. 10—17; John vi. 5—14.

This is the only miracle narrated by all the Evangelists. In St John it prepares the way for the memorable discourse on the 'Bread of Life.' St John also mentions, as a result of this miracle, the desire of the people 'to take him by force and make him a king.' There is a question as to the locality of the miracle. St Luke says (ch. ix. 10) that Jesus 'went aside privately into a desert place *belonging to a city called Bethsaida.*' St Mark (ch. vi. 45) describes the disciples as crossing to Bethsaida after the miracle. The general inference has been that there were two Bethsaidas; Bethsaida Julias, near the mouth of the Jordan (where the miracle is usually said to have taken place), and another Bethsaida, mentioned in the parallel passage in St Mark and possibly John i. 44. But the Sinaitic MS. omits the words in italics from Luke, and at John vi. 23 reads, 'When, therefore, the boats came from Tiberias, which was nigh unto the place where they did eat bread.' If these readings be accepted, the scene of the miracle must be placed near Tiberias; the Bethsaida of Mark, to which the disciples crossed, will be the well-known Bethsaida Julias, and the other supposed Bethsaida will disappear even from the researches of travellers.

13. πεζῇ (ὁδῷ), 'on foot,' i.e. not by boat; cp. Acts xx. 13, μέλλων αὐτὸς πεζεύειν.

15. ὀψίας γενομένης. In the Jewish division of the day there were two evenings. According to the most probable view the space of time called 'between the evenings' (Ex. xii. 6) was from the ninth to the twelfth hour (Jos. *B. J.* VI. 9. 3). Hence the first evening ended at 3 o'clock, the second began at sunset. In this verse the first evening is meant, in *v.* 23 the second.

The meaning of ἡ ὥρα is not quite clear, perhaps the usual hour for the mid-day meal.

16. ὑμεῖς. Emphatic.

17. οὐκ ἔχομεν κ.τ.λ. St John more definitely; ἔστιν παιδάριον ὧδε ὃς ἔχει πέντε ἄρτους κριθίνους, καὶ δύο ὀψάρια (vi. 9). Barley bread (ἄρτους κριθίνους), for which the classical word is μᾶζα, was the food of the very poorest. It seems probable that the English word *mass* is traceable to μᾶζα, a eucharistic significance having been given to this miracle from very early times. The ἄρτοι were a kind of biscuit, thin and crisp cakes which could be broken, hence κλάσας, κλάσματα, see note, ch. vi. 30. Cp. Juv. v. 67, 'quanto porrexit murmure panem | vix fractum.

19. ἀνακλιθῆναι ἐπὶ τοῦ χόρτου. St John has ἦν δὲ χόρτος πολὺς ἐν τῷ τόπῳ. St Mark and St Luke mention that they sat in companies, ἀνὰ ἑκατὸν καὶ ἀνὰ πεντήκοντα (Mark), ἀνὰ πεντήκοντα (Luke); to this St Mark adds the picturesque touch, καὶ ἀνέπεσαν πρασιαὶ πρασιαί. (ch. vi. 40). St John notes the time of year: ἦν δὲ ἐγγὺς τὸ πάσχα ἡ ἑορτὴ τῶν Ἰουδαίων.

ἔδωκεν. In Mark and Luke ἐδίδου: 'continued to give,' 'kept giving.'

20. τὸ περισσεῦον τῶν κλασμάτων. κλασμάτων connected with κλάσας, therefore not 'fragments' in the sense of crumbs of bread, but the 'portions' broken off for distribution.

δώδεκα κοφίνους. The same word is used for baskets in the four accounts of this miracle, and also by our Lord, when He refers to the miracle (ch. xvi. 9); whereas a different word (σπυρίδες) is used in describing the feeding of four thousand and in the reference made to that event by our Lord (ch. xvi. 10). Juvenal describes a large provision-basket of this kind, together with a bundle of hay, as being part of the equipment of the Jewish mendicants who thronged the grove of Egeria at Rome: 'Judæis quorum cophinus fœnumque supellex, III. 14,' 'cophino fœnoque relicto | arcanam Judæa tremens mendicat in aurem,' VI. 542. The motive for this custom was to avoid ceremonial impurity in eating or in resting at night.

22—33. THE DISCIPLES CROSS FROM THE SCENE OF THE MIRACLE TO BETHSAIDA.

Mark vi. 45—52; John vi. 15—21.

St Matthew alone narrates St Peter's endeavour to walk on the sea.

22. τὸ πλοῖον, *the* ship or *their* ship.

23. ὀψίας δὲ γενομένης. See v. 15.

μόνος ἦν ἐκεῖ. This is a simple but sublime thought:—the solitary watch on the lonely mountain, the communion in prayer with the Father throughout the beautiful Eastern night.

24. βασανιζόμενον. The expression is forcible, 'tortured by the waves,' writhing in throes of agony, as it were. These sudden storms are very characteristic of the Lake of Gennesaret.

25. τετάρτῃ δὲ φυλακῇ, i.e. early in the morning. Cp. 'Et jam quarta canit venturam buccina lucem,' Propert. IV. 4. 63. At this time the Jews had adopted the Greek and Roman custom of four night watches. Formerly they divided the night into three watches, or rather according to Lightfoot (*Hor. Heb.*) the Romans and Jews alike recognised four watches, but with the Jews the fourth watch was regarded as morning, and was not included in the three watches of

'deep night.' The four watches are named (Mark xiii. 35) 1 Even (ὀψέ), 2 Midnight (μεσονύκτιον), 3 Cockcrowing (ἀλεκτοροφωνίας), 4 Morning (πρωΐ). St John states that they had rowed 25 or 30 furlongs.

ἦλθεν πρὸς αὐτούς. Mark adds 'He would have passed by them.'

ἐπὶ τὴν θάλασσαν. ἐπί with accus. of motion over a surface, cp. ἐπὶ οἴνοπα πόντον ὁρᾶν περᾶν πλεῖν (Homer). See critical notes, *supra*.

26. ἀπὸ τοῦ φόβου ἔκραξαν. Note the article. Not merely cried out from fear, but *the* fear which necessarily resulted from the appearance made them cry out.

29. ὁ δὲ εἶπεν, ἐλθέ. The boat was so near that the voice of Jesus could be heard even through the storm, though the wind was strong and the oarsmen labouring and perhaps calling out to one another. The hand of the Saviour was quite close to the sinking disciple.

30. ἰσχυρόν. Predicate.

καταποντίζεσθαι. Here and ch. xviii. 6 only in N.T. 'to sink into the deep sea' (πόντος, the wide open sea, so the *deep* sea, connected with πάτος and *pons*, 'the watery way,' (Curtius), but according to others with βένθος, βάθος).

31. εἰς τί; Literal translation of the Hebr. *lammah*, 'with a view to what?' = ἱνατί, see note ch. xxvii. 46. ἐδίστασας, see ch. xxviii. 17.

32. ἐκόπασεν. κοπάζειν, properly to be weary or fatigued (κόπτω, κόπος), then to rest from weariness or suffering, used of a sick man Hipp. p. 1207, (so κόπος, of the pain of disease, Soph. *Phil.* 880,) then figuratively of the wind or a flood, cp. Herod. VII. 191, where speaking of the storm at Artemisium he says that the Magi stopped the wind by charms, ἢ ἄλλως κως αὐτὸς ἐθέλων ἐκόπασεν.

33. θεοῦ υἱὸς εἶ. A son of God. The higher revelation of *the* Son of the living God was not yet given. See ch. xvi. 16.

34—36. JESUS CURES SICK FOLK IN THE LAND OF GENNESARET.

Mark vi. 53—56, where the stir of the neighbourhood and eagerness of the people are vividly portrayed.

34. διαπεράσαντες. Having crossed the bay from Tiberias to the neighbourhood of Capernaum. See map and note on *vv*. 13—21.

εἰς Γεννησαρέτ. By this is meant the plain of Gennesaret, two miles and a half in length and about one mile in breadth. Modern travellers speak of 'its charming bays and its fertile soil rich with the scourings of the basaltic hills.' Josephus describes the district in glowing terms (*B. J.* III. 10. 8). See *Recovery of Jerusalem*, p. 351.

36. παρεκάλουν ἵνα ἅψωνται. For ἵνα in *petitio obliqua* for the classical ὅπως see note ch. i. 22, and Goodwin's *Greek Moods and Tenses*, p. 78.

The sequence of the subjunctive on a historical tense gives vividness to the narrative by retaining the mood originally used by the speaker. The usage is frequent in the classical period: ἐχώρουν ἐκ τῶν οἰκιῶν ὅπως μὴ κατὰ φῶς προσφέρωνται, Thuc. II. 3. καὶ περὶ τούτων ἐμνήσθην ἵνα μὴ ταὐτὰ πάθητε. Dem. *Olynth.* III. 30. 10. See note, ch. xii. 14.

τοῦ κρασπέδου. The hem of the garment had a certain sanctity attached to it. It was the distinguishing mark of the Jew: cp. Numbers xv. 38, 39, 'that they add to the fringes of the borders (or corners) a thread of blue.' At each corner of the robe there was a tassel; each tassel had a conspicuous blue thread symbolical of the heavenly origin of the Commandments. The other threads were white.

ὅσοι ἥψαντο διεσώθησαν. Cp. the case of the woman with an issue of blood, ch. ix. 20—22.

CHAPTER XV.

5. καὶ omitted before οὐ μὴ τιμ. on the most ancient authority.

6. τὸν λόγον for τὴν ἐντολὴν of *textus receptus;* τὸν νόμον the reading of Tischendorf has the authority of ℵ and C and some cursives, and would explain τὴν ἐντολήν. τὸν λόγον may have been introduced from Mark.

8. The words ἐγγίζει μοι...τῷ στόματι αὐτῶν καί, which fill up the quotation from the LXX., are omitted on the highest MS. authority.

16. Ἰησοῦς omitted and 30 τοῦ Ἰησοῦ for αὐτοῦ.

22. ἔκραζεν rightly replaces the rarer form ἐκραύγασεν.

25. προσεκύνει is probably right, though the evidence is evenly balanced between aor. and imperf.

35, 36. The omission of καί before εὐχαριστήσας makes the structure very harsh. It is the reading necessitated by the rules adopted for forming the present text. Tregelles omits the καί against Lachmann and Tischendorf. If the former had seen ℵ it can scarcely be doubted that he would have inserted the conjunction so necessary to the flow of the sentence.

39. Μαγαδάν for Μαγδαλά with the chief MSS. (ℵ B D) and versions; some ancient authorities have Μαγεδάν. Most of the later uncials read Μαγδαλά.

1—20. THE TRUE RELIGION AND THE FALSE. A DISCOURSE TO THE PHARISEES, THE PEOPLE, AND THE DISCIPLES.

Mark vii. 1—23.

These twenty verses sum up the great controversy of the N.T., that between the religion of the letter and external observances and the religion of the heart, between what St Paul calls 'the righteousness which is of the law and the righteousness which is of God by (or grounded upon) faith,' Phil. iii. 9.

1. ἀπὸ Ἱεροσολύμων Φαρισαῖοι καὶ γραμματεῖς. Probably a deputation from the Sanhedrin, such as was commissioned to question John the Baptist. Cp. John i. 19.

2. τὴν παράδοσιν τῶν πρεσβυτέρων. The elders, or presbyters, were the Jewish teachers, or scribes, such as Hillel and Shammai. The traditions were the rules or observances of the unwritten law, which they enjoined on their disciples. Many of these were frivolous; some actually subversive of God's law; yet such was the estimation in which these 'traditions' were held that, according to one Rabbinical saying, 'the words of the scribes are lovely, above the words of the law; for the words of the law are weighty and light but the words of the scribes are all weighty.'

3. διὰ τὴν παράδοσιν. 'For the sake of your tradition;' i.e. in order that ye may establish it: ἵνα τὴν παράδοσιν ὑμῶν τηρήσητε, Mark vii. 9.

4. ὁ γὰρ θεὸς ἐνετείλατο, answering to τὴν ἐντολὴν τοῦ θεοῦ, as in v. 5, ὑμεῖς λέγετε refers back to διὰ τὴν παράδοσιν ὑμῶν. St Mark has Μωϋσῆς γὰρ εἶπεν (vii. 10), an instructive variation.

ὁ κακολογῶν. As a classical word κακολογεῖν or κακῶς λέγειν—the preferable form (Lob. *Phryn.* 200), means to 'abuse,' 'revile;' so in LXX. θεοὺς οὐ κακολογήσεις, Ex. xxii. 28. In many passages the Hebrew word represented here by κακολογεῖν is translated by ἀτιμάζειν and means 'to treat with disrespect,' 'to despise.' In one form, however, of the Hebr. verb the meaning is 'to curse,' but the first sense is to be preferred here: 'whoever makes light of their claims to support,' &c. See Guillemard, *Hebraisms in N. T.*, ad loc.

5. δῶρον ὃ ἐὰν κ.τ.λ. 'Let that by whatsoever thou mayest be profited by me (i.e. the sum which might have gone to your support) be a 'gift' (κορβᾶν, Mark), or devoted to sacred purposes.'

The scribes held that these words, even when pronounced in spite and anger against parents who needed succour, excused the son from his natural duty, indeed bound him not to perform it; and, on the other hand, did not oblige him really to devote the sum to the service of God or of the temple.

οὐ μὴ τιμήσει. The omission of καὶ before these words (see critical notes) obviates the need of the awkward ellipse supplied in A.V. by the words 'he shall be free,' and throws out with far more force and clearness the contrast between the ἐντολὴ τοῦ θεοῦ and the παράδοσις τῶν πρεσβυτέρων. God's command was, 'honour thy father and thy mother;' ye say (in certain cases), 'a man shall not honour his father and mother.'

οὐ μὴ with future indicative or with subjunctive, is an emphatic denial. See note, ch. x. 42.

7. καλῶς ἐπροφήτευσεν. A common Jewish formula in quoting a saying of the prophets.

8, 9. Isaiah xxix. 13. The quotation nearly follows the LXX. The Hebrew has nothing answering to μάτην δὲ σέβονταί με.

9. ἐντάλματα ἀνθρώπων. 'Collections of ritual laws which were current in the times of the pre-exile prophets.' (Cheyne, Is. *ad loc.*) Thus Pharisaism had its counterpart in the old dispensation.

10. προσκαλεσάμενος τὸν ὄχλον. The moment our Lord turns to the people, His teaching is by parables.

This appeal to the multitude as worthier than the Pharisees to receive the divine truths is significant of the popular character of the Kingdom of heaven.

11. κοινοῖ. Literally, maketh common; cp. 'common or unclean,' Acts x. 14. 'The Pharisees esteemed "defiled men" for "*common and vulgar*" men; on the contrary, a religious man among men is "a *singular* man."' Lightfoot *ad loc.*

12. οἱ Φαρισαῖοι ἐσκανδαλίσθησαν. A proof of the influence of the Pharisees. The disciples believed that Christ would be concerned to have offended those who stood so high in popular favour.

13. πᾶσα φυτεία. Not a wild flower, but a cultivated plant or tree; the word occurs here only in N.T.; in LXX. version of O.T. it is used of the vine, the most carefully cultivated of all plants; 2 Kings xix. 29; Ezek. xvii. 7; Mic. i. 6; Aq. and Symm. have δένδρων φυτείαν in Gen. xxi. 33, of the tamarisk. Here the plant cultivated by human hands—the vine that is not the true vine of Israel—is the doctrine of the Pharisees.

14. ὁδηγοί εἰσιν τυφλοὶ τυφλῶν. The proverb which follows is quoted in a different connection, Luke vi. 39; cp. also ch. xxiii. 16.

εἰς βόθυνον πεσοῦνται Palestine abounded in dangers of this kind, from unguarded wells, quarries, and pitfalls; it abounded also in persons afflicted with blindness. See note ch. ix. 27.

16. ἀκμήν. Here only in N.T. Strictly, 'at the point of time,' in late authors, 'even now,' 'still.' Latin, *adhuc*. In the modern Greek versions ἔτι is used for ἀκμήν.

καὶ ὑμεῖς, as well as the crowds to whom the parables are spoken.

ἀσύνετοί ἐστε. Cp. συνέσει πνευματικῇ, Col. i. 9, and τὴν σύνεσιν μου ἐν τῷ μυστηρίῳ τοῦ Χριστοῦ, Ephes. iii. 4.

19. ἐκ γὰρ τῆς καρδίας κ.τ.λ. The enumeration follows the order of the Commandments. Evil thoughts—(διαλογισμοὶ πονηροί) 'harmful reasonings'—form a class under which the rest fall, indicating, too, that the transgression of the commandments is often in thought, by Christ's law, not in deed only.

The plurals 'murders, adulteries,' &c., as Meyer points out, denote the different instances and kinds of murder and adultery. Murder includes far more than the act of bloodshed.

21—28. THE DAUGHTER OF A CANAANITE WOMAN IS CURED.
Mark vii. 24—30.

This narrative of faith without external observance or knowledge of the Law affords a suggestive contrast to the preceding discourse. It is not related as we might have expected by the Gentile St Luke. St Mark has various points of particular description not given here.

21. ἀνεχώρησεν. Perhaps to avoid the hostility which this attack upon the Pharisees would arouse. St Mark preserves the connection ἀναστὰς ἀπῆλθεν as if He had been teaching (καθίσας).

εἰς τὰ μέρη Τύρου καὶ Σιδῶνος. The reading adopted by the leading editors, Mark vii. 31, ἦλθεν διὰ Σιδῶνος εἰς τὴν θάλασσαν τῆς Γαλιλαίας, makes it certain that Jesus crossed the borders of Palestine and passed through a Gentile land.

22. γυνὴ Χαναναία. In Mark ἡ δὲ γυνὴ ἦν Ἑλληνίς, Συροφοινίκισσα (vii. 26). The two expressions are in Hellenistic Greek identical. In Joshua v. 12, 'The land of Canaan' (Hebr.) appears in the LXX. version as τὴν χώραν τῶν Φοινίκων. Hecataeus (Tr. 254) states: Χνᾶ. [Canaan] οὕτω πρότερον ἡ Φοινίκη ἐκαλεῖτο. The term land of Canaan, literally the *low lands* or *netherlands*, at first applied to the whole of Palestine, was confined in later times to the maritime plain of Phœnicia. Still, according to Prof. Rawlinson, the Canaanites and Phœnicians were distinct races, possessing marked peculiarities. The former were the original occupants of the country, the latter 'immigrants at a comparatively recent date.' (Herod. Vol. IV. p. 199.) The relations between Phœnicia and Palestine had been with scarcely an exception peaceful and friendly. The importance of the narrative lies in the fact that this woman was a foreigner and a heathen—a descendant of the worshippers of Baal. She may have heard and seen Jesus in earlier days. Cp. Mark iii. 8, 'they about Tyre and Sidon...came unto him.' This instance of mercy extended to a Gentile points to the future diffusion of the Gospel beyond the Jewish race.

ἐλέησόν με. Identifying herself with her daughter. Cp. the prayer of the father of the lunatic child: 'Have compassion on *us* and help *us*,' Mark ix. 22.

υἱὸς Δαυείδ. A title that proves the expectation that the Messiah should spring from the house of David. It is the particular Messianic prophecy which would be most likely to reach foreign countries. The Tyrian woman's appeal to the descendant of Hiram's friend and ally has a special significance.

23. οὐκ ἀπεκρίθη αὐτῇ λόγον. Jesus, by this refusal, tries the woman's faith, that He may purify and deepen it. Her request must be won by earnest prayer, 'lest the light winning should make light the prize.'

Observe that Christ first refuses by silence, then by express words.

ἠρώτουν. For the form cp. νικοῦντι, Rev. ii. 7. the reading of Lachmann and Tischendorf (ed. 7); and see Winer, p. 104, note 3.

ἀπόλυσον αὐτήν. By granting what she asks, by yielding, like the unjust judge, to her importunity.

24. εἰς τὰ πρόβατα τὰ ἀπολωλότα κ.τ.λ. Jesus came to save all, but his personal ministry was confined, with few exceptions, to the Jews.

The thought of Israel as a flock of sheep lost upon the mountain is beautifully drawn out, Ezekiel xxxiv.; 'My flock was scattered upon all the face of the earth, and none did search or seek after them' (v. 6). Read the whole chapter.

26. τὸν ἄρτον τῶν τέκνων κ.τ.λ. The τέκνα are the Jews; the κυνάρια are the Gentiles. This was the name applied by the Jews to all outside the chosen race, the dog being in the East a symbol of impurity. St Paul, regarding the Christian Church as the true Israel, terms the Judaizing teachers τοὺς κύνας, Phil. iii. 2. The same religious hostility, and the same names of scorn, still exist in the East between Mussulman and Christian populations. Christ's words, as reported by St Mark (ch. vii. 27), contain a gleam of hope, ἄφες πρῶτον χορτασθῆναι τὰ τέκνα.

27. καὶ γάρ. 'For even' ('yet' of the A.V. is misleading). The woman takes Jesus at His word, admits the truth of what He says, accepts the name of reproach, and claims the little that falls even to the dogs. 'True, it is not good to cast the *children's* bread to the dogs, for even the dogs have their share,—the crumbs that fall from their master's table.'

τὰ κυνάρια ἐσθίει. St Mark has ἐσθίειν of the dogs and χορτασθῆναι of the children, so completely is the strict use of the two words reversed.

τῆς τραπέζης τῶν κυρίων. The 'Masters' must be interpreted to mean God, not, as by some, the Jewish people. Note the turn given by the introduction of the κύριοι. κυνάρια that have κύριοι are not the wretched outcasts of the streets—they have some one to care for them. Even the Gentiles may expect a blessing from the God of Israel.

28. St Mark has εὗρεν τὸ παιδίον βεβλημένον ἐπὶ τὴν κλίνην καὶ τὸ δαιμόνιον ἐξεληλυθός.

29—31. JESUS RETURNS TO THE HIGH LAND OF GALILEE, AND CURES MANY BLIND, DUMB, AND LAME.

Mark vii. 31—37, where, not content with the general statement, the Evangelist describes one special case of healing.

29. εἰς τὸ ὄρος. The mountain country; the high land, as distinguished from the low land, which He had left.

32—38. Four Thousand Men, besides Women and Children, are miraculously fed.

Mark viii. 1—9.

32. ἡμέραι τρεῖς. For this parenthetical introduction of the nominative see Winer, p. 704, § 2 and note 3.

36. εὐχαριστήσας. εὐχαριστεῖν does not occur before Polybius in the sense of *gratias agere*. The decree in Demosth. *de Cor.* p. 257, where the word is found, (see Lob. *Phryn.* 18) is probably spurious. The classical expression is χάριν εἰδέναι.

τὸ περισσεῦον τῶν κλασμάτων. See ch. xiv. 20. One side of the lesson is the lavishness of Providence. God gives even more than we require or ask for. But the leading thought is a protest against waste.

37. ἑπτὰ σπυρίδας. See note ch. xiv. 20, and Acts ix. 25, where St Paul is said to have been let down from the wall of Damascus in a σπυρίς, probably a large basket made of rope-net, possibly a fisherman's basket; in 2 Cor. xi. 33, where the same incident is related, the word σαργάνη is used. Why the people brought different kinds of baskets on the two occasions we cannot determine. The facts seem to point to a difference in nationality or in occupation. σπυρίς connected with σπείρω, 'to twist,' is the Lat. *sporta*, or *sportula*. σαργάνη in Æsch. *Suppl.* 769='the mesh of a net'.

39—XVI. 4. Jesus at Magdala, or Magadan, is tempted to give a Sign.

Mark viii. 10—12; Luke xii. 54—57.

39. Μαγαδάν. For the reading see critical note. It is probable that the familiar Magdala supplanted in the text the more obscure Magadan. Magdala or Migdol (a watch tower) is identified with the modern *Mejdel*, a collection of ruins and squalid huts at the S.E. corner of the plain of Gennesaret, opposite to K'hersa or Gergesa. This is the point where the lake is broadest. Prof. Rawlinson thinks that this Magdala may be the Magdolus of Herodotus, II. 159; unless indeed by a confusion curiously similar to that in the text, Herodotus has mistaken Migdol for Megiddo. Magdala was probably the home of Mary Magdalene.

CHAPTER XVI.

2 and 3. ὀψίας...οὐ δύνασθε. The genuineness of this passage is doubtful. It is omitted in several uncials (among them ℵB) and cursives. Origen passes over the passage in his Commentary, and Jerome notes its omission *in plerisque Codicibus*. Still the internal evidence is strong in its favour and it is retained by the leading editors, though bracketed by Tischendorf and Westcott and Hort. See Scrivener's *Introduction*, p. 49 (3).

3. ὑποκριταί omitted before τὸ μὲν πρόσωπον and (v. 4) τοῦ προφήτου after Ἰωνᾶ.

11. ἄρτων for ἄρτου, a certain correction.

20. Ἰησοῦς, though found in some important MSS. (not in אBL), is rightly omitted, the internal evidence against it is strong, and the insertion might easily be made by a mistake in transcription.

---

1. οἱ Φαρισαῖοι καὶ Σαδδουκαῖοι. In Mark οἱ Φαρισαῖοι alone. The coalition between these opposing sects can only be accounted for by the uniting influence of a strong common hostility against Jesus.

πειράζοντες. The participle sometimes expresses in a condensed form what might be expanded into a final or consecutive sentence. See Campbell's *Soph. Essay on the language*, &c., § 36. (5) b., ἔβας | τόσσον ἐν ποίμναις πίτνων (*Ajax*, 185) = τόσσον ὥστε πίτνειν. Cp. *Ant.* 752, ἢ κἀπαπειλῶν ὧδ' ἐπεξέρχει θρασύς; see Jebb's note on *Ajax*, *loc. cit.*

σημεῖον ἐκ τοῦ οὐρανοῦ. They could not conceive the inner beauty of Christ's teaching, but they would follow the rules of a Rabbi who, like one of the ancient prophets, should give an external sign—a darkening of the glowing sky—a flash of light—a peal of thunder. The answer of Christ teaches that the signs of the times, the events of the day, are the signs of God, the sign that Christ gives.

2. εὐδία...χειμών. For this contrast cp. ἀλλὰ νῦν μοι | γαιάοχος εὐδίαν ὄπασσεν | ἐκ χειμῶνος. Pind. *Isth.* (VII) VI. 37—39.

3. στυγνάζων, late. Polybius uses στυγνότης of the weather.

τὸ πρόσωπον τοῦ οὐρανοῦ. Perhaps Jesus and His questioners were looking across the lake towards the cliffs of Gergesa, with the sky red from the reflected sunset. In Luke the signs are 'a cloud rising in the west' and the blowing of the 'south wind.'

σημεῖα τῶν καιρῶν. The meaning of passing events—some of which point in many ways to the fulfilment of prophecy, and to the presence of Christ among men; others to the overthrow of the national existence through the misguided passions of the people, and the absence of true spiritual life. In Luke xiii., two events of typical importance are reported to Jesus who shews how they are σημεῖα τῶν καιρῶν: they were not, as the Jews interpreted them, instances of individual punishment for sin, but they were warnings to the nation. Perhaps no clearer proof of this want of political or spiritual insight, and of blindness to facts, could be given than the pretension to political liberty made by the Jews, John viii. 33, οὐδενὶ δεδουλεύκαμεν πώποτε. Neither Babylonish captivity, nor tribute to Caesar, nor presence of a Roman Procurator were σημεῖα to them.

The work and life of Christ were in the highest sense σημεῖα. He was Himself σημεῖον ἀντιλεγόμενον.

4. μοιχαλίς. See ch. xii. 39.

τὸ σημεῖον Ἰωνᾶ. See ch. xii. 39—41, where the same word occurs in the same connection. An estranged people cannot see signs. The words in Mark viii. 12 are 'there shall no sign be given unto this generation,' i.e. no such sign as they demanded.

5—12. THE LEAVEN OF THE PHARISEES AND OF THE SADDUCEES.

Mark viii. 14—21, where the rebuke of Christ is given more at length in stirring language; and Luke xii. 1, where the context and occasion are different. ἐπισυναχθεισῶν τῶν μυριάδων τοῦ ὄχλου ὥστε καταπατεῖν ἀλλήλους ἤρξατο λέγειν πρὸς τοὺς μαθητὰς αὐτοῦ πρῶτον.

6. τῆς ζύμης. Teaching, which like leaven is corrupt and penetrating, cp. 1 Cor. v. 7, ἐκκαθάρατε τὴν παλαιὰν ζύμην ἵνα ἦτε νέον φύραμα καθώς ἐστε ἄζυμοι, where the reference is to the putting away of leaven before the passover. See Schöttgen on 1 Cor. v. 7, and cp. Hos. vii. 4, and note ch. xiii. 33.

7. ὅτι ἄρτους οὐκ ἐλάβομεν. ὅτι, probably not causal but *recitativum* i.e. used to introduce the words of the speaker. εἰ μὴ ἕνα ἄρτον οὐκ εἶχον (Mark). It is possible that Jesus may have employed figurative language even more than was usual with Eastern teachers; certainly this special metaphorical use of leaven was new. See Lightfoot, *Hor. Hebr. ad loc.* Again, the Pharisees had rules of their own as to what kind of leaven it was lawful to use, and what kind it was right to avoid. Hence it was not strange that the disciples should imagine that their Master was laying down similar rules for their guidance.

8. ὀλιγόπιστοι. Their πίστις had failed in two respects: they had shown (1) want of *spiritual insight* by taking ζύμη in a literal sense. (2) Want of *loving trust* in thinking that Jesus intended a rebuke to their forgetfulness.

9. οὔπω νοεῖτε. In Mark the rebuke is conveyed by a reference to the prophecy quoted ch. xiii. 14, 15 (Is. vi. 9, 10), with the striking variation of πεπωρωμένην καρδίαν for ἐπαχύνθη ἡ καρδία.

κοφίνους...σπυρίδας. See notes ch. xiv. 20 and xv. 37.

12. συνῆκαν. See note on ἀσύνετοι, ch. xv. 16.

13—20. THE GREAT CONFESSION OF ST PETER, AND THE PROMISE GIVEN TO HIM.

Mark viii. 27—30: The question is put 'while they were on the way,' the words 'the Son of the living God' are omitted, as also the blessing on Peter. Luke ix. 18—21: Jesus was engaged in prayer alone; the words of the confession are 'the Christ of God;' the blessing on Peter is omitted.

13. Καισαρείας τῆς Φιλίππου. The most northerly point in the Holy Land reached by our Lord. The city was rebuilt by Herod Philip, who called it by his own name to distinguish it from Cæsarea Stratonis on the sea coast, the seat of the Roman government, and the scene of St Paul's imprisonment.

The Greek name of this Cæsarea was Paneas, which survives in the modern Banias. Cæsarea was beautifully placed on a rocky terrace under Mount Hermon, a few miles east of Dan, the old frontier city of Israel. The cliffs near this spot, where the Messiah was first acknowledged, bear marks of the worship of Baal and of Pan. See *Recovery of Jerusalem*, and Tristram's *Land of Israel*.

τὸν υἱὸν τοῦ ἀνθρώπου. See note ch. viii. 20. The question of Jesus is: In what sense do the people believe me to be the Son of man? In the sense which Daniel intended or in a lower sense? Observe the antithesis in Peter's answer:—the Son of man is the Son of God.

14. Ἰερεμίαν. Named by St Matthew only. The mention of Jeremiah as representative of the Prophets is explained by Lightfoot (*Hor. Hebr.* Matt. xxvii. 9) by reference to a Talmudic treatise, according to which the book of Jeremiah came first of the Prophets, following the books of Kings.

16. σὺ εἶ ὁ Χριστὸς ὁ υἱὸς τοῦ θεοῦ τοῦ ζῶντος. This confession not only sees in Jesus the promised Messiah, but in the Messiah recognises the divine nature. It was this claim that brought upon Jesus the hostility of the Jews. Trypho the Jew in his dialogue with Justin Martyr declares that his nation expected a human Messiah: such a claim made by Jesus might even have been admitted: it is the claim to divinity not to Messiahship that rouses the popular fury (John viii. 58, 59) and decides the judgment of the Sanhedrin (Matt. xxvi. 64, 65).

17. Βὰρ Ἰωνᾶ, 'son of Jonah,' or 'son of John.' The Greek form may stand for either name (see Bp. Lightfoot on a *Fresh Revision of N. T.*, pp. 159, 160); but the reading adopted by the best editors John i. 43, υἱὸς Ἰωάνου, seems conclusive in favour of the latter rendering. Bar is Aramaic for son; cp. Bar-abbas, Bar-tholomew, Bar-nabas.

ὅτι σὰρξ καὶ αἷμα κ.τ.λ. Not man, but God; 'flesh and blood' was a common Hebrew expression in this contrast. The recognition was not by material test or human judgment, but by the witness of the Holy Spirit.

18. σὺ εἶ Πέτρος κ.τ.λ. The precise meaning of πέτρα in relation to Πέτρος has been keenly disputed. To suppose no connection between Πέτρος and πέτρα is opposed to candid criticism. On the other hand, to view πέτρα as simply equivalent to Πέτρος, and to regard the *personal* Peter as the rock on which the Church is built, narrows the sense. Πέτρα is the central doctrine of the Christian Church— the Godhead of its Lord. Yet Peter is not named in connection with the πέτρα without cause. To Peter first was granted spiritual insight to discern, and courage to confess this great truth; and therefore it was his privilege to be the first scribe instructed to the kingdom of heaven, and to Peter as such the blessing is addressed. For an illustration of this view of Peter, regarded, not as an individual, but as a representative of a truth, cp. *Apol. Soc.*, p. 23 b., καὶ φαίνεται τοῦτ᾽ οὐ λέγειν

τὸν Σωκράτη, προσκεχρῆσθαι δὲ τῷ ἐμῷ ὀνόματι, ἐμὲ παραδεῖγμα ποιούμενος, ὥσπερ ἂν εἰ εἴποι ὅτι οὗτος ὑμῶν, ὦ ἄνθρωποι, σοφώτατός ἐστιν ὅστις ὥσπερ Σωκράτης ἔγνωκεν ὅτι οὐδενὸς ἄξιός ἐστι τῇ ἀληθείᾳ πρὸς σοφίαν.

On these words mainly rest the enormous pretensions of the Roman pontiff. It is therefore important (1) To remember that it is to Peter with the great confession on his lips that the words are spoken. The Godhead of Christ is the πέτρα—the keystone of the Church, and Peter is for the moment the representative of the belief in that truth among men. (2) To take the words in reference: (*a*) to other passages of Scripture. The Church is built on the foundation of the Apostles and Prophets, Eph. ii. 20, on Christ Himself, 2 Cor. iii. 11. (*b*) To history; Peter is not an infallible repository of truth. He is rebuked by Paul for Judaizing. Nor does he hold a chief place among the Apostles afterwards. It is James, not Peter, who presides at the Council at Jerusalem. (*c*) To reason: for even if Peter had precedence over the other Apostles, and if he was Bishop of Rome, which is not historically certain, there is no proof that he had a right of conferring such precedence on his successors.

μου τὴν ἐκκλησίαν. The word ἐκκλησία occurs twice in Matthew and not elsewhere in the Gospels. See note ch. xviii. 17 where the Jewish ἐκκλησία is meant. From the analogy of the corresponding Hebrew word, ἐκκλησία in a Christian sense may be defined as the congregation of the faithful throughout the world, united under Christ as their Head. The use of the word by Christ implied at least two things: (1) that He was founding an organized society, not merely preaching a doctrine: (2) That the Jewish ἐκκλησία was the point of departure for the Christian ἐκκλησία and in part its prototype. It is one among many links in this gospel between Jewish and Christian thought. The Greek word (ἐκκλησία) has passed into the language of the Latin nations; *église* (French), *chiesa* (Italian), *iglesia* (Spanish). The derivation of the Teutonic *Church* is very doubtful. That usually given—Κυριακόν (the Lord's house)—is abandoned by most scholars. The word is probably from a Teutonic root and may have been connected with heathen usages. See *Bib. Dict.* Art. *Church*.

πύλαι ᾅδου. Cp. Eur. *Hec.* 1., ἥκω νεκρῶν κευθμῶνα καὶ σκότου πύλας | λιπὼν ἵν' Ἅιδης χωρὶς ᾤκισται θεῶν. Theocr. *Idyll.* II. 159 (Schol.) τὴν τοῦ ᾅδου κρούει πύλην. τοῦτ' ἐστιν ἀποθανεῖται. Verg. *Aen.* VI. 126, Noctes atque dies patet atri janua Ditis. Here the expression symbolises the power of the unseen world, especially the power of death: cp. Rev. i. 18, καὶ ἔχω τὰς κλεῖς τοῦ θανάτου καὶ τοῦ ᾅδου. 1 Cor. xv. 55, ποῦ σου, θάνατε, τὸ κέντρον, ποῦ σου, ᾅδη (*var. lect.* θάνατε), τὸ νῖκος. Ἅιδης is used for the Hebrew *Sheol*, the abode of departed spirits in which were the two divisions, *Paradise* and *Gehenna*. The introduction of such Greek religious terms to translate Hebrew religious terms is full of interest. It may be thought to ratify in part, at least, Greek religious ideas, to blend and modify those ideas with Jewish doctrine, and to bring the result of both to be raised and enlightened by the teaching of the Master.

οὐ κατισχύσουσιν αὐτῆς. The gates of Hades prevail over all things human, but the Church shall never die.

19. τὰς κλεῖδας τῆς βασιλείας τῶν οὐρανῶν. This expression was not altogether new. To a Jew it would convey a definite meaning. A key was given to a Scribe when admitted to his office as a symbol of his authority to open the treasury of the divine oracles (ch. xiii. 52). Peter was to be a Scribe in the kingdom of heaven. He has received authority to teach the truths of the kingdom. Again the key was symbolic of office and authority generally; cp. Is. xxii. 22: 'The key of the house of David will I lay upon his shoulder, &c.'—words which are transferred to Christ Himself Rev. iii. 7. These words of his Lord would afterwards gain a fresh force for Peter, when he found that through him God had opened 'the door of faith to the Gentiles.' Acts xiv. 27.

ὃ ἐὰν δήσῃς κ.τ.λ. 'To bind' (cp. ch. xxiii. 4) is to impose an obligation as binding; 'to loose' is to declare a precept not binding. Such expressions as this were common: 'The school of Shammai binds it, the school of Hillel looses it.' The power is over things, not persons. The decisions of Peter, as an authorized Scribe of the Kingdom of God will be ratified in heaven. Such decisions of the Scribes of the Kingdom of Heaven were the sentence pronounced by James, Acts xv. 19, and the judgments of Paul in the Corinthian Church.

Compare with this passage John xx. 23, λάβετε πνεῦμα ἅγιον, ἄν τινων ἀφῆτε τὰς ἁμαρτίας ἀφέωνται αὐτοῖς· ἄν τινων κρατῆτε κεκράτηνται, where the reference is to the *judicial* authority of the apostles; here a *legislative* power is conferred. Observe carefully the force of the perfect ἀφέωνται and κεκράτηνται, 'whosesoever sins ye shall remit, they have been remitted.' Your spiritual σύνεσις will enable you to recognise and ratify the divine judgment on offending persons. So here note the future perfect ἔσται δεδεμένον. your decision will have been anticipated in heaven.

20. ἵνα μηδενὶ εἴπωσιν ὅτι αὐτός ἐστιν ὁ Χριστός. Lest the Galilæan enthusiasm should endeavour to make Him a king.

21—23. The Passion is foretold.

Mark viii. 31—33; Luke ix. 22. St Luke omits the rebuke to Peter. St Mark adds καὶ παρρησίᾳ (without reserve) τὸν λόγον ἐλάλει, both add καὶ ἀποδοκιμασθῆναι.

21. ἀπὸ τότε. An important note of time. Now that the disciples have learned to acknowledge Jesus to be the Messiah, He is able to instruct them in the true nature of the Kingdom.

δεῖ conveys the idea of duty, of a course of life not led haphazard, but determined by principle, of the divine plan which rules the life and work of Christ from first to last. This thought is specially prominent in the third gospel:—in His childhood, ἐν τοῖς τοῦ πατρός μου δεῖ εἶναί με. Luke ii. 49: in His preaching, καὶ ταῖς ἑτέραις πόλεσιν εὐαγγελίσασθαί με δεῖ τὴν βασιλείαν τοῦ θεοῦ ὅτι ἐπὶ τοῦτο ἀπεστάλην. iv. 43, in the fulfilment of the prophecies of His sufferings and death and exaltation, οὐχὶ ταῦτα ἔδει παθεῖν τὸν Χριστόν, καὶ εἰσελθεῖν εἰς τὴν δόξαν αὐτοῦ, xxiv. 26. Cp. Acts xvii. 3. The same thought is applied to St Paul's life and work in the Acts xviii. 21, xxiii. 11, and in other passages. It was felt to be the motive of noble lives before the gospel: οὗ ἄν τις ἑαυτὸν τάξῃ ἢ ἡγησάμενος βέλτιον εἶναι ἢ ὑπ' ἄρχοντος ταχθῇ, ἐνταῦθα δεῖ, ὡς ἐμοὶ δοκεῖ, μένοντα κινδυνεύειν, μηδὲν ὑπολογιζόμενον μήτε θάνατον μήτε ἄλλο μηδὲν πρὸ τοῦ αἰσχροῦ, Plato, *Apol. Socr.* p. 28.

πολλὰ παθεῖν. πάσχειν strictly means to 'feel,' or 'experience,' without any thought of pain or suffering. The history of the word is a melancholy comment on the experience of mankind. To feel was to suffer. In the language of Christianity πάσχειν is used specially of the sufferings and death of Christ, as here, and Luke xxii. 15, πρὸ τοῦ με παθεῖν. 1 Pet. ii. 21, Χριστὸς ἔπαθεν ὑπὲρ ἡμῶν. Hence through the Vulgate, 'passion' has passed with this technical sense into English as in 'Passion-tide,' 'Passion-week.'

τῶν πρεσβ. καὶ ἀρχ. καὶ γραμ. = the Sanhedrin. See ch. ii. 4, and xxvi. 3.

ἀποκτανθῆναι. As yet there is no mention of the Roman judge or of the death upon the cross; this truth is broken gradually, see *v*. 24.

ἀποκτανθῆναι. A rare late form. The Attic writers as a rule used θνήσκω and its compounds to supply the passive of κτείνω. Veitch cites ἐκτείνοντο, Thuc. III. 81, as the one known exception. In Homer the passive forms occur; e.g. aor. 1 ἐκτάθην, *Od.* IV. 537. Also rarely in late authors ἀπεκτάνθαι, Polyb. 7. 7, and in LXX. and N.T. (Veitch, *sub voc.* κτείνω).

τῇ τρίτῃ ἡμέρᾳ ἐγερθῆναι. How can the plainness of this intimation be reconciled with the slowness of the disciples to believe in the Resurrection? Not by supposing that obscure hints of the Passion were afterwards put into this explicit form; but rather (1) partly by the blindness of those who will not see; (2) partly by the constant use of metaphor by Jesus. "Might not," they would argue, "this 'death and rising again' be a symbol of a glorious visible kingdom about to issue from our present debasement?"

22. ἵλεώς σοι. Understand θεὸς γένοιτο or γένοιο, and translate literally: '*may God pity thee*,' i.e. '*give thee a better fate*,' or (2) '*pity thyself*.' ἵλεως is used of divine pity, in this way especially by late authors: σὺ δ' ἵλεως Ἀφροδίτη γενοῦ, Lucian. *Amor.* 30; δέσποτα Παλαῖμον, ἵλεως ἡμῖν γενοῦ, Eur. *Iph. T.* 271; ταῦτ' ὦ Λύκει' Ἄπολλον, ἵλεως κλύων | δὸς πᾶσιν κ.τ.λ., Soph. *El.* 655. Hence like Latin *di avertant* of events to be shunned or deprecated.

23. ὕπαγε ὀπίσω μου, σατανᾶ. Peter takes the place of the tempter, and argues for the false kingdom instead of for the true (see notes ch. iv. 8—10).

σκάνδαλον ἐμοῦ, i.e. a snare to allure me, as tempting me to forsake the divine plan of self-denial and sacrifice.

οὐ φρονεῖς τὰ τοῦ θεοῦ ἀλλὰ τὰ τῶν ἀνθρώπων. 'Thou mindest not the things of God but the things of men,' i.e. thine are not God's thoughts but man's thoughts. Cp. τὰ τῆς σαρκὸς φρονοῦσιν (have a carnal mind), Rom. viii. 5; τὰ ἄνω φρονεῖτε, Col. iii. 2. In the classics φρονεῖν is used of political partisanship: φρονεῖν τὰ Φιλίππου, or τὰ τοῦ δήμου (Dem.), 'to be on the side of Philip or on the side of the people.' μήτ' ἐμοὶ παρέστιος | γένοιτο μήτ' ἴσον φρονῶν (i.e. of the same party in the state) ὃς τάδ' ἔρδοι, Soph. *Ant.* 374. Thus the expression in the text='thou art not on God's side but on man's, and therefore a Satanas or διάβολος, an adversary of God thwarting his plan of humility'.

With the exception of the parallel passage in Mark, and Acts xxviii. 22, φρονεῖν is confined in N. T. to St Paul's epistles where it is frequent, especially in Romans and Philippians.

24—28. SELF-RENOUNCEMENT REQUIRED IN CHRIST'S FOLLOWERS. THEIR REWARD. Mark viii. 34—ix. 1; Luke ix. 23—27.

24. ἀράτω τὸν σταυρόν, 'take up his cross,' St Luke adds καθ' ἡμέραν. The expression, ch. x. 38, differs slightly, ὃς οὐ λαμβάνει τὸν σταυρὸν αὐτοῦ, where see note. ἀράτω τὸν σταυρὸν implies death; this explains the γὰρ (v. 15), let Christ's follower lose on the cross the lower life, as the Master lost His, crucify also his earthly affections, of which the ψυχή was the seat (ψυχή...ἀναπαύου, φάγε, πίε, εὐφραίνου, Luke xii. 19), and he shall win the higher spiritual life here and hereafter. Another thought of the Cross is slavery—it was especially a slave's death ('cives Romani servilem in modum cruciati et necati,' Cic. *in Verrem* I. 5); 'you must be slaves not kings;' cp. ch. xx. 25—28 and Phil. ii. 8, ἐταπείνωσεν ἑαυτόν, γενόμενος ὑπήκοος μέχρι θανάτου, θανάτου δὲ σταυροῦ.

For the thought of the Christian's crucifixion with Christ cp. among many other passages Gal. ii. 20, Χριστῷ συνεσταύρωμαι.

26. ἐὰν τὸν κόσμον ὅλον κερδήσῃ. One of the false Messianic notions was that the Christ should gain the whole world, i.e. the Roman Empire. This was the very temptation presented to our Lord Himself 'the kingdoms of the world and the glory of them.' What is the value of universal dominion, of the whole power of Cæsar, compared with life? ψυχή had a wide range of meaning to the Greek; it was 'life' in all its extent, from the mere vegetative existence to the highest intellectual life. Christianity has deepened the conception by adding to the connotation of ψυχή the spiritual life of the soul in union with Christ.

The higher and the lower sense are both present in these verses, it is true that the world is worthless if life be lost, still more true if the union of the soul with Christ should be sacrificed. The Greek poet discerned that there is a greater gain than external prosperity, ἐπεί σ' ἐφεύρηκα μοίρᾳ μὲν οὐκ ἐπ' ἐσθλᾷ | βεβῶσαν· ἃ δὲ μέγιστ' ἔβλαστε νόμιμα, τῶνδε φερομέναν | ἄριστα τᾷ Ζηνὸς εὐσεβείᾳ. Soph. *El.* 1094.

κερδήσῃ ζημιωθῇ. κέρδος and ζημία...are often thus opposed in the classics. Cp. Phil. iii. 7, ἀλλ' ἅτινα ἦν μοι κέρδος ταῦτα ἥγημαι διὰ τὸν Χριστὸν ζημίαν—a passage which reflects the thought of this.

ἀντάλλαγμα. Cp. κέκρισθε...μηδ' ἀνταλλάξασθαι μηδεμίας χάριτος μηδ' ὠφελείας τὴν εἰς τοὺς Ἕλληνας εὔνοιαν (Dem. *Phil.* II. 10); no external gain, it was felt, would tempt Athens to abandon her loyal and pro-Hellenic policy—for *that* she would make every sacrifice.

27. **γάρ.** The reason given why the higher life—the soul—is of priceless value: (1) The Judge is at hand who will condemn self-indulgence and all the works of the lower life, and will reward those who have denied themselves. (2) Further (*v.* 28) this judgment shall not be delayed—it is very near. The same motive for the Christian life is adduced by St Paul, Phil. iv. 5, τὸ ἐπιεικὲς ὑμῶν γνωσθήτω πᾶσιν ἀνθρώποις. ὁ Κύριος ἐγγύς. Cp. 1 Cor. xvi. 22.

28. **οὐ μὴ γεύσωνται θανάτου κ.τ.λ.** Compare

> The valiant never taste of death but once.
> SHAKSPEAR, *Jul. Cæs.* Act II, 2.

St Matthew's version of this 'hard saying' indicates more plainly than the other Synoptic Gospels the personal presence of Christ. St Luke has, ἕως ἂν ἴδωσιν τὴν βασιλείαν τοῦ θεοῦ: St Mark adds to these words, ἐληλυθυῖαν ἐν δυνάμει: but the meaning in each case is the same. Various solutions are given. The expression is referred to (1) the Transfiguration, (2) the Day of Pentecost, (3) the Fall of Jerusalem. The last best fulfils the conditions of interpretation—a judicial coming—a signal and visible event, and one that would happen in the lifetime of some, but not of all, who were present. To take ἐν τῇ βασιλείᾳ αὐτοῦ in a literal external sense would be to repeat St Peter's error, and to ignore the explanation of the Kingdom just given.

CHAPTER XVII.

4. **ποιήσω** (אBC*), for ποιήσωμεν, which is supported by all the later uncials—the more ancient evidence rightly prevails.

5. **ἀκούετε αὐτοῦ** for αὐτοῦ ἀκούετε on the authority of אBD.

9. **ἐκ** for ἀπό on decisive evidence; ἐκ from out the mountain, from the heart of it—a less usual expression than ἀπό.

10. **πρῶτον**, inserted to help the sense, appears in the majority of later uncials, not in אBD.

20. **ὀλιγοπιστίαν** for ἀπιστίαν, the term of gentler blame has the earliest evidence in its favour.

21. Here the received text has: τοῦτο δὲ τὸ γένος οὐκ ἐκπορεύεται εἰ μὴ ἐν προσευχῇ καὶ νηστείᾳ. The words are undisputed in the parallel passage, Mark ix. 29, with the exception of καὶ νηστείᾳ omitted by Tischendorf without decisive evidence. Here the omission is supported by אB* 33 and some important versions.

25. εἰσελθόντα, the reading of ℵ*. There is much variation in the MSS. ὅτε ἦλθεν is well supported, but looks like an explanation of the participle.

26. εἰπόντος δέ (ℵBCL) for λέγει αὐτῷ ὁ Πέτρος, not supported by the later uncials.

1—13. THE TRANSFIGURATION. Mark ix. 2—13; Luke ix. 28—36.

1. μεθ' ἡμέρας ἕξ. Within a week of Peter's confession. St Luke has 'about an eight days after,' according to the common Jewish reckoning, by which each part of a day is counted as a day. The note of time cannot be without a purpose. The link is intentional between the announcement of the Passion and the kingdom of utter sacrifice on the one hand, and the foretaste of glory on the other.

τὸν Πέτρον καὶ Ἰάκωβον καὶ Ἰωάννην. The three who were chosen to be with their Master on the two other occasions, (1) the raising of Jairus' daughter, (2) the agony in the Garden of Gethsemane.

εἰς ὄρος ὑψηλόν. A contrast suggests itself, between this mountain of the Kingdom of God, and the mountain of the kingdoms of the world, ch. iv. 8.

An old tradition placed the scene of the Transfiguration on Mount Tabor. It is known, however, that the summit of Tabor was at this period occupied by a fortress, and there is no hint given of Jesus being in that neighbourhood. Many regard one of the spurs of Hermon, or even its summit (Conder, *Tent Work*, &c. 266), as the most likely spot. Cæsarea Philippi, the last named locality, lies under Hermon, and its glittering cone of snow may have suggested the expression in Mark, λευκὰ λίαν ὡς χιών, if, indeed, the words ὡς χιών are to be admitted into the text.

2. μετεμορφώθη. 'Was transformed.' Here was a change (μετά) of μορφή, 'the abiding form,' 'the manner of existence.' μεταμορφοῦσθαι 'involves an inwardness of change, a change not external, not of accidents, but of essence.' Trench, *N. T. Syn.* Part II. p. 87. μετασχηματίζειν denotes change of external appearance. See Rom. xii. 2 and Phil. ii. 6—8, where see Bp Lightfoot's notes and separate note on μορφή and σχῆμα.

St Luke records that the change took place ἐν τῷ προσεύχεσθαι αὐτόν.

ὡς ὁ ἥλιος...ὡς τὸ φῶς. A hint that the Transfiguration took place at night, which is also rendered probable by the statement of St Luke that the three Apostles were 'heavy with sleep,' that they 'kept awake,' that they descended 'the next day,' ch. ix. 32 and 37.

3. Μωϋσῆς καὶ Ἠλίας (Elijah). The representatives of the Law and the Prophets. The whole history of the Jewish Church is brought in one glance, as it were, before the Apostles' eyes in its due relation to Christ. St Luke names the subject of converse: they 'spake of his decease which he should accomplish at Jerusalem' (ix. 31).

4. ποιήσω. So in the best MSS., 'let *me* make.' The transition to the singular is in keeping with Peter's temperament; *he* would like to make the tabernacles.—Meyer. By σκηναί are meant little huts made out of boughs of trees or shrubs, such as were made at the Feast of Tabernacles.

5. οὗτός ἐστιν ὁ υἱὸς κ.τ.λ. Words that recall the baptism of Jesus; ch. iii. 17, where see note. For the tense of εὐδόκησα, cp. παρεδόθη, ch. xi. 27.

8. τὸν Ἰησοῦν μόνον. Christ, who came to fulfil the Law and the Prophets, is left alone. To His voice alone the Church will listen.

9. τὸ ὅραμα. 'The thing seen,' not a 'vision' (A.V.) in the sense of a dream: it is equivalent to ἃ εἶδον (Mark), ἃ ἑώρακαν (Luke).

10. οὖν. Elijah had appeared to the chosen three Apostles. It seemed to them that this was a fulfilment of Malachi's prophecy and the necessary condition of the Messiah's Advent as explained by the Scribes. But they are forbidden to announce this to any one. Hence the inference expressed by οὖν. The Scribes must be mistaken. For surely the Messiah would allow His disciples to make known this clear token of His presence.

11. Ἡλίας ἔρχεται κ.τ.λ. 'Elijah cometh and will restore all things,' not *will* come *first* (A.V.). Our Lord's words point to a fulfilment of Malachi iv. 5, καὶ ἰδοὺ ἐγὼ ἀποστελῶ ὑμῖν Ἡλίαν τὸν Θεσβίτην, πρὶν ἐλθεῖν τὴν ἡμέραν Κυρίου τὴν μεγάλην καὶ ἐπιφανῆ ὃς ἀποκαταστήσει καρδίαν πατρὸς πρὸς υἱόν, καὶ καρδίαν ἀνθρώπου πρὸς τὸν πλησίον αὐτοῦ μὴ ἔλθω καὶ πατάξω τὴν γῆν ἄρδην. Note the concise form of the Lord's expression; it is not so much a citation as an allusion addressed to 'those that know the law.' By such ἀποκαταστήσει πάντα would naturally be interpreted by a reference to the precise words of Malachi. In the light of that prophecy the ἀποκατάστασις would signify a national restoration to unity under the influence of the Messenger of Jehovah.

ἀποκαταστήσει πάντα. Two questions arise in reference to these words, (1) How is the future to be explained? (2) In what sense were they fulfilled by John the Baptist? (1) If the prophecy be regarded as absolutely and finally fulfilled in John the Baptist the point of departure for the future ἀποκαταστήσει, and the present-future ἔρχεται must be taken, not from the time when the words were spoken, but from the time when the prophecy was first uttered. Christ cites and affirms the prediction of Malachi. (2) The answer to the second question must be sought in the angelic message to Zachariah, Luke i. 16, 17, πολλοὺς τῶν υἱῶν Ἰσραὴλ ἐπιστρέψει ἐπὶ Κύριον τὸν Θεὸν αὐτῶν· καὶ αὐτὸς προελεύσεται ἐνώπιον αὐτοῦ ἐν πνεύματι καὶ δυνάμει Ἡλίου ἐπιστρέψαι καρδίας πατέρων ἐπὶ τέκνα καὶ ἀπειθεῖς ἐν φρονήσει δικαίων, ἑτοιμάσαι Κυρίῳ λαὸν κατεσκευασμένον.

The view that regards the words as pointing to an event still in the future, and to the coming of another Elijah, of whom the first Elijah and John were types, is rendered improbable by the words quoted above, and by our Lord's words in the next verse, Ἡλίας ἤδη ἦλθεν.

12. οὐκ ἐπέγνωσαν, 'did not recognise.' ἐπὶ denotes 'further,' hence 'clear' recognition.

ἐν αὐτῷ ποιεῖν. In classical Greek ποιεῖν would be followed by two accusatives. ἐν αὐτῷ in him as the sphere or field of their action.

μέλλει πάσχειν, is destined to suffer, such is to be his experience also. πάσχειν refers to οὐκ ἐπέγνωσαν as well as to ἐποίησαν ἐν αὐτῷ ὅσα ἠθέλησαν.

14—21. A LUNATIC CHILD IS CURED.

Mark ix. 14—29, where the scene and the symptoms of the disease are described with great particularity. Luke ix. 37—42.

14. ἐλθόντων πρὸς τὸν ὄχλον. Some will recall Raphael's great picture of the Transfiguration, in which the contrast is powerfully portrayed between the scene on the mount, calm, bright, and heavenly, and the scene below of suffering, human passions, and failure.

15. σεληνιάζεται. This is the only special instance of cure in the case of a lunatic. They are mentioned as a class, ch. iv. 24. The word literally means 'affected by changes of the moon.' On the thought underlying the word, that there is an access of mania at the time of lunar changes, see Belcher, *Our Lord's Miracles of Healing*, p. 131.

St Mark describes the child as foaming, gnashing with his teeth, and pining away. St Luke mentions that he 'crieth out.' All these were epileptic symptoms; 'the child was a possessed epileptic lunatic.'

17. ὦ γενεὰ ἄπιστος καὶ διεστραμμένη, addressed to the scribes and the multitude thronging round, as representing the whole nation. The disciples, if not specially addressed, are by no means excluded from the rebuke. For this moral sense of διαστρέφω cp. Luke xxiii. 2, τοῦτον εὕρομεν διαστρέφοντα τὸ ἔθνος, Phil ii. 15 (Deut. xxxii. 5), γενεᾶς σκολιᾶς καὶ διεστραμμένης, and Polyb. VIII. 24. 3, διεστρέφετο ὑπὸ κόλακος.

20. ἐρεῖτε τῷ ὄρει τούτῳ κ.τ.λ. Such expressions are characteristic of the vivid imagery of Eastern speech generally. To 'remove mountains' is to make difficulties vanish. The Jews used to say of an eminent teacher, he is 'a rooter up of mountains.' See Lightfoot *ad loc.*

22, 23. THE SECOND ANNOUNCEMENT OF THE PASSION.

Mark ix. 31; Luke ix. 44.

Both St Mark and St Luke add that the disciples 'understood not this saying.' It was difficult for them to abandon cherished hopes of an earthly kingdom, and 'might not Jesus be speaking in parables of a figurative death and resurrection?' See note, ch. xvi. 21.

Observe here the various phases in the prediction of the Passion. The first (ch. xvi. 21) foretells the rejection of Jesus as the Messiah by the Jews, and his death in the indefinite passive, ἀποκτανθῆναι.

The second speaks of the betrayal into the hands of *men*, εἰς χεῖρας ἀνθρώπων (Matt., Mark, Luke); and 'they shall put him to death.'

The third (ch. xx. 17—19) particularises the share taken by Jew and Gentile. The Sanhedrin shall condemn and deliver to the Gentiles, εἰς τὸ ἐμπαῖξαι καὶ μαστιγῶσαι καὶ σταυρῶσαι.

24—27. JESUS PAYS THE HALF SHEKEL OF THE SANCTUARY.
Peculiar to St Matthew.

τὰ δίδραχμα. This was not a tribute levied by Cæsar or by Herod, but the half-shekel (Exod. xxx. 13) paid annually by every Jew into the Temple treasury. The 'sacred tax' was collected from Jews in all parts of the world. Josephus (*Ant.* xvi. 6) has preserved some interesting letters from Roman proconsuls and from Augustus himself, to Cyrene, Ephesus and other communities, directing that the Jews should be allowed to forward their contributions to the Temple without hindrance.

It would be interesting to know whether the Jewish Christians continued to pay the Temple-tax in accordance with the Lord's example.

After the fall of Jerusalem and the destruction of the Temple the Jews were obliged to pay the two drachmæ into the Roman treasury. Joseph. *B. J.* vii. 6. 6.

οὐ τελεῖ. Probably some who misunderstood or who wished to misrepresent Jesus had raised the doubt whether He would pay the tribute. It is possibly a hint that His claims to the Messiahship were becoming more widely known. Meyer remarks that the ναί of Peter makes it clear that Jesus had been in the habit of paying the tax.

25. προέφθασεν αὐτόν. 'Anticipated him' by answering his thoughts.

τέλη ἢ κῆνσον. Taxes (1) indirect and (2) direct; on (1) things and on (2) persons. κῆνσος, Lat. *census*: see ch. xxii. 17.

ἀπὸ τῶν υἱῶν κ.τ.λ., i.e. of their own sons, or of those who do not belong to the family, namely, subjects and tributaries.

26. ἐλεύθεροί εἰσιν οἱ υἱοί, 'the sons are exempt from tribute.' The deduction is, 'Shall he whom thou hast rightly named the Son of God pay tribute to the Temple of his Father?' The Romans called their sons free (*liberi*), as opposed to slaves.

27. στατῆρα (ἵστημι, 'to weigh'), 'a stater'; a Greek silver coin equivalent to the Hebrew shekel, or to four drachmæ in Greek money, hence sometimes called τετράδραχμος. 'In paying the temple-tax it is necessary that every one should have half a shekel to pay for himself. Therefore when he comes to the changer he is obliged to allow him some gain which is called κόλλυβος (see ch. xxi. 12). And when two pay one shekel between them each of them is obliged to allow the same gain or fee.' The collection of the Temple tax was

made in *Adar*, the month preceding the Passover. Lightfoot, *Hor. Hebr.*, Matt. xxi. 12.

ἀντὶ ἐμοῦ καὶ σοῦ. Cp. Ex. xxx. 12—16, 'The rich shall not give more, and the poor shall not give less than half a shekel, when they give an offering unto the Lord to make an atonement for your souls' (*v.* 15). It is in accordance with this thought of atonement or substitution that the preposition ἀντί is used.

CHAPTER XVIII.

6. περί (ℵBL and some of the Fathers) for ἐπί of *textus receptus*. εἰς is also strongly supported, and περί may have come from the parallel passages in Mark and Luke.

11. Here the *textus receptus* has: ἦλθε γὰρ ὁ υἱὸς τοῦ ἀνθρώπου σῶσαι τὸ ἀπολωλός. This is strongly supported by the later MSS. The omission rests on the evidence of ℵBL, and several versions and Fathers.

19. συμφωνήσουσιν has far higher authority than συμφωνήσωσιν, a grammatical correction.

29. εἰς τοὺς πόδας αὐτοῦ. Almost certainly a gloss, the weight of the earlier MSS. is in favour of the omission.

35. τὰ παραπτώματα αὐτῶν. After καρδιῶν ὑμῶν. These words have the support of C and 12 uncials, but are omitted in the earlier MSS.

1—4. A LESSON IN HUMILITY. THE KINGDOM OF HEAVEN AND LITTLE CHILDREN.

Mark ix. 33—37; Luke ix. 46—48.

1. ἐν ἐκείνῃ τῇ ὥρᾳ. The preceding incident and our Lord's words had again excited hopes of a glorious kingdom on earth. We may suppose that Jesus and St Peter were alone when the last incident happened, they had entered the house (probably Peter's) and were now joined by the other apostles who had been disputing on the way (ἐν τῇ ὁδῷ, Mark).

ὁ μείζων (τῶν ἄλλων) as distinct from the superlative, the comparative contrasts an object with but one standard of comparison, μέγιστος would have implied three or four degrees of rank among the Twelve. Winer, 303 and 305.

2. ἐν μέσῳ αὐτῶν. So Mark; St Luke has the more loving ἔστησεν αὐτὸ παρ' ἑαυτῷ. St Mark notes that Jesus first took the child in His arms (ἐγκαλισάμενος αὐτό).

3. στραφῆτε, 'be converted;' cp. John xii. 40, ἵνα μή...στραφῶσιν καὶ ἰάσομαι αὐτούς.

οὐ μὴ εἰσέλθητε, 'shall not enter,' much less be great therein.

4. ταπεινώσει ἑαυτόν. He who shall be most Christ-like in humility (see Phil. ii. 7, 8) shall be most like Christ in glory. Cp. ἐταπείνωσεν ἑαυτόν, γενομένος ὑπήκοος μέχρι θανάτου, θανάτου δὲ σταυροῦ. διὸ καὶ ὁ Θεὸς αὐτὸν ὑπερύψωσεν κ.τ.λ., Phil. ii. 8, 9. ταπεινώσει marks the particular point in which little children are an example to Christians, and the words of St Paul give the precise lesson of this incident taken in connection with the death upon the Cross just foretold. Jesus gives himself to His disciples as an example of ταπεινότης μέχρι θανάτου. See ch. xi. 29.

The expression ταπειν. ἑαυτὸν is more emphatic than the middle voice and implies greater self-mastery.

5, 6. CHRIST'S LITTLE ONES. Mark ix. 37—42.

The thought of Jesus passes from the dispute among His disciples to the care of his little ones, the young in faith, who, if they have the weakness, have also the humility of little children.

5. ὃς ἐὰν δέξηται. It is a sacrament of lovingkindness when Christ himself is received in the visible form of His little ones. δέχεσθαι is not only to welcome, show kindness to, but also to receive as a teacher (ἀποδέχεσθαι). The faithful see in the ταπεινότης of little children a symbol of the ταπεινότης of Christ.

6. πιστευόντων εἰς ἐμέ. For the distinction between πιστεύειν εἰς 'to believe in any one,' i.e. to put entire faith in him, and πιστεύειν τινί, 'to believe any one,' i.e. to give credit to his words, see Prof. Westcott on John viii. 30 (*Speaker's Commentary*). The first construction is characteristic of St John's gospel and in the Synoptics occurs only here, and in the parallel passage Mark ix. 42.

συμφέρει ἵνα, *expedit ut.* See note ch. i. 22.

μύλος ὀνικός. A millstone turned by an ass, and so larger than the ordinary millstone. Cp. Ovid (*Fasti* VI. 318): 'Et quæ pumiceas versat asella molas.'

The manner of death alluded to appears to have been unknown to the Jews. But Plutarch mentions this punishment as being common to Greece and Rome. Cp. Juv. *Sat.* VIII. 213, where, as in other places, it is named rather than the cross as a swift and terrible penalty for crime. The Scholiast on Aristoph. *Equites*, 1360, explains ὑπέρβολον, ὅταν γὰρ κατεπόντουν τινὰς βάρος ἀπὸ τῶν τραχήλων ἐκρέμων.

ἐν τῷ πελάγει τῆς θαλάσσης. πέλαγος does not in itself mean the 'deep sea,' but either 'the expanse of open water' (πλάξ, πλατύς, *flat*, &c.), or the 'tossing,' 'beating' sea (πλήσσω from root πλαγ). In this passage, therefore, the sense of depth is rather to be looked for in καταποντισθῇ, though the connection between πόντος and βένθος, βάθος, &c., is doubtful; Curtius prefers the etymology of πάτος, 'path,' and Lat. *pons*. (See Trench, *N. T. Syn.* 52, 53, and Curtius, *Etym.* 270 and 278.)

7—9. OF OFFENCES. Mark ix. 43—48.

From offences—snares and hindrances to the faith of Christ's little ones—the discourse proceeds to offences in general—everything that hinders the spiritual life.

7. οὐαί. Alexandrine, but corresponding to ὀά, Æsch., *Pers.* 115, 121, the Latin form is *vae*. ἀπό denotes that σκάνδαλα are the source of woes.

σκάνδαλα. Snares, allurements to evil, temptations. See notes on ch. v. 29, 30.

8. καλόν...ἤ. Cp. Luke xv. 7, χαρὰ ἔσται ἐπὶ ἑνὶ ἁμαρτωλῷ μετανοοῦντι ἢ ἐπὶ ἐνενηκονταεννέα δικαίοις. Instances are quoted from the classics, as Thuc. vi. 21, αἰσχρὸν βιασθέντας ἀπελθεῖν ἢ ὕστερον ἐπιμεταπέμπεσθαι, but it is better to refer the construction to the Hebrew usage, by which the comparative idea is expressed by the positive adjective followed by the preposition *min* (from). The construction is common in the LXX. and it may be noted that a rare classical usage tends to become frequent in Hellenistic Greek if it be found to correspond to a common Hebrew idiom. For another instance of this see note on τοῦ πυρός below.

9. μονόφθαλμον. In classical Greek a distinction is made: the Cyclops or the Arimaspi (Hdt. iii. 116) are μονόφθαλμοι. A man who has lost an eye is ἑτερόφθαλμος. Cp. Hdt. *loc. cit.* πείθομαι δὲ οὐδὲ τοῦτο, ὅκως μουνόφθαλμοι ἄνδρες φύονται.

τὴν γέενναν τοῦ πυρός. 'The fiery Gehenna.' This adjectival genitive may be paralleled from the classics: χόρτων εὐδένδρων Εὐρώπαν, *Iph. in Taur.* 134. See note ch. v. 22, and Donaldson, *Greek Grammar*, p. 481, for other instances. But the frequency of the usage in Hellenistic Greek is again attributable to the Hebrew idiom.

10—14. CHRIST'S CARE FOR HIS LITTLE ONES ILLUSTRATED BY A PARABLE. Luke xv. 3—7.

After a brief digression (*vv.* 7—9), Christ's love for His young disciples again breaks out in words. Let no one despise them. They have unseen friends in the court of heaven, who are ever in the presence of the King himself. There, at any rate, they are not despised. It was for them especially that the Son of Man came to earth.

10. οἱ ἄγγελοι αὐτῶν. In these words our Lord sanctions the Jewish belief in guardian angels. Cp. Acts xii. 15, ὁ ἄγγελός ἐστιν αὐτοῦ, and Hebr. i. 14, οὐχὶ πάντες εἰσὶν λειτουργικὰ πνεύματα εἰς διακονίαν ἀποστελλόμενα διὰ τοὺς μέλλοντας κληρονομεῖν σωτηρίαν; The reserve with which the doctrine is dwelt upon in the N.T. is in contrast with the general extravagance of Oriental belief on the subject.

βλέπουσιν τὸ πρόσωπον τοῦ πατρός μου. The image is drawn from the court of an Eastern king, where the favoured courtiers enjoy the right of constant approach to the royal presence; cp. Esther i. 14, 'Which saw the king's face and which sat the first in the kingdom.'

12. The expression and the imagery of the parable recall Ezek. xxxiv.; comp. also ch. xv. 24. In Luke the parable is spoken with direct reference to publicans and sinners, 'whom the Pharisees despised, and who are the 'little ones' of these verses. Such differences of context in the Gospels are very instructive; they are, indeed, comments by the Evangelists themselves on the drift and bearing of particular sayings of Christ.

This parable is followed in Luke by the parable of the Lost Drachma and that of the Prodigal Son which illustrate and amplify the same thought.

ἀφεὶς τὰ ἐνενήκοντα. St Luke adds ἐν τῇ ἐρήμῳ.

15—35. FORGIVENESS OF SINS. Luke xvii. 3, 4.

God's forgiveness of sinners suggests the duty of forgiveness among men.

15. ἔλεγξον αὐτὸν κ.τ.λ. 'Rebuke him.' See Levit. xix. 17, 'Thou shalt not hate thy brother in thine heart: thou shalt in any wise rebuke (ἐλέγξεις, LXX.) thy neighbour, and not suffer sin upon him' (rather, 'not bear sin on his account,' 'by bearing secret ill-will,' Ephes. iv. 26; or by 'encouraging him to sin by withholding due rebuke.' Speaker's Commentary *ad loc.*).

ἐκέρδησας, 'gained,' i.e. won over to a better mind,—to Christ. Cp. 1 Cor. ix. 19—22, and 1 Pet. iii. 1. The aorist is of the action just past. If he shall have heard thee thou didst (at that moment) gain thy brother.

17. εἰπὲ τῇ ἐκκλησίᾳ. The word ἐκκλησία is found only here and ch. xvi. 18 (where see note) in the Gospels. In the former passage the reference to the Christian Church is undoubted. Here either (1) the assembly or congregation of the Jewish synagogue, or rather, (2) the ruling body of the synagogue (collegium presbyterorum, *Schleusner*) is meant. This must have been the sense of the word to those who were listening to Christ. But what was spoken of the Jewish Church was naturally soon applied to the Christian Church. And the use of the term by Christ implied for the future an organised Church exercising discipline, organised too at least in part on the model of the synagogue.

ὁ ἐθνικὸς καὶ ὁ τελώνης. Jesus, the friend of publicans and sinners, uses the phrase of his contemporaries. What Jesus says, Matthew the publican records. ἐθνικός, the adjective of ἔθνη, in the special Jewish sense of 'Gentiles,' in Polybius ἐθνικὸς = 'national.'

18. ὅσα ἐὰν δήσητε κ.τ.λ. What was spoken to Peter alone is now spoken to all the disciples, representing the Church. 'Whatsoever you as a Church declare binding or declare not binding, that decision

shall be ratified in heaven.' Note the tense, ἔσται δεδεμένα...λελυμένα, 'shall have been bound...loosed,' and cp. note ch. ix. 2.

19. The slight digression is continued. Christ thinks of His Church. Not only shall your decisions be ratified, but your requests shall be granted, provided ye agree.

ἐὰν συμφωνήσουσιν. For this construction see Winer, p. 369. The close relation between the future indicative and the subjunctive moods easily accounts for the usage; in many passages the readings vary between the subjunctive and the future indicative; in Acts viii. 31, ἐὰν μή τις ὁδηγήσει is read by Tischendorf and Tregelles. It is more startling to find ἐὰν οἴδαμεν, 1 John v. 15. ὅταν ἐθεώρουν, Mark iii. 11. ὅταν ἤνοιξεν, Rev. viii. 1. See also the quotation from the Scholiast, v. 5, where ὅταν is followed by indicative.

20. δύο ἢ τρεῖς. In the smallest gathering of His followers Christ will be present.

συνηγμένοι. συνάγειν is used specially of the 'gathering' of the Church, as Acts xi. 26, συναχθῆναι ἐν τῇ ἐκκλησίᾳ. xx. 8, ἐν τῷ ὑπερῴῳ οὗ ἦμεν συνηγμένοι. Hence in later Ecclesiastical Greek σύναξις is 'a religious service,' συναξάριον a 'service book,' συνάξιμος ἡμέρα 'a day on which services are held.'

21. ἕως ἑπτάκις. The Rabbinical rule was that no one should ask forgiveness of his neighbour more than thrice. Peter, who asks as a scribe a scribe's question, thought he was making a great advance in liberality and shewing himself worthy of the kingdom of heaven. But the question itself indicates complete misunderstanding of the Christian spirit.

22. ἕως ἑβδομηκοντάκις ἑπτά, i.e. an infinite number of times. There is no limit to forgiveness.

23. ἠθέλησεν συνᾶραι λόγον μετὰ τῶν δούλων αὐτοῦ. The picture is drawn from an Oriental Court. The provincial governors, farmers of taxes, and other high officials, are summoned before a despotic sovereign to give an account of their administration.

ἠθέλησεν, 'chose,' 'resolved:' all is subject to his sole will.

δούλων, i.e. subjects, for all subjects of an Eastern monarch from the highest to the lowest are 'slaves.' Demosthenes frequently makes a point of this, e.g. *Phil.* III. 32, κἂν αὐτὸς μὴ παρῇ τοὺς δούλους ἀγωνοθετήσοντας πέμπει. This shade of meaning is perhaps present in the Apostolic title δοῦλος Ἰησοῦ Χριστοῦ, Rom. i. 1.

24. μυρίων ταλάντων. Even if silver talents are meant, the sum is enormous—at least two million pounds of our money. It was probably more than the whole annual revenue of Palestine at this time; see Joseph. *Ant.* XII. 4. 4. The modern kingdoms of Norway or Greece or Denmark hardly produce a larger national income.

It is the very sum which Demosthenes records with pride to have been stowed in the Acropolis at the height of Athenian prosperity: πλείω δ' ἢ μύρια τάλαντα εἰς τὴν ἀκρόπολιν ἀνήγαγον. *Olyn.* III. 24.

The vast amount implies the hopeless character of the debt of sin.

25. μὴ ἔχοντος, 'since he had not.' He had wasted in extravagance the provincial revenues, or the proceeds of taxation.

26. προσεκύνει. The imperfect tense denotes persistence.

27. τὸ δάνειον ἀφῆκεν αὐτῷ. With the almost reckless generosity of an Eastern Court that delights to exalt or debase with swift strokes. The pardon is free and unconditional.

28. εὗρεν, 'found,' perhaps even sought him out.

ἕνα τῶν συνδούλων. By this is meant the debt of man to man, offences which men are bound to forgive one another.

ἑκατὸν δηνάρια. The *denarius* was a day's wage (ch. xx. 2). The sum therefore is about three months' wages for an ordinary labourer, by no means a hopeless debt as the other was; see note, ch. xxvi. 7.

ἔπνιγεν, imperfect, not aor. 2, which does not appear to be used in the active. See Veitch and Lob. *Phryn.* 107.

29. παρεκάλει. Contrast this with προσεκύνει, v. 26. παρακαλεῖν would be used by an equal addressing an equal.

31. ἐλυπήθησαν σφόδρα. This seems to point to the common conscience of mankind approving or anticipating the divine sentence.

33. Cp. the Lord's Prayer, where forgiveness of others is put forward as the claim for divine pardon.

34. The acquittal is revoked—a point not to be pressed in the interpretation. The truth taught is the impossibility of the unforgiving being forgiven, but the chief lesson is the example of the divine spirit of forgiveness in the act of the king. This example the pardoned slave should have followed.

τοῖς βασανισταῖς. 'To the keepers of the prison,' the gaolers, part of whose duty it was to torture (βασανίζειν) the prisoners. Thus in the Greek version of Jer. xx. 2, by Symmachus, βασανιστήριον is 'a prison' (A.V. 'stocks'). Fischer, *de vitiis Lex. N.T.*, p. 458.

35. ἀπὸ τῶν καρδιῶν ὑμῶν. A different principle from the Pharisee's arithmetical rules of forgiveness.

CHAPTER XIX.

13. προσηνέχθησαν (א B C D L and others) for προσηνέχθη, an early grammatical change.

16, 17. Here the *textus receptus* has: Διδάσκαλε ἀγαθέ, τί ἀγαθὸν ποιήσω ἵνα ἔχω ζωὴν αἰώνιον; ὁ δὲ εἶπεν αὐτῷ· Τί με λέγεις ἀγαθόν; οὐδεὶς ἀγαθός, εἰ μὴ εἷς ὁ Θεός.

The omission of ἀγαθὲ has the most ancient evidence in its favour. τί με ἐρωτᾷς περὶ τοῦ ἀγαθοῦ rests on the authority of א B D L and other MSS., several versions and patristic quotations. The *textus receptus* is found in C and in many later uncials.

20. ἐφύλαξα (אBDL) for ἐφυλαξάμην (C and later uncials). The latter perhaps influenced by Mark; in Luke ἐφύλαξα should be read.

ἐκ νεότητός μου omitted in אBL. (D omits μου.) The insertion supported by א^cb CD, later uncials, some versions and Fathers, may be accounted for by the occurrence of the words in Mark and Luke.

29. After ἢ μητέρα the leading editors omit ἢ γυναῖκα with BD and some versions and on good patristic evidence.

πολλαπλασίονα (BL) for ἑκατονταπλασίονα (אCD and other uncials). The best editors adopt πολλ. notwithstanding the strong support of the other reading. ἑκατονταπ. probably introduced from Mark to explain the less definite πολλαπλασίονα.

1, 2. JESUS GOES TO JUDÆA FROM GALILEE.
Mark x. 1.

1. μετῆρεν ἀπὸ τῆς Γαλιλαίας κ.τ.λ. From the parallel passage in Mark we learn that this means: Came into Judæa by the trans-Jordanic route through Peræa, thus avoiding Samaria. It does not mean that any portion of Judæa lay beyond Jordan. St Matthew here omits various particulars, of which some are to be supplied from Luke ix. 51—xvii. 11; others from John—two visits to Jerusalem (vii. 8—10 and x. 22—39); the raising of Lazarus (xi. 1—46); the retirement to Ephraim (xi. 54).

μετῆρεν. In this sense late, in N. T. only here and ch. xiii. 51.

3—12. THE QUESTION OF MARRIAGE AND DIVORCE.
MARK x. 2—9.

vv. 10—12 are peculiar to Matthew. St Mark mentions the part of the conversation contained in v. 9 as having taken place 'in the house,' vv. 10—12.

3. πειράζοντες αὐτόν. For present participle containing an idea of purpose cp. Soph. *El.* 68, δέξασθέ μ' εὐτυχοῦντα ταῖσδε ταῖς ὁδοῖς.

εἰ ἔξεστιν ἀνθρώπῳ ἀπολῦσαι κ.τ.λ. The words 'for every cause' are omitted in Mark. In Matthew they contain the pith of the question: 'Is the husband's right to divorce his wife quite unlimited?' The school of Shammai allowed divorce in the case of adultery, the school of Hillel on any trivial pretext.

It was a question of special interest and of special danger in view of Herod's marriage with Herodias.

4. ἀπ' ἀρχῆς. An appeal from the law of Moses to a higher and absolute law, which has outlived the law of Moses.

5. ἕνεκα τούτου. The lesson of Nature is the lesson of God, 'Nunquam aliud Natura aliud Sapientia dicit.' Juv. *Sat.* XIV. 321.

κολληθήσεται. This word and the compound προσκ. in N. T. use are confined to St Paul and St Luke except Rev. xviii. 5. This passage and Mark x. 7 (where the reading is doubtful) are quotations.

The classical meaning of κολλᾶν is (1) to glue; (2) to inlay; (3) to join very closely: κεκόλληται γένος πρὸς ἄτᾳ, Æsch. *Ag*. 1566.

εἰς σάρκα μίαν. εἰς denotes the state or condition into which a thing passes. The construction follows the Hebrew idiom.

6. **ὅ**, the neuter strengthens the idea of complete fusion into a single being.

συνέζευξεν. The aorist of the divine action undetermined by time. Cp. εὐδόκησεν, ch. iii. 17, παρεδόθη, xi. 27, ἐδόθη, xxviii. 18.

7. **βιβλίον ἀποστασίου.** See ch. v. 31, 32.

8. **πρὸς τὴν σκληροκαρδίαν ὑμῶν.** Having respect to, with a view to the hardness of your hearts towards God. So the law was relatively good, not absolutely. A great principle. Even now all are not capable of the higher religious life or of the deepest truths. Some interpret 'hardness of heart,' of the cruelty of men towards their wives.

ἐπέτρεψεν, 'allowed,' a correction of ἐνετείλατο, v. 7. Moses did not *enjoin*, but merely *permitted* a bill of divorce.

οὐ γέγονεν. Not 'was not so,' A.V., but 'hath not been so' continuously from the beginning to the present time. It is not an original and continuous tradition.

9. See ch. v. 32.

10. It is difficult to fix the precise meaning of ἡ αἰτία. It is either: (1) the cause or principle of the conjugal union: 'If the union be so close as thou sayest;' or, (2) the cause or reason for divorce, namely adultery, referring to αἰτία, v. 3: 'If for this reason, and for this alone, divorce be allowed;' or (3) 'the case' in a legal sense like causa, res de qua in judicio agitur: 'If this be the only case with which a man may come into court.' A further meaning, sometimes assigned 'condition,' 'state of things,' may be rejected. On the whole (2), which is Meyer's view, seems preferable.

In D the reading is ἀνδρός, the correct word in contrast with γυναικός, but the reading is not supported. μετὰ is used to express relation generally, as in modern Greek.

οὐ συμφέρει γαμῆσαι. Nothing could prove more clearly the revolution in thought brought to pass by Christ than this. Even the disciples feel that such a principle would make the yoke of marriage unbearable.

γαμῆσαι. This aorist is used both in the sense of 'to give to wife' and 'to take to wife,' it is nearly confined to late authors. See Veitch *sub voc.* γαμέω.

11. χωρεῖν is to have or make room for, so (1) to contain: ὥστε μηκέτι χωρεῖν μηδὲ τὰ πρὸς τὴν θύραν, Mark ii. 2; ὑδρίαι χωροῦσαι ἀνὰ μετρητὰς δύο ἢ τρεῖς, John ii. 6; ὁ κρητὴρ χωρεῖ ἀμφορέας ἑξακοσίους, Hdt. I. 151; (2) to receive (in love): χωρήσατε ἡμᾶς, 2 Cor. vii. 2; (3) to receive intellectually, 'comprehend,' or 'accept;' (4) the Homeric meaning 'to withdraw,' i.e. to make room for another, is not found in

the N.T.; (5) the ordinary classical force, 'to advance,' i.e. to make room for oneself, 'to go,' is found ch. xv. 17 and 2 Pet. iii. 9, εἰς μετάνοιαν χωρῆσαι, and John viii. 37, ὁ λόγος ὁ ἐμὸς οὐ χωρεῖ ἐν ὑμῖν, 'makes no progress in you.'

It is better to refer τὸν λόγον τοῦτον to the last words of the disciples, οὐ συμφέρει γαμῆσαι, than to the whole preceding argument. The general sense will then be: 'Not all, but only those to whom it hath been given, make room for (i.e. accept and act upon) this saying.'

12. εἰσὶν γάρ. The γάρ explains οἷς δέδοται.

διὰ τὴν βασιλείαν τῶν οὐρανῶν. In old days some men abstained from marriage in order to devote themselves to the study of the law, in later times men have done so for the furtherance of Christianity.

ὁ δυνάμενος χωρεῖν χωρείτω. Let him accept the rule who can accept it—he to whom it has been given—he who belongs to either of the three classes named.

The disciples found difficulty in the pure and binding conditions of marriage laid down by Christ, and saw no escape save in abstaining from marriage like the Essenes of that day (Joseph. *B. J.*, γάμου μὲν ὑπεροψία παρ' αὐτοῖς, and *Antiq.* xviii. 1. 5, οὔτε γαμετὰς εἰσάγονται). Christ shews that there is difficulty there too. The limitations of Christ were forgotten in early days of Church history. False teachers arose, 'forbidding to marry' (1 Tim. iv. 3, κωλυόντων γαμεῖν).

As in so many of our Lord's important 'rules,' the principle of Hebrew parallelism is discernible here. The closing words—ὁ δυν. χωρ. χωρείτω—recall the opening words and respond to them—οὐ πάντες...οἷς δέδοται, the enclosed triplet rises to a climax—the highest motive is placed last.

13—15. LITTLE CHILDREN ARE BROUGHT TO CHRIST.
Mark x. 13—16. Luke xviii. 15—17.

In Luke the incident is placed immediately after the parable of the Pharisee and Publican; there it is an illustration of humility. Here, and in Mark, the connection between the purity of married life and the love of little children cannot be overlooked.

13. It appears that it was customary for Jewish infants to be taken to the synagogue to be blessed by the Rabbi. Smith's *Dict. of Bible*, Art. 'Synagogue,' note E.

ἵνα ἐπιθῇ. For the sequence of the subjunctive on historic tenses see note ch. xii. 14.

14. τῶν γὰρ τοιούτων κ.τ.λ. Love, simplicity of faith, innocence, and above all, humility, are the ideal characteristics of little children, and of the subjects of the kingdom.

15. ἐπιθεὶς τὰς χεῖρας. No unmeaning act, therefore infants are capable of receiving a blessing, though not *conscious* of an obligation. It is the authorization of infant baptism. St Mark, as often, records a further loving act of Jesus, ἐναγκαλισάμενος αὐτά.

16—22. THE YOUNG RICH RULER.

Mark x. 17—22. Luke xviii. 18—23.

From Luke alone we learn that he was a '*ruler;*' from Matthew alone that he was *young*. Each of the three Synoptists states that 'he was very rich' (Luke); 'had great possessions' (Matthew and Mark).

16. εἶς προσελθών. 'Came one running, and kneeled to him' (Mark). 'A certain ruler,' i.e. one of the rulers of the synagogue, like Jairus. The 'decemvirate' (see ch. iv. 23) of the synagogue were chosen from 'men of leisure' (Hebr. *Batlanin,* cp. the same thought in Greek σχολή, from which ultimately through Lat. *schola* comes Eng. *scholar*), who were free from the necessity of labour, and could devote themselves to the duties of the synagogue, and to study; of these the first three were called 'Rulers of the Synagogue.'

τί ἀγαθὸν ποιήσω κ.τ.λ. In Mark, τί ποιήσω ἵνα ζωὴν αἰώνιον κληρονομήσω; in Luke, τί ποιήσας ς. αἰ. κληρονομήσω; In this question, 'what shall I *do?*' the ruler touches the central error of the Pharisaic system—that goodness consisted in exact conformity to certain external rules of conduct. Jesus shews that it is not by *doing* anything whatever that a man can inherit eternal life, but by *being* something; not by observing Pharisaic rules, but by being childlike.

17. τί με ἐρωτᾷς περὶ τοῦ ἀγαθοῦ; The form in which our Lord's answer is reported in Mark and Luke is: τί με λέγεις ἀγαθόν; οὐδεὶς ἀγαθός, εἰ μὴ εἷς ὁ θεός. According to St Matthew's report, our Lord seizes upon the word ἀγαθόν in the ruler's question; according to the other gospels the reply turns on the use of the word as applied to himself, ἀγαθὲ διδάσκαλε. But though the reports differ in form, in effect they are identical. Christ's answer is so framed as to wake reflection. '*Why* do you put this question about "the *good*," *why* do you call me "*good?*" Do you understand the meaning of your own question?' It was not a simple question, as the ruler thought: two points are raised: (1) What is 'the good?' (2) How to enter life eternal. Then again the answer to the first is partly left to inference, and the answer to the second lies deeper than the young ruler's thoughts had gone. (1) There is one only who is good, therefore (the inference is) 'the good' can only be the will of God. (2) Then the way to enter into life eternal is to keep God's will as expressed in the commandments. Jesus shews that here too the questioner had not thought deeply enough. Keeping the commandments is not external observance of them, but being in heart what the commandments *mean*, and what the will of God is.

Note in this incident (1) the manner of Jesus adapting itself to the condition of the 'scholar,' one who had leisure to think, and who plumed himself on having thought. To such he points out the way to deeper reflection. (2) The mission of Jesus to 'fulfil the law.' (3) The spiritual use of the law (the ten commandments), as awakening the sense of sin, and so leading to repentance. Bengel says: 'Jesus securos ad Legem remittit, contritos evangelice consolatur.'

18. ποίας; What commandments? written or unwritten? human or divine? the law of Moses or the traditions of the elders? or perhaps the young ruler expected a specimen of the rules with which this new Rabbi would instruct his disciples to 'fence round' the law. In N. T. ποῖος may perhaps always be distinguished from τίς; in later Greek (see Sophocles, *Lex. sub voc.*) and in the modern vernacular the distinction is lost.

τὸ οὐ φονεύσεις κ.τ.λ. For the use of the article prefixed to a sentence cp. εἶπεν αὐτῷ· τὸ εἰ δύνῃ, Mark ix. 23; ὁ πᾶς νόμος ἐν ἑνὶ λόγῳ πεπλήρωται ἐν τῷ ἀγαπήσεις τὸν πλησίον σου, Gal. v. 14. See Winer, p. 135.

οὐ φονεύσεις. In Hebrew a negative is never used with the imperative; prohibitions being always expressed by means of the future (or imperfect). This idiom is here followed in the Greek, οὐ φον.—prohibition, τίμα—positive command (Rœd.-Gesen. *Hebr. Gram.*, p. 280) the future is however also used in pure Greek to express the imperative notion, as e.g. λέγ᾽ εἴ τι βούλει, χειρὶ δ᾽ οὐ ψαύσεις ποτέ, Eur *Med.* 1320 (Donaldson *Grk. Gram.* p. 407).

Comp. this enumeration with that in ch. xv. 19. Here, as there, the commandments proceed in order from the 6th to the 9th. Here, as there, the enumeration stops at covetousness—the rich ruler's special failing. The fifth commandment not named in ch. xv. had probably an individual application here. Neither St Mark nor St Luke preserve the same order

20. πάντα ταῦτα ἐφύλαξα. Like St Paul, he was κατὰ δικαιοσύνην τὴν ἐν νόμῳ ἄμεμπτος. Phil. iii. 6.

21. τέλειος. Used here in relation to τί ἔτι ὑστερῶ, 'complete;' not (1) in the deeper sense which the word sometimes bears in reference to the ancient mysteries, as 1 Cor. ii. 6, σοφίαν δὲ λαλοῦμεν ἐν τοῖς τελείοις (see also Col. i. 28); nor (2) in the sense of 'perfect' in manhood, opposed to babes, as Phil. iii. 15, ὅσοι οὖν τέλειοι τοῦτο φρονῶμεν (see also 1 Cor. xiv. 20; Eph. iv. 13; Heb. v. 14).

ὕπαγε, πώλησον κ.τ.λ. Jesus does indeed bid him do something, but to *do* that would be a proof of *being* perfect, it is *the* test for his special case, not a universal rule. With many it is more difficult to use wealth for Christ than to give it up for Christ. St Mark has the touching words 'Jesus beholding him loved him.' The incident recalls the parable of the 'merchant man seeking goodly pearls' (ch. xiii. 45, 46). Here is a seeker after good, the pearl is found: will he not sell all that he hath and buy it?

The aorist πώλησον indicates the single act, ἀκολούθει the continual following of Christ. Cp. Dem. *Phil.* I. 14, ἐπειδὰν ἅπαντα ἀκούσητε κρίνατε ('decide once for all'), μὴ πρότερον προλαμβάνετε ('don't be prejudging as I go on'); and Eur. *Med.* 1248, λαθοῦ βραχεῖαν ἡμέραν παίδων σέθεν κἄπειτα θρήνει. 'For one brief day forget, and then go on lamenting.'

22. λυπούμενος. A conflict of opposite desires vexed his soul. He wished to serve God and mammon. He was sorrowful because he saw that the special sacrifice required to win eternal life was too great for him. He was lost through the ἀπάτη τοῦ πλούτου (ch. xiii. 22).

23—26. OF RICHES, AND THE KINGDOM OF GOD.
Mark x. 23—27. Luke xviii. 24—27.

These reflections follow naturally on the last incident.

23. τὴν βασ. τῶν οὐρ. Comparing this with *vv.* 16 and 17, we note that ζωὴ αἰώνιος, ἡ ζωή and ἡ βασιλεία τῶν οὐρανῶν are used as synonyms.

24. κάμηλον διὰ τρυπήματος ῥαφίδος. An expression familiar to Jews of our Lord's time. The exaggeration is quite in the Eastern style. Some attempts however have been made to explain away the natural meaning of the words. κάμιλον, which is said to mean 'a thick rope,' has been read for κάμηλον. But the change has no MS. support, and κάμιλος, which does not occur elsewhere, is probably an invention of the Scholiast. Others have explained τρύπημα ῥαφίδος to be the name of a gate in Jerusalem. But the existence of such a gate is not established; and the variety of expression for 'a needle's eye,' τρύπημα ῥαφίδος (Matt.), τρυμαλιά ῥαφίδος (Mark), τρῆμα βελόνης (Luke), is against this view. The variation also indicates that the proverb was not current in Greek. The expression in Luke is the most classical. ῥαφίς is rejected by the Attic purists: ἡ δὲ ῥαφὶς τί ἐστιν οὐκ ἄν τις γνοίη (Lob. *Phryn.* p. 90). τρύπημα was a vernacular word and is found in Aristoph. *Pac.* 1234.

An eastern traveller has suggested that the association of ideas arose thus: every camel driver carries with him a large needle to mend his pack-saddle as occasion requires, hence the 'camel' and the 'needle.'

25. ἐξεπλήσσοντο σφόδρα. The extreme amazement of the disciples, which can find no echo in souls trained to Christianity, is not quite easy to understand. But there was present to the disciples, perhaps, a latent Jewish thought that external prosperity was a sign of the favour of heaven. Then in a town like Capernaum all the leading religious people would be rich (see note *v.* 16). There is always a tendency when religious life is at a low ebb to make disciples of the wealthy and to exalt their saintliness. One of the distinctive marks of Christ's mission was 'preaching to the poor.' Cp. St Paul's words: ἡ κατὰ βάθους πτωχεία αὐτῶν ἐπερίσσευσεν εἰς τὸ πλοῦτος τῆς ἁπλότητος αὐτῶν, 2 Cor. viii. 2. Read also St James v. 1—11.

τίς ἄρα δύναται σωθῆναι; The thought of the disciples still lives: for the guilt of detected wickedness is mainly brought home to the poor, the sins of the rich and educated seldom result in crime, accordingly wealth and intellect make men *seem* better, 'sometimes even supplying the absence of real good with what looks extremely like it.' See a Sermon by Prof. Mozley, on *The Reversal of Human Judgment*, pp. 85—87.

26. ἐμβλέψας. These heart-searching looks of Christ doubtless

gave an effect to His words which it is impossible to recall, but which would never be effaced from the memory of those who felt their meaning.

27—30. THE CLAIM OF THE DISCIPLES.
Mark x. 28—31. Luke xviii. 28—30.

27. ἀφήκαμεν...ἠκολουθήσαμεν. The aorists have their proper force, 'left,' 'followed.'

τί ἄρα ἔσται ἡμῖν; Peter, still not perfect in the Spirit of Christ, suggests a lower motive for following Christ. The answer of Christ shews that all true sacrifice shall have its reward, but all that looks like sacrifice is not really such, therefore 'Many that are first shall be last.' Among the Twelve there was a Judas.

28. ἐν τῇ παλινγενεσίᾳ. These words qualify καθίσεσθε, and are themselves defined by ὅταν καθίσῃ κ.τ.λ.

παλινγενεσία, 'a return to life,' a new birth. Late and rarely used. It expressed a Stoic thought, ἡ περιοδικὴ παλινγενεσία τῶν ὅλων, 'the periodic restitution of all things' (M. Antoninus XI. 1, quoted by Wetstein). Cicero speaks of his return from exile as a παλινγενεσία, *ad Attic.* VI. 6. Similarly Josephus writes: τὴν ἀνάκτησιν καὶ παλινγενεσίαν τῆς πατρίδος ἑορτάζοντες, *Ant.* XI. 3. 9. Both of these thoughts find a place in the N.T. meaning of the word. It is the renewed and higher life of the world regenerated by Christ, succeeding the birth-pangs (ὠδῖνες) which the present generation must suffer. Again, it is the spiritual return of Israel from the bondage of the law, which the Apostle calls ζωὴ ἐκ νεκρῶν, Rom. xi. 15.

Other meanings have been assigned to παλινγενεσία in this passage: (1) The Saviour's return to glory in His Father's kingdom. (2) The glorified life of the Apostles after death.

In Tit. iii. 5 παλινγενεσία is used of the new life the entrance to which is baptism: ἔσωσεν ἡμᾶς διὰ λουτροῦ παλινγενεσίας καὶ ἀνακαινώσεως πνεύματος ἁγίου κ.τ.λ.

καθίσεσθε καὶ αὐτοὶ κ.τ.λ. One aspect of the παλινγενεσία was the new birth of thought which spiritualised every conception. Israel became no longer Israel according to the flesh, to reign was to reign spiritually with Christ. In this spiritual Israel the Apostles have actually sat on thrones. They are the kings and judges of the Church of God.

τὰς δώδεκα φυλάς. Incidentally this expression confirms the connection between the number of the Apostles and the twelve tribes of Israel.

29. This saying would fulfil itself in many ways to the thoughts of the Apostles. (1) In the spiritual relationships, homes, children, and fathers in Christ that sprang up to them wherever the gospel was preached. In a deep sense the thought of '*omne solum forti patria est*' would come home to the first evangelists. (2) As Christ recognised his kindred in those who did the work of His Father, reciprocally His servants found in their brethren, wife, children and lands.

(3) Sometimes self-renouncement created intensified love for others: sometimes kinsfolk forsaken for Christ were in turn won for Christ, and thus increased manifold the gift and love of kinship.

πολλαπλασίονα λήμψεται. St Mark adds μετὰ διωγμῶν. Did this word that explains so much fall so softly at the end of the sentence as to be heard only by the nearest to the Saviour? Was it half forgotten till persecution came?

30. Note the connecting particles—δὲ in this verse, γάρ (xx. 1), οὕτως (xx. 16); δὲ marks the contrasting statement, γάρ introduces the illustration of it, οὕτως closing the illustration reverts to the statement illustrated.

CHAPTER XX.

6. ὥραν after ἑνδεκάτην and ἀργοὺς after ἑστῶτας omitted on the highest evidence.

7. After ἀμπελῶνα omit as אBDLZ the words καὶ ὃ ἐὰν ᾖ δίκαιον λήψεσθε. The thought of v. 4 was probably repeated in a marginal note.

12. The omission of ὅτι after λέγοντες is on the best evidence (אBC²DI versions and fathers).

16. After ἔσχατοι the *textus receptus* has: πολλοὶ γάρ εἰσι κλητοί, ὀλίγοι δὲ ἐκλεκτοί. Here the older MSS. are followed, but CD and the mass of later uncials and many versions and patristic quotations contain the clause, which is certainly genuine, in ch. xxii. 14.

19. ἐγερθήσεται for ἀναστήσεται. Here the evidence is conflicting, the two great uncials א and B are on opposite sides. ἐγερθήσεται (אC*L and other uncials), ἀναστήσεται (BDE and the majority of MSS.).

22. Omit καὶ τὸ βάπτισμα ὃ ἐγὼ βαπτίζομαι βαπτισθῆναι after πίνειν, and καὶ τὸ βάπτισμα ὃ ἐγὼ βαπτίζομαι βαπτισθήσεσθε after πίεσθε (v. 23) with אBDLZ and Origen. The words are genuine in Mark.

28. After this verse an early insertion is found in D and the Curetonian Syriac Version: the first words are ὑμεῖς δὲ ζητεῖτε ἐκ μικροῦ αὐξῆσαι καὶ ἐκ μείζονος ἔλαττον εἶναι, the rest reproduce to a great extent Luke xiv. 8—10. See Scrivener's *Introduction*, pp. 8 and 500.

34. αὐτῶν οἱ ὀφθαλμοὶ omitted (אBDLZ); the insertion is not very easy to account for.

1—16. THE PARABLE OF THE LABOURERS IN THE VINEYARD.
Peculiar to St Matthew.

1. ὁμοία γάρ ἐστιν κ.τ.λ. There are many possible applications of the parable, but the only true explanation of its meaning to the disciples at the time must be reached by considering the question to which it is an answer. The parable is addressed solely to the disciples. The thread of thought may be traced in this way: It is

impossible for a rich man, one who trusts in riches, to enter the kingdom of heaven. The disciples, through Peter, say 'We at any rate left all and followed thee; what shall we have therefore?' Our Lord's answer is (1) partly encouraging, (2) partly discouraging.

(1) All who have in a *true* sense given up all for Christ shall have a great reward (ch. xix. 28, 29).

(2) But (*v.* 30) priority of time is not everything. The parable is given in explanation of this point. Not only will the disciples not be the only called, but they may not reach a higher place or a higher reward than some who follow them at an apparent disadvantage. Still all who work shall have their reward. But they must beware of a spirit very prevalent among hard workers, and not think too much of their own labours, or be displeased because others are equally rewarded.

Possibly the element of time is introduced to illustrate in a parabolic form the *apparent* degrees of service, and to signify that no man can estimate the comparative merit of work for God.

ἀνθρώπῳ οἰκοδεσπότῃ. Cp. ἀνθρώπῳ ἐμπόρῳ, ch. xiii. 45. ἀνθρώπῳ βασιλεῖ, ch. xviii. 23.

ἅμα πρωΐ. This unclassical use of ἅμα with an adverb is modelled on such classical expressions as ἅμα ἕῳ, ἅμα ὄρθρῳ: cp. the late forms ἀπὸ τότε, ἀπὸ πέρυσι, and the classical ἐς ἀεί, ἐς ἔπειτα, ἐς ὀψέ. Winer, p. 525 and note 5.

2. ἐκ δηναρίου. 'On the terms of a denarius,' ἐκ indicates the point from which the bargaining proceeds, the starting point and so the basis of the compact. It is not = δηναρίου, *v.* 13, genitive of price or rate of pay. A *denarius* was the ordinary day's wage of a labourer, that of a common soldier was less, as we learn from Tac., *Annal.* I. 17: nec aliud levamentum quam si certis sub legibus militia iniretur, ut singulos denarios mererent.' A 'florin' or a 'half-crown' would represent the meaning to English readers far more accurately than the 'penny' of the A.V. which gives a wholly wrong impression. See ch. xviii. 28.

μετὰ τῶν ἐργατῶν. Later use of μετά. The classical construction is συμφωνεῖν τινί, or πρός τινα.

4. ὃ ἐὰν ᾖ δίκαιον. This time there is no stipulated sum. The labourers are invited to leave all to the justice of the householder. It is a lesson in faith and an implied rebuke to the spirit displayed in the question, τί ἄρα ἔσται ἡμῖν;

5. πάλιν δὲ ἐξελθών. The householder himself goes forth to summon labourers to his vineyard. Thus not only in the beginning of the gospel, but in every age Christ Himself calls labourers to His work. The Master never stands idle.

6. περὶ τὴν ἑνδεκάτην. The various hours may be referred in the first instance to the call of a Paul, a Barnabas, and a Timothy, who adopted the Cause later than the Twelve. In a secondary and less immediate sense they seem to indicate the successive periods at which the various nations were admitted to the Church of Christ. Was it

unjust that European nations should have equal privileges with the Jews in the Church of Christ, or that Paul should be equal to Peter?

Note the reproach conveyed by ἀργοί. Even they to whom no message has come may do some ἔργον for Christ. See Rom. ii. 10, 14.

8. τῷ ἐπιτρόπῳ. 'To his steward,' as in Luke viii. 3, Ἰωάννα γυνὴ Χουζᾶ ἐπιτρόπου Ἡρώδου. In the only other passage where the word occurs in the N. T., Gal. iv. 2, ἐπίτροποι, 'guardians' of a minor's person, are distinguished from οἰκόνομοι, stewards of his property. The word was Hebraized and used in both these senses by Rabbinical writers (Schöttgen *ad loc. cit.*).

9. ἀνὰ δηνάριον, 'a denarius each.'

11. γογγύζειν and γογγυσμός were ancient Ionic words synonymous with τονθυρίζειν and τονθυρισμός in the Attic dialect. Phrynichus quotes from Phocylides of Miletus χρή τοι τὸν ἑταῖρον ἑταίρῳ | φροντίζειν ἄσσ' ἂν περιγογγύζωσι πολῖται. The word was probably formed from the sound of the cooing of doves, and is therefore like τρύζειν both in original and derived meanings: cp. *Il.* ix. 311, ὡς μή μοι τρύζητε παρήμενοι ἄλλοθεν ἄλλοι. The verb occurs more frequently in St John's gospel, written in an Ionic city, than in any other book of the N. T. Verb and noun are found in the LXX. and in Epictetus and other late writers. See Lob. *Phryn.* 358.

12. μίαν ὥραν ἐποίησαν. Cp. Acts xv. 33, ποιήσαντες δὲ χρόνον ἀπελύθησαν. So *facere* in Latin, 'quamvis autem paucissimos una fecerimus dies tamen multi nobis sermones fuerunt.' Seneca, *Epist.* 67.

ὥραν. 'During the residence in Babylon the Hebrews adopted the division of the day into twelve hours whose duration varied with the length of the day.' Edersheim, *Temple, &c., in the Time of our Lord*, p. 174).

τοῖς βαστάσασι τὸ βάρος τῆς ἡμέρας καὶ τὸν καύσωνα. This may be regarded as man's estimate of his own merits, which is not the divine estimate. The words echo the tone of 'what shall we have?' ch. xix. 27. Man does not here acquiesce in the Judge's decision, as in the parable of the debtors, ch. xviii. What is just does not at first *seem* just, but, as in science many things that seemed untrue are proved to be true, what seems unjust will be proved just when we know all. Further, time is not the only element in service. An act of swift intelligence or of bravery wrought in the space of a single minute has saved an army or a people, and merited higher reward than a lifetime of ordinary service; a Romaic proverb says: τὰ φέρνει ἡ ὥρα ὁ χρόνος δὲν τὰ φέρνει, 'what an hour brings, a year brings not.'

βαστάσασι. Geldart, *Mod. Greek Lang.* pp. 191, 192, notices the frequent occurrence of βαστάζειν in N. T. as a modernism. No word has a longer literary history, it occurs in almost every Greek writer, from Homer to the N. T.

τὸ βάρος τῆς ἡμέρας καὶ τὸν καύσωνα. 'The burden of the day and the hot morning wind.' καύσωνα, emphatic by its position at the end of the sentence, heightens the effect of the picture, and gives reality to it. The labourers hired in the cool evening hours would escape the long toil, and what is more the scorching sirocco which blows from the desert at sunrise. Cp. ἀνέτειλεν γὰρ ὁ ἥλιος σὺν τῷ καύσωνι, James i. 11. It was from the combined influence of sun and sirocco that Jonah 'fainted and wished himself to die:' καὶ ἐγένετο ἅμα τῷ ἀνατεῖλαι τὸν ἥλιον καὶ προσέταξεν ὁ θεὸς πνεύματι καύσωνι συγκαίοντι. Jon. iv. 8. See also Ps. ciii. 16 and Is. xl. 6, and read Dr Thomson's account of the two kinds of sirocco (*Land and Book*, pp. 536, 537). Describing the effect of the sultry sirocco he says: 'The birds hide in thickest shades; the fowls pant under the walls with open mouth and drooping wings; the flocks and herds take shelter in caves and under great rocks; *the labourers retire from the fields*, and close the windows and doors of their houses.'

13. ἑταῖρος is used of any temporary connection, without the idea of affectionate friendship. It is used by a master to his slave; by a guest to a fellow-guest; as a general address on meeting. Cp. ch. xxii. 12 and xxvi. 50, where it is a term of reproachful rebuke.

15. ὀφθαλμὸς πονηρός. The belief in the evil eye still prevails in the East. The envious or malevolent glance is thought to have an injurious effect. Here the sense is: Art thou envious because I am just?

16. οἱ πρῶτοι. Not only as primarily in the parable the first called, but the first in position, knowledge and influence.

17—19. JESUS GOING UP TO JERUSALEM FORETELLS HIS PASSION FOR THE THIRD TIME.

See chs. xvi. 21, xvii. 22, 23; and Mark x. 32—34; Luke xviii. 31—34. St Mark and St Luke add 'shall spit upon him' (Mark); 'shall be spitted on' (Luke); St Matthew alone names 'crucifixion;' St Luke, who mentions only the share which the Gentiles had in the Passion, adds 'they understood none of these things, and this saying was hid from them, neither knew they the things which were spoken.'

The disciples, as Jews, still placed their hopes in the present world: 'what shall we have?' They still thought Jesus might be using a figure of speech. Jesus was alone in the certainty of His awful secret. He had no sympathy from His followers.

For distinctive points in the several predictions of the Passion see notes ch. xvii. 22, 23.

17. παρέλαβεν κατ' ἰδίαν. Cp. Plat. *Apol. Socr.* 26 A, ἰδίᾳ λαβόντα διδάσκειν καὶ νουθετεῖν.

18, 19. Observe the exactness of the prediction; the Sanhedrin shall condemn but not kill, the Gentiles shall scourge and crucify.

19. εἰς τὸ ἐμπαῖξαι κ.τ.λ. The use of εἰς with the infinitive is equivalent to a final clause. Thus the guilt of the crucifixion is fastened on the Jews. St Mark has (τὰ ἔθνη) ἐμπαίξουσιν...ἐμπτύσουσιν κ.τ.λ., denoting independent action on the part of the Gentiles. St Luke, the Gentile Evangelist, passes over in silence the guilt of the

Jewish chief priests and Scribes. That this is not accidental, but part of the evangelistic plan, seems proved by comparing the language of St Peter, Acts iii. 13, 14 (where the crime is pointedly brought home to Israel) with his speech in the house of Cornelius, Acts x. 39, ὃν καὶ ἀνεῖλαν κρεμάσαντες ἐπὶ ξύλου, where the subject of ἀνεῖλαν is tacitly dropped, and the Gentile mode of execution named.

20—28. SALOME'S PRAYER FOR HER SONS, AND THE ANSWER OF JESUS.

Mark x. 35—45. St Mark begins 'And James and John the sons of Zebedee came unto him, saying, &c.' For once St Matthew is more graphic and true to detail than St Mark.

20. ἡ μήτηρ τῶν υἱῶν Ζεβεδαίου. Her name was Salome, as we learn by comparing Matthew xxvii. 56 with Mark xv. 40.

'Among which was Mary Magdalene, and Mary the mother of James and Joses, and the mother of Zebedee's children.' Matthew xxvii. 56.

'Among whom was Mary Magdalene, and Mary the mother of James the less and of Joses, and Salome.' Mark xv. 40.

προσκυνοῦσα. The act of prostration before an Eastern King—though the word 'crucify' might have suggested a slave's death. The Kingdom of heaven introduces many such contrasts.

αἰτοῦσα. She dares not speak until her Lord addresses her.

21. εἰπὲ ἵνα καθίσωσιν κ.τ.λ. Cp. for the thought ch. xix. 28, for the construction ch. i. 22.

22. οὐκ οἴδατε. Observe, Jesus addresses the sons, not the mother.

τί αἰτεῖσθε. There is some force in the middle voice 'ask for yourselves,' or 'cause to be asked.'

πιεῖν...πίνειν. If the difference between the tenses be pressed, the aor. πιεῖν implies a single draught—a taste of the cup, the present πίνειν a continued drinking of the cup.

τὸ ποτήριον ὃ ἐγὼ μέλλω πίνειν, i.e. the destiny in store for me. Cp. among other passages, Is. li. 17, 'Thou hast drunken the dregs of the cup of trembling, and wrung them out,' and Ps. lxxv. 8; the prophets use the figure in reference to the vengeance of God and His wrath against sin. When the disciples afterwards recalled the image it would signify to them the mediation of Christ, who by His passion and death drank for man the cup of suffering. Maldonatus suggests the thought of 'the poison cup,' the cup of death. For the image, cp. 'quot bella *exhausta* canebat.' Verg. *Aen.* IV. 14.

23. τὸ μὲν ποτήριόν μου πίεσθε. James was slain by the sword of Herod Agrippa I. (Acts xii. 2). John suffered many persecutions, but died a natural death. The rebuke of Jesus is very gentle; his soul knew what suffering was in store for the two brothers.

ἀλλ' οἷς ἡτοίμασται. The A.V. is right in understanding δοθήσεται ἐκείνοις 'but it shall be given, &c.,' thus retaining the proper force of ἀλλά, which never = εἰ μή. In Mark ix. 8, οὐκέτι οὐδένα εἶδον ἀλλὰ τὸν Ἰησοῦν μόνον, εἶδον must be repeated in the second clause. See Winer, 566, 728.

24. οἱ δέκα ἠγανάκτησαν. *In his ingenuus Evangelistes.* Bengel. The indignation of the 'Ten' displayed the same spirit and motive as the request of the sons of Zebedee. It seemed as if the jealousies and intrigues of an earthly court were breaking out among the disciples of Jesus.

25. Jesus points out the inversion of earthly ideas in the Kingdom of heaven. This important 'rule' of the Master is thrown into the form of Hebrew parallelism. The antithesis is complete. In the Kingdom of heaven the ambition must be to serve not to reign; that Kingdom is in every way the reverse of the kingdoms of the world. In the latter the gradation of rank is (1) the supreme prince (ἄρχων); (2) the nobles (μεγάλοι); (3) the ministers or attendants (διάκονοι); (4) the slaves (δοῦλοι). In the Kingdom of heaven he that will be the noble must be the minister or attendant; he that will be supreme must be the slave. What Jesus teaches is the dignity of service in the Kingdom of heaven.

κατακυριεύουσιν. The word occurs in two other passages of the N.T. besides the parallel passage (Mark x. 42). In one there is probably a reference to our Lord's words here. St Peter, teaching the same lesson of humility, says (1 Pet. v. 3), μηδ᾽ ὡς κατακυριεύοντες τῶν κλήρων ἀλλὰ τύποι γενόμενοι τοῦ ποιμνίου. In Acts xix. 16 it is used in the account of the sons of Sceva, the possessed man, κατακυριεύσας ἀμφοτέρων ἴσχυσεν κατ᾽ αὐτῶν. Here it is used appropriately of supreme authority, just as κατεξουσιάζειν is appropriate to the delegated authority of the μέγας or subordinate governor. κατεξ. here only and in the parallel passage Mark x. 42. It is a novel compound formed perhaps for the sake of the parallelism.

28. οὐκ ἦλθεν κ.τ.λ. 'Came not to be ministered unto, but to minister,' i.e. (as the parallelism shews) came not to be a μέγας, 'a great one,' but to be a servant (διάκονος), καὶ δοῦναι τὴν ψυχὴν αὐτοῦ λύτρον ἀντὶ πολλῶν, a still further humiliation—to be a slave and render a slave's supreme service—to die a slave's death for others. This view, to which the poetical form of the whole paragraph points, brings the passage into close relation with St Paul's words: μορφὴν δούλου λαβών...ἐταπείνωσεν ἑαυτὸν γενόμενος ὑπήκοος μέχρι θανάτου θανάτου δὲ σταυροῦ (Phil. ii. 7, 8). The conception of a redemption from the slavery of sin through Christ is enriched by that of a life sacrificed to win life for us.

The bearing of such passages as this on the alleviation of slavery in the ancient world should be considered. Their influence towards the abolition of slavery in modern times might have been still greater if the translators had used the word 'slave' rather than 'servant' in the E.V.

λύτρον only here and Mark x. 45 in the N.T., a ransom or price paid for the redemption of a captive from slavery. For the thought cp. Rom. iii. 24; 1 Cor. vi. 20; 1 Pet. i. 19. The English word is derived through the French *rançon* from Lat. *redemptionem*. The act of redeeming is expressed by ἀπολύτρωσις, as δικαιούμενοι δωρεὰν τῇ αὐτοῦ χάριτι διὰ τῆς ἀπολυτρώσεως τῆς ἐν Χριστῷ Ἰησοῦ, Rom. iii. 24; ἐν ᾧ ἔχομεν τὴν ἀπολύτρωσιν διὰ τοῦ αἵματος αὐτοῦ τὴν ἄφεσιν τῶν ἁμαρτιῶν, Eph. i. 7. See also 1 Cor. vi. 20; 1 Pet. i. 19.

ἀντὶ πολλῶν. Cp. 1 Tim. ii. 6, ὁ δοὺς ἑαυτὸν ἀντίλυτρον ὑπὲρ πάντων. The difference between the πολλῶν and the πάντων in these two passages must be explained by the difference between the offer of salvation and the acceptance of it. It is offered to all, accepted by many. The preposition ἀντί denotes the vicarious nature of Christ's death.

29—34. TWO MEN CURED OF BLINDNESS.
Mark x. 46—52. Luke xviii. 35—43.

There are remarkable divergences in the Synoptic accounts of this miracle. Some indeed have supposed that different miracles are related by the Evangelists. St Mark speaks of one man, 'blind Bartimæus, the son of Timæus.' St Luke also mentions one only, but describes the incident as taking place 'when Jesus came nigh unto Jericho,' whereas St Matthew and St Mark state that the miracle was wrought 'as they departed from Jericho.'

It is of course possible that St Luke narrates a separate miracle. The only other solution is to suppose an inaccuracy in an unimportant detail.

29. ὄχλος πολύς. The caravan of Galilæans and others going up to Jerusalem for the Passover. Their numbers would protect them from attack in the dangerous mountain defiles leading to the capital.

Jericho was at this time a flourishing city. It was opulent even in the days of Joshua from the fertility of the surrounding plain, its extensive commerce, and from the metals found in the neighbourhood. Levelled to the ground and laid under a curse by Joshua, it was afterwards rebuilt by Hiel the Bethelite, and regained a portion of its former prosperity. At this period the balsam trade was a principal source of its wealth.

Herod the Great beautified the city with palaces and public buildings, and here he died. After Herod's death Jericho was sacked and burnt, but restored by his son Archelaus.

'Jericho was once more a 'City of Palms' when our Lord visited it. As the city that had so exceptionally contributed to His own ancestry; as the city which had been the first to fall, amidst so much ceremony, before 'the captain of the Lord's host and his servant Joshua,' we may well suppose that His eyes surveyed it with unwonted interest.'—Smith's *Bib. Dict.* Art. 'Jericho.'

30. υἱὲ Δαυείδ. An appeal which reflects the thought that especially signalizes this period of our Lord's ministry, the Son of David entering upon his kingdom.

34. ἠκολούθησαν αὐτῷ. It is probable that very many of those who had received sight and soundness of limb by the word or touch of Jesus followed Him to Jerusalem.

ἠκολούθησαν. Jesus Himself leads the procession. See Luke xix. 28.

CHAPTER XXI.

13. ποιεῖτε (ℵ B L) for ἐποιήσατε (C D E and the later uncials).

19. οὐ μηκέτι BL, whereas ℵ C D and later uncials omit οὐ. The accidental omission, however, is more probable than the insertion of οὐ, and the reading in Mark (μηκέτι without οὐ) may have influenced the text here.

23. ἐλθόντος αὐτοῦ (ℵ B C D L) for ἐλθόντι αὐτῷ, supported by the later authorities.

28—31. The *textus receptus* is here upheld. For a discussion of the *var. lect.* see Hammond, *Text. Crit.* 109.

41. ἐκδώσεται replaces ἐκδόσεται on decisive authority.

46. εἰς has the more ancient evidence, ὡς the more numerous later codices in its favour.

Nisan 9 (Palm Sunday).

1—10. THE ROYAL ENTRY INTO JERUSALEM.

Mark xi. 1—11. Luke xix. 29—40. John xii. 12—19. St Luke alone places here the incident of Christ weeping over Jerusalem (xix. 40—44).

1. εἰς Βηθφαγὴ εἰς τὸ ὄρος τῶν ἐλαιῶν. 'Unto Bethphage and Bethany at the mount of Olives' (Mark). 'Nigh to Bethphage and Bethany at the mount called the mount of Olives' (Luke). Bethany was about two miles from Jerusalem, at the S.E. base of the mount of Olives. Of Bethphage ('place of green or winter figs') no remains have been discovered, and its exact position is unknown. It was probably west of Bethany, and so near to Jerusalem as to be reckoned part of the Holy City. See Godet on St Luke xix. 28. Some have inferred from the order in which Bethphage and Bethany are named that Bethphage was east of Bethany.

2. ὄνον δεδεμένην καὶ πῶλον μετ' αὐτῆς. 'A colt tied whereon never man sat' (Mark and Luke). St Matthew notes the close correspondence with the words of the prophecy; see *v.* 5.

Oriental travellers describe the high estimation in which the ass is held in the East. The variety of Hebrew names for these animals indicates the many uses to which they are put. The prophecy from Zechariah quoted *v.* 4 contains three distinct Hebrew words for an 'ass.' 'Sitting upon an ass (*chamôr*, from a root meaning *red*) and a colt (*ayir*, 'a young male ass') the foal (lit. 'the son') of an ass (*athôn* = 'a she-ass,' from a root meaning 'slow').' 'His lot varies as does the lot of those he serves. The rich man's ass is a lordly beast. In size he is far ahead of anything of his kind we see here at home. His coat is as smooth and glossy as a horse's...His livery is shiny black, satiny white or sleek mouse colour. I never saw one of the dingy red of his Poitou brethren.' Zincke's *Egypt*.

3. The account leads to the inference that the owner of the ass was an adherent of Jesus who had perhaps not yet declared himself. The number of such secret followers was perhaps very large.

4. γέγονεν. 'Is come to pass:' the Evangelist speaks of an event still recent. Bp. Lightfoot points out (*On a Fresh Revision of the N. T.* p. 91) that for γέγονεν of the earlier and contemporary evangelist we find ἐγένετο in a similar expression in the later fourth Gospel.

ἴνα πληρωθῇ. See note ch. i. 22.

5. εἴπατε τῇ θυγατρὶ Σιών. The quotation is partly from Zechariah, partly from Isaiah. The first clause, εἴπατε τῇ θυγατρὶ Σιών, is the LXX. rendering of Is. lxii. 11. The remainder is an abbreviated citation from Zech. ix. 9, where the LXX. version is: [χαῖρε σφόδρα, θύγατερ Σιών, κήρυσσε, θύγατερ Ἱερουσαλήμ·] ἰδού, ὁ βασιλεὺς ἔρχεταί σοι [δίκαιος καὶ σώζων αὐτός] πραῢς καὶ ἐπιβεβηκὼς ἐπὶ ὑποζύγιον καὶ πῶλον νέαν. The words in brackets, omitted in the citation, occur in the Hebrew text as well as in the LXX. In the last clause, where St Matthew differs from the LXX., he agrees with the Hebrew text. It is a proof of St Matthew's feeling for poetical form that the parallelism does not suffer in the shortened form of quotation. The word σώζων which occurs in Zechariah, and ὁ σωτήρ which follows the words quoted from Isaiah, omitted here but suggested by the quotation, would recall 'hosanna' and the name Jesus (σωτήρ). See below.

πραῢς. Cp. ch. xi. 29 and 2 Cor. x. 1, παρακαλῶ ὑμᾶς διὰ τῆς πραΰτητος καὶ ἐπιεικείας τοῦ Χριστοῦ.

7. τὰ ἱμάτια. Their upper garments, the *abbas* of modern Arabs. Cp. with this the throne extemporised for Jehu, 2 Kings ix. 13.

8. ὁ πλεῖστος ὄχλος, the greater part of the crowd.

ἔστρωσαν ἑαυτῶν τὰ ἱμάτια. Instances are recorded of similar acts of respect shewn to Rabbis by their disciples. See Schöttgen, *ad loc.*

9. Ὡσαννά. Hebr. '*hoshiah-na*,' 'save now,' 'save I pray.' *Na* is a particle of entreaty added to imperatives. They are the first words of Ps. cxviii. 25, 'Save now, I beseech thee, O Lord; O Lord, I beseech thee, send now prosperity,' a verse which was sung in solemn procession round the altar at the feast of Tabernacles and on other occasions. As they sang these words it was the custom to carry young branches of palm, and the boughs of myrtle and willow, which were brandished or shaken at intervals. (See Lightfoot, *Hor. Hebr. ad loc.*)

τῷ υἱῷ Δ. Dative of general reference. The 'Salvation' is in some way connected with the Son of David as the cause or instrument of it. See Clyde's *Greek Synt.* § 15.

The multitude recognise the Messiah in Jesus and address to Him the strains and observe the ritual of their most joyous festival. The shouts of '*hosanna*' must have been significant in another way to the disciples. The verb is from the same root and had nearly the same sound as the name Jesus. See note *v.* 5.

The thought of 'salvation' is so closely connected with the feast of Tabernacles, that to this day the name 'hosanna' is given to the bundles of branches, to the prayers at the feast, and to the feast itself. See Wetstein *ad loc.*, and cp. Rev. vii. 9, 10.

St Luke paraphrases the expression for his Gentile readers, 'glory in the highest.'

εὐλογημένος ὁ ἐρχόμενος ἐν ὀνόματι κυρίου. 'According to the accents the rendering would be, "Blessed in the name of the Lord be he that cometh." Dean Perowne on Ps. cxviii. 26. 'He that cometh' (*Habba*) was a recognised Messianic title. St Mark adds 'Blessed be the kingdom of our father David, that cometh in the name of the Lord.' St Luke has 'Blessed be the king that cometh,' &c., and mentions that the multitude 'began to rejoice and praise God *with a loud voice* for all the mighty works that they had seen.' St John reports the words thus, 'Blessed is the King of Israel that cometh in the name of the Lord.' These shouts of triumph—which were the 'gospel' or heralding of the King—must have sounded across the valley of Kedron up to the precincts and porches of the Temple.

'Bethany stands in a shallow hollow scooped out of the shoulder of the hill. The path follows this till the descent begins at a turn where the first view of the Temple is caught. First appeared the castles and walls of the city of David; and immediately afterwards the glittering roof of the Temple and the gorgeous royal arcade of Herod with its long range of battlements overhanging the southern edge of Moriah.'—Tristram's *Topography of Holy Land*.

The entry into Jerusalem must not be regarded as an isolated fact. It was a culminating outburst of feeling. It is clear that the expectation of the kingdom was raised to the highest pitch. The prostration of Salome at the feet of the Prince; the request of her sons; the dispute among the ten; the gathering crowds; the cry of Bartimæus; the triumphal entry, are all signs of this feeling.

For us the Royal Entry is a figure, a parable through external sights and sounds of the true and inner secret kingdom of God.

10. From two passages of Josephus (*B. J.* II. 14. 3 and VI. 9. 3) it appears that 2,900,000, or even a greater number, were present at the passover, numbers encamping in the vicinity of the holy city. We may picture the narrow streets of Jerusalem thronged with eager inquisitive crowds demanding, with Oriental vivacity, in many tongues and dialects, 'Who is this?'

ἐσείσθη, was 'convulsed' or 'stirred' as by an earthquake, or by a violent wind.

(*Monday, Nisan* 10.)

The events of this day extend to v. 23 of this Chapter.

12—14. THE SECOND CLEANSING OF THE TEMPLE.
Mark xi. 15—18; Luke xix. 45, 46.

It is clear from the other Synoptists that the Cleansing of the Temple took place on Nisan 10, not on the day of the entry. St Mark says (xi. 11) that 'when he had looked round about on all things there, the eventide being come he went back to Bethany.' In point of time 'the cursing of the fig-tree' should precede the 'Cleansing of the Temple.' St Mark adds to this account 'would not suffer that any man should carry any vessel through the temple.' St Matthew alone mentions the healing of the lame and the blind, and omits the incident of 'the widow's mite,' recorded by the other Synoptists. The first 'Cleansing of the Temple,' at the commencement of our Lord's ministry, is recorded John ii. 13—17.

12. ἐξέβαλεν κ.τ.λ. It is probable that a look of divine authority, the enthusiasm of His Galilæan followers, and the consciousness of wrongdoing on the part of the traders, rather than any special exercise of miraculous power, effected this triumph of Jesus in His Father's House.

ἀγοράζοντας ἐν τῷ ἱερῷ. The traffic consisted in the sale of oxen and sheep, and such requisites for sacrifice as wine, salt, and oil. The merchandise took place in the Court of the Gentiles.

κολλυβιστής, 'a money changer,' for the classical ἀργυραμοιβός, from κόλλυβος, a small coin (Aristoph. *Pax*, 1200) taken as a fee, hence later 'rate of exchange.' Cp. Cic. *in Verr.* Act II. 3. 78, 'Ex omni pecunia...deductiones fieri solebant: primum pro spectatione et collybo.' Κόλλυβος, Hebr. *kolbon*, is said to be a Phœnician word, which spread with their trade, just as the Genoese or Venetian merchants brought the word *agio* into general use.

τὰς περιστεράς. The definite article here and in the parallel passage (Mark xi. 15) 'indicates the pen of a narrator, who was accustomed to the sight of the doves which might be purchased within the sacred precincts by worshippers'. [Bp Lightfoot, *On a Fresh Revision of the N. T.* p. 109.]

13. γέγραπται. See note, ch. ii. 5.

ὁ οἶκος κ.τ.λ. The passage is quoted from Is. lvi. 7, but, with the omission of the words πᾶσιν τοῖς ἔθνεσιν, these are included in the quotation by St Mark but not by St Luke. The context in Isaiah treats of the admission of the Gentiles: 'Yet will I gather others to him, beside those that are gathered unto him' (*v.* 8).

ποιεῖτε σπήλαιον λῃστῶν, 'are making it a cave of robbers or bandits,' cp. Jer. vii. 11, 'Is this house which is called by my name become a den of robbers in your eyes?' Thus two separate passages of the O. T. are combined in a contrasted or parallel form. The context of these words is strikingly suggestive: 'If ye thoroughly amend your ways and your doings...and *shed not innocent blood in this place*...then will I cause you to dwell in this place in the land that I gave to your fathers for ever and ever.' The caves of Palestine had always been refuges for the lawless, and in the reign of Herod the Great the robbers dwelling in caves had rebelled against him and resisted his power, Jos. *Ant.* I. 12. Possibly this thought may be present here: 'Ye have made my house a stronghold of rebels against God and the Messiah, when it ought to be a garrison of loyal subjects.' Also the disputes of the traffickers resembled the wrangling of bandits in their caves. Comp. $\sigma\pi\eta\lambda.\ \lambda\eta\sigma\tau\hat{\omega}\nu$ with the less severe $\text{o}\hat{i}\kappa o\nu\ \dot{\epsilon}\mu\pi o\rho\text{i}o\nu$ of the first 'cleansing' (John ii. 16).

15, 16. THE CHILDREN'S PRAISE. Peculiar to St Matthew.

15. οἱ ἀρχιερεῖς. (1) The high-priest, (2) those who had served that office, (3) the priests who were members of the high-priest's family, and (4) perhaps, the heads of the twenty-four priestly courses. See note ch. xxvi. 3.

τοὺς παῖδας τοὺς κράζοντας. Children were taught at an early age to join in the temple services. These caught the familiar feast-day strain from the Galilæan pilgrims, and unconscious of all that their words meant, saluted Jesus.

16. ἐκ στόματος νηπίων κ.τ.λ. The LXX. version is followed, the rendering of the Hebrew is: 'out of (or by) the mouths of children and sucklings hast thou founded strength'. Ps. viii. 2. The ruling thought of the opening verses is the glory of God set forth in His works. The 'scarcely articulate' cry of an infant proves, like the heaven and the stars, the power and providence of God. On all these God builds a stronghold against His adversaries, i.e. convinces them of His might. So also the children in the temple attest the truth of God. See Dean Perowne and *Speaker's Commentary* on the passage quoted.

17. Βηθανίαν. 'House of dates,' or, according to Caspari, 'Place of shops, or merchant tents,' on the S.E. of the Mount of Olives, see note *v.* 9. Here Jesus lodged with Lazarus and his sisters.

18—22. THE CURSING OF THE FIG-TREE.

Mark xi. 12—14, and 20—24. St Mark places this incident before the 'Cleansing of the Temple,' see note *vv.* 12—14. It is an interesting and leading instance of miracle and parable in one. The miracle is an acted parable.

18. ἐπείνασεν, late for ἐπείνησεν, the contraction of αε into α instead of η in πεινάω, διψάω and χράω against the Attic rule appears rarely in the later authors, Aristotle, Theophrastus, Plutarch, &c.

19. συκῆν μίαν. Probably a *single* fig-tree, standing alone, and so conspicuous. εἷς is, however, used in Alexandrine Greek for τις, cp. ch. viii. 19, εἷς γραμματεύς, and xviii. 24, εἷς ὀφειλέτης μυρίων ταλάντων, and in Hebrew the numeral 'one' is constantly no more than the indefinite article 'a'.

ἐπὶ τῆς ὁδοῦ. Either (1) *on* the road as ch. x. 27, ἐπὶ τῶν δωμάτων, or (2) hanging *over* the road.

εἰ μὴ φύλλα μόνον. The fig-tree loses its leaves in the winter: indeed it looks particularly bare with its white naked branches. Schöttgen, however, states *ad loc.*, that the Rabbis compared the fig-tree to the law because at every season fruit may be gathered from it; and one species (see Shaw's *Travels*, p. 370, and *Land and Book*, 23) if favoured by the season and in a good position, puts forth fruit and leaves in the very early spring, the fruit appearing before the leaves. This is the 'hasty fruit before the summer' (Is. xxviii. 4), 'the figs that are first ripe' (Jer. xxiv. 2); 'the first ripe in the fig-tree at her first time' (Hos. ix. 10). It was doubtless a fig-tree of this kind that Jesus observed, and seeing the leaves expected to find fruit thereon. At the time of the Passover the first leaf-buds would scarcely have appeared on the common fig-tree, while this year's ripe fruit would not be found till four months later.

The teaching of the incident depends on this circumstance (comp. Luke xiii. 6—9). The early fig-tree, conspicuous among its leafless brethren, seemed alone to make a show of fruit and to invite inspection. So Israel, alone among the nations of the world, held forth a promise. From Israel alone could fruit be expected; but none was found, and their harvest-time was past. Therefore Israel perished as a nation, while the Gentile races, barren hitherto, but now on the verge of their spring-time, were ready to burst into blossom and bear fruit.

ἐξηράνθη. From St Mark we gather that the disciples observed the effect of the curse on the day after it was pronounced by Jesus.

20. ἐθαύμασαν. It was rather the power and wonder of the act than the deeper significance of it that moved the disciples. The miracle was to them an 'act of power' (δύναμις), or a 'wonder' (τέρας), rather than a 'sign' (σημεῖον). Yet Jesus follows the turn their thoughts take, and teaches that prayer and faith will remove mountains of difficulty, see ch. xvii. 20.

21. διακριθῆτε. Passive form with meaning of middle voice; cp. ἀπεκρίθην. διακρίνειν, (1) lit. 'to separate:' (2) 'to discern' or 'discriminate.' See ch. xvi. 3, when it is used of discerning the face of the sky, and Acts xv. 9, οὐδὲν διέκρινεν μεταξὺ ἡμῶν τε καὶ αὐτῶν. (3) In a judicial sense 'to decide,' and in middle to 'get a question decided at law,' 'to litigate.' (4) Hence generally 'to dispute,' διεκρίνοντο πρὸς αὐτὸν οἱ ἐκ περιτομῆς, Acts xi. 2. (5) Thus 'to dispute or question with oneself,' 'to doubt,' as here and Rom. iv. 20, εἰς δὲ τὴν ἐπαγγελίαν τοῦ Θεοῦ οὐ διεκρίθη τῇ ἀπιστίᾳ; cp. Acts x. 20, where the context illustrates this passage. The last usage is not classical.

23—27. THE AUTHORITY OF CHRIST IS QUESTIONED.

Mark xi. 27—33; Luke xx. 1—8.

Tuesday, Nisan 11.

23. ἐν ποίᾳ ἐξουσίᾳ ταῦτα ποιεῖς; καὶ τίς σοι ἔδωκεν τὴν ἐξουσίαν ταύτην; The second question is not a mere repetition of the first.

Jesus is asked (1) what kind of authority He possesses—human or divine? (2) By whose agency this authority was bestowed? No one had a right to teach unless 'authority' had been conferred upon him by the scribes.

24. ἐρωτήσω ὑμᾶς κἀγὼ λόγον ἕνα. This form of argument was usual. The question of the Elders was really an attack. Jesus meets that attack by a counter-question which presented equal difficulties in three ways—whether they said from heaven or of men, or left it unanswered. To say from heaven was equivalent to acknowledging Jesus as Christ, to say from men was to incur the hostility of the people, to be silent was to resign their pretensions as spiritual chiefs of the nation.

26. διὰ τί οὐκ ἐπιστεύσατε αὐτῷ; A clear proof (1) that the priests had kept aloof from John though he was of the priestly caste; and (2) that John pointed to Jesus as the Messiah. For πιστεύειν αὐτῷ, cp. Dem. *Phil.* II. 6, οἱ θαρροῦντες καὶ πεπιστευκότες αὐτῷ, 'Those who have no fears and believe Philip.' See note ch. xviii. 6.

27. Note the sincerity of the οὐ λέγω in contrast with the evasion of οὐκ οἴδαμεν.

28—32. THE PARABLE OF THE TWO SONS, AND THE EXPLANATION OF IT. Peculiar to St Matthew.

St Luke omits the parable, perhaps as referring especially to Israel. The parable follows in close connection with the question as to the teaching of John.

The parables and discourses that follow deal no longer with the distant future of the Church, but with an immediate present. The subjects illustrated are—(1) The rejection of the Messiah. (2) The rejection of the Jews as a nation. (3) The Judgment, (*a*) which has already begun; (*b*) which will be enacted terribly at the siege of Jerusalem; and (*c*) finally fulfilled at the end of the world.

Observe throughout the *separation* which is implied in the Judgment—the dividing sword which Christ brings—the Jewish race and the world, each parted into two great divisions—the two sons—the two parties of husbandmen or of guests—the wise and foolish virgins—the sheep and the goats—the talents used and misused.

It is the last act in a divine drama of surpassing interest and full of contrasts. The nation, and especially the Pharisees, who are the leaders of thought, triumphant to external sight, are hurrying to destruction, impelled by a hidden fate in the face of clear warnings; while Christ the King, Who seems to be vanquished and done to death, is really winning an eternal victory.

28. τέκνα δύο, representing the sinners who first refused to do God's will, but repented at the preaching of John; and the Pharisees who, having 'the righteousness which is of the law' (Phil. iii. 9), professed to do God's will but did it not. Both are sons. God still cares for both. The Pharisees may follow the sinners into the kingdom of

God (v. 31). Paul was still a Pharisee; Nicodemus the Pharisee was still a secret follower of Christ.

29. μεταμεληθείς, 'having changed his mind,' felt regret but not repentance or *metanoia*, a deeper and more lasting feeling: see ch. iii. 2.

According to a well-supported reading (see Crit. Notes) the cases of the two sons are reversed. The first agrees but goes not, the second refuses but afterwards works in the vineyard. The variation is interesting, because it points to an interpretation by which the two sons represent Jew and Gentile.

30. ἐγὼ κύριε. Observe the alacrity and politeness of this answer compared with the blunt οὐ θέλω of the first: ἐγὼ draws attention to the contrast.

31. προάγουσιν. Are (now) going before you.

32. Ἰωάννης. The mention of John points to the connection between this parable and the preceding incident.

ἐν ὁδῷ δικαιοσύνης. A Hebrew expression. Cp. τὴν ὁδὸν τοῦ θεοῦ, ch. xxii. 16; ὁδὸν σωτηρίας, Acts xvi. 17. The Christian doctrine was called in a special sense ἡ ὁδός (Acts xix. 9, 23).

ἰδόντες, viz. that the publicans and the harlots believed him.

οὐ μετεμελήθητε. Did not even change your minds, much less repented in the deeper sense; see above, v. 29.

τοῦ πιστεῦσαι. For this consecutive formula see note ch. ii. 13.

33—46. THE WICKED HUSBANDMEN.
Mark xii. 1—12; Luke xx. 9—19.

No parable interprets itself more clearly than this. Israel is represented by an image which the prophets had made familiar and unmistakeable—the Vineyard of the Lord. The householder who planted the Vineyard and fenced it round signifies God the Father, Who created the nation for Himself—a peculiar and separate people. The husbandmen are the Jews, and especially the Pharisees, the spiritual leaders of the Jews. The servants are the prophets of God, the Son is the Lord Jesus Christ.

33. ἐφύτευσεν ἀμπελῶνα. Cp. the parable in Isaiah v. 1—7, where the description is very similar to this. See also Ps. lxxx. 8—16; Jer. ii. 21; Ezek. xv. 1—6. The vine was adopted as a national emblem on the Maccabean coins.

φραγμὸν αὐτῷ περιέθηκεν, defended it with a stone wall or with a fence of prickly pears. St Luke makes no mention of the separating hedge. Israel was separated throughout her history politically, and even physically, by the natural position of Palestine.

ὤρυξεν ἐν αὐτῷ ληνόν. The winepress was often dug or hewn out of the limestone rock in Palestine. There were two receptacles or vats.

The upper one was strictly the press or ληνός (Matthew), the lower one the winevat or ὑπολήνιον (Mark) into which the expressed juice of the grape passed. The two vats are mentioned together only in Joel iii. 13, 'The press (*gath*) is full, the vats (*yekabim*) overflow' (quoted in *Bibl. Dict.*, see art. 'Winepress').

πύργον. Probably a wooden booth raised on a high platform, in which a watcher was stationed to guard the grapes.

Neither the winepress nor the tower seems to have any special significance in the interpretation of the parable.

ἐξέδοτο αὐτὸν γεωργοῖς. This kind of tenancy prevails in many parts of Europe. It is known as the *metayer* system, the arrangement being that the occupier of the land should pay to the landlord a portion—originally half—of the produce. The system existed in England for about sixty years at the end of the fourteenth century. Before the Revolution of 1790 nearly the whole of the land of France was rented by metayers. At the time of our Lord's ministry it was customary for the Romans to restore conquered lands on condition of receiving a moiety of the produce. Fawcett's *Manual of Political Economy*, p. 223; Rogers' *Political Economy*, p. 168.

ἀπεδήμησεν. Left his home.

35. ὃν μὲν ἔδειραν, ὃν δὲ ἀπέκτειναν, κ.τ.λ. See ch. xxiii. 35.

δέρειν, (1) 'to flay,' (2) then, from the effect of scourging, 'to beat.' In the second sense it is classical only in the comic poets; cp. Vulgar English 'to hide.' In Acts xvi. 22 the Prætors bid the lictors 'scourge' (ῥαβδίζειν) Paul, who, referring to the outrage, says: δείραντες ἡμᾶς δημοσίᾳ (v. 37). λιθοβολεῖν, in LXX. for classical λεύειν.

37. ἐντραπήσονται. Non-classical future. ἐντρέπειν, (1) 'to turn,' (2) then 'turn a person,' cause him to avert his gaze through shame, fear, respect, &c., (3) so 'to put to shame:' οὐκ ἐντρέπων ὑμᾶς γράφω ταῦτα, 1 Cor. iv. 14. εἰς τοσοῦτον ἐνέτρεψαν τὴν σύγκλητον βουλήν, Ælian, *V. H.* 3. 17. And in passive, ἵνα ὁ ἐξ ἐναντίας ἐντραπῇ, Tit. ii. 8, 'that the adversary be put to shame;' (4) in middle voice, 'to let oneself be turned or influenced' by a person or thing, through some feeling of awe, reverence and the like; (*a*) with a genitive denoting the source of the action or feeling (Donaldson's *Greek Grammar*, 448), τί βαιὸν οὕτως ἐντρέπει τῆς συμμάχου, Soph. *Aj.* 90; (β) or later with an accusative denoting the object of reverence or concern, as here and Luke xviii. 2, τὸν θεὸν μὴ φοβούμενος καὶ ἄνθρωπον μὴ ἐντρεπόμενος.

38. σχῶμεν τὴν κληρ., 'seize on his inheritance,' ἔχειν being used in the technical sense which the English 'seize' also bears: cp. ἔχων τε καὶ κεκτημένος, *Antig.* 1265. Thomas Lawrence (1568—1583) suggested as a translation of this passage, 'take possession or seisin upon his inheritance.' (Moulton's *History of the English Bible*.)

39. ἐξέβαλον ἔξω τοῦ ἀμπελῶνος. Words that recall the crucifixion of Jesus outside the city of Jerusalem.

41. λέγουσιν αὐτῷ. An interruption from the listening crowd, which marks the intense interest with which these parables were heard. The indignation of the bystanders is aroused as if it were a tale of actual life.

κακοὺς κακῶς ἀπολέσει. Cp. εἰ μὴ φράσεις γὰρ ἀπό σ' ὀλῶ κακὸν κακῶς, Aristoph. *Plut.* 65. A frequent formula in the classics.

42. ἐν ταῖς γραφαῖς. Ps. cxviii. 22 (*vv.* 25, 26 of the same psalm are quoted above, *v.* 9, where see note); the psalm 'was probably composed for the first celebration of the Feast of Tabernacles after the completion of the Second Temple' (Neh. viii. 13—18). (Dean Perowne.) The original reference was to a stone used in the erection of the second Temple. The 'corner stone' is the Jewish nation rejected at first, afterwards restored from captivity. Christ transfers this image to His Church, formed of Jew and Gentile alike (see Meyer), which, though despised at first, was destined to succeed to the spiritual supremacy of Israel.

In Acts iv. 11, Eph. ii. 20, 1 Pet. ii. 6, Christ Himself is the head-corner-stone; but the two applications are not inconsistent, for Christ was the Representative first of the Jewish Nation (ch. iv. 15, ii. 1—11 (3)), then of the Church. Cp. also Isai. xxviii. 16, 'I lay in Zion for a foundation a stone, a tried stone, a precious corner stone, a sure foundation.'

λίθον. *A* stone rather than *the* stone. The builders probably rejected many stones.

κεφαλὴν γωνίας. The stone that connects the two walls at the top and supports the roof.

αὕτη. Either (1) agreeing with κεφαλή, or (2) a Hebraism. In Hebrew there is no neuter form, and it is possible that αὕτη of the LXX. may be due to the influence of Hebrew grammar. This corruption is found in some passages of the LXX., Ps. xxvi. 4, μίαν ᾐτησάμην παρὰ Κυρίου, ταύτην ἐκζητήσω τοῦ κατοικεῖν κ.τ.λ., where the Vulgate has 'unam petii a domino hanc requiram.' See Maldonatus *ad loc.*

43. διὰ τοῦτο. Because of this rejection.

44. ὁ πεσὼν ἐπὶ τὸν λίθον κ.τ.λ. Lightfoot, *Hor. Hebr.*, sees here a reference to the custom of stoning: 'the place of stoning was twice as high as a man. From the top of this one of the witnesses, striking him on his loins, fells him to the ground: if he died of this, well; if not, another witness threw a stone upon his heart.' The second process was inevitably fatal.

But it is perhaps better to refer the image to an earthenware vessel (1) falling to the ground when it would be shattered, or (2) crushed by a stone when it would be bruised into atoms.

συνθλασθήσεται. A late classical word, in N. T. here and Luke xx. 18 (the parallel passage). The simple verb θλάω is Epic (Homer and Hesiod) and Alexandrine (Theocritus).

λικμήσει· λικμᾶν. (1) 'to winnow,' Hom. *Il.* v. 499, ὡς δ' ἄνεμος ἄχνας φορέει ἱερὰς κατ' ἀλωάς, | ἀνδρῶν λικμώντων. (2) 'To cause to disappear' like chaff, so 'to destroy utterly,' ἀναλήψεται δὲ αὐτὸν καύσων καὶ ἀπελεύσεται καὶ λικμήσει αὐτὸν ἐκ τοῦ τόπου αὐτοῦ, Job xxvii. 21. Cp. Dan. ii. 44, where the rendering in Theodotion's version is λεπτυνεῖ καὶ λικμήσει πάσας τὰς βασιλείας, in the LXX. πατάξει καὶ ἀφανίσει τὰς βασιλείας ταύτας. λικμήσει therefore = ἀφανίσει. The translation of the A.V., 'grind to powder,' which probably is due to *conteret* of the Vulgate, cannot be justified. The Vulgate rendering may be due to a confusion between the nearly simultaneous processes of threshing and winnowing. '*Conterere*' is very applicable to the former process. See a good description in 'Conder's *Tent Work in Palestine*, II. 259.

The meaning as applied to Christ appears to be: Those to whom Jesus is a 'rock of offence' (1 Peter ii. 8; Isai. viii. 14) in the days of his humiliation shall have great sorrow: but to incur his wrath when He comes to judge the earth will be utter destruction.

43, 44. For remarks on the poetical form of these verses see Bp Jebb's *Sacred Literature*, pp. 127—130. The climax is perfect. The first couplet (ἀρθήσεται...καρποὺς αὐτῆς) expresses loss, the second (καὶ ὁ πεσὼν...λικμήσει αὐτόν) infliction of pain: in the first the sense of loss is enhanced by the sight of the possession passing to another, in the second pain is succeeded by utter destruction.

46. ζητοῦντες αὐτὸν κρατῆσαι. The Sanhedrin aimed at two things: (1) to seize Jesus quickly, for the Passover (during which no hostile measures could be taken) was close at hand; and because Jesus might be expected to quit Jerusalem after the feast. (2) To seize Him apart from the people; for the Galilæans would suffer no one to lay hands on their King and Prophet. Treachery alone enabled the Jews to secure their end.

CHAPTER XXII.

10. νυμφῶν for γάμος on the evidence of אB*L.

13. ἄρατε αὐτὸν καὶ omitted before ἐκβάλετε on the highest authority. Alford suggests that the insertion was made from 'the difficulty presented by a person bound hand and foot being cast out, without some expression implying his being taken up by the hands of others.'

23. λέγοντες for οἱ λέγοντες, on the best authority—אBD (C is defective here), and many other uncials.

25. γήμας replaces the unclassical γαμήσας, probably an insertion when the latter form became the usual one.

32. Against the repeated θεός, θεός the most ancient testimony is conclusive; between ὁ θεός and θεός the great MSS. are divided, θεός (אD), ὁ θεός (BLΔ). Tischendorf omits the article, Lachmann and Tregelles retain it.

35. Omit καὶ λέγων before διδάσκαλε with אBL, versions, and patristic evidence.

38. The article before μεγάλη is a gain to the sense. It is strongly supported.

44. ὑποκάτω for ὑποπόδιον on conclusive evidence.

1—14. THE PARABLE OF THE ROYAL MARRIAGE FEAST.
Peculiar to St Matthew.

The parable recorded by St Luke (xiv. 16—24), though similar to this in some respects, differs in its context and special teaching and in many details.

As of the other parables of the Passion, the primary intention of this regards the present and the immediate future. The parable falls into two divisions, (1) *vv.* 1—7; (2) *vv.* 8—14. In the first (1) the servants are John Baptist and the first disciples of Christ; the feast is the Kingdom of God, or the Christian Church; the invited guests, who refuse to come, are the Jews; the vengeance taken was literally fulfilled at the siege of Jerusalem, A.D. 70. (2) This division relates to the preaching of the Gospel to the Gentiles. As in the Net (ch. xiii. 47) or in the Corn-field (ch. xiii. 24), worthy and unworthy are mingled until the King separates.

2. γάμους, 'a marriage feast.' εἰλαπίνη ἠὲ γάμος; ἐπεὶ οὐκ ἔρανος τάδε γ' ἐστίν, *Od.* I. 226.

3. ἀπέστειλεν τοὺς δούλους. This was in accordance with Eastern custom. Cp. Esther v. 8, and vi. 14.

οὐκ ἤθελον, 'refused,' the imperfect expresses the successive refusals: cp. singuli introducebantur, Livy x. 38.

7. ὠργίσθη. For a subject to scorn the summons to the royal feast implied disloyalty and rebellion.

τὰ στρατεύματα, 'troops.' Cp. Luke xxiii. 11, where the word is used of Herod's soldiers, σὺν τοῖς στρατεύμασιν αὐτοῦ, and Rev. ix. 16. The soldiers of Titus literally achieved the purposes of God.

9. τὰς διεξόδους τῶν ὁδῶν. διεξ. here only in N.T. Either (1) the outlets of the streets, i.e. the central place into which the streets converge. This has the authority of Chrysostom. Hom. 69, *in Matt.* (see Trench, *Parables*, p. 230, and cp. Schleusner). Or (2) roads leading out of the city into the country. Cp. αἱ διέξοδοι τοῦ θανάτου (Ps. lxvii. 20), 'the means of escape from death.' (3) Cross-roads or through passages connecting the main streets. Hdt. I. 199, διέξοδοι πάντα τρόπον ὁδῶν. Cp. Eur. *Andr.* 1086, φαεννὰς ἡλίου διεξόδους, 'the sun's path across the sky,' and Ps. i. 3, τὰς διεξ. τῶν ὑδάτων, 'streams branching out in several directions.' (1) and (2) are perhaps most suggestive in the interpretation of the parable. The gospel should pass into the regions beyond the city of the king, or be preached in such meeting places of the nations as Rome, Antioch and Corinth.

10. ἐξελθόντες οἱ δοῦλοι. The 'servants' are the earliest Christian missionaries, Paul, Silas, Barnabas and others.

εἰς τὰς ὁδούς. Cp. this with εἰς τὰς διεξόδους above. The servants' performance did not rise to the thoroughness of the Master's command. See Bp Lightfoot, *On a Fresh Revision of the N.T.*, p. 68.

πονηρούς τε καὶ ἀγαθούς. Who will always co-exist in the Church on earth.

11. ἔνδυμα γάμου. The festive robe (χλανὶς γαμική, Arist. *Av.* 1693) which in this instance it is supposed the master of the feast himself provided, so that there was no excuse. The supposition is required by the conditions of the parable, and gifts of robes were, and still are, too common in the East to make this a difficulty, though no clear evidence of this practice appears in books of Eastern travel. This man is the representative of a class—the bad (v. 10), who are not clothed in righteousness.

12. ἑταῖρε. See note, ch. xx. 13.

πῶς εἰσῆλθες. 'How didst thou presume to enter'.

ἐφιμώθη. See v. 34.

13. τὸ σκότος τὸ ἐξώτερον. The dark wild night without moon or stars, the cold and gloom of which would contrast terribly with the warmth and light within; or perhaps the dark dungeon outside the brightness of the banqueting-hall.

ὁ κλαυθμὸς κ.τ.λ. See note ch. viii. 12.

15—22. THE TEMPTATION OF THE HERODIANS. THE TRIBUTE MONEY.
Mark xii. 13—17; Luke xx. 20—26.

15. παγιδεύειν, 'to ensnare,' as a fowler ensnares birds: used here only in N. T.

All the previous attempts had been to discredit Jesus as a religious teacher; the present is an attempt to expose Him to the hostility of the Roman government. Will He follow Judas the Gaulonite, in disowning all human authority? or will He acquiesce in the Roman rule? In the one case He would incur the condemnation of Pilate, in the other the scorn of His Galilæan followers.

16. τοὺς μαθητὰς αὐτῶν μετὰ τῶν Ἡρωδ. An unnatural coalition, for the Pharisees represented the patriotic resistance to all foreign power; whereas the Herodians, as their name implies, supported the Herodian dynasty, and, as the context shews, acquiesced in the Roman rule. With the form of the name cp. Cassiani, Sertoriani, the partisans of Cassius, Sertorius; so also Christiani. The Herodians are not named except in the first two Gospels; nor does Josephus include them in his account of Jewish sects. They were probably numerically insignificant,

and may indeed have consisted merely of a few renegade Jews, who belonged to Herod's court. See ch. xi. 8.

οἴδαμεν ὅτι ἀληθὴς εἶ. Nothing could exceed the insidious hypocrisy of this attack on Jesus. His enemies approach Him as a teacher whom they trust.

οὐ γὰρ βλέπεις εἰς πρόσωπον, i.e. 'Thou art not moved by external appearance; neither wealth, power, nor prestige will influence thy decision.' In the parallel passage St Luke has οὐ λαμβάνεις πρόσωπον, a rendering of a Hebrew expression meaning literally 'to raise the face,' or 'to accept the face.' So in O.T., in a good sense, 'to receive kindly;' in N.T., always in a bad sense, 'to look on the outside of things,' external condition, or 'to shew partiality.'

17. ἔξεστιν δοῦναι κῆνσον Καίσαρι ἢ οὔ; The injunction, 'thou mayest not set a stranger over thee' (Deut. xvii. 15), was interpreted to mean that the Jews should pay tribute to no foreign power. But their history exhibits them as tributary in turn to Assyria, Babylon, Egypt and Persia.

The question was an attempt to see whether Jesus would adopt the watchword of the Zealots—'there is no king but God.' This special tribute, the poll-tax levied on each individual, was particularly offensive to the patriotic party among the Jews. The foreign word (*censum*) would in itself have a hateful sound to Jewish ears, and was probably purposely used by the Pharisees and Herodians for that reason. The translator of the Aramaic gospel (see Introd. ch. ii.) does not suffer the point to be lost by giving a Greek equivalent for *censum*.

18. γνούς, 'having recognised.'

19. τὸ νόμισμα τοῦ κήνσου. The current coin of the census, i.e. the coin in which the tax is paid.

δηνάριον. A *denarius*, bearing probably the image of Tiberius. The Jewish coins were not impressed with the effigy of their kings. Herod Philip, alone of his family, out of flattery to the Emperor, had caused his coins to be stamped with the likeness of Cæsar.

20. ἐπιγραφή. 'Inscription' or 'legend.'

21. ἀπόδοτε οὖν τὰ Καίσαρος Καίσαρι. 'Pay back *therefore*.' The Jewish doctors laid down the principle that 'He is king whose coin passes current.' St Paul expands this principle, which underlies our Lord's answer (Rom. xiii. 1 foll.). The claim of earthly rulers to obedience rests on the delegated authority of God. Cæsar has a claim to tribute because his ἐξουσία is of God—he is God's viceroy. In the providence of God the Jews had become subject to Cæsar, therefore the lower duty of tribute was due to Cæsar, the higher duty of obedience was due to God. 'Cæsar and God' are not therefore opposed terms, as they are often taken to be. Submission is due to Cæsar *because* submission is due to God. It is the Suzerain enjoining proper submission to his vassal-prince, 'the powers that be are ordained of God.'

καὶ τὰ τοῦ θεοῦ τῷ θεῷ. The claim of the kingdom of heaven is equally cogent. As the subjects and 'husbandmen' of God, the Jews owe Him service and fruit. Neither in regard to Cæsar nor to God do the facts of the case leave any doubt as to what is due, and to whom, nor does obedience to the one of necessity clash with obedience to the other.

The deep importance of the words consists in this. They define the nature of the Kingdom of God. It is not a Jewish theocracy excluding Rome, but a divine supreme kingdom existing side by side with the Roman empire, or any other empire or kingdom, not an *imperium in imperio*, but an *imperium supra imperium*.

23—33. THE SADDUCEES TEMPT JESUS. THE CONDITION OF THE FUTURE LIFE.

Mark xii. 18—27; Luke xx. 27—39.

23. Σαδδουκαῖοι. See note ch. iii. 7. This is the only direct contact of the Sadducees with Jesus.

λέγοντες. 'Then came Sadducees saying,' i.e. with their argument that, &c. For the omission of article before λέγοντες see Crit. Notes *supra*; its absence before Σαδδουκαῖοι implies that they did not come as a class. Cp. οἱ Φαρισαῖοι, v. 15.

24. ἐπιγαμβρεύσει ὁ ἀδελφὸς κ.τ.λ. This is sometimes called the 'levirate law,' from Lat. *levir*, a brother-in-law; see Deut. xxv. 5. 'The law on this subject is not peculiar to the Jews, but is found amongst various Oriental nations, ancient and modern.' *Speaker's Comment.*, Deut. xxv. 5.

29. μὴ εἰδότες, i.e. 'because ye do not know' (μὴ states the ground or reason of the mistake) (1) *the Scriptures*, which affirm the doctrine; nor (2) *the power of God*, which is able to effect the resurrection, and after the resurrection to create a new order of things in the new world.

30. ἐν τῇ ἀναστάσει, i.e. in that world or that phase of existence which begins with the resurrection.

The logical difficulty vanishes; for in this respect the analogy between the present world and the next does not hold good. The danger of the argument from analogy always lies in the fallacy that the things compared are alike at each point.

32. Jesus appeals to the Pentateuch when arguing with the Sadducees, with whom the books of Moses had the greatest authority.

Stated in a logical form the argument is: God is a God of the living *only*, but He is the God of Abraham, therefore Abraham is living. The same deduction from the words was made by the later Rabbinical writers.

The principle on which the proposition 'God is the God of the living' rests, lies deeper. It depends upon the close relation between the life of God and the life of His children. The best illustration of the truth is the parable of the Vine (John xv. 1—8). The connection between the living God and the patriarchs, whose God He is, is as close as that between the vine and its branches. If the vine lives its branches live. If God is living and immortal the patriarchs are living and immortal. If the branches die they cease to belong to the vine; if the patriarchs were dead they would have ceased to have any relation to God, or God to them. Cp. John xiv. 19, ὅτι ἐγὼ ζῶ καὶ ὑμεῖς ζήσετε, and Rom. v. 10, σωθησόμεθα ἐν τῇ ζωῇ αὐτοῦ. Hence in a deep sense God is termed ὁ ζῶν, 'the living One,' in whom all live.

So far there has been proof of immortality.

The communion of saints in and with God carries with it immortality.

The resurrection of the body is not expressly proved. But as Maldonatus observes *ad loc.* those only denied the resurrection of the body who denied immortality; therefore one argument proved both. In Jewish thought to raise the dead implied reunion of soul and body. This appears from Hebr. xi. 19 λογισάμενος ὅτι καὶ ἐκ νεκρῶν ἐγείρειν δυνατὸς ὁ θεός, ὅθεν αὐτὸν καὶ ἐν παραβολῇ ἐκομίσατο. Bengel adds the thought that God is God not of Abraham's spirit only, but also of his body on which the seal of the promise was set, ...'ergo ii qui Deum habent vivere debent et qua parte vivere intermiserant reviviscere in perpetuum.'

33. διδαχῇ. Teaching.

ἐξεπλήσσοντο. The imperfect well expresses the thrill of amazement passing through the crowd from one to another.

34—40. THE GREATEST COMMANDMENT.

Mark xii. 28—34; comp. Luke x. 25—28.

In Luke the question is asked at an earlier period of the ministry, after the return of the Seventy; and the meaning of 'neighbour' is illustrated by the parable of the 'Good Samaritan.'

34. ἐφίμωσεν. Literally 'gagged' or 'muzzled,' hence silenced completely, not only for the moment. φιμός is a muzzle for dogs, or a nose-band in a horse's bridle: φιμοὶ δὲ συρίζουσι βάρβαρον τρόπον. Æsch. *Sep. c. Th.* 463. The verb is rare in the classics, ἤν...φιμώσητε τούτου τῷ ξύλῳ τὸν αὐχένα, Arist. *Nubes* 592, 'fasten in the stocks.' The figurative sense is Hellenistic. φιμοῦν is used (v. 12) of the guest; Mark i. 25 and Luke iv. 35, of silencing a demon; Mark iv. 39, of silencing a storm; 1 Cor. ix. 9 and 1 Tim. v. 18, of muzzling an ox.

35. εἷς ἐξ αὐτῶν νομικός, i.e. an interpreter of the written law, as distinguished from the 'traditions' or unwritten law.

37. See Deut. vi. 5.

καρδίᾳ...ψυχῇ...διανοίᾳ. St Mark and St Luke add ἰσχύς. In Deut. the words are heart...soul...might. καρδία includes the emotions, will, purpose; ψυχή, the spiritual faculties; διάνοια the intellect, the thinking faculty. This greatest commandment was written on the phylactery which the 'lawyer' was probably wearing. See ch. xxiii. 5.

St Mark (vv. 32—34) adds the lawyer's rejoinder and the commendation of Jesus, 'thou art not far from the Kingdom of God.'

40. ἐν ταύταις κρέμαται. The classical expression would be ἐκ τούτων κρέμανται.

41—46. THE SON OF DAVID.

Mark xii. 35—37; Luke xx. 41—44.

44. κύριος τῷ κυρίῳ μου. Ps. cx. 1. According to the Hebrew, 'Jehovah said to Adoni,' i.e. to my sovereign Lord, the Messiah, the Son of David. The repeated κύριος...κυρίῳ seems to be an indication of what must certainly have been the fact, that Jesus avoided (as all Jews do now) the pronunciation of the name Jehovah, using instead Adonai, which is represented by Κύριος.

εἶπεν. The Hebrew word translated 'said' implies divine inspiration, hence 'in spirit' (v. 43). Dean Perowne translates, 'the oracle of Jehovah unto my Lord.'

Κάθου ἐκ δεξιῶν μου. As My co-regent, having power equal to Mine. This verse is quoted in 1 Cor. xv. 25; Heb. i. 13, and x. 12, 13. (Cp. for the expression ch. xx. 21.) The Psalm was always regarded by the Jews as Messianic, hence their silence and inability to answer without acknowledging the divinity of Jesus.

κάθου for κάθησο in late prose and in comedy, see Veitch, sub voc. κάθημαι, and Winer, p. 98, with Dr Moulton's note. The same form occurs Luke xx. 42; Acts ii. 34; Jas. ii. 3; and in LXX.

CHAPTER XXIII.

3. τηρεῖν, omitted after εἴπωσιν ὑμῖν.

ποιήσατε καὶ τηρεῖτε for τηρεῖτε καὶ ποιεῖτε.

4. καὶ δυσβάστακτα omitted after βαρέα. The grounds of omission are not quite decisive. ℵ (μεγάλα βαρέα) and L omit the words but BD and the majority of uncials and versions retain them.

αὐτοὶ δὲ τῷ δακτύλῳ αὐτῶν] The restoration of αὐτοὶ to the text emphasises the contrast.

5. In textus receptus τῶν ἱματίων αὐτῶν follows κράσπεδα. Rightly omitted.

7. ῥαββί, twice in textus receptus against best evidence.

8. διδάσκαλος, for καθηγητής. All the leading editors against ℵ*DL, and others following ℵ^caB and a majority of codices.

13. The *textus receptus* here inserts the words which stand for certain in Mark xii. 40; Luke xx. 47. Rejected on decisive evidence here.

17. ἁγιάσας for ἁγιάζων. The aorist, which is well established, gives a more accurate sense.

19. μωροὶ καὶ before τυφλοί. The omitted words were probably inserted from *v*. 17. They occur in the important MSS. B and C.

23. τὸ ἔλεος for τὸν ἔλεον, ἀφεῖναι for ἀφιέναι; and 30, ἤμεθα for ἦμεν twice; 35, ἐκχυννόμενον for ἐκχυνόμενον: all well supported changes.

35. The difficult words υἱοῦ Βαραχίου are omitted in ℵ and in two *evangelistaria* or service books, viz. 6, 13 and in 59 first hand only, also by Eus. Jerome *ad loc.* says: 'in Evangelio quo utuntur Nazareni Barachiæ filium Joiadæ reperimus scriptum.'

CH. XXIII. 1—36. A PROPHETIC ODE, DENOUNCING THE PHARISEES AND THE RELIGIOUS HYPOCRISY OF THE AGE. Each division is marked by its special beauty of poetical form.

1—7. STRENGTH AND WEAKNESS OF THE PHARISEES. They are the successors of Moses, *v*. 2; but they say and do not, 3—7.

Only a part of this discourse appears in the other Synoptics; for this portion cp. Mark xii. 38—40; Luke xi. 43—46, xx. 46, 47.

2. ἐπὶ τῆς Μωϋσέως καθέδρας ἐκάθισαν. i.e. succeed him as teachers. For sitting as the posture of a teacher cp. ch. v. 1.

3. ποιήσατε. 'Do the special act enjoined.' τηρεῖτε, 'continue to observe.'

4. δεσμεύουσιν...κινῆσαι αὐτά. The picture is of the merciless camel- or ass-driver, who makes up (δεσμεύειν) burdens, not only heavy but unwieldy and so difficult to carry, and then placing them on the animals' shoulders, stands by indifferent, raising no finger to lighten or even adjust the burden.

The three steps or degrees in the triplet answer to three points in the Pharisaic condemnation. They make hard rules, they impose them upon others, and themselves fail to observe them. Contrast with this the Saviour's invitation ch. xi. 30, ὁ ζυγός μου χρηστός, καὶ τὸ φορτίον μου ἐλαφρόν ἐστιν.

δεσμεύειν, is to tie in bundles, as corn into sheafs: ᾤμην ὑμᾶς δεσμεύειν δράγματα ἐν μέσῳ τῷ πεδίῳ, Gen. xxxvii. 7. That this is the correct force of δεσμεύειν, rather than that of binding on the shoulder (Schleusner), appears partly from the parallelism which requires the three acts, and partly by the thing meant—the procedure of the Pharisees.

5. τὰ φυλακτήρια. Literally, 'defences,' and in late Greek 'amulets' or 'charms.' The Hebrew name, *tephillin*, which is still in use, signifies 'prayers.' They were slips of parchment inscribed with four portions of the Law (Ex. xii. 3—10, 11—17; Deut. vi. 4—9; xi. 13—21) enclosed in little cases or boxes made of calf-skin, and fastened by leather straps to the left arm and on the forehead, in accordance with a literal interpretation of Ex. xiii. 16 and Deut. vi. 8. To make the phylacteries, or rather the cases which contained them, broad and conspicuous was to assume a character of superior piety, for the phylacteries were symbols of devotion.

Jesus does not prohibit the practice of wearing phylacteries, but the ostentatious enlargement of them. It is thought by many that our Saviour Himself wore phylacteries.

μεγαλύνουσιν τὰ κράσπεδα. Strictly, the fringe of the tallith, or cloak: another instance of ostentation; the blue threads in the fringe the colour of the sky—were a type of heavenly purity. Our Lord Himself wore the fringed tallith (see ch. ix. 20); the offence of the Pharisees consisted in enlarging the symbolical fringes.

τὰ κράσπεδα. Cp. Theocr. II. 53, τοῦτ' ἀπὸ τᾶς χλαίνας τὸ κράσπεδον ὤλεσε Δέλφις. The singular is rare.

6. τὴν πρωτοκλισίαν. The most honourable place at the triclinium. It was at this period the Jewish custom for men to recline at meals in Roman fashion on couches (triclinia), each containing three seats, and each seat having its special dignity. See Becker's *Gallus Excursus* II., Hor. *Sat.* II. 8.

τὰς πρωτοκαθεδρίας. 'The chief seats;' the same word is translated 'uppermost seats' (Luke xi. 43), and 'highest seats' (Luke xx. 46). They were seats or 'stalls' placed in the highest part of the synagogue in front of the ark containing the roll of the law, and opposite to the entrance. The Elders sat facing the people, a fact which gives force to πρὸς τὸ θεαθῆναι τοῖς ἀνθρώποις. See Dr Ginsburg's Art. in *Bib. Educator*, Vol. II. pp. 263, 264. The poor had no seats in the synagogue. From James ii. 1 foll. we learn that the same evil distinction soon invaded the Christian Church: Σὺ κάθου ὧδε καλῶς, καὶ τῷ πτωχῷ εἴπητε· Σὺ στῆθι ἐκεῖ, ἢ κάθου ὑπὸ τὸ ὑποπόδιόν μου. James ii. 3.

7. τοὺς ἀσπασμούς. The customary greetings. The article is disregarded in A.V.

ῥαββί. Literally, my great [one], lord. This title, with which the great doctors of the law were saluted, was quite modern, not having been introduced before the time of Hillel. The true teaching on this point is found in the Talmud, 'Love the work but hate the title.'

8—11. THE CONTRAST OF CHRISTIAN CONDUCT.

8. ὑμεῖς δὲ μὴ κληθῆτε ῥαββί. The emphasis is on ὑμεῖς. Ye as Scribes of the Kingdom of Heaven must not be as the Jewish Scribes.

ὑμεῖς ἀδελφοί ἐστε. How completely the Church accepted her Founder's words may be seen by the frequent use of ἀδελφοί in the

Epistles, and the very rare use of διδάσκαλοι, though it appears from 1 Cor. xii. 13 that διδάσκαλος was adopted as a title in the Christian Church.

One result has been the levelling of all distinctions in Christ; another the sense of a common brotherhood, slowly spreading, not yet perfect in achievement, gradually making slavery impossible, gradually linking nations in a common sympathy.

10. καθηγητής. 'A guide,' then a dignified name for 'a teacher,' used in this sense by Plutarch of one who did not care to be called a παιδαγωγός and so adopted the more high-sounding title of καθηγητής· τροφεὺς Ἀλεξάνδρου καὶ καθηγητὴς καλούμενος. Strabo, p. 674, says of one of the Stoic philosophers at Tarsus, καίσαρος καθηγήσατο καὶ τιμῆς ἔτυχε μεγάλης. In the N.T. the word does not occur again. It is discarded as a title. In Soph. *Greek Lex.* it is said to be used for an abbot or prior of a monastery in a *Synaxarion* (see note ch. xviii. 20). καθηγητής is modern Greek for 'professor.'

11. Cp. ch. xx. 26, 27.

Seven woes denounced against the Scribes and Pharisees. 13—36. The leading words are ὑποκριταί—τυφλοί—μωροί.

14. κλείετε τὴν βασιλείαν τῶν οὐρανῶν. In allusion to the symbolic 'key of knowledge' given to the Scribe on admission to the order. They use their keys to shut rather than to open the doors of the Kingdom.

15. περιάγετε, 'go about,' 'traverse.' The word is used of our Lord's 'circuits' in Galilee, ch. iv. 23; ix. 35.

προσήλυτον. Literally, one who approaches, hence, 'a worshipper,' (cp. Heb. x. 1), 'a convert.' The word occurs in three other passages Acts ii. 11, vi. 5, xiii. 43. Elsewhere proselytes are called οἱ σεβόμενοι, εὐλαβεῖς and οἱ φοβούμενοι θεόν. The word occurs in no classical author. It is used in the LXX. for 'one who comes,' i.e. a stranger (Hebr. *ger*), like the classical ἐπήλυτος and ἔπηλυς. Cp. Ex. xii. 48, νόμος εἷς ἔσται τῷ ἐγχωρίῳ καὶ τῷ προσελθόντι προσηλύτῳ ἐν ὑμῖν. The passage shows the word would easily pass from the meaning of 'stranger' to that of one who conforms to the law—a convert. The Pharisee, St Paul, carried with him into his new faith the same zeal, with a higher motive. He describes (2 Cor. xi. 26) 'the perils by water, perils in the city, and perils in the wilderness,' which this eager 'compassing of land and sea' brought to him.

Judaism has been classed among the non-missionary religions. This is true at the present day, and through most of its history. Indeed, Rabbinical sayings display jealousy of proselytes. On the other hand, John Hyrcanus imposed Judaism on Edom at the point of the sword (1 Macc. v. 65, 66). The conversion is recorded of whole tribes in Arabia, and on the shores of the Caspian. Also, it appears from the Acts that the number of proselytes in Asia Minor and in Greece was considerable. And in later days Solomon Malco, a Portuguese Jew, was burnt to death under Charles V. on a charge of proselytizing.

Probably the proselytism in the text is connected with the charge of rapacity; the Pharisees seeking to convert wealthy Gentiles, over whom they obtained influence.

The decrees recorded by Tacitus and Suetonius against the introduction of Jewish rites point to the same spirit of proselytism: 'actum et de sacris Ægyptiis Judaicisque pellendis,' Tacit. *Ann.* II. 85. The result was the deportation of 6000 'libertini generis' to Sardinia. 'Extimas cæremonias Ægyptios Judaicosque ritus compescuit (Tiberius)', Suet. *Tib.* 36.

υἱὸν γεέννης διπλότερον ὑμῶν. In accordance with a tendency in new converts to exaggerate the external points of the creed which they adopt, Gentile proselytes strained to the utmost the worst features of Pharisaism.

υἱὸν γεέννης. 'Subject to the doom of Gehenna,' i.e. either (1) to the severest sentence known to the Jewish law—to be slain and then flung into the accursed valley of Hinnom; or (2) worthy of being cast into the Gehenna of the after world—that division of Sheol (Hades) into which the accursed were thrown. But the two thoughts were so closely connected in the Jewish mind as scarcely to be separable. In neither view should the expression be literally pressed. Oriental speech delights in strong expressions, and the absence of superlatives in Hebrew necessitated the use of such phrases. Comp. 'a son of death,' i.e. 'worthy of death,' or 'doomed to die.'

Observe the contrast between verses 14 and 15. The Pharisee suffers not those who are entering the kingdom to come in, to their salvation—whereas he spares no effort to bring in a single proselyte, to his ruin. The verbal correspondence between τοὺς εἰσερχομένους... εἰσελθεῖν and προσήλυτον is probably not unintentional though it does not appear to have been noticed.

16. ὁμόσῃ ἐν τῷ ναῷ. In classical Greek the thing on which the oath is taken is in the accusative or genitive with κατά. (τι or κατά τινος.) ναός, the 'holy place,' not as in A.V. the temple.

ἐν τῷ χρυσῷ τοῦ ναοῦ, i.e. the offerings made to the Temple, called 'Corban,' or 'devoted;' the use of that word made an oath binding, see ch. xv. 5. Tacitus (*Hist.* v. 8) says of the Temple at Jerusalem: 'illic immensæ opulentiæ templum.'

18. θυσιαστηρίῳ, 'altar of sacrifice.' This word is an instance of the care taken to exclude certain heathen associations from Jewish and Christian religious thought. βωμὸς is used once only in N.T., Acts xvii. 22, and then of a pagan altar. In the LXX. θυσιαστήριον is used of the altar of Jehovah except Judges vi. 25, where the altar of Baal is called θυσιαστήριον. The altar 'Ed' is called βωμός, this however being not a sacrificial altar but 'a heap of witness.' The two words are distinguished, 1 Macc. i. 54, ᾠκοδόμησαν βδέλυγμα ἐρημώσεως ἐπὶ τὸ θυσιαστήριον· καὶ ἐν πόλεσιν Ἰούδα κύκλῳ ᾠκοδόμησαν βωμούς. Elsewhere βωμὸς is used of the 'high places' of paganism, ἀπολεῖται καὶ Δηβὼν οὗ ὁ βωμὸς ὑμῶν, Is. xv. 2. Josephus does not observe the distinction; he uses βωμὸς of the altar in the temple.

23. ἀποδεκατοῦτε τὸ ἡδύοσμον καὶ τὸ ἄνηθον κ.τ.λ. 'Mint and rue and all manner of herbs,' (Luke xi. 42). Zeal in paying tithes was one of the points of reform under the Maccabees.

ἀποδεκατοῦν. Unclassical, (1) 'to pay tithes,' here and Luke xviii. 12, ἀποδεκατῶ πάντα ὅσα κτῶμαι. (2) 'to exact tithes,' καὶ τὰ σπέρματα ὑμῶν καὶ τοὺς ἀμπελῶνας ὑμῶν ἀποδεκατώσει, 1 Sam. viii. 15 and Heb. vii. 5.

According to Lightfoot (*Hor. Hebr. ad loc.*) the tithes required by law were: (1) A fifth for the priests. (2) A tenth of the remainder for the Levites. (3) A further tenth of the remainder either to be eaten at Jerusalem or to be redeemed. Other views however are taken; see Smith's *Bib. Dict.* III. 1517. These payments would be often evaded, and to be able to say ἀποδεκατῶ πάντα ὅσα κτῶμαι implied an exceptional strictness.

τὸ ἄνηθον, either = 'anise' as in E.V., or 'dill,' a plant similar in appearance, and used like anise as a sedative medicine and for cooking purposes.

τὸ κύμινον. See Isaiah xxviii. 25, 27, where the special method of beating out cummin seeds is named. 'It is used as a spice, both bruised to mix with bread, and also boiled in the various messes and stews which compose an Oriental banquet.' Tristram, *Nat. Hist. of Bible*.

τὰ βαρύτερα τοῦ νόμου. The distinction between great and small precepts of the law is found in the Talmud. Schöttgen gives many instances, p. 183. One saying is: 'Observance of the lesser precepts is rewarded on earth; observance of the greater precepts is rewarded in heaven.' The rival schools differed in their classification. Note, therefore, the Saviour's enumeration of the 'weightier precepts,'—κρίσις, ἔλεος, πίστις. Cp. Luke xi. 42, παρέρχεσθε τὴν κρίσιν καὶ τὴν ἀγάπην τοῦ θεοῦ. (ἔλεος and πίστις represent two aspects of ἀγάπη τοῦ θεοῦ.)

24. διϋλίζοντες. Wetstein quotes from Galen: εἶτα ἄρας ἀπὸ τοῦ πυρὸς καὶ διυλίσας εἰς ἕτερον ἀγγεῖον ἐᾷ ψυγῆναι.

The sense of contrast and the humour of the illustration are brought out by the antithetic position of the words. In the first respect the illustration, ch. vii. 3—5, is somewhat similar; for the contrast of opposites cp. ch. xiii. 31 and xix. 24.

25. παροψίς, 'a side dish on which viands are served.' The classical meaning is 'a side dish' in the sense of the viands themselves. See Lob. *Phryn.* 176. The word was introduced into Latin: 'quam multa magnaque paropside cenat.' Juv. *Sat.* III. 142.

ἔσωθεν δὲ γέμουσιν κ.τ.λ. Observe how swiftly and naturally Eastern speech passes from the figurative to the literal. The outside of the cup and platter is the external behaviour and conduct of the Pharisee, the inside of the cup is his heart and real life.

ἐξ ἁρπαγῆς καὶ ἀκρασίας, 'of rapacity and incontinence.' ἀκρασία occurs also 1 Cor. vii. 5. It is opposed to ἐγκράτεια, Arist. *Eth. Nic.* VII. 4. 2. ἐκ is either (1) redundant, denoting that out of which the vessel is filled, and helping out the meaning of the genitive (comp. the gradual introduction of *de* to express the Latin genitive, resulting in the French genitive with *de*), or (2) denotes result, 'are full as the result of' &c. With either meaning cp. John xii. 3, ἡ δὲ οἰκία ἐπληρώθη ἐκ τῆς ὀσμῆς τοῦ μύρου.

26. φαρισαῖε τυφλέ. The change to the singular number indicates a personal and individual self-examination.

τυφλέ. Schöttgen notes that certain among the Pharisees veiled their faces in order that no glimpse of the wicked world or of evil men or of any other thing might tempt them to sin. Sometimes they even injured themselves by self-imposed blindness; these were called Pharisæi percutientes vel illidentes. This would give point to the expression in the text and be another sign of that earnest humour that results from a profound sense of the discrepancy between things as they really are and as they seem to be.

27. τάφοις κεκονιαμένοις. In Luke the comparison is to 'graves that appear not,' by walking over which men unconsciously defile themselves. To avoid this ceremonial defilement the Jews carefully whitewashed the graves or marked them with chalk on a fixed day every year—the fifteenth of Adar. The custom still exists in the East. One of the spiteful devices of the Samaritans against the Jews was to remove the whitewash from sepulchres in order that the Jews might be contaminated by walking over them.

29. κοσμεῖτε τὰ μνημεῖα τῶν δικαίων. Lightfoot (*Hor. Hebr. ad loc.*) quotes from the Jerusalem Gemara: 'They do not adorn the sepulchres of the righteous, for their own sayings are their memorial.' Yet it appears, on the same authority (Lightfoot, *Hor. Hebr.*), that a portion of the Temple-offerings was devoted to the purpose of building the tombs of the prophets. So that the Jews with a show of reverence disobeyed the noble precepts of their own traditions.

30. ἤμεθα. The same form occurs Acts xxvii. 37 and Gal. iv. 3 (ℵD*) and Eph. ii. 3 (ℵB). In the classics ἤμεθα is not found, and the instances of the sing. ἤμην (the usual form in N. T.) are rare and doubtful. See Veitch, p. 195.

31. μαρτυρεῖτε ἑαυτοῖς. You call yourselves children, and indeed you *are* children of those who slew the prophets. You inherit their wickedness in compassing the death of the Prophet of the Lord. See note ch. iii. 7.

32. καὶ nearly = 'and so.' See Dr Moulton's note, Winer, p. 540, cp. Phil. iv. 9, 12.

33. γεννήματα ἐχιδνῶν. See note ch. iii. 7.

34. ἀποστέλλω...προφήτας καὶ σοφοὺς καὶ γραμματεῖς. Marking the continuity of the Christian with the Jewish Church.

ἀποκτενεῖτε καὶ σταυρώσετε. Kill, directly as Stephen (Acts vii. 59), indirectly as James (Acts xii. 2), and crucify, by means of the Roman power, as Symeon, second Bishop of Jerusalem (Eus. *H. E.* III. 32).

μαστιγώσετε ἐν ταῖς συν. See note ch. iv. 23.

ἀπὸ πόλεως εἰς πόλιν. As Paul pursued Christians to Damascus; as he was himself driven from Antioch in Pisidia, from Iconium, from Philippi, and from Thessalonica.

35. ἐκχυννόμενον. For the form see ch. x. 28 crit. notes.

ἀπὸ τοῦ αἵματος Ἄβελ κ.τ.λ. If the reading υἱοῦ Βαραχίου be retained (it is omitted in the Sinaitic MS.) a difficulty arises; for the Zacharias, whose death 'in the court of the house of the Lord' is recorded 2 Chron. xxiv. 20—22, was the son of Jehoiada. The words, however, do not occur in Luke xi. 51, and are possibly interpolated. Zechariah the prophet was a son of Barachias: but of his death no record is preserved. Another explanation has been offered. At the commencement of the Jewish War with Vespasian a Zacharias, son of Baruch, was slain in the Temple by two zealots (Jos. *B. J.* IV. 5. 4). Accordingly many commentators have thought that Jesus spoke prophetically of that event. The coincidence is remarkable, but the aorist ἐφονεύσατε is decisively against the explanation. The deed had already been accomplished.

The space from Abel to Zacharias, son of Jehoiada, covers the whole written history of the Jews; for the Jewish Canon, not being arranged in order of time, began with Genesis and closed with the second book of Chronicles.

ἐφονεύσατε. The present generation shares in the guilt of that murder.

μεταξὺ τοῦ ναοῦ καὶ τοῦ θ. 'Between the sanctuary and the altar.' Even the priests were not allowed at all times to tread that sacred part of the Temple Courts.

37—39. The Fate of Jerusalem.

37. Ἰερουσαλήμ, Ἰερουσαλήμ. From Luke xiii. 34, it appears that our Lord spoke these words in a different connection at an earlier period of His ministry. For the pathetic reiteration of the name, cp. ch. xxvii. 46.

Ἰερουσαλήμ. See note ch. ii. 3. The Aramaic form for Jerusalem appears here only in Matthew; it is the usual form in Luke. The use of the termination -ήμ in this one passage by St Matthew indicates the exact reproduction of our Lord's words. Probably the very form— Aramaic, not Greek—employed by our Lord is retained. Cp. the use of the Hebrew form Σαούλ rather than Σαῦλε, Acts ix. 4 and xxvi. 14, for the same reason.

ἀποκτείνουσα...λιθοβολοῦσα. Recalling the precise expressions of ch. xxi. 35.

ὑπὸ τὰς πτέρυγας. Schöttgen *ad loc.* observes that converts to Judaism were said to come 'under the wings of the Shechinah.' That thought may be contained in the words of Christ. Many times by His prophets He called the children of Jerusalem to Himself—the true Shechinah—through whom the latter glory of the house was greater than the former.

οὐκ ἠθελήσατε. Note the change to the plural.

38. ὁ οἶκος ὑμῶν, i.e. Jerusalem, rather than the Temple. ὑμῶν, 'yours,' no longer God's.

ἔρημος. Omitted in the Vatican Codex, but too strongly supported to be removed from the text.

39. γάρ explains ἔρημος of v. 38. The Temple is desolate, for Christ, who is the Lord of the Temple, leaves it for ever.

ἕως ἂν εἴπητε. Till, like the children in these Temple-courts, ye recognise Me as the Messiah. See ch. xxi. 15. The words of Jesus, and the place, and the anger of the Scribes, may have recalled to some the scene in which Jeremiah, on the same spot, denounced the sin of Israel, called them to repentance, and foretold the destruction of the Temple: 'then will I make this house like Shiloh'...'and all the people took him, saying, Thou shalt surely die,' Jer. xxvi. 1—8.

CHAPTER XXIV.

1. ἐπορεύετο, placed after ἀπὸ τοῦ ἱεροῦ. The change is certain and much improves the sense.

2. Ἰησοῦς, omitted before εἶπεν, and ἀποκριθεὶς brought in.

3. τῆς, omitted before συντελείας (אBCL). The omission has the effect of bringing the παρουσία into closer connection with the συντέλεια τοῦ αἰῶνος.

7. καὶ λοιμοί, omitted after λιμοί. Probably an insertion from Luke, not in the oldest MSS.

36. After οὐρανῶν Lachmann and Tischendorf add οὐδὲ ὁ υἱός. The reading is supported by אBD, many cursives and Latin codices, but is probably an insertion from Mark.

41. μύλῳ, for μύλωνι. The authority for the latter is weak. μυλών is the commoner word, strictly = 'a place for a mill,' μύλος a 'mill' or a 'millstone.'

43. The unclassical διορυγῆναι, which however is read in B and several uncials, gives place to διορυχθῆναι (Hdt. Plat. Xen.).

45. οἰκετείας, for θεραπείας (Luke xii. 42) on good authority. The rare word οἰκετείας could not have been inserted as an explanation, whereas this may well have been the case with θεραπείας. א reads οἰκίας.

49. ἐσθίῃ...πίνῃ, for ἐσθίειν...πίνειν, on quite decisive evidence.

CH. XXIV. 1—22. PREDICTION OF THE FALL OF JERUSALEM.

Mark xiii. 1—end. Luke xxi. 5—36.

This chapter opens with the great discourse of Jesus, which is continued to the end of ch. xxv. That discourse contains (1) a prediction of the fall of Jerusalem, (2) a prediction of the end of the world, (3) Parables in relation to these predictions.

It is difficult to determine the limits of the several portions.

(1) Some of the earliest Fathers referred the whole prophecy to the end of the world. (2) Others held that the fall of Jerusalem was alone intended down to the end of v. 22. (Chrysostom, Theophylact, Euthymius.)

In an interesting monograph founded on this view the Rev. W. Sherlock has shown a parallelism between the two divisions:

THE FALL OF JERUSALEM (*vv.* 5—22).
1. False Christs and false prophets (*vv.* 5, 11).
2. Persecution and apostasy (*vv.* 9, 10, 12).
3. Wars, famine, pestilence (*vv.* 6, 7).
4. Great tribulation (*v.* 21).
5. The abomination of desolation (*v.* 15).
6. The escape of the Christians (*vv.* 16—18).

THE SECOND ADVENT (*vv.* 23—31).
1. False Christs and false prophets (*vv.* 23, 24).
2. Dangers even to the elect (*v.* 24).
3. Distress of nations (*v.* 29).
4. The sun and moon darkened (*v.* 29).
5. The sign of the Son of man (*v.* 30).
6. The salvation of the elect (*v.* 31).

(3) Augustine, Jerome, and Beda, followed by Maldonatus, receive this view in a modified form, holding that while the two events were conceived by the Apostles as coincident in point of time, and while our Lord's words appeared to them to be describing a single great catastrophe, it is now possible in the light of the past history to detect the distinctive references to the first and the second event.

(4) Another arrangement of the prophecy is: (i) A general answer of the question to the end of *v.* 14; (ii) a specific reference to the fall of Jerusalem, 15—28; (iii) in *v.* 29 a resumption of the subject of (i).

1. ἐπορεύετο. For the reading see critical notes. He was going on his way across the Valley of Kidron, when his disciples came to Him and stopped Him, and prayed Him to look at the buildings of the Temple where full in view it rose with its colonnades of dazzling white marble, surmounted with golden roof and pinnacles, and founded on a substructure of huge stones. It was in the freshness of recent building, 'white from the mason's hand,' still indeed incomplete, but seeming by its very beauty and solidity to protest against the words of doom just spoken.

Josephus (*B. J.* v. 2) gives a full description of the Temple which is well worth reading in the original. He speaks of the brilliant effect of 'the golden plates of great weight which at the first rising of the sun reflected back a very fiery splendour, causing the spectator to turn away his eyes as he would have done at the sun's own rays. At a distance the whole Temple looked like a mount of snow fretted with golden pinnacles.'

τὰς οἰκοδομὰς τοῦ ἱεροῦ. 'The various parts of the Temple-building.' οἰκοδομή, according to Phrynichus, non-Attic, either (1) 'a building' for the more usual and classical οἰκοδόμημα, a form not found in N.T., or

(2) 'act of building,' for which the classical and older forms οἰκοδομία (or οἰκοδομιά) and οἰκοδόμησις do not occur in the N.T., or (3) 'edification.' This beautiful figure for the orderly and continuous growth of religious life in individuals and in a society appears to be a purely Christian thought; it is a frequent one with St Paul, ἄρα οὖν τὰ τῆς εἰρήνης διώκωμεν καὶ τὰ τῆς οἰκοδομῆς τῆς εἰς ἀλλήλους, Rom. xiv. 19; εἰς οἰκοδομὴν καὶ οὐκ εἰς καθαίρεσιν ὑμῶν, 2 Cor. x. 8. If the image did not actually spring from the Temple, it gained force and frequency from the building, the stately growth of which must have been an ever prominent sight and thought with the existing generation of Jews; the perfect joining of the stones (πᾶσα οἰκοδομὴ συναρμολογουμένη), —which gave the appearance of one compact mass of rock,—and the exceeding beauty of the whole, suggested an inspiring figure for the progress and unity of the Church.

2. **οὐ μὴ ἀφεθῇ ὧδε λίθος ἐπὶ λίθον.** Compare with the complete ruin of the Temple at Jerusalem, the still magnificent remains of temples at Karnak and Luxor, Baalbec and Athens. The Temple was destroyed by fire, notwithstanding every effort made to save it by Titus. For a vivid description of this last awful scene in the history of the Temple, see Milman, *History of the Jews*, II. Bk. xvi.

3. **οἱ μαθηταί.** St Mark names the four, Peter and James and John and Andrew.

τῆς σῆς παρουσίας. 'Thy presence,' used with the same special meaning, 1 Thess. ii. 19. Jas. v. 7. 2 Pet. i. 16. 1 John ii. 28. The precise word 'coming,' or 'advent,' which the Church has adopted in reference to the second 'presence' of Christ, has no exact equivalent in this prophecy.

συντελείας τοῦ αἰῶνος. See ch. xiii. 39, 40.

5. **ἐγώ εἰμι ὁ Χριστός.** The Christ, the Messiah. The appearance of false Messiahs shall be the first sign. St John bears witness to the fulfilment of this sign: 'Even now are there many antichrists, whereby we know that it is the last time.' 1 John ii. 18.

6. **πολέμους καὶ ἀκοὰς πολέμων.** The second sign. Philo and Josephus describe the disturbed state of Judæa from this date to the siege of Jerusalem. Massacres of the Jews were perpetrated at Cæsarea, at Alexandria, in Babylonia and in Syria.—See Milman's *History of the Jews*, Bks. xii.—xv. Tacitus, characterising the same period, says 'opus adgredior opimum casibus, atrox præliis, discors seditionibus, ipsa etiam pace sævum.' *Hist.* I. 2.

ὁρᾶτε μὴ θροεῖσθε. 'Look,' i.e. observe, 'be not afraid.' Not as in A.V., see that ye be not troubled.

The classical meaning of θροεῖν is 'to cry aloud,' hence 'to speak,' 'declare.' The later use of θροεῖσθαι is connected either with the womanish shrieks of fear (mid. voice), cp. θρέομαι, or with the thought of terrifying with a shout (passive voice). The word occurs Mark xiii. 7, the parallel passage to this, and 2 Thess. ii. 2, where it is also used in relation to the παρουσία, and probably in direct reference to this passage: ἐρωτῶμεν δὲ ὑμᾶς, ἀδελφοί, ὑπὲρ τῆς παρουσίας τοῦ Κυρίου ἡμῶν Ἰησοῦ Χριστοῦ καὶ ἡμῶν ἐπισυναγωγῆς ἐπ' αὐτὸν εἰς τὸ μὴ ταχέως σαλευθῆναι ὑμᾶς ἀπὸ τοῦ νοός, μηδὲ θροεῖσθαι κ.τ.λ.

δεῖ expresses divine necessity, conformity to God's plan; cp. ch. xxvi. 54.

7. **λιμοὶ καὶ σεισμοὶ κατὰ τόπους.** The commentators enumerate instances of all these calamities recorded by the contemporary historians.

8. **ὠδίνων.** Literally, pains of travail, that preceded the birth of a new order of things, a fresh *æon*, the παλινγενεσία.

9. **θλίψιν.** Rare in the classics, the figurative sense is late in the noun but appears in the verb, Aristoph. *Vespæ* 1289 and elsewhere. In Phil. i. 17 the literal 'pressure' of the chain is thought of: θλίψιν ἐγείρειν, 'to make my chain gall me' (Bp. Lightfoot). θλίψις is preferable to θλῖψις, though the latter is the Attic accentuation. The tendency of later Greek was to shorten the penultimate. See Winer, pp. 56, 57 and Dr Moulton's note.

10. **σκανδαλισθήσονται.** Shall fall, fail in loyalty, be tempted to forsake the faith.

μισήσουσιν ἀλλήλους. Disappointed hopes will bring about a disruption of Christian unity and love.

11. **ψευδοπροφῆται.** At the siege of Jerusalem 'false prophets suborned by the Zealots kept the people in a state of feverish excitement, as though the appointed Deliverer would still appear.' Milman's *History of the Jews*, II. 371. Cp. 1 John iv. 1, 2, 3.

12. **ψυγήσεται ἡ ἀγάπη τῶν πολλῶν.** 'The love of the majority shall grow cold.' The use by our Lord in this passage of a word which expressed the highest and most enduring (1 Cor. xiii. 8, 13) of Christian graces, and which was the bond of the future Christian society is in itself prophetic. ἀγάπη in this sense occurs here only in the Synoptic gospels (τὴν ἀγάπην τοῦ θεοῦ, Luke xi. 42, is not an exception). Yet from the fourth gospel we learn that this word or its Aramaic equivalent was very frequently on the Lord's lips. In the Epistles no word meets us more often, though the occurrence of ἀγάπη in the LXX. seems to imply that it was a vernacular word before it took its place in literature; its absence from classical Greek enabled it to enter Christian thought and literature unstained (ἔρως has no place in the vocabulary of the N.T.). To the Greek, however (though Christianity raised ἀγάπη far above the range of pagan thought), it would recall the purest and highest conceptions of Greek poets—the pure love of brother and sister—the devotion of a child to her father—duty to the living—respect for the dead. The drama of *Antigone* is the story of ἀγάπη triumphant: οὔτοι συνέχθειν ἀλλὰ συμφιλεῖν ἔφυν (Soph. *Ant.* 523) breathes the spirit of Christianity. As a Christian word ἀγάπη meant the love of the Christian brotherhood to one another and to God, and the outward symbols of that love in the Eucharist (ἀγάπην ποιεῖν 'to celebrate the "love-feast"') in 'charity'

or 'alms' (see note on δικαιοσύνη, ch. vi. 1) in the salutation or holy kiss (see Sophocles' *Lex.*, *sub voc.*).

13. ὁ ὑπομείνας. 'He that endureth.' The meaning of ὑπομένειν and ὑπομονή like ἀγάπη grows with the growth of the Church. As classical words they conveyed noble thoughts of constancy in danger, and heroic endurance: ὑπεμείνατε ὑπὲρ τῶν δικαίων τὸν πρὸς ἐκείνους πόλεμον, Dem. *Phil.* I. 3. See also Polyb. IV. 51. 1. Josephus uses ὑπομονή of the heroic endurance of the Maccabees. There, as in the N.T., it is closely and necessarily connected with immortality, it contains the promise of the life to come: ἐν τῇ ὑπομονῇ ὑμῶν κτήσεσθε τὰς ψυχὰς ὑμῶν, 'by your constancy ye shall win your souls,' i.e. your higher lives, Luke xxi. 19. The noun occurs in Luke alone of the Gospels, in John neither verb nor noun; there the thought of ἀγάπη is predominant. In the Epistle to the Hebrews, in the Epistle of St James, and in the Apocalypse (ὑπομονή, not ὑπομένειν), these words are frequent; in the Epistles of St Paul, ὑπομονή takes its place in the category of the Christian excellencies: εἰδότες ὅτι ἡ θλῖψις ὑπομονὴν κατεργάζεται ἡ δὲ ὑπομονὴ δοκιμήν, ἡ δὲ δοκιμὴ ἐλπίδα, ἡ δὲ ἐλπὶς οὐ καταισχύνει ὅτι ἡ ἀγάπη τοῦ θεοῦ ἐκκέχυται ἐν ταῖς καρδίαις ἡμῶν κ.τ.λ., Rom. v. 4.

14. ὅλῃ τῇ οἰκουμένῃ. The frequent and increasing use of ὅλος for πᾶς must be regarded as a modernism. See Geldart's *Modern Greek*, p. 184, 187. Possibly the similarity in sound to Hebr. *Col* may have had an influence.

ἡ οἰκουμένη (γῆ). 'The inhabited earth' originally the Hellenic portion of the world, (Dem. and Æsch.), later the Roman Empire, and the whole world: τὸ τῆς ὅλης οἰκουμένης σχῆμα, Polyb. I. 4. 6; in Hebr. ii. 5, of the future age—the world of Christianity: οὐ γὰρ ἀγγέλοις ὑπέταξεν τὴν οἰκουμένην τὴν μέλλουσαν. The adjective οἰκουμενικός, not in N.T., is frequent in later ecclesiastical use.

15. βδέλυγμα. Hellenistic from βδελύσσομαι, 'feel disgust for,' 'detest,' Aristoph. *Ach.* 586 and elsewhere in Comedy. The noun is used especially of idols, τὰ βδελύγματα τῶν Ἀιγυπτίων θύσομεν Κυρίῳ τῷ θεῷ ἡμῶν, Ex. ix. 26. ᾠκοδόμησαν βδέλυγμα ἐρημώσεως ἐπὶ τὸ θυσιαστήριον, 1 Macc. i. 54, referring to the Statue of Jupiter Olympius.

βδέλυγμα τῆς ἐρημώσεως. i.e. 'the abomination that maketh desolate,' 'the act of sacrilege, which is a sign and a cause of desolation.' What special act of sacrilege is referred to cannot be determined for certain. The expression may refer (1) to the besieging army; cp. the parallel passage in Luke, 'When ye shall see Jerusalem compassed with armies.' Lightfoot, *Hor. Hebr.*, translates Dan. ix. 27 in this sense: 'Until the wing (or army) of abominations shall make desolate.' (2) The Roman eagles; the A.V. margin, Dan. ix. 27, reads: 'Upon the battlements shall be the idols of the desolator.' (3) The excesses of the Zealots. See Josephus, *B. J.* IV. 6. 3, 'They (the Zealots) caused the fulfilment of the prophecies against their own country; for there was a certain ancient saying that the city would be taken at that time......for sedition would arise, and their own hands would pollute the Temple of God.'

ἐν τόπῳ ἁγίῳ. i.e. within the Temple area.

ὁ ἀναγινώσκων νοείτω. These words are almost beyond a doubt an insertion of the Evangelist, and not part of our Lord's discourse.

16. **φευγέτωσαν ἐπὶ τὰ ὄρη.** Many Christians, warned by this prediction (according to Eusebius, *H.E.* III. 5, 'by a certain oracle'), took refuge at Pella in Peræa during the siege of Jerusalem. The mountains would be the natural place of refuge: cp. Thuc. VIII. 41, τήν τε πόλιν ἐκπορθεῖ τῶν ἀνθρώπων ἐς τὰ ὄρη πεφευγότων. Arrian. *in Indic.* c. 24, καὶ διέφυγον ἐς τὰ ὄρεα.

17. **μὴ καταβάτω κ.τ.λ.** i.e. either (1) pass from the roof to the entrance, and thence to the street, without entering any apartments, or (2) escape along the flat roofs from house to house.

ἆραι τὰ ἐκ τῆς οἰκίας, for ἆραι ἐκ τῆς οἰκίας τὰ ἐν τῇ οἰκίᾳ. Cp. Plato, *Symp.* IV. 31, τὰ ἐκ τῆς οἰκίας πέπραται, and Luke xi. 13, ὁ πατὴρ ὁ ἐξ οὐρανοῦ δώσει πνεῦμα ἅγιον. See Winer, p. 784.

18. **ἆραι τὸ ἱμάτιον αὐτοῦ.** τὸ ἱμάτιον, the outer garment, which the field labourer would throw off while at work, wearing the tunic only. Cp. 'Nudus ara, sere nudus.' *Georg.* I. 299.

20. **χειμῶνος.** When swollen streams, bitter cold and long nights would increase the misery and danger of the fugitives.

σαββάτῳ. When religious scruples might delay the flight. The extent of a Sabbath day's journey was 2000 cubits. Here, however, the question meets us, how far Jewish observances would affect the Christians. Probably the early Christians observed both the Sabbath and the Lord's day. But in any case many impediments would arise against flight on the Sabbath day. St Matthew alone records these words of warning.

21. **θλίψις μεγάλη.** 'Jerusalem, a city that had been liable to so many miseries during the siege, that had it enjoyed as much happiness from its first foundation, it would certainly have been the envy of the world.' Josephus, *B. J.* VIII. 6. 5.

No words can describe the unequalled horrors of this siege. It was the Passover season, and Jews from all parts were crowded within the walls. Three factions, at desperate feud with each other, were posted on the heights of Sion and on the Temple Mount. These only united to fling themselves at intervals upon the Roman entrenchments, and then resumed their hate. The Temple-courts swam with the blood of civil discord, which was literally mingled with the blood of the sacrifices. Jewish prisoners were crucified by hundreds in view of their friends, while within the city the wretched inhabitants were reduced by famine to the most loathsome of food and to deeds of unspeakable cruelty. Jerusalem was taken on the 10th August, A.D. 70. 1,100,000 Jews perished in the siege, 100,000 were sold into slavery. With the fall of Jerusalem, Israel ceased to exist as a nation. It was truly the end of an *æon*.

οὐδ' οὐ μὴ γένηται. Note the triple negative. The regular construction would be οὐδὲ μὴ γένηται, οὐ being redundant. The form of the sentence is not strictly logical, but θλίψις μεγάλη is excluded from the predication of οὐ μὴ γένηται. When the last great tribulation does come it will prove to be unparalleled.

22. εἰ μὴ ἐκολοβώθησαν κ.τ.λ. 'Unless those days had been shortened.' The event still future, is by the divine prescience looked upon as past. κολοβόω, lit. 'to cut off,' 'mutilate' (Aristotle and Polyb.), here 'to abridge.'

Several circumstances concurred to shorten the duration of the siege, such as the scanty supply of provisions, the crowded state of the city, the internal dissensions, and the abandonment of important defences. So strong did the place seem to Titus that he exclaimed, 'We have certainly had God on our side in this war; and it was God alone who ejected the Jews from these fortifications.' Josephus VI. 9. 1.

οὐκ ἂν ἐσώθη πᾶσα σάρξ. In this construction οὐ coalesces with the verb, so that οὐκ ἐσώθη = ἀπώλετο: when οὐ is joined to πᾶς the meaning is 'not every' as οὐ πᾶς ὁ λέγων Κύριε Κύριε, εἰσελεύσεται εἰς τὴν βασιλείαν, ch. vii. 12.

23—31. THE SECOND COMING OF CHRIST.
Mark xiii. 21—27; Luke xxi. 24—28.

23. τότε. According to Chrysostom, Jerome and others who make the division at v. 22 τότε marks a transition, and the description which follows is applicable to the end of the world not to the fall of Jerusalem.

24. ὥστε πλανῆσαι. ὥστε indicates here not only a possible result—the usual classical form of ὥστε with infinitive—but *intention*, for which use of ὥστε see Goodwin's *Greek Moods and Tenses*, § 98. 2. Translate 'with the view of deceiving if possible (εἰ δυνατόν), i.e. by every possible means, even the elect.' The A.V. is misleading here, (1) by so connecting εἰ δυνατόν as to infer the impossibility of πλανῆσαι; (2) by translating πλανῆσαι as a future.

τοὺς ἐκλεκτούς. Cp. Rom viii. 33 and Tit. i. 1, ἐκλεκτῶν Θεοῦ. The term, like many others, ἅγιοι, ἠγαπημένοι, πιστοί, is transferred from the O.T. to the N.T., from Israel according to the flesh to the true spiritual Israel. The church is heir to the titles as well as to the promises of the old dispensation. ἐκλεκτοί and ἐκλογή imply election, choice, appointment to a special work or office, as of Jesus to the Messiahship, 1 Pet. ii. 4—6; of Isaac and Jacob to the fathership of the faithful, Rom. ix. 11, of Paul to the office of evangelist σκεῦος ἐκλογῆς, Acts ix. 15—of persons to Church-membership, εἰδότες τὴν ἐκλογὴν ὑμῶν, 1 Thess. i. 4. Thus the thoughts of final salvation and irreversible decree, to say the least, do not necessarily enter into the word. Bp. Lightfoot observes in his note on Col. iii. 12, that κλητοί and ἐκλεκτοί are distinguished in the gospels as an outer and inner circle (Matt. xxii. 14), but that in St Paul there is no such distinction. The same persons are 'called' to Christ and 'chosen out' of the world.

25. ἰδοὺ προείρηκα ὑμῖν. These words solemnly call attention to the warning—the disciples as the Church, the ἐκλεκτοί, must take heed, for the signs are calculated and intended to deceive even them.

26. ἐν τῇ ἐρήμῳ. Cp. Joseph. *B. J.* II. 13. 4.

ἐν τοῖς ταμείοις. Here probably 'the lecture rooms' of the synagogue, so that the meaning of the verse would be, 'whether the false Christ come like John the Baptist in the desert, or like a great Rabbi in the schools of the synagogue, be not deceived.'

27. φαίνεται, 'appeareth,' not 'shineth,' A.V. The flash is instantly visible in the opposite quarter of the heaven. Like lightning all-pervading, swift, sudden and of dazzling brightness, shall be the coming of the Son of man.

28. ὅπου ἐὰν ᾖ τὸ πτῶμα. The spiritual perception will discern wherever the Lord comes, by a subtle sense like that by which the vulture is cognisant of his distant prey.

Another interpretation fixes upon the idea of corruption in the body, and reads the sense thus: 'where the corrupt body of sin lies, wherever there is the corruption of moral death and decay, there the vultures of judgment will gather upon the carrion.'

29. ὁ ἥλιος σκοτισθήσεται κ.τ.λ. Such figurative language is frequent with the Hebrew prophets; it implies (1) the perplexity and confusion of a sudden revolution, a great change; the very sources of light become darkness. Cp. Isaiah xiii. 10, 'For the stars of heaven and the constellations thereof shall not give their light: the sun shall be darkened in his going forth, and the moon shall not cause her light to shine;' and (2) the darkness of distress as Ezek. xxxii. 7, 8, 'All the bright lights of heaven will I make dark over thee, and set darkness upon thy land, saith the Lord God.' Cp. also Joel ii. 28—32 quoted Acts ii. 19, 20.

30. τὸ σημεῖον τοῦ υἱοῦ τοῦ ἀνθρώπου. What this shall be it is vain to conjecture, but when it appears its import will be instantly recognised by the faithful.

ἐπὶ τ. ν. *On* the clouds, not, as in A. V., *in* the clouds.

31. μετὰ σάλπιγγος φωνῆς μεγάλης. The image would be suggestive to the Jews, who were called together in the camp by silver trumpets (Numb. x. 2 foll.). Moreover, the great festivals, the commencement of the year, and other celebrations were announced by trumpets. There will be once again a marshalling of the host of Jehovah, of God's Church.

ἐπισυνάξουσιν. Cp. ch. xxiii. 37 and 2 Thess. ii. 1, ἐρωτῶμεν δὲ ὑμᾶς, ἀδελφοί, ὑπὲρ τῆς παρουσίας τοῦ κυρίου ἡμῶν Ἰησοῦ Χριστοῦ καὶ ἡμῶν ἐπισυναγωγῆς ἐπ' αὐτόν.

32—35. THE PARABLE OF THE FIG TREE.

Mark xiii. 28—31; Luke xxi. 29—33.

32. ἀπὸ δὲ τῆς συκῆς μάθετε τὴν παραβολήν. Learn from the fig-tree its parable, the lesson that the fig-tree teaches. The parable relates to the siege of Jerusalem and the ruin of the Jewish nationality, illustrating *vv.* 4—22.

It was spring time, and the fig-tree was putting forth its leaf-buds; no more certainly does that natural sign foretell the coming harvest than the signs of Christ shall foretell the fall of the Holy City. The sequence of historical events is as certain as the sequence of natural events. And the first, at least to some extent, is within the range of the same human intelligence that discerns the promise of summer. Thus Jesus rebuked the Pharisees for not discerning the signs of the times as they discerned the face of the sky.

The facts of botany throw fresh light on our Lord's illustration. The season of spring is described by botanists as one of the greatest stir and vital activity throughout the plant organism, a general but secret internal movement preceding the outburst of vegetation. A true figure of political movement. See Thomé's *Struct. and Phys. Botany* (translation), pp. 196—208.

ὅταν ἤδη ὁ κλάδος αὐτῆς γένηται ἁπαλός. 'As soon as its branch becomes tender,' i.e. ready to sprout.

γινώσκετε, 'ye recognise;' as also in the following verse.

ἐγγὺς τὸ θέρος, 'that harvest time is nigh,' i.e. the corn-harvest, not the fig-harvest (Meyer). This is a probable rendering, because the sprouting of the fig-tree would coincide with the barley harvest, rather than with the summer; it gives force to our Lord's words, when it is remembered that the barley harvest was actually nigh; the omer, or first sheaf, being offered on the day following the Passover. Again, the siege of Jerusalem, prefigured by this 'parable,' took place at the time of harvest (see note, *v.* 21).

33. ὅτι ἐγγύς ἐστιν. The harvest-time of God—the end of this *æon* or period at the fall of Jerusalem.

34. ἡ γενεὰ αὕτη. See note, ch. xvi. 28.

36—End of CHAP. XXV. PARABLES AND TEACHINGS CONCERNING THE SECOND ADVENT.

36—51. THE COMING OF CHRIST; THE NEED OF WATCHFULNESS.

More briefly reported in Mark xiii. 32—37; Luke xxi. 34—36.

36. τῆς ἡμέρας ἐκείνης. The Day of Judgment. The discourse turns from the type—the fall of Jerusalem—to the antitype—the Day of Judgment, and continues on this subject to the end of the following chapter.

37. ὥσπερ δὲ αἱ ἡμέραι τοῦ Νῶε κ.τ.λ. As at other critical times in history—the days before the flood—the eve of the destruction of

Sodom and Gomorrah—so before the parousia of Christ the world will be given up to enjoyment (τρώγοντες καὶ πίνοντες), it will rest its hopes in the present, and plan for the continuance of the existing order (γαμοῦντες καὶ ἐκγαμίζοντες), it will be immersed in business (ἠγόραζον ἐπώλουν ἐφύτευον ᾠκοδόμουν, Luke xvii. 28), all which things are the perils of the religious life—the cares (μέριμναι), riches (πλοῦτος), pleasures (ἡδοναί), that choke the good seed (Luke viii. 14).

For τρώγοντες καὶ πίνοντες, implying luxurious living, cp. ch. xi. 19, ἐσθίων καὶ πίνων and see v. 49 of this chap. and Luke xii. 45. Cp. Eur. *Cycl.* 335, πιεῖν καὶ φαγεῖν τοὔφ' ἡμέραν. But the use of τρώγοντες rather than ἐσθίοντες adds force to the picture of a world plunged in animal delights. τρώγειν is said to be formed from the sound; Eustath. *Od.* VI. 60, cp. 'Feeding like horses when you hear them feed,' (Tennyson, *Œnid*). It is used in Homer of mules and of mice, then in Hdt. and vernacular speech of men 'to eat vegetables or fruit,' (cp. τρωγάλια, τρωκτά,) and not till quite late in a general sense. With the exception of this passage τρώγειν occurs in the fourth Gospel only. This use of τρώγειν to the exclusion of ἐσθίειν is one of the interesting specialisms in St John's Gospel; in ch. xiii. 18, ὁ τρώγων is substituted for ὁ ἐσθίων of the LXX., Ps. xli. 9, and the completely settled use of the word is shown by its occurrence in the solemn connection ch. vi. 54, ὁ τρώγων μου τὴν σάρκα. Compare generally the use of χορτάζειν.

40, 41. Instances like these serve to bring out the reflection that the world's work will be going on then as now; there is also the thought of a real separation in this life beneath an external sameness.

40. παραλαμβάνεται, 'is taken or withdrawn.' For this present for future of certainty see ch. xxvii. 63.

41. δύο ἀλήθουσαι ἐν τῷ μύλῳ. In southern Palestine, where there are no mill-streams, hand-mills are to be seen and heard in every village. 'Two women sit at the mill facing each other; both having hold of the handle by which the upper is turned round on the nether mill-stone.' *Land and Book*, p. 526.

43—45. THE LORD COMETH AS A THIEF IN THE NIGHT.

Luke xii. 39, 40.

43. γιγνώσκειν, 'to observe,' 'learn,' 'recognise,' not 'to know' (εἰδέναι, ἐπίστασθαι). Here the verb is either (1) *imperative*, like γρηγορεῖτε and γίνεσθε, or (2) *indicative*, 'ye recognise' while I speak.

οἰκοδεσπότης. A late word (Plut. Epictet.) for the classical οἰκίας δεσπότης. οἰκοδεσπότης, οἰκοδεσποτεῖν came into use as technical terms in astrology: οἶκος is the 'house' of the ruling planet. 'Goodman' (A.V.) is probably a corruption for *gummann* or *guma* A.S., a man (*Bible Word Book*).

ποίᾳ φυλακῇ. See ch. xiv. 25.

ὁ κλέπτης ἔρχεται. Cp. αὐτοὶ γὰρ ἀκριβῶς οἴδατε ὅτι ἡ ἡμέρα Κυρίου ὡς κλέπτης ἐν νυκτὶ οὕτως ἔρχεται, 1 Thess. v. 2; see also 2 Pet. iii. 10.

διορυχθῆναι. See ch. vi. 19, 20.

45—51. The Stewards of God.

Luke xii. 41—48, where this parable is joined on to the preceding one by a question of St Peter, 'Lord, speakest thou this parable unto us, or even to all?' Mark xiii. 37 has 'what I say unto you I say unto all, Watch.' Here, and throughout the discourse, the disciples are specially addressed.

οἰκετείας, the correct reading, according to the best criticism, is strictly speaking wider than θεραπείας, including not only the θεράποντες, but also the γυνή and τέκνα, here however it means the household of slaves, Lat. *familia*.

The imagery is drawn from a large estate (latifundium) or household, over which an honest and intelligent slave would be appointed as steward (οἰκονόμος, Lat. *vilicus* or *dispensator*), part of his duty being to give the daily allowance (τροφήν, or σιτομέτριον, Luke. Lat. *diarium*, Hor. *Ep.* I. 14. 41) to the slaves.

From this short parable springs the conception of the stewardship of the Christian ministry expanded in the Epistles and indelibly fixed in religious thought. Cp. 1 Cor. iv. 1, 2, οὕτως ἡμᾶς λογιζέσθω ἄνθρωπος, ὡς ὑπηρέτας Χριστοῦ καὶ οἰκονόμους μυστηρίων θεοῦ. ὧδε λοιπὸν ζητεῖται ἐν τοῖς οἰκονόμοις ἵνα πιστός τις εὑρεθῇ κ.τ.λ. Tit. i. 7, δεῖ γὰρ τὸν ἐπίσκοπον ἀνέγκλητον εἶναι ὡς θεοῦ οἰκονόμον. 1 Pet. iv. 10, ὡς καλοὶ οἰκονόμοι ποικίλης χάριτος θεοῦ. And from the Latin Version of this and parallel passages such expressions as 'the present dispensation,' 'the Christian dispensation,' are derived. It is deeply interesting to trace in a few and simple words of Christ the genesis of such great and fruitful thoughts which are the very life of the Church and of society.

51. διχοτομήσει. See Dan. ii. 5 and iii. 29. μένει γὰρ ὁ ἄγγελος τοῦ θεοῦ τὴν ῥομφαίαν ἔχων πρίσαι σε μέσον, (Susanna, 59.) Comp. also 'Multos honesti ordinis aut ad bestias condemnavit, aut serra dissecuit.' Sueton. *Calig.* 17, quoted by Wetstein, who gives other instances.

μετὰ τῶν ὑποκριτῶν. St Luke has μετὰ τῶν ἀπίστων. Such adaptations of the Gentile Evangelist to his readers are always interesting. Hypocrisy was especially a Jewish sin. St Luke adds our Lord's words on the degrees of punishment, varying with the degrees of responsibility.

CHAPTER XXV.

1. ὑπάντησιν, (אBC) for ἀπάντησιν, see v. 6.

2. The order μωραί...φρόνιμοι on decisive evidence. The striking and unexpected fact was that there were *foolish* virgins in the group.

6. ἔρχεται, omitted after ὁ νυμφίος according to all the important codices greatly enhances the vividness of the narrative.

9. οὐκ ἀρκέσῃ is upheld with אALZ of the uncials against οὐ μὴ ἀρκέσῃ with BCD and several late uncials. See Winer, p. 632, and Dr Moulton's note 3. This is the first appeal to Codex A.

13. The *textus receptus* after ὥραν reads ἐν ᾗ ὁ υἱὸς τοῦ ἀνθρώπου ἔρχεται. But all the ancient testimony is against the insertion.

22. λαβών after τάλαντα omitted (ABCL, &c.), inserted (אD, &c.).

31. ἅγιοι, omitted before ἄγγελοι (אBDL and others). A heads the evidence for the retention of ἅγιοι.

41. κατηραμένοι. Without the article (אBL) against AD and many other uncials and fathers. The participle alone gives a reason, or indicates a state or condition, 'under your curse;' with the article it denotes a class.

1—13. The Parable of the Ten Virgins.
In St Matthew only.

1. τότε. In the Last Day—the time just spoken of.

ὁμοιωθήσεται 'shall be like,' not, 'shall be compared (by me).' The condition of the Church at the End of the World shall be like the condition of the ten virgins described in the parable.

This parable is another warning for the disciples of Christ 'to watch.' Like the rest of the discourse it is primarily addressed to the Apostles, and after them to the pastors of the Church, who are posted as sentinels for the coming of Christ; lastly, to all Christians. Whatever interpretation may be put on the lesser incidents they must be subordinated to the lesson of the parable—vigilance, and the reason for vigilance—the certainty of the event, and the uncertainty as to the time of its occurrence.

αἵτινες. The more frequent use of ὅστις in the N.T. may be regarded as a tendency to modern idiom: for in Romaic the relative ὅς is rarely used, but ὅστις frequently occurs in the nominative, both singular and plural (Corfe's *Modern Greek Grammar*, p. 67). But in most cases where ὅστις occurs in N. T. the classical usage is observed. Here αἵτινες denotes the kind or class of persons to whom the similitude relates, giving a reason for the analogy. Cp. Æsch. *Prom. V.* 37, 38, τί τὸν θεοῖς ἔχθιστον οὐ στυγεῖς θεόν | ὅστις τὸ σὸν θνητοῖσι προὔδωκεν γέρας; 'one who has betrayed;' see Paley's note. For the distinction between ὅς and ὅστις see Winer, pp. 209, 210; and Ellicott on Gal. iv. 24.

λαμπάδας. 'Torches,' the only meaning which the word bears in Greek literature early or late. Lat. *lampas* sometimes signifies a 'lamp,' as Juv. III. 285 'aenea lampas.'

εἰς ὑπάντησιν κ.τ.λ. The usual Jewish custom was for the 'friends of the bridegroom' to conduct the bride to her husband's home; and when the procession arrived, the bridegroom went forth to lead the bride across the threshold (Lightfoot, *Hor. Hebr.* ad loc., and Dr Ginsburg in Kitto's *Cycl. of Bib. Lit.*). The imagery of the parable, however, implies that the bridegroom himself went to fetch his bride perhaps from a great distance, while a group of maidens await his return ready to welcome him in Oriental fashion with lamps and flambeaux.

εἰς ὑπάντησιν. εἰς denotes purpose. For ὑπάντησιν see ch. viii. 28.

2. φρόνιμοι. Used of prudence or practical intelligence, a characteristic of the steward, ch. xxiv. 45, and Luke xvi. 8.

3. αἱ γὰρ μωραὶ κ.τ.λ. All watch for their Lord, but some only—'the wise'—with true intensity and with due provision for the watch. The foolish virgins have sufficient oil if the Lord come quickly; not sufficient for long and patient expectation. It is a rebuke to shallow religion that dies away when the excitement passes.

The oil seems to mean generally the spiritual life or preparedness for the Lord's coming.

5. τοῦ νυμφίου. The thought of Christ as the Bridegroom of the Church is hardly appropriate here, for in the parable the maidens, and not the bride, are the expectant Church. The thought of the 'children of the bridechamber,' ch. ix. 15, is a nearer parallel.

ἐνύσταξαν πᾶσαι κ.τ.λ. 'Nodded from drowsiness, and fell asleep.' The two stages of sleep are noted in Plato, *Apol. Socr.*, p. 31, ὑμεῖς δ' ἴσως τάχ' ἂν ἀχθόμενοι ὥσπερ οἱ νυστάζοντες ἐγειρόμενοι...εἶτα τὸν λοιπὸν βίον καθεύδοντες διατελοῖτ' ἄν. Sleep represents the ignorance as to the time of Christ's coming; it is not to be interpreted of unwatchfulness, it is not a guilty or imprudent sleep, as in the parable of the thief coming by night (ch. xxiv. 43).

6. κραυγὴ γέγονεν. 'A cry is raised'. *fit sonus* (Verg.). The tense gives vividness.

ἐξέρχεσθε. The Codex Alexandrinus commences at this word.

7. ἐκόσμησαν. 'Trimmed,' by addition of oil, and by clearing the fibres with a needle.

8. σβέννυνται. 'Are going out,' not 'are gone out,' A.V. A picture in the newly discovered Codex Rossanensis (sixth cent.) gives this point accurately. Three of the foolish virgins hold torches nearly extinguished, but still burning. This parable is a favourite subject in the catacombs.

9. Μήποτε οὐκ ἀρκέσῃ ἡμῖν καὶ ὑμῖν. The bridal procession was still to be made in which there would be need of burning lamps. The wise cannot impart their oil:—an incident necessary to the leading idea of the parable;—nothing can make up for unreadiness at the last moment. This point has been adduced as an argument against works of supererogation.

μήποτε οὐκ ἀρκέσῃ. 'Lest haply it suffice not.' There is an ellipse of a refusal or of a word signifying fear. The reading οὐ μὴ ἀρκ. need

XXV. 16.]   NOTES.   277

not alter the construction, οὐ μή being merely a strengthened negative; but by some μήποτε is taken by itself, 'no, in no wise.'

10. **εἰς τοὺς γάμους.** To the marriage feast, as ch. xxii. 2. The happiness of the blest is often described by the image of a great supper, cp. ch. xxvi. 29.

11. **Κύριε κύριε.** Cp. ch. vii. 22, 23.

13. **γρηγορεῖτε οὖν.** Our Lord's explanation of the parable, shewing the true purport of it.

14—30. THE PARABLE OF THE TALENTS, in this Gospel only.

The parable of the Pounds, Luke xix. 12—27, is similar, but there are important points of distinction; (1) in regard to the occasions on which the two parables are given; (2) in the special incidents of each.

The lesson is still partly of watchfulness, it is still in the first instance for the apostles. And mainly always for those who bear office in the Church. But fresh thoughts enter into this parable: (1) There is work to be done in the time of waiting; the watching must not be idle or unemployed; (2) Even the least talented is responsible.

14. **παρέδωκεν αὐτοῖς τὰ ὑπάρχοντα αὐτοῦ.** Cp. Mark xiii. 34. 'A man taking a far journey, who left his house and gave authority (rather, his authority) to his servants, and to every man his work.' Christ in his absence gives to each a portion of his own authority and of his own work on earth.

A great deal of the commerce of antiquity was managed by slaves, who were thus often entrusted with responsible functions (cp. ch. xxiv. 45). In this case they are expected to use their Master's money in trade or in cultivation of the soil, and to make as large an increase as possible.

15. **ᾧ μὲν ἔδωκεν κ.τ.λ.** In the parable of the Pounds or 'minæ' (Luke xix.), each subject receives one pound. Here the truth is indicated that there is variety in the services wrought for God in respect of dignity and of difficulty. More will be required of the influential and enlightened than of the ignorant and poor. 'Nemo urgetur ultra quam potest' (Bengel).

ᾧ μὲν...ᾧ δέ. See note on ch. xiii. 4.

τάλαντα. See ch. xviii. 24. It is from this parable that the word 'talents' has passed into modern languages in the sense of 'abilities,' or 'mental gifts,' though it seems properly to mean 'opportunities' or 'spheres of duty.'

16. **πορευθεὶς...εἰργάσατο.** The ideas of trade and travelling were very nearly connected in ancient times, as the Greek words for traffic shew: ἔμπορος, ἐμπορία, ἐμπορεύομαι, πωλέω. Cp. also the connection between *venio, veneo* and *vendito, ventito*. See James iv. 13, "Ἄγε νῦν οἱ λέγοντες· Σήμερον ἢ αὔριον πορευσόμεθα εἰς τήνδε τὴν πόλιν καὶ ποιήσωμεν ἐκεῖ ἐνιαυτὸν καὶ ἐμπορευσόμεθα καὶ κερδήσομεν. Contrast therefore πορευθεὶς here with ἀπελθὼν v. 18.

εἰργάσατο ἐν αὐτοῖς. 'Traded with them.' Made money (χρήματα) by them. A technical use of the word, cp. Demosth., *Contr. Dionys.*, καὶ δὶς ἢ τρὶς ὑπῆρχεν αὐτοῖς εἰργάσασθαι τῷ αὐτῷ ἀργυρίῳ; Aristoph. *Eq.* 840, ἢ πολλὰ χρήματ' ἐργάσει σείων τε καὶ ταράττων.

19. μετὰ πολὺν χρόνον. Another hint that the second coming of Christ would be long deferred.

συναίρει λόγον. 'Reckoneth with them,' in order to have his stipulated share of the profits. συναίρ. λόγ. Not a classical expression; it appears in this Gospel only, and may have been a business phrase familiar to Matthew the publican.

21. ἐπὶ ὀλίγα πιστός. Accusative from notion of extending over. ἐπὶ πολλῶν, over or upon, without the closer connection indicated by ἐπὶ with the dative.

εἴσελθε εἰς τὴν χαρὰν τοῦ κυρίου σου. Either (1) share the life of happiness which thy lord enjoys, and which shall be the reward of thy zeal; or (2) the joyous feast; as in the last parable; cp. also Esther ix. 18, 19. (See especially the LXX. version.)

24. ὁ εἰληφώς. A variety from ὁ λαβών, v. 16.

εἶπεν κ.τ.λ. This slave anticipates his lord's condemnation; 'qui s'excuse s'accuse.'

σκληρός. ἄνθρωπον μὲν σκληρὸν λέγουσι τὸν μονότροπον καὶ δυσπειθῆ καὶ πρὸς ἅπαν ἀντιτείνοντα. Galen, quoted by Wetstein.

συνάγων ὅθεν οὐ διεσκόρπισας. i.e. 'gathering into the garner from another's threshing-floor where thou hast not winnowed' (Meyer); so, 'exacting interest where thou hast invested no money.' The accusation was false, but the Lord takes his slave at his word, 'thou oughtest *therefore*,' for that very reason.

συνάγειν is used of the Israelites gathering straw in Egypt; αὐτοὶ πορευέσθωσαν καὶ συναγαγέτωσαν ἑαυτοῖς ἄχυρα, Ex. v. 7; σκορπίζων is used of the sower: ὁ σκορπίζων τὸν σῖτον σπορεύς ἐστιν (Eustathius, quoted by Wetstein). This verb and its compounds are Ionic, and do not belong to the Attic dialect. Lob. *Phryn.*, p. 218.

26. ᾔδεις ὅτι...διεσκόρπισα; 'Thou knewest that I was,' &c.? It is an interrogation *ex concesso*. The Lord does not admit the truth of this description, but judges the slave from his own standpoint. Even a low conception of the divine nature brings some responsibility, and has some promise of reward. This view brings this picture into agreement with the other descriptions of the last judgment.

27. τὸ ἀργύριόν μου. It was not thine own.

τοῖς τραπεζίταις. To the bankers, who set up tables or counters (τράπεζαι) for the purpose of lending or exchanging money. In the cities of eastern Russia Jewish bankers (τραπεζῖται) are still to be seen seated at their tables in the market-place. Such bankers' tables in the ἀγορά were places of resort. Socrates asks his judges not to be surprised if he should use the same arguments, δι' ὧνπερ εἴωθα λέγειν καὶ ἐν ἀγορᾷ ἐπὶ τῶν τραπεζῶν, *Apol. Socr.*, p. 17; cp. also κἀμοὶ μὲν τὰ προειρημένα διείλεκτο ἐπὶ τῇ φιλίου τραπέζῃ, Lysias, ix. 5, p. 114.

σὺν τόκῳ. τόκος, lit. 'offspring,' then the offspring of money 'interest,' or usury. Aristotle playing upon the word argues against usury as being a birth contrary to nature (παρὰ φύσιν), Arist. *Pol.* I. 10. 5. Shakespeare has the same thought when he calls 'interest' 'the breed of barren metal,' and Bacon who terms it 'the bastard use of money.' The high rates of interest in the ancient world and the close connection between debt and slavery naturally brought usury into odium. The Jew was forbidden to lend money upon usury to his brother (Deut. xxiii. 20); in later times, however, the practice of usury was reduced to a system and carried on without restriction of race. See *Bib. Dict.*, Articles 'Loan' and 'Usury.'

This was the very least the slave could have done: to make money in this way required no personal exertion.

29. The thought conveyed by this verse is true, even in worldly matters: talents not used pass away from their possessor: and the strenuous worker seems to gather to himself what is lost by the idle. Demosthenes says (*Phil.* I. 5) 'the possessions of the negligent belong of right to those who will endure toil and danger.'

31—46. THE DAY OF JUDGMENT.

32. πάντα τὰ ἔθνη. Either (1) all the nations of the world, including the Jews; or (2) all the Gentiles. The almost invariable use of τὰ ἔθνη to signify the Gentiles; the unconsciousness of service to Christ shewn by just and unjust alike; the simplicity of the standard proposed by the Judge, favour the second interpretation. On the other hand the special warning to the Apostles, and to the Jewish race, in the previous parts of the discourse render it probable that Jews and Christians are not excluded from this picture of the judgment. The unconsciousness of the judged may be referred not to ignorance of Christ, but to unconsciousness that in relieving the distressed they were actually relieving Christ. The simplicity of the standard may be intended to include what is called 'natural' religion, as well as revealed religion. The nations are judged by a standard of justice which *all* recognise. (Read Rom. i. 18—20, ii. 9—16.)

ὥσπερ ὁ ποιμὴν κ.τ.λ. Cp. Ezek. xxxiv. 17, 'And as for you, O my flock, thus saith the Lord God; Behold, I judge between cattle and cattle, between the rams and the he goats.' 'The sheep and goats are always seen together under the same shepherd and in company; yet they never trespass on the domain of each other...When folded together at night they may always be seen gathered in distinct groups; and so, round the wells they appear instinctively to classify themselves apart, as they wait for the troughs to be filled.'—Tristram.

34—46. These verses are constructed according to the rules of Hebrew poetry: they fall into two divisions, the *first* extends from v. 34—40, the *second* from v. 41—46.

Each division consists of a triplet or stanza of three lines containing the sentence of the Judge (v. 34 answering to v. 41), followed by a stanza of six lines, which in the form of a climax state the reason of the sentence (*vv.* 35, 36 answering to 42, 43), then the response of those who receive the sentence (*vv.* 37—39 answering to *v.* 44), then the reply of the Judge (*v.* 40 answering to 44), lastly the concluding couplet describing the passage to their doom of just and unjust.

The contrast between the sentences is impressively shown in the corresponding verses:

(1) (a) τότε ἐρεῖ ὁ βασιλεὺς τοῖς ἐκ δεξιῶν αὐτοῦ.

(β) τότε ἐρεῖ καὶ τοῖς ἐξ εὐωνύμων.

The form of Hebrew poetry emphasizes differences in the corresponding lines.

Note *first* here the absence in (β) of the subject to ἐρεῖ (Bengel says of ὁ βασιλεύς, 'appellatio majestatis plena solisque piis laeta') and *secondly* the absence of the qualifying genitive αὐτοῦ. That the omission of the subject is not unintentional appears to be proved by the repeated omission in *vv.* 40 and 45. The meaning of these two points of difference seems to be that at this dread moment the connection is severed between God and those whom He had sought in vain. He is now no King to them, no longer their God.

(2) (a) Δεῦτε οἱ εὐλογημένοι τοῦ πατρός μου | κληρονομήσατε τὴν ἡτοιμασμένην ὑμῖν βασιλείαν ἀπὸ καταβολῆς κόσμου.

(β) πορεύεσθε ἀπ' ἐμοῦ οἱ κατηραμένοι | εἰς τὸ πῦρ τὸ αἰώνιον τὸ ἡτοιμασμένον τῷ διαβόλῳ καὶ τοῖς ἀγγέλοις αὐτοῦ.

Observe here that the righteous are said to be blessed of the Father, but the unrighteous are not cursed of the Father.

Then note the righteous as Sons of the Father inherit of right the Kingdom that has been prepared for *them*, whereas the disinherited children pass into the fire of the ages prepared not for them but for the devil and his angels.

In the parallel passages that follow the respective sentences contrast the brief agitated questions of the doomed with the words of the righteous lingering over the particulars of their unconscious service to Christ. Rather their words do not breath service (διηκονήσαμεν, *v.* 44) but friendship (ἐθρέψαμεν ἐποτίσαμεν κ.τ.λ.). See on the whole of this passage Jebb, *Sacred Lit.*, pp. 363—367.

35, 36. There is a climax in this enumeration. The first three are recognised duties, the last three are voluntary acts of self-forgetting love. Common humanity would move a man to relieve his bitterest foe when perishing by hunger or by thirst (see Rom. xii. 20). Oriental custom required at least a bare hospitality. But to clothe the naked implies a liberal and loving spirit, to visit the sick is an act of spontaneous self-sacrifice, to go to the wretched outcasts in prison was perhaps an unheard of act of charity in those days; it was to enter places horrible and foul beyond description; Sallust, speaking of the Tullianum (the state prison at Rome), says: 'incultu, tenebris, odore foeda atque terribilis ejus facies est.'

40. ἐφ' ὅσον. 'So far as,' ἐπί denotes the point to which the action extends.

ἐμοὶ ἐποιήσατε. This unconscious personal service of Christ may be contrasted with the conscious but unreal knowledge of Christ assumed by false prophets; see Luke xiii. 26.

Christ identifies Himself with his Church, as in his words to Saul, τί με διώκεις; (Acts ix. 4).

44. σοι. The position of the personal pronouns throughout is emphatic.

45. ἐφ' ὅσον κ.τ.λ. Men will be judged not only for evil done, but for good left undone. In this view sins are regarded as debts (ὀφειλήματα) unpaid.

46. οὗτοι. Those on the left are unnamed here and throughout the description, but the parallel δίκαιοι infuses a meaning into οὗτοι. Compare with this the unnamed rich man in the parable of Lazarus, Luke xvi. 19—31.

In this important passage αἰώνιος is translated in A.V. *everlasting* (punishment) and (life) *eternal;* in each case the adjective in the text follows the noun, though in A.V. it precedes one noun and follows the other. αἰώνιος = of or belonging to (1) an *æon* or period, (a) past, (b) present, (c) future, or (2) to a succession of αἰῶνs or periods. In αἰών the idea of time is subordinate. It is the period required for the accomplishment of a specific result. τὰ τέλη τῶν αἰώνων (1 Cor. x. 11) are the results of the æons since the world began. A man's life is an αἰών not because it endures a certain number of years, but because it is complete in itself—with the life the life's work ends. It does not, therefore, in itself = 'unending,' but 'lasting through the required epoch.' But life eternal, which is 'to know the true God and Jesus Christ' (John xvii. 3), can only be conceived of as unending and infinite; cp. 'Art thou not from everlasting, O Lord my God, mine Holy One? we shall not die' (Hab. i. 12).

κόλασις (der. from a root meaning to lop, prune, &c.) is 'correction,' punishment that checks and reforms, not vengeance (τιμωρία). The two are distinguished, Arist. *Rhet.* I. 10. 17. The rare occurrence of κόλασις draws attention to its use here. The only other passage where it is found in N.T. is 1 John iv. 18, where the Apostle speaks of 'perfect love' (ἡ τελεία ἀγάπη) giving confidence in the day of judgment (ἐν τῇ ἡμέρᾳ τῆς κρίσεως); fear is inconsistent with that perfect love, because φόβος ἔχει κόλασιν—'hath the remedial correcting punishment even now, and so separates from good while it lasts.' In a profound sense that passage is cognate to this. Cp. also the use of κολάζεσθαι, 2 Pet. ii. 9, ἀδίκους εἰς ἡμέραν κρίσεως κολαζομένους (suffering punishment now) τηρεῖν. Cp. Acts iv. 21, μηδὲν εὑρίσκοντες τὸ πῶς κολάσωνται αὐτούς, where the notion of restraint and reform is evident. Two passages of Aristotle's *Ethics* which exhibit the use of κόλασις agree with these instances: μηνύουσι δὲ καὶ αἱ κολάσεις γινόμεναι διὰ τούτων· ἰατρεῖαι γάρ τινές εἰσιν, *Eth. Nic.* II. 3. 5, 'they are a sort of remedies.'

ἀπειθοῦσι δὲ καὶ ἀφυεστέροις οὖσι κολάσεις τε καὶ τιμωρίας ἐπιτιθέναι τοὺς δὲ ἀνιάτους (the incurable) ὅλως ἐξορίζειν, Eth. Nic. 10.

The rebuke of the king is the beginning of the κόλασις.

CHAPTER XXVI.

3. καὶ οἱ γραμματεῖς, omitted with all the best MSS. Insertion from Mark and Luke.

7. πολυτίμου for βαρυτίμου, which has the support of B, but the evidence for πολυτ. is very strong.

9. The weight of evidence is against τὸ μύρον after τοῦτο.

26. ἄρτον for τὸν ἄρτον on very strong evidence, though the article is found in A and several other uncials. The evidence is more evenly divided between ποτήριον and τὸ ποτήριον (v. 27). The former has the support, among others, of ℵ and B.

26. For ἐδίδου...καὶ the true reading is δούς.

28. Tischendorf omits καινῆς with ℵBLZ, but it has the testimony of ACD and other uncials.

39. προσελθών for προελθών. Here B is opposed to all the other important uncials.

50. ἐφ' ὅ for ἐφ' ᾧ on conclusive grounds.

53. ἄρτι placed after παραστήσει μοι on the evidence of ℵBL against the other important uncials, in which it precedes παρακαλέσαι. The omission of ἢ before δώδεκα gives the classical idiom. Here AC and a large majority of MSS. retain ἢ against ℵBDL.

55. ἐν τῷ ἱερῷ follows διδάσκων in the *textus receptus*. The most ancient authority favours the change.

59. The *textus receptus* adds καὶ οἱ πρεσβύτεροι with AC, and the preponderance of later authority, against ℵBDL, some Versions and Fathers.

θανατώσουσιν for θανατώσωσι.

60. καὶ after οὐχ εὗρον, and a second οὐχ εὗρον after ψευδομαρτύρων, deleted on the authority of the oldest but not the majority of MSS. and Versions. Among those which support the *textus receptus* are A and E.

ψευδομάρτυρες after δύο is almost certainly a gloss, though found in A²CD and a mass of later MSS.

74. καταθεματίζειν for καταναθεματίζειν of *textus receptus* with preponderating authority. The second word is scarcely supported.

1—5. WEDNESDAY, NISAN 12. THE APPROACH OF THE PASSOVER. JESUS AGAIN FORETELLS HIS DEATH. THE SANHEDRIN MEET.

Mark xiv. 1, 2; Luke xxii. 1, 2.

Cp. John xi. 55—57, where we read that 'the chief priests and Pharisees had given a commandment, that, if any man knew where he were, he should shew it, that they might take him.'

That Jesus should be able for so many days to 'speak openly in the Temple,' and shew Himself to the people without fear of capture is a proof of the deep hold He had taken on the enthusiasm and affection of His fellow-countrymen. The words of St John (quoted above) imply a combination of the priestly and aristocratic party—the Sadducees—with the democratic Pharisees, against the despised Galilæan, and yet it requires treachery of the deepest dye and a deed of darkness to secure Him.

2. μετὰ δύο ἡμέρας. According to the Jewish reckoning, any length of time including part of two days.

τὸ πάσχα. (1) The *word* is interesting in its (*a*) Hebrew, (*b*) Greek, and (*c*) English form. (*a*) The Hebrew *pesach* is from a root meaning 'to leap over,' and, figuratively, to 'save,' 'shew mercy.' (*b*) The Greek πάσχα represents the Aramaic or later Hebrew form of the same word, but the affinity in sound and letters to the Greek word πάσχειν, 'to suffer,' led to a connection in thought between the Passover and the Passion of our Lord: indeed, some of the early Christian writers state the connection as if it were the true etymology. (*c*) Tyndale has the merit of introducing into English the word 'passover,' which keeps up the play on the words in the original Hebrew (Exod. xii. 11 and 13). Before Tyndale the word '*paske*' (for πάσχα) was transferred from the Vulgate, with an explanation: 'For it is paske, that is, the passyng of the Lord' (Wyclif).

the feast of the passover commemorated the deliverance of Israel from the Egyptian bondage. The ordinances of the first Passover are narrated Exod. xii. 1—14, but some of those were modified in later times. It was no longer necessary to choose the lamb on the 10th of Nisan. The blood was sprinkled on the altar, not on the door-post, those who partook of the paschal meal no longer 'stood with loins girded, with shoes on their feet, with staff in hand,' but reclined on couches, as at an ordinary meal; it was no longer unlawful to leave the house before morning (Exod. xii. 22). The regular celebration of the Passover was part of the religious revival after the return from Captivity. During the kingly period only three celebrations of the Passover are recorded; in the reigns of Solomon, of Hezekiah and of Josiah. For the relation of the Last Supper to the Passover and for further notes on the paschal observance, see below.

The date of this Passover was probably April 3 (old style), A.D. 33 (Mr J. W. Bosanquet in *Trans. Soc. Bib. Arch.*, Vol. IV. 2). See note, ch. ii. 1.

παραδίδοται, either (1) the present for the future, denoting greater certainty, or (2) the full relative present 'is in the act of being betrayed;' the treacherous scheme of Judas is already afoot.

3. οἱ ἀρχιερεῖς κ.τ.λ. i.e. the Sanhedrin, the supreme council, legislative and administrative, of the Jewish people. Sanhedrin is strictly a plural form, the old poetical plural termination, -*in* having become the ordinary form in later Hebrew in place of -*im*. But from similarity of sound *Sanhedrin* came to represent συνέδριον rather than σύνεδροι, and is used as a singular noun of multitude.

A. The history of the Sanhedrin. Many learned Rabbis endeavoured to trace the origin of the Sanhedrin to the council of 70 elders whom Moses, by the advice of Jethro, appointed to assist him. But it is improbable that this council existed before the Macedonian conquest. (1) The name is Greek, not Hebrew. (2) It finds its equivalent among the political institutions of Macedonia; finally, (3) no allusion to the Sanhedrin is to be found in the Historical Books or in the Prophets. Cp. Livy, XLV. 32, Pronuntiatum, quod ad statum Macedoniæ pertinebat, Senatores quos synedros vocant, legendos esse, quorum consilio res publica administraretur.

B. Constitution. The President or *Nasi* (prince) was generally, though not always, the high priest; next in authority was the vice-president or *Ab Beth Din* (father of the house of judgment); the third in rank was the *Chacham* (sage or interpreter). The members were 71 in number, and consisted (1) of the chief priests, see note ch. xxi. 15; (2) the scribes or lawyers; (3) the elders of the people or heads of families, who were the representatives of the laity.

C. Authority and functions. The Sanhedrin formed the highest court of the Jewish commonwealth. It originally possessed the power of life and death, but this power no longer belonged to it; John xviii. 31, 'It is not lawful for us to put any man to death,' a statement which agrees with a tradition in the Talmud, 'forty years before the temple was destroyed judgment in capital causes was taken away from Israel.'

All questions of the Jewish law, and such as concerned the ecclesiastical polity, religious life of the nation and discipline of the priests fell under the jurisdiction of the Sanhedrin.

This authority extended to settlements of Jews in foreign countries; *e.g.* it is exercised in Damascus. Acts ix. 1, 2.

D. Place of meeting. In the present instance the Sanhedrin met at the high priest's house; from ch. xxvii. 6 we may conjecture that the Temple was sometimes the place of meeting, but their usual house of assembly at this particular epoch was called the 'Halls of Purchase,' on the east of the Temple Mount (Dr Ginsburg in Kitto's *Encyc. Bib. Lit.* and Lightfoot's *Hor. Hebr.*).

τοῦ λεγομένου κ.τ.λ. Joseph Caiaphas, the son-in-law of Annas, was appointed high priest by the Procurator Valerius Gratus A.D. 26, and was deposed A.D. 38. The high priesthood had long ceased to be held for life and to descend from father to son; appointments were made at the caprice of the Roman government. Annas who had been high priest was still regarded as such by popular opinion, which did not recognise his deposition; cp. Luke iii. 2, where the correct reading is ἐπ' ἀρχιερέως Ἅννα καὶ Καϊάφα, and Acts iv. 6, Ἅννας ὁ ἀρχιερεὺς καὶ Καϊάφας.

4. ἵνα δόλῳ κ.τ.λ. It was no longer possible (1) to entrap Him by argument (xxii. 46); (2) to discredit Him with the Roman government (xxii. 22); or (3) to take Him by force.

5. ἐν τῇ ἑορτῇ. During the feast, including the Passover and the seven days of unleavened bread.

ἵνα μὴ θόρυβος κ.τ.λ. The great danger at the time of the Passover, when the people, numbering hundreds of thousands, filled the city and encamped in tents outside the walls like a vast army. At a Passover, less than 30 years before, the people, partly to avenge the death of two Rabbis, rose against Archelaus, and were cruelly repressed with a slaughter of 3000 men (Joseph. *Ant.* XVII. 9. 3); see also XVII. 10. 2, where a similar rising against Sabinus, during the feast of Pentecost, is described.

6—13. THE FEAST IN THE HOUSE OF SIMON THE LEPER.
Mark xiv. 3—9; John xii. 1—8.

St John's narrative places this incident on the evening of the Sabbath—the last Sabbath spent by Jesus on earth—before the triumphal entry. St Matthew has here disregarded the strictly chronological order. A comparison with St Mark will shew how accurately the words of Jesus are remembered, the rest of the incident is told in somewhat different language.

Compare a similar act of devotion on the part of a 'woman that was a sinner' (Luke vii. 36—39).

6. τοῦ λεπροῦ. i.e. he had been a leper. St John, in the parallel passage, says 'they made him a supper, and Martha served; but Lazarus was one of them that sat at the table with him.' Nothing further is known of Simon. He was evidently a disciple of Jesus and probably a near friend of Lazarus and his sisters.

7. ἀλάβαστρον κ.τ.λ. ἀλάβαστρον μύρου νάρδου πιστικῆς πολυτελοῦς (Mark). λίτραν μύρου νάρδου πιστικῆς πολυτίμου (John). The 'alabaster box' was 'a flask of fragrant oil;' the special kind of ointment named by the Evangelists—nard or spikenard—was extracted from the blossoms of the Indian and Arabian nard-grass (Becker's *Gallus*).

These *alabastra* or unguent-flasks were usually made of the Oriental or onyx alabaster, with long narrow necks, which let the oil escape drop by drop, and could easily be broken (Mark xiv. 3). But the shape and material varied. Herodotus (III. 20) mentions a μύρου ἀλάβαστρον—the precise expression in the text—sent among other royal gifts of gold and purple by Cambyses to the king of Æthiopia.

The costliness of Mary's offering may be judged from this. The other Evangelists name three hundred pence or *denarii* as the price (St Mark says, 'more than three hundred pence'). Now a denarius was a day's wages for a labourer (see ch. xx. 2); equivalent, therefore, to two shillings at least of English money; hence, relatively to English ideas, Mary's offering would amount to £30. It was probably the whole of her wealth.

8. ἠγανάκτησαν. 'There were some that had indignation' (Mark); 'Then said one of his disciples, Judas Iscariot' (John).

ἡ ἀπώλεια. Cp. Polyb. vi. 59. 5, πρὸς τὴν ἀπώλειαν εὐφυεῖς, where ἀπώλ. is opposed to ἡ τήρησις.

10. γνοὺς δὲ ὁ Ἰησοῦς. The murmurings had been whispered at first. St Mark says, 'had indignation *within themselves*, and said, &c.'

ἔργον καλόν. A noble and beautiful work, denoting a delicate and refined sense of the fitness of things, which was lacking to the blunter perception of the rest.

The Lord passes a higher commendation on this than on any other act recorded in the N.T.; it implied a faith that enabled Mary to see, as no one else then did, the truth of the Kingdom. She saw that Jesus was still a King, though destined to die. The same thought—the certainty of the death of Jesus—that estranged Judas made her devotion more intense.

12. πρὸς τὸ κ.τ.λ. For this use of perfumes cp. 2 Chron. xvi. 14, 'They laid him (Asa) in the bed which was filled with sweet odours and divers kinds of spices prepared by the apothecaries' art.'

13. εἰς μνημόσυνον qualifies λαληθήσεται (not ἐποίησεν) as a final or consecutive clause. So either (1) 'to be a record or memorial of her'—something by which she will be remembered. Cp. Hdt. ii. 135, τοῦτο ἀναθεῖναι ἐς Δελφοὺς μνημόσυνον ἑωυτῆς. Or (2) with a sacrificial sense, 'for her memorial offering,' a meaning which μνημόσυνον bears in the only other passage where (with the exception of the parallel Mark xiv. 9) the word occurs in N.T., Acts x. 4, αἱ προσευχαί σου καὶ αἱ ἐλεημοσύναι σου ἀνέβησαν εἰς μνημόσυνον ἔμπροσθεν τοῦ θεοῦ. In the LXX. μνημόσυνον is used of the portion of the *minchah*, or flour-offering, which was burnt upon the altar: ἐπιθήσει ὁ ἱερεὺς τὸ μνημόσυνον αὐτῆς ἐπὶ τὸ θυσιαστήριον· θυσία ὀσμὴ εὐωδίας τῷ Κυρίῳ, Lev. ii. 2. Cp. the expression in John xii. 3, ἡ δὲ οἰκία ἐπληρώθη ἐκ τῆς ὀσμῆς τοῦ μύρου, where, though the word μνημόσυνον does not occur, ὀσμὴ suggests the odour of sacrificial incense. See Levit. xxiv. 7. 'Thou shalt put pure frankincense upon each row that it may be upon the bread for a memorial (ἀνάμνησιν, LXX.), even an offering by fire unto the Lord;' and Phil. iv. 18. τὰ παρ' ὑμῶν ὀσμὴν εὐωδίας θυσίαν δεκτήν, εὐάρεστον τῷ θεῷ.

14—16. THE TREACHERY OF JUDAS.
Mark xiv. 10, 11; Luke xxii. 3—6.

St Mark, like St Matthew, connects the treachery of Judas with the scene in Simon's house. His worldly hopes fell altogether at the thought of 'burial.' It is a striking juxtaposition: as Mary's is the highest deed of loving and clear-sighted faith, Judas' is the darkest act of treacherous and misguided hate.

The motive that impelled Judas was probably not so much avarice as disappointed worldly ambition. Jesus said of him that he was a 'devil' (*diabolus* or *Satan*), the term that was on a special occasion applied to St Peter, and for the same reason. Peter for a moment allowed the thought of the earthly kingdom to prevail; with Judas it was the predominant idea which gained a stronger and stronger hold on his mind until it forced out whatever element of good he once possessed. 'When the manifestation of Christ ceased to be attractive it became *repulsive;* and more so every day' (Neander, *Life of Christ*, Bohn's trans., p. 424).

15. κἀγώ. Here the form of the sentence is probably an example of colloquial simplicity, but the use of καί where in classical Greek the sentences would be joined by a consecutive (ὥστε) or final (ἵνα, ὅπως) particle, is a mark of Hebrew influence. Such sentences are connected by coordinate particles, and the relation between them is left to inference from the context.

ἔστησαν αὐτῷ τριάκοντα ἀργύρια. 'Weighed out for him thirty pieces of silver.' For this use of ἵστημι, cp. μὴ στήσῃς αὐτοῖς ταύτην τὴν ἁμαρτίαν, Acts vii. 60, and στατήρ, which, like its equivalent 'shekel,' originally meant 'a weight.'

τριάκοντα ἀργύρια. 'Thirty silver shekels.' St Matthew alone names the sum, which = 120 denarii. The shekel is sometimes reckoned at three shillings, but for the real equivalent in English money see note on *v.* 7. Thirty shekels was the price of a slave (Ex. xxi. 32); a fact which gives force to our Lord's words, ch. xx. 28, and to the passage there cited from Phil. ii. 7, 8.

16. εὐκαιρίαν. See Lob. *Phryn.* 126. εὐκαιρία is admitted as a classical word, but the verb εὐκαιρεῖν is rejected. προκόπτειν and προκοπή are an instance of the reverse. Cp. Cic. *de Offic.* I. 40, 'Tempus actionis opportunum Græce εὐκαιρία, Latine appellatur occasio.'

17—19. PREPARATIONS FOR THE LAST SUPPER.
Mark xiv. 12—16; Luke xxii. 7—13.

Nisan 13—from the sunset of Wednesday to the sunset of Thursday —Jesus seems to have passed in retirement; no events are recorded.

17. τῇ δὲ πρώτῃ κ.τ.λ. This was the 14th of Nisan, which commenced after sunset on the 13th; it was also called the preparation (παρασκευή) of the passover. The feast of unleavened bread followed the passover, and lasted seven days, from the 15th to the 21st of Nisan. Hence the two feasts are sometimes included in the term 'passover,' sometimes in that of 'unleavened bread.' On the evening of 13th of Nisan every head of the family carefully searched for and collected by the light of a candle all the leaven, which was kept and destroyed before midday on the 14th. The offering of the lamb took place on the 14th at the evening sacrifice, which on this day commenced at 1.30; or if the *preparation* fell on a Friday, at 12.30. The paschal meal was celebrated after sunset on the 14th, i.e. strictly on the 15th of Nisan.

The events of the Passover are full of difficulty for the harmonist. It is however almost certain that the 'Last Supper' was not the paschal meal, but was partaken of on the 14th, that is after sunset on the 13th of Nisan. It is quite certain, from John xviii. 28, that Jesus was crucified on the *preparation*, and although the synoptic narratives seem at first sight to disagree with this, it is probably only the want of a complete knowledge of the facts that creates the apparent discrepancy.

The order of events in the 'Passion' was as follows: when the 14th commenced, at sunset, Jesus sent two disciples to prepare the feast for that evening, instead of for the following evening. A sign of hastening on the meal may be detected in the words ὁ καιρός μου ἐγγύς ἐστιν, v. 18, cp. Luke xxii. 15, 'with desire I have desired to eat this passover with you *before I suffer*.' The supper succeeds, which bears a paschal character, and follows the paschal ceremonial. Early in the morning of the 14th of Nisan the irregular sitting of the Sanhedrin took place. Then followed the formal sitting of the Sanhedrin, and the trial before Pilate, the 'remission' to Herod, and, finally, the Crucifixion. This view meets the typical requirements of our Lord's death completely. During the very hours when our Great High Priest was offering Himself as a sacrifice for our sins upon the cross, the Jewish people were engaged in slaying thousands of lambs in view of the paschal feast about to commence.

18. πρὸς τὸν δεῖνα. 'To a certain man' (one who is known, but not named), with whom the arrangements had been previously made. He was doubtless a follower of Jesus. It was usual for the inhabitants of Jerusalem to lend guestchambers to the strangers who came to the feast, and no other payment was accepted save the skin of the paschal lamb.

20—30. THE LAST SUPPER.

Mark xiv. 17—26; Luke xxii. 14—38, where the dispute as to who should be the greatest is recorded, and the warning to Peter related as happening before Jesus departed for the Mount of Olives. St John omits the institution of the Eucharist, but relates the washing of the disciples' feet by our Lord, and has preserved the discourses of Jesus, chs. xiii.—xvii. end. 1 Cor. xi. 23—26; where the institution of the Eucharist is narrated nearly in St Luke's words.

20. ἀνέκειτο κ.τ.λ. Reclined with the Twelve. ἀνακεῖσθαι in this sense is late for the classical κατακεῖσθαι. This posture had not only become customary at ordinary meals, but was especially enjoined in the passover ritual. The Paschal ceremonial, so far as it bears on the Gospel narrative, may be described as follows:

(*a*) The meal began with a cup of red wine mixed with water: this is the *first* cup mentioned, Luke xxii. 17. After this the guests washed their hands. Here probably must be placed the washing of the disciples' feet, John xiii.

(*b*) The bitter herbs, symbolic of the bitter bondage in Egypt, were then brought in together with unleavened cakes, and a sauce called *charoseth*, made of fruits and vinegar, into which the unleavened bread and bitter herbs were dipped. This explains 'He it is, to whom I shall give a *sop*,' John xiii. 26.

(*c*) The *second* cup was then mixed and blessed like the first. The father then explained the meaning of the rite (Exod. xiii. 8). This was the *haggadah* or 'shewing forth,' a term transferred by St Paul to the Christian meaning of the rite (1 Cor. xi. 26). The first part of the '*hallel*' (Psalms cxiii. and cxiv.) was then chanted by the company.

(*d*) After this the paschal lamb was placed before the guests. This is called in a special sense 'the supper.' But at the Last Supper there was no paschal lamb. There was no need now of the typical lamb without blemish, for the antitype was there. Christ Himself was our Passover 'sacrificed for us' (1 Cor. v. 7). He was there being slain for us—His body was being given, His blood being shed. At this point, when according to the ordinary ritual the company partook of the paschal lamb, Jesus 'took bread and blessed it, and gave it to his disciples' (*v.* 26).

(*e*) The *third* cup, or 'cup of blessing,' so called because a special blessing was pronounced upon it, followed: 'after *supper* he took the cup' (Luke). 'He took the cup *when he had supped*' (Paul). This is the 'cup' named in *v.* 27.

(*f*) After a *fourth* cup the company chanted (see *v.* 30) the second part of the '*hallel*' (Psalms cxv.—cxviii.). (Lightfoot *Hor. Hebr.*, Dr Ginsburg in *Kitto's Encycl.*, Dr Edersheim *Temple Services*.)

22. λυπούμενοι σφόδρα. St John (xiii. 22) has the graphic words Ἔβλεπον οὖν εἰς ἀλλήλους οἱ μαθηταὶ ἀπορούμενοι περὶ τίνος λέγει. It is this moment of intense and painful emotion which Leonardo da Vinci has interpreted by his immortal picture, so true to the spirit of this scene, so unlike the external reality of it.

23. ὁ ἐμβάψας μετ' ἐμοῦ κ.τ.λ. John xiii. 26, Ἐκεῖνός ἐστιν ᾧ ἐγὼ βάψω τὸ ψωμίον καὶ δώσω αὐτῷ; here we have the words of the disciple who heard the reply of Jesus, which was probably whispered and not heard by the rest.

Ὁ ἐμβάψας...ἐν τῷ τρυβλίῳ τὴν χεῖρα. i.e. in the *charoseth*, see above, *v.* 20 (*b*).

24. καλὸν ἦν αὐτῷ κ.τ.λ. A familiar phrase in the Rabbinical Schools, used here with awful depth of certainty. The omission of ἄν makes the expression more emphatic. The condition is unfulfilled, but assuredly it would have been well if it had been fulfilled. In later Greek the tendency to this omission grows: cp. εἰ μὴ ἦν οὗτος παρὰ θεοῦ οὐκ ἠδύνατο ποιεῖν οὐδέν, John ix. 33. In modern Greek ἄν is always omitted in such cases. The same construction occurs in Latin. 'Antoni gladios potuit contemnere si sic | omnia dixisset,' Juv. Sat. x. 123. 'Me truncus illapsus cerebro | sustulerat nisi Faunus ictum | dextra levasset,' Hor. Od. II. 17. 27 (Winer, p. 382; Goodwin, pp. 96, 97).

εἰ οὐκ ἐγεννήθη. οὐ not μή after εἰ. Here οὐκ so entirely coalesces with ἐγεννήθη as to form with it a single verbal notion and to remain uninfluenced by εἰ. Cp. εἰ καὶ οὐ δώσει, Luke xi. 8, where οὐ δώσει = 'will refuse.' Cp. also 1 Cor. xi. 6, εἰ γὰρ οὐ κατακαλύπτεται γυνή, καὶ κειράσθω. Soph. Aj. 1131, εἰ τοὺς θανόντας οὐκ ἐᾷς θάπτειν. Plat. Apol. Socr. 25 B, ἐάν τε σὺ καὶ Ἄνυτος οὐ φῆτε ἐάν τε φῆτε. (Winer, p. 599 foll.; Goodwin, p. 88.)

25. Σὺ εἶπας. This is a formula of assent both in Hebrew and Greek, and is still used in Palestine in that sense. These words seem also to have been spoken in a low voice inaudible to the rest.

The special mention of Judas is omitted by St Mark and St Luke.

26. τοῦτό ἐστιν κ.τ.λ. Accurately, 'this is the body of me;' St Luke adds, 'which is in the act of being given for you' (τὸ ὑπὲρ ὑμῶν διδόμενον); St Paul, 'which is in the act of being broken for you' (τὸ ὑπὲρ ὑμῶν κλώμενον. Lachmann and Tischendorf omit κλώμενον); the sacrifice had begun, the body of Christ was already being offered. The expression may be paraphrased: 'This—the bread—and not the paschal lamb, represents—*is* to the faithful—the body of Me, who am even now being offered a sacrifice for you.' Without entering on the great controversy of which these four words have been the centre, we may note that; (1) the thought is not presented now for the first time to the disciples. It was the 'hard saying' which had turned many from Christ, see John vi. 51—57, 66. (2) The special form of the controversy is due to a mediæval philosophy which has passed away leaving 'the dispute of the sacraments' as a legacy. St Luke and St Paul have the addition, 'this do in remembrance of me'—now, as a memorial of *Me*, not of the Passover deliverance.

27. ποτήριον. See note v. 20 (e).

28. τοῦτο γάρ κ.τ.λ. The blood of the sacrifice was the seal and assurance of the old covenant, so wine, which is the blood of Christ once shed, is the seal of the new covenant.

The thought of shedding of blood would certainly connect itself with the ratification of a covenant in the minds of the apostles. From a covenant ratified by the victim's blood (Gen. xv. 18) began the divine and glorious history of the Jewish race. By sprinkling of blood the covenant was confirmed in the wilderness: see Ex. xxiv. 8, where the very expression occurs τὸ αἷμα τῆς διαθήκης (cp. 1 Pet. i. 2, ῥαντισμὸν αἵματος Ἰησοῦ Χριστοῦ), and now a new *B'rith* or covenant (cp. Jer. xxxi. 33) confirmed by the victim's blood is destined to be the starting point of a still more divine and glorious history. The Mediator of the New Covenant is ratifying it with the Princes of the New Israel.

καινῆς. See critical notes and ch. ix. 17.

διαθήκη means either (1) a 'covenant,' 'contract,' or (2) 'a will.' The first is the preferable sense here, as in most passages where the word occurs in N.T. the new covenant is contrasted with 'the covenant which God made with our fathers,' Acts iii. 25. For this reason it is to be regretted that the title 'new testament' rather than 'new covenant' has been adopted. The effect has been partly to obscure the continuity of the earlier and later dispensations.

περὶ πολλῶν, i.e. 'to save many:' this force of περί comes from the thought of encircling a thing or person, or fighting round him for the sake of protecting him: cp. ἀμύνεσθαι περὶ πάτρης, *Il.* xii. 243. ἀμυνέμεναι περὶ Πατρόκλοιο θανόντος, *Il.* xvii. 182.

πολλῶν. See note ch. xx. 23.

ἐκχυννόμενον. Now being shed. The sacrifice has already begun.

εἰς ἄφεσιν ἁμαρτιῶν. St Matthew alone records these words in this connection. Cp. Hebr. ix. 22, χωρὶς αἱματεκχυσίας οὐ γίνεται ἄφεσις—a passage which bears closely upon this. For the expression cp. βάπτισμα μετανοίας εἰς ἄφεσιν ἁμαρτιῶν, 'having for its end forgiveness.' The figure in ἄφεσις is either (1) that of forgiving a debt, the word being frequently used of the year of release: ἔσται ἡ πρᾶσις ἕως τοῦ ἕκτου ἔτους τῆς ἀφέσεως καὶ ἐξελεύσεται ἐν τῇ ἀφέσει, Levit. xxv. 28, or (2) from 'letting go' the sacrificial dove or scape-goat to symbolise the putting away of sins.

29. ὅταν αὐτὸ πίνω κ.τ.λ. The reference is to the feast, which is a symbol of the glorified life, cp. Luke xxii. 30. The new wine signifies the new higher existence (ch. ix. 17), which Christ would share with his Saints. The expression may also symbolize the Christian as distinguished from the Jewish dispensation, and be referred specially to the celebration of the Eucharist, in which Christ joins with the faithful in the feast of the Kingdom of God on earth.

30. ὑμνήσαντες. 'Having chanted' the second part of the *hallel*. See note on v. 20 (*f*).

31—35. ALL SHALL BE OFFENDED.

Mark xiv. 27—31; Luke xxii. 31—34. Cp. John xiii. 36—38 and xvi. 32.

31. γέγραπται. See note ch. ii. 5.

πατάξω κ.τ.λ. Zech. xiii. 7. The words do not literally follow the Hebrew. Both Hebrew and LXX. have imperative for future. The difference in form is as slight in Hebrew as in Greek (πατάξω, πάταξον). The context describes the purification of Jerusalem in the last days—'in that day there shall be a fountain opened to the house of David and to the inhabitants of Jerusalem'—the discomfiture of the false prophets, and the victory of Jehovah on the Mount of Olives.

It may be fitly remembered that the Valley of Jehoshaphat (in N.T. the Valley of Kedron) according to the most probable view derived its name—the Valley of the Judgment of Jehovah—not from the king of Judah, but from the vision of Joel (iii. 2 and 9—17), of which the prophecy of Zechariah is the repetition in a later age. If so, there is deep significance in the words recurring to the mind of Christ, as He trod the very field of Jehovah's destined victory. The prophecy carried on from age to age rested here in its fulfilment. Nor is it irreverent to believe that the thought of this vision brought consolation to the human heart of Jesus as he passed to his supreme self-surrender with the knowledge that He would be left alone, deserted even by his chosen followers.

32. The expression, προάξω, lit., 'I will lead you as a shepherd,' falls in with the thought of the quotation.

34. πρὶν ἀλέκτορα κ.τ.λ. 'This day, even in this night, before the cock crow twice, thou shalt deny me thrice' (Mark). A curious difficulty has been raised here from the fact that it was unlawful for Jews to keep fowls in the Holy City. Such rules, however, could not be applied to the Romans.

35. κἂν δέῃ με κ.τ.λ. Accurately, 'Even if I shall be obliged to die with thee.' σύν denotes the closest possible union. Contrast σὺν σοὶ ἀποθανεῖν with γρηγορῆσαι μετ' ἐμοῦ (v. 38). He who swore to die by the side of (σύν) Christ could not even watch in his company (μετά).

36—46. The Agony in the Garden of Gethsemane.
Mark xiv. 32—42; Luke xxii. 39—46; John xviii. 1.

In St Luke's account verses 43, 44 are peculiar to his Gospel. The use of ἀγωνία (ἅπαξ λεγ. in N.T.) by the same Evangelist has given the title to this passage.

St Luke also relates that 'there appeared an angel unto him from heaven, strengthening him.' There is, however, some reason for doubting the genuineness of these verses.

36. Γεθσημανεί = 'the oil press;' πέραν τοῦ χειμάρρου τῶν Κέδρων ὅπου ἦν κῆπος (John xviii. 1), χωρίον is an enclosed place or garden, answering to κῆπος.

37. τὸν Πέτρον κ.τ.λ. See ch. xvii. 1 and Mark v. 37. The Evangelist, St John, was thus a witness of this scene; hence, as we should expect, his narrative of the arrest of Jesus is very full of particulars.

ἀδημονεῖν. This word is found in the parallel passage, Mark xiv. 33 and in Phil. ii. 26, not elsewhere in N.T. Buttmann, *Lex.* p. 29 *foll.* connects it with ἄδημος, as if the train of thought were,—absence from home—perplexity—distress. It is better however to recur to the older derivation connecting it with ἄδην, ἀδῆσαι (see Bp. Lightfoot, on Phil. ii. 26), where the idea of the word would be either (1) 'satiety,' so painful weariness of life and life's work; cp. the use of the rare word ἄδος of the weary woodcutter: ἐπεί τ' ἐκορέσσατο χεῖρας | τάμνων δένδρεα μακρά ἄδος τέ μιν ἵκετο θυμόν (Π. xi. 88), loathing of his work, dislike to go on with it. Or (2) from the sense of physical derangement transferred to mental pain, 'distress,' 'agony of mind,' which agrees very well with the instance quoted by Buttmann of a woman threatened with violence: ἀδημονούσης τῆς ἀνθρώπου, Dem. de F. L. p. 402. The old lexicons give as synonyms, ἀγωνιᾶν, ἀλύειν, ἀπορεῖν, ἀμηχανεῖν.

38. ἡ ψυχή μου. Comp. John xii. 27, the only other passage in which Jesus ascribes to Himself a human ψυχή in this particular sense—the seat of the feelings and emotions.

γρηγορεῖτε μετ' ἐμοῦ. The Son of man in this dark hour asks for human sympathy.

μετ' ἐμοῦ. Only in Matthew.

39. προσελθὼν μικρόν. The paschal full moon would make deep shadow for the retirement of Jesus.

Πάτερ μου. St Mark has the Aramaic *Abba* as well as πάτερ.

τὸ ποτήριον τοῦτο. See note, ch. xx. 22. Were these words overheard by the sons of Zebedee? Christ was probably praying aloud, according to the usual custom. If so, the thought of their ambition and of their Master's answer would surely recur to them (ch. xx. 20—23).

οὐχ ὡς ἐγὼ θέλω. In the 'Agony,' as in the Temptation, the Son submits Himself to his Father's will.

40. οὐκ ἰσχύσατε; Had you not the ἰσχύς—the physical strength to watch? This was an instance of failing to serve God with their strength (ἐξ ὅλης τῆς ἰσχύος, Mark xii. 30). ἰσχύω, not a mere synonym of δύναμαι, seems always to retain some sense of physical power, cp. οἱ ἰσχύοντες, ch. ix. 12; ὥστε μὴ ἰσχύειν τινὰ παρελθεῖν διὰ τῆς ὁδοῦ ἐκείνης, ch. viii. 28; σκάπτειν οὐκ ἰσχύω, Luke xvi. 3, 'am not strong enough to dig.'

Note that the verb is in the plural. As Peter took the lead in the promise of devotion, Jesus by naming him singles him out for rebuke. St Mark has 'Simon (the name of the old life), sleepest thou? Couldest not thou watch one hour?'

41. τὸ μὲν πνεῦμα πρόθυμον κ.τ.λ. The touch of clemency mingled with the rebuke is characteristic of the gentleness of Jesus.

44. τὸν αὐτὸν λόγον εἰπών. This repetition of earnestness must be distinguished from the vain repetitions of ch. vi. 7.

45, 46. Καθεύδετε...ἐγείρεσθε κ.τ.λ. The sudden transition may be explained either (1) by regarding the first words as intended for a rebuke, or else (2) at that very moment Judas appeared, and the time for action had come. The short, quick sentences, especially as reported by St Mark, favour the second suggestion. The words ὁ υἱὸς τοῦ ἀνθρώπου παραδίδοται mark the approach of the band, ἰδοὺ ἤγγικεν ὁ παραδιδούς με that of Judas himself, who is now distinctly seen.

47—56. THE ARREST OF JESUS.

St Mark xiv. 43—50; St Luke xxii. 47—53; St John xviii. 3—11.

47. ὄχλος πολὺς κ.τ.λ. St John more definitely, 'having received a (strictly, *the*) band (of men) and officers from the chief priests and Pharisees' (xviii. 3). The band of men here = the maniple of Roman soldiers, placed at the service of the Sanhedrin by the Procurator. The same word is used Acts x. 1, xxi. 32, xxvii. 1. St Luke names the 'captains of the Temple' (xxii. 52). Hence the body, guided by Judas, consisted of (1) a maniple (σπεῖρα, see note ch. xxvii. 27) of Roman soldiers; (2) a detachment of the Levitical temple-guard (Luke); (3) certain members of the Sanhedrin and Pharisees.

ξύλων. 'clubs,' as Hdt. II. 63, μάχη ξύλοισι καρτέρη γίνεται. So also Polybius, Lucian, and other late authors. St John has μετὰ φανῶν καὶ λαμπάδων καὶ ὅπλων, xviii. 3.

49. Χαῖρε, ῥαββί. The joyous Greek salutation 'be glad,' and the Jewish term of respect 'my master.'

κατεφίλησεν αὐτόν, 'kissed him with fervour, or repeatedly;' cp. Xen. *Mem.* II. 6. 33, ὡς τοὺς μὲν καλοὺς φιλήσοντός μου, τοὺς δὲ ἀγαθοὺς καταφιλήσοντος.

50. Ἑταῖρε. See ch. xx. 13. In relation to the word ῥαββί (*v.* 49) the meaning of ἑταῖρε would be: 'thou, my disciple.'

ἐφ' ὅ. The sentence is best explained by an ellipse of ποίησον or some equivalent word, 'Do that for which thou art come.' ὅς is never used for τίς in the N.T. unless this be an instance. St Luke preserves the question to Judas: φιλήματι τὸν υἱὸν τὸν ἀνθρώπου παραδίδως;

ἐπέβαλον τὰς χεῖρας. ἐπιβάλλειν τὰς χεῖρας is a technical term, 'to arrest,' so frequently in the Acts: ἐπέβαλον αὐτοῖς τὰς χεῖρας καὶ ἔθεντο εἰς τήρησιν (Acts iv. 3).

τότε προσελθόντες ἐπέβαλον τὰς χεῖρας ἐπὶ τὸν Ἰησοῦν. St John, who does not mention the kiss of Judas, sets the self-surrender of Jesus in a clear light: 'I have told you that I am he: if therefore ye seek me, let these go their way.'

51. εἷς τῶν μετὰ Ἰησοῦ. This was St Peter, named by St John, but not by the earlier Evangelists, probably from motives of prudence.

τὴν μάχαιραν. Probably a short sword or dirk, worn in the belt.

τὸν δοῦλον. *The* servant, or rather slave. St John gives his name, Malchus. St Luke alone records the cure of Malchus.

τὸ ὠτίον. ὠτάριον (Mark). Lobeck, *on Phryn.* p. 211, remarks the tendency in common speech to express parts of the body by diminution, as τὰ ῥινία—τὸ ὀμμάτιον—στηθίδιον—χελύνιον—σαρκίον.

52—54. These verses are peculiar to Matthew; each Evangelist has recorded sayings unnoticed by the others. It is easy to understand that in these exciting moments each bystander should perceive a part only of what was said or done.

52. πάντες γάρ κ.τ.λ. To this reason for non-resistance Christ added another, 'The cup which my Father has given me shall I not drink it?' (John.)

λαβόντες μάχαιραν, i.e. against rightful authority. There may be some force in λαβόντες, 'take' the sword, handle it of their own pleasure and impulse; λαβή is a sword-hilt. Cp. οὐ γὰρ εἰκῇ τὴν μάχαιραν φορεῖ, Rom. xiii. 4, where φορεῖν the legitimate wearing of the sword may be contrasted with λαβεῖν. The truth of this saying was exemplified by the slaughter of nearly a million and a half of Jews, who 'took the sword' against Rome A.D. 67—70.

ἐν μαχαίρῃ. For instrumental ἐν see note, ch. iii. 11.

53. δοκεῖς ὅτι οὐ δύναμαι...καὶ παραστήσει. The form of the sentence is Aramaic, the real subject of the whole sentence being ὁ πατήρ: a regular Greek construction would express the thought of παρακαλέσαι by a participle or by a conditional clause. But though the form is irregular it throws into emphasis the certainty that the prayer would be granted. 'Can I not summon my Father to my aid as an ally in my extremity, and swiftly He will draw up by my side twelve legions of angels against the single maniple of the Roman guard.' παρακαλεῖν and παριστάναι are both military terms: cp. Hdt. vii. 158, ἐτολμήσατε ἐμὲ σύμμαχον παρακαλέοντες ἐλθεῖν, *advocantes socium*, 'Summoning me to be your ally.' For παριστάναι cp. Polyb. iii. 72. 9, τοὺς ἱππεῖς διελὼν ἐφ' ἑκάτερον παρέστησε τὸ κέρας, 'posted them,' &c., and Hdt. viii. 80, ἔδεε γὰρ ὅτε οὐκ ἑκόντες ἤθελον ἐς μάχην κατίστασθαι, ἄκοντας παραστήσασθαι. For the omission of ἤ after πλείω, the usual Attic construction, cp. Plato, *Apol. Socr.*, p. 17, ἔτη γεγονὼς πλείω ἐβδομήκοντα. So also in Latin, 'plus septima ducitur aestas,' Verg. *Georg.* iv. 207. For the neuter pl. πλείω (instead of πλείον), standing independent of the construction, see Lob. *Phryn*, p. 410, where several instances are given of constructive laxity in the case of numerals, e.g. οὐσίᾳ πλείον ἢ δέκα ταλάντων, Dem. c. *Aphob.* ii. 341; ὑπὲρ τετρακισχίλιοι ὄντες, Joseph. *Ant.* xviii. 1. 871. But none of the instances there given precisely meet this case.

δώδεκα λεγεῶνας κ.τ.λ. It is characteristic of this gospel that the authority and kingly majesty of Jesus should be suggested at a moment when every hope seemed to have perished.

λεγεῶνας. One of the few Latin words in this gospel, perhaps used with a special reason, as in the case of κῆνσον (ch. xxii. 17). Here probably the intention was to preserve the very term used by Jesus. The word might be suggested by the sight of the maniple (σπεῖρα) of the Roman soldiers; see note above.

55. λῃστήν, 'a robber,' not 'thief,' as A.V. Cp. St John x. 1, where the two words are distinguished. See note, ch. xxi. 13.

ἐκαθεζόμην διδάσκων. See note, ch. v. 1 (καθίσαντος).

According to St Luke these words were addressed to 'the chief priests, and captains of the temple, and elders,' where it appears that some members of the Sanhedrin had in their evil zeal joined in the capture. The same Evangelist adds, 'this is your hour, and the power of darkness' (xxii. 53).

56. τοῦτο δὲ ὅλον γέγονεν κ.τ.λ. These are probably the words of Christ, and not a reflection by the Evangelist (cp. Mark xiv. 49); if so, they were, for most of the disciples, their Master's last words.

For the tense of γέγονεν see notes, ch. i. 22, xxi. 4.

τότε, closely connected with the preceding words. If *this* was the fulfilment of prophecy, *their* interpretation was indeed mistaken. It was the death-blow to temporal hopes.

τότε...ἔφυγον. Note the beauty and nervous strength of this short clause. Each word has its special force and its true position. ἔφυγον 'fled,' as though by the capture of the leader the whole enterprise had failed. 'Quantæ in periculis fugæ proximorum!' (Cicero.)

57—68. JESUS IS BROUGHT BEFORE CAIAPHAS. THE FIRST AND INFORMAL MEETING OF THE SANHEDRIN.

St Mark xiv. 53—65; St Luke xxii. 54 and 63—65.

St Luke reports this first irregular trial with less detail than the other synoptists, but gives the account of the second *formal* sitting at greater length.

It is not clear whether the private examination, related by St John xviii. 19—23, was conducted by Annas or Caiaphas. Jesus was first taken to the house of Annas, whose great influence (he was still high priest in the eyes of the people) would make it necessary to have his sanction for the subsequent measures. Possibly 'the high priest' (John xviii. 19) was Caiaphas, but the expression 'therefore Annas sent him bound unto Caiaphas' (*v.* 24) makes this improbable.

The subjoined order of events is certainly not free from difficulties, but is the most probable solution of the question:

(1) From the garden Gethsemane Jesus was taken to Annas; thence, after brief questioning (St John xviii. 19—23),

(2) To Caiaphas, in another part of the Sacerdotal palace, where some members of the Sanhedrin had hastily met, and the *first* irregular trial of Jesus took place at night; Matt. xxvi. 57—68; Mark xiv. 52—65; Luke xxii. 54 and 63—65.

(3) Early in the morning a *second* and formal trial was held by the Sanhedrin. This is related by St Luke ch. xxii. 66—71; and is mentioned by St Matthew ch. xxvii. 1; and in St Mark xv. 1.

(4) The trial before Pontius Pilate, consisting of two parts: (*a*) a preliminary examination (for which there is a technical legal phrase in St Luke xxiii. 14); (*b*) a final trial and sentence to death.

(5) The *remission* to Herod, recorded by St Luke only, xxiii. 7—11; between the two Roman trials, (*a*) and (*b*).

The question is sometimes asked, Was the trial of Jesus fair and legal according to the rules of Jewish law? The answer must be that the proceedings against Jesus violated both (1) the spirit, and (2) the express rules of Hebrew jurisdiction, the general tendency of which was to extreme clemency.

(1) The Talmud states: 'The Sanhedrin is to save, not to destroy life.' No man could be condemned in his absence, or without a majority of two to one; the penalty for procuring false witnesses was death; the condemned was not to be executed on the day of his trial. This clemency was violated in the trial of Jesus Christ.

(2) But even the ordinary legal rules were disregarded in the following particulars: (*a*) The examination by Annas without witnesses. (*b*) The trial by night. (*c*) The sentence on the first day of trial. (*d*) The trial of a capital charge on the day before the Sabbath. (*e*) The suborning of witnesses. (*f*) The direct interrogation by the High Priest.

57. ἀπήγαγον. ἀπάγειν is used technically of carrying off to prison. Cp. Acts xii. 19, ἐκέλευσεν ἀπαχθῆναι, 'to be led off to execution.'

συνήχθησαν. St Mark describes the members of the Sanhedrin entering with Jesus (συνέρχονται αὐτῷ) to this pre-arranged irregular meeting.

58. τῶν ὑπηρετῶν. 'Attendants,' 'retinue.'

59. ἐζήτουν κ.τ.λ. See above (1): to *seek* witnesses at all was against the spirit of the law. The imperfect ἐζήτουν implies anxious and continued search.

61. δύναμαι καταλῦσαι κ.τ.λ. The actual words of Jesus spoken (John ii. 19) in the first year of his ministry were, λύσατε τὸν ναὸν τοῦτον καὶ ἐν τρισὶν ἡμέραις ἐγερῶ αὐτόν, not 'I am able to destroy' (note that ἐγερῶ is appropriate to raising from the dead, and is very different from οἰκοδομῆσαι). The attempt was to convict Jesus of blasphemy in asserting a superhuman power.

63. ἐξορκίζω. Here only in N.T. Used in classical authors in the sense of 'to administer an oath,' especially the military oath (sacramentum). Possibly the word may be used here in reference to the charge against Jesus, δαιμόνιον ἔχει.

ὁ υἱὸς τοῦ θεοῦ. The Jews might have recognised Jesus as the Messiah, but not as the Son of God.

64. σὺ εἶπας. See note, *v*. 25.

ἀπ' ἄρτι ὄψεσθε κ.τ.λ. Cp. Dan. vii. 13; ch. xvi. 27, xxiv. 30, xxv. 31.

ἐπὶ τῶν νεφ. See ch. xxiv. 30.

65. διέρρηξεν. This act was enjoined by the Rabbinical rules. When the charge of blasphemy was proved 'the judges standing on their feet rend their garments, and do not sew them up again.' τὰ ἱμάτια in the plural, because according to Rabbinical directions all the *under*garments were to be rent, 'even if there were ten of them.'

66. ἔνοχος κ.τ.λ. i.e. 'has incurred the penalty of death.' The Sanhedrin do not pass sentence, but merely re-affirm their foregone conclusion, and endeavour to have sentence passed and judgment executed by the Procurator. For ἔνοχος see note, ch. v. 22.

67. κολαφίζειν, 'to strike with clenched fist,' from κόλαφος, late for Attic κονδυλίζειν (κόνδυλος). Cp. ποῖον γὰρ κλέος εἰ ἁμαρτάνοντες καὶ κολαφιζόμενοι ὑπομενεῖτε, 1 Pet. ii. 20. See also 1 Cor. iv. 11; 2 Cor. xii. 7.

ῥαπίζειν, from ῥαπίς, 'a rod,' 'to strike with cudgels' (Hdt. Xen. Dem. Polyb. *al.*), later, to strike with the flat of the hand.

For οἱ δὲ with οἱ μὲν of the first clause suppressed cp. οἱ δὲ ἐδίστασαν, ch. xxviii. 17.

68. προφήτευσον ἡμῖν. Observe the coarse popular idea of prophecy breaking out, according to which prophecy is a meaningless exhibition of miraculous power. A similar vein of thought shews itself in the second temptation (ch. iv. 6).

69—75. The Denial of Peter.

St Mark xiv. 66—72; Luke xxii. 54—62; John xviii. 15—18, and 25—27.

The accounts differ slightly, and exactly in such a way as the evidence of honest witnesses might be expected to differ in describing the minor details (which at the time would appear unimportant) in a scene full of stir and momentous incidents. Discrepancies of this kind form the strongest argument for the independence of the different gospels. St Luke mentions that 'the Lord turned and looked upon Peter.' St John states that the third question was put by a kinsman of Malchus.

69. ἐν τῇ αὐλῇ. In the court. In Oriental houses the street door opens into an entrance hall or passage: this is the 'porch' (πυλῶνα) of v. 71; beyond this is a central court (αὐλή) open to the sky and surrounded by pillars. The reception rooms are usually on the ground floor, and are built round the central court. Probably the hall or room in which Jesus was being tried opened upon the court. Thus Jesus was able to look upon Peter.

73. λαλιά. An Aristophanic word, λαλιὰν ἀσκῆσαι, 'to talk (practise), gossip.' The same notion of contempt underlies the word, John iv. 42, οὐκέτι διὰ τὴν σὴν λαλιὰν πιστεύομεν. Here thy 'talk' or 'speech,' as in A.V., not definitely 'a dialect' (Schleusner). In the LXX. it is used generally for 'word' or 'speech.'

ἡ λαλιά σου κ.τ.λ. Peter was discovered by his use of the Galilæan dialect. The Galilæans were unable to pronounce the gutturals distinctly, and they lisped, pronouncing *sh* like *th*. Perhaps Peter said, 'I know not the *ith*,' instead of, 'I know not the *ish*' (man).

74. καταθεματίζειν. See critical notes *supra*. Cp. Rev. xxii. 3, where κατάθεμα is restored for κατανάθεμα. No other instance is cited either of noun or verb. They appear to be used as synonymous with ἀνάθεμα, 'an accursed thing,' and ἀναθεματίζειν, 'to devote to destruction,' 'to curse.' Two explanations may be given: (1) the meanings of ἀνά and κατά in composition so often coincide that an interchange of the two prepositions in noun- or verb-forms is quite explicable; (2) the original forms may have been κατανάθεμα, καταναθεματίζειν, and have fallen by usage to κατάθεμα, καταθεματίζειν, the Greek language shrinking from the union of κατά and ἀνά in composition, of which the instances are extremely rare.

75. ἔκλαυσεν, of loud and bitter wailing, in distinction from δακρύειν, 'to weep silently.' The latter verb is found once only in N. T., John xi. 35, ἐδάκρυσεν ὁ Ἰησοῦς.

CHAPTER XXVII.

2. אBL, several Versions and Fathers omit Ποντίῳ before Πιλάτῳ. The majority of MSS. give both names. Josephus generally has Πιλᾶτος only.

4. ὄψῃ has far higher authority than ὄψει. The Ionic termination of 2nd person in -ῃ was the usual form in late Attic, but the older termination in -ει was retained in three verbs—βούλει—οἴει—ὄψει, even after -ῃ became common in other instances, hence the variation in the MSS.

5. εἰς τὸν ναόν for ἐν τῷ ναῷ (אBL). In favour of ἐν τ. ν. AC and many uncials. The variation and evenly-balanced evidence is another proof of the close relationship between εἰς and ἐν. If εἰς τ. ν. be the true reading a very early copyist finds ἐν τ. ν. to be more intelligible or more natural.

16. Origen notes that in some Codices Ἰησοῦν was read before λεγόμενον in this verse and before Βαραββᾶν in the next. There is, however, no good evidence for the insertion, and (as Tregelles remarks) *vv.* 20 and 26 are fatal to it. Possibly, according to the same critic, the reading arose from the repetition in an uncial of the last letters of ὑμῖν, which would appear as IN and so resemble the ordinary contraction for Ἰησοῦν.

29. ἐν τῇ δεξιᾷ for ἐπὶ τὴν δεξιάν.

34. οἶνον for ὄξος, with the more ancient MSS. A and many uncials have the reading of the *textus receptus*.

35. Here the *textus receptus* has: ἵνα πληρωθῇ τὸ ῥηθὲν ὑπὸ τοῦ προφήτου· Διεμερίσαντο τὰ ἱμάτιά μου ἑαυτοῖς καὶ ἐπὶ τὸν ἱματισμόν μου ἔβαλον κλῆρον. The omission is made on quite decisive evidence, the authorities being headed by אABDL.

49. After this verse the important MSS. אBCL insert these words: ἄλλος δὲ λαβὼν λόγχην ἔνυξεν αὐτοῦ τὴν πλευράν, καὶ ἐξῆλθεν ὕδωρ καὶ αἷμα. Cp. John xix. 34. Evidence from the Fathers points to the very early existence of this important reading, which states that the Saviour was pierced while still living. The words are, however, rightly rejected by the best textual criticism. See Tischendorf and Meyer *ad loc.*, and Scrivener (*Introduction*, &c. p. 472, 480), who well points out the danger of following without discrimination the reading of even the oldest and most authoritative MSS.

54. γινόμενα, BD, some cursives and Origen; for γενόμενα אACL and many other uncials.

56. Ἰωσὴφ for Ἰωσῆ: the first is supported by א*DL, Versions and Origen, and the second by ABC, many other uncials and Fathers.

64. νυκτός, almost certainly a gloss, with very small support.

Ch. XXVII. 1. The Second and formal Meeting of the Sanhedrin.

St Mark xv. 1; St Luke xxii. 66—71; not mentioned by St John.

2. The Delivery to Pontius Pilate.

St Mark xv. 1; St Luke xxiii. 1; St John xviii. 28: 'then led they Jesus from Caiaphas unto the hall of Judgment (or *Prætorium*), and it was early.'

2. Πιλάτῳ. Pontius Pilatus was the governor, or more accurately, the Procurator of Judæa, which after the banishment of Archelaus (see ch. ii. 22) had been placed under the direct government of Rome, and attached as a dependency to Syria. Pilate filled this office during the last ten years of the reign of Tiberius, to whom as Procurator in an imperial province he was directly responsible. In the year A.D. 35 or 36, he was sent to Rome on a charge of cruelty to the Samaritans. The death of Tiberius probably deferred his trial, and according to Eusebius, 'wearied with his misfortunes,' he put himself to death. In character Pilate appears to have been impolitic, cruel and weak. On three signal occasions he had trampled on the religious feelings of the Jews, and repressed their resistance with merciless severity. A further instance of cruelty, combined with profanation, is alluded to, St Luke xiii. 1: 'the Galilæans, whose blood Pilate had mingled with their sacrifices.' The name Pontius connects Pilate with the *gens* of the Pontii, to which the great Samnite General, C. Pontius Telesinus, belonged. The *cognomen* Pilatus probably signifies 'armed with a *pilum*' (javelin). Tacitus mentions Pontius Pilate in a well-known passage (*Ann.* xv. 44), 'Auctor nominis ejus Christus Tiberio imperitante per procuratorem Pontium Pilatum supplicio affectus erat.' 'Christus, from whom the Christians are called, suffered death in the reign of Tiberius, under the procurator P. Pilate.' Many traditions have gathered round the name of Pontius Pilate. According to one, he was banished to Vienne in the south of France; according to another, he ended a restless life by plunging into a deep and gloomy lake on Mount Pilatus, near Lucerne. The shallow pool, often dry in the summer months, sufficiently disproves this story. The usual residence of the Roman Procurator in Judæa was Cæsarea Stratonis (see map).

The wish of the Sanhedrin in delivering Jesus to Pilate was to have their sentence confirmed without enquiry, see ch. xxvi. 66.

τῷ ἡγεμόνι. Pilate's special title as dependent governor of an imperial province was ἐπίτροπος (*procurator*), or 'high steward.' In the plural ἡγεμόνες is used as a general term. Cp. ἐπὶ ἡγεμόνας, ch. x. 18, and 1 Peter ii. 14. In the singular ἡγεμών is applied in the N.T. to the Procurators of Judæa, as here and elsewhere to Pilate, in Acts xxiii. 24 and elsewhere to Felix. In Luke iii. 1, ἡγεμονία means the imperium of Cæsar, ἡγεμονεύειν is used of the Proprætor Quirinus, Luke ii. 2. In the Acts St Luke distinguishes with great historical accuracy the various titles of the provincial governors. See note, ch. x. 18.

3—10. THE REMORSE OF JUDAS. HE RETURNS THE SILVER SHEKELS. THE USE MADE OF THEM. Peculiar to St Matthew.

3. ἰδὼν ὅτι κ.τ.λ. It has been argued from these words that Judas had not expected this result of his treachery. He had hoped that Jesus would by a mighty manifestation of His divine power usher in at once the Kingdom whose coming was too long delayed. The whole tenour of the narrative, however, contradicts such an inference.

μεταμεληθείς implies no change of heart or life, but merely remorse or regret that a wiser course had not been followed. Cp. καὶ μετεμέλοντο τὰς σπονδὰς οὐ δεξάμενοι, Thuc. IV. 27; οὐ μεταμέλομαι εἰ καὶ μετεμελόμην, 2 Cor. vii. 8; ὤμοσεν θεὸς καὶ οὐ μεταμεληθήσεται, Hebr. vii. 21; also ἀμεταμέλητα γὰρ τὰ χαρίσματα καὶ ἡ κλῆσις τοῦ Θεοῦ, Rom. xi. 29. See note, ch. xxi. 29, 30.

4. ἀθῷον, 'innocent,' here and v. 24 only in N.T., der. from θωή (Homeric), 'a penalty:' σοὶ δέ, γέρον, θωὴν ἐπιθήσομεν, *Od.* II. 192. In the classics it is used (1) absolutely, ἀθῷον ἐᾶν, 'free from penalty,' or (2) with a genitive, ἀθῷος πληγῶν, Aristoph. *Nub.* 1413. In the LXX., after the Hebrew idiom, it is constructed with ἀπό as in v. 24. The expression αἷμα ἀθῷον occurs Ps. xliii. 21, and is frequent in Jeremiah; cp. the expression νίψομαι ἐν ἀθῴοις τὰς χεῖράς μου, Ps. xxv. 6.

ὄψῃ. 'Thou shalt see,' it shall be thy concern. Cp. τάδε μὲν θεὸς ὄψεται, Soph. *Phil.* 839, 'This shall be the care of heaven.' Bengel's comment is: 'Impii in facto consortes post factum deserunt.' For the form ὄψῃ see critical notes.

5. εἰς τὸν ναόν. 'Into the holy place, which only the priests could enter.

ἀπελθὼν ἀπήγξατο. A different account of the end of Judas is given Acts i. 18, either by St Peter, or by St Luke in a parenthetical insertion. It is there stated (1) that Judas, not the Priests, bought the field; (2) that 'falling headlong he burst asunder in the midst, and all his bowels gushed out;' (3) that the field was called Aceldama for that reason, not for the reason stated in this passage. The two accounts are not actually inconsistent, but the key to their concordance is lost. No entirely satisfactory solution of the discrepancy has been given.

6. **εἰς τὸν κορβανᾶν.** For the prohibition cp. Deut. xxiii. 18.

7. **τὸν ἀγρὸν κ.τ.λ.** Tradition places *Aceldama* (Acts i. 19) in the valley of Hinnom, south of Jerusalem. The Athenians also had their κεραμεικός, the Potters' Quarter, in the most beautiful suburb of their city, where the illustrious dead were buried.

τοῖς ξένοις. i.e. for the Jews of the dispersion, Hellenists and proselytes. It is a note of the exclusiveness of those Jews whose home was still the Holy Land, that a plot of ground should be set apart for the burial of all who were not *par excellence* Hebrews. See Phil. iii. 5.

At the time of the Passover, when hundreds of thousands were crowded in a confined space, the question of burying strangers was doubtless urgent.

8. **ἕως τῆς σήμερον (ἡμέρας).** Cp. Latin, 'hodierno die,' Cic. *Cat.* III. 9. 21, and frequently.

9. **τὸ ῥηθὲν κ.τ.λ.** The citation is from Zech. xi. 12, but neither the Hebrew nor the LXX. version is followed exactly. The Hebrew literally translated is: "And Jehovah said to me, 'Cast it into the treasury;' a goodly price that I was prised at by them. And I took the thirty pieces of silver, and cast them into the treasury in the house of Jehovah." Zechariah, under the image of a shepherd, refuses any longer to lead the disobedient and divided flock, and asks for the price of his hire, which he then casts into the treasury. The discrepancy is probably due to the citation being made from memory. The ascription of the words to Jeremiah instead of to Zechariah may be assigned (1) to the same cause, or (2) explained, with Lightfoot (*Hor. Hebr. ad loc.*), by supposing that Jeremiah, who begins the Book of the Prophets according to one tradition, is intended to indicate the whole of that division of the Scriptures (see note ch. xvi. 14). Two other conjectures have been made: (3) That chs. ix., x. and xi. of Zechariah in the present Canon are the work of Jeremiah. (4) That in the original text the words διὰ τοῦ προφήτου stood alone and the name was added by an early copyist. The fact that St Matthew not unfrequently quotes in this manner without naming the book from which the citation is made is in favour of the conjecture. See chs. i. 22, ii. 5, xiii. 35, and xxi. 4 (Horne's *Introd.*, P. I. ch. 9, § 1.)

11—26. THE TRIAL BEFORE PONTIUS PILATE.

St Mark xv. 2—15; St Luke xxiii. 2—5 and 13—24; St John xviii. 29—xix. 16.

St Luke states the threefold charge most clearly: 'We found this [fellow] (1) perverting the nation; (2) and forbidding to give tribute to Cæsar; (3) saying that he himself is Christ a King.'

Pilate, true to the Roman sense of justice, refused merely to confirm the sentence of the Sanhedrin. 'He asked, what accusation bring ye against this man?' (John xviii. 29), being determined to try the case. This accusation amounted to a charge of treason—the greatest crime known to Roman law. Of the three points of accusation, (2) was utterly false; (1) and (3) though *in a sense* true, were not true in the sense intended. The answer or defence of Jesus is that He is a King, but that His 'kingdom is not of this world,' therefore (it is inferred) the 'perversion of the people' was not a rebellion that threatened the Roman government; see note v. 11. The defence was complete, as Pilate admits: 'I find no fault in him.'

11. Σὺ εἶ ὁ βασιλεὺς κ.τ.λ.; The answer of Jesus to this question, and His explanation to Pilate of the Kingdom of God are given at length, John xviii. 33—37; observe especially that the servants of the kingdom would fight, if they fought at all, not against Rome but against Israel who had rejected the Messiah: 'If my Kingdom were of this world, then would my servants fight that I should not be delivered to the *Jews*.'

Σὺ λέγεις. See note, ch. xxvi. 25.

12. ἀπεκρίνατο. 1 aor. mid. for the more usual 1 aor. passive. Of this form four instances occur in the Synoptic gospels, three in the parallel accounts of the Passion, the fourth Luke iii. 16.

14. Note the emphatic position of λίαν. Reserve during his trial was the last thing that Pilate's experience had led him to expect from a Jew.

15. ἀπολύειν κ.τ.λ. The origin of this custom is quite unknown; St Mark says, 'as he had ever done unto them,' as if the custom originated with Pilate; St Luke has, 'of necessity he must release;' St John, 'Ye have a custom.'

No trace of this custom is found in the Talmud. But the release of prisoners was usual at certain festivals at Rome, and at Athens during the Panathenaic festival prisoners enjoyed temporary liberty. It is not, therefore, improbable that Herod the Great, who certainly familiarised the Jews with other usages of Greece and Rome, introduced this custom, and that the Roman governor, finding the custom established and gratifying to the Jews, in accordance with Roman practice (see Introd. p. 22 (3)) retained the observance of it.

16. Βαραββᾶν = 'Son of a father,' or perhaps 'Son of a Rabbi.' The reading, Ἰησοῦν Βαραββᾶν, which appears in some copies, is rightly rejected by the best editors; see critical notes. As Alford remarks,

v. 20 is fatal to the insertion. St Mark and St Luke add that Barabbas had committed murder in the insurrection.

17. συνηγμένων κ.τ.λ. In accordance, probably, with the custom named, *v.* 15, an appeal was made to the *people*, not to the Sanhedrin. Pilate was sitting on the tribunal to ascertain the popular decision; at this point he was interrupted by his wife's messengers, and while he was engaged with them, the chief priests employed themselves in persuading the people to demand Barabbas rather than Christ.

19. ἐπὶ τοῦ βήματος. The βῆμα, or *tribunal*, was generally a raised platform in the Basilica or court where the judges sat; here a portable tribunal, from which the sentence was pronounced; it was placed on a tesselated pavement called Gabbatha (John xix. 13).

ἡ γυνὴ αὐτοῦ. Claudia Procula or Procla: traditions state that she was a proselyte of the gate, which is by no means unlikely, as many of the Jewish proselytes were women. By an imperial regulation provincial governors had been prohibited from taking their wives with them. But the rule gradually fell into disuse, and an attempt made in the Senate (A.D. 21) to revive it completely failed. 'Severus Cæcina censuit ne quem magistratum cui provincia obvenisset uxor comitaretur...paucorum hæc assensu audita plures obturbabant, neque relatum de negotio neque Cæcinam dignum tantæ rei censorem.' Tac. *Ann.* III. 33, 34. The dream of Pilate's wife is recorded by St Matthew only.

πολλὰ ἔπαθον. Not 'suffered many things' in the sense of suffering pain, but 'experienced many sensations,' i.e. 'felt much.'

20. ἵνα αἰτήσωνται κ.τ.λ. St Peter brings out the full meaning of this choice: 'ye denied the Holy One and the Just, and desired a murderer to be granted unto you; and killed the Prince of life' (Acts iii. 14, 15). They saved the murderer, and slew the Saviour.

21. τίνα θέλετε κ.τ.λ.; Once more the question is put to the people (see *v.* 17). His wife's message had made Pilate anxious to acquit Jesus. But the very form of the question implied condemnation. Jesus was classed with Barabbas in the category of condemned prisoners.

22. τί οὖν ποιήσω τὸν Ἰησοῦν; ποιεῖν has the classical construction τι τινά (instead of the usual τι τινί) here only for certain. In the parallel passage, Mark xv. 12, the reading of Lachm. and Treg. (ὃν λέγετε *om.*) gives another instance, and the reading of Tisch. is not inconsistent with this construction. The coincidence would imply an exact reproduction of Pilate's words, (the trial would be conducted in Greek), and the correctness of structure in this single instance seems to indicate the higher culture of an educated Roman.

23. οἱ δὲ περισσῶς κ.τ.λ. There is no further question even of a show of legality or justice: the traditional clemency is quite forgotten; the fanatical crowd, pressing round the doors of the Prætorium, which they cannot enter, join with excited gesticulation in one loud and furious cry for the blood of Jesus.

It is a forecast of the brutal popular cry 'Christianos ad leones,' which in that or more subtle forms doomed many martyrs in all ages.

This is often quoted as an instance of the fickleness of popular favour, and a contrast is drawn between the shouts of 'hosanna' a few days before and the cries of σταυρωθήτω now. But when the Jews present at the feast were numbered by hundreds of thousands, it is not necessary to think that the same crowds who hailed Jesus as the Messiah were now demanding his death.

24. ἰδὼν δὲ κ.τ.λ. St Luke relates a further attempt on Pilate's part to release Jesus, 'I will chastise Him and let Him go' (Luke xxiii. 22). Will not the cruel torture of a Roman scourging melt their hearts?

St John, at still greater length, narrates the struggle in Pilate's mind between his sense of justice and his respect for Jesus on the one hand, and on the other his double fear of the Jews and of Cæsar. (1) He tried to stir their compassion by shewing Jesus to them crowned with thorns and mangled with the scourging; (2) hearing that Jesus called Himself the 'Son of God,' he 'was the more afraid;' (3) at length he even 'sought to release Him,' but the chief priests conquered his scruples by a threat that moved his fears, 'If thou let this man go thou art not Cæsar's friend.' This was the charge of treason which Tacitus says (*Ann.* III. 39) was 'omnium accusationum complementum.' The vision of the implacable Tiberius in the background clenched the argument for Pilate. It is the curse of despotism that it makes fear stronger than justice.

λαβὼν ὕδωρ κ.τ.λ. Recorded by St Matthew only. In so doing Pilate followed a Jewish custom which all would understand. Deut. xxi. 6; Ps. xxvi. 6.

ὑμεῖς ὄψεσθε. See note *v.* 4.

25. τὸ αἷμα αὐτοῦ κ.τ.λ. Also peculiar to Matthew. St Peter finds as the sole excuse for his fellow countrymen, 'I wot that through ignorance ye did it, as did also your rulers' (Acts iii. 17). The prayer of Jesus on the cross for his murderers was meant for these as well as for the Roman soldiers.

26. φραγελλώσας. Here and Mark xv. 15, from Latin '*flagello.*' Scourging usually preceded crucifixion. It was in itself a cruel and barbarous torture, under which the victim often perished.

27—30. JESUS IS MOCKED BY THE ROMAN SOLDIERS.
Mark xv. 16—19. John xix. 1—3.

St Luke, who records the mockery of Herod's soldiers, makes no mention of these insults on the part of the Roman guard.

27. οἱ στρατιῶται τοῦ ἡγεμόνος. The Procurator's body-guard as opposed to ὅλην τὴν σπεῖραν.

τὸ πραιτώριον meant originally (1) the general's tent; (2) it was then used for the residence of the governor or prince, cp. Acts xxiii. 35; (3) then for an official Roman villa or country house; (4) barracks especially for the Prætorian guard; (5) the Prætorian guard itself (Phil. i. 13). The second meaning (2) is to be preferred here.

ὅλην τὴν σπεῖραν, 'the whole maniple.' The article is explained by a passage of Josephus, B. J. v. 5. 8, where it is stated that during the great festivals a 'maniple' (σπεῖρα or τάγμα, see Schweighäuser's *Lex.* Polyb. *sub voc.* τάγμα) was kept under arms to quell any disturbance that might arise. It was this body that was sent to arrest Jesus λαβὼν τὴν σπεῖραν, John xviii. 3. Cp. Acts xxi. 31, where allusion is made to the same force, ἀνέβη φάσις τῷ χιλιάρχῳ τῆς σπείρης ὅτι ὅλη συγχύννεται Ἱερουσαλήμ. The *manipulus* was the thirtieth part of the Roman legion, and the third part of a cohort, consisting therefore nominally of 200 men. Cp. Theophylact (quoted by Wetstein), κουστωδία ξ' (60) ἐστι στρατιωτῶν ἡ δὲ σπεῖρα σ' (200). This agrees with the number of the escort sent to conduct Paul to Cæsarea, Acts xxiii. 23. There seems to be no good reason for translating σπεῖρα 'cohort,' in Acts x. 1. Polyb. says expressly (XI. 23. 1) τρεῖς σπείρας· τοῦτο δὲ καλεῖται τὸ σύνταγμα τῶν πεζῶν παρὰ Ῥωμαίοις κόορτις.

The word itself, σπεῖρα, anything *twisted round* like a ball of thread, is a translation of 'manipulus' (a wisp of hay).

28. χλαμύδα κοκκίνην. A soldier's scarf, Lat. *chlamys:* it was generally worn by superior officers, but its use was not confined to them. This may have been a worn-out scarf belonging to Pilate; it is different from ἐσθῆτα λαμπράν, (Luke xxiii. 11), which Herod's soldiers put on Jesus. Scarlet was the proper colour for the military chlamys; cp. 'coccum imperatoriis dicatum paludamentis.' Plin. *H. N.* XXII. 10. (See *Dict. of Ant.*) St Mark has the less definite πορφύραν; St John ἱμάτιον πορφυροῦν. *Purpureus*, however, is used by Latin writers to denote any bright colour.

29. στέφανον κ.τ.λ. It cannot be ascertained what especial kind of thorn was used. The soldiers, as Bp. Ellicott remarks, would take what first came to hand, utterly careless whether it was likely to inflict pain or no.

ὁ βασιλεὺς τῶν Ἰουδαίων. Cp. ch. ii. 2, and xxvii. 37.

31, 32. Jesus is led to Crucifixion.
Mark xv. 20, 21; Luke xxiii. 26—32; John xix. 16, 17.

St Luke has several particulars of what happened on the way to Golgotha, omitted in the other Gospels. The great company of people and of women who followed Him; the touching address of Jesus to the women; the last warning of the coming sorrows; the leading of two malefactors with Him.

31. ἀπήγαγον. See note ch. xxvi. 57. St Mark has φέρουσιν, possibly implying that Jesus through physical weakness needed support on the way to the Cross.

32. ἄνθρωπον Κυρηναῖον. (1) 'coming out of the country' (Mark and Luke), (2) the father of Alexander and Rufus (Mark).

(1) This has been thought to imply that Simon was returning from work, and hence that it cannot have been the actual day of the Feast. Simon was probably coming into the city for the Paschal sacrifice, the hour for which was close at hand. (2) Rufus is probably the Christian named Rom. xvi. 13, who would be known to St Mark's readers. May not Simon have been one of those 'Men of Cyrene' who preached the word to Greeks when others preached to the Jews only? (Acts xi. 20.) The inference that he was already an adherent of Christ is quite uncertain.

For an account of the foundation of Cyrene see Hdt. III. 158 *foll.* For the origin of the Jewish colony there see Joseph. *c. Apion.* II. 4: Πτολεμαῖος ὁ Λάγου...Κυρήνης ἐγκρατῶς ἄρχειν βουλόμενος καὶ τῶν ἄλλων τῶν ἐν τῇ Λιβύῃ πόλεων εἰς αὐτὰς μέρος Ἰουδαίων ἔπεμψε κατοικῆσον. The expression in Acts ii. 10, τὰ μέρη τῆς Λιβύης τῆς κατὰ Κυρήνην, points to its position as metropolis of the district. The Cyrenians had a synagogue in Jerusalem (Acts vi. 9), of which Simon was probably a member. Lucius of Cyrene is named among the 'prophets and teachers' at Antioch (Acts xiii. 1) who bidden by the Holy Ghost separated Barnabas and Saul for the work, and laid their hands on them and sent them away. This Lucius, according to tradition, was first bishop of Cyrene. The district was however connected politically with Crete, together with which it formed a Roman Province—this arrangement would probably, as in other cases, determine the ecclesiastical jurisdiction.

ἠγγάρευσαν. See note ch. v. 41, where the same word is used, and the custom referred to of which this is an instance. If, as was probable, Simon became a Christian, it would be his pride to have been 'pressed into the service' of the Great King.

33—50. THE CRUCIFIXION AND DEATH OF JESUS.

Mark xv. 22—37; Luke xxiii. 33—46; John xix. 18—30.

St Mark's account differs little from St Matthew's. St Luke names the mockery of the soldiers and the words of the robbers to one another and to Jesus. Three of the sayings on the cross are related by St Luke only: 'Father, forgive them; for they know not what they do;' —'Verily, I say unto thee, To day shalt thou be with me in paradise;' —'Father, into thy hands I commend my spirit.' Among other particulars recorded by St John alone are the attempt to alter the superscription—the commendation of His mother to John—the breaking of the malefactors' legs—the piercing of Jesus—three sayings from the cross: 'Woman, behold thy son!' and to the disciple, 'Behold thy mother!'—'I thirst'—'It is finished.' St Matthew and St Mark alone record the cry of loneliness: 'Eli, Eli, lama sabachthani?'

33. εἰς τόπον κ.τ.λ. The site of Golgotha is not known for certain, but see notes to Plan of Jerusalem; it was outside the walls, but 'nigh to the city' (John xix. 20), probably near the public road where people passed by (*v.* 39), it contained a garden (John xix. 41). The name, which = 'place of a skull,' is generally thought to be derived from the shape and appearance of the hillock or mound on which the crosses were reared. This, however, is uncertain. Pictures often mislead by representing the crucifixion as taking place on a lofty hill at a considerable distance from the city.

The English 'Calvary' comes from the Vulgate translation of Luke xxiii. 33, 'Et postquam venerunt in locum qui vocatur Calvariæ.' Calvaria = 'a bare skull.'

34. οἶνον κ.τ.λ. 'Wine mingled with myrrh' (Mark). This was the 'sour wine,' or *posca*, ordinarily drunk by the Roman soldiers. 'Vinum atque acetum milites nostros solere accipere: uno die vinum, alio die acetum' (Ulpian, quoted by Wetstein). The potion was a stupefying draught given to criminals to deaden the sense of pain. 'Some of the wealthy ladies of Jerusalem charged themselves with this office of mercy' (Lightfoot, *ad loc.*). Jesus refuses this alleviation of his sufferings.

35. σταυρώσαντες. From the fact of the *titulus* or inscription being placed over the Saviour's head, it is inferred that the cross on which He suffered was such as is usually shewn in pictures, the *crux immissa* (†) or Latin cross as distinguished from the *crux commissa* (T) or the *crux decussata* (×), the form of cross on which St Andrew is said to have suffered. The height was from 9 to 12 feet; at a short distance from the ground a projecting rest supported the sufferer's feet, which, as well as the hands, were nailed to the cross.

According to St Mark (xv. 25) the Crucifixion took place at the third hour—nine o'clock. St John (xix. 14) says it was about the sixth hour when Pilate delivered Jesus to be crucified.

This discrepancy has received no entirely satisfactory solution. It has however been suggested that St John, writing at a later period and in a different part of the world, may have followed a different mode of reckoning time. How easily such difficulties may arise can be seen by the curious fact that *noon*, which means the ninth hour (*nona hora*) or three o'clock, is now used for twelve o'clock. The explanation would be difficult to those who did not know the historical facts.

διεμερίσαντο κ.τ.λ. St John describes the division more accurately; they divided His ἱμάτια, or outer garments, but cast lots for the seamless χιτών, or tunic. The latter is said to have been a dress peculiar to Galilæan peasants.

The Greek of the quotation from Ps. xxii. 18 (see below) does not convey the same distinction.

36. ἐτήρουν αὐτόν, fearing lest a rescue should be attempted by the friends of Jesus.

37. τὴν αἰτίαν κ.τ.λ. It was the Roman custom to place on the cross over the criminal's head, a *titulus*, or placard, stating the crime for which he suffered. St John records Pilate's refusal to alter the inscription, and mentions that the title was written in Hebrew and Greek and Latin.

ὁ βασιλεὺς τῶν Ἰουδαίων. See note ch. ii. 2.

The inscription is given with slight variations by the four Evangelists. ὁ βασιλεὺς τῶν Ἰουδαίων (Mark xv. 26). ὁ βασιλεὺς τῶν Ἰουδαίων οὗτος (Luke xxiii. 38). Ἰησοῦς ὁ Ναζωραῖος ὁ βασιλεὺς τῶν Ἰουδαίων (John xix. 19). This variation points to the independence of the different Gospels, and also indicates that a real though not a verbal accuracy should be looked for in the records of the Evangelists.

38. δύο λῃσταί, 'Two robbers'; in all probability partners in the crime of Barabbas. The mountain robbers, or banditti, were always ready to take part in such desperate risings against the Roman power. In the eyes of the Jews they would be patriots.

Josephus tells of one leader of robbers who burnt the palaces in Jericho (*B. J.* II. 6), and of another who for twenty years had wasted the country with fire and sword.

Note the absence of αὐτοῦ after δεξιῶν and εὐωνύμων. See notes, ch. xxv. 31 (1).

39. See Ps. xxii. 7. This was not a Psalm of David, but was probably 'composed by one of the exiles during the Babylonish Captivity... who would cling to the thought that he suffered not only as an individual, but as one of the chosen of God. But it has more than an individual reference. It looks forward to Christ.' Dean Perowne on Ps. xxii.

40. ὁ καταλύων κ.τ.λ. This is the mockery of the Jewish populace, who have caught up the charges brought against Jesus before the Sanhedrin. The taunts of the soldiers are named by St Luke alone: 'If thou be the King of the Jews, save thyself' (xxiii. 37).

41. οἱ ἀρχιερεῖς κ.τ.λ. Members of the Sanhedrin, the 'rulers' of Luke xxiii. 35.

42. ἄλλους ἔσωσεν κ.τ.λ. These words in the original would recall the 'hosannas' in the Temple which had enraged the chief priests; see note, ch. xxi. 9. They also connect themselves with the name of Jesus (σωτήρ).

βασιλεὺς Ἰσραήλ. Comp. ὁ βασιλεὺς τῶν Ἰουδ. *supra* v. 37, and see John i. 49, xii. 13.

43. πέποιθεν κ.τ.λ. See Ps. xxii. 8 [LXX. xxi. 9]: ἤλπισεν ἐπὶ Κύριον, ῥυσάσθω αὐτὸν σωσάτω αὐτὸν ὅτι θέλει αὐτόν. The chief priests unconsciously apply to the true Messiah the very words of a Messianic psalm.

εἰ θέλει αὐτόν. A late construction frequent in LXX. Cp. the quotation chs. ix. 13 and xii. 7: ἔλεον θέλω καὶ οὐ θυσίαν (Hos. vi. 6). On the still more unclassical idiom, θέλων ἐν ταπεινοφροσύνῃ, Col. ii. 18, see Bp. Lightfoot *ad loc.*

44. τὸ δ' αὐτὸ κ.τ.λ. They would naturally catch at the thought that the deliverer failed to give deliverance. St Luke alone relates that 'one of the malefactors which were hanged railed on him...the other answering rebuked him.' It is by no means impossible that the penitent robber may have seen and heard Jesus in Galilee.

45. ἀπὸ δὲ ἕκτης κ.τ.λ. From 12 to 3 o'clock in the afternoon, the hours of the Paschal sacrifice.

σκότος ἐγένετο κ.τ.λ. Not the darkness of an eclipse, for it was the time of the Paschal full moon, but a miraculous darkness symbolic of that solemn hour, and veiling the agonies of the Son of Man, when human soul and body alike were enduring the extremity of anguish and suffering for sin

46. Ἠλὶ ἠλί, λεμὰ σαβαχθανεί; (Ps. xxii. 1). Sh'baktani is an Aramaic form and occurs in the Chaldee paraphrase for the Hebrew 'azabtani. Such quotations of the Aramaic are very valuable and interesting as evidence of the language most familiar to Jesus, and also of the reverent accuracy of the Evangelists.

The repetition, θεέ μου, θεέ μου, gives a deeply pathetic force; cp. ch. xxiii. 37. It is an expression of utter loneliness and desolation, the depth of which it is not for man to fathom. Yet, 'it is going beyond Scripture to say that a sense of God's wrath extorted that cry. For to the last breath He was the well-beloved of the Father, and the repeated 'My God! My God!' is a witness even then to His confidence in His Father's Love' (Dean Perowne. Ps. xxii. 1).

Just as we are permitted to know that a particular passage of Zechariah was passing through the Saviour's mind as He crossed the valley of Kedron, so now we learn that Jesus, who in his human agony on the Cross had watched the various incidents that brought the words of that particular Psalm to his soul, found no words more fit to express the sense of awful desolation in that dark hour than the cry of the unknown psalmist—a captive perhaps by the waters of Babylon—in whose breast was such deep sorrow that it was like the sorrow of the Son of Man.

θεέ. Noticeable as perhaps the only instance of this—the regular form of the vocative of θεός.

ἱνατί; Elliptical for ἵνα τί γένηται; 'in order that what may happen?' So 'to what end?' precisely synonymous with εἰς τί (Mark xv. 34).

ἐγκατέλιπες; Cp. John xvi. 32: ἰδοὺ ἔρχεται ὥρα καὶ ἐλήλυθεν ἵνα σκορπισθῆτε ἕκαστος εἰς τὰ ἴδια κἀμὲ μόνον ἀφῆτε· καὶ οὐκ εἰμὶ μόνος ὅτι ὁ πατὴρ μετ' ἐμοῦ ἐστίν. Now even the sense of the Father's presence was lost.

This was probably the fourth word from the cross; the fifth 'I thirst' (John); the sixth 'It is finished' (John); the seventh 'Father, into thy hands I commend my spirit' (Luke). It is thought by some that after these words the darkness, which had lasted to the ninth hour, rolled away; others think that it lasted till the death of Jesus.

The thought of the Saviour's loneliness upon the cross has perhaps never been more feelingly expressed than in the smaller of Vandyke's two pictures of 'Christ on the Cross' in the Museum at Antwerp—the single figure dimly seen with none beside Him, or near, and a background of impenetrable darkness.

47. Ἠλίαν κ.τ.λ. This was probably spoken in pure mockery, not in a real belief that Jesus expected the personal reappearance of Elijah,

Wetstein notes that there were tales current among the Jews of the intervention of Elijah to rescue persons from the imminent peril of death.

48. λαβὼν σπόγγον κ.τ.λ. The soldiers' sour wine (*posca*), the reed, or hyssop stalk (John), and the sponge, were kept in readiness to quench the sufferers' thirst.

49. ἄφες ἴδωμεν. We must understand this to mean either (1) leave *him*, do not assist him; or (2) leave *it*, do not give the draught to him; or (3) ἄφες coalesces with the verb following as in modern Greek, and = 'let us see.' For the construction cp. ch. vii. 4 and Luke vi. 42. In Mark the words ἄφετε ἴδωμεν are put in the mouth of him who offered the wine to the Saviour. There ἄφετε may mean, 'let me alone.'

50. κράξας φωνῇ μεγάλῃ. Perhaps an inarticulate cry is meant, or perhaps the sixth word from the cross, τετέλεσται. John xix. 30.

ἀφῆκεν κ.τ.λ. As in classical Greek, Hdt. IV. 190, φυλάσσοντες ἐπεὰν ἀπίῃ τὴν ψυχήν: and Eur. *Hec.* 571, ἐπεὶ δ' ἀφῆκε πνεῦμα. St Luke preserves the exact words, πάτερ, εἰς χεῖράς σου παρατίθεμαι τὸ πνεῦμά μου (xxiii. 46).

51—56. EVENTS THAT FOLLOWED THE CRUCIFIXION. (1) THE VEIL OF THE TEMPLE RENT; (2) THE EARTHQUAKE; (3) THE SAINTS ARISE; (4) THE CENTURION AT THE CROSS; (5) THE WATCHING OF THE WOMEN.

Of these, (2) and (3) are peculiar to St Matthew. Mark xv. 38—41; Luke xxiii. 45, 47—49, where the grief of the spectators is an additional fact. St John omits these incidents, but records the breaking of the malefactors' legs and the piercing of Jesus' side.

51. τὸ καταπέτασμα κ.τ.λ. The veil meant is that which separated the holy of holies from the holy place. The rending of the veil signifies that henceforth there is free access for man to God the Father through Jesus Christ. Cp. 'Having therefore, brethren, boldness to enter into the holiest by the blood of Jesus, by a new and living way, which he hath consecrated for us, through the veil, that is to say, his flesh' (Heb. x. 19, 20). The incident would be observed and made known to the Church by the priests, of whom afterwards 'a great company were obedient unto the faith' (Acts vi. 7).

ἐσχίσθη...εἰς δύο. Examples of this expression are given from Polybius, Lucian, and other late authors. St Luke has the more classical idiom, ἐσχίσθη τὸ καταπ. τοῦ ναοῦ μέσον.

52. τῶν κεκοιμημένων ἁγίων. κοιμᾶσθαι twice in this gospel, here figuratively of death; ch. xxviii. 13, of literal sleep. The figure is quite classical, as ὣς ὁ μὲν αὖθι πεσὼν κοιμήσατο χάλκεον ὕπνον, *Il.* λ. 241. Cp. the beautiful lines of Moschus, *Id.* III. 109—111:

> ἄμμες δ' οἱ μεγάλοι καὶ καρτεροὶ ἢ σοφοὶ ἄνδρες
> ὁππότε πρᾶτα θάνωμες ἀνάκοοι ἐν χθονὶ κοίλᾳ
> εὕδομες εὖ μάλα μακρὸν ἀτέρμονα νήγρετον ὕπνον.

and Verg. *Æn.* VII. 277, 'et consanguineus leti sopor.' With Christianity it became the usual word to express the sleep of death, see 1 Cor. xv. 6, 18; hence κοιμητήριον (cemetery), the resting-place of the dead.

53. ἐκ τῶν μνημείων. There were doubtless other tombs besides Joseph's near Golgotha.

ἔγερσιν, late in this sense.

54. ἑκατόνταρχος. The centurion in command of the guard of four soldiers who watched the execution. It is interesting to think that this officer would in all probability generally be quartered in the garrison town of Cæsarea, where the centurion Cornelius (Acts x. 1) was also stationed.

As the Roman centurions were not chosen so much for impetuous courage as for judgment, firmness and presence of mind, there were doubtless many noble and thoughtful characters among them; cp. (especially the last phrase): βούλονται δὲ εἶναι τοὺς ταξιάρχους (centurions) οὐχ οὕτω θρασεῖς καὶ φιλοκινδύνους ὡς ἡγεμονικοὺς καὶ στασίμους καὶ βαθεῖς μᾶλλον ταῖς ψυχαῖς κ.τ.λ. Polyb. VI. 24. 9.

ἀληθῶς θεοῦ υἱὸς ἦν οὗτος. In Luke xxiii. 47, ὄντως ὁ ἄνθρωπος οὗτος δίκαιος ἦν—a translation of St Matthew's phrase for Gentile readers.

διακονοῦσαι. The beginning of the ministry of women—the female diaconate—in the Christian Church. The loving tendance of these women is a relief to the dark picture of the 'afflictions of Christ,' a relief recognised and feelingly expressed by all the great mediæval painters.

56. St Mark (xv. 40) specifies the group as 'Mary Magdalene, and Mary the mother of James the less (rather, *the little*) and of Joses, and Salome.'

Μαρία ἡ Μαγδαληνή. Mentioned here for the first time by St Matthew. She was probably named from Magdala (*Mejdel*) on the Lake of Gennesaret; see map. She had been a victim of demoniacal possession, but was cured by Jesus (Luke viii. 2), and then joined the company of faithful women who followed Him with the Twelve. Mary Magdalene is named by St John as standing by the cross of Jesus, together with 'his mother, and his mother's sister, Mary the wife of Cleophas' (xix. 25). With these she watched the entombment of the Lord, and, after the Sabbath rest, early in the morning she was present at the sepulchre with sweet spices to anoint Him.

The great Italian painters have identified Mary Magdalene either with the 'woman that was a sinner' who anointed Jesus in the house of Simon the Pharisee (Luke vii. 36—50), or with Mary the sister of Lazarus. But neither identification can be sustained on critical grounds.

Μαρία κ.τ.λ. Perhaps the same Mary who was the wife of Cleophas, Clopas, or Alphæus (different forms of one name), mentioned John xix. 25. If so, according to *one* interpretation of the passage in John, the sister of the Blessed Virgin.

ἡ μήτηρ κ.τ.λ. Salome. See ch. xx. 20.

The record of the names of these women and the special note of their presence seems intended to be an express testimony to their high courage and devotion, which kept them on the scene of danger when the disciples had fled. The deed of them contrasts with the words of Peter and of all the Apostles (ch. xxvi. 35).

57—66. THE ENTOMBMENT.

Mark xv. 42—47; Luke xxiii. 50—56; John xix. 38—42.

Vv. 62—66 are peculiar to St Matthew. St Mark notes the wonder of Pilate that Jesus was already dead, and the evidence of the centurion to the fact. St John mentions the co-operation of Nicodemus—like Joseph, a member of the Sanhedrin, who 'consented not to the deed of them;' who brought 'a mixture of myrrh and aloes about a hundred pound weight.'

57. Arimathæa is generally identified with Ramathaim-zophim, on Mount Ephraim, the birth-place of Samuel (1 Sam. i. 1), the site of which is undetermined. Many authorities place it much nearer to Jerusalem than the position indicated in the map.

Ἰωσήφ. From the other two Synoptic Gospels we learn that he was 'an honourable (Mark) counsellor (Mark and Luke),' i.e. a member of the Sanhedrin. Like Nicodemus, he was a secret disciple of Jesus, and must undoubtedly have absented himself from the meetings of the Sanhedrin when Jesus was condemned. He 'had not consented to the counsel and deed of them' (Luke).

An ancient but groundless legend has connected Joseph of Arimathæa with Glastonbury, where, it is said, he built of osier-twigs the first Christian Church in England. It is with this legend that the 'Quest of the San Grail' is connected.

58. ἐκέλευσεν ἀποδοθῆναι, after having ascertained from the centurion that Jesus was dead. Usually those who suffered crucifixion lingered for days upon the cross. By Roman law the corpse of a crucified person was not buried except by express permission of the Emperor. A concession was made in favour of the Jews, whose law did not suffer a man to hang all night upon a tree. Deut. xxi. 23. (See Jahn, *Bib. Ant.* 296.) 'The readiness of Pilate to grant Joseph's request is quite in accordance with his anxiety to release Jesus and his displeasure against the Jews. If Joseph had not made this request, the body of Jesus would have been placed in one of the common burying-places appointed by the Council' (Lightfoot, *Hor. Hebr. ad loc.*).

59. ἐντυλίσσειν, an Aristophanic word, meaning, 'to wrap or envelope closely,' so to swathe the dead body with bandages. Cp. Acts v. 6, where συστέλλειν is used in a similar sense, and John xi. 44, δεδεμένος τοὺς πόδας καὶ τὰς χεῖρας κειρίαις, καὶ ἡ ὄψις αὐτοῦ σουδαρίῳ περιεδέδετο.

σινδόνι καθαρᾷ, 'fine linen.' σινδών, as Professor Rawlinson shews (Hdt. II. 86, note 6), was in itself a general term, meaning any stuff of a very fine texture; Josephus even speaks of a σινδών of goats' hair (*Ant.* III. 5. 4). Here, however, σινδών is certainly the βυσσίνη σινδών, in strips (τελαμῶσι) of which the mummy was wrapped (Hdt. II. 86); and that the mummy cloths are of linen has been proved by microscopic examination. The derivation of σινδών is uncertain, possibly from Ἰνδός, or Egyptian *shevit* or Hebr. *sâdin*.

60. ἔθηκεν αὐτὸ κ.τ.λ. καινῷ, 'new,' in the sense of not having been used. St John mentions that the tomb was 'in a garden in the place where he was crucified' (xix. 41). It was probably hewn out of the face of the rock near the ground (John xx. 11), and the body of Jesus would lie horizontally in it.

προσκυλίσας κ.τ.λ., assisted by Nicodemus. This stone was technically called *golal*.

This was the first instance and a signal one of the power of the Cross of Christ to inspire enthusiasm and courage at the darkest hour. Up to this time Joseph had been a secret disciple, now he braves everything for the *dead* Christ.

61. ἡ ἄλλη Μαρία. The mother of James the less (or little, ὁ μικρός) and Joses (Mark xv. 47).

τοῦ τάφου. St Matthew is the only writer in the N.T. who uses the word τάφος (Rom. iii. 13 is a quotation): τάφος is strictly, the place where the dead is 'laid or put away with care.' See Curtius, *Etym.* 502. The Jews preferred to call the tomb 'a memorial' (μνημεῖον).

62. τῇ δὲ ἐπαύριον κ.τ.λ. It was after sunset on Nisan 14. The preparation (παρασκευή) was over, the Sabbath and the Paschal feast had commenced. This explanation of the somewhat unusual phrase accords with the view already taken of the Last Supper and the Passover.

While Christ's enemies were busy this Sabbath day, his friends rested according to the commandment (Luke xxiii. 56).

63. ἐμνήσθημεν. 'We remembered,' it occurred to us, aorist of an action just past.

πλάνος...πλάνη, 'deceiver'...'deceit.' The relation between the two words is lost in A.V.

Μετὰ τρεῖς κ.τ.λ. For this present cp. ch. xxiv. 41, xxvi. 2.

It appears from this that the priests and Pharisees understood the true import of Christ's words, 'Destroy this temple, and after three days I will raise it up,' which they wilfully misinterpreted to the people.

64. τῷ λαῷ. As frequently in N.T. in a special sense, the people of Israel, the Jews.

Ἠγέρθη. 'He rose.'

65. ἔχετε κουστωδίαν. The meaning is either (1) that Pilate refuses the request; 'Ye have a watch of your own'—(*a*) the Levitical

temple guard, or more probably (*b*) a small body of soldiers whom Pilate may have already placed at their disposal—or (2) he grants it curtly and angrily, 'Take a watch; begone.'

The latter view is generally adopted now; but it involves a meaning of ἔχειν ('to take') of which no clear example appears either in classical or Hellenistic Greek. See, however, Alford on 1 Tim. ii. 13, who argues for such a meaning in that passage: ὑποτύπωσιν ἔχε ὑγιαινόντων λόγων, 'have (take) an ensample of (the) healthy words,' &c. It should also be mentioned that in modern Greek ἔχειν and λαμβάνειν are so nearly connected in meaning that the defective parts of ἔχειν (aor. and 2nd future) are supplied from λαμβάνω. Still the argument in favour of retaining the ordinary meaning of ἔχειν in this passage is strong, and the objection that we have no record of a body of Roman soldiers being placed occasionally under the orders of the Sanhedrin need not have great weight. In this case Pilate may well have held it to be a measure on the side of order.

It seems quite clear from ch. xxviii. 14 that the guard was of Roman soldiers.

In any view the *asyndeton* ἔχετε ὑπάγετε ἀσφαλίσασθε indicates impatience on the part of Pilate.

κουστωδίαν appears to have meant a guard of 60 men. See quotation from Theophylact, note on *v.* 27 of this chapter.

ἀσφαλίσασθε...ἠσφαλίσαντο. The middle voice has its proper form, 'secure for yourselves.' A providential point, for if the Roman soldiers had secured the sepulchre the Jews might still have affirmed that deceit had been practised.

ἀσφαλίζειν is a Polybian word which does not seem to have been used earlier. Cp. Acts xvi. 24, τοὺς πόδας ἠσφαλίσατο αὐτῶν εἰς τὸ ξύλον. The verb does not occur elsewhere in N.T.

66. σφραγίσαντες. 'The sealing was by means of a cord or string passing across the stone at the mouth of the sepulchre and fastened at either end to the rock by sealing clay' (Alford). Cp. Dan. vi. 17: καὶ ἐσφραγίσατο ὁ βασιλεὺς ἐν τῷ δακτυλίῳ αὐτοῦ καὶ ἐν τῷ δακτυλίῳ τῶν μεγιστάνων αὐτοῦ (sc. τὸν λίθον ὃν ἐπέθηκαν ἐπὶ τὸ στόμα τοῦ λάκκου).

σφραγίζειν is used in various figurative senses, all more or less nearly connected with this literal signification. See John iii. 33 and 2 Cor. i. 2, 'certify.' Eph. i. 13, iv. 30, 'assure.' Rom. xv. 28, 'secure,' 'authenticate.' Rev. x. 4, xxii. 10, 'conceal.' In Ecclesiastical Greek it is used of making the sign of the Cross in baptism and other rites.

CHAPTER XXVIII.

2. ἀπὸ τῆς θύρας after λίθον omitted ℵBD, some versions and Origen. The words are found in the later authorities, ACE and other uncials, some versions and Fathers.

9. In *textus receptus* the verse begins: ὡς δὲ ἐπορεύοντο ἀπαγγεῖλαι τοῖς μαθηταῖς αὐτοῦ. The clause is omitted in ℵBD, many versions and Fathers; appears in AC and some versions. The leading editors reject the words.

20. The evidence against the final ἀμήν is very strong: ℵABD, many versions and Fathers.

Ch. XXVIII. 1—8. The Resurrection.
Mark xvi. 1—8; Luke xxiv. 1—12; John xx. 1—18.

The discrepancies are slight, and may be accounted for by the agitation of the witnesses of this momentous scene. To the women named in this Gospel St Mark adds Salome; St Luke, Joanna and other women; St John names Mary Magdalene only. St Luke and St John mention the visit of Peter to the sepulchre, St John adding 'that other disciple.' This Evangelist also records the appearance of Jesus to Mary Magdalene in the garden.

The order of events was probably this: First, Mary Magdalene and the other Mary, having come early to the tomb, were addressed by the Angel and saw the empty sepulchre; they hasten to inform Peter and the other disciples; Peter and John visit the tomb and depart; Mary Magdalene, left alone, beholds her Lord, whom at first she does not recognise; soon afterwards the Lord appears a second time to Mary Magdalene, now in the company of other women.

1. ὀψέ denotes a longer interval after sunset than ἑσπέρα.

σάββατα. Plural in both senses, 'sabbath' and 'week.'

τῇ ἐπιφωσκούσῃ. Cp. Luke xxiii. 54, σάββατον ἐπέφωσκεν, the only other passage where the word occurs, the cognate form ἐπιφαύσκειν is classical, and occurs four times in the LXX. version of Job: ἢ οὐχ ὁρῶμεν ἥλιον τὸν ἐπιφαύσκοντα, Job xxxi. 26. In Luke *loc. cit.* the word ἐπιφώσκειν is used not of the natural daybreak, but of the commencement of the sabbath after sunset on the παρασκευή. Here, as we see from the parallel passages (Luke xxiv. 1, ὄρθρου βαθέως; Mark xvi. 2, λίαν πρωὶ μιᾷ τῶν σαββάτων; John xx. 1, πρωί, σκοτίας ἔτι οὔσης), it means the early dawn.

θεωρῆσαι τὸν τάφον. Both St Mark and St Luke mention that they brought spices and ointments.

2. σεισμὸς ἐγένετο μέγας. Peculiar to St Matthew.

ἄγγελος κυρίου. ἄνδρες δύο ἐπέστησαν αὐταῖς ἐσθῆτι ἀστραπτούσῃ (Luke xxiv. 4). δύο ἀγγέλους ἐν λευκοῖς καθεζομένους (John xx. 12).

3. εἰδέα. Here only in N.T., not 'countenance,' but 'appearance,' 'species sub oculos cadens,' not the thing itself but the thing as beholden, 'ἰδέα τοῦ προσώπου, 'the look of the countenance.' (Trench, *N.T. Syn.* 2nd series, p. 93.)

4. ἀπὸ φόβου...ὡς νεκροί. Cp. οἱ δὲ σύμμαχοι τεθνᾶσι τῷ δέει τοὺς τοιούτους ἀποστόλους, Dem. *Phil.* I. 45.

5. μὴ φοβεῖσθε ὑμεῖς. The pronoun is emphatic; a contrast with the alarm of the soldiers is implied.

τὸν ἐσταυρωμένον. 'Who hath been crucified,' not 'which was crucified,' A.V.

6. ἠγέρθη. As in ch. xxvii. 64, He rose. So also in next verse.
καθώς. Non-Attic for classical καθά. See Lob. *Phryn.* p. 426.
ἴδετε κ.τ.λ. In order that they might be convinced of the fact.

It is hardly possible for us even to conceive the overwhelming joy that the conviction of this truth must have brought to these holy women, whose recollection of the divine words and looks and love-inspiring sweetness of character would be quickened by the painful watching and the passionate sorrow for their seeming loss.

7. εἴπατε κ.τ.λ. 'And Peter' (Mark). Peter, more than the rest, would be longing for the Lord's return to win forgiveness.

9, 10. THE APPEARANCE OF JESUS TO MARY MAGDALENE AND THE OTHER MARY.

Recorded by St Matthew only.

Jesus had already appeared to Mary Magdalene *alone*. We must suppose that she was now joined by the other Mary, and perhaps by Salome, Joanna, and others; and while these were going to announce the great news to the rest of the disciples [Peter and John already knew] the Lord Jesus met them.

The following is a list of the different recorded appearances of Jesus during the forty days:—(1) To Mary Magdalene alone (John xx. 14 foll.; Mark xvi. 9). (2) To Mary Magdalene, the other Mary, and perhaps other women (Matthew xxviii. 9, 10). (3) To Peter (Luke xxiv. 34; 1 Cor. xv. 5). (4) To Cleophas and another on the way to Emmaus (Luke xxiv. 13—35). (5) To the apostles, in the absence of Thomas, at Jerusalem (Mark xvi. 14; Luke xxiv. 36; John xx. 19). (6) To the eleven apostles at Jerusalem (John xx. 26). (7) To seven disciples at the Sea of Tiberias (John xxi. 1—24). (8) To the eleven on the highland of Galilee (Matthew xxviii. 16). (9) To five hundred brethren at once—possibly the same appearance as 8 (1 Cor. xv. 6). (10) To James, the Lord's brother (1 Cor. xv. 7). (11) To the eleven in the neighbourhood of the Holy City (Mark xvi. 19, 20; Luke xxiv. 50; Acts i. 3—12; 1 Cor. xv. 7).

9. ὑπήντησεν. See note, ch. viii. 28.

Χαίρετε. The Greek salutation, both on meeting and on parting.

ἐκράτησαν αὐτοῦ τοὺς πόδας κ.τ.λ. The immemorial usage in the East in obeisance to a sovereign prince.

In the interesting clay cylinder of Cyrus he says of the subject kings: 'they brought me their full tribute and kissed my feet.' (Canon Rawlinson, *Cont. Rev.* Jan. 1880).

10. ἀπαγγείλατε κ.τ.λ. i.e. tell my brethren (of my Resurrection), in order that they may go.

ἀδελφοῖς μου. The disciples; 'He named them brethren, as being Himself a man and their kinsman according to man's nature' (Euthymius quoted by Ellicott, *Life of our Lord*); comp. Heb. ii. 11, ὅ τε γὰρ ἁγιάζων καὶ οἱ ἁγιαζόμενοι ἐξ ἑνὸς πάντες· δι' ἣν αἰτίαν οὐκ ἐπαισχύνεται ἀδελφοὺς αὐτοὺς καλεῖν. The name of 'brethren' is not directly applied by Christ to his disciples, until after the Resurrection (cp. John xx. 17). He had clearly manifested the power of the Godhead, and there was special need of reminding his disciples that He was still man, and that they were brethren.

11—15. THE ROMAN GUARDS ARE BRIBED. This important testimony is given by St Matthew only.

11. τινὲς τῆς κουστωδίας. An expression that implies more than the traditional number of four guards. The full complement of a κουστωδία appears to have been 60 men. See note, ch. xxvii. 65.

12. ἀργύρια ἱκανά. Many pieces of silver, a *largesse*.

13. ἡμῶν κοιμωμένων. The penalty for which would be death.

14. ἐπὶ τοῦ ἡγεμόνος. 'Before the governor.' With this use of ἐπί comp. ἐπὶ μαρτύρων, 1 Tim. v. 19; ἐπὶ τῶν ἀδίκων...ἐπὶ τῶν ἁγίων, 1 Cor. vi. 1, 'at the bar of,' and the common phrases ἐπὶ δικαστῶν, δικαστηρίων. These expressions are closely connected with the physical notion of ἐπί, 'upon.' A matter may be said to rest upon witnesses or judges, i.e. depend upon their evidence or decision. This use explains the expression in the text, which means either, (1) 'If the matter should be heard in the Procurator's Court'—come before him officially. (2) Or perhaps in a more general sense; 'If rumours of it should come before him'—if he should hear of it.

πείσομεν. 'Will persuade' (by bribes). Cp. Eur. *Medea* 964, μή μοι σύ, πείθειν δῶρα καὶ θεοὺς λόγος· | χρυσὸς δὲ κρείσσων μυρίων λόγων βροτοῖς. Hdt. VIII. 134, ξεῖνόν τινα καὶ οὐ Θηβαῖον χρήμασι πείσας.

ἀμερίμνους. At Rome, in Cicero's time, judicial bribery was so organized that contracts were taken to secure acquittal by this means. And the whole process of bribery had a special vocabulary, in which this very word ἀμέριμνος appears to have had a place, Curio meeting Verres and assuring him that he has won his acquittal by bribery: 'hunc jubet *sine cura* esse: renuntio inquit tibi te hodiernis comitiis esse absolutum.' ἀμέριμνος here and 1 Cor. vii. 32 only in N.T.

15. διεφημίσθη μέχρι τῆς σήμερον. Hence St Matthew found it especially needful to narrate the true facts. An aorist qualified by an adverb of present time has the force of a perfect definite. The note of time therefore, like the use of γέγονεν (ch. i. 22, xxii. 4), implies that the events described were still of comparatively recent memory.

16, 17. JESUS APPEARS TO THE ELEVEN IN GALILEE.
Peculiar to St Matthew.

16. τὸ ὄρος. The mountain. Perhaps the highland behind Tell Hum or Capernaum (see map), the scene of their earliest intercourse with Christ, and the very spot where the New Law was first proclaimed. There the brethren, possibly five hundred in number [see *vv.* 9, 10 (8) (9)], besides the Eleven, awaited the coming of the Great Shepherd (*v.* 7). As the sacred form appeared on the familiar mountain side they threw themselves on the ground, doing homage to their Lord and God. But some doubted still. Then He drew more near and spake. And as the words sounded in their ears, we may believe they 'knew his voice' and dismissed their doubts.

17. προσεκύνησαν. See note, ch. xx. 20. It is characteristic of St Matthew's Gospel that this word, which indicates the homage and prostration before a king, should occur twelve times, whereas it is found twice only in each of the other Synoptics.

οἱ δέ. Probably not some of the Apostles, but some of the five hundred who had not previously seen the Lord.

For οἱ δέ when οἱ μέν is omitted in the first clause see note, ch. xxvi. 67. *Il.* xi. 536, ἀφ' ἱππείων ὁπλέων ῥαθάμιγγες ἔβαλλον, | αἱ δ' ἀπ' ἐπισσώτρων (Winer, p. 131, and Riddell on Plato, *Apol. Soc.*, p. 18, note 3, and Dig. 241).

ἐδίστασαν. The same word is used of St Peter's doubt, ch. xiv. 31, and in these passages only in N.T.; there too the doubt is followed by adoration, *v.* 33.

18—20. THE LAST CHARGE TO THE APOSTLES.

18. προσελθὼν ἐλάλησεν. Came up to them, near to them, and spake.

Ἐδόθη, 'was given,'—the aorist of an eternal fact, so undefined and independent of time-notion, cp. ch. iii. 17 and xi. 27, and Phil. ii. 8—10. These words, in which the infallible King Himself announces His eternal possession of the Kingdom, St Matthew, who is essentially the historian of the Kingdom, alone records.

19. μαθητεύσατε. Make disciples of. Cp. Acts xiv. 21, μαθητεύσαντες ἱκανούς, and see ch. xiii. 52, xxvii. 57, where the same word is used. διδάσκοντες, *v.* 20, = 'instructing.' 'Make disciples of all the Gentiles πάντα τὰ ἔθνη) by baptism and by instruction in all my commands to you' (πάντα ὅσα ἐνετειλάμην).

εἰς τὸ ὄνομα. 'Into the name.' Jewish proselytes were baptized into the name of the Father; Jesus adds the name of the Son and of the Holy Ghost. In the instances of baptism recorded in the Acts, ii. 38, viii. 16, x. 48, xix. 5, the name of Jesus Christ (or the Lord Jesus) alone occurs in the baptismal formula, but the promise of the Holy Ghost is given (ii. 38), or the gift of the Holy Ghost follows the rite (viii. 17, xix. 6), or precedes it (x. 44, 47).

20. μεθ' ὑμῶν εἰμί. The Lord Jesus had already taught His disciples during the forty days how He could be present with them and yet be unseen by them. They could then the more easily believe this promise.

πάσας τὰς ἡμέρας. 'All the days,' not at intervals during the days (δι' ἡμερῶν τεσσεράκοντα ὀπτανόμενος, Acts i. 3), but continuously on each and all the days between now and the completion of the Æon.

ἕως τῆς κ.τ.λ. See note ch. xiii. 39. The last words of St Matthew's Gospel fall solemnly on the ear, the sense of the continual presence of Christ is not broken even by an account of the Ascension. No true subject can doubt that the King is enthroned in Heaven.

INDEX TO NOTES.

I. ENGLISH.

Abomination of desolation, 268
Accentuation, 138, 267
Aceldama, 302
Æon, end of the, 192
Agony in the Garden, 292
Ahimelech, 177
Almsgiving, 126
Analysis of Gospel, xxii.
Andrew, call of, 109; name, 161
Anise, 261
Annas, 296
Aorist, use of in N. T., 175; see also 119, 130, 134, 143, 150, 227, 257, 319
— imperative, 99
— late form of, 114, 118
Apostles, meaning of word, 160; mission of, 160; list of, 160
Appearances of our Lord after the Resurrection, 317
Arimathæa, 313
Arrest of Jesus, 294
Article, the definite, 105, 150, 151, 230, 306
Asaph the Seer, 191
Ass, 240
Augment, 142

Banks, 133, 278
Banquet, kingdom of heaven compared to a, 147
Baptism, of John, 97; meaning of, 97; our Lord's, 102; form of enjoined by Christ, 319

Bar, meaning of, 210
Barabbas, 303
Bartholomew, meaning of name, 161; identified with Nathanael, 161
Baskets, different words for, 200, 207
Beelzebub, meaning of, 166
Bethany, 240, 242, 244
Bethlehem, 86, 88, 92
Bethphagé, 240
Bethsaida, 173; question of two places called, 199
Betrayal of Jesus, 287. *See* Arrest of Jesus
Binding and loosing, meaning of, 212, 223
Birds, 134, 135, 164, 167
Blasphemy, 297
Blindness, cause of prevalence in the East, 157; cure of, 157, 239
Brethren of the Lord, theories concerning, 184, 194
Bushel, 118

Cæsarea Philippi, 209, 210
Caiaphas, 284, 296
Calvary, 307
Camel's hair, 97
Canaanite woman, the, 205
Cananite, Simon the, 161; meaning of word, 161
Candle. *See* Lamp
Capernaum, 108, 173

INDEX

Centurion in Herod's army, 146; Roman, 312
Charoseth, 289
Chief Priests, 244, 284
Chorazin, 173
Christ, meaning of, 82
Church of the future, 164; Christian, 211; meaning of word, 211; Jewish, 223
Cleansing of the Temple, 243
Clothes, 124, 241, 269; rending of, 297
Commandments, the, in regard to the New Law, 119; enumerated, 230; the greatest, 255
Comparative degree, 220
Corban, 121, 203
Corn, plucking ears of, 177
Cowardice, 150
Cross, 168; different kinds of, 308
Crown of thorns, 306
Cummin, 261
Cup, meaning of, 237

Dative case, 197
David and the shewbread, 177
David, son of, 205, 239, 256
Decapolis, 111
Demoniacs, 150, 157
Denarius, 225, 234, 253
Destruction, miracles of, 151, 244
Devil, meaning of name, 105
Devils, Greek word for, 111, 151
Disciples of John, 154
Discourses peculiar to Matthew, xxi.
Divorce, 83, 122, 226, 227
Dogs, 206
Drachmæ, 219
Drowning, 221

Egypt, 91
Elijah, 216, 217
Epilepsy, 218
Eternal, 281
Eucharist, 290
Evenings, between the, 199
Evil eye, 133, 236

Fasting, 105, 132, 154

Fig-tree, cursing of, 244; early kind of, 245; parable of, 272
Final infinitive, 104, 167
Final sentences, 84
Five thousand fed, 199
Flowers, 135
Forgiveness, 224
Four thousand fed, 207
Fragments, proper meaning of, 200
Friend, meaning of, as an address, 236, 294
Future tense, 126, 224

Gadara, 150
Galilæans, dialect of, 298
Galilee, ministry in, 107; meaning and history of, 107
Garment, hem or fringe of the, 202, 258
Gehenna, 120, 211, 260
Genitive case, 120, 177
— of infinitive, 91
Gennesaret, Lake of, 108, 185; land of, 201
Gerasa, 150
Gergesa, 150
Gesture and looks of Jesus, 231, 243
Gethsemane, 292
Goats, 279
Golgotha, 307
Gospel, meaning of word, 80
Greek names among the apostles, 161
Guards at the Cross, 312; at the Sepulchre, 318

Habba as a Messianic title, 83, 242
Hebraisms, 168, 169, 174, 177, 230, 247, 249
Hebrew original of St Matthew's Gospel, xviii.
Hell, two Greek words for, 211, and see *Gehenna*
Herod the Great, 86, 239; Antipas, 196, 226; Archelaus, 239; Philip, 196
Herodian family, xxxii.
Herodians, 252
Herodias, 196, 226

INDEX. 323

High-priesthood, no longer hereditary, 284
Hinnom, valley of, 120
History, external during Christ's ministry on earth, xxvii.
Holy Ghost promised to the Apostles, 165; sin against the, 181
Hosanna, meaning of word, 241
Hosea quoted, 93, 154, 178

Immortality, proof of, 254
Imperative (Hebrew), 230; aor. and pres., 230
Imperfect tense, 102, 143, 145, 156, 197, 200
Infinitive, final, 104, 118
Innocents, massacre of, 93
Inscription, or title on the Cross, 308
Irenæus' testimony concerning St Matthew, xviii.
Isaiah quoted, 84, 85, 95, 108, 179, 187, 204, 241, 243
Iscariot, meaning of, 162
Ish, 299
Itacism, 151

Jairus, daughter of, 156
James, different persons called, 161
Jeremiah quoted, 92
Jericho, 239
Jerusalem, fall of as a type of the end of the world, 215, 265; population during passover, 242; Jesus weeps over, 263; Aramaic form for used once by St Matthew, 263; horrors of siege, 269
Jesus, meaning of name, 84; date of birth, 86; Baptism, 101; Temptation, 104; Crucifixion, 308; Resurrection, 316
John the son of Zebedee, call, 109; one of the three present at the raising of Jairus' daughter, 156; at Transfiguration, 216; at Agony in the garden, 292
John the Baptist, preaching, 95; imprisonment, 170; death, 198
Jonah, the sign of the prophet, 183, 209

Jordan, fords of the, 102
Joseph, husband of the Virgin Mary, both genealogies shew descent of, 80, 82; son of Heli, and probably first cousin to Mary, 82
Joseph of Arimathæa, 313
Jot, 119
Judas Iscariot, probably a non-Galilæan, 162; betrays Jesus, 294; remorse of, 301; end of, 214, 302
Judas or Jude, three persons named, 161
Jude the apostle, also called Lebbæus and Thaddæus, 161
Judgment on others, 138
Judgment, day of, 279

Kedron, valley of, pinnacle overlooking, 105; Jesus crosses in triumph, 242; and on His way to Gethsemane, 292
Keys, significance of, 212, 259
Kingdom of God, or of heaven, meaning of, 96; relation of, to sermon on the Mount, 112; compared to a banquet, 147; keys of, 212; rank in, 238

Lamp, 118
Last Supper, 288
Leaven, 190, 209
Lebbæus, 161
Leper and leprosy, 145, 163
Levi. *See* Matthew
Life, different senses of word, 168, 214
Lilies, 135
Little ones, meaning of, 169, 221
Locusts, 97
Lord's prayer, 128—132
Love or *agapé*, 267
Lunatic, 111; cure of, 218

Machærus, scene of John the Baptist's imprisonment, 107; and death, 197
Magdala, or Mejdel, 207
Magdalene. *See* Mary
Magi, 87

324 INDEX.

Malachi quoted, 171, 217
Malchus, his ear cut off by St Peter, 294
Mammon, 134
Marriage, 226; customs of, 82, 154, 226, 252, 275
Marriage-feast, parable of, 251
Mary Magdalene, account of, 312; at the Cross, 312; at the resurrection, 316
Mary the Virgin, genealogy of, 82; her betrothal, 83; subject of prophecy, 85
Mary, sister of Lazarus, anoints Christ, 285
Mary, mother of James and Joses, 312
Matthew, life of, xi.; call, 153; change of name, xi.; service under Herod Antipas, xii.; preaches to the Jews in Palestine, xiv.; and in other countries, xiv.; character, xiv.; death, xiv.
Matthew, Gospel according to; origin, authorship, and date, xv.; special reference to Jews, xvi.; style, xvi.; Hebrew original, xviii.; analysis of, xxii.
Messiah, meaning and origin of title, 82; false, 266
Metayer system, 248
Micah, quoted, 89
Middle voice, 135
Mills in Palestine, 273
Millstone, 221
Miracles peculiar to Matthew, xxi.
———— names for, 245
Money, different kinds and value of, 121, 163, 225, 234, 253, 286, 287
Money-changers, 243
Moses, 216
Mount of Transfiguration, 216
Mustard seed, 190

Nathanael identified with Bartholomew, 161
Nativity, date of, 85
Nazarene, meaning of expression, 94, 95
Nazareth, 85, 93, 94, 108

New Testament, 291
Nicodemus, a secret disciple of Jesus, 313; assists at the burial, 313

Oaths, 123
Optative mood, 179
Oven, description of, 136

Painters and pictures, illustrations from, 102, 198, 218, 310, 312
Paneas, 210
Pantænus, } testimony as to St
Papias,   } Matthew, xviii.
Parables, peculiar to Matthew, xxi.; meaning of word, 186; reason for teaching by, 186, 187, 191
Paralysis, } 146, 152
Paralytic, }
Parousia, 266
Participles, 83, 208
Passion foretold, 212, 218, 236
Passover, account of; meaning of word, 283; account of ritual, 289
Pearls, 139
Peræa, 226
Perfect tense, 116, 152, 193, 241
Periblem, 136
Persecution, 116, 165
Peter, confession, 210; one of the Three at raising of Jairus' daughter, 156; at Transfiguration, 216; at Garden of Gethsemane, 292; denial of Christ by, 298
Pharisees, 98, 153; coalition with Sadducees, 208
Phylacteries, 257
Pilate, procurator of Judæa; history; character; name; traditions concerning, 300; trial of Jesus before, 303; attempts to save Jesus, 305; gives the body of Jesus to Joseph, 313
Pilate's wife, 304
Plant life, 190, 272
Plural, 135, 143, 198
Poetical element in N. T., xxxv.
Prætorium, 306
Prayer, 127; the Lord's, 128
Present tense, 89, 134, 152, 273, 314

INDEX. 325

Prisons, 280
Procurator, 300
Prophecies, how fulfilled, 84
Psalms quoted, 106, 115, 310
Publicans, 125, 153, 223, 247
Punctuation, 169
Purple robe. *See* Scarlet robe

Rabbi, 258
Rabbinical sayings, 122, 203, 212, 218, 258, 261
Raca, 120
Ransom, meaning and derivation, 239
Release of prisoners at Passover, 303
Restoration of all things, 217, 232
Resurrection, proof of, 254; our Lord's, 316; foretold, 213, 218, 236
Riches, 231
Robbers or bandits, 243, 309
Rome, Archelaus and Antipas resided at, 196
Rooms, uppermost, 258
Rulers of synagogue, 110, 229

Sabbath, observance of the, 177; flight on the, 269
Sabbath day's journey, 269
Sadducees, account of, 98; tempt Jesus, 254
Salome, mother of Zebedee's children, 237, 313
Salome, daughter of Herodias, 196
Salt, 117
Samaritans, 162
Sanhedrin or Sanhedrim, 89, 284; first meeting at our Lord's trial, 296; second meeting, 300
Satan, meaning of name, 105
Scarlet robe, 306
Scourging, 305
Scribes, 143; of the Kingdom of heaven, 193
Seine or drag net, 193
Sermon on the Mount, 112—143
Shekel, 219, 301
Shewbread, 177
Simon of Cyrene, 307

Simon Peter. *See* Peter
Simon the leper, 285
Sins, forgiveness of, 152
Sitting, the position of a teacher, 113, 257; on the right hand, 256
Slaves and slavery, 100, 133, 147, 238, 287
Sleep of Jesus, 150
Son of man, 149
Sower, parable of, 186
Speira, 306
Spikenard, 285
Star, in the east, 87; appearance of the Messiah connected with, 88
Subjunctive mood, sequence of on historical tenses, 178, 201; relation of with future, 188, 224
Supper, the last, 287; order and incidents of, 288
Swine, destruction of, 151
Synagogue, account of, 110; allusion to, 166
Syrophœnician. *See* Canaanite

Tabor, 216
Talents, value of, 224; parable of, 277
Tallith, fringe of, 202, 258
Tares, meaning of parable of, 189
Tax-gatherers. *See* Publicans
Temple, cleansing of the, 243; destruction of, foretold, 264; veil of, rent in twain, 311
Temptation, different accounts of, 103; how to be viewed, 104
Tetrarch, meaning of, 196
Thaddæus, 161
Thief. *See* Robber
Thirty pieces of silver. *See* Shekel
Tiberias, 199
Time, divisions of, 199, 200, 235; reckoning of, 216
Title on the Cross, 308
Tombs at Gergesa, 150
Trade, 277
Traditional sayings of Christ, 136, 164
Traditions, 203
Transfiguration, 216
Transitional particles, 90

Treasury. *See* Corban
Trial of Jesus Christ, order of the, 296
Tribute money or Temple tax, 219; Roman, 253
Triclinia, 258
Trumpet, 127
Tunic, 124

Vespasian, 90
Vinegar, 308
Vineyard, parable of labourers in the, 233
Virgin, the. *See* Mary
Virgins, parable of the ten, 275
Voice from heaven, 102

Watch at the Sepulchre, 315
Watches, division of night into, 200
Wilderness of Judæa, 95, 104
Wine, 155
Words from the Cross, 307, 310

Yoke, meaning of, 176

Zealot, Zealots, 98; Simon, the, 161; excesses of at siege of Jerusalem, 268
Zebedee, sons of, 237
Zechariah, the prophet, 241, 291 302; the priest, 263

II. GREEK.

ἀγαπᾶν, 125
ἀγάπη, 103, 267
ἀγαπητός, 103
ἀγγαρεύειν, 124, 307
ἄγναφος, 155
ἀδελφός, 258, 318
ἀδημονεῖν, 292
ᾅδης, 211
ἀθῷος, 301
αἰτεῖν, 140
αἰών, 192
αἰώνιος, 281
ἄκανθα, 141
ἀκέραιος, 164
ἀκριβοῦν, 90
ἀλάβαστρον, 285
ἅλας, 117
ἁλιεῖς, 109
ἅλων, 101
ἀμέριμνος, 318
ἀμήν, 119
ἀμφίβληστρον, 109
ἄν omitted, 290
ἀναιρεῖν, 93
ἀνάστασις, 254
ἀνατολή, 88
ἀναχωρεῖν, 92
ἀντάλλαγμα, 214
ἀντί, 220, 239
ἄνυδρος, 184
ἀπάγειν, 297
ἅπαξ λεγόμενα, 129, 167, 179, 238
ἀπέχειν, 127
ἀπό, 98, 138, 141, 201
ἀποδεκατοῦν, 261
ἀποκατάστασις, 217

ἀποκρίνεσθαι, 102, 174, 303
ἀπόστολος, 160
ἄρτος, 129, 136, 177, 199
ἀρχιερεῖς, 244, 284
ἀσφαλίζειν, 315
αὐλή, 298
αὐληταί, 156
αὐτός, 100, 110, 115
ἀφανίζειν, 132
ἄφες, 138, 311
ἄφεσις, 130, 291
ἄχυρον, 101

βαπτίζειν, 97
βασανίζειν, 146, 200
βασανιστής, 225
βάσανος, 110
βασίλισσα, 183
βαττολογεῖν, 128
βδέλυγμα, 268
βεβηλοῦν, 178
Βεελζεβούλ, 166
βῆμα, 304
βιάζεσθαι, 172
βλασφημεῖν, 153
βλασφημία, 153
βλέπειν, 138
βρέχειν, 125
βρῶσις, 133

γέεννα, 120, 260
γενέσια, 198
γογγύζειν, 235
γογγυσμός, 235

δαιμόνιον, 157

δαίμων, 151
δεῖ, 267
δειγματίσαι, 83
δειλός, 150
δέρειν, 248
δεσμεύειν, 257
δεῦτε, 109
δηνάριον, 225, 234
διά, 89, 203
διάβολος, 105
διαθήκη, 291
διακονεῖν, 107
διακρίνεσθαι, 245
διάνοια, 255
δίδραχμα, 219
διέξοδοι, 251
δίκαιος, 83
δικαιοσύνη, 119, 126, 136
διχάσαι, 167
δοκός, 188
δοῦλος, 224, 238

ἐάν with fut. indic. 224
εἰ, followed by οὐ, 290
εἰδέα, 316
εἰ δὲ μήγε, 155
εἰρήνη, 116, 164
εἰς, 99, 123, 183, 236
εἷς, 244
ἐκ, 138, 262
ἑκατόνταρχος, 146, 312
ἐκβάλλειν, 159, 180, 182
ἐκκλησία, 211, 223
ἐκλεκτοί, 270
ἐλέγχειν, 223
ἐλεήμονες, 178
ἔλεος, 154, 178
ἐμβριμᾶσθαι, 157
ἐν, 99, 123, 139, 183
ἐνεργεῖν, 197
ἔνοχος, 120
ἐντρέπειν, 248
ἐντυλίσσειν, 313
ἐξετάζειν, 90
ἐξομολογεῖσθαι, 174
ἐπανιστάναι, 165
ἐπί, 81, 136, 166, 176, 189, 201, 218, 278, 281, 318
ἐπιβάλλειν, 294
ἐπικαλεῖν, 166

ἐπιούσιος, 129
ἐπίτροπος, 235, 301
ἐπιφώσκειν, 316
ἐργάζεσθαι, 277
ἐρεύγεσθαι, 191
ἐρωτᾶν, 140
ἑταῖρος, 236, 294
εὐαγγελίζεσθαι, 170
εὐαγγέλιον, 80
εὐδοκεῖν, 103
εὐκαιρία, 287
ἔχειν, 197, 248, 314

ζηλωτής, 161
ζιζάνια, 189
ζυγός, 176
ζύμη, 190, 209
ζώνη, 163

ἡγεμών, 165, 301
ἡλικία, 135

θεέ, 310
θέλω, 154, 309
θησαυρός, 91
θλίψις, 138, 269
θυσιαστήριον, 121, 260

ἰδού, 151
Ἱεροσόλυμα, 89
Ἱερουσαλήμ, 263
ἵλεως, 213
ἱμάτιον, 241
ἵνα, 84, 146, 201
ἵνα τί; 310
ἰσχύειν, 154, 293
ἰῶτα, 119

καθαρός, 116
καθεύδειν, 156
καθηγητής, 259
καθίζειν, 113
καθοῦ, 256
καί, 83, 287
καὶ γάρ, 206
καινός, 155, 193
κακολογεῖν, 203
καλεῖν, 154
καλεῖσθαι, 116
Καναναῖος, 161

INDEX.

κατά, 80, 157, 294
καταθεματίζειν, 299
κατακυριεύειν, 238
καταπέτασμα, 311
καταποντίζεσθαι, 201
κατασκηνοῦν, 190
καρδία, 255
κάρφος, 138
καύσων, 235
κεραία, 119
κῆνσος, 253
κλαίειν, 299
κλίβανος, 136
κοδράντης, 121
κοιμᾶσθαι, 156, 311
κοινοῦν, 204
κόλασις, 281
κολαφίζειν, 298
κολλυβιστής, 243
κοπάζειν, 201
κοπιᾶν, 176
κόσμος, 117, 214
κουστωδία, 314
κόφινος, 200
κράσπεδον, 202, 258
κρίμα, 138

λαλιά, 298
λαός, 314
λεγεών, 295
ληνός, 247
ληστής, 295, 309
λικμᾶν, 250
λόγος, distinguished from ῥῆμα, 182
λύκος, 141
λύτρον, 238

μάγοι, 87
μαθητεύειν, 319
μαμωνᾶς, 134
μαργαρίτης, 139
μάχαιρα, 295
μεριμνᾶν, 134
μετά, 89, 216, 292
μεταίρειν, 194
μεταμεληθείς, 301
μεταμορφοῦσθαι, 216
μετανοεῖν, 96
μετάνοια, 247
μή, 83, 180, 225

μνημόσυνον, 121, 286
μονόφθαλμος, 222
μυστήριον, 187

ν ἐφελκυστικόν, 79
ναός, 260, 263
νεκρός, 149
νέος, 155
νυστάζειν, 276

ξύλον, 294

οἰκοδεσπότης, 273
οἰκοδομαί, 265
οἶνος, 308
ὅλος, 84
ὄνος, 240
ὀργή, 98
ὅρος, τό, 113
ὅς μὲν...ὅς δέ, 186, 277
ὅστις, 275
οὐ μή, 169
οὐ...πᾶς, 270
ὀφείλημα, 130
ὄφις, 164
ὄψῃ, 299, 301
ὀψία, 199

παῖς, 146, 179
παλινγενεσία, 232
παραβολή, 186, 191
παραδιδόναι, 107
παρακαλεῖν, 295
παραλαβεῖν, 84
παράπτωμα, 132
παριστάναι, 295
παρουσία, 266
πάσχα, 283
πάσχειν, 213, 218, 283, 304
πείθειν, 318
πεινῆν, 244
πίναξ, 198
πίστις, 209
πλήν, 173
πνεῦμα, 100
ποιεῖν, 304
πόντος, 221
ποτήριον, 237
πραότης, 115, 176
πραΰς, 176

INDEX.

προσέχειν, 141
προσήλυτος, 259
προσκυνεῖν, 88, 237, 319
προφητεύειν, 142, 298
πτερύγιον, 105
πτύον, 101
πτῶμα, 199
πτωχοί, 115
πύλαι ᾅδου, 211

ῥαββί, 258
ῥαπίζειν, 124, 298
ῥῆμα, 182
ῥύεσθαι, 131

σάββατον, 177, 269, 316
σαγήνη, 193
σὰρξ καὶ αἷμα, 210
σεληνιαζόμενοι, 111
σημεῖα τῶν καιρῶν, 208
σινδών, 314
σκανδαλίζειν,} 122, 171, 188
σκάνδαλον,   } 213
σκληρός, 278
σκορπίζειν, 181
σκύλλειν, 159
σοφία, σοφός, 173, 174
σπεῖρα, 306
σπλάγχνα,
σπλαγχνίζεσθαι,} 158
σπυρίς, 207
στατήρ, 219
σταυρός, 168, 214, 308
σύν, 292
συνάγειν, 224, 278
συνέχειν, 111
συντέλεια, 192
σφραγίζειν, 315
σχίσμα, 155
σχολάζειν, 184
σώζειν, 165

τάλαντον, 224
ταμιεῖον, 128, 271

ταπεινός, 176
ταπεινοῦν, 221
τάφος, 314
τελῶναι, 125, 153, 223
τετράρχης, 196
τόκος, 279
τότε, 90
τρίβολος, 142
τρύπημα ῥαφίδος, 231
τρώγειν, 273

υἱὸς Δαυείδ, 205
ὑπάντησις, 151, 275
ὑπό, 89, 151
ὑποδήματα, 100, 163
ὑποκρίτης, 127
ὑπομένειν,}
ὑπομονή, } 165, 268

φθάνειν, 180
φιμοῦν, 255
φραγελλοῦν, 305
φρονεῖν τὰ τοῦ θεοῦ, 214
φρόνιμοι, 164
φυλακή, 200
φυλακτήρια, 257
φωλεός, 148

χαῖρε, 294
χιτών, 124, 163
χλαμύς, 306
χορτάζειν, 115
χόρτος, 135
χρηματίζειν, 91
χριστός, 82
χωρεῖν, 227
χωρίον, 292

ψυχή, 168, 255, 293

ὥρα, 235
ὥστε, 270
ὠτίον, 294

CAMBRIDGE: PRINTED BY J. & C. F. CLAY, AT THE UNIVERSITY PRESS.

THE PITT PRESS SERIES.

COMPLETE LIST.

1. GREEK.

Author	Work	Editor	Price
Aristophanes	Aves—Plutus—Ranae	Green	3/6 each
,,	Vespae	Graves	3/6
,,	Nubes	,,	In the Press
Demosthenes	Olynthiacs	Glover	In the Press
Euripides	Heracleidae	Beck & Headlam	3/6
,,	Hercules Furens	Gray & Hutchinson	2/-
,,	Hippolytus	Hadley	2/-
,,	Iphigeneia in Aulis	Headlam	2/6
,,	Hecuba	Hadley	2/6
,,	Alcestis	,,	2/6
,,	Orestes	Wedd	4/6
Herodotus	Book V	Shuckburgh	3/-
,,	,, VI, VIII, IX	,,	4/- each
,,	,, VIII 1—90, IX 1—89	,,	2/6 each
Homer	Odyssey IX, X	Edwards	2/6 each
,,	,, XXI	,,	2/-
,,	Iliad VI, XXII, XXIII, XXIV	,,	2/- each
Lucian	Somnium, Charon, etc.	Heitland	3/6
,,	Menippus and Timon	Mackie	3/6
Plato	Apologia Socratis	Adam	3/6
,,	Crito	,,	2/6
,,	Euthyphro	,,	2/6
,,	Protagoras	J. & A. M. Adam	4/6
Plutarch	Demosthenes	Holden	4/6
,,	Gracchi	,,	6/-
,,	Nicias	,,	5/-
,,	Sulla	,,	6/-
,,	Timoleon	,,	6/-
Sophocles	Oedipus Tyrannus	Jebb	4/6
Thucydides	Book III	Spratt	5/-
,,	Book VII	Holden	5/-
Xenophon	Agesilaus	Hailstone	2/6
,,	Anabasis Vol. I. Text.	Pretor	3/-
,,	,, Vol. II. Notes.	,,	4/6
,,	,, I, II	,,	4/-
,,	,, I, III, IV, V	,,	2/- each
,,	,, II, VI, VII	,,	2/6 each
,,	,, II	Edwards	1/6
,,	Cyropaedeia I, II (2 vols.)	Holden	6/-
,,	,, III, IV, V	,,	5/-
,,	,, VI, VII, VIII	,,	5/-

2. LATIN.

Author	Work	Editor	Price
Caesar	De Bello Gallico Com. I, III, VI, VIII	Peskett	1/6 each
,,	,, II–III, and VII	,,	2/- each
,,	,, I–III	,,	3/-
,,	,, IV–V	,,	1/6
,,	De Bello Gallico I ch. 1–29	Shuckburgh	1/6
,,	De Bello Civili. Com. I	Peskett	3/-
,,	,, ,, Com. III	,,	In the Press
Cicero	Actio Prima in C. Verrem	Cowie	1/6
,,	De Amicitia	Reid	3/6
,,	De Senectute	,,	3/6
,,	Div. in Q. Caec. et Actio Prima in C. Verrem	Heitland & Cowie	3/-
,,	Philippica Secunda	Peskett	3/6
,,	Pro Archia Poeta	Reid	2/-
,,	,, Balbo	,,	1/6
,,	,, Milone	,,	2/6
,,	,, Murena	Heitland	3/-
,,	,, Plancio	Holden	4/6
,,	,, Sulla	Reid	3/6
,,	Somnium Scipionis	Pearman	2/-
Cornelius Nepos	Miltiades, Themistocles, Aristides, Pausanias, Cimon	Shuckburgh	1/6
,,	Hannibal, Cato, Atticus	,,	1/6
,,	Lysander, Alcibiades, Thrasybulus, Conon, Dion, Iphicrates, Chabrias	,,	1/6
Horace	Epistles. Bk I	,,	2/6
,,	Odes and Epodes	Gow	5/-
,,	Odes. Books I, III	,,	2/- each
,,	,, Book II, IV	,,	1/6 each
,,	Epodes	,,	1/6
Livy	Books IV, VI, IX, XXVII	Stephenson	2/6 each
,,	,, V	Whibley	2/6
,,	,, XXI, XXII	Dimsdale	2/6 each
Lucan	Pharsalia. Bk I	Heitland & Haskins	1/6
,,	Pharsalia. Bk VII	Postgate	2/-
Lucretius	Book V	Duff	2/-
Ovid	Fasti. Book VI	Sidgwick	1/6
,,	Metamorphoses, Bk I.	Dowdall	1/6
Plautus	Epidicus	Gray	3/-
,,	Stichus	Fennell	2/6
Quintus Curtius	Alexander in India	Heitland & Raven	3/6
Tacitus	Agricola and Germania	Stephenson	3/-
,,	Hist. Bk I	Davies	2/6
Terence	Hautontimorumenos	Gray	3/-
Vergil	Aeneid I to XII	Sidgwick	1/6 each
,,	Bucolics	,,	1/6
,,	Georgics I, II, and III, IV	,,	2/- each
,,	Complete Works, Vol. I, Text	,,	3/6
,,	,, ,, Vol. II, Notes	,,	4/6

3. FRENCH.

Author	Work	Editor	Price
About	Le Roi des Montagnes	Ropes	2/-
Biart	Quand j'étais petit, Pt I	Boïelle	2/-
Corneille	La Suite du Menteur	Masson	2/-
,,	Polyeucte	Braunholtz	2/-
De Bonnechose	Lazare Hoche	Colbeck	2/-
,,	Bertrand du Guesclin	Leathes	2/-
,,	,, Part II (*With Vocabulary*)	,,	1/6
Delavigne	Louis XI	Eve	2/-
,,	Les Enfants d'Edouard	,,	2/-
D'Harleville	Le Vieux Célibataire	Masson	2/-
De Lamartine	Jeanne d'Arc	Clapin & Ropes	1/6
De Vigny	La Canne de Jonc	Eve	1/6
Erckmann-Chatrian	La Guerre	Clapin	3/-
Guizot	Discours sur l'Histoire de la Révolution d'Angleterre	Eve	2/6
Lemercier	Frédégonde et Brunehaut	Masson	2/-
Mme de Staël	Le Directoire	Masson & Prothero	2/-
,,	Dix Années d'Exil	,,	2/-
Merimée	Colomba	Ropes	2/-
Michelet	Louis XI & Charles the Bold	,,	2/6
Molière	Le Bourgeois Gentilhomme	Clapin	1/6
,,	L'École des Femmes	Saintsbury	2/6
,,	Les Précieuses ridicules	Braunholtz	2/-
,,	,, (*Abridged Edition*)	,,	1/-
,,	Le Misanthrope	,,	2/6
,,	L'Avare	,,	2/6
Piron	La Métromanie	Masson	2/-
Ponsard	Charlotte Corday	Ropes	2/-
Racine	Les Plaideurs	Braunholtz	2/-
,,	,, (*Abridged Edition*)	,,	1/-
Sainte-Beuve	M. Daru. (Causeries du Lundi, Vol. IX)	Masson	2/-
Saintine	Picciola	Clapin	2/-
Scribe & Legouvé	Bataille de Dames	Bull	2/-
Scribe	Le Verre d'Eau	Colbeck	2/-
Sédaine	Le Philosophe sans le savoir	Bull	2/-
Souvestre	Un Philosophe sous les Toits	Eve	2/-
,,	Le Serf & Le Chevrier de Lorraine	Ropes	2/-
,,	Le Serf (*With Vocabulary*)	,,	1/6
Thierry	Lettres sur l'histoire de France (XIII—XXIV)	Masson & Prothero	2/6
,,	Récits des Temps Mérovingiens, I—III	Masson & Ropes	3/-
Villemain	Lascaris ou les Grecs du XVᵉ Siècle	Masson	2/-
Voltaire	Histoire du Siècle de Louis XIV, Pt I, Ch. I—XIII	Masson & Prothero	2/6
,,	Pt II, Ch. XIV—XXIV	,, ,,	2/6
,,	Pt III, Ch. XXV—end	,, ,,	2/6
Xavier de Maistre	La Jeune Sibérienne. Le Lépreux de la Cité d'Aoste	Masson	1/6

THE PITT PRESS SERIES.

4. GERMAN.

Author	Work	Editor	Price
	Ballads on German History	Wagner	2/-
Benedix	Dr Wespe	Breul	3/-
Freytag	Der Staat Friedrichs des Grossen	Wagner	2/-
	German Dactylic Poetry	,,	3/-
Goethe	Knabenjahre (1749—1761)	Wagner & Cartmell	2/-
,,	Hermann und Dorothea	,, ,,	3/6
,,	Iphigenie	Breul	*In the Press*
Grimm	Selected Tales	Rippmann	3/-
Gutzkow	Zopf und Schwert	Wolstenholme	3/6
Häcklander	Der geheime Agent	E. L. Milner Barry	3/-
Hauff	Das Bild des Kaisers	Breul	3/-
,,	Das Wirthshaus im Spessart	Schlottmann & Cartmell	3/-
,,	Die Karavane	Schlottmann	3/-
Immermann	Der Oberhof	Wagner	3/-
Klee	Die deutschen Heldensagen	Wolstenholme	3/-
Kohlrausch	Das Jahr 1813	,,	2/-
Lessing	Minna von Barnhelm	Wolstenholme	*In the Press*
Lessing & Gellert	Selected Fables	Breul	3/-
Mendelssohn	Selected Letters	Sime	3/-
Raumer	Der erste Kreuzzug	Wagner	2/-
Riehl	Culturgeschichtliche Novellen	Wolstenholme	3/-
,,	Die Ganerben & Die Gerechtigkeit Gottes	,,	3/-
Schiller	Wilhelm Tell	Breul	2/6
,,	,, (*Abridged Edition*)	,,	1/6
,,	Geschichte des dreissigjährigen Kriegs Book III.	,,	3/-
,,	Maria Stuart	,,	3/6
,,	Wallenstein I. (Lager and Piccolomini)	,,	3/6
,,	Wallenstein II. (Tod)	,,	3/6
Uhland	Ernst, Herzog von Schwaben	Wolstenholme	3/6

5. ENGLISH.

Author	Work	Editor	Price
Mayor	A Sketch of Ancient Philosophy from Thales to Cicero		3/6
Wallace	Outlines of the Philosophy of Aristotle		4/6
Bacon	History of the Reign of King Henry VII	Lumby	3/-
,,	Essays	West	3/6 & 5/-
Cowley	Essays	Lumby	4/-
Gray	Poems	Tovey	*In the Press*
Macaulay	Lord Clive	Innes	1/6
More	History of King Richard III	Lumby	3/6
,,	Utopia	,,	3/6
Milton	Arcades and Comus	Verity	3/-
,,	Ode on the Nativity, L'Allegro, Il Penseroso & Lycidas	,,	2/6
,,	Samson Agonistes	,,	2/6
,,	Paradise Lost, Bks I, II	,,	2/-
,,	,, Bks III, IV	,,	2/-
,,	,, Bks V, VI	,,	2/-
,,	,, Bks VII, VIII	,,	2/-
,,	,, Bks IX, X	,,	2/-
,,	,, Bks XI, XII	,,	2/-
Pope	Essay on Criticism	West	2/-
Scott	Marmion	Masterman	2/6
,,	Lady of the Lake	,,	2/6
,,	Lay of the last Minstrel	Flather	2/-
,,	Legend of Montrose	Simpson	2/6
Shakespeare	A Midsummer-Night's Dream	Verity	1/6
,,	Twelfth Night	,,	1/6
,,	Julius Caesar	,,	1/6
,,	The Tempest	,,	1/6
,,	King Lear	,,	*In the Press*
Shakespeare & Fletcher	Two Noble Kinsmen	Skeat	3/6
Sidney	An Apologie for Poetrie	Shuckburgh	3/-

West	Elements of English Grammar		2/6
,,	English Grammar for Beginners		1/-
Carlos	Short History of British India		1/-
Mill	Elementary Commercial Geography		1/6
Bartholomew	Atlas of Commercial Geography		3/-

Robinson	Church Catechism Explained		2/-

6. EDUCATIONAL SCIENCE.

Author	Work	Editor	Price
Colbeck	Lectures on the Teaching of Modern Languages		2/-
Comenius	Life and Educational Works	Laurie	3/6
	Three Lectures on the Practice of Education		
Eve	I. On Marking	} 1 Vol.	2/-
Sidgwick	II. On Stimulus		
Abbott	III. On the teaching of Latin Verse Composition		
Farrar	General Aims of the Teacher	} 1 Vol.	1/6
Poole	Form Management		
Locke	Thoughts on Education	Quick	3/6
Milton	Tractate on Education	Browning	2/-
Sidgwick	On Stimulus		1/-
Thring	Theory and Practice of Teaching		4/6

7. MATHEMATICS.

Ball	Elementary Algebra		4/6
Euclid	Books I—VI, XI, XII	Taylor	5/-
,,	Books I—VI	,,	4/-
,,	Books I—IV	,,	3/-
	Also separately		
,,	Books I, & II; III, & IV; V, & VI; XI, & XII		1/6 each
,,	Solutions to Bks I—IV	W. W. Taylor	6/-
Hobson & Jessop	Elementary Plane Trigonometry		4/6
Loney	Elements of Statics and Dynamics		7/6
	Part I. Elements of Statics		4/6
	,, II. Elements of Dynamics		3/6
,,	Solutions of Examples, Statics and Dynamics		7/6
,,	Mechanics and Hydrostatics		4/6
Smith, C.	Arithmetic for Schools, with or without answers		3/6
,,	Part I. Chapters I—VIII. Elementary, with or without answers		2/-
,,	Part II. Chapters IX—XX, with or without answers		2/-
Hale, G.	Key to Smith's Arithmetic		7/6

LONDON: C. J. CLAY AND SONS,
CAMBRIDGE UNIVERSITY PRESS WAREHOUSE,
AVE MARIA LANE.
GLASGOW: 263, ARGYLE STREET.

The Cambridge Bible for Schools and Colleges.

GENERAL EDITORS:
J. J. S. PEROWNE, D.D., BISHOP OF WORCESTER,
A. F. KIRKPATRICK, D.D., REGIUS PROFESSOR OF HEBREW.

Extra Fcap. 8vo. cloth, with Maps when required.

Book of Joshua. Rev. G. F. MACLEAR, D.D. 2s. 6d.
Book of Judges. Rev. J. J. LIAS, M.A. 3s. 6d.
First Book of Samuel. Prof. KIRKPATRICK, D.D. 3s. 6d.
Second Book of Samuel. Prof. KIRKPATRICK, D.D. 3s. 6d.
First & Second Books of Kings. Prof. LUMBY, D.D. 3s. 6d. each.
Books of Ezra & Nehemiah. Prof. RYLE, D.D. 4s. 6d.
Book of Job. Prof. DAVIDSON, D.D. 5s.
Psalms. Book I. Prof. KIRKPATRICK, D.D. 3s. 6d.
Psalms. Books II and III. Prof. KIRKPATRICK, D.D. 3s. 6d.
Book of Ecclesiastes. Very Rev. E. H. PLUMPTRE, D.D. 5s.
Book of Isaiah. Chaps. I.–XXXIX. Rev. J. SKINNER, D.D. 4s.
Book of Jeremiah. Rev. A. W. STREANE, D.D. 4s. 6d.
Book of Ezekiel. Prof. DAVIDSON, D.D. 5s.
Book of Hosea. Rev. T. K. CHEYNE, M.A., D.D. 3s.
Books of Joel and Amos. Rev. S. R. DRIVER, D.D.
In the Press.
Books of Obadiah and Jonah. Arch. PEROWNE. 2s. 6d.
Book of Micah. Rev. T. K. CHEYNE, M.A., D.D. 1s. 6d.
Nahum, Habakkuk & Zephaniah. Prof. DAVIDSON, D.D. 3s.
Books of Haggai, Zechariah & Malachi. Arch. PEROWNE. 3s. 6d.
Book of Malachi. Archdeacon PEROWNE. 1s.
First Book of Maccabees. Rev. W. FAIRWEATHER and Rev. J. S. BLACK, LL.D.
In the Press.
Gospel according to St Matthew. Rev. A. CARR, M.A. 2s. 6d.
Gospel according to St Mark. Rev. G. F. MACLEAR, D.D. 2s. 6d.
Gospel acc. to St Luke. Very Rev. F. W. FARRAR, D.D. 4s. 6d.
Gospel according to St John. Rev. A. PLUMMER, D.D. 4s. 6d.
Acts of the Apostles. Prof. LUMBY, D.D. 4s. 6d.
Epistle to the Romans. Rev. H. C. G. MOULE, D.D. 3s. 6d.
First and Second Corinthians. Rev. J. J. LIAS, M.A. 2s. each.
Epistle to the Galatians. Rev. E. H. PEROWNE, D.D. 1s. 6d.
Epistle to the Ephesians. Rev. H. C. G. MOULE, D.D. 2s. 6d.
Epistle to the Philippians. Rev. H. C. G. MOULE, D.D. 2s. 6d.
Colossians and Philemon. Rev. H. C. G. MOULE, D.D. 2s.
Epistles to the Thessalonians. Rev. G. G. FINDLAY, B.A. 2s.
Epistles to Timothy & Titus. Rev. A. E. HUMPHREYS, M.A. 3s.
Epistle to the Hebrews. Very Rev. F. W. FARRAR, D.D. 3s. 6d.
Epistle of St James. Very Rev. E. H. PLUMPTRE, D.D. 1s. 6d.
St Peter and St Jude. Very Rev. E. H. PLUMPTRE, D.D. 2s. 6d.
Epistles of St John. Rev. A. PLUMMER, D.D. 3s. 6d.
Book of Revelation. Rev. W. H. SIMCOX, M.A. 3s.

Other Volumes Preparing.

LONDON: C. J. CLAY AND SONS,
CAMBRIDGE UNIVERSITY PRESS WAREHOUSE,
AVE MARIA LANE.

The Smaller Cambridge Bible for Schools.

Now Ready. With Maps. Price 1s. each volume.

Book of Joshua. Rev. J. S. BLACK, LL.D.
Book of Judges. Rev. J. S. BLACK, LL.D.
First Book of Samuel. Prof. KIRKPATRICK, D.D.
Second Book of Samuel. Prof. KIRKPATRICK, D.D.
First Book of Kings. Prof. LUMBY, D.D.
Second Book of Kings. Prof. LUMBY, D.D.
Gospel according to St Matthew. Rev. A. CARR, M.A.
Gospel according to St Mark. Rev. G. F. MACLEAR, D.D.
Gospel according to St Luke. Very Rev. F. W. FARRAR, D.D.
Gospel according to St John. Rev. A. PLUMMER, D.D.
Acts of the Apostles. Prof. LUMBY, D.D.

The Cambridge Greek Testament
for Schools and Colleges

GENERAL EDITOR: J. J. S. PEROWNE, D.D.

Gospel according to St Matthew. Rev. A. CARR, M.A. With 4 Maps. 4s. 6d.
Gospel according to St Mark. Rev. G. F. MACLEAR, D.D. With 3 Maps. 4s. 6d.
Gospel according to St Luke. Very Rev. F. W. FARRAR. With 4 Maps. 6s.
Gospel according to St John. Rev. A. PLUMMER, D.D. With 4 Maps. 6s.
Acts of the Apostles. Prof. LUMBY, D.D. 4 Maps. 6s.
First Epistle to the Corinthians. Rev. J. J. LIAS, M.A. 3s.
Second Epistle to the Corinthians. Rev. J. J. LIAS, M.A. 3s.
Epistle to the Hebrews. Very Rev. F. W. FARRAR, D.D. 3s. 6d.
Epistles of St John. Rev. A. PLUMMER, D.D. 4s.

GENERAL EDITOR: Prof. J. A. ROBINSON, D.D.

Epistle to the Philippians. Rev. H. C. G. MOULE, D.D. 2s. 6d.
Epistle of St James. Rev. A. CARR, M.A. 2s. 6d.
Pastoral Epistles. Rev. J. H. BERNARD, D.D. [*In Preparation.*
Book of Revelation. Rev. W. H. SIMCOX, M.A. 5s.

London: C. J. CLAY AND SONS,
CAMBRIDGE WAREHOUSE, AVE MARIA LANE.
Glasgow: 263, ARGYLE STREET.
Leipzig: F. A. BROCKHAUS.
New York: THE MACMILLAN CO.

CAMBRIDGE: PRINTED BY J. & C. F. CLAY, AT THE UNIVERSITY PRESS.

www.ingramcontent.com/pod-product-compliance
Lightning Source LLC
Chambersburg PA
CBHW051247300426
44114CB00011B/930